Advances in Behavioral Finance

VOLUME II

The Roundtable Series in Behavioral Economics

The Roundtable Series in Behavioral Economics aims to advance research in the new interdisciplinary field of behavioral economics. Behavioral economics uses facts, models, and methods from neighboring sciences to establish descriptively accurate findings about human cognitive ability and social interaction and to explore the implications of these findings for economic behavior. The most fertile neighboring science in recent decades has been psychology, but sociology, anthropology, biology, and other fields can usefully influence economics as well. The Roundtable Series publishes books in economics that are deeply rooted in empirical findings or methods from one or more neighboring sciences and advance economics on its own terms—generating theoretical insights, making more accurate predictions of field phenomena, and suggesting better policy.

Colin Camerer and Ernst Fehr, editors

OTHER VOLUMES IN THE SERIES

Behavioral Game Theory: Experiments in Strategic Interaction by Colin F. Camerer

Microeconomics: Behavior, Institutions, and Evolution by Samuel Bowles

Advances in Behavioral Economics, edited by Colin F. Camerer, George Loewenstein, and Matthew Rabin

Advances in Behavioral Finance: Volume II, edited by Richard H. Thaler

The Behavioral Economics Roundtable

Henry Aaron
George Akerlof
Linda Babcock
Colin Camerer
Peter Diamond
Jon Elster
Ernst Fehr
Daniel Kahneman
David Laibson

George Loewenstein
Sendhil Mullainathan
Matthew Rabin
Thomas Schelling
Eldar Shafir
Robert Shiller
Cass Sunstein
Richard Thaler
Richard Zeckhauser

Advances in Behavioral Finance

VOLUME II

Edited by
Richard H. Thaler

RUSSELL SAGE FOUNDATION
NEW YORK

PRINCETON UNIVERSITY PRESS
PRINCETON AND OXFORD

Copyright © 2005 by Russell Sage Foundation

Published by Princeton University Press, 41 William Street, Princeton, New Jersey 08540
In the United Kingdom: Princeton University Press, 3 Market Place, Woodstock,
Oxfordshire OX20 1SY

and Russell Sage Foundation
112 East 64th Street, New York, New York 10021

All Rights Reserved

ISBN 0-691-12174-5

0-691-12175-3 (paper)

Library of Congress Control Number 93012149

British Library Cataloging-in-Publication Data is available

This book has been composed in Sabon

Printed on acid-free paper. ∞

pup.princeton.edu

www.russellsage.org

Printed in the United States of America

3   5   7   9   10   8   6   4   2

ISBN-13: 978-0-691-12174-1 (cloth)
ISBN-10: 0-691-12174-5 (cloth)

ISBN-13: 978-0-691-12175-8 (pbk.)
ISBN-10: 0-691-12175-3 (pbk.)

This book is dedicated to the memory of Fischer Black (1938–1995) and Amos Tversky (1937–1996).

CONTENTS

PART III *Empirical Studies of Overreaction and Underreaction*

PART IV *Theories of Overreaction and Underreaction*

PART V *Investor Behavior*

PART VI *Corporate Finance*

PREFACE

It has been a decade since the first volume in this series was published. That volume documented the birth of a new approach to studying financial markets. This volume illustrates some of what has been going on during the second decade of behavioral finance research. It has been an exciting time both for financial markets and for financial market research. I think that many economists began to take behavioral approaches to finance more seriously on October 19, 1987, when stock prices fell over 20 percent on a day without any important news (other than the crash itself). If that is the case, then the rise and fall of the Internet bubble has surely solidified the view that rational models have trouble explaining all that we see in financial markets. It is quite hard to claim that NASDAQ was rationally priced at both 5000 and 1300 within a couple years. Indeed, I think it is now generally accepted that it is essential to understand how investors behave if we are to truly understand how prices behave.

Since the first chapter of the book presents an extensive review of behavioral finance research to date, in this preface I will just provide a brief outline of what is to come. In selecting the papers to include, I have drawn on what I consider to be the five major themes of research over the past decade.[1]

I. LIMITS TO ARBITRAGE

It has long been known by researchers in behavioral economics that the importance of less than fully rational behavior depends on the extent to which rational actors can profit from the suboptimal choices of others, especially if in the act of profiting, rational individuals push the quasi-rational

---

[1] Of course, in choosing these papers I have had to make many hard choices in order to keep the volume to a manageable size. My apologies to the authors of the excellent ones that have been left out. Serious scholars should use this book as an entry point to the field; the book is not meant to be complete. One explicit choice I made was not to include articles from critics of behavioral finance. This is not meant to suggest that behavioral finance is without critics (though, in fact, there are not many examples of comprehensive critiques of the whole field). Readers interested in a critical appraisal of some of the empirical papers in this book could start with Eugene Fama's (1998). And, to be explicit about something that should be obvious, the field of behavioral finance could not exist without the building blocks of traditional (rational) financial theorizing, including the efficient market hypothesis, the capital asset pricing model, the Modigliani-Miller theorem, and so forth. Behavioral economics (of which behavioral finance is a subset) builds upon (does not replace) standard economics analyses.

agents to behave more rationally.[2] In many important economic choices (e.g., career choice, marriage, saving for retirement), if one agent makes a poor choice (picks the wrong career or spouse, saves too little) no profit opportunity is created. You may think that my wife will soon realize what a mistake she has made in marrying me, but (as far as I know) there is no way for you to sell my marriage prospects short, and even if you could, it might not alter the behavior of me or my unlucky wife. Missing markets prevent arbitrage, thus allowing irrationality to persist.

For years, many financial economists believed that in the financial world, the existence of well-functioning markets (including opportunities to sell short) implies that irrational agents will not affect asset prices. If I (and other confused investors) buy the wrong stock and drive up the price too high, smart investors like you can sell that stock short (unlike my marriage). In a series of papers Brad DeLong et al. started to undercut this notion (see their chapter in Volume I), but I think scope of "limits to arbitrage" was much better understood after the paper by Andrei Shleifer and Robert Vishny (Chapter 2) appeared. Shleifer and Vishny show that arbitrageurs need long horizons to be able to bet successfully on slow-moving market mispricing, and since real-world arbitrageurs need to bet with other people's money in order to have sufficient capital to affect prices, they need their investors to have long horizons. Shleifer and Vishny show that in the annoying circumstances in which prices temporarily move even further away from rationality, arbitrageurs lose money and, as a result, their investors may withdraw funds. The chapter contains what now appears to be an uncanny prediction of events that soon followed, especially the downfall of Long Term Capital Management (LTCM).

Chapters 3 and 4 document two particularly dramatic illustrations of limits to arbitrage, namely violation of the law of one price. Kenneth Froot and Emil Dabora discuss so-called twin stocks, such as Royal Dutch and Shell, whose prices should be linked by a simple formula (since by charter the earnings are divided according to a 60:40 ratio). Nevertheless, prices have diverged from this true fundamental value by as much as 35 percent. (Ironically, one of the trades that LTCM had on when they collapsed was a bet on the Royal Dutch Shell spread to converge.) Owen Lamont and I discuss the equally bizarre case of Palm and 3Com in Chapter 4. In the midst of the Internet bubble, 3Com announced a spin-off of their Palm division, maker of spiffy handheld computers. 3Com held a wildly successful IPO for Palm, in which a small portion of the shares were sold, the rest were to be distributed in a few months to 3Com shareholders. The weird part was that the market value of 3Com was, for several months, less than the value of the Palm shares they owned. Several other similar negative valuations were observed around the same time.

[2] See for example, Arrow (1982), Akerlof and Yellen (1985), Russell and Thaler (1985), and Haltiwanger and Waldman (1985).

II. Stock Returns and the Equity Premium

The second section of the book discusses the overall stock market and two distinct puzzles. The first puzzle is the long-term predictability of the stock market. Although the stock market was long thought to be a random walk, and thus unpredictable, numerous researchers have found that over long horizons (several years) the returns on the stock market are at least somewhat predictable. Specifically, when stock prices are very high, as judged by price/earnings or price/dividends ratios, then subsequent returns tend to be low. John Campbell and Robert Shiller review this evidence in Chapter 5. Their analysis suggests that stock prices were too high by the mid-1990s, and they were predicting (albeit too early) the bear market that eventually arrived. In fact they are indirectly responsible for one of the most famous phrases to emerge from the 1990s. The story is that Campbell and Shiller presented an early version of this chapter to the Federal Reserve Board a few days before Chairman Alan Greenspan made a speech containing the words "irrational exuberance." Neither John nor Bob recall using that phrase in their talk, but they did seem to give Greenspan the idea. In a fair exchange, Shiller then borrowed the phrase back for the title of his best-selling book.

The other puzzle discussed in this section is the "equity premium" puzzle. Briefly put, the historical difference between the return on equities and the risk free rate has been judged too big to be explained within traditional asset pricing models of expected utility maximization. In Chapter 6 Shlomo Benartzi and I offer a behavioral explanation for part of this puzzle based on two concepts from the psychology of decision making: *loss aversion* (the tendency to weigh losses much more heavily than gains) and *narrow framing* (the tendency to consider returns over brief periods of time rather than the long run. We show that the equity premium can be understood if people weigh losses twice as much as gains and evaluate their portfolios roughly once a year. In the appendix to the chapter, added for this book, we review a few experimental studies offering empirical tests of myopic loss aversion. In Chapter 7 loss aversion is incorporated into a much more sophisticated equilibrium model by Nick Barberis, Ming Huang, and Tano Santos. They also incorporate a third behavioral concept: the house money effect,[3] the idea that when investors consider themselves to be "ahead" in the game they are playing, they are more willing to take risks (since they are playing with the "house money," in gambling parlance).

---

[3] See Thaler and Johnson, 1990

III. Empirical Studies of Overreaction and Underreaction

The third section contains four important empirical papers. Chapter 8, by Josef Lakonishok, Andrei Shleifer, and Robert Vishny (LSV), offer, the definitive study of value investing, a theme of behavioral finance since Benjamin Graham. De Bondt and Thaler (1985, 1987) had shown that simple value strategies, such as buying stocks that had greatly underperformed in the market for 3–5 years, or had extremely low ratios of price to book value, earn excess returns. We hypothesized that these excess returns could be attributed to investor overreaction. Efficient market adherents, such as Eugene Fama and Kenneth French conducted a series of studies that confirmed the basic facts of the De Bondt and Thaler findings, but offered a different interpretation, namely that the apparent excess returns to value stocks were attributable to risk. In this chapter LSV respond to the Fama-French challenge in various ways. Specifically, they show that value stocks do not appear to be riskier than growth stocks (e.g., do not underperform in down markets or recessions). They also find that value stocks do particularly well in the days around earnings announcements, suggesting that investors had biased expectations of earnings, as the behavioral theory predicts.

The question of whether the returns to value strategies can be attributed to risk is also addressed by Kent Daniel and Sheridan Titman in Chapter 9. The heart of their paper is an investigation of whether there is a "distress factor" shared by value firms that can explain their excess returns. Daniel and Titman reject this interpretation. Instead, they find that value stocks tend to move together because stocks with similar factor loadings tend to become distressed (i.e., cheap) at the same time.

Value strategies are long-term phenomena. Stocks that have done well or poorly over a period of years subsequently show mean-reverting returns. But over shorter horizons, such as six months or a year, just the opposite is true. That is, the best performers over the past year tend to keep outperforming over the subsequent year. Over the past decade much attention has been given to this phenomenon, that has come to be known as *momentum*. Narasimhan Jegadeesh and Sheridan Titman summarize the research in this area in Chapter 10. They find the evidence supporting the existence of excess returns to be quite strong, and judge that it is very difficult to claim that these excess returns can be attributed to risk.

The final empirical paper in this section addresses a topic of growing concern, namely the role of brokerage stock recommendations. Roni Michaely and Kent Womack survey this important field in Chapter 11. Specifically they cover two important topics: first, do recommendations have information content? (Yes); second, is there evidence of biases stemming from either cognitive biases or from conflicts of interests? (Yes and yes).

IV. Theories of Overreaction and Underreaction

The chapters in the previous section document some of the anomalies that be-havioral finance researchers identified. All are troubling to the efficient mar-ket hypothesis, but as my Chicago colleagues like to say, "It takes a theory to beat a theory." This section contains three attempts by leading theorists to offer an account of the anomalous facts, specifically, the apparent finding that stock prices display mean reversion over long horizons but positive serial cor-relation over short to medium horizons. The first two chapters, by Barberis, Shleifer, and Vishny (BSV), and by Daniel, David Hirshleifer, and Avanidhar Subrahmanyam (DHS) were written in parallel, and both adopt a representa-tive agent formulation. In BSV agents at times believe that earnings are trend-ing and at other times think that they are mean-reverting. The model is based on the psychological principles of representativeness and conservatism. DHS build their model around overconfidence, specifically overconfidence about the validity of what investors treat as private information. The third chapter in the section, by Harrison Hong and Jeremy Stein, followed shortly after the first two, and instead of modeling a single representative agent they envision a world with two different types of boundedly rational agents. "Newswatch-ers" make forecasts based on what they consider private information but do not condition properly on past prices. "Momentum traders" condition only on past price movements. In the version of the paper included in this book, Hong and Stein also report some empirical evidence supporting some of the predictions of their model.

V. Investor Behavior

Behavioral finance during most of its first decade was more finance than be-havior. In recent years that emphasis has begun to change as researchers have obtained data sets of actual behavior by investors. Using such data re-searchers have been able to show that the same biases discovered by psy-chologists in laboratory experiments at low or zero stakes also emerge in the field at high stakes. The pioneer of this style of research was Terry Odean, who as a graduate student obtained a large data set of trading in-formation from a large discount brokerage firm. Writing first on his own and then later in collaboration with Brad Barber, he has documented how investors behave. Barber and Odean summarize this research in Chapter 15. They stress two findings: First, investors are reluctant to sell stocks that have declined in value (compared to stocks that have appreciated) even though the effect of taxes is to push investors to do just the opposite; sec-ond, investors display overconfidence in the sense that they trade too much. Women will not be surprised to learn that this overconfident behavior is more pronounced among men.

Another domain in which investor behavior can be observed is in their defined contribution savings plans such as 401(k)s. In Chapter 16 Benartzi and I investigate how investors handle diversification in such plans. We show that investors have very naïve notions of diversification, and at least some investors behave as if they were choosing funds from their plan at random. This implies that when plan sponsors add new funds to the plan, they inadvertently induce participants to alter their asset allocation.

VI. CORPORATE FINANCE

The final section of the book concerns corporate finance, another new direction for behavioral finance researchers. In Chapter 17 Jeremy Stein starts the ball rolling on an important question: How should firms behave if market efficiency is no longer taken for granted? Specifically, professors of corporate finance have been teaching their students to use the CAPM beta to determine hurdle rates for corporate investments; what should they be teaching now if beta is dead? This is a tough problem, but Stein makes a good start at thinking about it. He shows that factors such as time horizon and financial constraints come into play in determining how a firm should handle this problem.

In Chapter 18, Francois Degeorge, Jayendu Patel, and Richard Zeckhauser (DPZ) document some corporate behavior of the unsavory kind. Just as Shleifer and Vishny's paper on limits to arbitrage foretold the meltdown of some hedge funds, DPZ offers an eerie warning of future headlines in their essay on earnings manipulations. The authors hypothesize that management has certain earnings targets that serve as salient aspiration levels for themselves, their shareholders, and the analysts that follow the stock. In particular, DPZ suggest three particularly important goals: make a profit, make more than last year, and beat the analyst's forecasts. They then show that the distributions of reported earnings display odd discontinuities at precisely the points suggested by the threshold model. For example, firms are much more likely to make a penny more a share than last year than a penny less. Since Enron, we now know that such earnings manipulations can, at least occasionally, be just the small tip of a big iceberg.

Finally, in the last chapter of the book, J. B. Heaton approaches corporate finance from a different behavioral perspective. In Chapter 19 he starts by assuming that markets are efficient and then asks how much of the empirical literature in corporate finance can be understood by using one behavioral assumption about managers: optimism. He shows that much of what we know about corporate behavior can be explained with this one assumption (as opposed to rational models based on asymmetric information and/or agency costs).

Final Thoughts

Many of the papers in this volume were presented at the semiannual meetings at the National Bureau of Economics research that I have been organizing with Bob Shiller for many years. As I glance through the past programs of these meetings, and compare this volume with the first one, I am struck at how the field is becoming both more mainstream and more behavioral. More mainstream because the questions raised by these papers have been at the very heart of many of the debates financial economists have been having in recent years. More behavioral because the research has moved beyond just documenting anomalies to getting on with a constructive research agenda.

I am optimistic, as J. B. Heaton would predict, about the future. I am optimistic for two reasons. First, it must be the case that building models with agents that more closely resemble actual people has to be the right way, long term, of increasing the explanatory power of economics. The only excuse for doing otherwise is the bounded rationality of the investigator (fully rational models are easier to play with). But, this brings me to my second reason for optimism: some of the very best young minds in financial economics have taken up this subject. Many of the authors represented in this book were just out of graduate school when they wrote these papers. They are now getting tenure at the top finance and economics departments in the world, and are training the next crop. I can't wait to see Volume III. What will it contain? Speculating about the new directions of a field is always risky, but my guess (and hope) is that behavioral finance will continue to broaden, at least in two ways. First, the range of psychological complexities that are incorporated will be extended beyond the judgment and decision-making field. Issues such as emotion are surely important in understanding how markets work. Second, the emphasis on asset pricing (and mostly equity pricing) is likely to be diminished as researchers study other security markets using behavioral tools. Young scholars should not get the impression that the work is done. It has just started.

REFERENCES

Akerlof, George and Janet Yellen, 1985, Can Small Deviations from Rationality Make Significant Differences to Economic Equilibria?, *The American Economic Review* 75(4)(Sep.), 708–20.

Arrow, Kenneth, 1982, Risk Perception in Psychology and Economics, *Economic Inquiry* 20, 1–9.

Fama, Eugene F., 1998, Market Efficiency, Long-term Returns, and Behavioral Finance, *Journal of Financial Economics* 49, 283–306.

Haltiwanger, John, and Michael Waldman, 1985, Rational Expectations and the Limits of Rationality: An Analysis of Heterogeneity, *American Economics Review* 75, 326–40.

Russell, Thomas, and Richard H. Thaler, 1985, The Relevance of Quasi-Rationality in Competitive Markets, *American Economics Review* 75, 1071–82.

Thaler, Richard H., and Eric J. Johnson, 1990, Gambling with the House Money and Trying to Break Even: The Effects of Prior Outcomes on Risky Choice, *Management Science* 36, 643–60.

Werner F., M. De Bondt, and Richard H. Thaler, 1985, Does the Stock Market Overreact?, *Journal of Finance* 40, 793–808.

Werner F., M. De Bondt, and Richard H. Thaler, 1987, Further Evidence on Investor Overreaction and Stock Market Seasonality, *Journal of Finance* 42, 557–81.

ACKNOWLEDGMENTS

Preface: Richard H. Thaler, "Preface," © 2004 Russell Sage Foundation. Reprinted with permission.

Chapter 1: Nicholas Barberis and Richard H. Thaler, "A Survey of Behavioral Finance." From George Constantinides, Milton Harris, and Rene Stulz, eds. *Handbook of the Economics of Finance*, vol. 1B, "Financial Markets and Asset Pricing" (Amsterdam: North-Holland, 2003), pp. 1051–1121.

Chapter 2: Andrei Shleifer and Robert W. Vishny, "The Limits of Arbitrage," *Journal of Finance* 52(1) (March 1997), pp. 35–55. Used by permission of Black Publishing.

Chapter 3: Kenneth Froot et al., "How Are Stock Prices," reprinted from the *Journal of Financial Economics*, 53, pp. 189–216, © 1999, with permission from Elsevier.

Chapter 4: Owen A. Lamont and Richard H. Thaler, "Can the Market Add and Subtract? Mispricing in Tech Price Carve-Outs," *Journal of Political Economy* (forthcoming). Copyright by The University of Chicago. All rights reserved. Reprinted with permission.

Chapter 5: John Y. Campbell and Robert J. Shiller, "Valuation Rations and the Long-Run Stock Market Outlook." © 2004 Russell Sage Foundation. Reprinted with permission.

Chapter 6: Shlomo Benartzi and Richard H. Thaler, "Myopic Loss Aversion and the Equity Premium Puzzle," *Quarterly Journal of Economics* 110:1 (February, 1995), pp. 73–92. © 1995 by the President and Fellows of Harvard College and the Massachusetts Institute of Technology. Used by permission.

Chapter 7: Nicholas Barberis, Ming Huang, and Tano Santos, "Prospect Theory and Asset Prices," *Quarterly Journal of Economics* 116:1 (February 2001), pp. 1–53. © 2001 by the President and Fellows of Harvard College and the Massachusetts Institute of Technology. Used by permission.

Chapter 8: Josef Lakonishok, Andrei Shleifer, and Robert W. Vishny, "Contrarian Investment, Extrapolation, and Risk," *Journal of Finance* 49(5) (December 1994), pp. 1541–78. Used by permission of Blackwell Publishing.

Chapter 9: Kent Daniel and Sheridan Titman, "Evidence on the Characteristics of Cross Sectional Variation in Stock Returns," *Journal of Finance* 52(1) (March 1997), pp. 1–33. Used by permission of Blackwell Publishing.

Chapter 10: Narasimhan Jegadeesh and Sheridan Titman, "Momentum." © Russell Sage Foundation. Reprinted with permission.

Chapter 11: Roni Michaely and Kent L. Womack, "Market Efficiency and Biases in Brokerage Recommendations." © 2004 Russell Sage Foundation. Reprinted with permission.

Chapter 12: Andrei Shleifer, "Model of Investor Sentiment," reprinted from the *Journal of Financial Economics*, Vol 49, pp. 307–43, © 1998, with permission from Elsevier.

Chapter 13: Kent Daniel, David Hirshleifer, and Avanidhar Subrahmanyam, "Investor Psychology and Security Market Under- and Overreaction," *Journal of Finance* 52(1) (March 1997), pp. 1–33. Used by permission of Blackwell Publishing.

Chapter 14: Harrison Hong and Jeremy C. Stein, "A Unified Theory of Underreaction, Momentum Trading, and Overreaction in Asset Markets," *Journal of Finance* 54(6) (December 1999), pp. 2143–84. Used by permission of Blackwell publishing.

Chapter 15: Brad M. Barber and Terrance Odean, "Individual Investors." © 2004 Russell Sage Foundation. Reprinted with permission.

Chapter 16: Shlomo Benartzi and Richard H. Thaler, "Naive Diversification Strategies in Defined Contribution Savings Plans," *American Economic Review* (2001). Used by permission.

Chapter 17: Jeremy C. Stein, "Rational Capital Budgeting in an Irrational World," *Journal of Business* 69 (1996), pp. 429–55. © 1996 by The University of Chicago. All rights reserved. Reprinted with permission.

Chapter 18: François Degeorge, Jayendu Patel, and Richard Zeckhauser, "Earnings Management to Exceed Thresholds," *Journal of Business* 72

(1999), pp. 1–34. © 1999 by The University of Chicago. All rights reserved. Reprinted with permission.

Chapter 19: J. B. Heaton, "Managerial Optimism and Corporate Finance," reprinted from *Financial Management*, 31 (summer 2002), pp. 33–45. Reprinted with permission of Financial Management Association International, University of South Florida, College of Business Administration #3331, Tampa, FL 33620, (813) 974-2084.

ABBREVIATIONS

ACT	advance corporation tax
APT	arbitrage pricing theory
B/M	book-to-market
CAPM	capital asset pricing model
CARA	constant absolute risk aversion
CRSP	Center for Research in Security Prices
C/P	cash flow to price
EM	earnings management
E/P	earnings-to-price
EMH	efficient markets hypothesis
EU	expected utility framework
FAR	fundamental assert risk
GAAP	generally accepted accounting
GIC	guaranteed investment contracts
GS	growth in sales
LTCM	long-term capital management
NAV	net asset value
NEER	new estimator of expected returns
NPV	net present value
PBA	performance-based arbitrage
PGR	proportion of gains realized
PLR	proportion of losses realized
RBOC	regional Bell operating company
REE	rational expectations equilibrium
SEO	seasoned equity offerings
SEU	subjective expected utility
SUE	standardized unexpected earnings
TR	threshold-regarding
VAR	vector autoregressions
WRSS	weighted relative strength strategy

Advances in Behavioral Finance

Volume II

Chapter 1

A SURVEY OF BEHAVIORAL FINANCE

Nicholas Barberis and Richard Thaler

1. Introduction

The traditional finance paradigm, which underlies many of the other articles in this handbook, seeks to understand financial markets using models
in which agents are "rational." Rationality means two things. First, when
they receive new information, agents update their beliefs correctly, in the
manner described by Bayes's law. Second, given their beliefs, agents make
choices that are normatively acceptable, in the sense that they are consistent with Savage's notion of Subjective Expected Utility (SEU).

This traditional framework is appealingly simple, and it would be very
satisfying if its predictions were confirmed in the data. Unfortunately, after
years of effort, it has become clear that basic facts about the aggregate
stock market, the cross-section of average returns and individual trading
behavior are not easily understood in this framework.

Behavioral finance is a new approach to financial markets that has
emerged, at least in part, in response to the difficulties faced by the traditional paradigm. In broad terms, it argues that some financial phenomena
can be better understood using models in which some agents are *not* fully
rational. More specifically, it analyzes what happens when we relax one, or
both, of the two tenets that underlie individual rationality. In some behavioral finance models, agents fail to update their beliefs correctly. In other
models, agents apply Bayes's law properly but make choices that are normatively questionable, in that they are incompatible with SEU.[1]

We are very grateful to Markus Brunnermeier, George Constantinides, Kent Daniel, Milt Harris, Ming Huang, Owen Lamont, Jay Ritter, Andrei Shleifer, Jeremy Stein and Tuomo
Vuolteenaho for extensive comments.

[1] It is important to note that most models of asset pricing use the Rational Expectations
Equilibrium framework (REE), which assumes not only individual rationality but also *consistent beliefs* (Sargent 1993). Consistent beliefs means that agents' beliefs are correct: the
subjective distribution they use to forecast future realizations of unknown variables is indeed the distribution that those realizations are drawn from. This requires not only that
agents process new information correctly, but that they have *enough* information about the
structure of the economy to be able to figure out the correct distribution for the variables of
interest.

This review essay evaluates recent work in this rapidly growing field. In section 2, we consider the classic objection to behavioral finance, namely that even if some agents in the economy are less than fully rational, rational agents will prevent them from influencing security prices for very long, through a process known as arbitrage. One of the biggest successes of behavioral finance is a series of theoretical papers showing that in an economy where rational and irrational traders interact, irrationality *can* have a substantial and long-lived impact on prices. These papers, known as the literature on "limits to arbitrage," form one of the two buildings blocks of behavioral finance.

To make sharp predictions, behavioral models often need to specify the form of agents' irrationality. How exactly do people misapply Bayes's law or deviate from SEU? For guidance on this, behavioral economists typically turn to the extensive experimental evidence compiled by cognitive psychologists on the biases that arise when people form *beliefs*, and on people's *preferences*, or on how they make decisions, given their beliefs. Psychology is therefore the second building block of behavioral finance, and we review the psychology most relevant for financial economists in section 3.[2]

In sections 4–8, we consider specific applications of behavioral finance: to understanding the aggregate stock market, the cross-section of average returns, and the pricing of closed-end funds in sections 4, 5 and 6 respectively; to understanding how particular groups of investors choose their portfolios and trade over time in section 7; and to understanding the financing and investment decisions of firms in section 8. Section 9 takes stock and suggests directions for future research.[3]

Behavioral finance departs from REE by relaxing the assumption of individual rationality. An alternative departure is to retain individual rationality but to relax the consistent beliefs assumption: while investors apply Bayes's law correctly, they lack the information required to know the actual distribution variables are drawn from. This line of research is sometimes referred to as the literature on bounded rationality, or on structural uncertainty. For example, a model in which investors do not know the growth rate of an asset's cash flows but learn it as best as they can from available data, would fall into this class. Although the literature we discuss also uses the term bounded rationality, the approach is quite different.

[2] The idea, now widely adopted, that behavioral finance rests on the two pillars of limits to arbitrage and investor psychology is originally due to Shleifer and Summers (1990).

[3] We draw readers' attention to two other recent surveys of behavioral finance. Shleifer (2000) provides a particularly detailed discussion of the theoretical and empirical work on limits to arbitrage, which we summarize in section 2. Hirshleifer's (2001) survey is closer to ours in terms of material covered, although we devote less space to asset pricing, and more to corporate finance and individual investor behavior. We also organize the material somewhat differently.

2. Limits to Arbitrage

2.1. Market Efficiency

In the traditional framework where agents are rational and there are no frictions, a security's price equals its "fundamental value." This is the discounted sum of expected future cash flows, where in forming expectations, investors correctly process all available information, and where the discount rate is consistent with a normatively acceptable preference specification. The hypothesis that actual prices reflect fundamental values is the Efficient Markets Hypothesis (EMH). Put simply, under this hypothesis, "prices are right," in that they are set by agents who understand Bayes's law and have sensible preferences. In an efficient market, there is "no free lunch": no investment strategy can earn excess risk-adjusted average returns, or average returns greater than are warranted for its risk.

Behavioral finance argues that some features of asset prices are most plausibly interpreted as deviations from fundamental value, and that these deviations are brought about by the presence of traders who are not fully rational. A long-standing objection to this view that goes back to Friedman (1953) is that rational traders will quickly undo any dislocations caused by irrational traders. To illustrate the argument, suppose that the fundamental value of a share of Ford is $20. Imagine that a group of irrational traders becomes excessively pessimistic about Ford's future prospects and through its selling, pushes the price to $15. Defenders of the EMH argue that rational traders, sensing an attractive opportunity, will buy the security at its bargain price and at the same time, hedge their bet by shorting a "substitute" security, such as General Motors, that has similar cash flows to Ford in future states of the world. The buying pressure on Ford shares will then bring their price back to fundamental value.

Friedman's line of argument is initially compelling, but it has not survived careful theoretical scrutiny. In essence, it is based on two assertions. First, as soon as there is a deviation from fundamental value—in short, a mispricing—an attractive investment opportunity is created. Second, rational traders will immediately snap up the opportunity, thereby correcting the mispricing. Behavioral finance does not take issue with the second step in this argument: when attractive investment opportunities come to light, it is hard to believe that they are not quickly exploited. Rather, it disputes the first step. The argument, which we elaborate on in sections 2.2 and 2.3, is that even when an asset is wildly mispriced, strategies designed to correct the mispricing can be both risky and costly, rendering them unattractive. As a result, the mispricing can remain unchallenged.

It is interesting to think about common finance terminology in this light. While irrational traders are often known as "noise traders," rational traders are typically referred to as "arbitrageurs." Strictly speaking, an arbitrage is an investment strategy that offers riskless profits at no cost. Presumably, the rational traders in Friedman's fable became known as arbitrageurs because of the belief that a mispriced asset immediately creates an opportunity for riskless profits. Behavioral finance argues that this is *not* true: the strategies that Friedman would have his rational traders adopt are not necessarily arbitrages; quite often, they are very risky.

An immediate corollary of this line of thinking is that "prices are right" and "there is no free lunch" are *not* equivalent statements. While both are true in an efficient market, "no free lunch" can also be true in an inefficient market: just because prices are away from fundamental value does not necessarily mean that there are any excess risk-adjusted average returns for the taking. In other words,

$$\text{"prices are right"} \Rightarrow \text{"no free lunch"}$$

but

$$\text{"no free lunch"} \nRightarrow \text{"prices are right"}.$$

This distinction is important for evaluating the ongoing debate on market efficiency. First, many researchers still point to the inability of professional money managers to beat the market as strong evidence of market efficiency (Rubinstein 2001, Ross 2001). Underlying this argument, though, is the assumption that "no free lunch" implies "prices are right." If, as we argue in sections 2.2 and 2.3, this link is broken, the performance of money managers tells us little about whether prices reflect fundamental value.

Second, while some researchers accept that there is a distinction between "prices are right" and "there is no free lunch," they believe that the debate should be more about the latter statement than about the former. We disagree with this emphasis. As economists, our ultimate concern is that capital be allocated to the most promising investment opportunities. Whether this is true or not depends much more on whether prices are right than on whether there are any free lunches for the taking.

2.2 Theory

In the previous section, we emphasized the idea that when a mispricing occurs, strategies designed to correct it can be both risky and costly, thereby allowing the mispricing to survive. Here we discuss some of the risks and costs that have been identified. In our discussion, we return to the example of Ford, whose fundamental value is $20, but which has been pushed down to $15 by pessimistic noise traders.

Fundamental Risk.   The most obvious risk an arbitrageur faces if he buys Ford's stock at $15 is that a piece of bad news about Ford's fundamental value causes the stock to fall further, leading to losses. Of course, arbitrageurs are well aware of this risk, which is why they short a substitute security such as General Motors at the same time that they buy Ford. The problem is that substitute securities are rarely perfect, and often highly imperfect, making it impossible to remove all the fundamental risk. Shorting General Motors protects the arbitrageur somewhat from adverse news about the car industry as a whole, but still leaves him vulnerable to news that is specific to Ford—news about defective tires, say.[4]

Noise Trader Risk. Noise trader risk, an idea introduced by De Long et al. (1990a) and studied further by Shleifer and Vishny (1997), is the risk that the mispricing being exploited by the arbitrageur worsens in the short run. Even if General Motors is a perfect substitute security for Ford, the arbitrageur still faces the risk that the pessimistic investors causing Ford to be undervalued in the first place become even more pessimistic, lowering its price even further. Once one has granted the possibility that a security's price can be different from its fundamental value, then one must also grant the possibility that future price movements will increase the divergence.

Noise trader risk matters because it can force arbitrageurs to liquidate their positions early, bringing them potentially steep losses. To see this, note that most real-world arbitrageurs—in other words, professional portfolio managers—are not managing their own money, but rather managing money for other people. In the words of Shleifer and Vishny (1997), there is "a separation of brains and capital."

This agency feature has important consequences. Investors, lacking the specialized knowledge to evaluate the arbitrageur's strategy, may simply evaluate him based on his returns. If a mispricing that the arbitrageur is trying to exploit worsens in the short run, generating negative returns, investors may decide that he is incompetent, and withdraw their funds. If this happens, the arbitrageur will be forced to liquidate his position prematurely. Fear of such premature liquidation makes him less aggressive in combating the mispricing in the first place.

These problems can be severely exacerbated by creditors. After poor short-term returns, creditors, seeing the value of their collateral erode, will call their loans, again triggering premature liquidation.

In these scenarios, the forced liquidation is brought about by the worsening of the mispricing itself. This need not always be the case. For example, in their efforts to remove fundamental risk, many arbitrageurs sell securities short. Should the original owner of the borrowed security want it back, the arbitrageur may again be forced to close out his position if he cannot find other shares to borrow. The risk that this occurs during a temporary

---

[4] Another problem is that even if a substitute security exists, it may itself be mispriced. This can happen in situations involving industry-wide mispricing: in that case, the only stocks with similar future cash flows to the mispriced one are themselves mispriced.

worsening of the mispricing makes the arbitrageur more cautious from the start.

Implementation Costs. Well-understood transaction costs such as commissions, bid–ask spreads and price impact can make it less attractive to exploit a mispricing. Since shorting is often essential to the arbitrage process, we also include short-sale constraints in the implementation costs category. These refer to anything that makes it less attractive to establish a short position than a long one. The simplest such constraint is the fee charged for borrowing a stock. In general these fees are small—D'Avolio (2002) finds that for most stocks, they range between 10 and 15 basis points—but they can be much larger; in some cases, arbitrageurs may not be able to find shares to borrow at *any* price. Other than the fees themselves, there can be legal constraints: for a large fraction of money managers—many pension fund and mutual fund managers in particular—short-selling is simply not allowed.[5]

We also include in this category the cost of finding and learning about a mispricing, as well as the cost of the resources needed to exploit it (Merton 1987). Finding mispricing, in particular, can be a tricky matter. It was once thought that if noise traders influenced stock prices to any substantial degree, their actions would quickly show up in the form of predictability in returns. Shiller (1984) and Summers (1986) demonstrate that this argument is completely erroneous, with Shiller calling it "one of the most remarkable errors in the history of economic thought." They show that even if noise trader demand is so strong as to cause a large and persistent mispricing, it may generate so little predictability in returns as to be virtually undetectable.

In contrast, then, to straightforward-sounding textbook arbitrage, real world arbitrage entails both costs and risks, which under some conditions will limit arbitrage and allow deviations from fundamental value to persist. To see what these conditions are, consider two cases.

Suppose first that the mispriced security does *not* have a close substitute. By definition then, the arbitrageur is exposed to fundamental risk. In this case, sufficient conditions for arbitrage to be limited are: (1) that arbitrageurs are risk averse and (2) that the fundamental risk is systematic, in that it cannot

---

[5] The presence of per-period transaction costs like lending fees can expose arbitrageurs to another kind of risk, *horizon risk*, which is the risk that the mispricing takes so long to close that any profits are swamped by the accumulated transaction costs. This applies even when the arbitrageur is certain that no outside party will force him to liquidate early. Abreu and Brunnermeier (2002) study a particular type of horizon risk, which they label *synchronization risk*. Suppose that the elimination of a mispricing requires the participation of a sufficiently large number of separate arbitrageurs. Then in the presence of per-period transaction costs, arbitrageurs may hesitate to exploit the mispricing because they don't know how many *other* arbitrageurs have heard about the opportunity, and therefore how long they will have to wait before prices revert to correct values.

be diversified by taking many such positions. Condition (1) ensures that the mispricing will not be wiped out by a single arbitrageur taking a large position in the mispriced security. Condition (2) ensures that the mispricing will not be wiped out by a large number of investors each adding a *small* position in the mispriced security to their current holdings. The presence of noise trader risk or implementation costs will only limit arbitrage further.

Even if a perfect substitute does exist, arbitrage can still be limited. The existence of the substitute security immunizes the arbitrageur from fundamental risk. We can go further and assume that there are no implementation costs, so that only noise trader risk remains. De Long et al. (1990a) show that noise trader risk is powerful enough, that even with this single form of risk, arbitrage can sometimes be limited. The sufficient conditions are similar to those above, with one important difference. Here arbitrage will be limited if: (1) arbitrageurs are risk averse *and have short horizons* and (2) the noise trader risk is systematic. As before, condition (1) ensures that the mispricing cannot be wiped out by a single, large arbitrageur, while condition (2) prevents a large number of small investors from exploiting the mispricing. The central contribution of Shleifer and Vishny (1997) is to point out the real-world relevance of condition (1): the possibility of an early, forced liquidation means that many arbitrageurs effectively have short horizons.

In the presence of certain implementation costs, condition (2) may not even be necessary. If it is costly to learn about a mispricing, or the resources required to exploit it are expensive, that may be enough to explain why a large number of different individuals do not intervene in an attempt to correct the mispricing.

It is also important to note that for particular types of noise trading, arbitrageurs may prefer to trade in the *same* direction as the noise traders, thereby exacerbating the mispricing, rather than against them. For example, De Long et al. (1990b) consider an economy with positive feedback traders, who buy more of an asset this period if it performed well last period. If these noise traders push an asset's price above fundamental value, arbitrageurs do not sell or short the asset. Rather, they *buy* it, knowing that the earlier price rise will attract more feedback traders next period, leading to still higher prices, at which point the arbitrageurs can exit at a profit.

So far, we have argued that it is not easy for arbitrageurs like hedge funds to exploit market inefficiencies. However, hedge funds are not the only market participants trying to take advantage of noise traders: firm managers also play this game. If a manager believes that investors are overvaluing his firm's shares, he can benefit the firm's existing shareholders by issuing extra shares at attractive prices. The extra supply this generates could potentially push prices back to fundamental value.

Unfortunately, this game entails risks and costs for managers, just as it does for hedge funds. Issuing shares is an expensive process, both in terms of underwriting fees and time spent by company management. Moreover, the manager can rarely be sure that investors are overvaluing his firm's shares. If he issues shares, thinking that they are overvalued when in fact they are not, he incurs the costs of deviating from his target capital structure, without getting any benefits in return.

2.3. Evidence

From the theoretical point of view, there is reason to believe that arbitrage is a risky process and therefore that it is only of limited effectiveness. But is there any *evidence* that arbitrage is limited? In principle, any example of persistent mispricing is immediate evidence of limited arbitrage: if arbitrage were not limited, the mispricing would quickly disappear. The problem is that while many pricing phenomena can be interpreted as deviations from fundamental value, it is only in a few cases that the presence of a mispricing can be established beyond any reasonable doubt. The reason for this is what Fama (1970) dubbed the "joint hypothesis problem." In order to claim that the price of a security differs from its properly discounted future cash flows, one needs a model of "proper" discounting. Any test of mispricing is therefore inevitably a *joint* test of mispricing and of a model of discount rates, making it difficult to provide definitive evidence of inefficiency.

In spite of this difficulty, researchers have uncovered a number of financial market phenomena that are almost certainly mispricings, and persistent ones at that. These examples show that arbitrage is indeed limited, and also serve as interesting illustrations of the risks and costs described earlier.

2.3.1. TWIN SHARES

In 1907, Royal Dutch and Shell Transport, at the time completely independent companies, agreed to merge their interests on a 60:40 basis while remaining separate entities. Shares of Royal Dutch, which are primarily traded in the United States and in the Netherlands, are a claim to 60 percent of the total cash flow of the two companies, while Shell, which trades primarily in the United Kingdom, is a claim to the remaining 40 percent. If prices equal fundamental value, the market value of Royal Dutch equity should always be 1.5 times the market value of Shell equity. Remarkably, it isn't.

Figure 1.1, taken from Froot and Dabora's (1999) analysis of this case, shows the ratio of Royal Dutch equity value to Shell equity value relative to the efficient markets benchmark of 1.5. The picture provides strong evidence of a persistent inefficiency. Moreover, the deviations are not small. Royal Dutch is sometimes 35 percent underpriced relative to parity, and sometimes 15 percent overpriced.

This evidence of mispricing is simultaneously evidence of limited arbitrage, and it is not hard to see why arbitrage might be limited in this case. If an arbitrageur wanted to exploit this phenomenon—and several hedge funds, Long-Term Capital Management included, did try to—he would buy the

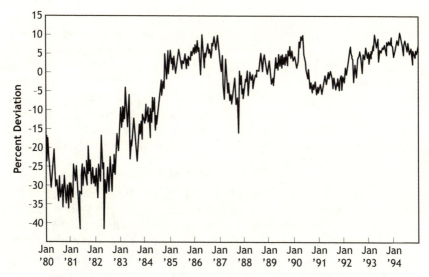

Figure 1.1. Log deviations from Royal Dutch/Shell parity. *Source*: Froot and Dabora (1999).

relatively undervalued share and short the other. Table 1.1 summarizes the risks facing the arbitrageur. Since one share is a good substitute for the other, fundamental risk is nicely hedged: news about fundamentals should affect the two shares equally, leaving the arbitrageur immune. Nor are there any major implementation costs to speak of: shorting shares of either company is an easy matter.

The one risk that remains is noise trader risk. Whatever investor sentiment is causing one share to be undervalued relative to the other could also cause that share to become *even more* undervalued in the short term. The graph shows that this danger is very real: an arbitrageur buying a 10 percent undervalued Royal Dutch share in March 1983 would have seen it drop still further in value over the next six months. As discussed earlier,

TABLE 1.1
Arbitrage Costs and Risks That Arise in Exploiting Mispricing

Example	Fundamental Risk (FR)	Noise Trader Risk (NTR)	Implementation Costs (IC)
Royal Dutch/Shell	×	√	×
Index Inclusions	√	√	×
Palm/3Com	×	×	√

when a mispriced security has a perfect substitute, arbitrage can still be limited if (1) arbitrageurs are risk averse and have short horizons and (2) the noise trader risk is systematic, or the arbitrage requires specialized skills, or there are costs to learning about such opportunities. It is very plausible that both (1) and (2) are true, thereby explaining why the mispricing persisted for so long. It took until 2001 for the shares to finally sell at par.

This example also provides a nice illustration of the distinction between "prices are right" and "no free lunch" discussed in section 2.1. While prices in this case are clearly *not* right, there are no easy profits for the taking.

2.3.2. INDEX INCLUSIONS

Every so often, one of the companies in the S&P 500 is taken out of the index because of a merger or bankruptcy, and is replaced by another firm. Two early studies of such index inclusions, Harris and Gurel (1986) and Shleifer (1986), document a remarkable fact: when a stock is added to the index, it jumps in price by an average of 3.5 percent, and much of this jump is permanent. In one dramatic illustration of this phenomenon, when Yahoo was added to the index, its shares jumped by 24 percent in a single day.

The fact that a stock jumps in value upon inclusion is once again clear evidence of mispricing: the price of the share changes even though its fundamental value does not. Standard and Poor's emphasizes that in selecting stocks for inclusion, they are simply trying to make their index representative of the U.S. economy, not to convey any information about the level or riskiness of a firm's future cash flows.[6]

This example of a deviation from fundamental value is also evidence of limited arbitrage. When one thinks about the risks involved in trying to exploit the anomaly, its persistence becomes less surprising. An arbitrageur needs to short the included security and to buy as good a substitute security as he can. This entails considerable fundamental risk because individual stocks rarely have good substitutes. It also carries substantial noise trader risk: whatever caused the initial jump in price—in all likelihood, buying by S&P 500 index funds—may continue, and cause the price to rise still further in the short run; indeed, Yahoo went from $115 prior to its S&P inclusion announcement to $210 a month later.

Wurgler and Zhuravskaya (2002) provide additional support for the limited arbitrage view of S&P 500 inclusions. They hypothesize that the jump

---

[6] After the initial studies on index inclusions appeared, some researchers argued that the price increase might be rationally explained through information or liquidity effects. While such explanations cannot be completely ruled out, the case for mispricing was considerably strengthened by Kaul, Mehrotra, and Morck (2000). They consider the case of the TS300 index of Canadian equities, which in 1996 changed the weights of some of its component stocks to meet an innocuous regulatory requirement. The reweighting was accompanied by significant price effects. Since the affected stocks were already in the index at the time of the event, information and liquidity explanations for the price jumps are extremely implausible.

upon inclusion should be particularly large for those stocks with the worst substitute securities, in other words, for those stocks for which the arbitrage is riskiest. By constructing the best possible substitute portfolio for each included stock, they are able to test this, and find strong support. Their analysis also shows just how hard it is to find good substitute securities for individual stocks. For most regressions of included stock returns on the returns of the best substitute securities, the R^2 is below 25 percent.

2.3.3. INTERNET CARVE-OUTS

In March 2000, 3Com sold 5 percent of its wholly owned subsidiary Palm Inc. in an initial public offering, retaining ownership of the remaining 95 percent. After the IPO, a shareholder of 3Com indirectly owned 1.5 shares of Palm. 3Com also announced its intention to spin-off the remainder of Palm within nine months, at which time they would give each 3Com shareholder 1.5 shares of Palm.

At the close of trading on the first day after the IPO, Palm shares stood at $95, putting a lower bound on the value of 3Com at $142. In fact, 3Com's price was $81, implying a market valuation of 3Com's substantial businesses outside of Palm of about –$60 per share!

This situation surely represents a severe mispricing, and it persisted for several weeks. To exploit it, an arbitrageur could buy one share of 3Com, short 1.5 shares of Palm, and wait for the spin-off, thus earning certain profits at no cost. This strategy entails no fundamental risk and no noise trader risk. Why, then, is arbitrage limited? Lamont and Thaler (2003), who analyze this case in detail, argue that implementation costs played a major role. Many investors who tried to borrow Palm shares to short were either told by their broker that no shares were available, or else were quoted a very high borrowing price. This barrier to shorting was not a legal one, but one that arose endogenously in the marketplace: such was the demand for shorting Palm, that the supply of Palm shorts was unable to meet it. Arbitrage was therefore limited, and the mispricing persisted.[7]

Some financial economists react to these examples by arguing that they are simply isolated instances with little broad relevance.[8] We think this is an overly complacent view. The "twin shares" example illustrates that in situations where arbitrageurs face only one type of risk—noise trader risk—securities can become mispriced by almost 35 percent. This suggests that if a typical stock trading on the NYSE or NASDAQ becomes subject to investor sentiment, the mispricing could be an order of magnitude larger. Not

---

[7] See also Mitchell, Pulvino, and Stafford (2002) and Ofek and Richardson (2003) for further discussion of such "negative stub" situations, in which the market value of a company is less than the sum of its publicly traded parts.

[8] During a discussion of these issues at a University of Chicago seminar, one economist argued that these examples are "the tip of the iceberg," to which another retorted that "they *are* the iceberg."

only would arbitrageurs face noise trader risk in trying to correct the mis-pricing, but fundamental risk as well, not to mention implementation costs.

3. Psychology

The theory of limited arbitrage shows that if irrational traders cause devia-tions from fundamental value, rational traders will often be powerless to do anything about it. In order to say more about the structure of these devi-ations, behavioral models often assume a specific form of irrationality. For guidance on this, economists turn to the extensive experimental evidence compiled by cognitive psychologists on the systematic biases that arise when people form beliefs, and on people's preferences.[9]

In this section, we summarize the psychology that may be of particular interest to financial economists. Our discussion of each finding is necessar-ily brief. For a deeper understanding of the phenomena we touch on, we refer the reader to the surveys of Camerer (1995) and Rabin (1998) and to the edited volumes of Kahneman, Slovic, and Tversky (1982), Kahneman and Tversky (2000) and Gilovich, Griffin, and Kahneman (2002).

3.1. Beliefs

A crucial component of any model of financial markets is a specification of how agents form expectations. We now summarize what psychologists have learned about how people appear to form beliefs in practice.

Overconfidence. Extensive evidence shows that people are overconfident in their judgments. This appears in two guises. First, the confidence inter-vals people assign to their estimates of quantities—the level of the Dow in a year, say—are far too narrow. Their 98 percent confidence intervals, for ex-ample, include the true quantity only about 60 percent of the time (Alpert and Raiffa 1982). Second, people are poorly calibrated when estimating probabilities: events they think are certain to occur actually occur only around 80 percent of the time, and events they deem impossible occur ap-proximately 20 percent of the time (Fischhoff, Slovic, and Lichtenstein 1977).[10]

---

[9] We emphasize, however, that behavioral models do not *need* to make extensive psycho-logical assumptions in order to generate testable predictions. In section 6, we discuss Lee, Shleifer, and Thaler's (1991) theory of closed-end fund pricing. That theory makes numerous crisp predictions using only the assumptions that there are noise traders with correlated senti-ment in the economy, and that arbitrage is limited.

[10] Overconfidence may in part stem from two other biases, self-attribution bias and hind-sight bias. Self-attribution bias refers to people's tendency to ascribe any success they have in some activity to their own talents, while blaming failure on bad luck, rather than on their

Optimism and Wishful Thinking.   Most people display unrealistically rosy views of their abilities and prospects (Weinstein 1980). Typically, over 90 percent of those surveyed think they are above average in such domains as driving skill, ability to get along with people, and sense of humor. They also display a systematic planning fallacy: they predict that tasks (such as writing survey papers) will be completed much sooner than they actually are (Buehler, Griffin, and Ross 1994).

Representativeness.   Kahneman and Tversky (1974) show that when people try to determine the probability that a data set A was generated by a model B, or that an object A belongs to a class B, they often use the representativeness heuristic. This means that they evaluate the probability by the degree to which A reflects the essential characteristics of B.

Much of the time, representativeness is a helpful heuristic, but it can generate some severe biases. The first is *base rate neglect*. To illustrate, Kahneman and Tversky present this description of a person named Linda:

> *Linda is thirty-one years old, single, outspoken, and very bright. She majored in philosophy. As a student, she was deeply concerned with issues of discrimination and social justice, and also participated in antinuclear demonstrations.*

When asked which of "Linda is a bank teller" (statement A) and "Linda is a bank teller and is active in the feminist movement" (statement B) is more likely, subjects typically assign greater probability to B. This is, of course, impossible. Representativeness provides a simple explanation. The description of Linda *sounds* like the description of a feminist—it is representative of a feminist—leading subjects to pick B. Put differently, while Bayes's law says that

$$p(\text{statement B}|\text{description}) = \frac{p(\text{description}|\text{statement B})\, p(\text{statement B})}{p(\text{description})},$$

people apply the law incorrectly, putting too much weight on p (description | statement B), which captures representativeness, and too little weight on the base rate, p (statement B).

Representativeness also leads to another bias, *sample-size neglect*. When judging the likelihood that a data set was generated by a particular model,

---

ineptitude. Doing this repeatedly will lead people to the pleasing but erroneous conclusion that they are very talented. For example, investors might become overconfident after several quarters of investing success (Gervais and Odean 2001). Hindsight bias is the tendency of people to believe, after an event has occurred, that they predicted it before it happened. If people think they predicted the past better than they actually did, they may also believe that they can predict the future better than they actually can.

people often fail to take the size of the sample into account: after all, a small sample can be just as representative as a large one. Six tosses of a coin resulting in three heads and three tails are as representative of a fair coin as 500 heads and 500 tails are in a total of 1,000 tosses. Representativeness implies that people will find the two sets of tosses equally informative about the fairness of the coin, even though the second set is much more so.

Sample-size neglect means that in cases where people do not initially know the data-generating process, they will tend to infer it too quickly on the basis of too few data points. For instance, they will come to believe that a financial analyst with four good stock picks is talented because four successes are not representative of a bad or mediocre analyst. It also generates a "hot hand" phenomenon, whereby sports fans become convinced that a basketball player who has made three shots in a row is on a hot streak and will score again, even though there is no evidence of a hot hand in the data (Gilovich, Vallone, and Tversky 1985). This belief that even small samples will reflect the properties of the parent population is sometimes known as the "law of small numbers" (Rabin 2002).

In situations where people *do* know the data-generating process in advance, the law of small numbers leads to a gambler's fallacy effect. If a fair coin generates five heads in a row, people will say that "tails are due." Since they believe that even a short sample should be representative of the fair coin, there have to be more tails to balance out the large number of heads.

Conservatism. While representativeness leads to an underweighting of base rates, there are situations where base rates are over-emphasized relative to sample evidence. In an experiment run by Edwards (1968), there are two urns, one containing 3 blue balls and 7 red ones, and the other containing 7 blue balls and 3 red ones. A random draw of 12 balls, with replacement, from one of the urns yields 8 reds and 4 blues. What is the probability the draw was made from the first urn? While the correct answer is 0.97, most people estimate a number around 0.7, apparently overweighting the base rate of 0.5.

At first sight, the evidence of conservatism appears at odds with representativeness. However, there may be a natural way in which they fit together. It appears that if a data sample is representative of an underlying model, then people overweight the data. However, if the data is not representative of any salient model, people react too little to the data and rely too much on their priors. In Edwards's experiment, the draw of 8 red and 4 blue balls is not particularly representative of either urn, possibly leading to an overreliance on prior information.[11]

---

[11] Mullainathan (2001) presents a formal model that neatly reconciles the evidence on underweighting sample information with the evidence on overweighting sample information.

Belief Perseverance. There is much evidence that once people have formed an opinion, they cling to it too tightly and for too long (Lord, Ross, and Lepper 1979). At least two effects appear to be at work. First, people are reluctant to search for evidence that contradicts their beliefs. Second, even if they find such evidence, they treat it with excessive skepticism. Some studies have found an even stronger effect, known as confirmation bias, whereby people misinterpret evidence that goes against their hypothesis as actually being in their favor. In the context of academic finance, belief perseverance predicts that if people start out believing in the Efficient Markets Hypothesis, they may continue to believe in it long after compelling evidence to the contrary has emerged.

Anchoring. Kahneman and Tversky (1974) argue that when forming estimates, people often start with some initial, possibly arbitrary value, and then adjust away from it. Experimental evidence shows that the adjustment is often insufficient. Put differently, people "anchor" too much on the initial value.

In one experiment, subjects were asked to estimate the percentage of United Nations countries that are African. More specifically, before giving a percentage, they were asked whether their guess was higher or lower than a randomly generated number between 0 and 100. Their subsequent estimates were significantly affected by the initial random number. Those who were asked to compare their estimate to 10, subsequently estimated 25 percent, while those who compared to 60, estimated 45 percent.

Availability Biases. When judging the probability of an event—the likelihood of getting mugged in Chicago, say—people often search their memories for relevant information. While this is a perfectly sensible procedure, it can produce biased estimates because not all memories are equally retrievable or "available," in the language of Kahneman and Tversky (1974). More recent events and more salient events—the mugging of a close friend, say—will weigh more heavily and distort the estimate.

Economists are sometimes wary of this body of experimental evidence because they believe (1) that people, through repetition, will learn their way out of biases; (2) that experts in a field, such as traders in an investment bank, will make fewer errors; and (3) that with more powerful incentives, the effects will disappear.

While all these factors can attenuate biases to some extent, there is little evidence that they wipe them out altogether. The effect of learning is often muted by errors of application: when the bias is explained, people often understand it, but then immediately proceed to violate it again in specific applications. Expertise, too, is often a hindrance rather than a help: experts, armed with their sophisticated models, have been found to exhibit *more* overconfidence than laymen, particularly when they receive only limited feedback about their predictions. Finally, in a review of dozens of studies on the topic, Camerer and Hogarth (1999, p. 7) conclude that while incentives can sometimes reduce the biases people display, "no replicated study has made rationality violations disappear purely by raising incentives."

3.2. Preferences

3.2.1. PROSPECT THEORY

An essential ingredient of any model trying to understand asset prices or trading behavior is an assumption about investor preferences, or about how investors evaluate risky gambles. The vast majority of models assume that investors evaluate gambles according to the expected utility framework, EU henceforth. The theoretical motivation for this goes back to von Neumann and Morgenstern (1944), VNM henceforth, who show that if preferences satisfy a number of plausible axioms—completeness, transitivity, continuity, and independence—then they can be represented by the expectation of a utility function.

Unfortunately, experimental work in the decades after VNM has shown that people systematically violate EU theory when choosing among risky gambles. In response to this, there has been an explosion of work on so-called non-EU theories, all of them trying to do a better job of matching the experimental evidence. Some of the better known models include weighted-utility theory (Chew and MacCrimmon 1979, Chew 1983), implicit EU (Chew 1989, Dekel 1986), disappointment aversion (Gul 1991), regret theory (Bell 1982, Loomes and Sugden 1982), rank-dependent utility theories (Quiggin 1982; Segal 1987, 1989; Yaari 1987), and prospect theory (Kahneman and Tversky 1979, Tversky and Kahneman 1992).

Should financial economists be interested in any of these alternatives to expected utility? It may be that EU theory is a good approximation to how people evaluate a risky gamble like the stock market, even if it does not explain attitudes to the kinds of gambles studied in experimental settings. On the other hand, the difficulty the EU approach has encountered in trying to explain basic facts about the stock market suggests that it may be worth taking a closer look at the experimental evidence. Indeed, recent work in behavioral finance has argued that some of the lessons we learn from violations of EU are central to understanding a number of financial phenomena.

Of all the non-EU theories, prospect theory may be the most promising for financial applications, and we discuss it in detail. The reason we focus on this theory is, quite simply, that it is the most successful at capturing the experimental results. In a way, this is not surprising. Most of the other

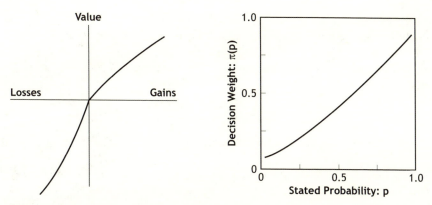

Figure 1.2. The two panels show Kahneman and Tversky's (1979) proposed value function v and probability weighting function π.

non-EU models are what might be called quasi-normative, in that they try to capture some of the anomalous experimental evidence by slightly weakening the VNM axioms. The difficulty with such models is that in trying to achieve two goals—normative and descriptive—they end up doing an unsatisfactory job at both. In contrast, prospect theory has no aspirations as a normative theory: it simply tries to capture people's attitudes to risky gambles as parsimoniously as possible. Indeed, Tversky and Kahneman (1986) argue convincingly that normative approaches are doomed to failure, because people routinely make choices that are simply impossible to justify on normative grounds, in that they violate dominance or invariance.

Kahneman and Tversky (1979), KT henceforth, lay out the original version of prospect theory, designed for gambles with at most two nonzero outcomes. They propose that when offered a gamble

$$(x, p; y, q),$$

to be read as "get outcome x with probability p, outcome y with probability q," where $x \leq 0 \leq y$ or $y \leq 0 \leq x$, people assign it a value of

$$\pi(p)v(x) + \pi(q)v(y), \tag{1}$$

where v and π are shown in figure 1.2. When choosing between different gambles, they pick the one with the highest value.

This formulation has a number of important features. First, utility is defined over gains and losses rather than over final wealth positions, an idea first proposed by Markowitz (1952). This fits naturally with the way gambles are often presented and discussed in everyday life. More generally, it is consistent with the way people perceive attributes such as brightness, loudness, or temperature relative to earlier levels, rather than in absolute terms.

Kahneman and Tversky (1979) also offer the following violation of EU as evidence that people focus on gains and losses. Subjects are asked:[12]

In addition to whatever you own, you have been given 1000. Now choose between

$$A = (1000, 0.5)$$
$$B = (500, 1).$$

B was the more popular choice. The same subjects were then asked:

In addition to whatever you own, you have been given 2000. Now choose between

$$C = (-1000, 0.5)$$
$$D = (-500, 1).$$

This time, *C* was more popular.

Note that the two problems are identical in terms of their final wealth positions and yet people choose differently. The subjects are apparently focusing only on gains and losses. Indeed, when they are not given any information about prior winnings, they choose *B* over *A* and *C* over *D*.

The second important feature is the shape of the value function v, namely its concavity in the domain of gains and convexity in the domain of losses. Put simply, people are risk averse over gains, and risk-seeking over losses. Simple evidence for this comes from the fact just mentioned, namely that in the absence of any information about prior winnings[13]

$$B \succ A, \quad C \succ D.$$

The v function also has a kink at the origin, indicating a greater sensitivity to losses than to gains, a feature known as *loss aversion*. Loss aversion is introduced to capture aversion to bets of the form:

$$E = (110, \tfrac{1}{2}; \quad -100, \tfrac{1}{2}).$$

It may seem surprising that we need to depart from the expected utility framework in order to understand attitudes to gambles as simple as *E*, but it is nonetheless true. In a remarkable paper, Rabin (2000) shows that if an expected utility maximizer rejects gamble *E* at all wealth levels, then he will also reject

$$(20000000, \tfrac{1}{2}; \quad -1000, \tfrac{1}{2}),$$

an utterly implausible prediction. The intuition is simple: if a smooth, increasing, and concave utility function defined over final wealth has sufficient

---

[12] All the experiments in Kahneman and Tversky (1979) are conducted in terms of Israeli currency. The authors note that at the time of their research, the median monthly family income was about 3,000 Israeli lira.

[13] In this section $G_1 \succ G_2$ should be read as "a statistically significant fraction of Kahneman and Tversky's subjects preferred G_1 to G_2."

local curvature to reject E over a wide range of wealth levels, it must be an extraordinarily concave function, making the investor extremely risk averse over large stakes gambles.

The final piece of prospect theory is the nonlinear probability transformation. Small probabilities are overweighted, so that $\pi(p) > p$. This is deduced from KT's finding that

$$(5000, 0.001) \succ (5, 1),$$

and

$$(-5, 1) \succ (-5000, 0.001),$$

together with the earlier assumption that v is concave (convex) in the domain of gains (losses). Moreover, people are more sensitive to differences in probabilities at higher probability levels. For example, the following pair of choices,

$$(3000, 1) \succ (4000, 0.8; 0, 0.2),$$

and

$$(4000, 0.2; 0, 0.8) \succ (3000, 0.25),$$

which violate EU theory, imply

$$\frac{\pi(0.25)}{\pi(0.2)} < \frac{\pi(1)}{\pi(0.8)}.$$

The intuition is that the 20 percent jump in probability from 0.8 to 1 is more striking to people than the 20 percent jump from 0.2 to 0.25. In particular, people place much more weight on outcomes that are certain relative to outcomes that are merely probable, a feature sometimes known as the "certainty effect."

Along with capturing experimental evidence, prospect theory also simultaneously explains preferences for insurance and for buying lottery tickets. Although the concavity of v in the region of gains generally produces risk aversion, for lotteries which offer a small chance of a large gain, the overweighting of small probabilities in figure 1.2 dominates, leading to risk-seeking. Along the same lines, while the convexity of v in the region of losses typically leads to risk-seeking, the same overweighting of small probabilities induces risk aversion over gambles which have a small chance of a large loss.

Based on additional evidence, Tversky and Kahneman (1992) propose a generalization of prospect theory which can be applied to gambles with more than two outcomes. Specifically, if a gamble promises outcome x_i with probability p_i, Tversky and Kahneman (1992) propose that people assign the gamble the value

$$\sum_i \pi_i v(x_i), \tag{2}$$

where

$$v = \begin{cases} x^\alpha & \text{if } x \geq 0 \\ -\lambda(-x)^\alpha & \text{if } x < 0 \end{cases}$$

and

$$\pi_i = w(P_i) - w(P_i^*),$$

$$w(P) = \frac{P^\gamma}{(P^\gamma + (1-P)^\gamma)^{1/\gamma}}.$$

Here, P_i (P_i^*) is the probability that the gamble will yield an outcome at least as good as (strictly better than) x_i. Tversky and Kahneman (1992) use experimental evidence to estimate $\alpha = 0.88$, $\lambda = 2.25$, and $\gamma = 0.65$. Note that λ is the coefficient of loss aversion, a measure of the relative sensitivity to gains and losses. Over a wide range of experimental contexts λ has been estimated in the neighborhood of 2.

Earlier in this section, we saw how prospect theory could explain why people made different choices in situations with identical final wealth levels. This illustrates an important feature of the theory, namely that it can accommodate the effects of problem description, or of *framing*. Such effects are powerful. There are numerous demonstrations of a 30 to 40 percent shift in preferences depending on the wording of a problem. No normative theory of choice can accommodate such behavior since a first principle of rational choice is that choices should be independent of the problem description or representation.

Framing refers to the way a problem is posed for the decision maker. In many actual choice contexts the decision maker also has flexibility in how to think about the problem. For example, suppose that a gambler goes to the race track and wins $200 in his first bet, but then loses $50 on his second bet. Does he code the outcome of the second bet as a loss of $50 or as a reduction in his recently won gain of $200? In other words, is the utility of the second loss $v(-50)$ or $v(150) - v(200)$? The process by which people formulate such problems for themselves is called *mental accounting* (Thaler 2000). Mental accounting matters because in prospect theory, v is nonlinear.

One important feature of mental accounting is *narrow framing*, which is the tendency to treat individual gambles separately from other portions of wealth. In other words, when offered a gamble, people often evaluate it as if it is the only gamble they face in the world, rather than merging it with pre-existing bets to see if the new bet is a worthwhile addition.

Redelmeier and Tversky (1992) provide a simple illustration, based on the gamble

$$F = (2000, \tfrac{1}{2}; \ -500, \tfrac{1}{2}).$$

Subjects in their experiment were asked whether they were willing to take this bet; 57 percent said they would not. They were then asked whether they would prefer to play F five times or six times; 70 percent preferred the six-fold gamble. Finally they were asked:

Suppose that you have played F five times but you don't yet know your wins and losses. Would you play the gamble a sixth time?

Sixty percent rejected the opportunity to play a sixth time, reversing their preference from the earlier question. This suggests that some subjects are framing the sixth gamble narrowly, segregating it from the other gambles. Indeed, the 60 percent rejection level is very similar to the 57 percent rejection level for the one-off play of F.

3.2.2. AMBIGUITY AVERSION

Our discussion so far has centered on understanding how people act when the outcomes of gambles have known objective probabilities. In reality, probabilities are rarely objectively known. To handle these situations, Savage (1964) develops a counterpart to expected utility known as subjective expected utility, SEU henceforth. Under certain axioms, preferences can be represented by the expectation of a utility function, this time weighted by the individual's subjective probability assessment.

Experimental work in the last few decades has been as unkind to SEU as it was to EU. The violations this time are of a different nature, but they may be just as relevant for financial economists.

The classic experiment was described by Ellsberg (1961). Suppose that there are two urns, 1 and 2. Urn 2 contains a total of 100 balls, 50 red and 50 blue. Urn 1 also contains 100 balls, again a mix of red and blue, but the subject does not know the proportion of each.

Subjects are asked to choose one of the following two gambles, each of which involves a possible payment of $100, depending on the color of a ball drawn at random from the relevant urn

a_1: a ball is drawn from Urn 1, $100 if red, $0 if blue,
a_2: a ball is drawn from Urn 2, $100 if red, $0 if blue.

Subjects are then also asked to choose between the following two gambles:

b_1: a ball is drawn from Urn 1, $100 if blue, $0 if red,
b_2: a ball is drawn from Urn 2, $100 if blue, $0 if red.

a_2 is typically preferred to a_1, while b_2 is chosen over b_1. These choices are inconsistent with SEU: the choice of a_2 implies a subjective probability that *fewer* than 50 percent of the balls in Urn 1 are red, while the choice of b_2 implies the opposite.

The experiment suggests that people do not like situations where they are uncertain about the probability distribution of a gamble. Such situations are known as situations of ambiguity, and the general dislike for them, as ambiguity aversion.[14] SEU does not allow agents to express their degree of confidence about a probability distribution and therefore cannot capture such aversion.

Ambiguity aversion appears in a wide variety of contexts. For example, a researcher might ask a subject for his estimate of the probability that a certain team will win its upcoming football match, to which the subject might respond 0.4. The researcher then asks the subject to imagine a chance machine, which will display 1 with probability 0.4 and 0 otherwise, and asks whether the subject would prefer to bet on the football game—an ambiguous bet—or on the machine, which offers no ambiguity. In general, people prefer to bet on the machine, illustrating aversion to ambiguity.

Heath and Tversky (1991) argue that in the real world, ambiguity aversion has much to do with how competent an individual feels he is at assessing the relevant distribution. Ambiguity aversion over a bet can be strengthened by highlighting subjects' feelings of incompetence, either by showing them other bets in which they have more expertise, or by mentioning other people who are more qualified to evaluate the bet (Fox and Tversky 1995).

Further evidence that supports the competence hypothesis is that in situations where people feel especially competent in evaluating a gamble, the opposite of ambiguity aversion, namely a "preference for the familiar," has been observed. In the example above, people chosen to be especially knowledgeable about football often prefer to bet on the outcome of the game than on the chance machine. Just as with ambiguity aversion, such behavior cannot be captured by SEU.

4. APPLICATION: THE AGGREGATE STOCK MARKET

Researchers studying the aggregate U.S. stock market have identified a number of interesting facts about its behavior. Three of the most striking are:

The Equity Premium.   The stock market has historically earned a high excess rate of return. For example, using annual data from 1871 to 1993, Campbell and Cochrane (1999) report that the average log return on the

---

[14] An early discussion of this aversion can be found in Knight (1921), who defines risk as a gamble with known distribution and uncertainty as a gamble with unknown distribution, and suggests that people dislike uncertainty more than risk.

S&P 500 index is 3.9 percent higher than the average log return on short-term commercial paper.

Volatility.   Stock returns and price–dividend ratios are both highly variable. In the same data set, the annual standard deviation of excess log returns on the S&P 500 is 18 percent, while the annual standard deviation of the log price/dividend ratio is 0.27.

Predictability.   Stock returns are forecastable. Using monthly, real, equal-weighted NYSE returns from 1941 to 1986, Fama and French (1988) show that the dividend/price ratio is able to explain 27 percent of the variation of cumulative stock returns over the subsequent four years.[15]

All three of these facts can be labelled puzzles. The first fact has been known as the equity premium puzzle since the work of Mehra and Prescott (1985) (see also Hansen and Singleton 1983). Campbell (1999) calls the second fact the volatility puzzle and we refer to the third fact as the predictability puzzle. The reason they are called puzzles is that they are hard to rationalize in a simple consumption-based model.

To see this, consider the following endowment economy, which we come back to a number of times in this section. There are an infinite number of identical investors, and two assets: a risk-free asset in zero net supply, with gross return $R_{f,t}$ between time t and $t+1$, and a risky asset—the stock market—in fixed positive supply, with gross return R_{t+1} between time t and $t+1$. The stock market is a claim to a perishable stream of dividends $\{D_t\}$, where

$$\frac{D_{t+1}}{D_t} = \exp[g_D + \sigma_D \varepsilon_{t+1}], \qquad (3)$$

and where each period's dividend can be thought of as one component of a consumption endowment C_t, where

$$\frac{C_{t+1}}{C_t} = \exp[g_C + \sigma_C \eta_{t+1}], \qquad (4)$$

and

$$\begin{pmatrix} \varepsilon_t \\ \eta_t \end{pmatrix} \sim N\left(\begin{pmatrix} 0 \\ 0 \end{pmatrix}, \begin{pmatrix} 1 & \omega \\ \omega & 1 \end{pmatrix} \right), \quad \text{i.i.d. over time.} \qquad (5)$$

---

[15] These three facts are widely agreed on, but they are not completely uncontroversial. A large literature had debated the statistical significance of the time series predictability, while others have argued that the equity premium is overstated due to survivorship bias (Brown, Goetzmann and Ross 1995).

TABLE 1.2
Parameter Values for a Simple Consumption-based Model

Parameter	g_C	σ_C	g_D	σ_D	ω	γ	ρ
Value	1.84%	3.79%	1.5%	12.0%	0.15	1.0	0.98

Investors choose consumption C_t and an allocation S_t to the risky asset to maximize

$$E_0 \sum_{t=0}^{\infty} \rho^t \frac{C_t^{1-\gamma}}{1-\gamma},$$ (6)

subject to the standard budget constraint.[16] Using the Euler equation of optimality,

$$1 = \rho E_t \left[\left(\frac{C_{t+1}}{C_t} \right)^{-\gamma} R_{t+1} \right],$$ (7)

it is straightforward to derive expressions for stock returns and prices. The details are in the Appendix.

We can now examine the model's quantitative predictions for the parameter values in table 1.2. The endowment process parameters are taken from U.S. data spanning the twentieth century, and are standard in the literature. It is also standard to start out by considering *low* values of γ. The reason is that when one computes, for various values of γ, how much wealth an individual would be prepared to give up to avoid a large-scale timeless wealth gamble, low values of γ match best with introspection as to what the answers should be (Mankiw and Zeldes 1991). We take $\gamma = 1$, which corresponds to log utility.

In an economy with these parameter values, the average log return on the stock market would be just 0.1 percent higher than the risk-free rate, not the 3.9 percent observed historically. The standard deviation of log stock returns would be only 12 percent, not 18 percent, and the price/dividend ratio would be constant (implying, of course, that the dividend/price ratio has no forecast power for future returns).

It is useful to recall the intuition for these results. In an economy with power utility preferences, the equity premium is determined by risk aversion γ and by risk, measured as the covariance of stock returns and consumption growth. Since consumption growth is very smooth in the data, this covariance is very low, thus predicting a very low equity premium.

---

[16] For $\gamma = 1$, we replace $C_t^{1-\gamma}/1 - \gamma$ with $\log(C_t)$.

Stocks simply do not appear risky to investors with the preferences in Eq. (6) and with low γ, and therefore do not warrant a large premium. Of course, the equity premium predicted by the model can be increased by using higher values of γ. However, other than making counterintuitive predictions about individuals' attitudes to large-scale gambles, this would also predict a counterfactually high risk-free rate, a problem known as the risk-free rate puzzle (Weil 1989).

To understand the volatility puzzle, note that in the simple economy described above, both discount rates and expected dividend growth are constant over time. A direct application of the present value formula implies that the price/dividend ratio, P/D henceforth, is constant. Since

$$R_{t+1} = \frac{D_{t+1} + P_{t+1}}{P_t} = \frac{1 + P_{t+1}/D_{t+1}}{P_t/D_t} \frac{D_{t+1}}{D_t}, \tag{8}$$

it follows that

$$r_{t+1} = \Delta d_{t+1} + \text{const.} \equiv d_{t+1} - d_t + \text{const.}, \tag{9}$$

where lower case letters indicate log variables. The standard deviation of log returns will therefore only be as high as the standard deviation of log dividend growth, namely 12 percent.

The particular volatility puzzle seen here illustrates a more general point, first made by Shiller (1981) and LeRoy and Porter (1981), namely that it is difficult to explain the historical volatility of stock returns with any model in which investors are rational and discount rates are constant.

To see the intuition, consider the identity in Eq. (8) again. Since the volatility of log dividend growth is only 12 percent, the only way for a model to generate an 18 percent volatility of log returns is to introduce variation in the P/D ratio. But if discount rates are constant, a quick glance at a present-value formula shows that the only way to do that is to introduce variation in investors' forecasts of the dividend growth rate: a higher forecast raises the P/D ratio, a lower forecast brings it down. There is a catch here, though: if investors are rational, their expectations for dividend growth must, on average, be confirmed. In other words, times of higher (lower) P/D ratios should, on average, be followed by higher (lower) cash-flow growth. Unfortunately, price/dividend ratios are *not* reliable forecasters of dividend growth, neither in the United States nor in most international markets (see Campbell 1999, for recent evidence).

Shiller and LeRoy and Porter's results shocked the profession when they first appeared. At the time, most economists felt that discount rates *were* close to constant over time, apparently implying that stock market volatility could only be fully explained by appealing to investor irrationality. Today, it is well understood that rational variation in discount rates can help explain the volatility puzzle, although we argue later that models with irrational beliefs also offer a plausible way of thinking about the data.

Both the rational and behavioral approaches to finance have made progress in understanding the three puzzles singled out at the start of this section. The advances on the rational side are well described in other articles in this handbook. Here, we discuss the behavioral approaches, starting with the equity premium puzzle and then turning to the volatility puzzle.

We do not consider the predictability puzzle separately, because in any model with a stationary P/D ratio, a resolution of the volatility puzzle is simultaneously a resolution of the predictability puzzle. To see this, recall from Eq. (8) that any model which captures the empirical volatility of returns must involve variation in the P/D ratio. Moreover, for a model to be a *satisfactory* resolution of the volatility puzzle, it should not make the counterfactual prediction that P/D ratios forecast subsequent dividend growth. Now suppose that the P/D ratio is higher than average. The only way it can return to its mean is if cash flows D subsequently go up, or if prices P fall. Since the P/D ratio is not allowed to forecast cash flows, it must forecast lower returns, thereby explaining the predictability puzzle.

4.1. The Equity Premium Puzzle

The core of the equity premium puzzle is that even though stocks appear to be an attractive asset—they have high average returns and a low covariance with consumption growth—investors appear very unwilling to hold them. In particular, they appear to demand a substantial risk premium in order to hold the market supply.

To date, behavioral finance has pursued two approaches to this puzzle. Both are based on preferences: one relies on prospect theory, the other on ambiguity aversion. In essence, both approaches try to understand what it is that is missing from the popular preference specification in Eq. (6) that makes investors fear stocks so much, leading them to charge a high premium in equilibrium.

4.1.1. PROSPECT THEORY

One of the earliest papers to link prospect theory to the equity premium is Benartzi and Thaler (1995), BT henceforth. They study how an investor with prospect theory-type preferences allocates his financial wealth between T-Bills and the stock market. Prospect theory argues that when choosing between gambles, people compute the gains and losses for each one and select the one with the highest prospective utility. In a financial context, this suggests that people may choose a portfolio allocation by computing, for each allocation, the potential gains and losses in the value of their holdings, and then taking the allocation with the highest prospective utility. In other words, they choose ω, the fraction of financial wealth in stocks, to maximize

$$E_\pi \upsilon[(1 - \omega)R_{f,t+1} + \omega R_{t+1} - 1], \tag{10}$$

where π and υ are defined in Eq. (2). In particular, υ captures loss aversion, the experimental finding that people are more sensitive to losses than to gains. $R_{f,t+1}$ and R_{t+1} are the gross returns on T-Bills and the stock market between t and $t + 1$, respectively, making the argument of υ the return on financial wealth.

In order to implement this model, BT need to stipulate how often investors evaluate their portfolios. In other words, how long is the time interval between t and $t + 1$? To see why this matters, compare two investors: energetic Nick who calculates the gains and losses in his portfolio every day, and laid-back Dick who looks at his portfolio only once per decade. Since, on a daily basis, stocks go down in value almost as often as they go up, the loss aversion built into υ makes stocks appear unattractive to Nick. In contrast, loss aversion does not have much effect on Dick's perception of stocks since, at ten-year horizons, stocks offer only a small risk of losing money.

Rather than simply pick an evaluation interval, BT calculate how often investors would have to evaluate their portfolios to make them indifferent between stocks and T-Bills: in other words, given historical U.S. data on stocks and T-Bills, for what evaluation interval would substituting $\omega = 0$ and $\omega = 1$ into Eq. (10) give the same prospective utility? Roughly speaking, this calculation can be thought of as asking what kind of equity premium might be sustainable in equilibrium: how often would investors need to evaluate their gains and losses so that even in the face of the large historical equity premium, they would still be happy to hold the market supply of T-Bills.

BT find that for the parametric forms for π and υ estimated in experimental settings, the answer is one year, and they argue that this is indeed a natural evaluation period for investors to use. The way people frame gains and losses is plausibly influenced by the way information is presented to them. Since we receive our most comprehensive mutual fund reports once a year, and do our taxes once a year, it is not unreasonable that gains and losses might be expressed as annual changes in value.

The BT calculation therefore suggests a simple way of understanding the high historical equity premium. If investors get utility from annual changes in financial wealth and are loss averse over these changes, their fear of a major drop in financial wealth will lead them to demand a high premium as compensation. BT call the combination of loss aversion and frequent evaluations *myopic loss aversion*.

BT's result is only *suggestive* of a solution to Mehra and Prescott's equity premium puzzle. As emphasized at the start of this section, that puzzle is in large part a consumption puzzle: given the low volatility of consumption growth, why are investors so reluctant to buy a high return asset, stocks, especially when that asset's covariance with consumption growth is so low? Since BT do not consider an intertemporal model with consumption choice, they cannot address this issue directly.

To see if prospect theory can in fact help with the equity premium puzzle, Barberis, Huang, and Santos (2001), BHS henceforth, make a first attempt at building it into a dynamic equilibrium model of stock returns. A simple version of their model, an extension of which we consider later, examines an economy with the same structure as the one described at the start of section 4, but in which investors have the preferences

$$E_0 \sum_{t=0}^{\infty} \left[\rho^t \frac{C_t^{1-\gamma}}{1-\gamma} + b_0 \overline{C}_t^{\gamma} \hat{v}(X_{t+1}) \right]. \qquad (11)$$

The investor gets utility from consumption, but over and above that, he gets utility from changes in the value of his holdings of the risky asset between t and $t + 1$, denoted here by X_{t+1}. Motivated by BT's findings, BHS define the unit of time to be a year, so that gains and losses are measured annually.

The utility from these gains and losses is determined by $\hat{v}$ where

$$\hat{v}(X) = \begin{cases} X \\ 2.25X \end{cases} \quad \text{for} \quad \begin{matrix} X \geq 0, \\ X < 0. \end{matrix} \qquad (12)$$

The 2.25 factor comes from Tversky and Kahneman's (1992) experimental study of attitudes to timeless gambles. This functional form is simpler than the one used by BT, v. It captures loss aversion, but ignores other elements of prospect theory, such as the concavity (convexity) over gains (losses) and the probability transformation. In part this is because it is difficult to incorporate all these features into a fully dynamic framework; but also, it is based on BT's observation that it is mainly loss aversion that drives their results.[17]

BHS show that loss aversion can indeed provide a partial explanation of the high Sharpe ratio on the aggregate stock market. However, how much of the Sharpe ratio it can explain depends heavily on the importance of the

---

[17] The $b_0 \overline{C}_t^{\gamma}$ coefficient on the loss aversion term is a scaling factor which ensures that risk premia in the economy remain stationary even as aggregate wealth increases over time. It involves per capita consumption $\overline{C}_t$ which is exogeneous to the investor, and so does not affect the intuition of the model. The constant b_0 controls the importance of the loss aversion term in the investor's preferences; setting $b_0 = 0$ reduces the model to the much studied case of power utility over consumption. As $b_0 \to \infty$, the investor's decisions are driven primarily by concern about gains and losses in financial wealth, as assumed by Benartzi and Thaler.

second source of utility in Eq. (11), or in short, on b_0. As a way of thinking about this parameter, BHS note that when $b_0 = 0.7$, the psychological pain of losing $100 in the stock market, captured by the second term, is roughly equal to the consumption-related pain of having to consume $100 less, captured by the first term. For this b_0, the Sharpe ratio of the risky asset is 0.11, about a third of its historical value.

BT and BHS are both effectively assuming that investors engage in narrow framing, both cross-sectionally and temporally. Even if they have many forms of wealth, both financial and nonfinancial, they still get utility from changes in the value of one specific component of their total wealth: financial wealth in the case of BT, and stock holdings in the case of BHS. And even if investors have long investment horizons, they still evaluate their portfolio returns on an annual basis.

The assumption about cross-sectional narrow framing can be motivated in a number of ways. The simplest possibility is that it captures nonconsumption utility, such as regret. Regret is the pain we feel when we realize that we would be better off if we had not taken a certain action in the past. If the investor's stock holdings fall in value, he may regret the specific decision he made to invest in stocks. Such feelings are naturally captured by defining utility directly over changes in the investors' financial wealth or in the value of his stock holdings.

Another possibility is that while people actually care only about consumption-related utility, they are boundedly rational. For example, suppose that they are concerned that their consumption might fall below some habit level. They know that the right thing to do when considering a stock market investment is to merge the stock market risk with other pre-existing risks that they face—labor income risk, say—and then to compute the likelihood of consumption falling below habit. However, this calculation may be too complex. As a result, people may simply focus on gains and losses in stock market wealth alone, rather than on gains and losses in total wealth.

What about temporal narrow framing? We suggested above that the way information is presented may lead investors to care about annual changes in financial wealth even if they have longer investment horizons. To provide further evidence for this, Thaler, Tversky, Kahneman, and Schwartz (1997) provide an experimental test of the idea that the manner in which information is presented affects the frame people adopt in their decision making.[18]

In their experiment, subjects are asked to imagine that they are portfolio managers for a small college endowment. One group of subjects—Group I, say—is shown monthly observations on two funds, Fund A and Fund B. Returns on Fund A (B) are drawn from a normal distribution calibrated to mimic bond (stock) returns as closely as possible, although subjects are not given this information. After each monthly observation, subjects are asked

---

[18] See also Gneezy and Potters (1997) for a similar experiment.

to allocate their portfolio between the two funds over the next month. They are then shown the realized returns over that month, and asked to allocate once again.

A second group of investors—Group II—is shown exactly the same series of returns, except that it is aggregated at the annual level; in other words, these subjects do not see the monthly fund fluctuations, but only cumulative annual returns. After each annual observation, they are asked to allocate their portfolio between the two funds over the next year.

A final group of investors—Group III—is shown exactly the same data, this time aggregated at the five-year level, and they too are asked to allocate their portfolio after each observation.

After going through a total of 200 months worth of observations, each group is asked to make one final portfolio allocation, which is to apply over the next 400 months. Thaler et al. (1997) find that the average final allocation chosen by subjects in Group I is much lower than that chosen by people in Groups II and III. This result is consistent with the idea that people code gains and losses based on how information is presented to them. Subjects in Group I see monthly observations and hence more frequent losses. If they adopt the monthly distribution as a frame, they will be more wary of stocks and will allocate less to them.

4.1.2. AMBIGUITY AVERSION

In section 3, we presented the Ellsberg paradox as evidence that people dislike ambiguity, or situations where they are not sure what the probability distribution of a gamble is. This is potentially very relevant for finance, as investors are often uncertain about the distribution of a stock's return.

Following the work of Ellsberg, many models of how people react to ambiguity have been proposed; Camerer and Weber (1992) provide a comprehensive review. One of the more popular approaches is to suppose that when faced with ambiguity, people entertain a range of possible probability distributions and act to maximize the minimum expected utility under any candidate distribution. In effect, people behave as if playing a game against a malevolent opponent who picks the actual distribution of the gamble so as to leave them as worse off as possible. Such a decision rule was first axiomatized by Gilboa and Schmeidler (1989). Epstein and Wang (1994) showed how such an approach could be incorporated into a dynamic asset-pricing model, although they did not try to assess the quantitative implications of ambiguity aversion for asset prices.

Quantitative implications *have* been derived using a closely related framework known as robust control. In this approach, the agent has a reference probability distribution in mind, but wants to ensure that his decisions are good ones even if the reference model is misspecified to some extent. Here too, the agent essentially tries to guard against a "worst-case" misspecification. Anderson, Hansen, and Sargent (1998) show how such a framework can be used for portfolio choice and pricing problems, even when state equations and objective functions are nonlinear.

Maenhout (1999) applies the Anderson et al. framework to the specific issue of the equity premium. He shows that if investors are concerned that their model of stock returns is misspecified, they will charge a substantially higher equity premium as compensation for the perceived ambiguity in the probability distribution. He notes, however, that to explain the full 3.9 percent equity premium requires an unreasonably high concern about misspecification. At best then, ambiguity aversion is only a partial resolution of the equity premium puzzle.

4.2. The Volatility Puzzle

Before turning to behavioral work on the volatility puzzle, it is worth thinking about how rational approaches to this puzzle might proceed. Since, in the data, the volatility of returns is higher than the volatility of dividend growth, Eq. (8) makes it clear that we have to make up the gap by introducing variation in the price/dividend ratio. What are the different ways we might do this? A useful framework for thinking about this is a version of the present value formula originally derived by Campbell and Shiller (1988). Starting from

$$R_{t+1} = \frac{P_{t+1} + D_{t+1}}{P_t}, \tag{13}$$

where P_t is the value of the stock market at time t, they use a log-linear approximation to show that the log price/dividend ratio can be written

$$p_t - d_t = E_t \sum_{j=0}^{\infty} \rho^t \Delta d_{t+1+j} - E_t \sum_{j=0}^{\infty} \rho^t r_{t+1+j} + E_t \lim_{j \to \infty} \rho^j (p_{t+j} - d_{t+j}) + \text{const.},$$

$$\tag{14}$$

where lower case letters represent log variables—$P_t = \log P_t$, for example—and where $\Delta d_{t+1} = d_{t+1} - d_t$.

If the price/dividend ratio is stationary, so that the third term on the right is zero, this equation shows clearly that there are just two reasons price/dividend ratios can move around: changing expectations of future dividend growth or changing discount rates. Discount rates, in turn, can change because of changing expectations of future risk-free rates, changing forecasts of risk or changing risk aversion.

While there appear to be many ways of introducing variation in the P/D ratio, it has become clear that most of them cannot form the basis of a rational explanation of the volatility puzzle. We cannot use changing forecasts of dividend growth to drive the P/D ratio: restating the argument of Shiller (1981) and LeRoy and Porter (1981), if these forecasts are indeed rational, it must be that P/D ratios predict cash-flow growth in the time series, which they do not.[19] Nor can we use changing forecasts of future risk-free rates: again, if the forecasts are rational, P/D ratios must predict interest rates in the time series, which they do not. Even changing forecasts of risk cannot work, as there is little evidence that P/D ratios predict changes in risk in the time series. The only story that remains is therefore one about changing risk aversion, and this is the idea behind the Campbell and Cochrane (1999) model of aggregate stock market behavior. They propose a habit formation framework in which changes in consumption relative to habit lead to changes in risk aversion and hence variation in P/D ratios. This variation helps to plug the gap between the volatility of dividend growth and the volatility of returns.

Some rational approaches try to introduce variation in the P/D ratio through the third term on the right in Eq. (14). Since this requires investors to expect explosive growth in P/D ratios forever, they are known as models of rational bubbles. The idea is that prices are high today because they are expected to be higher next period; and they are higher next period because they are expected to be higher the period after that, and so on, forever. While such a model might initially seem appealing, a number of papers, most recently Santos and Woodford (1997), show that the conditions under which rational bubbles can survive are extremely restrictive.[20]

We now discuss some of the behavioral approaches to the volatility puzzle, grouping them by whether they focus on beliefs or on preferences.

4.2.1. BELIEFS

One possible story is that investors believe that the mean dividend growth rate is more variable than it actually is. When they see a surge in dividends, they are too quick to believe that the mean dividend growth rate has increased. Their exuberance pushes prices up relative to dividends, adding to the volatility of returns.

A story of this kind can be derived as a direct application of representativeness and in particular, of the version of representativeness known as the

[19] There is an important caveat to the statement that changing cash-flow forecasts cannot be the basis of a satisfactory solution to the volatility puzzle. A large literature on structural uncertainty and learning, in which investors do not know the parameters of the cash-flow process but learn them over time, has had some success in matching the empirical volatility of returns (Brennan and Xia 2001, Veronesi 1999). In these models, variation in price/dividend ratios comes precisely from changing forecasts of cash-flow growth. While these forecasts are not subsequently confirmed in the data, investors are not considered irrational—they simply don't have enough data to infer the correct model. In related work, Barsky and De Long (1993) generate return volatility in an economy where investors forecast cash flows using a model that is wrong, but not easily rejected with available data.

[20] Brunnermeier (2001) provides a comprehensive review of this literature.

law of small numbers, whereby people expect even short samples to reflect the properties of the parent population. If the investor sees many periods of good earnings, the law of small numbers leads him to believe that earnings growth has gone up, and hence that earnings will continue to be high in the future. After all, the earnings growth rate cannot be "average." If it were, then according to the law of small numbers, earnings should *appear* average, even in short samples: some good earnings news, some bad earnings news, but not several good pieces of news in a row.

Another belief-based story relies more on private, rather than public information, and in particular, on overconfidence about private information. Suppose that an investor has seen public information about the economy, and has formed a prior opinion about future cash-flow growth. He then does some research on his own and becomes overconfident about the information he gathers: he overestimates its accuracy and puts too much weight on it relative to his prior. If the private information is positive, he will push prices up too high relative to current dividends, again adding to return volatility.[21]

Price/dividend ratios and returns might also be excessively volatile because investors extrapolate *past returns* too far into the future when forming expectations of future returns. Such a story might again be based on representativeness and the law of small numbers. The same argument for why investors might extrapolate past cash flows too far into the future can be applied here to explain why they might do the same thing with past returns.

The reader will have noticed that we do not cite any specific papers in connection with these behavioral stories. This is because these ideas were originally put forward in papers whose primary focus is explaining *cross-sectional* anomalies such as the value premium, even though they also apply here in a natural way. In brief, many of those papers—which we discuss in detail in section 5—generate certain cross-sectional anomalies by building excessive time series variation into the price/earnings ratios of individual stocks. It is therefore not surprising that the mechanisms proposed there might also explain the substantial time series variation in *aggregate*-level price/earnings ratios. In fact, it is perhaps satisfying that these behavioral theories simultaneously address both aggregate and firm-level evidence.

---

[21] Campbell (2000), among others, notes that behavioral models based on cash-flow forecasts often ignore potentially important interest rate effects. If investors are forecasting excessively high cash-flow growth, pushing up prices, interest rates should also rise, thereby dampening the price rise. One response is that interest rates are governed by expectations about *consumption* growth, and in the short run, consumption and dividends can be somewhat delinked: even if dividend growth is expected to be high, this need not necessarily trigger an immediate interest rate response. Alternatively, one can try to specify investors' expectations in such a way that interest rate effects become less important. Cecchetti, Lam, and Mark (2000) take a step in this direction.

We close this section with a brief mention of "money illusion," the confusion between real and nominal values first discussed by Fisher (1928),
and more recently investigated by Shafir et al. (1997). In financial markets,
Modigliani and Cohn (1979) and more recently, Ritter and Warr (2002),
have argued that part of the variation in P/D ratios and returns may be due
to investors mixing real and nominal quantities when forecasting future
cash flows. The value of the stock market can be determined by discounted
real cash flows at real rates, or nominal cash flows at nominal rates. At
times of especially high or especially low inflation though, it is possible that
some investors mistakenly discount *real* cash flows at *nominal* rates. If inflation increases, so will the nominal discount rate. If investors then discount the same set of cash flows at this higher rate, they will push the value
of the stock market down. Of course, this calculation is incorrect: the same
inflation which pushes up the discount rate should also push up future cash
flows. On net, inflation should have little effect on market value. Such real
versus nominal confusion may therefore cause excessive variation in P/D
ratios and returns and seems particularly relevant to understanding the low
market valuations during the high inflation years of the 1970s, as well as
the high market valuations during the low inflation 1990s.

4.2.2. PREFERENCES

Barberis, Huang, and Santos (2001) show that a straightforward extension
of the version of their model discussed in section 4.1 can explain both the
equity premium and volatility puzzles. To do this, they appeal to experimental evidence about dynamic aspects of loss aversion. This evidence suggests that the degree of loss aversion is not the same in all circumstances
but depends on prior gains and losses. In particular, Thaler and Johnson
(1990) find that after prior gains, subjects take on gambles they normally
do not, and that after prior losses, they refuse gambles that they normally
accept. The first finding is sometimes known as the "house money effect,"
reflecting gamblers' increasing willingness to bet when ahead. One interpretation of this evidence is that losses are less painful after prior gains because
they are cushioned by those gains. However, after being burned by a
painful loss, people may become more wary of additional setbacks.[22]

To capture these ideas, Barberis, Huang, and Santos (2001) modify the
utility function in Eq. (11) to

$$E_0 \sum_{t=0}^{\infty} \left[\rho^t \frac{C_t^{1-\gamma}}{1-\gamma} + b_0 \overline{C}_t^{\gamma} \tilde{v}(X_{t+1}, z_t) \right]. \tag{15}$$

---

[22] It is important to distinguish Thaler and Johnson's (1990) evidence from other evidence
presented by Kahneman and Tversky (1979) and discussed in section 3, showing that people
are risk averse over gains and risk-seeking over losses. One set of evidence pertains to one-shot
gambles, the other to sequences of gambles. Kahneman and Tversky's (1979) evidence suggests

Here, z_t is a state variable that tracks past gains and losses on the stock market. For any fixed z_t, the function $\bar{v}$ is a piecewise linear function similar in form to $\hat{v}$, defined in Eq. (12). However, the investors' sensitivity to losses is no longer constant at 2.25, but is determined by z_t, in a way that reflects the experimental evidence described above.

A model of this kind can help explain the volatility puzzle. Suppose that there is some good cash-flow news. This pushes the stock market up, generating prior gains for investors, who are now less scared of stocks: any losses will be cushioned by the accumulated gains. They therefore discount future cash flows at a lower rate, pushing prices up still further relative to current dividends and adding to return volatility.

5. APPLICATION: THE CROSS-SECTION OF AVERAGE RETURNS

While the behavior of the aggregate stock market is not easy to understand from the rational point of view, promising rational models have nonetheless been developed and can be tested against behavioral alternatives. Empirical studies of the behavior of *individual* stocks have unearthed a set of facts which is altogether more frustrating for the rational paradigm. Many of these facts are about the *cross-section* of average returns: they document that one group of stocks earns higher average returns than another. These facts have come to be known as "anomalies" because they cannot be explained by the simplest and most intuitive model of risk and return in the financial economist's toolkit, the Capital Asset Pricing Model (CAPM).

We now outline some of the more salient findings in this literature and then consider some of the rational and behavioral approaches in more detail.

The Size Premium. This anomaly was first documented by Banz (1981). We report the more recent findings of Fama and French (1992). Every year from 1963 to 1990, Fama and French group all stocks traded on the NYSE, AMEX, and NASDAQ into deciles based on their market capitalization, and then measure the average return of each decile over the next year. They find that for this sample period, the average return of the smallest stock decile is 0.74 percent per month higher than the average return of the largest stock decile. This is certainly an anomaly relative to the CAPM: while stocks in the smallest decile do have higher betas, the difference in risk is not enough to explain the difference in average returns.[23]

---

that people are willing to take risks in order to avoid a loss; Thaler and Johnson's (1990) evidence suggests that if these efforts are unsuccessful and the investor suffers an unpleasant loss, he will *subsequently* act in a more risk-averse manner.

[23] The last decade of data has served to reduce the size premium considerably. Gompers and Metrick (2001) argue that this is due to demand pressure for large stocks resulting from the growth of institutional investors, who prefer such stocks.

Long-term Reversals.   Every three years from 1926 to 1982, De Bondt and Thaler (1985) rank all stocks traded on the NYSE by their prior three-year cumulative return and form two portfolios: a "winner" portfolio of the thirty-five stocks with the best prior record and a "loser" portfolio of the thirty-five worst performers. They then measure the average return of these two portfolios over the three years subsequent to their formation. They find that over the whole sample period, the average annual return of the loser portfolio is higher than the average return of the winner portfolio by almost 8 percent per year.

The Predictive Power of Scaled-price Ratios.   These anomalies, which are about the cross-sectional predictive power of variables like the book-to-market (B/M) and earnings-to-price (E/P) ratios, where some measure of fundamentals is scaled by price, have a long history in finance going back at least to Graham (1949), and more recently Dreman (1977), Basu (1983), and Rosenberg, Reid, and Lanstein (1985). We concentrate on Fama and French's (1992) more recent evidence.

Every year, from 1963 to 1990, Fama and French group all stocks traded on the NYSE, AMEX, and NASDAQ into deciles based on their book-to-market ratio, and measure the average return of each decile over the next year. They find that the average return of the highest B/M-ratio decile, containing so called "value" stocks, is 1.53 percent per month higher than the average return on the lowest B/M-ratio decile, "growth" or "glamour" stocks, a difference much higher than can be explained through differences in beta between the two portfolios. Repeating the calculations with the earnings–price ratio as the ranking measure produces a difference of 0.68 percent per month between the two extreme decile portfolios, again an anomalous result.[24]

Momentum.   Every month from January 1963 to December 1989, Jegadeesh and Titman (1993) group all stocks traded on the NYSE into deciles based on their prior six-month return and compute average returns of each decile over the six months after portfolio formation. They find that the decile of biggest prior winners outperforms the decile of biggest prior losers by an average of 10 percent on an annual basis.

Comparing this result to De Bondt and Thaler's (1985) study of prior winners and losers illustrates the crucial role played by the length of the prior ranking period. In one case, prior winners continue to win; in the

---

[24] Ball (1978) and Berk (1995) point out that the size premium and the scaled-price ratio effects emerge naturally in any model where investors apply different discount rates to different stocks: if investors discount a stock's cash flows at a higher rate, that stock will typically have a lower market capitalization and a lower price-earnings ratio, but also higher returns. Note, however, that this view does not shed any light on whether the variation in discount rates is rationally justifiable or not.

other, they perform poorly.[25] A challenge to both behavioral and rational approaches is to explain why extending the formation period switches the result in this way.

There is some evidence that tax-loss selling creates seasonal variation in the momentum effect. Stocks with poor performance during the year may later be subject to selling by investors keen to realize losses that can offset capital gains elsewhere. This selling pressure means that prior losers continue to lose, enhancing the momentum effect. At the turn of the year, though, the selling pressure eases off, allowing prior losers to rebound and weakening the momentum effect. A careful analysis by Grinblatt and Moskowitz (1999) finds that on net, tax-loss selling may explain part of the momentum effect, but by no means all of it. In any case, while selling a stock for tax purposes is rational, a model of predictable price movements based on such behavior is not. Roll (1983) calls such explanations "stupid" since investors would have to be stupid not to buy in December if prices were going to increase in January.

A number of studies have examined stock returns following important corporate announcements, a type of analysis known as an event study.

Event Studies of Earnings Announcements. Every quarter from 1974 to 1986, Bernard and Thomas (1989) group all stocks traded on the NYSE and AMEX into deciles based on the size of the surprise in their most recent earnings announcement. "Surprise" is measured relative to a simple random walk model of earnings. They find that on average, over the sixty days after the earnings announcement, the decile of stocks with surprisingly good news outperforms the decile with surprisingly bad news by an average of about 4 percent, a phenomenon known as post-earnings announcement drift. Once again, this difference in returns is not explained by differences in beta between the two portfolios. A later study by Chan, Jegadeesh, and Lakonishok (1996) measures surprise in other ways—relative to analyst expectations, and by the stock price reaction to the news—and obtains similar results.[26]

Event Studies of Dividend Initiations and Omissions. Michaely, Thaler, and Womack (1995) study firms that announced initiation or omission of a dividend payment between 1964 and 1988. They find that on average, the shares of firms initiating (omitting) dividends significantly outperform (underperform) the market portfolio over the year after the announcement.

---

[25] In fact, De Bondt and Thaler (1985) also report that one-year big winners outperform one-year big losers over the following year, but do not make much of this finding.

[26] Vuolteenaho (2002) combines a clean-surplus accounting version of the present value formula with Campbell's (1991) log-linear decomposion of returns to estimate a measure of cash-flow news that is potentially more accurate than earnings announcements. Analogous to the post-earnings announcement studies, he finds that stocks with good cash-flow news subsequently have higher average returns than stocks with disappointing cash-flow news.

Event Studies of Stock Repurchases.   Ikenberry, Lakonishok, and Vermaelen (1995) look at firms that announced a share repurchase between 1980
and 1990, while Mitchell and Stafford (2001) study firms which did either
self-tenders or share repurchases between 1960 and 1993. The latter study
finds that on average, the shares of these firms outperform a control group
matched on size and B/M by a substantial margin over the four-year period
following the event.

Event Studies of Primary and Secondary Offerings.   Loughran and Ritter
(1995) study firms that undertook primary or secondary equity offerings
between 1970 and 1990. They find that the average return of shares of
these firms over the five-year period after the issuance is markedly below
the average return of shares of non-issuing firms matched to the issuing
firms on size. Brav and Gompers (1997) and Brav, Geczy, and Gompers
(2000) argue that this anomaly may not be distinct from the scaled-price
anomaly listed above: when the returns of event firms are compared to
the returns of firms matched on both size and B/M, there is very little
difference.

Long-term event studies like the last three analyses summarized above raise
some thorny statistical problems. In particular, conducting statistical inference with long-term buy-and-hold post-event returns is a treacherous business. Barber and Lyon (1997), Lyon, Barber, and Tsai (1999), Brav (2000),
Fama (1998), Loughran and Ritter (2000), and Mitchell and Stafford
(2001) are just a few of the papers that discuss this topic. Cross-sectional
correlation is one important issue: if a certain firm announces a share repurchase shortly after another firm does, their four-year post-event returns
will overlap and cannot be considered independent. Although the problem
is an obvious one, it is not easy to deal with effectively. Some recent attempts to do so, such as Brav (2000), suggest that the anomalous evidence
in the event studies on dividend announcements, repurchase announcements, and equity offerings is statistically weaker than initially thought, although how much weaker remains controversial.
     A more general concern with *all* the above empirical evidence is data-
mining. After all, if we sort and rank stocks in enough different ways, we
are bound to discover striking—but completely spurious—cross-sectional
differences in average returns.
     A first response to the data-mining critique is to note that the above stud-
ies do not use the kind of obscure firm characteristics or marginal corporate
announcements that would suggest data-mining. Indeed, it is hard to think
of an important class of corporate announcements that has not been associated with a claim about anomalous post-event returns. A more direct check
is to perform out-of-sample tests. Interestingly, a good deal of the above evidence has been replicated in other data sets. Fama, French, and Davis (2000)

show that there is a value premium in the subsample of U.S. data that precedes the data set used in Fama and French (1992), while Fama and French (1998) document a value premium in international stock markets. Rouwenhorst (1998) shows that the momentum effect is alive and well in international stock market data.

If the empirical results are taken at face value, then the challenge to the rational paradigm is to show that the above cross-sectional evidence emerges naturally from a model with fully rational investors. In special cases, models of this form reduce to the CAPM, and we know that this does not explain the evidence. More generally, rational models predict a multifactor pricing structure,

$$\bar{r}_i - r_f = \beta_{i,1}(\bar{F}_1 - r_f) + \cdots + \beta_{i,K}(\bar{F}_K - r_f), \qquad (16)$$

where the factors proxy for marginal utility growth and where the loadings $\beta_{i,k}$ come from a time series regression of excess stock returns on excess factor returns,

$$r_{i,t} - r_{f,t} = \alpha_i + \beta_{i,1}(F_{1,t} - r_{f,t}) + \cdots + \beta_{i,K}(F_{K,t} - r_{f,t}) + \varepsilon_{i,t}. \qquad (17)$$

To date, it has proved difficult to derive a multifactor model that explains the cross-sectional evidence, although this remains a major research direction.

Alternatively, one can skip the step of *deriving* a factor model, and simply try a specific model to see how it does. This is the approach of Fama and French (1993, 1996). They show that a certain three-factor model does a good job explaining the average returns of portfolios formed on size and B/M rankings. Put differently, the α_i intercepts in regression (17) are typically close to zero for these portfolios and for their choice of factors. The specific factors they use are the return on the market portfolio, the return on a portfolio of small stocks minus the return on a portfolio of large stocks—the "size" factor—and the return on a portfolio of value stocks minus the return on a portfolio of growth stocks—the "book-to-market" factor. By constructing these last two factors, Fama and French are isolating common factors in the returns of small stocks and value stocks, and their three factor model can be loosely motivated by the idea that this co-movement is a systematic risk that is priced in equilibrium.

The low α_i intercepts obtained by Fama and French (1993, 1996) are not necessarily cause for celebration. After all, as Roll (1977) emphasizes, in any specific sample, it is always possible to mechanically construct a one factor model that prices average returns *exactly*.[27] This sounds a cautionary

---

[27] For any sample of observations on individual returns, choose any one of the ex-post mean-variance efficient portfolios. Roll (1977) shows that there is an exact linear relationship between the sample mean returns of the individual assets and their betas, computed with respect to the mean-variance efficient portfolio.

note: just because a factor model happens to work well does not necessarily mean that we are learning anything about the economic drivers of average returns. To be fair, Fama and French (1996) themselves admit that their results can only have their full impact once it is explained what it is about investor preferences and the structure of the economy that leads people to price assets according to their model.

One general feature of the rational approach is that it is loadings or betas, and not firm characteristics, that determine average returns. For example, a risk-based approach would argue that value stocks earn high returns not because they have high B/M ratios, but because such stocks happen to have a high loading on the B/M factor. Daniel and Titman (1997) cast doubt on this specific prediction by performing double sorts of stocks on both B/M ratios and loadings on B/M factors, and showing that stocks with different loadings but the same B/M ratio do *not* differ in their average returns. These results appear quite damaging to the rational approach, but they have also proved controversial. Using a longer data set and a different methodology, Fama, French, and Davis (2000) claim to reverse Daniel and Titman's findings.

More generally, rational approaches to the cross-sectional evidence face a number of other obstacles. First, rational models typically measure risk as the covariance of returns with marginal utility of consumption. Stocks are risky if they fail to pay out at times of high marginal utility—in "bad" times—and instead pay out when marginal utility is low—in "good" times. The problem is that for many of the above findings, there is little evidence that the portfolios with anomalously *high* average returns do poorly in bad times, whatever plausible measure of bad times is used. For example, Lakonishok, Shleifer, and Vishny (1994) show that in their 1968 to 1989 sample period, value stocks do well relative to growth stocks even when the economy is in recession. Similarly, De Bondt and Thaler (1987) find that their loser stocks have higher betas than winners in up markets and lower betas in down markets—an attractive combination that no one would label "risky."

Second, some of the portfolios in the above studies—the decile of stocks with the lowest B/M ratios for example—earn average returns below the risk-free rate. It is not easy to explain why a rational investor would willingly accept a lower return than the T-Bill rate on a volatile portfolio.

Third, Chopra, Lakonishok, and Ritter (1992) and La Porta et al. (1997) show that a large fraction of the high (low) average returns to prior losers (winners) documented by De Bondt and Thaler (1985), and of the high (low) returns to value (growth) stocks, is earned over a very small number of days around earnings announcements. It is hard to tell a rational story for why the premia should be concentrated in this way, given that there is no evidence of changes in *systematic* risk around earnings announcements.

Finally, in some of the examples given above, it is not just that one port-folio outperforms another on average. In some cases, the outperformance is present in almost every period of the sample. For example, in Bernard and Thomas's (1989) study, firms with surprisingly good earnings outperform those with surprisingly poor earnings in 46 out of the 50 quarters studied. It is not easy to see any risk here that might justify the outperformance.

5.1. Belief-based Models

There are a number of behavioral models which try to explain some of the above phenomena. We classify them based on whether their mechanism centers on beliefs or on preferences.

Barberis, Shleifer, and Vishny (1998), BSV henceforth, argue that much of the above evidence is the result of systematic errors that investors make when they use public information to form expectations of future cash flows. They build a model that incorporates two of the updating biases from section 3: conservatism, the tendency to underweight new information rela-tive to priors; and representativeness, and in particular the version of repre-sentativeness known as the law of small numbers, whereby people expect even short samples to reflect the properties of the parent population.

When a company announces surprisingly good earnings, conservatism means that investors react insufficiently, pushing the price up too little. Since the price is too low, subsequent returns will be higher on average, thereby generating both post-earnings announcement drift and momentum. After a series of good earnings announcements, though, representativeness causes people to overreact and push the price up too high. The reason is that after many periods of good earnings, the law of small numbers leads investors to believe that this is a firm with particularly high earnings growth, and hence to forecast high earnings in the future. After all, the firm cannot be "average." If it were, then according to the law of small num-bers, its earnings should appear average, even in short samples. Since the price is now too high, subsequent returns are too low on average, thereby generating long-term reversals and a scaled-price ratio effect.

To capture these ideas mathematically, BSV consider a model with a rep-resentative risk-neutral investor in which the true earnings process for all assets is a random walk. Investors, however, do not use the random-walk model to forecast future earnings. They think that at any time, earnings are being generated by one of two regimes: a "mean-reverting" regime, in which earnings are more mean-reverting than in reality, and a "trending" regime in which earnings trend more than in reality. The investor believes that the regime generating earnings changes exogenously over time and sees his task as trying to figure out which of the two regimes is currently gener-ating earnings.

This framework offers one way of modeling the updating biases described above. Including a "trending" regime in the model captures the effect of representativeness by allowing investors to put more weight on trends than they should. Conservatism suggests that people may put too little weight on the latest piece of earnings news relative to their prior beliefs. In other words, when they get a good piece of earnings news, they effectively act as if part of the shock will be reversed in the next period, in other words, as if they believe in a "mean-reverting" regime. BSV confirm that for a wide range of parameter values, this model does indeed generate post-earnings announcement drift, momentum, long-term reversals and cross-sectional forecasting power for scaled-price ratios.[28]

Daniel, Hirshleifer, and Subrahmanyam (1998, 2001), DHS henceforth, stress biases in the interpretation of private, rather than public information. Imagine that the investor does some research on his own to try to determine a firm's future cash flows. DHS assume that he is overconfident about this information; in particular, they argue that investors are more likely to be overconfident about private information they have worked hard to generate than about public information. If the private information is positive, overconfidence means that investors will push prices up too far relative to fundamentals. Future public information will slowly pull prices back to their correct value, thus generating long-term reversals and a scaled-price effect. To get momentum and a post-earnings announcement effect, DHS assume that the public information alters the investor's confidence in his original private information in an asymmetric fashion, a phenomenon known as self-attribution bias: public news which confirms the investor's research strongly increases the confidence he has in that research. Disconfirming public news, though, is given less attention, and the investor's confidence in the private information remains unchanged. This asymmetric response means that initial overconfidence is on average followed by even greater overconfidence, generating momentum.

If, as BSV and DHS argue, long-term reversals and the predictive power of scaled-price ratios are driven by excessive optimism or pessimism about future cash flows followed by a correction, then most of the correction should occur at those times when investors find out that their initial beliefs were too extreme, in other words, at earnings announcement dates. The findings of Chopra, Lakonishok, and Ritter (1992) and La Porta et al. (1997), who show that a large fraction of the premia to prior losers and to value stocks is earned around earnings announcement days, strongly confirm this prediction.

Perhaps the simplest way of capturing much of the cross-sectional evidence is positive feedback trading, where investors buy more of an asset

---

[28] Poteshman (2001) finds evidence of a BSV-type expectations formation process in the options market. He shows that when pricing options, traders appear to underreact to individual daily changes in instantaneous variance, while overreacting to longer sequences of increasing or decreasing changes in instantaneous variance.

that has recently gone up in value (De Long et al. 1990b, Barberis and Shleifer 2003). If a company's stock price goes up this period on good earnings, positive feedback traders buy the stock in the following period, causing a further price rise. On the one hand, this generates momentum and post-earnings announcement drift. On the other hand, since the price has now risen above what is justified by fundamentals, subsequent returns will on average be too low, generating long-term reversals and a scaled-price ratio effect.

The simplest way of motivating positive feedback trading is extrapolative expectations, where investors' expectations of future returns are based on past returns. This in turn, may be due to representativeness and to the law of small numbers in particular. The same argument made by BSV as to why investors might extrapolate past cash flows too far into the future can be applied here to explain why they might extrapolate past *returns* too far into the future. De Long et al. (1990b) note that institutional features such as portfolio insurance or margin calls can also generate positive feedback trading.

Positive feedback trading also plays a central role in the model of Hong and Stein (1999), although in this case it emerges endogenously from more primitive assumptions. In this model, two boundedly rational groups of investors interact, where bounded rationality means that investors are only able to process a subset of available information. "Newswatchers" make forecasts based on private information, but do not condition on past prices. "Momentum traders" condition only on the most recent price change.

Hong and Stein also assume that private information diffuses slowly through the population of newswatchers. Since these investors are unable to extract each others' private information from prices, the slow diffusion generates momentum. Momentum traders are then added to the mix. Given what they are allowed to condition on, their optimal strategy is to engage in positive feedback trading: a price increase last period is a sign that good private information is diffusing through the economy. By buying, momentum traders hope to profit from the continued diffusion of information. This behavior preserves momentum, but also generates price reversals: since momentum traders cannot observe the extent of news diffusion, they keep buying even after price has reached fundamental value, generating an overreaction that is only later reversed.

These four models differ most in their explanation of momentum. In two of the models—BSV, and Hong and Stein (1999)—momentum is due to an initial underreaction followed by a correction. In De Long et al. (1990b) and DHS, it is due to an initial overreaction followed by even more overreaction. Within each pair, the stories are different again.[29]

---

[29] In particular, the models make different predictions about how individual investors would trade following certain sequences of past returns. Armed with transaction-level data, Hvidkjaer (2001) exploits this to provide initial evidence that may distinguish the theories.

Hong, Lim, and Stein (2000) present supportive evidence for the view of Hong and Stein (1999) that momentum is due simply to slow diffusion of private information through the economy. They argue that the diffusion of information will be particularly slow among small firms and among firms with low analyst coverage, and that the momentum effect should therefore be more prominent there, a prediction they confirm in the data. They also find that among firms with low analyst coverage, momentum is almost entirely driven by prior losers continuing to lose. They argue that this, too, is consistent with a diffusion story. If a firm not covered by analysts is sitting on good news, it will do its best to convey the news to as many people as possible, and as quickly as possible; bad news, however, will be swept under the carpet, making its diffusion much slower.

5.2. Belief-based Models with Institutional Frictions

Some authors have argued that models which combine mild assumptions about investor irrationality with institutional frictions may offer a fruitful way of thinking about some of the anomalous cross-sectional evidence.

The institutional friction that has attracted the most attention is short-sale constraints. As mentioned in section 2.2, these can be thought of as anything which makes investors less willing to establish a short position than a long one. They include the direct cost of shorting, namely the lending fee; the risk that the loan is recalled by the lender at an inopportune moment; as well as legal restrictions: a large fraction of mutual funds are not allowed to short stocks.

Several papers argue that when investors differ in their beliefs, the existence of short-sale constraints can generate deviations from fundamental value and in particular, explain why stocks with high price/earnings ratios earn lower average returns in the cross-section. The simplest way of motivating the assumption of heterogeneous beliefs is overconfidence, which is why that assumption is often thought of as capturing a mild form of irrationality. In the absence of overconfidence, investors' beliefs converge rapidly as they hear each other's opinions and hence deduce each other's private information.

There are at least two mechanisms through which differences of opinion and short-sale constraints can generate price/earnings ratios that are too high, and thereby explain why price/earnings ratios predict returns in the cross-section.

Miller (1977) notes that when investors hold different views about a stock, those with bullish opinions will, of course, take long positions. Bearish investors, on the other hand, want to short the stock, but being unable to do so, they sit out of the market. Stock prices therefore reflect only the opinions of the most optimistic investors which, in turn, means that they are too high and that they will be followed by lower returns.

Harrison and Kreps (1978) and Scheinkman and Xiong (2003) argue that in a dynamic setting, a second, speculation-based mechanism arises. They show that when there are differences in beliefs, investors will be happy to buy a stock for more than its fundamental value in anticipation of being able to sell it later to other investors even more optimistic than themselves. Note that short-sale constraints are essential to this story: in their absence, an investor can profit from another's greater optimism by simply shorting the stock. With short-sale constraints, the only way to do so is to buy the stock first, and then sell it on later.

Both types of models make the intriguing prediction that stocks which investors disagree about more will have higher price/earnings ratios and lower subsequent returns. Three recent papers test this prediction, each using a different measure of differences of opinion.

Diether, Malloy, and Scherbina (2002) use IBES data on analyst forecasts to obtain a direct measure of heterogeneity of opinion. They group stocks into quintiles based on the level of dispersion in analysts' forecasts of current year earnings and confirm that the highest dispersion portfolio earns lower average returns than the lowest dispersion portfolio.

Chen, Hong, and Stein (2002) use "breadth of ownership"—defined roughly as the fraction of mutual funds that hold a particular stock—as a proxy for divergence of opinion about the stock. The more dispersion in opinions there is, the more mutual funds will need to sit out the market due to short sales constraints, leading to lower breadth. Chen et al. predict, and confirm in the data, that stocks experiencing a decrease in breadth subsequently have lower average returns compared to stocks whose breadth increases.

Jones and Lamont (2002) use the cost of short-selling a stock—in other words, the lending fee—to measure differences of opinion about that stock. The idea is that if there is a lot of disagreement about a stock's prospects, many investors will want to short the stock, thereby pushing up the cost of doing so. Jones and Lamont confirm that stocks with higher lending fees have higher price/earnings ratios and earn lower subsequent returns. It is interesting to note that their data set spans the years from 1926 to 1933. At that time, there existed a centralized market for borrowing stocks and lending fees were published daily in *The Wall Street Journal*. Today, by contrast, stock lending is an over-the-counter market, and data on lending fees is harder to come by.

In other related work, Hong and Stein (2003) show that short-sale constraints and differences of opinion also have implications for higher order moments, in that they can lead to skewness. The intuition is that when a stock's price goes down, more information is revealed: by seeing at what point they enter the market, we learn the valuations of those investors whose pessimistic views could not initially be reflected in the stock price, because of short-sale constraints. When the stock market goes up, the sidelined investors stay out of the market and there is less information revelation. This increase in volatility after a downturn is the source of the skewness.

One prediction of this idea is that stocks which investors disagree about more should exhibit greater skewness. Chen, Hong, and Stein (2001) test this idea using increases in turnover as a sign of investor disagreement. They show that stocks whose turnover increases subsequently display greater skewness.

5.3. Preferences

Earlier, we discussed Barberis, Huang, and Santos (2001), which tries to explain *aggregate* stock market behavior by combining loss aversion and narrow framing with an assumption about how the degree of loss aversion changes over time. Barberis and Huang (2001) show that applying the same ideas to individual stocks can generate the evidence on long-term reversals and on scaled-price ratios. The key idea is that when investors hold a number of different stocks, narrow framing may induce them to derive utility from gains and losses in the value of *individual* stocks. The specification of this additional source of utility is exactly the same as in BHS, except that it is now applied at the individual stock level instead of at the portfolio level: the investor is loss averse over individual stock fluctuations and the pain of a loss on a specific stock depends on that stock's past performance.

To see how this model generates a value premium, consider a stock which has had poor returns several periods in a row. Precisely because the investor focuses on individual stock gains and losses, he finds this painful and becomes especially sensitive to the possibility of further losses on the stock. In effect, he perceives the stock as riskier, and discounts its future cash flows at a higher rate: this lowers its price/earnings ratio and leads to higher subsequent returns, generating a value premium. In one sense, this model is narrower than those in the "beliefs" section, section 5.1, as it does not claim to address momentum. In another sense, it is broader, in that it simultaneously explains the equity premium and derives the risk-free rate endogenously.

The models we describe in sections 5.1, 5.2, and 5.3 focus primarily on momentum, long-term reversals, the predictive power of scaled-price ratios and post-earnings announcement drift. What about the other examples of anomalous evidence with which we began section 5? In section 7, we argue that the long-run return patterns following equity issuance and repurchases may be the result of rational managers responding to the kinds of noise traders analyzed in the preceding behavioral models. In short, if investors cause prices to swing away from fundamental value, managers may try to time these cycles, issuing equity when it is overpriced, and repurchasing it when it is cheap. In such a world, equity issues will indeed be followed by low returns, and repurchases by high returns. The models we have discussed so far do not, however, shed light on the size anomaly, nor on the dividend announcement event study.

6. Application: Closed-end Funds and Comovement

6.1. Closed-end Funds

Closed-end funds differ from more familiar open-end funds in that they only issue a fixed number of shares. These shares are then traded on exchanges: an investor who wants to buy a share of a closed-end fund must go to the exchange and buy it from another investor at the prevailing price. By contrast, should he want to buy a share of an open-end fund, the fund would create a new share and sell it to him at its net asset value, or NAV, the per share market value of its asset holdings.

The central puzzle about closed-end funds is that fund share prices differ from NAV. The typical fund trades at a discount to NAV of about 10 percent on average, although the difference between price and NAV varies substantially over time. When closed-end funds are created, the share price is typically above NAV; when they are terminated, either through liquidation or open-ending, the gap between price and NAV closes.

A number of rational explanations for the average closed-end fund discount have been proposed. These include expenses, expectations about future fund manager performance, and tax liabilities. These factors can go some way to explaining certain aspects of the closed-end fund puzzle. However, none of them can satisfactorily explain all aspects of the evidence. For example, management fees can explain why funds usually sell at discounts, but not why they typically initially sell at a premium, nor why discounts tend to vary from week to week.

Lee, Shleifer, and Thaler (1991), LST henceforth, propose a simple behavioral view of these closed-end fund puzzles. They argue that some of the individual investors who are the primary owners of closed-end funds are noise traders, exhibiting irrational swings in their expectations about future fund returns. Sometimes they are too optimistic, while at other times, they are too pessimistic. Changes in their sentiment affect fund share prices and hence also the difference between prices and net asset values.[30]

This view provides a clean explanation of all aspects of the closed-end fund puzzle. Owners of closed-end funds have to contend with two sources of risk: fluctuations in the value of the funds' assets, and fluctuations in noise trader sentiment. If this second risk is systematic—we return to this

---

[30] For the noise traders to affect the *difference* between price and NAV rather than just price, it must be that they are more active traders of closed-end fund shares than they are of assets owned by the funds. As evidence for this, LST point out that while funds are primarily owned by individual investors, the funds' assets are not.

issue shortly—rational investors will demand compensation for it. In other words, they will require that the fund's shares trade at a discount to NAV.

This also explains why new closed-end funds are often sold at a premium. Entrepreneurs will choose to create closed-end funds at times of investor exuberance, when they know that they can sell fund shares for more than they are worth. On the other hand, when a closed-end fund is liquidated, rational investors no longer have to worry about changes in noise trader sentiment because they know that at liquidation, the fund price will equal NAV. They therefore no longer demand compensation for this risk, and the fund price rises towards NAV.

An immediate prediction of the LST view is that prices of closed-end funds should comove strongly, even if the cash-flow fundamentals of the assets held by the funds do not: if noise traders become irrationally pessimistic, they will sell closed-end funds across the board, depressing their prices regardless of cash-flow news. LST confirm in the data that closed-end fund discounts are highly correlated.

The LST story depends on noise trader risk being systematic. There is good reason to think that it is. If the noise traders who hold closed-end funds also hold other assets, then negative changes in sentiment, say, will drive down the prices of closed-end funds *and* of their other holdings, making the noise trader risk systematic. To check this, LST compute the correlation of closed-end fund discounts with another group of assets primarily owned by individuals, small stocks. Consistent with the noise trader risk being systematic, they find a significant positive correlation.

6.2. Comovement

The LST model illustrates that behavioral models can make interesting predictions not only about the *average* level of returns, but also about patterns of comovement. In particular, it explains why the prices of closed-end funds comove so strongly, and also why closed-end funds as a class comove with small stocks. This raises the hope that behavioral models might be able to explain other puzzling instances of comovement as well.

Before studying this in more detail, it is worth setting out the traditional view of return comovement. This view, derived from economies without frictions and with rational investors, holds that comovement in prices reflects comovement in fundamental values. Since, in a frictionless economy with rational investors, price equals fundamental value—an asset's rationally forecasted cash flows discounted at a rate appropriate for their risk—any comovement in prices must be due to comovement in fundamentals. There is little doubt that many instances of return comovement can be explained by fundamentals: stocks in the automotive industry move together primarily because their earnings are correlated.

The closed-end fund evidence shows that the fundamentals-based view of comovement is at best, incomplete: in that case, the prices of closed-end funds comove even though their fundamentals do not.[31] Other evidence is just as puzzling. Froot and Dabora (1999) study "twin stocks," which are claims to the same cash-flow stream, but are traded in different locations. The Royal Dutch/Shell pair, discussed in section 2, is perhaps the best known example. If return comovement is simply a reflection of comovement in fundamentals, these two stocks should be perfectly correlated. In fact, as Froot and Dabora show, Royal Dutch comoves strongly with the S&P 500 index of U.S. stocks, while Shell comoves with the FTSE index of U.K. stocks.

Fama and French (1993) uncover salient common factors in the returns of small stocks, as well as in the returns of value stocks. In order to test the rational view of comovement, Fama and French (1995) investigate whether these strong common factors can be traced to common factors in news about the earnings of these stocks. While they do uncover a common factor in the earnings news of small stocks, as well as in the earnings news of value stocks, these cash-flow factors are weaker than the factors in returns and there is little evidence that the return factors are driven by the cash-flow factors. Once again, there appears to be comovement in returns that has little to do with fundamentals-based comovement.[32]

In response to this evidence, researchers have begun to posit behavioral theories of comovement. LST is one such theory. To state their argument more generally, they start by observing that many investors choose to trade only a subset of all available securities. As these investors' risk aversion or sentiment changes, they alter their exposure to the particular securities they hold, thereby inducing a common factor in the returns of these securities. Put differently, this "habitat" view of comovement predicts that there will be a common factor in the returns of securities that are the primary holdings of a specific subset of investors, such as individual investors. This story

---

[31] Bodurtha et al. (1993) and Hardouvelis et al. (1994) provide further interesting examples of a delinking between fundamentals-based comovement and return comovement in the closed-end fund market. They study closed-end *country* funds, whose assets trade in a different location from the funds themselves and find that the funds comove as much with the national stock market in the country where they are traded as with the national stock market in the country where their *assets* are traded. For example, a closed-end fund invested in German equities but traded in the United States typically comoves as much with the U.S. stock market as with the German stock market.

[32] In principle, comovement can also be rationally generated through changes in discount rates. However, changes in interest rates or risk aversion induce a common factor in the returns on *all* stocks, and do not explain why a particular group of stocks comoves. A common factor in news about the risk of certain assets may also be a source of comovement for those assets, but there is little direct evidence to support such a mechanism in the case of small stocks or value stocks.

seems particularly appropriate for thinking about closed-end funds, and also for Froot and Dabora's evidence.

A second behavioral view of comovement was recently proposed by Barberis and Shleifer (2003). They argue that to simplify the portfolio allocation process, many investors first group stocks into categories such as small-cap stocks or automotive industry stocks, and then allocate funds across these various categories. If these categories are also adopted by noise traders, then as these traders move funds from one category to another, the price pressure from their coordinated demand will induce common factors in the returns of stocks that happen to be classified into the same category, even if those stocks' cash flows are largely uncorrelated. In particular, this view predicts that when an asset is added to a category, it should begin to comove more with that category than before.

Barberis, Shleifer, and Wurgler (2001) test this "category" view of comovement by taking a sample of stocks that have been added to the S&P 500, and computing the betas of these stocks with the S&P 500 both before and after inclusion. Based on both univariate and multivariate regressions, they show that upon inclusion, a stock's beta with the S&P 500 rises significantly, as does the fraction of its variance that is explained by the S&P 500, while its beta with stocks outside the index falls.[33] This result does not sit well with the cash-flow view of comovement—addition to the S&P 500 is not intended to carry any information about the covariance of a stock's cash flows with other stocks' cash flows—but emerges naturally from a model where prices are affected by category-level demand shocks.

7. Application: Investor Behavior

Behavioral finance has also had some success in explaining how certain groups of investors behave, and in particular, what kinds of portfolios they choose to hold and how they trade over time. The goal here is less controversial than in the previous three sections: it is simply to explain the actions of certain investors, and not necessarily to claim that these actions also affect prices. Two factors make this type of research increasingly important. First, now that the costs of entering the stock market have fallen, more and more individuals are investing in equities. Second, the worldwide trend toward defined contribution retirement savings plans, and the possibility of individual accounts in social security systems mean that individuals are more responsible for their own financial well-being in retirement. It is therefore natural to ask how well they are handling these tasks.

[33] Similar results from univariate regressions can also be found in earlier work by Vijh (1994).

We now describe some of the evidence on the actions of investors and the behavioral ideas that have been used to explain it.

7.1. Insufficient Diversification

A large body of evidence suggests that investors diversify their portfolio holdings much less than is recommended by normative models of portfolio choice.

First, investors exhibit a pronounced "home bias." French and Poterba (1991) report that investors in the United States, Japan, and the United Kingdom allocate 94 percent, 98 percent, and 82 percent of their overall equity investment, respectively, to *domestic* equities. It has not been easy to explain this fact on rational grounds (Lewis 1999). Indeed, normative portfolio choice models that take human capital into account typically advise investors to *short* their national stock market, because of its high correlation with their human capital (Baxter and Jermann 1997).

Some studies have found an analog to home bias within countries. Using an especially detailed data set from Finland, Grinblatt, and Keloharju (2001) find that investors in that country are much more likely to hold and trade stocks of Finnish firms which are located close to them geographically, which use their native tongue in company reports, and whose chief executive shares their cultural background. Huberman (2001) studies the geographic distribution of shareholders of U.S. Regional Bell Operating Companies (RBOCs) and finds that investors are much more likely to hold shares in their local RBOC than in out-of-state RBOCs. Finally, studies of allocation decisions in 401(k) plans find a strong bias towards holding own company stock: over 30 percent of defined contribution plan assets in large U.S. companies are invested in employer stock, much of this representing voluntary contributions by employees (Benartzi 2001).

In section 3, we discussed evidence showing that people dislike ambiguous situations, where they feel unable to specify a gamble's probability distribution. Often, these are situations where they feel that they have little competence in evaluating a certain gamble. On the other hand, people show an excessive liking for familiar situations, where they feel they are in a better position than others to evaluate a gamble.

Ambiguity and familiarity offer a simple way of understanding the different examples of insufficient diversification. Investors may find their national stock markets more familiar—or less ambiguous—than foreign stock indices; they may find firms situated close to them geographically more familiar than those located further away; and they may find their employer's stock more familiar than other stocks.[34] Since familiar assets are attractive,

---

[34] Particularly relevant to this last point is survey data showing that people consider their own company stock less risky than a diversified index (Driscoll et al. 1995).

people invest heavily in those, and invest little or nothing at all in ambiguous assets. Their portfolios therefore appear undiversified relative to the
predictions of standard models that ignore the investor's degree of confidence in the probability distribution of a gamble.

Not all evidence of home bias should be interpreted as a preference for the
familiar. Coval and Moskowitz (1999) show that U.S. mutual fund managers tend to hold stocks whose company headquarters are located close to
their funds' headquarters. However, Coval and Moskowitz's (2001) finding
that these local holdings subsequently perform well suggests that an information story is at work here, not a preference for the familiar. It is simply
less costly to research local firms and so fund managers do indeed focus on
those firms, picking out the stocks with higher expected returns. There is no
obvious information-based explanation for the results of French and Poterba
(1991), Huberman (2001), or Benartzi (2001), while Grinblatt and Keloharju
(2001) argue against such an interpretation of their findings.

7.2. Naive Diversification

Benartzi and Thaler (2001) find that when people *do* diversify, they do so in
a naive fashion. In particular, they provide evidence that in 401(k) plans,
many people seem to use strategies as simple as allocating $1/n$ of their savings to each of the n available investment options, whatever those options
are. Some evidence that people think in this way comes from the laboratory. Benartzi and Thaler ask subjects to make an allocation decision in
each of the following three conditions: first, between a stock fund and a
bond fund; next, between a stock fund and a balanced fund, which invests
50 percent in stocks and 50 percent in bonds; and finally, between a bond
fund and a balanced fund. They find that in all three cases, a 50:50 split
across the two funds is a popular choice, although of course this leads to very
different effective choices between stocks and bonds: the average allocation
to stocks in the three conditions was 54 percent, 73 percent, and 35 percent,
respectively.

The $1/n$ diversification heuristic and other similar naive diversification
strategies predict that in 401(k) plans which offer predominantly stock
funds, investors will allocate more to stocks. Benartzi and Thaler test this in
a sample of 170 large retirement savings plans. They divide the plans into
three groups based on the fraction of funds—low, medium, or high—they
offer that are stock funds. The allocation to stocks increases across the
three groups, from 49 to 60 to 64 percent, confirming the initial prediction.

7.3. Excessive Trading

One of the clearest predictions of rational models of investing is that there
should be very little trading. In a world where rationality is common

knowledge, I am reluctant to buy if you are ready to sell. In contrast to this prediction, the volume of trading on the world's stock exchanges is very high. Furthermore, studies of individuals and institutions suggest that both groups trade more than can be justified on rational grounds.

Barber and Odean (2000) examine the trading activity from 1991 to 1996 in a large sample of accounts at a national discount brokerage firm. They find that after taking trading costs into account, the average return of investors in their sample is well below the return of standard benchmarks. Put simply, these investors would do a lot better if they traded less. The underperformance in this sample is largely due to transaction costs. However, there is also some evidence of poor security selection: in a similar data set covering the 1987 to 1993 time period, Odean (1999) finds that the average gross return of stocks that investors buy, over the year after they buy them, is lower than the average gross return of stocks that they sell, over the year after they sell them.

The most prominent behavioral explanation of such excessive trading is overconfidence: people believe that they have information strong enough to justify a trade, whereas in fact the information is too weak to warrant any action. This hypothesis immediately predicts that people who are more overconfident will trade more and, because of transaction costs, earn lower returns. Consistent with this, Barber and Odean (2000) show that the investors in their sample who trade the most earn by far the lowest average returns. Building on evidence that men are more overconfident than women, and using the same data as in their earlier study, Barber and Odean (2001) predict and confirm that men trade more and earn lower returns on average.

Working with the same data again, Barber and Odean (2002a) study the subsample of individual investors who switch from phone-based to online trading. They argue that for a number of reasons, the switch should be accompanied by an increase in overconfidence. First, better access to information and a greater degree of control—both features of an online trading environment—have been shown to increase overconfidence. Moreover, the investors who switch have often earned high returns prior to switching, which may only increase their overconfidence further. If this is indeed the case, they should trade more actively after switching and perform worse. Barber and Odean confirm these predictions.

7.4. The Selling Decision

Several studies find that investors are reluctant to sell assets trading at a loss relative to the price at which they were purchased, a phenomenon labelled the "disposition effect" by Shefrin and Statman (1985). Working with the same discount brokerage data used in the Odean (1999) study from above, Odean (1998) finds that the individual investors in his sample are more likely to sell stocks that have gone up in value relative to their purchase price, rather than stocks that have gone down.

It is hard to explain this behavior on rational grounds. Tax considerations point to the selling of losers, not winners.[35] Nor can one argue that investors rationally sell the winners because of information that their future performance will be poor. Odean reports that the average performance of stocks that people sell is better than that of stocks they hold on to.

Two behavioral explanations of these findings have been suggested. First, investors may have an irrational belief in mean-reversion. A second possibility relies on prospect theory and narrow framing. We have used these ingredients before, but this time it is not loss aversion that is central, but rather the concavity (convexity) of the value function in the region of gains (losses).

To see the argument, suppose that a stock that was originally bought at $50 now sells for $55. Should the investor sell it at this point? Suppose that the gains and losses of prospect theory refer to the sale price minus the purchase price. In that case, the utility from selling the stock now is $v(5)$. Alternatively, the investor can wait another period, whereupon we suppose that the stock could go to $50 or $60 with equal probability; in other words, we abstract from belief-based trading motives by saying that the investor expects the stock price to stay flat. The expected value of waiting and selling next period is then $\frac{1}{2}v(0) + \frac{1}{2}v(10)$. Since the value function v is concave in the region of gains, the investor sells now. In a different scenario, the stock may currently be trading at $45. This time, the comparison is between $v(-5)$ and $\frac{1}{2}v(-10) + \frac{1}{2}v(0)$, assuming a second period distribution of $40 and $50 with equal probability. Convexity of v pushes the investor to wait. Intuitively, by not selling, he is gambling that the stock will eventually break even, saving him from having to experience a painful loss.

The disposition effect is not confined to individual stocks. In an innovative study, Genesove and Mayer (2001) find evidence of a reluctance to sell at a loss in the housing market. They show that sellers whose expected selling price is below their original purchase price, set an asking price that exceeds the asking price of other sellers with comparable houses. Moreover, this is not simply wishful thinking on the sellers' part that is later corrected by the market: sellers facing a possible loss do actually transact at considerably higher prices than other sellers.

Coval and Shumway (2000) study the behavior of professional traders in the Treasury Bond futures pit at the CBOT. If the gains and losses of prospect theory are taken to be daily profits and losses, the curvature of the value function implies that traders with profits (losses) by the middle of the

---

[35] Odean (1998) does find that in December, investors prefer to sell past losers rather than past winners, but overall, this effect is swamped by a strong preference for selling past winners in the remaining eleven months.

trading day will take less (more) risk in their afternoon trading. This prediction is borne out in the data.

Grinblatt and Han (2001) argue that the investor behavior inherent in the disposition effect may be behind a puzzling feature of the cross-section of average returns, namely momentum in stock returns. Due to the concavity of the value function in the region of gains, investors will be keen to sell a stock which has earned them capital gains on paper. The selling pressure that results may initially depress the stock price, generating higher returns later. On the other hand, if the holders of a stock are facing capital losses, convexity in the region of losses means that they will only sell if offered a price premium; the price is therefore initially inflated, generating lower returns later. Grinblatt and Han provide supportive evidence for their story by regressing, in the cross-section, a stock's return on its past twelve-month return as well as on a measure of the capital gain or loss faced by its holders. This last variable is computed as the current stock price minus investors' average cost basis, itself inferred from past volume. They find that the capital gain or loss variable steals a substantial amount of explanatory power from the past return.

7.5. The Buying Decision

Odean (1999) presents useful information about the stocks the individual investors in his sample choose to buy. Unlike "sells," which are mainly prior winners, "buys" are evenly split between prior winners and losers. Conditioning on the stock being a prior winner (loser) though, the stock is a big prior winner (loser). In other words, a good deal of the action is in the extremes.

Odean argues that the results for stock purchases are in part due to an attention effect. When buying a stock, people do not tend to systematically sift through the thousands of listed shares until they find a good "buy." They typically buy a stock that has caught their attention and perhaps the best attention draw is extreme past performance, whether good or bad.

Among individual investors, attention is less likely to matter for stock sales because of a fundamental way in which the selling decision differs from the buying decision. Due to short-sale constraints, when individuals are looking for a stock to sell, they limit their search to those stocks that they currently own. When buying stocks, though, people have a much wider range of possibilities to choose from, and factors related to attention may enter the decision more.

Using the same discount brokerage data as in their earlier papers, Barber and Odean (2002b) test the idea that for individual investors, buying decisions are more driven by attention than are selling decisions. On any particular day, they create portfolios of "attention-getting" stocks using a number of different criteria: stocks with abnormally high trading volume, stocks with abnormally high or low returns, and stocks with news announcements. They find that the individual investors in their sample are more likely, on the following day, to be purchasers of these high-attention stocks than sellers.

8. Application: Corporate Finance

8.1. Security Issuance, Capital Structure and Investment

An important strand of research in behavioral finance asks whether irrational investors such as those discussed in earlier sections affect the financing and investment decisions of firms.

We first address this question theoretically, and ask how a rational manager interested in maximizing true firm value—in other words, the stock price that will prevail once any mispricing has worked its way out of valuations—should act in the face of irrational investors. Stein (1996) provides a useful framework for thinking about this, as well as about other issues that arise in this section. He shows that when a firm's stock price is too high, the rational manager should issue more shares so as to take advantage of investor exuberance. Conversely, when the price is too low, the manager should repurchase shares. We refer to this model of security issuance as the "market timing" view.

What evidence there is to date on security issuance appears remarkably consistent with this framework. First, at the aggregate level, the share of new equity issues among total new issues—the "equity share"—is higher when the overall stock market is more highly valued. In fact, Baker and Wurgler (2000) show that the equity share is a reliable predictor of future stock returns: a high share predicts low, and sometimes negative, stock returns. This is consistent with managers timing the market, issuing more equity at its peaks, just before it sinks back to more realistic valuation levels.

At the individual firm level, a number of papers have shown that the B/M ratio of a firm is a good cross-sectional predictor of new equity issuance (see Korajczyk, Lucas, and McDonald 1991; Jung, Kim, and Stulz 1996; Loughran, Ritter, and Rydqvist 1994; Pagano, Panetta, and Zingales 1998; Baker and Wurgler 2002a). Firms with high valuations issue more equity while those with low valuations repurchase their shares. Moreover long-term stock returns after an IPO or SEO are low (Loughran and Ritter 1995), while long-term returns after the announcement of a repurchase are high (Ikenberry, Lakonishok, and Vermaelen 1995). Once again, this evidence is consistent with managers timing the market in their own securities.

More support for the market-timing view comes from survey evidence. Graham and Harvey (2001) report that 67 percent of surveyed CFOs said that "the amount by which our stock is undervalued or overvalued" was an important consideration when issuing common stock.

The success of the market-timing framework in predicting patterns of equity issuance offers the hope that it might also be the basis of a successful theory of capital structure. After all, a firm's capital structure simply represents its cumulative financing decisions over time. Consider, for example, two firms which are similar in terms of characteristics like firm size, profitability, fraction of tangible assets, and current B/M ratio, which have traditionally been thought to affect capital structure. Suppose, however, that in the past, the B/M ratio of firm A has reached much higher levels than that of firm B. Since, under the market timing theory, managers of firm A may have issued more shares at that time to take advantage of possible overvaluation, firm A may have more equity in its capital structure today.

In an intriguing recent paper, Baker and Wurgler (2002a) confirm this prediction. They show that all else equal, a firm's weighted-average historical B/M ratio, where more weight is placed on years in which the firm made an issuance of some kind, whether debt or equity, is a good cross-sectional predictor of the fraction of equity in the firm's capital structure today.

There is some evidence, then, that irrational investor sentiment affects financing decisions. We now turn to the more critical question of whether this sentiment affects actual investment decisions. Once again, we consider the benchmark case in Stein's (1996) model, in which the manager is both rational and interested in maximizing the firm's true value.

Suppose that a firm's stock price is too high. As discussed above, the manager should issue more equity at this point. More subtly, though, Stein shows that he should *not* channel the fresh capital into any actual new investment, but instead keep it in cash or in another fairly priced capital market security. While investors' exuberance means that, in *their* view, the firm has many positive net present value (NPV) projects it could undertake, the rational manager knows that these projects are not, in fact, positive NPV and that in the interest of true firm value, they should be avoided. Conversely, if the manager thinks that his firm's stock price is irrationally low, he should repurchase shares at the advantageously low price but not scale back actual investment. In short, irrational investors may affect the timing of security issuance, but they should not affect the firm's investment plans.

Once we move beyond this simple benchmark case, though, there emerge several channels through which sentiment might affect investment after all. First, the above argument properly applies only to *non-equity dependent* firms; in other words, to firms which because of their ample internal funds and borrowing capacity do not need the equity markets to finance their marginal investments.

For equity-dependent firms, however, investor sentiment and, in particular, excessive investor pessimism, may distort investment: when investors are excessively pessimistic, such firms may have to forgo attractive investment opportunities because it is too costly to finance them with undervalued equity. This thinking leads to a cross-sectional prediction, namely that the investment of equity-dependent firms should be more sensitive to gyrations in stock price than the investment of non-equity dependent firms.

Other than this equity-dependence mechanism, there are other channels through which investor sentiment might distort investment. Consider the case where investors are excessively optimistic about a firm's prospects. Even if a manager is in principle interested in maximizing true value, he faces the danger that if he refuses to undertake projects investors perceive as profitable, they may depress stock prices, exposing him to the risk of a takeover, or more simply, try to have him fired.[36]

Even if the manager is rational, this does not mean he will choose to maximize the firm's true value. The agency literature has argued that some managers may maximize other objectives—the size of their firm, say—as a way of enhancing their prestige. This suggests another channel for investment distortion: managers might use investor exuberance as a cover for doing negative NPV "empire building" projects.

Finally, investor sentiment can also affect investment if managers put some weight on investors' opinions, perhaps because they think investors know something they do not. Managers may then mistake excessive optimism for well-founded optimism and get drawn into making negative NPV investments.

An important goal of empirical research, then, is to try to understand whether sentiment does affect investment, and if so, through which channel. Early studies produced little evidence of investment distortion. In aggregate data, Blanchard, Rhee, and Summers (1993) find that movements in price apparently unrelated to movements in fundamentals have only weak forecasting power for future investment: the effects are marginally statistically significant and weak in economic terms. To pick out two particular historical episodes: the rise in stock prices through the 1920s did not lead to a commensurate rise in investment, nor did the crash of 1987 slow investment down appreciably. Morck, Shleifer, and Vishny (1990) reach similar conclusions using firm level data, as do Baker and Wurgler (2002a): in their work on capital structure, they show that not only do firms with higher B/M ratios in their past have more equity in their capital structure today, but also that the equity funds raised are typically used to increase cash balances and *not* to finance new investment.

More recently though, Polk and Sapienza (2001) report stronger evidence of investment distortion. They identify overvalued firms as firms with

---

[36] Shleifer and Vishny (2003) argue that in a situation such as this, where the manager feels forced to undertake some kind of investment, the best investment of all may be an acquisition of a less overvalued firm, in other words, one more likely to retain its value in the long run. This observation leads to a parsimonious theory of takeover waves, which predicts, among other things, an increase in stock-financed acquisitions at times of high dispersion in valuations.

high accruals, defined as earnings minus actual cash flow, and as firms with high net issuance of equity. Firms with high accruals may become overvalued if investors fail to understand that earnings are overstating actual cash flows, and Chan et al. (2001) confirm that such firms indeed earn low returns. Overvalued firms may also be identified through their opportunistic issuance of equity, and we have already discussed the evidence that such firms earn low long-run returns. Controlling for actual investment opportunities as accurately as possible, Polk and Sapienza find that the firms they identify as overvalued appear to invest more than other firms, suggesting that sentiment does influence investment.

Further evidence of distortion comes from Baker, Stein, and Wurgler's (2003) test of the cross-sectional prediction that equity-dependent firms will be more sensitive to stock price gyrations than will non-equity dependent firms. They identify equity-dependent firms on the basis of their low cash balances, among other measures, and find that these firms have an investment sensitivity to stock prices about three times as high as that of non-equity dependent firms. This study therefore provides initial evidence that for some firms at least, sentiment may distort investment, and that it does so through the equity-dependence channel.

8.2. Dividends

A major open question in corporate finance asks why firms pay dividends. Historically, dividends have been taxed at a higher rate than capital gains. This means that stockholders who pay taxes would always prefer that the firm repurchase shares rather than pay a dividend. Since the tax exempt shareholders would be indifferent between the dividend payment and the share repurchase, the share repurchase is a Pareto improving action. Why then, do investors seem perfectly happy to accept a substantial part of their return in the form of dividends? Or, using behavioral language, why do firms choose to frame part of their return as an explicit payment to stockholders, and in so doing, apparently make some of their shareholders worse off?

Shefrin and Statman (1984) propose a number of behavioral explanations for why investors exhibit a preference for dividends. Their first idea relies on the notion of self-control. Many people exhibit self-control problems. On the one hand, we want to deny ourselves an indulgence, but on the other hand, we quickly give in to temptation: today, we tell ourselves that tomorrow we will not overeat, and yet, when tomorrow arrives, we again eat too much. To deal with self-control problems, people often set rules, such as "bank the wife's salary, and only spend from the husband's paycheck." Another very natural rule people might create to prevent themselves from overconsuming their wealth is "only consume the dividend, but don't touch the portfolio capital." In other words, people may like dividends because dividends help them surmount self-control problems through the creation of simple rules.

A second rationale for dividends is based on mental accounting: by designating an explicit dividend payment, firms make it easier for investors to segregate gains from losses and hence to increase their utility. To see this, consider the following example. Over the course of a year, the value of a firm has increased by $10 per share. The firm could choose *not* to pay a dividend and return this increase in value to investors as a $10 capital gain. Alternatively, it could pay a $2 dividend, leaving an $8 capital gain. In the language of prospect theory, investors will code the first option as $v(10)$. They may also code the second option as $v(10)$, but the explicit segregation performed by the firm may encourage them to code it as $v(2) + v(8)$. This will, of course, result in a higher perceived utility, due to the concavity of v in the domain of gains.

This manipulation is equally useful in the case of losses. A firm whose value has declined by $10 per share over the year can offer investors a $10 capital loss or a $12 capital loss combined with a $2 dividend gain. While the first option will be coded as $v(-10)$, the second is more likely to be coded as $v(2) + v(-12)$, again resulting in a higher perceived utility, this time because of the convexity of v in the domain of losses.

The utility enhancing trick in these examples depends on investors segregating the overall gain or loss into different components. The key insight of Shefrin and Statman is that by paying dividends, firms make it easier for investors to perform this segregation.

Finally, Shefrin and Statman argue that by paying dividends, firms help investors avoid regret. Regret is a frustration that people feel when they imagine having taken an action that would have led to a more desirable outcome. It is stronger for errors of commission—cases where people suffer because of an action they took—than for errors of omission—where people suffer because of an action they failed to take.

Consider a company that does not pay a dividend. In order to finance consumption, an investor has to sell stock. If the stock subsequently goes up in value, the investor feels substantial regret because the error is one of commission: he can readily imagine how not selling the stock would have left him better off. If the firm had paid a dividend and the investor was able to finance his consumption out of it, a rise in the stock price would not have caused so much regret. This time, the error would have been one of omission: to be better off, the investor would have had to reinvest the dividend.

Shefrin and Statman try to explain why firms pay dividends at all. Another question asks how dividend paying firms decide on the size of their dividend. The classic paper on this subject is Lintner (1956). His treatment is based on extensive interviews with executives of large American companies in which he asked the respondent, often the CFO, how the firm set dividend policy. Based on these interviews Lintner proposed what we would now call a behavioral model. In his model, firms first establish a target dividend payout rate based on notions of fairness, in other words, on what portion of the earnings it is fair to return to shareholders. Then, as earnings increase and the dividend payout ratio falls below the target level, firms increase dividends only when they are confident that they will not have to reduce them in the future.

There are several behavioral aspects to this model. First, the firm is not setting the dividend to maximize firm value or shareholder after-tax wealth. Second, perceptions of fairness are used to set the target payout rate. Third, the asymmetry between an increase in dividends and a decrease is explicitly considered. Although fewer firms now decide to start paying dividends, for those that do Lintner's model appears to be valid to this day (Benartzi, Michaely, and Thaler 1997; Fama and French 2001).

Baker and Wurgler (2004) argue that changes in dividend policy may also reflect changing investor sentiment about dividend-paying firms relative to their sentiment about nonpaying firms. They argue that for some investors, dividend-paying firms and nonpaying firms represent salient categories and that these investors exhibit changing sentiment about the categories. For instance, when investors become more risk averse, they may prefer dividend-paying stocks because of a confused notion that these firms are less risky (the well-known "bird in the hand" fallacy). If managers are interested in maximizing short-run value, perhaps because it is linked to their compensation, they may be tempted to change their dividend policy in the direction favored by investors.

Baker and Wurgler find some supportive evidence for their theory. They measure relative investor sentiment about dividend-paying firms as the log B/M ratio of paying firms minus the log B/M ratio of nonpaying firms, and find that in the time series, a high value of this measure one year predicts that in the following year, a higher fraction of nonpaying firms initiate a dividend and a larger fraction of newly-listed firms choose to pay one. Similar results obtain for other measures of sentiment about dividend-paying firms.

8.3. Models of Managerial Irrationality

The theories we have discussed so far interpret the data as reflecting actions taken by rational managers in response to irrationality on the part of investors. Other papers have argued that some aspects of managerial behavior are the result of irrationality on the part of managers themselves.

Much of section 2 was devoted to thinking about whether rational agents might be able to correct dislocations caused by irrational traders. Analogously, before we consider models of irrational managers, we should ask to what extent rational agents can undo their effects.

On reflection, it doesn't seem any easier to deal with irrational managers than irrational investors. It is true that many firms have mechanisms in place designed to solve agency problems and to keep the manager's mind focused on maximizing firm value: giving him stock options for example, or saddling him with debt. The problem is that these mechanisms are unlikely to have much of an effect on irrational managers. These managers *think* that they are maximizing firm value, even if in reality, they are not. Since they think that they are already doing the right thing, stock options or debt are unlikely to change their behavior.

In the best known paper on managerial irrationality, Roll (1986) argues that much of the evidence on takeover activity is consistent with an economy in which there are *no* overall gains to takeovers, but in which managers are overconfident, a theory he terms the "hubris hypothesis." When managers think about taking over another firm, they conduct a valuation analysis of that firm, taking synergies into account. If managers are overconfident about the accuracy of their analysis, they will be too quick to launch a bid when their valuation exceeds the market price of the target. Just as overconfidence among individual investors may lead to excessive trading, so overconfidence among managers may lead to excessive takeover activity.

The main predictions of the hubris hypothesis are that there will be a large amount of takeover activity, but that the total combined gain to bidder and target will be zero; and that on the announcement of a bid, the price of the target will rise and the value of the bidder will fall by a similar amount. Roll examines the available evidence and concludes that it is impossible to reject any of these predictions.

Heaton (2002) analyses the consequences of managerial optimism whereby managers overestimate the probability that the future performance of their firm will be good. He shows that it can explain pecking order rules for capital structure: since managers are optimistic relative to the capital markets, they believe their equity is undervalued, and are therefore reluctant to issue it unless they have exhausted internally generated funds or the debt market. Managerial optimism can also explain the puzzlingly high correlation of investment and cash flow: when cash flow is low, managers' reluctance to use external markets for financing means that they forgo an unusually large number of projects, lowering investment at the same time.

Malmendier and Tate (2001) test Heaton's model by investigating whether firms with excessively optimistic CEOs display a greater sensitivity of investment to cash flow. They detect excessive optimism among CEOs by examining at what point they exercise their stock options: CEOs who hold on to their options longer than recommended by normative models of optimal exercise are deemed to have an overly optimistic forecast of their stock's future price. Malmendier and Tate find that the investment of these CEOs' firms is indeed more sensitive to cash flow than the investment of other firms.[37]

9. Conclusion

Behavioral finance is a young field, with its formal beginnings in the 1980s. Much of the research we have discussed was completed in the past decade. Where do we stand? Substantial progress has been made on numerous fronts.

Empirical Investigation of Apparently Anomalous Facts.   When De Bondt and Thaler's (1985) paper was published, many scholars thought that the best explanation for their findings was a programming error. Since then their results have been replicated numerous times by authors both sympathetic to their view and by those with alternative views. At this stage, we think that most of the empirical facts are agreed upon by most of the profession, although the interpretation of those facts is still in dispute. This is progress. If we all agree that the planets do orbit the sun, we can focus on understanding why.

Limits to Arbitrage.   Twenty years ago, many financial economists thought that the Efficient Markets Hypothesis had to be true because of the forces of arbitrage. We now understand that this was a naive view, and that the limits to arbitrage can permit substantial mispricing. It is now also understood by most that the absence of a profitable investment strategy does not imply the absence of mispricing. Prices can be very wrong without creating profit opportunities.

Understanding Bounded Rationality.   Thanks largely to the work of cognitive psychologists such as Daniel Kahneman and Amos Tversky, we now have a long list of robust empirical findings that catalog some of the ways in which actual humans form expectations and make choices. There has also been progress in writing down formal models of these processes, with prospect theory being the most notable. Economists once thought that behavior was either rational or impossible to formalize. We now know that models of bounded rationality are both possible and also much more accurate descriptions of behavior than purely rational models.

---

[37] Another paper that can be included in the managerial irrationality category is Loughran and Ritter's (2002) explanation for why managers issuing shares appear to leave significant amounts of money "on the table," as evidenced by the high average return of IPOs on their first day of trading. The authors note that the IPOs with good first day performance are often those IPOs in which the price has risen far above its filing range, giving the managers a sizeable wealth gain. One explanation is therefore that since managers are already enjoying a major windfall, they do not care too much about the fact that they could have been even wealthier.

Behavioral Finance Theory Building.   In the past few years there has been a burst of theoretical work modelling financial markets with less than fully rational agents. These papers relax the assumption of individual rationality either through the belief formation process or through the decision-making process. Like the work of psychologists discussed above, these papers are important existence proofs, showing that it is possible to think coherently about asset pricing while incorporating salient aspects of human behavior.

Investor Behavior.   We have now begun the important job of trying to document and understand how investors, both amateurs and professionals, make their portfolio choices. Until recently such research was notably absent from the repertoire of financial economists.

This is a lot of accomplishment in a short period of time, but we are still much closer to the beginning of the research agenda than we are to the end. We know enough about the perils of forecasting to realize that most of the future progress of the field is unpredictable. Still, we cannot resist venturing a few observations on what may be coming next.

First, much of the work we have summarized is narrow. Models typically capture something about investors' beliefs, or their preferences, or the limits to arbitrage, but not all three. This comment applies to most research in economics, and is a natural implication of the fact that researchers are boundedly rational too. Still, as progress is made, we expect theorists to begin to incorporate more than one strand into their models.

An example can, perhaps, illustrate the point. The empirical literature repeatedly finds that the asset pricing anomalies are more pronounced in small- and mid-cap stocks than in the large-cap sector. It seems likely that this finding reflects limits to arbitrage: the costs of trading smaller stocks are higher, keeping many potential arbitrageurs uninterested. While this observation may be an obvious one, it has not found its way into formal models. We expect investigation of the interplay between limits to arbitrage and cognitive biases to be an important research area in the coming years.

Second, there are obviously competing behavioral explanations for some of the empirical facts. Some critics view this as a weakness of the field. It is sometimes said that the long list of cognitive biases summarized in section 3 offer behavioral modelers so many degrees of freedom that anything can be explained. We concede that there are numerous degrees of freedom, but note that rational modelers have just as many options to choose from. As Arrow (1986) has forcefully argued, rationality per se does not yield many predictions. The predictions in rational models often come from auxiliary assumptions.

There is really only one scientific way to compare alternative theories, behavioral or rational, and that is with empirical tests. One kind of test looks for novel predictions the theory makes. For example, Lee, Shleifer, and Thaler (1991) test their model's prediction that small firm returns will be correlated with closed-end fund discounts, while Hong, Lim, and Stein (2000) test the implication of the Hong and Stein (1999) model that momentum will be stronger among stocks with thinner analyst coverage.

Another sort of test is to look for evidence that agents actually behave the way a model claims they do. The Odean (1998) and Genesove and Mayer (2001) investigations of the disposition effect using actual market behavior fall into this category. Bloomfield and Hales (2002) offers an experimental test of the behavior theorized by Barberis, Shleifer, and Vishny (1998). Of course, such tests are never airtight, but we should be skeptical of theories based on behavior that is undocumented empirically. Since behavioral theories claim to be grounded in realistic assumptions about behavior, we hope behavioral finance researchers will continue to give their assumptions empirical scrutiny. We would urge the same upon authors of rational theories.[38]

We have two predictions about the outcome of direct tests of the assumptions of economic models. First, we will find that most of our current theories, both rational and behavioral, are wrong. Second, substantially better theories will emerge.

[38] Directly testing the validity of a model's assumptions is not common practice in economics, perhaps because of Milton Friedman's influential argument that one should evaluate theories based on the validity of their predictions rather than the validity of their assumptions. Whether or not this is sound scientific practice, we note that much of the debate over the past twenty years has occurred precisely because the evidence has not been consistent with the theories, so it may be a good time to start worrying about the assumptions. If a theorist wants to claim that fact X can be explained by behavior Y, it seems prudent to check whether people actually do Y.

Appendix A

We show that for the economy laid out in Equations (3–6), there is an equilibrium in which the risk-free rate is constant and given by

$$R_f = \frac{1}{\rho} \exp[\gamma g_C - \tfrac{1}{2}\gamma^2 \sigma_C^2], \tag{18}$$

and in which the price/dividend ratio is a constant f, and satisfies

$$1 = \rho \frac{1+f}{f} \exp[g_D - \gamma g_C + \tfrac{1}{2}(\sigma_D^2 + \gamma^2 \sigma_C^2 - 2\gamma\sigma_C\sigma_D\omega)]. \tag{19}$$

In this equilibrium, returns are therefore given by

$$R_{t+1} = \frac{D_{t+1} + P_{t+1}}{P_t} = \frac{1 + P_{t+1}/D_{t+1}}{P_t/D_t} \cdot \frac{D_{t+1}}{D_t} = \frac{1+f}{f} \exp[g_D + \sigma_D \varepsilon_{t+1}]. \tag{20}$$

To see this, start from the Euler equations of optimality, obtained through the usual perturbation arguments,

$$1 = \rho R_f E_t \left[\left(\frac{C_{t+1}}{C_t} \right)^{-\gamma} \right], \tag{21}$$

$$1 = \rho E_t \left[R_{t+1} \left(\frac{C_{t+1}}{C_t} \right)^{-\gamma} \right]. \tag{22}$$

Computing the expectation in Eq. (21) gives Eq. (18). We conjecture that in this economy, there is an equilibrium in which the price/dividend ratio is a constant f, so that returns are given by Eq. (20). Substituting this into Eq. (22) and computing the expectation gives Eq. (19), as required. For given parameter values, the quantitative implications for *P/D* ratios and returns are now easily computed.

REFERENCES

Abreu, D., and M. Brunnermeier, 2002, Synchronization risk and delayed arbitrage, *Journal of Financial Economics* 66, 341–60.

Alpert, M., and H. Raiffa, 1982, A progress report on the training of probability assessors, in D. Kahneman, P. Slovic and A. Tversky (eds), *Judgment Under Uncertainty: Heuristics and Biases*, Cambridge University Press, 294–305.

Anderson, E., L. Hansen, and T. Sargent, 1998, Risk and robustness in equilibrium, Working Paper, University of Chicago.

Arrow, K., 1986, Rationality of self and others, in R. Hogarth and M. Reder (eds.), *Rational Choice* (University of Chicago Press, Chicago), 201–15.

Baker, M., and J. Wurgler, 2000, The equity share in new issues and aggregate stock returns, *Journal of Finance* 55, 2219–57.

Baker, M., and J. Wurgler, 2002, Market timing and capital structure, *Journal of Finance* 57, 1–32.

——, 2004, A catering theory of dividends, *Journal of Finance* 59, 1125–65.

Baker, M., J. Stein, and J. Wurgler, 2003, When does the market matter? Stock prices and the investment of equity dependent firms, *Quarterly Journal of Economics*, 118, 969–1006.

Ball, R., 1978, Anomalies in relations between securities' yields and yield surrogates, *Journal of Financial Economics* 6, 103–26.

Banz, R., 1981, The relation between return and market value of common stocks, *Journal of Financial Economics* 9, 3–18.

Barber, B., and J. Lyon, 1997, Detecting long-run abnormal stock returns: the empirical power and specification of test statistics, *Journal of Financial Economics* 43, 341–72.

Barber, B., and T. Odean, 2000, Trading is hazardous to your wealth: the common stock performance of individual investors, *Journal of Finance* 55, 773–806.

Barber, B., and T. Odean, 2001, Boys will be boys: gender, overconfidence, and common stock investment, *Quarterly Journal of Economics* 141, 261–92.

Barber, B., and T. Odean, 2002a, Online investors: do the slow die first?, *Review of Financial Studies* 15, 455–87.

Barber, B., and T. Odean, 2002b, All that glitters: the effect of attention and news on the buying behavior of individual and institutional investors, Working Paper, University of California.

Barberis, N., and M. Huang, 2001, Mental accounting, loss aversion and individual stock returns, *Journal of Finance* 56, 1247–92.

Barberis, N., and A. Shleifer, 2003, Style investing, *Journal of Financial Economics* 68, 161–99.

Barberis, N., A. Shleifer, and R. Vishny, 1998, A model of investor sentiment, *Journal of Financial Economics* 49, 307–45.

Barberis, N., M. Huang, and T. Santos, 2001, Prospect theory and asset prices, *Quarterly Journal of Economics* 116, 1–53.

Barberis, N., A. Shleifer, and J. Wurgler, 2001, Comovement, *Journal of Financial Economics*, forthcoming.

Barsky, R., and B. De Long, 1993, Why does the stock market fluctuate?, *Quarterly Journal of Economics* 107, 291–311.

Basu, S., 1983, The relationship between earnings yield, market value and return for NYSE common stocks: further evidence, *Journal of Financial Economics* 12, 129–56.

Baxter, M., and U. Jermann, 1997, The international diversification puzzle is worse than you think, *American Economic Review* 87, 170–80.

Bell, D., 1982, Regret in decision making under uncertainty, *Operations Research* 30, 961–81.

Benartzi, S., 2001, Excessive extrapolation and the allocation of 401(k) accounts to company stock, *Journal of Finance* 56, 1747–64.

Benartzi, S., and R. Thaler, 1995, Myopic loss aversion and the equity premium puzzle, *Quarterly Journal of Economics* 110, 75–92.

————, 2001, Naïve diversification strategies in defined contribution savings plans, *American Economic Review* 91, 79–98.

Benartzi, S., R. Michaely, and R. Thaler, 1997, Do changes in dividends signal the future or the past?, *Journal of Finance* 52, 1007–34.

Berk, J., 1995, A critique of size related anomalies, *Review of Financial Studies* 8, 275–86.

Bernard, V., and J. Thomas, 1989, Post-earnings announcement drift: delayed price response or risk premium?, *Journal of Accounting Research* (Supplement), 1–36.

Blanchard, O., C. Rhee, and L. Summers 1993, The stock market, profit, and investment, *Quarterly Journal of Economics* 108, 115–36.

Bloomfield, R., and J. Hales, 2002, Predicting the next step of a random walk: experimental evidence of regime-shifting beliefs, *Journal of Financial Economics* 65, 397–414.

Bodurtha, J., D. Kim, and C. M. Lee, 1993, Closed-end country funds and U.S. market sentiment, *Review of Financial Studies* 8, 879–918.

Brav, A., 2000, Inference in long-horizon event studies, *Journal of Finance* 55, 1979–2016.

Brav, A., and P. Gompers, 1997, Myth or reality? The long-run underperformance of initial public offerings: evidence from venture and non-venture-backed companies, *Journal of Finance* 52, 1791–1821.

Brav, A., C. Geczy, and P. Gompers, 2000, Is the abnormal return following equity issuances anomalous?, *Journal of Financial Economics* 56, 209–49.

Brennan, M., and Y. Xia, 2001, Stock return volatility and the equity premium, *Journal of Monetary Economics* 47, 249–83.

Brown, S., W. Goetzmann, and S. Ross, 1995, Survival, *Journal of Finance* 50, 853–73.

Brunnermeier, M., 2001, Asset Pricing under Asymmetric Information—Bubbles, Crashes, Technical Analysis, and Herding, Oxford University Press.

Buehler, R., D. Griffin, and M. Ross, 1994, Exploring the planning fallacy: why people underestimate their task completion times, *Journality of Personality and Social Psychology* 67, 366–81.

Camerer, C., 1995, Individual decision making, in J. Kagel and A. Roth (eds.), *Handbook of Experimental Economics*, Princeton University Press.

Camerer, C., and R. Hogarth, 1999, The effects of financial incentives in experiments: a review and capital-labor production framework, *Journal of Risk and Uncertainty* 19, 7–42.

Camerer, C., and M. Weber, 1992, Recent developments in modeling preferences: uncertainty and ambiguity, *Journal of Risk and Uncertainty* 5, 325–70.

Campbell, J. Y. (1991), "A variance decomposition for stock returns," Economic Journal 101:157–179.

———, 1999, Asset prices, consumption and the business cycle, in J. Taylor and M. Woodford (eds.), Handbook of Macroeconomics, Elsevier, 1231–1303.

———, 2000, Asset pricing at the millenium, Journal of Finance 55, 1515–67.

Campbell, J. Y., and J. Cochrane, 1999, By force of habit: a consumption-based explanation of aggregate stock market behavior, Journal of Political Economy 107, 205–51.

Campbell, J. Y., and R. Shiller, 1988, Stock prices, earnings and expected dividends, Journal of Finance 43, 661–76.

Cecchetti, S., P. Lam, and N. Mark, 2000, Asset pricing with distorted beliefs: are equity returns too good to be true?, American Economic Review 90, 787–805.

Chan, K., L. Chan, N. Jegadeesh, and J. Lakonishok, 2001, Earnings quality and stock returns, Working Paper, University of Illinois.

Chan, L., N. Jegadeesh, and J. Lakonishok, 1996, Momentum strategies, Journal of Finance 51, 1681–1713.

Chen, J., H. Hong, and J. Stein, 2001, Forecasting crashes: trading volume, past returns and conditional skewness in stock prices, Journal of Financial Economics 61, 345–81.

———, 2002, Breadth of ownership and stock returns, Journal of Financial Economics 66, 171–205.

Chew, S., 1983, A generalization of the quasilinear mean with applications to the measurement of income inequality and decision theory resolving the allais paradox, Econometrica 51, 1065–92.

———, 1989, Axiomatic utility theories with the betweenness property, Annals of Operations Research 19, 273–98.

Chew, S., and K. MacCrimmon, 1979, Alpha-nu choice theory: an axiomatization of expected utility, Working Paper, University of British Columbia.

Chopra, N., J. Lakonishok, and J. Ritter, 1992, Measuring abnormal performance: do stocks overreact?, Journal of Financial Economics 31, 235–68.

Coval, J., and T. Moskowitz, 1999, Home bias at home: local equity preference in domestic portfolios, Journal of Finance 54, 2045–73.

———, 2001, The geography of investment: informed trading and asset prices, Journal of Political Economy 109, 811–41.

Coval, J., and T. Shumway, 2000, Do behavioral biases affect prices?, Working Paper, University of Michigan.

Daniel, K., and S. Titman, 1997, Evidence on the characteristics of cross-sectional variation in stock returns, Journal of Finance 52, 1–33.

Daniel, K., D. Hirshleifer, and A. Subrahmanyam, 1998, Investor psychology and security market under- and overreactions, Journal of Finance 53, 1839–85.

———, 2001, Overconfidence, arbitrage and equilibrium asset pricing, Journal of Finance 56, 921–65.

D'Avolio, G., 2002, The market for borrowing stock, Journal of Financial Economics 66, 271–306.

De Bondt, W., and R. Thaler, 1985, Does the stock market overreact?, Journal of Finance 40, 793–808.

———, 1987, Further evidence on investor overreaction and stock market seasonality, Journal of Finance 42, 557–81.

De Long, J. B., A. Shleifer, L. Summers, and R. Waldmann, 1990a, Noise trader risk in financial markets, *Journal of Political Economy* 98, 703–38.

———, 1990b, Positive feedback investment strategies and destabilizing rational speculation, *Journal of Finance* 45, 375–95.

Dekel, E., 1986, An axiomatic characterization of preferences under uncertainty: weakening the independence axiom, *Journal of Economic Theory* 40, 304–18.

Diether, K., C. Malloy, and A. Scherbina, 2002, Stock prices and differences of opinion: empirical evidence that stock prices reflect optimism, *Journal of Finance* 57, 2113–41.

Dreman, D., 1977, *Psychology and the Stock Market: Investment Strategy Beyond Random Walk*, Warner Books.

Driscoll, K., J. Malcolm, M. Sirul, and P. Slotter, 1995, Gallup Survey of Defined Contribution Plan Participants, John Hancock Financial Services.

Edwards, W., 1968, Conservatism in human information processing, in B. Kleinmutz (ed.), *Formal Representation of Human Judgment*, Wiley, 17–52.

Ellsberg, D., 1961, Risk, ambiguity, and the savage axioms, *Quarterly Journal of Economics* 75, 643–69.

Epstein, L., and T. Wang, 1994, Intertemporal asset pricing under Knightian uncertainty, *Econometrica* 62, 283–322.

Fama, E., 1970, Efficient capital markets: a review of theory and empirical work, *Journal of Finance* 25, 383–417.

———, 1998, Market efficiency, long-term returns and behavioral finance, *Journal of Financial Economics* 49, 283–307.

Fama, E., and K. French, 1988, Dividend yields and expected stock returns, *Journal of Financial Economics* 22, 3–25.

———, 1992, The cross-section of expected stock returns, *Journal of Finance* 47, 427–65.

———, 1993, Common risk factors in the returns of bonds and stocks, *Journal of Financial Economics* 33, 3–56.

———, 1995, Size and book-to-market factors in earnings and returns, *Journal of Finance* 50, 131–55.

———, 1996, Multifactor explanations of asset pricing anomalies, *Journal of Finance* 51, 55–84.

———, 1998, Value vs. growth: the international evidence, *Journal of Finance* 53, 1975–99.

———, 2001, Disappearing dividends: changing firm characteristics or lower propensity to pay?, *Journal of Financial Economics* 60, 3–43.

Fama, E., K. French, and J. Davis, 2000, Characteristics, covariances and average returns 1929–1997, *Journal of Finance* 55, 389–406.

Fischhoff, B., P. Slovic, and S. Lichtenstein, 1977, Knowing with certainty: the appropriateness of extreme confidence, *Journal of Experimental Psychology: Human Perception and Performance* 3, 552–64.

Fisher, I., 1928, *Money Illusion* (Adelphi, New York).

Fox, C., and A. Tversky, 1995, Ambiguity aversion and comparative ignorance, *Quarterly Journal of Economics* 110, 585–603.

French, K., and J. Poterba, 1991, Investor diversification and international equity markets, *American Economic Review* 81, 222–26.

Friedman, M., 1953, The case for flexible exchange rates, in *Essays in Positive Economics*, University of Chicago Press, 157–203.

Froot, K., and E. Dabora, 1999, How are stock prices affected by the location of trade?, *Journal of Financial Economics* 53, 189–216.

Genesove, D., and C. Mayer, 2001, Loss aversion and seller behavior: evidence from the housing market, *Quarterly Journal of Economics* 116, 1233–60.

Gervais, S., and T. Odean, 2001, Learning to be overconfident, *Review of Financial Studies* 14, 1–27.

Gilboa, I., and D. Schmeidler, 1989, Maxmin expected utility with a non-unique prior, *Journal of Mathematical Economics* 18, 141–53.

Gilovich, T., R. Vallone, and A. Tversky, 1985, The hot hand in basketball: on the misperception of random sequences, *Cognitive Psychology* 17, 295–314.

Gilovich, T., D. Griffin, and D. Kahneman, eds., 2002, *Heuristics and Biases: The Psychology of Intuitive Judgment*, Cambridge University Press.

Gneezy, U., and J. Potters, 1997, An experiment on risk taking and evaluation periods, *Quarterly Journal of Economics* 112, 631–45.

Gompers, P., and A. Metrick, 2001, Institutional investors and equity prices, *Quarterly Journal of Economics* 116, 229–59.

Graham, B., 1949, *The Intelligent Investor: A Book of Practical Counsel*, Harper and Row.

Graham, J., and C. Harvey, 2001, The theory and practice of corporate finance: evidence from the field, *Journal of Financial Economics* 60, 187–243.

Grinblatt, M., and B. Han, 2001, The disposition effect and momentum, Working Paper, University of California, Los Angeles.

Grinblatt, M., and M. Keloharju, 2001, How distance, language, and culture influence stockholdings and trades, *Journal of Finance* 56, 1053–73.

Grinblatt, M., and T. Moskowitz, 1999, The cross-section of expected returns and its relation to past returns, Working Paper, University of Chicago.

Gul, F., 1991, A theory of disappointment in decision making under uncertainty, *Econometrica* 59, 667–86.

Hansen, L., and K. Singleton, 1983, Stochastic consumption, risk aversion and the temporal behavior of asset returns, *Journal of Political Economy* 91, 249–68.

Hardouvelis, G., R. La Porta, and T. Wizman, 1994, What moves the discount on country equity funds?, in J. Frankel (ed.), *The Internationalization of Equity Markets*, University of Chicago Press, 345–97.

Harris, L., and E. Gurel, 1986, Price and volume effects associated with changes in the S&P 500: new evidence for the existence of price pressure, *Journal of Finance* 41, 851–60.

Harrison, J. M., and D. Kreps, 1978, Speculative investor behavior in a stock market with heterogeneous expectations, *Quarterly Journal of Economics* 92, 323–36.

Heath, C., and A. Tversky, 1991, Preference and belief: ambiguity and competence in choice under uncertainty, *Journal of Risk and Uncertainty* 4, 5–28.

Heaton, J. B., 2002, Managerial optimism and corporate finance, *Financial Management* (Summer), 33–45.

Hirshleifer, D., 2001, Investor psychology and asset pricing, *Journal of Finance* 56, 1533–97.

Hong, H., and J. Stein, 1999, A unified theory of underreaction, momentum trading, and overreaction in asset markets, *Journal of Finance* 54, 2143–84.

Hong, H., and J. Stein, 2003, Differences of opinion, short-sale constraints and market crashes, *Review of Financial Studies*, 16, 487–525.

Hong, H., T. Lim, and J. Stein, 2000, Bad news travels slowly: size, analyst coverage, and the profitability of momentum strategies, *Journal of Finance* 55, 265–95.

Huberman, G., 2001, Familiarity breeds investment, *Review of Financial Studies* 14, 659–80.

Hvidkjaer, S., 2001, A trade-based analysis of momentum, Working Paper, University of Maryland, College Park.

Ikenberry, D., J. Lakonishok, and T. Vermaelen, 1995, Market underreaction to open market share repurchases, *Journal of Financial Economics* 39, 181–208.

Jegadeesh, N., and S. Titman, 1993, Returns to buying winners and selling losers: implications for stock market efficiency, *Journal of Finance* 48, 65–91.

Jones, C., and O. Lamont, 2002, Short-sale constraints and stock returns, *Journal of Financial Economics* 66, 207–39.

Jung, K., Y. Kim, and R. Stulz, 1996, Timing, investment opportunities, managerial discretion, and the security issue decision, *Journal of Financial Economics* 42, 159–85.

Kahneman, D., and A. Tversky, 1974, Judgment under uncertainty: heuristics and biases, *Science* 185, 1124–31.

Kahneman, D., and A. Tversky, 1979, Prospect theory: an analysis of decision under risk, *Econometrica* 47, 263–91.

Kahneman, D., and A. Tversky, eds., 2000, *Choices, Values and Frames*, Cambridge University Press.

Kahneman, D., P. Slovic and A. Tversky, eds., 1982, *Judgment Under Uncertainty: Heuristics and Biases*, Cambridge University Press.

Kaul, A., V. Mehrotra, and R. Morck, 2000, Demand curves for stocks do slope down: new evidence from an index weights adjustment, *Journal of Finance* 55, 893–912.

Knight, F., 1921, *Risk, Uncertainty and Profit*, Houghton Mifflin.

Korajczyk, R., D. Lucas, and R. McDonald, 1991, The effects of information releases on the pricing and timing of equity issues, *Review of Financial Studies* 4, 685–708.

La Porta, R., J. Lakonishok, A. Shleifer, and R. Vishny, 1997, Good news for value stocks: further evidence on market efficiency, *Journal of Finance* 49, 1541–78.

Lakonishok, J., A. Shleifer, and R. Vishny, 1994, Contrarian investment, extrapolation and risk, *Journal of Finance* 49, 1541–78.

Lamont, O., and R. Thaler, 2003, Can the market add and subtract? Mispricing in tech stock carve-outs, *Journal of Political Economy* 111, 227–68.

Lee, C., A. Shleifer, and R. Thaler, 1991, Investor sentiment and the closed-end fund puzzle, *Journal of Finance* 46, 75–110.

LeRoy, S., and R. Porter, 1981, The present-value relation: tests based on implied variance bounds, *Econometrica* 49, 97–113.

Lewis, K., 1999, Trying to explain home bias in equities and consumption, *Journal of Economic Literature* 37, 571–608.

Lintner, J., 1956, Distribution of incomes of corporations among dividends, retained earnings and taxes, *American Economic Review* 46, 97–113.

Loomes, G., and R. Sugden, 1982, Regret theory: an alternative theory of rational choice under uncertainty, *The Economic Journal* 92, 805–24.

Lord, C., L. Ross, and M. Lepper, 1979, Biased assimilation and attitude polarization: the effects of prior theories on subsequently considered evidence, *Journal of Personality and Social Psychology* 37, 2098–2109.

Loughran, T., and J. Ritter, 1995, The new issues puzzle, *Journal of Finance* 50, 23–50.

———, 2000, Uniformly least powerful tests of market efficiency, *Journal of Financial Economics* 55, 361–89.

———, 2002, Why don't issuers get upset about leaving money on the table?, *Review of Financial Studies* 15, 413–43.

Loughran, T., J. Ritter, and K. Rydqvist, 1994, Initial public offerings: international insights, *Pacific Basin Finance Journal* 2, 165–99.

Lyon, J., B. Barber, and C. Tsai, 1999, Improved methods for tests of long-run abnormal stock returns, *Journal of Finance* 54, 165–201.

Maenhout, P., 1999, Robust portfolio rules and asset pricing, Working Paper (INSEAD, Paris).

Malmendier, U., and G. Tate, 2001, CEO overconfidence and corporate investment, Working Paper (Harvard University).

Mankiw, N.G., and S. Zeldes, 1991, The consumption of stockholders and non-stockholders, *Journal of Financial Economics* 29, 97–112.

Markowitz, H., 1952, The utility of wealth, *Journal of Political Economy* 60, 151–58.

Mehra, R., and E. Prescott, 1985, The equity premium: a puzzle, *Journal of Monetary Economics* 15, 145–61.

Merton, R., 1987, A simple model of capital market equilibrium with incomplete information, *Journal of Finance* 42, 483–510.

Michaely, R., R. Thaler, and K. Womack, 1995, Price reactions to dividend initiations and omissions, *Journal of Finance* 50, 573–608.

Miller, E., 1977, Risk, uncertainty and divergence of opinion, *Journal of Finance* 32, 1151–68.

Mitchell, M., and E. Stafford, 2001, Managerial decisions and long-term stock price performance, *Journal of Business* 73, 287–329.

Mitchell, M., T. Pulvino, and E. Stafford, 2002, Limited arbitrage in equity markets, *Journal of Finance* 57, 551–84.

Modigliani, F., and R. Cohn, 1979, Inflation and the stock market, *Financial Analysts Journal* 35, 24–44.

Morck, R., A. Shleifer, and R. Vishny, 1990, The stock market and investment: is the market a sideshow?, Brookings Papers on Economic Activity 0:157–202.

Mullainathan, S., 2001, Thinking through categories, Working Paper, MIT.

Odean, T., 1998, Are investors reluctant to realize their losses?, *Journal of Finance* 53, 1775–98.

———, 1999, Do investors trade too much?, *American Economic Review* 89, 1279–98.

Ofek, E., and M. Richardson, 2003, Dot-com mania: market inefficiency in the internet sector, *Journal of Finance* 58, 1113–37.

Pagano, M., F. Panetta, and L. Zingales, 1998, Why do companies go public? An empirical analysis, *Journal of Finance* 53, 27–64.

Polk, C., and P. Sapienza, 2001, The real effects of investor sentiment, Working Paper, Northwestern University.

Poteshman, A., 2001, Underreaction, overreaction and increasing misreaction to information in the options market, *Journal of Finance* 56, 851–76.

Quiggin, J., 1982, A theory of anticipated utility, *Journal of Economic Behavior and Organization* 3, 323–43.

Rabin, M., 1998, Psychology and economics, *Journal of Economic Literature* 36, 11–46.

———, 2000, Risk aversion and expected utility theory: a calibration theorem, *Econometrica* 68, 1281–92.

———, Inference by believers in the law of small numbers, *Quarterly Journal of Economics* 117, 775–816.

Redelmeier, D., and A. Tversky, 1992, On the framing of multiple prospects, *Psychological Science* 3, 191–93.

Ritter, J., and R. Warr, 2002, The decline of inflation and the bull market of 1982 to 1997, *Journal of Financial and Quantitative Analysis* 37, 29–61.

Roll, R., 1977, A critique of the asset pricing theory's tests: part I, *Journal of Financial Economics* 4, 129–74.

———, 1983, Vas ist das?, *Journal of Portfolio Management* 9, 18–28.

———, 1986, The hubris hypothesis of corporate takeovers, *Journal of Business* 59, 197–216.

Rosenberg, B., K. Reid, and R. Lanstein, 1985, Persuasive evidence of market inefficiency, *Journal of Portfolio Management* 11, 9–17.

Ross, S., 2001, *Lectures Notes on Market Efficiency*, MIT.

Rouwenhorst, G., 1998, International momentum strategies, *Journal of Finance* 53, 267–84.

Rubinstein, M., 2001, Rational markets: yes or no? The affirmative case, *Financial Analysts Journal* (May–June), 15–29.

Santos, M., and M. Woodford, 1997, Rational asset pricing bubbles, *Econometrica* 65, 19–58.

Sargent, T., 1993, *Bounded Rationality in Macroeconomics*, Oxford University Press.

Savage, L., 1964, *The Foundations of Statistics*, Wiley.

Scheinkman, J., and W. Xiong, 2003, Overconfidence and speculative bubbles, *Journal of Political Economy*, 111, 1183–219.

Segal, U., 1987, Some remarks on Quiggin's anticipated utility, *Journal of Economic Behavior and Organization* 8, 145–54.

Segal, U., 1989, Anticipated utility: a measure representation approach, *Annals of Operations Research* 19, 359–73.

Shafir, E., P. Diamond, and A. Tversky, 1997, Money illusion, *Quarterly Journal of Economics* 112, 341–74.

Shefrin, H., and M. Statman, 1984, Explaining investor preference for cash dividends, *Journal of Financial Economics* 13, 253–82.

———, 1985, The disposition to sell winners too early and ride losers too long, *Journal of Finance* 40, 777–90.

Shiller, R., 1981, Do stock prices move too much to be justified by subsequent changes in dividends?, *American Economic Review* 71, 421–36.

———, 1984, Stock prices and social dynamics, Brookings Papers on Economic Activity 2: 457–98.

Shleifer, A., 1986, Do demand curves for stocks slope down, *Journal of Finance* 41, 579–90.

———, 2000, *Inefficient Markets: An Introduction to Behavioral Finance*, Oxford University Press.

Shleifer, A., and L. Summers, 1990, The noise trader approach to finance, *Journal of Economic Perspectives* 4, 19–33.

Shleifer, A., and R. Vishny, 1997, The limits of arbitrage, *Journal of Finance* 52, 35–55.

———, 2003, Stock market driven acquisitions, *Journal of Financial Economics*, 70, 295–311.

Stein, J., 1996, Rational capital budgeting in an irrational world, *Journal of Business* 69, 429–55.

Summers, L., 1986, Does the stock market rationally reflect fundamental values?, *Journal of Finance* 41, 591–601.

Thaler, R., 2000, Mental accounting matters, in: D. Kahneman and A. Tversky (eds.), *Choice Values and Frames*, Cambridge University Press, 241–68.

Thaler, R., and E. Johnson, 1990, Gambling with the house money and trying to break even: the effects of prior outcomes on risky choice, *Management Science* 36, 643–60.

Thaler, R., A. Tversky, D. Kahneman, and A. Schwartz, 1997, The effect of myopia and loss aversion on risk-taking: an experimental test, *Quarterly Journal of Economics* 112, 647–61.

Tversky, A., and D. Kahneman, 1986, Rational choice and the framing of decisions, *Journal of Business* 59, 251–78.

Tversky, A., and D. Kahneman, 1992, Advances in prospect theory: cumulative representation of uncertainty, *Journal of Risk and Uncertainty* 5, 297–323.

Veronesi, P., 1999, Stock market overreaction to bad news in good times: a rational expectations equilibrium model, *Review of Financial Studies* 12, 975–1007.

Vijh, A., 1994, S&P 500 trading strategies and stock betas, *Review of Financial Studies* 7, 215–51.

von Neumann, J., and O. Morgenstern, 1944, *Theory of Games and Economic Behavior*, Princeton University Press.

Vuolteenaho, T., 2002, What drives firm-level stock returns?, *Journal of Finance* 57, 233–64.

Weil, P., 1989, The equity premium puzzle and the risk-free rate puzzle, *Journal of Monetary Economics* 24, 401–21.

Weinstein, N., 1980, Unrealistic optimism about future life events, *Journal of Personality and Social Psychology* 39, 806–20.

Wurgler, J., and K. Zhuravskaya, 2002, Does arbitrage flatten demand curves for stocks?, *Journal of Business* 75, 583–608.

Yaari, M., 1987, The dual theory of choice under risk, *Econometrica* 55, 95–115.

PART I

Limits to Arbitrage

Chapter 2

THE LIMITS OF ARBITRAGE

Andrei Shleifer and Robert W. Vishny

ONE OF THE FUNDAMENTAL concepts in finance is arbitrage, defined as "the simultaneous purchase and sale of the same, or essentially similar, security in two different markets for advantageously different prices" (Sharpe and Alexander 1990). Theoretically speaking, such arbitrage requires no capital and entails no risk. When an arbitrageur buys a cheaper security and sells a more expensive one, his net future cash flows are zero for sure, and he gets his profits up front. Arbitrage plays a critical role in the analysis of securities markets, because its effect is to bring prices to fundamental values and to keep markets efficient. For this reason, it is extremely important to understand how well this textbook description of arbitrage approximates reality. This chapter argues that the textbook description does not describe realistic arbitrage trades, and, moreover, the discrepancies become particularly important when arbitrageurs manage other people's money.

Even the simplest realistic arbitrages are more complex than the textbook definition suggests. Consider the simple case of two Bund futures contracts to deliver DM250,000 in face value of German bonds at time T, one traded in London on LIFFE and the other in Frankfurt on DTB. Suppose for the moment, counter factually, that these contracts are exactly the same. Suppose finally that at some point in time t the first contract sells for DM240,000 and the second for DM245,000. An arbitrageur in this situation would sell a futures contract in Frankfurt and buy one in London, recognizing that at time T he is perfectly hedged. To do so, at time t, he would have to put up some good faith money, namely DM3,000 in London and DM3,500 in Frankfurt, leading to a net cash outflow of DM6,500. However, he does not get the DM5,000 difference in contract prices at the time he puts on the trade. Suppose that prices of the two contracts both converge to DM242,500 just after t, as the market returns to efficiency. In this case, the arbitrageur would immediately collect DM2,500 from each exchange, which would simultaneously charge the counter parties for their losses. The arbitrageur can then close out his position and get back his

Nancy Zimmerman and Gabe Sunshine have helped us to understand arbitrage. We thank Yacine Aït Sahalia, Douglas Diamond, Oliver Hart, Steve Kaplan, Raghu Rajan, Jésus Saa-Requejo, Luigi Zingales, Jeff Zwiebel, and especially Matthew Ellman, Gustavo Nombela, René Stulz, and an anonymous referee (*The Journal of Finance*) for helpful comments.

good faith money as well. In this near textbook case, the arbitrageur required only DM6,500 of capital and collected his profits at some point in time between t and T.

Even in this simplest example, the arbitrageur need not be so lucky. Suppose that soon after t, the price of the futures contract in Frankfurt rises to DM250,000, thus moving further away from the price in London, which stays at DM240,000. At this point, the Frankfurt exchange must charge the arbitrageur DM5,000 to pay to his counter party. Even if eventually the prices of the two contracts converge and the arbitrageur makes money, in the short run he loses money and needs more capital. The model of capital-free arbitrage simply does not apply. If the arbitrageur has deep enough pockets to always access this capital, he still makes money with probability one. But if he does not, he may run out of money and have to liquidate his position at a loss.

In reality, the situation is more complicated since the two Bund contracts have somewhat different trading hours, settlement dates, and delivery terms. It may easily happen that the arbitrageur has to find the money to buy bonds so that he can deliver them in Frankfurt at time T. Moreover, if prices are moving rapidly, the value of bonds he delivers and the value of bonds delivered to him may differ, exposing the arbitrageur to additional risks of losses. Even this simplest trade then becomes a case of what is known as risk arbitrage. In risk arbitrage, an arbitrageur does not make money with probability one, and may need substantial amounts of capital to both execute his trades and cover his losses. Most real world arbitrage trades in bond and equity markets are examples of risk arbitrage in this sense. Unlike in the textbook model, such arbitrage is risky and requires capital.

One way around these concerns is to imagine a market with a very large number of tiny arbitrageurs, each taking an infinitesimal position against the mispricing in a variety of markets. Because their positions are so small, capital constraints are not binding and arbitrageurs are effectively risk neutral toward each trade. Their collective actions, however, drive prices toward fundamental values. This, essentially, is the model of arbitrage implicit in Fama's (1965) classic analysis of efficient markets and in models such as CAPM (Sharpe 1964) and APT (Ross 1976).

The trouble with this approach is that the millions of little traders are typically not the ones who have the knowledge and information to engage in arbitrage. More commonly, arbitrage is conducted by relatively few professional, highly specialized investors who combine their knowledge with resources of outside investors to take large positions. The fundamental feature of such arbitrage is that brains and resources are separated by an agency relationship. The money comes from wealthy individuals, banks, endowments, and other investors with only a limited knowledge of individual markets, and is invested by arbitrageurs with highly specialized knowledge of these markets. In this chapter, we examine such arbitrage and its effectiveness in achieving market efficiency.

In particular, the implications of the fact that arbitrage—whether it is ultimately risk-free or risky—generally requires capital become extremely important in the agency context. In models without agency problems, arbitrageurs are generally more aggressive when prices move further from fundamental values (see Grossman and Miller 1988, De Long et al. 1990, Campbell and Kyle 1993). In our Bund example above, an arbitrageur would in general increase his positions if London and Frankfurt contract prices move further out of line, as long as he has the capital. When the arbitrageur manages other people's money, however, and these people do not know or understand exactly what he is doing, they will only observe him losing money when futures prices in London and Frankfurt diverge. They may therefore infer from this loss that the arbitrageur is not as competent as they previously thought, refuse to provide him with more capital, and even withdraw some of the capital—even though the expected return from the trade has increased.

We refer to the phenomenon of responsiveness of funds under management to past returns as performance-based arbitrage. Unlike arbitrageurs using their own money, who allocate funds based on expected returns from trades, investors may rationally allocate money based on past returns of arbitrageurs. When arbitrage requires capital, arbitrageurs can become most constrained when they have the best opportunities, that is, when the mispricing they have bet against gets even worse. Moreover, the fear of this scenario would make them more cautious when they put on their initial trades, and hence less effective in bringing about market efficiency. This chapter argues that this feature of arbitrage can significantly limit its effectiveness in achieving market efficiency.

We show that performance-based arbitrage is particularly ineffective in extreme circumstances, where prices are significantly out of line and arbitrageurs are fully invested. In these circumstances, arbitrageurs might bail out of the market when their participation is most needed. Performance-based arbitrage, then, is even more limited than arbitrage described in earlier models of inefficient markets, such as Grossman and Miller (1988), De Long et al. (1990), and Campbell and Kyle (1993).

Ours is obviously not the first study of the consequences of delegated portfolio management. Early articles in this area include Allen (1990) and Bhattacharya, Pfleiderer (1985). Scharfstein and Stein (1990) model herding by money managers operating on incentive contracts. Lakonishok, Shleifer, Thaler, and Vishny (1991) and Chevalier and Ellison (1995) consider the possibility that money managers "window dress" their portfolios to impress investors. In two interesting recent articles, Allen and Gorton (1993) and Dow and Gorton (1994) show how money managers can churn assets to mislead their investors, and how such churning can sustain inefficient asset prices. Unlike this work, our essay does not focus as much on the distortions in the behavior of arbitrageurs, as on their limited effectiveness in bringing prices to fundamental values.

The next section of the chapter presents a very simple model that illustrates the mechanics of arbitrage. For simplicity, our model focuses on the case where mispricing may deepen in the short run, even though there is no long-run fundamental risk in the trade. We thus focus on a case that is closest to pure arbitrage, as opposed to risk arbitrage. Section II establishes the main results of the essay, including our results on the effectiveness of arbitrage in extreme circumstances when prices are very far from fundamentals. Section III explores the performance-based arbitrage assumption in more detail. In section IV, we examine some empirical implications of the model. In particular, we extend the logic of the model to the more realistic case of risk arbitrage, rather than the pure arbitrage case modeled in the article. We first ask what are the characteristics of markets in which we expect risk arbitrage resources to be concentrated. We then analyze return predictability and pricing anomalies more generally. Section V concludes.

1. An Agency Model of Limited Arbitrage

The structure of the model follows Shleifer and Vishny (1990). We focus on the market for a specific asset, in which we assume there are three types of participants: noise traders, arbitrageurs, and investors in arbitrage funds who do not trade on their own. Arbitrageurs specialize in trading only in this market, whereas investors allocate funds between arbitrageurs operating in both this and many other markets. The fundamental value of the asset is V, which arbitrageurs, but not their investors, know. There are three time periods: 1, 2, and 3. At time 3, the value V becomes known to arbitrageurs and noise traders, and hence the price is equal to that value. Since the price is equal to V at $t = 3$ for sure, there is no long-run fundamental risk in this trade (this is not risk arbitrage). For $t = 1, 2$, the price of the asset at time t is p_t. For concreteness, we only consider pessimistic noise traders. In each of periods 1 and 2, noise traders may experience a pessimism shock S_t, which generates for them, in the aggregate, the demand for the asset given by:

$$QN(t) = [V - S_t]/p_t. \tag{1}$$

At time $t = 1$, the first-period noise trader shock, S_1, is known to arbitrageurs, but the second-period noise trader shock is uncertain. In particular, there is some chance that $S_2 > S_1$, i.e., that noise trader misperceptions deepen before they correct at $t = 3$. De Long et al. (1990) stressed the importance of such noise trader risk for the analysis of arbitrage.

Both arbitrageurs and their investors are fully rational. Risk-neutral arbitrageurs take positions against the mispricing generated by the noise traders. Each period, arbitrageurs have cumulative resources under management (including their borrowing capacity) given by F_t. These resources are limited, for reasons we describe below. We assume that F_1 is exogenously given, and specify the determination of F_2 below.

At time $t = 2$, the price of the asset either recovers to V, or it does not. If it recovers, arbitrageurs invest in cash. If noise traders continue to be confused, then arbitrageurs want to invest all of F_2 in the underpriced asset, since its price rises to V at $t = 3$ for sure. In this case, the arbitrageurs' demand for the asset $QA(2) = F_2/p_2$ and, since the aggregate demand for the asset must equal the unit supply, the price is given by:

$$p_2 = V - S_2 + F_2. \tag{2}$$

We assume that $F_2 < S_2$, so the arbitrage resources are not sufficient to bring the period 2 price to fundamental value, unless of course noise trader misperceptions have corrected anyway.

In period 1, arbitrageurs do not necessarily want to invest all of F_1 in the asset. They might want to keep some of the money in cash in case the asset becomes even more underpriced at $t = 2$, so they could invest more in that asset. Accordingly, denote by D_1 the amount that arbitrageurs invest in the asset at $t = 1$. In this case, $QA(1) = D_1/p_1$, and

$$p_1 = V - S_1 + D_1. \tag{3}$$

We again assume that, in the range of parameter values we are focusing on, arbitrage resources are not sufficient to bring prices all the way to fundamental values, that is, $F_1 < S_1$.

To complete the description of the model, we need to specify the organization of the arbitrage industry and the relationship between arbitrageurs and their investors, which determines F_2. Recall that we are focusing on a particular narrow market segment in which a given set of arbitrageurs specialize. A "segment" here should be interpreted as a particular arbitrage strategy. We assume that there are many such segments and that within each segment there are many arbitrageurs, so that no arbitrageur can affect asset prices in a segment. For simplicity, we can think of T investors each with one dollar available for investment with arbitrageurs. We are concerned with the aggregate amount $F_2 \ll T$ that is invested with the arbitrageurs in a particular segment.

Arbitrageurs compete in the price they charge for their services. For simplicity, we assume constant marginal cost per dollar invested, such that all arbitrageurs in all segments have the same marginal cost. We also assume that each arbitrageur has at least one competitor who is viewed as a perfect substitute, so that Bertrand competition drives price to marginal cost. Each of the T risk-neutral investors allocates his $1 investment to maximize expected consumer surplus, that is, the difference between the expected return on his dollar and the price charged by the arbitrageur. Investors are Bayesians, who have prior beliefs about the expected return of each arbitrageur. Since prices are equal, an investor gives his dollar to the arbitrageur with the

highest expected return according to his beliefs. Different investors hold
different beliefs about various arbitrageurs' abilities, so one arbitrageur
does not end up with all the funds. The market share of each arbitrageur is
just the total fraction of investors who believe that he has the highest expected return. The total share of money allocated to a given segment is just
the sum of these market shares across all arbitrageurs in the segment. Importantly, we assume that arbitrageurs across many segments have, on average, earned high enough returns to convince investors to invest with them
rather than to index.[1]

The key remaining question is how investors update their beliefs about
the future expected returns of an arbitrageur. We assume that investors have
no information about the structure of the model-determining asset prices in
any segment. In particular, they do not know the trading strategy employed
by any arbitrageur. This assumption is meant to capture the idea that arbitrage strategies are difficult to understand, and a lot of specialized knowledge
is needed for investors to evaluate them. In part, this is because arbitrageurs
do not share all their knowledge with investors, and cultivate secrecy to protect their knowledge from imitation. Even if the investors were told more
about what arbitrageurs were doing, they would have a difficult time deciding whether what they heard was true. Implicitly, we are assuming that the
underlying structural model is sufficiently nonstationary and high dimen-
sional that investors are unable to infer the underlying structure of the model
from past returns data. As a result, they only use simple updating rules based
on past performance. In particular, investors are assumed to form posterior
beliefs about future returns of the arbitrageur based only on their prior and
any observations of his arbitrage returns.

Under these informational assumptions, individual arbitrageurs who experience relatively poor returns in a given period lose market share to those
with better returns. Moreover, since all arbitrageurs in a given segment are
taking the same positions, they all attract or lose investors simultaneously,
depending on the performance of their common arbitrage strategy. Specifically, investors' aggregate supply of funds to the arbitrageurs in a particular
segment at time 2 is an increasing function of arbitrageurs' gross return between time 1 and time 2 (call this performance-based arbitrage or PBA).
Denoting this function by G, and recognizing that the return on the asset is
given by p_2/p_1, the arbitrageurs' supply of funds at $t = 2$ is given by:

$$F_2 = F_1 * G\{(D_1/F_1) * (p_2/p_1) + (F_1 - D_1)/F_1\},$$

$$\text{with} \quad G(1) = 1, \quad G' \geq 1, \quad \text{and} \quad G'' \leq 0. \tag{4}$$

If arbitrageurs do as well as some benchmark given by performance of arbitrageurs in other markets, which for simplicity we assume to be zero return,
they neither gain nor lose funds under management. However, they gain

---

[1] See Lakonishok, Shleifer, and Vishny (1992) for a description of the agency problems in
the money management industry.

(lose) funds if they outperform (under perform) that benchmark. Because of the extremely poor quality of investors' information, past performance of arbitrageurs completely determines the resources they get to manage, regardless of the actual opportunities available in their market.

The responsiveness of funds under management to past performance (as measured by G') is the solution to a signal extraction problem in which investors are trying to ascribe an arbitrageur's poor performance to one of three causes: (1) a random error term (2) a deepening of noise trader sentiment (bad luck), and (3) inferior ability. High cross-sectional variation in ability across arbitrageurs will tend to increase the responsiveness of invested funds to past performance. On the other hand, if the variance of the noise trader sentiment term is high relative to the variation in (unobserved) ability, this will tend to decrease the responsiveness to past performance. In the limit, if ability is known or does not vary across arbitrageurs, poor performance could be ascribed only to a deepening of the noise trader shock (or a pure noise term), which would only increase the investor's estimate of the arbitrageur's future return. The seemingly perverse behavior of taking money away from an arbitrageur after noise trader sentiment deepens, that is, precisely when his expected return is greatest, is a rational response to the problem of trying to infer the arbitrageur's (unobserved) ability and future opportunities jointly from past returns.

Since our results do not rely on the concavity of the G function, we focus on a linear G, given by

$$G(x) = ax + 1 - a, \qquad \text{with} \quad a \geq 1, \tag{5}$$

where x is arbitrageur's gross return. In this case, equation (4) becomes:

$$F_2 = a \{D_1 * (p_2/p_1) + (F_1 - D_1)\} + (1 - a)F_1 = F_1 - aD_1(1 - p_2/p_1). \tag{6}$$

With this functional form, if $p_2 = p_1$, that is, the arbitrageur earns a zero net return, he neither gains nor loses funds under management. If $p_2 > p_1$, he gains funds and if $p_2 < p_1$, he loses funds. Note also that the higher is a, the more sensitive are the resources under management to past performance. The case of $a = 1$ corresponds to the arbitrageur not getting any more money when he loses some, whereas if $a > 1$, funds are actually withdrawn in response to poor performance.

One could in principle imagine more complicated incentive contracts that would allow arbitrageurs to signal their opportunities or abilities and attract funds based not just on past performance. For example, arbitrageurs who feel that they have superior investment opportunities might try to offer investors contracts that pay arbitrageurs a fixed price below marginal cost and a share of the upside. That is, if, at a particular point of time, arbitrageurs believe that they can earn extremely high returns with a high probability (as happens artificially at $t = 2$ in our model), they can try to attract investors by partially insuring them against further losses. We do not consider such "separating" contracts in our model, since they are unlikely to emerge in equilibrium under plausible circumstances. First, with limited liability or risk aversion, arbitrageurs might be unwilling or unable after mispricing worsens to completely retain (or increase) funds under management by insuring the investor against losses, or pricing below marginal cost. Second, these contracts are less attractive when the risk-averse arbitrageur himself is highly uncertain about his own ability to produce a superior return. We could model this more realistically by adding some noise into the third period return. In sum, under plausible conditions, the use of incentive contracts does not eliminate the effect of past performance on the market shares of arbitrageurs.[2] Empirically, most money managers in the pension and mutual fund industries work for fees proportional to assets under management and rarely get a percentage of the upside.[3] As documented by Ippolito (1992) and Warther (1995), for example, mutual fund managers lose funds under management when they perform poorly. Interestingly, Warther (1995) also shows that fund flows in and out of mutual funds affect contemporaneous returns of securities these funds hold, consistent with the results established below.

PBA is critical to our model. In conventional arbitrage, capital is allocated to arbitrageurs based on expected returns from their trades. Under PBA, in contrast, capital is allocated based on past returns, which, in the model, are low precisely when expected returns are high. At that time, arbitrageurs face fund withdrawals, and are not very effective in betting against the mispricing. Breaking the link between greater mispricing and higher expected returns perceived by those allocating capital drives our main results.

To complete the model, we need to set up an arbitrageur's optimization problem. For simplicity, we assume that the arbitrageur maximizes expected time 3 profits. Since arbitrageurs are price-takers in the market for investment services and marginal cost is constant, maximizing expected time 3 profit is equivalent to maximizing expected time 3 funds under management. For concreteness, we examine a specific form of uncertainty about S_2. We assume that, with probability q, $S_2 = S > S_1$, that is, noise trader misperceptions deepen. With a complementary probability $1 - q$, noise traders recognize the true value of the asset at $t = 2$, so $S_2 = 0$ and $p_2 = V$.

---

[2] Our research assistant, Matthew Ellman of Harvard University, has solved a model in which allowing arbitrageurs to offer high-powered incentive contracts does not permit the arbitrageurs with better investment opportunities to separate themselves. The result is driven by two factors: first, limited liability precludes contracts from discouraging imitators through large penalties for poor performance, which are more likely to be levied against imitators, and, second, better arbitrageurs have more valuable alternative uses of their time, making it difficult to discourage the imitators by paying only for success since, at the contract necessary to meet the individual rationality constraint of the better arbitrageurs, the imitators still earn enough by sheer luck to cover their lower opportunity costs.

[3] Hedge fund managers typically do get a large incentive component in their compensation, but we are not aware of increases in that component, and cuts in fees, to avert withdrawal of funds.

When $S_2 = 0$, arbitrageurs liquidate their position at a gain at $t = 2$, and hold cash until $t = 3$. In this case, $W = a(D_1 * V/p_1 + F_1 - D_1) + (1 - a)F_1$. When $S_2 = S$, in contrast, arbitrageurs third-period funds are given by $W = (V/p_2) * [a\{D_1 * p_2/p_1 + F_1 - D_1\} + (1 - a)F_1]$. Arbitrageurs then maximize:

$$EW = (1 - q)\left\{a\left(\frac{D_1 * V}{p_1} + F_1 - D_1\right) + (1 - a)F_1\right\}$$
$$+ q\left(\frac{V}{p_2}\right) * \left\{a\left(\frac{D_1 * p_2}{p_1} + F_1 - D_1\right) + (1 - a)F_1\right\} \qquad (7)$$

2. Performance-Based Arbitrage and Market Efficiency

Before analyzing the pattern of prices in our model, we specify what the benchmarks are. The first benchmark is efficient markets, in which arbitrageurs have access to all the capital they want. In this case, since noise trader shocks are immediately counteracted by arbitrageurs, $p_1 = p_2 = V$. An alternative benchmark is one in which arbitrageurs resources are limited, but PBA is inoperative, that is, arbitrageurs can always raise F_1. Even if they lose money, they can replenish their capital up to F_1. In this case, $p_1 = V - S_1 + F_1$ and $p_2 = V - S + F_1$. Prices fall one for one with noise trader shocks in each period. This case corresponds most closely to the earlier models of limited arbitrage. There is one final interesting benchmark in this model, namely the case of $a = 1$. This is the case in which arbitrageurs cannot replenish the funds they have lost, but do not suffer withdrawals beyond what they have lost. We will return to this special case below.

The first-order condition to the arbitrageur's optimization problem is given by:

$$(1 - q)\left(\frac{V}{p_1} - 1\right) + q\left(\frac{p_2}{p_1} - 1\right)\frac{V}{p_2} \geq 0 \qquad (8)$$

with strict inequality holding if and only if $D_1 = F_1$, and equality holding if $D_1 < F_1$. The first term of Eq. (8) is an incremental benefit to arbitrageurs from an extra dollar of investment if the market recovers at $t = 2$. The second term is the incremental loss if the price falls at $t = 2$ before recovering at $t = 3$, and so they have foregone the option of being able to invest more in that case. Condition (8) holds with a strict equality if the risk of price deterioration is high enough, and this deterioration is severe enough, that arbitrageurs choose to hold back some funds for the option to invest more at time 2. On the other hand, Eq. (8) holds with a strict inequality if q is low, if p_1 is low relative to V (S_1 is large), if p_2 is not too low relative to p_1

(S not too large relative to S_1). That is to say, the initial displacement must be very large and prices should be expected to recover with a high probability rather than fall further. If they do fall, it cannot be by too much. Under these circumstances, arbitrageurs choose to be fully invested at $t = 1$ rather than hold spare reserves for $t = 2$. We describe the case in which mispricing is so severe at $t = 1$ that arbitrageurs choose to be fully invested as "extreme circumstances," and discuss it at some length.

This discussion can be summarized more formally in:

> **Proposition 1:** For a given V, S_1, S, F_1, and a, there is a q^* such that, for $q > q^*$, $D_1 < F_1$, and for $q < q^*$, $D_1 = F_1$.

If Eq. (8) holds with equality, the equilibrium is given by Eq. (2), (3), (6), and (8). If Eq. (8) holds with inequality, then equilibrium is given by $D_1 = F_1$, $p_1 = V - S_1 + F_1$, as well as Eq. (2) and (6). To illustrate the fact that both types of equilibria are quite plausible, consider a numerical example. Let $V = 1$, $F_1 = 0.2$, $a = 1.2$, $S_1 = 0.3$, $S_2 = 0.4$. For this example, $q^* = 0.35$. If $q < 0.35$, then arbitrageurs are fully invested and $D_1 = F_1 = 0.2$, so that the first-period price is 0.9. In this case, regardless of the exact value of q, we have $F_2 = 0.1636$ and $p_2 = 0.7636$ if noise trader sentiment deepens, and $F_2 = 0.227$ and $p_2 = V = 1$ if noise trader sentiment recovers. On the other hand, if $q > 0.35$, then arbitrageurs hold back some of the funds at time 1, with the result that p_1 is lower than it would be with full investment. For example, if $q = 0.5$, then $D_1 = 0.1743$ and $p_1 = 0.8743$ (arbitrage is less aggressive at $t = 1$). If noise trader shock deepens, then $F_2 = 0.1766$, and $p_2 = 0.7766$ (arbitrageurs have preserved more funds to invest at $t = 2$), whereas if noise trader sentiment recovers then $F_2 = 0.23$ and price returns to $V = 1$. This example illustrates that both the corner solution and the interior equilibrium are quite plausible in our model. In fact, both occur for most parameters we have tried.

In this simple model, we can show that the larger the shocks, the further the prices are from fundamental values.[4]

> **Proposition 2:** At the corner solution ($D_1 = F_1$), $dp_1/dS_1 < 0$, $dp_2/dS < 0$, and $dp_1/dS = 0$. At the interior solution, $dp_1/dS_1 < 0$, $dp_2/dS < 0$, and $dp_1/dS < 0$.

This proposition captures the simple intuition, common to all noise trader models, that arbitrageurs' ability to bear against mispricing is limited, and larger noise trader shocks lead to less efficient pricing. Moreover, at the interior solution, arbitrageurs spread out the effect of a deeper period 2 shock by holding more cash at $t = 1$ and thus allowing prices to fall more

---

[4] The proof of this proposition is straightforward, but requires some tedious calculations, which are omitted.

at $t = 1$. As a result, they have more funds at $t = 2$ to counter mispricing at that time.

A more interesting question is how prices behave as a function of the parameter a. In particular, we would want to know whether the market becomes less efficient when PBA intensifies (a rises). Unfortunately, we do not believe that general conclusions can be drawn about how ex ante market efficiency (say, as measured by volatility) varies with a. The behavior of time 1 and time 2 prices with respect to a is very sensitive to the distribution of noise trader shocks.

In our current model, prices return to fundamentals at time 3 irrespective of the behavior of arbitrageurs. Also, the noise at time 2 either disappears or gets worse; it does not adjust part of the way toward fundamentals. Under these circumstances, we can show that a higher a makes the market less efficient. As a increases, the equilibrium exhibits the same or lower p_1 (if arbitrageurs hold back at time 1), and a strictly lower p_2 when the noise trader shock intensifies. In particular, arbitrage under PBA ($a > 0$) gives less efficient prices than limited arbitrage without PBA ($a = 0$).

On the other hand, if we modify the model to allow prices to adjust more slowly toward fundamentals, a higher a could actually make prices adjust more quickly by giving arbitrageurs more funds after a partial reversal of the noise trader shock. A partial adjustment toward fundamentals would be self-reinforcing through increased funds allocated to arbitrageurs along the way. Depending on the distribution of shocks over time, this could be the dominant effect. In general, we cannot draw any robust conclusions about ex ante market efficiency and the intensity of PBA.

However, we can say more about the effectiveness of arbitrage under extreme circumstances. In particular, we can analyze whether arbitrageurs become more aggressive when mispricing worsens. There are two ways to measure this. One is to ask whether arbitrageurs invest more total dollars in the asset at $t = 2$ than at $t = 1$, that is, is $D_1 < F_2$? The second is whether arbitrageurs actually hold proportionally more of the asset at $t = 2$, that is, is $D_1/p_1 < F_2/p_2$? In principle, it is possible that because $p_2 < p_1$, arbitrageurs hold more of the asset at $t = 2$ even though they spend less on it. Perhaps the clearest evidence of less aggressive arbitrage at $t = 2$ would be to show that arbitrageurs actually hold fewer shares at $t = 2$, and are liquidating their holdings, even though prices have fallen from $t = 1$. In the rest of this section, we focus on these liquidation problems.

We focus on a sufficient condition for liquidation at $t = 2$ when the noise trader shock deepens, namely, that arbitrageurs are fully invested at $t = 1$. Specifically, we have:

Proposition 3: If arbitrageurs are fully invested at $t = 1$, and noise trader misperceptions deepen at $t = 2$, then, for $a > 1$, $F_2 < D_1$ and $F_2/p_2 < D_1/p_1$.

Proposition 3 describes the extreme circumstances in our model, in which fully invested arbitrageurs experience an adverse price shock, face equity withdrawals, and therefore liquidate their holdings of the extremely underpriced asset. Arbitrageurs bail out of the market when opportunities are the best.

Before analyzing this case in more detail, we note that full investment at $t = 1$ is a sufficient, but not a necessary condition for liquidation at $t = 2$. In general, for q's in the neighborhood above q^*, where $F_1 - D_1$ is positive but small, investors would still liquidate some of their holdings when $a > 1$. The reason is that their cash holdings are not high enough to maintain their holdings of the asset despite equity withdrawals. The cash holdings ameliorate these withdrawals, but do not eliminate them. For higher q's, however, D_1 is high enough that $F_2/p_2 > D_1/p_1$.

We can illustrate this with our numerical example from Section II, with $V = 1$, $S_1 = 0.3$, $S_2 = 0.4$, $F_1 = 0.2$, $a = 1.2$. Recall that in this example, we had $q^* = 0.35$. One can show for this example that asset liquidations occur for $q < 0.39$, that is, when arbitrageurs are fully invested as well as in a small region where they are not fully invested. For $q > 0.39$, arbitrageurs increase their holdings of the asset at $t = 2$.

For concreteness, it is easier to focus on the case of Proposition 3, when arbitrageurs are fully invested. In this case, we have that

$$p_2 = [V - S - aF_1 + F_1]/[1 - aF_1/p_1], \qquad (9)$$

as long as $aF_1 < p_1$. The condition that $aF_1 < p_1$ is a simple stability condition in this model, which basically says that arbitrageurs do not lose so much money that in equilibrium they bail out of the market completely. If $aF_1 > p_1$, then at $t = 2$ the only equilibrium price is $p_2 = V - S$, and arbitrageurs bail out of the market completely. In the stable equilibrium, arbitrageurs lose funds under management as prices fall, and hence liquidate some holdings, but they still stay in the market.

For this equilibrium, simple differentiation yields the following result:

Proposition 4: At the fully invested equilibrium, $dp_2/dS < -1$ and $d^2p_2/dadS < 0$.

This proposition shows that when arbitrageurs are fully invested at time 1, prices fall more than one for one with the noise trader shock at time 2. Precisely when prices are furthest from fundamental values, arbitrageurs take the smallest position. Moreover, as PBA intensifies, that is, as a rises, the price decline per unit increase in S gets greater. If we think of dp_2/dS as a measure of the resiliency of the market (equal to zero for an efficient market and to -1 when $a = 0$ and there is no PBA), then Proposition 4 says that a market driven by PBA loses its resiliency in extreme circumstances. The analysis thus shows that the arbitrage process can be quite ineffective in bringing prices back to fundamental values in extreme circumstances.

This result contrasts with the more standard models, in which arbitrageurs are most aggressive when prices are furthest away from fundamentals. This point relates to Friedman's (1953) famous observation that "to say that arbitrage is destabilizing is equivalent to saying that arbitrageurs lose money on average," which is implausible. Our model is consistent with Friedman in that, on average, arbitrageurs make money and move prices toward fundamentals. However, the fact that they make money on average does not mean that they make money always. Our model shows that the times when they lose money are precisely the times when prices are far away from fundamentals, and in those times the trading by arbitrageurs has the weakest stabilizing effect.

These results are closely related to the recent studies of market liquidity (Shleifer and Vishny 1992, Stein 1995). As in these studies, an asset here is liquidated involuntarily at a time when the best potential buyers—other arbitrageurs of this asset—have limited funds and external capital is not easily forthcoming. As a result of such fire sales, the price falls even further below fundamental value (holding the noise trader shock constant). The implication of limited resiliency for arbitrage is that arbitrage does not bring prices close to fundamental values in extreme circumstances.

The problem here may be even more severe than in operating firms. In such firms, the withdrawal/liquidation of assets is limited to the amount of debt that the firm has. In the case of arbitrage funds, unless they have a specific prohibition against withdrawals, even the equity capital can cash out because the assets themselves are liquid, as opposed to the hard assets of an operating firm. This difference in governance structures makes arbitrage funds much more susceptible to costly liquidations. In addition, investors probably understand the structure of industry downturns in operating companies better than they understand why arbitrageurs have lost their money. From this perspective as well, funds are at a greater risk of forced liquidation.

This analysis has one more interesting implication. The sensitivity to past returns of funds under management must be higher for young, unseasoned arbitrage (hedge) funds than for older, more established funds, with a long reputation for performance. As a result, the established funds will be able to earn higher returns in the long run, since they have more funds available when prices have gotten way out of line, which is when the returns to arbitrage are the greatest. In contrast, new arbitrageurs lose their funds precisely when the potential returns are the highest, and hence their average returns are lower than those of the older funds.

3. DISCUSSION OF PERFORMANCE-BASED ARBITRAGE

In our model, performance-based arbitrage, by delinking the expected return on the asset and arbitrageurs' demand for it at $t = 2$, generates the results that arbitrage is very limited. Although it is difficult to deny that PBA plays some role in the world, the question remains whether its consequences are as significant as our model suggests.

For example, one might argue that, even if funds under management decline in response to poor performance, they decline with a lag. For moderate price moves, arbitrageurs may be able to hold out and not liquidate until the price recovers. Moreover, if arbitrageurs are at least somewhat diversified, not all of their holdings lose money at the same time, suggesting again that they might be able to avoid forced liquidations.

Despite these objections, we continue to believe that, especially in extreme circumstances, PBA has significant consequences for prices. In many arbitrage funds, investors have the option to withdraw at least some of their funds at will, and are likely to do so quite rapidly if performance is poor. To some extent, this problem is mitigated by contractual restrictions on withdrawals, which are either temporary (as in the case of hedge funds that do not allow investors to take the money out for one to three years) or permanent (as in the case of closed-end funds). However, these restrictions expose investors to being stuck with a bad fund manager for a long time, which explains why they are not common.[5] Moreover, creditors usually demand immediate repayment when the value of the collateral falls below (or even close to) the debt level, especially if they can get their money back before equity investors are able to withdraw their capital. Fund withdrawal by creditors is likely to be as or even more important as that by equity investors in precipitating liquidations (e.g., Orange County, December 1994). Last but not least, there may be an agency problem inside an arbitrage organization. If the boss of the organization is unsure of the ability of the subordinate taking a position, and the position loses money, the boss may force a liquidation of the position before the uncertainty works itself out. All these forces point to the likelihood that liquidations become important in extreme circumstances.

Our model shows how arbitrageurs might be forced to liquidate their positions when prices move against them. One effect that our model does not capture is that risk-averse arbitrageurs might choose to liquidate in this situation even when they don't have to, for fear that a possible further adverse price move will cause a really dramatic outflow of funds later on. Such risk aversion by arbitrageurs, which is not modeled here, would make them likely to liquidate rather than double-up when prices are far away from fundamentals, making the problem we are identifying even worse. In this way, the fear of future withdrawals might have a similar effect as withdrawals themselves. We therefore expect that, even when arbitrageurs are

---

[5] According to the New York Stock Exchange (NYSE) Fact Book for 1993, the total dollar value of U.S. equities held by closed-end funds was only $20.1 billion compared to $617 billion for (open-end) mutual funds, $1,038 billion for private pension funds (who typically have an open-end arrangement with their outside managers), and $6,006 billion in total U.S. equities.

not fully invested in a particular arbitrage strategy, significant losses in that strategy will induce voluntary liquidation behavior in extreme circumstances that looks very much like the involuntary liquidation behavior of the model.

The likelihood that risk-averse arbitrageurs voluntarily liquidate their positions in extreme circumstances is even larger if arbitrageurs are Bayesians with an imprecise posterior about the true distribution of returns on the arbitrage strategy. In that case, a sequence of poor returns may cause an arbitrageur to update his posterior and abandon his original strategy. The precision of the arbitrageur's posterior depends on the amount of past data available to estimate the return on the arbitrage strategy and on how much extra weight (if any) is placed on the more recent data. If arbitrageurs (correctly or not) believe that the world is nonstationary, they will use a shorter time series of data. This will cause their beliefs about the profitability of their strategies to be less precise (Heaton 1994), and to change more in response to the most recent returns. This would further limit the effectiveness of arbitrage in extreme circumstances.

Finally, PBA supposes that all arbitrageurs have the same sensitivity of funds under management to performance, and that all invest in the mispriced asset from the beginning. In fact, arbitrageurs differ. Some may have access to resources independent of past performance, and as a result might be able to invest more when prices diverge further from fundamentals. The introduction of a substantial number of such arbitrageurs can undo the effects of performance-based liquidations. If the new arbitrageurs reverse the price decline, the already invested arbitrageurs make money and hence no longer need to liquidate their holdings. However, after a very large noise trader shock that we have in the model, most arbitrageurs operating in a market are likely to find themselves fully committed. Even if some of them have held back initially, at some point most of them entered and even accumulated substantial debts to bet against the mispricing. As the mispricing gets deeper, withdrawals, as well as feared future withdrawals, cause them to liquidate. Admittedly, the total amount of capital available for arbitrage is huge, and perhaps outsiders can come in when insiders liquidate. But in practice, arbitrage markets are specialized, and arbitrageurs typically lack the experience and reputations to engage in arbitrage across multiple markets with other people's money. For this reason, outside capital does not come in to stabilize a market. In extreme circumstances, then, PBA is likely to be important and little fresh capital will be available to stabilize the market.

4. EMPIRICAL IMPLICATIONS

The model presented in this article deals with the case of pure arbitrage, in which arbitrageurs do not need to bear any long-run fundamental risk.

While even such arbitrage must deal with problems of possible interim liquidations, in most real-world situations arbitrageurs also face some long-run fundamental risk. In other words, their positions pay off only on average, and not with probability one. Most data that financial economists deal with, such as stock market data, come from markets in which informed investors at best make advantageous bets. In this section, we describe some possible implications of the specialized arbitrage approach for financial markets in which arbitrageurs bear some fundamental risk, including both systematic and idiosyncratic risk. In particular, we show that this approach delivers different implications than those of noise trader models with many well-diversified arbitrageurs, such as DeLong et al. (1990).

A. Which Markets Attract Arbitrage Resources?

Casual empiricism suggests that a great deal of professional arbitrage activity, such as that of hedge funds, is concentrated in a few markets, such as the bond market and the foreign exchange market. These also tend to be the markets where extreme leverage, short-selling, and performance-based fees are common. In contrast, there is much less evidence of such activity in the stock market, either in the United States or abroad.[6] Why is that so? Which markets attract arbitrage?

Part of the answer is the ability of arbitrageurs to ascertain value with some confidence and to be able to realize it quickly. In the bond market, calculations of relative values of different fixed-income instruments are doable, since future cash flows of securities are (almost) certain. As a consequence, there is almost no fundamental risk in arbitrage. In foreign exchange markets, calculations of relative values are more difficult, and arbitrage becomes riskier. However, arbitrageurs put on their largest trades, and appear to make the most money, when central banks attempt to maintain nonmarket exchange rates, so it is possible to tell that prices are not equal to fundamental values and to make quick profits. In stock markets, in contrast, both the absolute and the relative values of different securities are much harder to calculate. As a consequence, arbitrage opportunities are harder to identify in stock markets than in bond and foreign exchange markets.

The discussion in this chapter suggests a further reason why some markets are more attractive for arbitrage than others. Unlike the well-diversified arbitrageurs of the conventional models, the specialized arbitrageurs of our model might avoid extremely volatile markets if they are risk averse.

---

[6] Some of these activities, such as short-selling and use of leverage, are limited by government regulations or by fund charters. Many institutions, such as mutual funds, are also restricted in the degree to which their positions can be concentrated in a small number of securities and in their ability to keep their positions confidential.

At first this claim seems counterintuitive, since high volatility may be associated with more frequent extreme mispricing, and hence more attractive opportunities for arbitrage. Assume that all volatility is due to noise trader sentiment and that the average out-performance of the arbitrageur relative to the benchmark, typically called alpha, is roughly proportional to the standard deviation of the noise trader demand shock. This means that if the arbitrageur switches to a market with twice the noise trader volatility, he also can expect twice the alpha per $1 investment. In such a market, by cutting his investment in half, the arbitrageur gets the same expected alpha and the same volatility as in the first market. He is indifferent to trading in these two markets because alpha per unit of risk is the same and he can always adjust his position to achieve the desired level of risk. This assumes that outside borrowing by the arbitrageur is limited not by the total dollar value of the investment, but by the dollar volatility of investment, which also seems plausible. In this simplified environment, the volatility of the market does not matter for the attractiveness of entry by the marginal arbitrageur.

High volatility *does*, however, make arbitrage less attractive if expected alpha does not increase in proportion to volatility. This would be true in particular when fundamental risk is a substantial part of volatility. For example, increasing one's equity position in an industry that is perceived to be underpriced carries substantial fundamental risk, and hence reduces the attractiveness of the trade. Another important factor determining the attractiveness of any arbitrage concerns the horizon over which mispricing is eliminated. While greater volatility of noise trader sentiment may increase long-run returns to arbitrage, over short horizons the ratio of expected alpha to volatility may be low. Once again, this may be true for securities like equities where the resolution of uncertainty is slow and where noise trader sentiment can push prices a long way away from fundamentals before disconfirming evidence becomes available. In this case, the long-run ratio of expected alpha to volatility may be high, but the ratio over the horizon of a year may be low. Markets in which fundamental uncertainty is high and slowly resolved are likely to have a high long-run, but a low short-run ratio of expected alpha to volatility. For arbitrageurs who care about interim consumption and whose reputations are permanently affected by their performance over the next year or two, the ratio of reward to risk over shorter horizons may be more relevant. All else equal, high volatility will deter arbitrage activity.

To specialized arbitrageurs, both systematic and idiosyncratic volatility matters. In fact, idiosyncratic volatility probably matters more, since it cannot be hedged and arbitrageurs are not diversified. Ours is not the first article to emphasize that idiosyncratic risk matters in a world of information costs and specialization.[7] Merton (1987) suggests that idiosyncratic risk

---

[7] The importance of idiosyncratic risk in our framework is a consequence of the assumed specialization, and not of the agency problem per se. The agency problem itself is also a natural consequence of the returns to specialization.

raises expected returns when security markets are segmented and investors must incur a fixed cost to become informed and participate in each market. Our view of risky arbitrage activity is easy to distinguish empirically from Merton's view of idiosyncratic risk in segmented markets. In Merton's model, there are no noise traders. As a result, stocks with higher idiosyncratic risk are rationally priced to earn a higher expected return. In our model, in contrast, stocks are not rationally priced, and idiosyncratic risk deters arbitrage. In particular, some stocks with high idiosyncratic variance may be overpriced, and this overpricing is not eliminated by arbitrage because shorting them is risky. These volatile overpriced stocks earn a lower expected return, unlike in Merton's model. A good example is so-called glamour stocks, or stocks of firms with higher market prices relative to various measures of fundamentals, such as earnings or book value of assets (see, for example, Lakonishok, Shleifer, and Vishny 1994). Since these stocks have a higher than average variance of returns, a rational pricing model with segmented markets would predict higher expected returns for these stocks. In contrast, if we take the view that these stocks are overpriced, then their expected returns are lower despite the higher variance. The evidence supports the latter interpretation.

B. Anomalies

Recent research in finance has identified a number of so-called anomalies, in which particular investment strategies have historically earned higher returns than those justified by their systematic risk. One such anomaly, already mentioned, is that value stocks have earned higher returns than glamour stocks, but there are many others. Our analysis offers a different approach to understanding these anomalies than does the standard efficient markets theory.

The efficient markets approach to these anomalies is to argue that higher returns must be compensation for higher systematic risk, and therefore the model of asset pricing that made the evidence look anomalous must have been misspecified. It must be possible to explain the anomalies away by finding a covariance between the returns on the anomalous portfolio and some fundamental factor from the intertemporal capital asset pricing model or arbitrage pricing theory.

The efficient markets approach is based on the assumption that most investors, like the economists, see the available arbitrage opportunities and take them. Excess returns are eliminated by the action of a large number of such investors, each with only a limited extra exposure to any one set of securities. Excess returns to particular securities persist only if they are negatively correlated with state variables such as the aggregate marginal utility of consumption or wealth.

As we argue in this article, the theoretical underpinnings of the efficient markets approach to arbitrage are based on a highly implausible assumption of many diversified arbitrageurs. In reality, arbitrage resources are heavily concentrated in the hands of a few investors that are highly specialized in trading a few assets, and are far from diversified. As a result, these investors care about total risk, and not just systematic risk. Since the equilibrium excess returns are determined by the trading strategies of these investors, looking for systematic risk as the only potential determinant of pricing is inappropriate. Idiosyncratic risk as well deters arbitrageurs, whether it is fundamental or noise trader idiosyncratic risk.

Our essay suggests a different approach to understanding anomalies. The first step is to understand the source of noise trading that might generate the mispricing in the first place. Specifically, it is essential to examine the demand of the potential noise traders, whether such demand is driven by sentiment or institutional restrictions on holdings. The second step is to evaluate the costs of arbitrage in the market, especially the total volatility of arbitrage returns. For a given noise trading process, volatile securities will exhibit greater mispricing and a higher average return to arbitrage in equilibrium. (Other costs of arbitrage, such as transaction costs, are also important [Pontiff 1996.])

We can illustrate the difference between the two approaches using the value/glamour anomaly. To justify an efficient markets approach to explaining this anomaly, Fama and French (1992) argue that the capital asset pricing model is misspecified, and that high (low) book-to-market stocks earn a high (low) return because the former have a high loading on a different risk factor than the market. Although they don't precisely identify a macroeconomic factor to which the high B/M stocks are particularly exposed, they argue that the portfolio of high B/M stocks is itself a proxy for such a factor, which they call the distress factor.

Our approach instead would be to identify the pattern of investor sentiment responsible for this anomaly, as well as the costs of arbitrage that would keep it from being eliminated. To begin, the glamour-value evidence is consistent with some investors extrapolating past earnings growth of companies and failing to recognize that extreme earnings growth is likely to revert to the mean (Lakonishok, Shleifer, and Vishny 1994, LaPorta 1996). With respect to risk, the conventional arbitrage of the glamour-value anomaly, that is, simply taking a long position in a diversified portfolio of value (high book-to-market) stocks, has been roughly a 60:40 proposition over a one-year horizon. That is, the odds of outperforming the S&P 500 index over one year have been only 60 percent, although over 5 years the superior performance has been much more likely.[8] Over a short horizon, then,

---

[8] The exact odds depend on what sample period and what universe of stocks is used.

arbitrage returns on the value portfolio are volatile. Even though this risk may be idiosyncratic, it cannot be hedged by arbitrageurs specializing in this segment of the market. Because of the high volatility of the hedge strategy, and the relatively long horizon it relies on to secure positive returns with a high probability, it is likely to be shunned by arbitrageurs, particularly those with a short track record.

Our approach further implies that, in extreme situations, arbitrageurs trying to eliminate the glamour/value mispricing might lose enough money that they have to liquidate their positions. In this case, arbitrageurs may become the least effective in reducing the mispricing precisely when it is the greatest. Something along these lines occurred with the stocks of commercial banks between 1990 and 1991. As the prices of these stocks fell sharply, many traditional value arbitrageurs invested heavily in these stocks. However, the prices kept falling, and many value arbitrageurs lost most of their funds under management. As a consequence, they had to liquidate their positions, which put further pressure on the prices of banking stocks. After this period, the returns on banking stocks have been very high, but many value funds did not last long enough to profit from this recovery.

The glamour/value anomaly is one of several that our approach might explain. The analysis actually predicts what types of market anomalies can persist over the long-term. These anomalies must have a high degree of unpredictability, which makes betting against them risky for specialized arbitrageurs. However, unlike in the efficient markets model, this risk need not be correlated with any macroeconomic factors, and can be purely idiosyncratic fundamental or noise trader risk.

Finally, the specialized arbitrage approach assumes that only a relatively small number of specialists understand the return anomaly well enough to exploit it. This may be questionable in the case of anomalies like the value-glamour anomaly or the small firm anomaly about which there is now much published work. As more investors begin to understand an anomaly, the superior returns to the trading strategy may be diminished by the actions of a larger number of investors who each tilt their portfolios toward the underpriced assets. Alternatively, investors may become more knowledgeable about the strategies being used and judge arbitrageurs relative to a more accurate benchmark of their peers (e.g., other value managers or a value index), thereby diminishing some of the withdrawals when an entire peer group is performing poorly. The specialized arbitrage approach is clearly more appropriate for difficult-to-understand new arbitrage opportunities than it is for well-understood anomalies (which should presumably not be anomalies for long).

We would nonetheless argue that anomalies become understood very slowly and that investors do not take definitive action on their information until long after a phenomenon has been exposed to public scrutiny. The anomaly is more easily accepted when the pattern of returns is not very noisy and the payoff horizon is short (such as the small firm effect in January). A "noisy" anomaly like the value-glamour anomaly is accepted only slowly, even by relatively sophisticated investors.

5. Conclusion

Our chapter describes the workings of markets in which specialized arbitrageurs invest the capital of outside investors, and where investors use arbitrageurs' performance to ascertain their ability to invest profitably. We show that such specialized performance-based arbitrage may not be fully effective in bringing security prices to fundamental values, especially in extreme circumstances. More generally, specialized, professional arbitrageurs may avoid extremely volatile "arbitrage" positions. Although such positions offer attractive average returns, the volatility also exposes arbitrageurs to risk of losses and the need to liquidate the portfolio under pressure from the investors in the fund. The avoidance of volatility by arbitrageurs also suggests a different approach to understanding persistent excess returns in security prices. Specifically, we expect anomalies to reflect not some exposure of securities to difficult-to-measure macroeconomic risks, but rather, high idiosyncratic return volatility of arbitrage trades needed to eliminate the anomalies. In sum, this more realistic view of arbitrage can shed light on a variety of observations in securities markets that are difficult to understand in more conventional models.

References

Allen, Franklin, 1990, The market for information and the origin of financial intermediation, *Journal of Financial Intermediation* 1, 3–30.

Allen, Franklin, and Gary Gorton, 1993, Churning bubbles, *Review of Economic Studies* 60, 813–836.

Bhattacharya, Sudipto, and Paul Pfleiderer, 1985, Delegated portfolio management, *Journal of Economic Theory* 36, 1–25.

Campbell, John, and Albert Kyle, 1993, Smart money, noise trading, and stock price behavior, *Review of Economic Studies* 60, 1–34.

Chevalier, Judith, and Glenn Ellison, 1995, Risk taking by mutual funds as a response to incentives, manuscript.

DeLong, J. Bradford, Andrei Shleifer, Lawrence Summers, and Robert Waldmann, 1990, Noise trader risk in financial markets, *Journal of Political Economy* 98, 703–38.

Dow, James, and Gary Gorton, 1994, Noise trading, delegated portfolio management, and economic welfare, NBER Working paper 4858.

Fama, Eugene, 1965, The behavior of stock market prices, *Journal of Business* 38, 34–105.

Fama, Eugene, and Kenneth French, 1992, The cross-section of expected stock returns, *Journal of Finance* 46, 427–66.

Friedman, Milton, 1953, The case for flexible exchange rates, in *Essays in Positive Economics*, University of Chicago Press.

Grossman, Sanford, and Merton Miller, 1988, Liquidity and market structure, *Journal of Finance* 43, 617–33.

Heaton, John, 1994, Learning and the belief in low-scaled price portfolio strategies, 1940–1993, manuscript, University of Chicago.

Ippolito, Richard, 1992, Consumer reaction to measures of poor quality: evidence from the mutual fund industry, *Journal of Law and Economics* 35, 45–70.

Lakonishok, Josef, Andrei Shleifer, Richard Thaler, and Robert Vishny, 1991, Window dressing by pension fund managers, *American Economic Review Papers and Proceedings* 81, 227–31.

Lakonishok, Josef, Andrei Shleifer, and Robert Vishny, 1992, The structure and performance of the money management industry, *Brookings Papers on Economic Activity: Microeconomics*, 339–91.

———, 1994, Contrarian investment, extrapolation, and risk, *Journal of Finance* 49, 1541–78.

LaPorta, Rafael, 1996, Expectations and the cross-section of stock returns, *Journal of Finance* 51, 1715–42.

Merton, Robert, 1987, A simple model of capital market equilibrium with incomplete information, *Journal of Finance* 42, 483–510.

Pontiff, Jeffrey, 1996, Costly arbitrage: Evidence from closed-end funds. *Quarterly Journal of Economics* 111, 1135–52.

Ross, Steven, 1976, The arbitrage theory of capital asset pricing, *Journal of Economic Theory* 13, 341–60.

Scharfstein, David, and Jeremy Stein, 1990, Herd behavior and investment, *American Economic Review* 80, 465–89.

Sharpe, William, 1964, Capital asset prices: A theory of market equilibrium under conditions of risk, *Journal of Finance* 19, 425–42.

Sharpe, William, and Gordon Alexander, 1990, Investments, 4th edition, Prentice Hall.

Shleifer, Andrei, and Robert Vishny, 1990, Equilibrium short horizons of investors and firms, *American Economic Review Papers and Proceedings* 80, 148–53.

———, 1992, Liquidation values and debt capacity: A market equilibrium approach, *Journal of Finance* 47, 1343–66.

Stein, Jeremy, 1995, Prices and trading volume in the housing market: A model with downpayment effects, *Quarterly Journal of Economics*, 110, 379–406.

Warther, Vincent, 1995, Aggregate mutual fund flows and security returns, *Journal of Financial Economics* 39, 209–36.

Chapter 3

HOW ARE STOCK PRICES AFFECTED BY THE LOCATION OF TRADE?

KENNETH A. FROOT AND EMIL M. DABORA

1. INTRODUCTION

The classical finance paradigm predicts that an asset's price is unaffected by its location of trade. If international financial markets are perfectly integrated, then a given set of risky cash flows has the same value and risk characteristics when its trade is redistributed across markets and investors.

This essay provides a stark example in which the location of trade and ownership appears to influence prices. We show that the stock prices of three of the world's largest and most liquid multinational companies are strongly influenced by locational factors. Specifically, we test whether location matters by examining "Siamese-twin" company stocks, or pairs of corporations whose charter fixes the division of current and future equity cash flows to each twin. The twins each have their own stock, with its own distinct trading habitat. We examine three examples of Siamese twins: Royal Dutch Petroleum and Shell Transport and Trading, PLC; Unilever N.V. and Unilever PLC; and SmithKline Beecham. At face value, twin charters imply that the twins' stock prices should move in lockstep, in a ratio given by the proportional division of cash flows. Surprisingly, the stock prices of twins do not behave in this manner. Rosenthal and Young (1990) show that the stock prices of Royal Dutch-Shell and Unilever N.V./PLC exhibit persistent and strikingly large deviations from the ratio of adjusted cash flows. To this, we add that the stock prices of SmithKline Beecham exhibit similar types of deviations.

The main contribution of this essay is to show that the relative price of twin stocks is highly correlated with the relative stock market indexes of the countries where the twins' stocks are traded most actively. For example, when the U.S. market moves up relative to the U.K. market, the price of

We thank Richard Meyer, André Perold, Leonard Rosenthal, Rick Ruback, Jeremy Stein, an anonymous referee, and numerous practitioners for helpful conversations and commentary, Chris Allen and Philip Hamilton for help in obtaining data, and the Q-Group, the New York Stock Exchange, and the Division of Research at Harvard Business School for financial support. All errors and opinions are our own.

Royal Dutch (which trades relatively more in New York) tends to rise relative to the price of its twin Shell (which trades relatively more in London). Similarly, when the dollar appreciates against the pound, the price of Royal Dutch tends to increase relative to that of Shell. We consider a number of obvious potential explanations for this behavior, but find that none is able to fully explain it.

A similar sort of phenomenon occurs with closed-end country funds, which invest in emerging markets but are financed by issuing shares on developed-country markets. It is well known that the prices of these shares differ from the net asset values of the fund portfolios. In particular, it appears that closed-end fund share prices comove most strongly with the stock market on which they trade, while net asset values comove most strongly with their local stock markets.[1]

We believe our Siamese-twin stocks provide a more clear-cut example of "excess comovement" for several reasons. First, the twins we examine are among the largest and most liquid stocks in the world. By contrast, closed-end funds (and many of the stocks they hold) are relatively illiquid, so their prices are not as "clean." Second, our Siamese-twin stocks represent claims on exactly the same underlying cash flows. Closed-end shares, on the other hand, are claims not only to a portfolio of foreign stocks, but also to the dynamic trading strategy followed by fund managers. The differences between fund share prices and net asset values might be explained by the perceived value of this strategy. Third, arbitrage between closed-end fund shares and net assets is costly or even forbidden.[2] Indeed, closed-end funds profit by enabling investors to better internationalize their portfolios, so funds tend to open where investment barriers are relatively high. By contrast, the stocks of our twins can be arbitraged easily. They trade on major world stock exchanges, and the twins' stock can both be purchased locally by many investors. For example, a U.S. (Dutch) investor can buy Royal Dutch *and* Shell in New York (Amsterdam). As a consequence, the *additional* costs and informational advantages commonly associated with cross-border trading cannot be used to explain our results.[3]

---

[1] Hardouvelis et al. (1995) chronicle the behavior of thirty-five country funds. They find that the funds trade, on average, at a discount and that fund discounts are sensitive to movements in the host country, U.S., and world stock markets. Similarly, Bodurtha et al. (1993) find that the movement of closed-end country funds prices on U.S. markets is correlated with the U.S. market, while the underlying share prices are correlated with the foreign markets on which they trade. These papers build on Lee et al. (1991), which argues that closed-end fund discounts reflect the sentiment on small stocks (see also Chen et al. 1993; Chopra et al. 1993).

[2] Pontiff (1993) shows that the size and persistence of closed-end fund discounts are cross-sectionally related to measures of arbitrage costs between the net asset values and the fund shares.

[3] This argument assumes that the law of one price holds around the world for each stock. Our data support this assumption, as each individual stock trades for approximately the same price in all markets at the same time.

What sources of international segmentation might explain our findings? One hypothesis, which we discuss below, is that of cross-border tax rules. Withholding taxes on dividends differ across countries and investor clienteles. In most instances, however, the withholding taxes for any given investor are the same for the stocks of any pair of twins. Thus, while helpful, tax-driven stories cannot fully account for our findings.

A second possible source of segmentation is country-specific noise. Suppose that a noise shock hitting, say, U.S. stocks, disproportionately affects the twin that trades relatively more in New York. In other words, stocks that trade more actively in the local market are more sensitive to local noise shocks and less sensitive to foreign noise shocks. This story has an interesting implication: the component of market movements explained by changes in twin's relative prices is likely to be noise. Twin price disparities, which are readily observable, may therefore be informative about market-wide noise shocks, which are not directly observable.

Finally, the comovement patterns we observe might result from institutional frictions involving informational and contractual inefficiencies. Principals must control the agents who invest on their behalf. To do this, it might be optimal to narrowly define agents' discretionary authority or to write contracts that provide incentives for agents to limit discretion. As a result, equity fund managers may be restricted to invest in U.S. or international stocks, or they may be benchmarked against a widely accepted index, such as the S&P 500 (which includes Royal Dutch and Unilever N.V.) or the *Financial Times* Allshare index (which includes Shell and Unilever PLC), even if that index does not exhibit optimal risk/return characteristics. All else equal, these arrangements can create a bias toward certain stocks and away from others, but the arrangements could be optimal given the information and agency problems in investing.

The rest of this chapter is organized as follows. Section 2 briefly describes the organizational structure of the twins. Section 3 presents our tests of comovement and cointegration of price twin differentials. Section 4 discusses the data. Section 5 presents our findings on comovement. Section 6 discusses several possible explanations for the results. Section 7 offers conclusions.

2. THE RELATIONS BETWEEN PAIRS OF CORPORATE TWINS

2.1. *Royal Dutch Petroleum and Shell Transport and Trading, PLC*

Royal Dutch and Shell are independently incorporated in the Netherlands and England, respectively. The structure has grown "out of a 1907 alliance" between Royal Dutch and Shell Transport by which the two companies agreed to merge their interests on a 60:40 basis while remaining separate and distinct entities (Royal Dutch 20F, 1994, p. 1). All sets of cash flows,

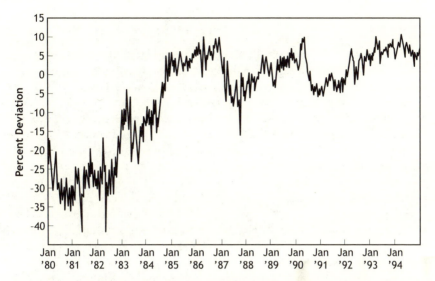

Figure 3.1. Log deviations from Royal Dutch/Shell parity. Note: This figure shows on a percentage basis the deviations from theoretical parity of Royal Dutch and Shell shares and ADRs traded on the NYSE. Data are from the Center for Research in Security Pricing (CRSP).

adjusting for corporate tax considerations and control rights, are effectively split in the proportion of 60:40.[4] Information clarifying the linkages between the two parent companies is widely available. In addition to being explained at the beginning of each Annual Report, the connections are detailed in 20F submissions to the SEC and are the subject of an analyst/ investor guide (Royal Dutch Shell 1994). There is also considerable public information about the relative pricing of Royal Dutch and Shell, and "switch" trades are known by traders as those that seek to take advantage of price disparities between Royal Dutch and Shell.

Royal Dutch and Shell trade on nine exchanges in Europe and the United States, but Royal Dutch trades primarily in the United States and the Netherlands (it is in the S&P 500 and virtually every index of Dutch shares) and Shell trades predominantly in the United Kingdom (it is in the *Financial Times* Allshare Index, or FTSE). Geographical ownership and trading information for Royal Dutch and Shell is shown in table 3.1. Log deviations from the expected price ratio are graphed in figure 3.1.

---

[4] Royal Dutch and Shell Transport shall share in the aggregate net assets and in the net aggregate dividends and interest received from Group companies in the proportion of 60:40. It is further arranged that the burden of all taxes in the nature of or corresponding to an income tax leveeable in respect of such dividends and interest shall fall in the same proportion (Royal Dutch 20F, 1993, pp. 1–2). See also Rosenthal and Young (1990).

2.2. Unilever N.V. and Unilever PLC

Unilever N.V. and Unilever PLC are independently incorporated in the Netherlands and England, respectively. In 1930, the two companies established an equalization agreement of cash flows. According to this agreement, the two companies act as a single group company and use the same board of directors. In the case of liquidation, all assets are to be pooled and divided evenly among shareholders. The intent of the agreement is to make the shares as similar as possible, as if all shareholders held shares of a single company. The Equalization Agreement states that distributions are "made on the basis that the sum paid as dividends on every 1 pound nominal amount of PLC capital is equal . . . to the sum paid as dividends on every 12 fl. nominal amount of ordinary capital of N.V." The PLC shares are listed as 5 pence per share, and the N.V. shares are listed at 4 fl per share. Thus earnings per share (expressed in a common currency) are equated by $(1/5)$ PLC EPS $= (12/4)$ N.V. EPS.[5]

Unilever trades on eight exchanges in Europe and the United States. N.V. trades mostly in the Netherlands, then in Switzerland and the United States (it is in the S&P 500). PLC trades predominantly in the United Kingdom (it is in the FTSE). Geographical ownership data are given in table 3.1. Log deviations from the expected price ratio are graphed in figure 3.2.

2.3. SmithKline Beecham

SmithKline Beckman and Beecham Group merged to form SmithKline Beecham on July 26, 1989. The former holders of Beecham (a U.K. company) received class A ordinary shares while former holders of SmithKline Beckman (a U.S. corporation) received Equity Units (class E shares) comprised of five shares of SmithKline Beecham B ordinary shares and one preferred share of SmithKline Beecham Corporation. The equity units receive their dividends from SB Corp., a wholly owned American subsidiary. The dividends are equalized, so that one class E share provides the same dividend flow as one class A share.[6]

Geographic ownership data are unavailable, so table 3.1 lists trading as a percentage of yearly trading volume. A shares are traded predominantly in the U.K., while H (the ADR on A shares) and E shares are traded in the U.S. Log deviations from parity are graphed in figure 3.3.

---

[5] The 1993 Unilever N.V. 20F submission to the SEC (1993, p. 2) states: "Since 1930 N.V. and PLC have operated as nearly as is practical as a single entity . . . they have agreed to cooperate in every way for the purpose of maintaining a common policy in every field of operations." See also Rosenthal and Young (1990).

[6] Dividends on Equity Units, which are paid by SmithKline Beecham Corporation (SB Corp.), are equivalent to the dividends on the A shares of the Company together with the related tax credit, and include the cumulative preference dividends on the Participating Preferred Shares of SB Corp. up to the date of payment (SmithKline Beecham Annual Report and Accounts, 1993).

TABLE 3.1
Distribution of Share Ownership and Trading Volume Across Markets

Panel A: Ownership (average 1980–1992)

Company	Percent Owned in		
	U.S.	U.K.	Netherlands
Royal Dutch	33	4	34
Shell	3	96	<1
Unilever N.V.	16	10	46
Unilever PLC	<1	99	<1

Panel B: Trading volume (average 1991–1995)

Company	Percent of Average Daily Volume Traded in		
	U.S.	U.K.	Netherlands
Royal Dutch	70	NA	30
Shell (ADR)	32	68	NA
SmithKline	83	17	NA

Sources: Royal Dutch and Shell 20-F statements, 1980–1992; Unilever N.V., 20-F, 1980–1983; a booklet published by Unilever N.V. entitled 'Charts 1984–1994'; Trading volume data are from the NYSE and London Stock Exchange.

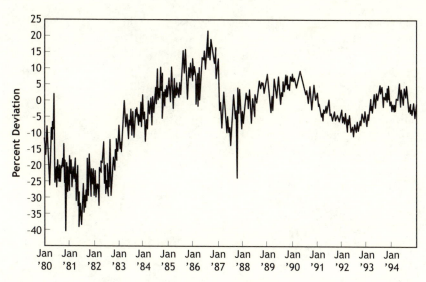

Figure 3.2. Log deviations from Unilever N.V./Unilever PLC parity. *Note*: This figure shows on a percentage basis the deviations from theoretical parity of Unilever N.V. and PLC shares and ADRs traded on the NYSE. Data are from the Center for Research in Security Pricing (CRSP).

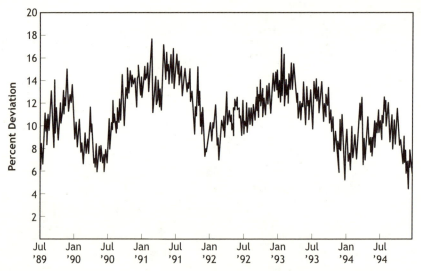

Figure 3.3. Log deviations from SmithKline Beecham parity. *Note*: This figure shows on a percentage basis the deviations from theoretical parity of SmithKline Beecham H and E shares are traded on the NYSE. Data are from the Center for Research in Security Pricing (CRSP).

3. EMPIRICAL HYPOTHESES AND TESTS

Our null hypothesis is that relative twin prices should be uncorrelated with everything. Our alternative hypothesis is that markets are segmented, so that relative market shocks explain movements in the price differential. Specifically, we hypothesize that stocks that are most intensively traded on a given market will comove excessively with that market's return and currency.

To measure the relative comovement of twin prices, we regress the twins' log return differential on U.S., U.K., and Dutch market index log returns plus the relevant log currency changes:

$$
r_{\text{A-B},t} = \alpha + \sum_{i=-1}^{1} \beta_i S\&P_{t+i} + \sum_{j=-1}^{1} \delta_j FTSE_{t+j} + \sum_{k=-1}^{1} \lambda_k DI_{t+k}
$$

$$
+ \sum_{l=-1}^{1} \gamma_l gl/\$_{t+l} + \sum_{m=-1}^{1} \upsilon_m gl/\pounds_{t+m} + \varepsilon_t, \tag{1}
$$

where A and B represent the twin pair. Because of the cross-border aspects of these markets, we include currency changes as well as local-currency stock returns as market factors in Eq. (1). The null hypothesis is that all of the slope coefficients are zero. Under the alternative hypothesis, the more a stock trades on a given market, the higher its estimated slope. So for example, since Unilever N.V. trades relatively less intensively in the United Kingdom than Unilever PLC, the relative return of N.V. over PLC should generate a negative coefficient on the FTSE, and a positive coefficient on the S&P and Dutch markets (where N.V. trades relatively more intensively). Similarly, the N.V./PLC differential should exhibit a negative coefficient on the guilder/dollar and guilder/pound exchange rates. For given local-currency stock returns, an appreciation of the guilder increases the return on the Dutch index relative to other indexes, and therefore should increase the N.V./PLC differential.

Clearly, the log dollar return on a foreign stock index can be written as the sum of the local-currency stock return plus the log currency change. We use this additive decomposition to give each market and currency factor its own coefficient in Eq. (1), which is preferred to imposing the same coefficient for several reasons. First, currency values and local-currency stock prices are typically recorded at different times of day, inducing measurement error in the dollar returns. By separating out the two factors, we keep any measurement error in one of the variables from infecting the coefficient on the other currency change and local-market stock return are nearly uncorrelated). Second, any change in the dollar value of foreign stocks must be due to some combination of currency change and local stock return. It is useful to know if the relative twin returns have differential exposures to these two factors. For example, if local residents drive up the local currency value of local stocks (caused by, say, a decline in risk aversion or by noise), they may drive up the price of the "home" twin relative to the "foreign" twin. We would therefore expect to find a positive beta on the appropriate local currency stock index in Eq. (1). But, changes in the local currency may be driven by entirely different factors, so that the beta on the currency change could be zero.

The data in table 3.1 suggest that under the alternative hypothesis, Royal Dutch should have higher correlation with the U.S. and Dutch markets, while Shell should have higher correlation with the U.K. market. The same is true for the relative returns on Unilever N.V. and PLC. For SmithKline Beecham, the A (or H) share/E share differential should vary positively with the U.S. market and negatively with the U.K. market.

We estimate Eq. (1) using return horizons of 1, 2, 5, 15, and 50 days. The lower frequency regressions are less affected by imperfect synchronization of price observations (e.g., prices are observed at the closes of the New York and European markets, which occur with a five-hour difference), staleness, bid/ask bounce, etc. Furthermore, these tests can help differentiate among the underlying causes of segmentation. For example, if liquidity shocks explain the comovement of local market stocks, they should do so predominantly at higher frequencies.

We also examine the twin price differential for evidence of univariate mean reversion at very low frequencies. Specifically, we test to see whether we can reject the hypothesis that twin price disparities contain unit roots:

$$\Delta P_{A-B,t} = \alpha + \delta t + \beta P_{A-B,t-1} + \gamma(\Delta P_{A,t-1} - \Delta P_{B,t-1}) + \varepsilon_t, \qquad (2)$$

where $P_{A-B,t}$ is the difference in the logs of twin prices, and Δ is the first-difference operator. The null hypothesis of a unit root in price differentials is given by $\beta = 0$. Naturally, this null hypothesis is unlikely to be true: it is hard to accept the notion that the price differential contains a unit root, so that over sufficient time, the probability that the differential becomes arbitrarily large equals one. However, we use Eq. (2) to get a point estimate of the rate at which price differentials decay. We also investigate the multivariate comovement of price disparities and market indexes. In particular, we test whether price disparities are cointegrated with some linear combination of stock indexes.

4. DATA

European stock prices for Shell and Unilever PLC are taken from the London Stock Exchange, while the prices of Royal Dutch and Unilever N.V. are from the Amsterdam Exchange.[7] Royal Dutch, Shell, Unilever PLC, and Unilever N.V. are traded as American Depository Receipts (ADRs) in the U.S. Royal Dutch trades in the U.S. market as a regular security.[8] U.S. return data are from Center for Research in Security Prices (CRSP). The sample period is January 1, 1980 to December 31, 1995. European prices for SmithKline Beecham A shares are from Interactive Data Corporation and dividend data are from Bloomberg Data Services. SmithKline Beecham E shares and ADRs of the A shares (H shares) are from CRSP. The sample period follows the merger of SmithKline and Beecham, July 26, 1989 to December 31, 1995. All returns are expressed in log form.

For U.S. and U.K. market returns, we use log returns of the S&P 500 and FTSE indexes, respectively. The use of these popular indexes creates some ambiguity because Royal Dutch and Unilever N.V. are in the S&P 500 and Shell, Unilever PLC, and SmithKline Beecham are in the FTSE. Consequently, the regression coefficients are slightly biased relative to what they would be on indexes that exclude these stocks. The bias is minor since these

---

[7] Data for Royal Dutch, Shell, and Unilever PLC are total returns from Datastream. For Unilever N.V., we use price data from Interactive Data Corporation, and total return data from Datastream (January 1, 1993 to December 31, 1995). We obtain dividend information for Unilever N.V. from Rosenthal and Young (January 1, 1980 to May 16, 1986), corporate annual reports (May 17, 1986 to May 4, 1989), and Bloomberg (May 5, 1989 to December 31, 1992).

[8] Shell Oil U.S. handles shareholder servicing responsibilities for Royal Dutch in the United States, making ADRs unnecessary.

stocks comprise only a small part of index capitalization. To see this, one can estimate the approximate bias in the coefficient relative to what it would be in the absence of an own-stock effect. Using data on capitalizations, covariances, and variances from 1994, for example, we calculate an upward bias of 0.032 in the coefficient for Shell, which has the largest capitalization of the three stocks in the FTSE.[9] This source of bias is too small to affect the results presented below.[10]

The own-stock effect is more severe in the case of the Netherlands stock index. Royal Dutch is by far the largest native stock traded on the Amsterdam Exchange. To eliminate any confusion, we remove Royal Dutch from the standard CBS Allshare General Price index. Data for this index and all other European indexes and exchange rates are obtained from Datastream.

Another important consideration is where returns are measured. In the tables below, we estimate the relative return on the twins by taking the difference of their log returns *in the markets where they trade most actively*. For example, we use the returns of Royal Dutch and Shell in Amsterdam and London. The basic results are unaffected if we use instead the relative return of Royal Dutch and Shell observed in, say, New York. In other words, the results we report are not sensitive to geographic deviations in the law of one price for any given stock.

A final issue concerns the currency denomination of returns. We leave all return variables in local currencies and then add exchange-rate changes as separate independent variables on the right-hand side of the regressions. To the extent that exchange rates and local-currency equity returns are uncorrelated, any error in exchange-rate changes from nonsynchroneities will not bias the coefficients.[11]

---

[9] The bias in beta is given by

$$\beta_w - \beta_{w/o} = \left(\frac{Cov(r_{sh}, r_{ftse})}{Var(r_{ftse})} \right) - \left(\frac{Cov(r_{sh}, r) - \alpha Var(r_{sh})}{Var(r_{ftse}) - \alpha^2 Var(r_{sh}) - 2\alpha Cov(r_{sh}, r_{ftse})} \right),$$

where β_w and $\beta_{w/o}$ are regression coefficients with and without Shell included in the FTSE, and α is Shell's fraction of the FTSE's capitalization (equal to 0.030 in 1994). Using data from 1994 to estimate the variances and covariances above, β_w and $\beta_{w/o}$ are estimated as 0.913 and 0.891, respectively. This suggests that the beta estimate is approximately 0.02 too high.

[10] In some tests (not reported), we create our own value-weighted U.K. stock index of the 20 largest U.K. stocks (as of 1993) excluding Shell, Unilever PLC, and SmithKline Beecham. The coefficients on this index are nearly identical to those on the FTSE.

[11] Exchange-rate changes and local-currency stock returns show little correlation in our data. In an earlier version of this work (available from the authors), we provide a second method of dealing with currencies. We convert all returns into a common currency, and omit exchange-rate changes from the right-hand side of the regressions. In principle this method is inferior, because nonsynchronous measurement of currency rates and stock prices introduce measurement error into the right-hand side variables. However, in practice the two methodologies yield very similar results.

5. Results

5.1. Alternative Specifications

Tables 3.2–3.4 report estimates of Eq. (1) for Royal Dutch/Shell, Unilever N.V./PLC, and SmithKline Beecham, respectively.[12] Each line in the tables represents a slight variant of the general specification of the regression. The first four specifications use one-day return horizons, while specifications 5–8 use longer return horizons. For the one-day returns, specifications 1 and 2 represent slightly different lead/lag variants. In specification 1, the independent variables have one lead and one lag of all right-hand side variables. In specification 2, we restrict the leads and lags to those suggested by the actual market timing differences. For example, in table 3.2, the dependent variable, the relative return of Royal Dutch over Shell, is observed daily at the close of European trading. Since the European markets close before the U.S. market, only the earlier day's U.S. market return is included on the right-hand side of specification 2. Specifications 3 and 4 are analogous to specifications 1 and 2, except that a lagged dependent variable is added to the right-hand side. This allows us to estimate the short-run versus long-run effects of a change in the market indicators on the twin price disparity:[13]

$$r_{A-B,s} = \alpha + \theta r_{A-B,s-1} + \beta r_{S\&P,s} + \delta r_{FTSE,s} + \lambda r_{DI,s}$$
$$+ \gamma g l / \$_s + \upsilon g l / £_s + \varepsilon_{A-B,s}. \tag{3}$$

The coefficient β can be interpreted as the short-run response of the return differential to a shock to the S&P 500, and $\beta/(1 - \theta)$ can be interpreted as the long-run response. If prices tend to revert toward parity, then we should find that long-run responses are smaller than short-run responses, so that $\theta < 0$.

Specifications 5–8 report results for return horizons of 2, 5, 15, and 50 days using specification 2. Because low power does not appear to be a problem at these horizons, we use nonoverlapping returns to make inferences more reliable.[14]

---

[12] In the tables, twin equity returns are observed in the country where each twin is most liquid. We tried using returns from a common market (e.g., Royal Dutch and Shell both measured on the NYSE). See the earlier version of this chapter for details. The results were qualitatively similar to those presented here. Small differences in coefficients (particularly in the 1-day regressions) occur, however, due to transient deviations from the law of one price for any given stock.

[13] Leads and lags in (3) are identical to those in (1) for all variables other than the lagged dependent variable. They are omitted to keep the notation simple.

[14] Nonoverlapping returns fail to utilize all the information in the data. However, they generate higher quality standard errors because the residuals are serially uncorrelated under the null hypothesis.

5.2. Estimates

The results in tables 3.2–3.4 strongly reject the perfect-integration hypothesis. The signs of virtually all coefficients line up with our alternative hypothesis, and most are significantly different from zero at the 1 percent level.[15] The estimates are also economically large. In table 3.2, for example, the one-day Royal Dutch/Shell return differential yields coefficients of about 0.15 on the S&P, −0.50 on the FTSE, and 0.30 on the Dutch index. The coefficients on the exchange rate changes are also large, at −0.10 and −0.50 for the guilder/dollar and guilder/pound exchange rates. A 1 percent appreciation of the guilder against the dollar and pound, respectively, increases the relative price of Royal Dutch over Shell by about 10 and 50 basis points. These coefficient values also imply that a 1 percent appreciation of the dollar relative to the pound increases the relative price of Royal Dutch over Shell by about 40 basis points.

It is also interesting to note that much of the variation in return differentials (which have an average annualized standard deviation of about 17 percent) is explained by Eq. (1). The R^2s in table 3.2 are surprisingly high, around 20 percent for one-day returns and up to 50 percent for longer-horizon returns.

The coefficient estimates appear reasonably stable over time. Interestingly, a large change in Shell ownership occurred in 1985, when U.S. holdings rose to 8 percent from under 1 percent. Table 3.2 suggests that this change in ownership was associated with a decline in the S&P coefficient, consistent with our alternative hypothesis. Specifications 3 and 4 yield estimates of the lagged-dependent variable coefficient, θ_{AB}, of about −0.2, which is strongly statistically significant. This implies that the short-horizon beta coefficients are about 20 percent greater than their long-horizon counterparts. While this estimate is not small economically, it suggests that the comovements we measure persist over longer return horizons.

Tables 3.3 and 3.4 reveal a similar story for Unilever N.V./PLC and SmithKline Beecham. We reject the null hypothesis in most cases at the 1 percent level.

These results provide evidence of comovement between relative twin prices and market indexes for both short and long horizons. The data actually reveal an even stronger finding: in our sample, we find no statistical evidence that the comovement is at all transient. Specifically, we cannot reject the hypotheses that: (1) the price differentials contain unit roots, and (2) the price differentials and stock indexes are cointegrated.

In table 3.5 we investigate whether the price differentials contain unit roots using the augmented Dickey–Fuller test. The data cannot reject the

---

[15] The significance tests are F-tests on the sum of the lead, current, and lag coefficients for each index.

TABLE 3.2
Royal Dutch/Shell Price Differentials and Market Movements

This table reports regression estimates of the equation:

$$r_{RD-SH,t} = \alpha + \sum_{i=-1}^{1} \beta_i S\&P_{t+i} + \sum_{j=-1}^{1} \delta_j FTSE_{t+j} + \sum_{k=-1}^{1} \lambda_k DI_{t+k} + \sum_{l=-1}^{1} \gamma_l\, gl/\$_{t+l} + \sum_{m=-1}^{1} v_m\, gl/£_{t+m} + \varepsilon_t$$

where $r_{RD-SH,t}$ is the difference between the log returns of Royal Dutch (Amsterdam) and Shell (London); S&P, FTSE, and DI are returns on the S&P, *Financial Times* Allshare index, and Dutch stock indexes, respectively, expressed in their native currencies; and $gl/\$$ and $gl/£$ represent log changes in the guilder-to-dollar and guilder-to-pound exchange rates. Specification 1 includes leads and lags (shown) to allow for nonsynchronous trading. Specification 2 employs a more restricted set of leads and lags (based on actual time differentials). Specifications 3 and 4 are the same as Specifications 1 and 2, but include a lagged dependent variable on the right-hand side. Durbin's Alternate H (DAH) is reported in place of the Durbin–Watson (DW) statistic for Specifications 3 and 4. Specifications 5, 6, 7, 8 employ 2-, 5-, 15-, and 50-day returns. For these specifications, leads and lags of independent variables are dropped. All regressions are OLS, with standard errors that allow for serial correlation and heteroskedasticity. Where there is only a single coefficient, standard errors are in parentheses.

Specification	Return Horizon	R^2	DW or DAH	DOF	Lagged Dep. Var.	S&P	FTSE	Dutch Index	gl/$	gl/£
1, 1980–1995	1 day	0.247	2.37	4155		0.207[c]	−0.428[c]	0.150[c]	−0.102[c]	−0.345[c]
2, 1980–1995	1 day	0.218	2.35	4164		0.135[c]	−0.516[c]	0.365[c]	−0.123[c]	−0.612[c]
3, 1980–1995	1 day	0.271	−0.39[c]	4154		0.205[c]	−0.516[c]	0.213[c]	−0.113[c]	−0.439[c]
4, 1980–1995	1 day	0.262	0.19	4164	−0.174[c]	0.146[c]	−0.536[c]	0.359[c]	−0.121[c]	−0.612[c]
5, 1980–1995	2 days	0.204	2.42	1950	−0.209[c]	0.064[b]	−0.451[c]	0.292[c]	−0.041[a]	−0.502[c]
						(0.032)	(0.038)	(0.032)	(0.030)	(0.047)
6, 1980–1995	5 days	0.244	2.29	776		0.087[b]	−0.409[c]	0.246[c]	−0.068[a]	−0.440[c]
						(0.038)	(0.042)	(0.041)	(0.046)	(0.070)

7, 1980–1995	15 days	0.233	2.49	254	0.116^c	−0.370^c	0.213^c	−0.126^b	−0.287^c
					(0.048)	(0.048)	(0.053)	(0.059)	(0.070)
8, 1980–1995	50 days	0.521	2.35	71	0.184^c	−0.489^c	0.285^c	−0.170^c	−0.385^c
					(0.078)	(0.066)	(0.060)	(0.072)	(0.102)
2, 1980	1 day	0.187	2.40	250	0.074	−0.636^c	0.450^c	−0.114	−0.629^c
2, 1981	1 day	0.274	2.33	253	0.483^b	−0.882^c	0.817^c	−0.449^b	0.885^c
2, 1982	1 day	0.188	2.29	253	0.186	−0.540^c	0.356^c	−0.152	−0.846^c
2, 1983	1 day	0.265	2.05	253	0.291^c	−0.500^c	0.141^a	−0.065	−0.779^c
2, 1984	1 day	0.305	2.19	253	0.206	−0.556^c	0.364^c	0.024	−0.752^c
2, 1985	1 day	0.158	2.39	253	−0.036	−0.307^c	0.158^b	−0.050	−0.562^c
2, 1986	1 day	0.295	2.02	253	0.131^c	−0.323^c	0.198^c	−0.067	−0.564^c
2, 1987	1 day	0.293	2.38	253	0.048^c	−0.496^c	0.484^c	0.212	−0.656^c
2, 1988	1 day	0.270	2.69	253	0.084^b	−0.630^c	0.437^c	−0.178	−0.583^c
2, 1989	1 day	0.362	2.16	253	0.069	−0.722^c	0.464^c	−0.177^b	−0.345^c
2, 1990	1 day	0.256	2.43	253	0.091^b	−0.306^c	0.247^c	−0.182	−0.695^c
2, 1991	1 day	0.189	2.09	253	0.033	−0.562^c	0.499^c	−0.005	−0.328^a
2, 1992	1 day	0.242	2.23	253	0.151	−0.428^c	0.289^c	−0.187^b	−0.430^c
2, 1993	1 day	0.323	2.27	253	−0.097	−0.475^c	0.266^c	−0.009	−0.659^c
2, 1994	1 day	0.376	2.45	253	0.224^c	−0.698^c	0.388^c	0.260^c	−0.556^c
2, 1995	1 day	0.183	2.65	252	0.059	−0.270^c	0.186^b	−0.169^b	−0.357^c

[a] Significant at the 10% level for F-tests that the sum of all coefficients (leads and lags) equals zero.
[b] Significant at the 5% level.
[c] Significant at the 1% level.

TABLE 3.3

Unilever N.V./Unilever PLC Price Differentials and Market Movements

This table reports regressions estimates of the equation:

$$r_{NV-PLC,t} = \alpha + \sum_{i=-1}^{1} \beta_i S\&P_{t+i} + \sum_{j=-1}^{1} \delta_j FTSE_{t+j} + \sum_{k=-1}^{1} \lambda_k DI_{t+k} + \sum_{l=-1}^{1} \gamma_l gl/\$_{t+l} + \sum_{m=-1}^{1} \upsilon_m gl/\pounds_{t+m} + \varepsilon_t$$

where $r_{NV-PLC,t}$ is the difference between the log returns of Unilever N.V. (Amsterdam) and PLC (London); $S\&P$, $FTSE$, and DI are returns on the S&P, *Financial Times* Allshare index, and Dutch stock indexes, respectively, expressed in their native currencies; and $gl/\$$ and $gl/\pounds$, represent log changes in the guilder-to-dollar and guilder-to-pound exchange rates. Specification 1 includes leads and lags (shown above) to allow for nonsynchronous trading. Specification 2 employs a more restricted set of leads and lags (based on actual time differentials). Specifications 3 and 4 are the same as Specifications 1 and 2, but include a lagged dependent variable on the right-hand side. Durbin's Alternate H (DAH) is reported in place of the Durbin–Watson (DW) statistic for Specifications 3 and 4. Specifications 5, 6, 7, 8 employ 2-, 5-, 15-, and 50-day returns. For these specifications, leads and lags of independent variables are dropped. All regressions are OLS, with standard errors that allow for serial correlation and heteroskedasticity. Where there is only a single coefficient, standard errors are in parentheses.

Specification	Return Horizon	R^2	DW or DAH	DOF	Lagged Dep. Var.	S&P	FTSE	Dutch Index	gl/$	gl/£
1, 1980–1995	1 day	0.290	2.27	4124		0.098c	-0.490c	0.328c	-0.138c	-0.463c
2, 1980–1995	1 day	0.259	2.25	4133		0.046c	-0.624c	0.556c	-0.125c	-0.658c
3, 1980–1995	1 day	0.298	-0.30b	4091	-0.131c	0.098c	-0.571c	0.394c	-0.157c	-0.552c
4, 1980–1995	1 day	0.287	0.13c	4101	-0.182c	0.085c	-0.640c	0.544c	-0.667c	-0.132c
5, 1980–1995	2 days	0.258	2.26	1950		0.041b (0.024)	-0.550c (0.033)	0.467c (0.032)	-0.090c (0.033)	-0.565c (0.052)
6, 1980–1995	5 days	0.244	2.26	776		0.034 (0.042)	-0.470c (0.044)	0.341c (0.048)	-0.123c (0.039)	-0.374c (0.072)

7, 1980–1995	15 days	0.239	2.44	254	0.095[b] (0.057)	−0.436[c] (0.059)	0.253[c] (0.050)	−0.146[b] (0.068)	−0.291[c] (0.102)
8, 1980–1995	50 days	0.352	2.16	71	0.017 (0.082)	−0.376[c] (0.065)	0.274[c] (0.068)	−0.090[a] (0.070)	−0.255[c] (0.099)
2, 1980	1 day	0.300	2.06	247	0.073	−0.596[c]	0.847[c]	−0.401	−0.862[c]
2, 1981	1 day	0.313	2.18	250	0.014	−0.752[c]	0.760[c]	0.009	−0.705[c]
2, 1982	1 day	0.331	2.03	250	−0.092	−0.687[c]	0.725[c]	−0.145	−0.777[c]
2, 1983	1 day	0.163	2.32	250	0.166	−0.392[c]	0.247[c]	−0.070	−0.468[c]
2, 1984	1 day	0.355	2.29	250	−0.007	−0.546[c]	0.547[c]	−0.120	−0.755[c]
2, 1985	1 day	0.235	1.73	251	0.074	−0.506[c]	0.390[c]	0.064	−0.799[c]
2, 1986	1 day	0.355	2.05	251	−0.010	−0.442[c]	0.512[c]	−0.417[c]	−0.940[c]
2, 1987	1 day	0.291	2.34	251	−0.060	−0.744[c]	0.695[c]	−0.093	−0.886[c]
2, 1988	1 day	0.395	2.45	252	0.167[c]	−0.778[c]	0.715[c]	0.101	−0.510[c]
2, 1989	1 day	0.469	2.00	252	0.040[b]	−0.696[c]	0.688[c]	−0.214[a]	−0.838[c]
2, 1990	1 day	0.346	2.21	250	0.188[a]	−0.629[c]	0.548[c]	−0.106	−0.454[c]
2, 1991	1 day	0.256	2.16	250	0.080[a]	−0.635[c]	0.502[c]	−0.116	−0.432[b]
2, 1992	1 day	0.220	2.21	251	0.199	−0.369[c]	0.309[c]	−0.127	−0.450[c]
2, 1993	1 day	0.176	2.58	253	0.002[b]	−0.493[c]	0.202[a]	−0.069	−0.688[c]
2, 1994	1 day	0.200	2.59	253	0.513[c]	−0.775[c]	0.199	−0.668[c]	−0.845[c]
2, 1995	1 day	0.160	2.67	252	0.015[b]	−0.456[c]	0.230[b]	−0.213	−0.464[b]

[a] Significant at the 10% level for F-tests that the sum of all coefficients (leads and lags) equals zero.
[b] Significant at the 5% level.
[c] Significant at the 1% level.

TABLE 3.4

SmithKline Beecham Price Differentials and Market Movements

This table reports regressions estimates of the equation:

$$r_{\text{SKA-SKB},t} = \alpha + \sum_{i=-1}^{1} \beta_i S \wedge P_{t+i} + \sum_{j=-1}^{1} \delta_j FTSE_{t+j} + \sum_{l=-1}^{1} \gamma_l \$/\pounds_{t+l} + \varepsilon_t$$

where $r_{\text{SKA-SKB},t}$ is the difference between the log returns of SmithKline Beecham A shares (London) and E shares (New York); S&P and FTSE, are returns on the S&P and *Financial Times* Allshare index, respectively, expressed in their native currencies; and $\$/\pounds$ represents log changes in the dollar-to-pound exchange rate. Specification 1 includes leads and lags (shown above) to allow for nonsynchronous trading. Specification 2 employs a more restricted set of leads and lags (based on actual time differentials). Specifications 3 and 4 are the same as Specifications 1 and 2, but include a lagged dependent variable on the right-hand side. Durbin's Alternate H (DAH) is reported in place of the Durbin–Watson (DW) statistic for Specifications 3 and 4. Specifications 5–8 employ 2-, 5-, 15-, and 50-day returns. For these specifications, leads and lags of independent variables are dropped. All regressions are OLS, with standard errors that allow for serial correlation and heteroskedasticity. Where there is only a single coefficient, standard errors are in parentheses.

Specification	Return Horizon	R^2	DW or DAH	DOF	Lagged Dep. Var.	S&P	FTSE	$\$/\pounds$
1, 7/89–12/95	1 day	0.221	2.70	1665		−0.270[c]	0.291[c]	0.119[c]
2, 7/89–12/95	1 day	0.216	2.69	1668		−0.390[c]	0.390[c]	0.215[c]
3, 7/89–12/95	1 day	0.311	−0.54[c]	1665		−0.508[c]	0.458[c]	0.212[c]
4, 7/89–12/95	1 day	0.307	−0.43[c]	1667	−0.335[c]	−0.541[c]	0.365[c]	0.214[c]
5, 7/89–12/95	2 days	0.118	2.70	834	−0.318[c]	−0.466[c]	0.409[c]	0.184[c]

6, 7/89–12/95	5 days	0.167	2.68	330	−0.460c (0.064)	0.380c (0.053)	0.136c (0.045)
7, 7/89–12/95	15 days	0.112	2.57	106	−0.275c (0.069)	0.216c (0.055)	0.092a (0.051)
8, 7/89–12/95	50 days	0.217	1.98	28	−0.299b (0.085)	0.120a (0.058)	−0.057 (0.067)
2, 7/89–7/90	1 day	0.450	2.35	253	−0.713c (0.133)	0.629c (0.085)	0.309c (0.085)
2, 7/90–7/91	1 day	0.302	2.57	256	−0.400b	0.242c	0.331b
2, 7/91–7/92	1 day	0.282	2.50	256	−0.167c	0.213c	0.232c
2, 7/92–7/93	1 day	0.214	2.88	256	−0.278c	0.544c	0.237
2, 7/93–7/94	1 day	0.122	2.85	256	−0.235c	0.382c	−0.137a
2, 7/94–7/95	1 day	0.113	2.57	256	−0.060c	0.154c	0.104c
2, 7/95–12/95	1 day	0.143	2.41	107	−0.457c	0.285a	0.035c

[a] Significant at the 10% level for F-tests that the sum of all coefficients (leads and lags) equals zero.
[b] Significant at the 5% level.
[c] Significant at the 1% level.

TABLE 3.5
Cointegration and Unit Root Tests
Augmented Dickey-Fuller Tests of Log Price Differentials and Log Prices

Variable	Coefficient	P-value	Results
$P_{RD,t} - P_{Shell,t}$	−0.0034	0.2926	Fail to reject unit root
$P_{UNV,t} - P_{Uplc,t}$	−0.0042	0.8729	Fail to reject unit root
$P_{SKA,t} - P_{SKE,t}$	−0.0052	0.6212	Fail to reject unit root
Dutch index	−0.0002	0.9845	Fail to reject unit root
FTSE index	−0.0006	0.4106	Fail to reject unit root
S&P index	−0.0007	0.6735	Fail to reject unit root

Variables are relative log prices of twin stocks, e.g., $P_{RD,t} - P_{Shell,t}$ is the log price of Royal Dutch relative to that of Shell. Index variables are stock market total return indexes. Coefficients are estimates of β from the augmented Dickey-Fuller regression, $\Delta P_{A-B,t} = \alpha + \delta t + \beta P_{A-B,t-1} + \gamma(\Delta P_{A,t-1} - \Delta P_{B,t-1}) + \varepsilon_t$.

unit root hypothesis for any of the twins. The estimates from the Dickey–Fuller test also give us a sense for the half-life of price deviations, as measured from daily data. With a coefficient on the lagged twin price differential of 0.004, the half-life of price deviations works out to be almost exactly one-half year. However, this estimate is imprecise, and we cannot reject the hypothesis that the half-life is infinite.

In addition, we test for cointegration between the twin price differentials and arbitrary linear combinations of market indexes. The data reject the null hypothesis of no cointegration for all three sets of twins.[16] This suggests that we would need a longer time series to make even the minimal claim that price differentials do not grow with stock markets differentials over the long run, but instead revert back toward zero.

The basic interpretation of these unit root tests is that price deviations and their relations with market variables are highly durable—so much so that we cannot detect evidence that the price deviations mean revert, or that the price differentials do not follow differentials in market indexes. While we do not take the null hypotheses of these tests too literally, the tests do demonstrate the high degree of persistence in the twin price differentials.

6. Explaining the Comovement of Relative Prices and Market Indexes

In this section we analyze several potential explanations for the price deviations and their comovements with market indexes. In order to conserve

---

[16] To save space, we do not repeat the results here. See Froot and Dabora (1998) for details.

space, we focus on the largest twin pair, Royal Dutch/Shell, although similar results obtain for all three twin pairs. While each explanation could be a
source of slippage between relative prices, it appears none can explain a
meaningful fraction of the price differentials or comovement patterns.

6.1. Preliminary Issue: The Mechanics of Splitting Cash Flow

The Royal Dutch/Shell Group splits net income in the proportion 60:40.
The Group's charter includes an arrangement for offsetting corporate taxes
across countries, so that the 60:40 split applies on an after-corporate-tax
basis. This policy was tested in 1972 when the United Kingdom introduced
a tax system aimed at eliminating double taxation of dividend income, the
Advance Corporation Tax (ACT). ACT provided dividend holders an offset
against corporate taxes on dividends. Specifically, under ACT shareholders
received dividends plus a tax credit from the government. Over time, the
tax credit has varied slightly, but has typically been about 20 percent of the
gross dividend (dividend plus credit).

The Group's response to ACT was to split the value of the credit 60:40,
thereby neutralizing the distributional effects of ACT.[17] To see how this
works, note that any credit going to Royal Dutch shareholders must come
through the company (since the U.K. government credits under ACT apply
only to Shell shareholders). Thus, the Group pays more than 60 percent of
distributed dividends to Royal Dutch shareholders. Inclusive of ACT, the
precise split is 652:435—still a 60:40 ratio—where the ACT credit is 8.7
percent (i.e., 20 percent of the Shell gross dividend of $0.435). Sixty per-
cent of the credit ($0.052) goes to Royal Dutch shareholders, bringing their
payment to $0.652. The remaining $0.348 ($1.000 − $0.652) goes to Shell
shareholders. Thus, the Group's direct shareholder payments are split
652:348, but Shell shareholders also receive the 8.7 percent credit to bring
their after-tax share to $0.348 + $0.087 = $0.435.[18]

---

[17] The 1907 merger agreement anticipated that income taxes paid by parent companies on
group dividends would have to be split 60:40. However, taxes on dividends paid by *shareholders* were not included. Because the ACT behaves both as a group tax on dividends and as
a Shell shareholder credit, there was a dispute within the group companies as to whether Shell
shareholders were entitled, in the spirit of the original merger agreement, to the entire ACT
credit or only 40 percent of that credit. From the inception of the ACT in 1972, the group held
to a 60:40 split of the ACT credit. In 1977, the group resolved the dispute by deciding that the
60:40 split would continue, but that Shell shareholders were to receive supplementary dividends of 15 percent of normal dividends for the 1977–1984 period, in consideration of their
claims (January 13, 1977 press releases by parent companies).

[18] The split can be obtained as follows. Let a represent the fraction of distributed dividends
received by Shell shareholders and b represent the after-tax credit value per unit of distributed
dividends. Royal Dutch shareholders must receive $0.6b = 1 - a$. Shell shareholders receive b
augmented by their tax credit, $b = 1 + a\tau/(1 - \tau)$, where τ is the corporate income tax rate. If
$\tau = 0.20$, then $a = 0.348$.

The larger point here is simply that Royal Dutch/Shell actively maintains its 60:40 policy, even intervening to offset asymmetries in the two countries' corporate tax regimes.

6.2. Discretion in the Use of Dividend Income

One possible explanation for the price behavior is that the parent companies do not pass dividends directly to shareholders, but instead invest a portion of the funds independently. If this is the case, we would expect parent company prices to deviate from the calculated expected price ratio as investment returns varied. However, this does not appear to be the case. The 1907 merger agreement specifies that the parent companies are not to make their own investments, and that they are to pass the dividends received directly along to shareholders.[19]

However, neither company pays out *all* distributed group earnings as shareholder dividends. Both parents maintain a cash reserve account to promote ease in rounding and "to provide a cushion against extreme currency fluctuations"[20] (*Guidance Notes For Investors and Analysts*: 1994, p. 23). The policy is to keep reserves low, but the size of the reserve cushion varies from year to year. Annual reports and company interviews suggest that the reserve account is invested either in cash at a bank or in the form of short-term deposits with a duration of less than three months. To see if the reserve is important, we can cumulate dividends in a common currency, adjusting for splits and short-term interest rates. This provides us with a crude measure of deviations from a common reserve investment policy. If reserve funds withheld by the parents are invested at riskless interest rates, then the ratio of cumulative dividends would be constant. In fact, the ratio of cumulated dividends did deviate from the 60:40 ratio, but only by a maximum of about 75 basis points (see figure 3.4). Such deviations are far too small to explain the magnitude and volatility of the price differentials. Nevertheless, figure 3.4 is interesting since cumulated dividends appear to be correlated with the price differential at low frequencies.

[19] "Royal Dutch Petroleum has no operations of its own and virtually the whole of its income derives from its 60 percent interest in the companies collectively known as the Royal Dutch/Shell Group of Companies . . . ." (Royal Dutch 1994 Annual Report). "The Shell Transport and Trading Company, PLC has no operations of its own and virtually the whole of its income derives from its 40 percent interest in the companies collectively known as the Royal Dutch/Shell Group of Companies" (Shell Transport and Trading 1994 Annual Report).

[20] "As the amounts dealt with under the investment reserve have been, or will be, substantially reinvested by the companies concerned, it is not meaningful to provide for taxes on possible future distributions out of earnings retained by those companies; it is furthermore not practicable to estimate the full amount of the tax or the withholding tax element" (Royal Dutch Shell, 1994 Annual Report).

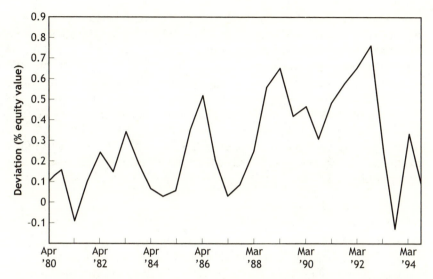

Figure 3.4. Cumulative present value of dividends on Royal Dutch shares relative to those of Shell. *Note*: This figure shows, on a present value basis, the cumulative dividends for Royal Dutch relative to Shell as a percentage of the average stock price. Dividends of Royal Dutch are converted into a common currency and cumulated using short-term interest rates.

6.3. Differences between the Parent Companies' Expenditures

Another potential explanation for the price disparities is that parent company expenses differ. If expenses deviated substantially from the 60:40 ratio, then the net receipts of shareholders would deviate as well. However, expense deviations from 60:40 are far too small to explain our findings. Differential expenses for 1993, for example, impact each share by approximately 6 basis points. A generous capitalization of these expense differentials would yield share price differentials of only about 1 percent.

6.4. Voting Rights

Differences in corporate control might explain price disparities. Royal Dutch has a 60 percent share in both cash flows as well as voting power, so it could use this power to damage Shell shareholders interests.[21] Fluctuations

---

[21] The internal control of the companies is set up as follows. Each parent has its own independent management. The members of the Board of Managers of Royal Dutch and the Managing Directors of Shell are also Group Managing Directors. They maintain positions on the boards of the three Group Holding Companies. The ratio of members on this Group Board is 60:40.

in the value of control would lead to fluctuations in relative prices. The biggest problem with this story is that it fails to explain how Shell can be expensive relative to Royal Dutch, which was the case between 1980 and 1986. Furthermore, a control premium on Royal Dutch would explain the correlation with market indexes only if economy-wide changes in the value of control explain a large fraction of market movements. Finally, anti takeover provisions make it difficult to accumulate large blocks of control of Royal Dutch or Shell. For example, ordinary shareholders of Royal Dutch face a cap on the number of shareholder votes at 12,000. This limits attacks on the management board, which can in principle alter the 60:40 relationship.

6.5. Dividends and Currencies

Dividends are announced by both parents on the same day. At that time, dividend allocations for Royal Dutch (Shell) are converted into guilders (pounds) at prevailing spot exchange rates. In the time between the announcement and payment dates, fluctuations in the pound/guilder rate change the relative value of the dividend payments to Royal Dutch and Shell shareholders.

These factors can explain movements in the price differential, but only very minor ones. Exchange-rate changes matter only during the window between the announcement and ex-dividend dates. Furthermore, they can matter only for the value of the current dividend, not the present value of dividends. For example, assuming that the dividend/price ratio is 5 percent, dividend payments are made semi-annually, pound/guilder volatility is 1 percent per day, and actual payment periods corresponding to those in practice, currency differences in dividend denomination add at most 40 basis points to total return volatility over a year. This is very small relative to the large observed fluctuations in relative twin prices. Note also that we control for currency fluctuations in our regressions. Thus, currency fluctuations cannot explain comovements with local-currency market indexes.

6.6. Ex-dividend Date Structure

Royal Dutch and Shell shares can go ex-dividend on different dates. For example, between 1991 and 1993, the difference between ex-dividend dates for Royal Dutch and Shell was 13 and 63 days, respectively, for interim and final dividend payments. This implies that there will be a price wedge between the two securities if one security is past its ex-dividend date but the other is not. This effect is also small. At a dividend/price ratio of 5 percent, of which approximately 3 percent is the final dividend and 2 percent is the interim dividend, the price differential would be at most a few percentage points. There is also no reason to think that the ex-dividend patterns are correlated with market movements.

6.7. Tax-induced Investor Heterogeneity

Perhaps the most promising explanation for the price behavior is tax distortions. In the presence of such distortions, country-specific shocks to investor preferences or taxation could lead to correlation between relative twin returns and market indicators. However, for this explanation to succeed, taxes not only must segment one country from another, but within each country, taxes must also segment the twin pair.

To see this, suppose that there are differences in dividend taxation across countries and that, within any given country, dividends on twin stocks are treated identically by the local tax authority. Under these circumstances, a reduction in local dividend taxation might well move the local market up relative to the foreign market. However, there is no reason for the twin price differential to change, since from any given investor's perspective there is no change in the after-tax cash flows of one twin relative to the other. Thus, the tax treatment of one twin relative to the other must be different for at least some investor classes for the tax explanation to work.

To address this issue, we examine the tax burdens borne by specific investor groups in the United States, United Kingdom, and Netherlands. Taxation of international dividends is clearly complex. For example, a U.S. shareholder of a U.K. security might pay withholding tax, receive the ACT tax credit, and receive a credit from the U.S. Treasury on the withholding tax.[22] The actual rates paid may be altered through financial contracting or institutional restructuring. In spite of such complications, the tax laws are generally clear on how dividends ought to be treated for investor classes in different countries. Table 3.6 shows dividend withholding tax rates inclusive of ACT for shareholders by country and by investor class (private investors, companies and investment trusts, and pension funds).

The table shows that private investors in all countries should be indifferent toward investing in Royal Dutch and Shell.[23] Companies and investment

---

[22] This ignores taxes that affect both twins identically (e.g., personal income taxes).

[23] When holding Royal Dutch, U.K. residents pay a 25 percent withholding tax, but 10 percent is reclaimable under the U.K./Netherlands double taxation agreement. The United Kingdom also levees a supplemental 5 percent dividend tax, bringing the total tax to 20 percent. The Shell shareholder also pays a net tax of 20 percent on dividends, so that the taxation on Royal Dutch and Shell are the same. Netherlands investors are subject to a 25 percent withholding tax on Royal Dutch dividends, which is creditable against their Netherlands income tax liability on the dividends. Shell shareholders that invest through a U.K. nominee company receive the full U.K. tax credit, but then must pay a 15 percent U.K. withholding tax. The withholding tax is creditable against Netherlands income taxes, so that the effective tax rates are equal on both sources of dividend income.

TABLE 3.6
Taxation of Different Investor Classes in Different Countries, 1993[a]

Country	Investor Class	Tax Rate on Royal Dutch Dividends	Tax Rate on Shell Dividends	Preference	Difference in Annual Return from Tax Differential[b]
UK	Private investors	20%	20%	Indifferent	—
	Companies	33%	20%	Shell	−0.64%
	Pension funds	15%	—	Shell	−0.74%
Nether	Private investors	25%	25%	Indifferent	—
	Companies	25%	25%	Indifferent	—
	Pension funds	—	25%	Royal Dutch	1.23%
US[c]	Private investors	15%	15%	Indifferent	—
	Companies	15%	15%	Indifferent	—
	Pension funds[d]	15%	15%	Indifferent	—

[a] Taxes represented withholding tax, dividend tax, and ACT. Tax treatment of capital gains on Royal Dutch and Shell were equivalent for all shareholder groups, and are therefore not reported.

[b] Average of Royal Dutch and Shell dividend/price ratios (4.92% in 1993) times the difference between Shell and Royal Dutch rates of dividend taxation.

[c] In the U.S., withholding taxes were reclaimable from income tax for corporations and individuals. Withholding taxes on foreign securities could either be deducted against U.S. personal or corporate income taxes, or, under current tax treaties, refunded directly from the U.K. and Netherlands tax authorities.

[d] Historically, U.S. pension and endowment funds were not able to deduct foreign taxes paid against U.S. tax obligations. Following January 1, 1994, U.S. pension funds were able to obtain withholding-tax refunds on Netherlands stocks, such as Royal Dutch, reducing the effective tax rate to zero.

trusts in the Netherlands and United States should also be indifferent between Royal Dutch and Shell, while U.K. companies and investment trusts should slightly prefer holding Shell. Pension funds, however, should not be indifferent between the twins. U.K. pension (or "gross") funds pay no taxes on investments in Shell, but face 15 percent net withholding taxes on Royal Dutch dividends.[24] In contrast, Netherlands pension funds face no taxation on Royal Dutch, but pay 15 percent withholding taxes on Shell. Prior to January 1, 1994, U.S. pensions were indifferent to holding Royal Dutch and Shell, as they faced 15 percent withholding tax for both stocks. After January 1, 1994, the Double Taxation treaty between the United States and the Netherlands became effective, which gives United States pension funds a preference for Royal Dutch.

These facts have several implications. First, there is at least one group of investors in each country that is indifferent to the tax effect. This group

[24] Under U.K. law, tax-exempt investors, including pension funds in the United States, United Kingdom, and Netherlands, are entitled to a full credit against ACT.

could act as the marginal investor to equalize prices. For example, we expect private investors and companies in the Netherlands to hold shares in Shell when it is cheap relative to Royal Dutch. However, we find no discernible increase in the net holdings of Shell in the Netherlands during these periods.

Second, during all but the last two years of the sample period, *all* U.S. investors were indifferent to Royal Dutch and Shell on a tax basis. Thus, we expect to see holding patterns in the United States move toward the cheaper security. For example, Shell was relatively cheap from 1985 through 1992. Nevertheless, very few Shell shares were held in the United States during this period, yet at the same time Royal Dutch holdings in the United States were large and increasing. Furthermore, the tax indifference makes it difficult to explain the correlation of relative prices with either U.S. market returns or the U.S. dollar.

Third, even though some investors may have had tax-induced differences in reservation prices, it is not clear that these differences would be large enough to explain price deviations of 30 percent or more. Thus, tax issues, while potentially helpful, are unlikely to explain all of the components of the price deviations.

7. CONCLUSIONS

This chapter presents evidence that stock prices are affected by the location of trade. It shows that twin stocks, which have nearly identical cash flows, move more like the markets where they trade most intensively than they should. The comovements between price differentials and market indexes are present at long as well as short horizons. Location of trade therefore appears to matter for pricing.

Our study suggests three possible sources of segmentation. The first source is tax-induced investor heterogeneity. This explanation seems incomplete. It does not explain correlations of twin price differentials with the U.S. market, since during the bulk of our sample all major U.S. investor groups faced equivalent tax treatment on twin stocks, and it does not explain why U.S. holdings of the cheap stock did not grow and why holdings of the expensive stock did not shrink.

The second possible source of segmentation is noise. Market-wide noise shocks from irrational traders, which infect locally traded stocks more than foreign traded stocks, can explain the comovements. Indeed, this story suggests that the portion of market movements that is correlated with fluctuations in twins' relative prices is attributable to noise. The main problem with this story—here and more generally—is that the source of noise or persistent irrationality is difficult to identify.

Third, institutional inefficiencies might explain comovements. By virtue of higher liquidity or inclusion in domestic-market indexes, one twin may be classified as a "domestic" stock. (Note that causality here could easily run the other way, suggesting the possibility of multiple equilibria.) Classification as "domestic" or "foreign" appears to be important in practice, and could help resolve informational asymmetries and agency problems in the investment process.

Finally, there is the question of how arbitrage disciplines the price gap. In a frictionless world, it is clear that arbitrage would occur—any single investor could finance sufficiently large long positions to drive prices to parity.[25] But lack of disciplinary arbitrage does not explain why there are deviations in the first place.

---

[25] Specific data on transactions costs and strategies are explored by Froot and Perold (1996).

References

Bodurtha, J., D. S. Kim, C. Lee, 1993, Closed-end country funds and U.S. market sentiment. University of Michigan and Sang Yong Research Institute.

Chen, N. F., R. Kan, M. Miller, 1993, Are the discounts on closed-end funds a sentiment index? Working Paper. *Journal of Finance* 48, 795–800.

Chopra, N., C. Lee, A. Shleifer, R. Thaler, 1993, Yes, discounts on closed-end funds are a sentiment index. *Journal of Finance* 48, 801–8.

Froot, K. A., E. Dabora, 1998, How are stock prices affected by the location of trade. Working Paper no. 6572. National Bureau of Economic Research, Cambridge, MA.

Froot, K. A., A. Perold, 1996, Global equity markets: the case of Royal Dutch and Shell. Case no. 296-077. Harvard Business School.

Hardouvelis, G., R. La Porta, T. Wizman, 1995, What moves the discount on country equity funds. Working paper no. 4571. National Bureau of Economic Research, Cambridge, MA.

Lee, C., A. Shleifer, R. Thaler, 1991, Investor sentiment and the closed-end fund puzzle. *Journal of Finance* 46, 75–109.

Pontiff, J., 1993, Costly arbitrage and closed-end fund discounts. Working Paper, University of Washington.

Rosenthal, L., C. Young, 1990, The seemingly anomalous price behavior of royal dutch shell and unilever N. V./PLC. *Journal of Financial Economics* 26, 123–41.

Royal Dutch Petroleum Company, Shell Transport and Trading, 1994, Guidance Notes for Investors and Analysts.

Chapter 4

CAN THE MARKET ADD AND SUBTRACT?

MISPRICING IN TECH STOCK CARVE-OUTS

OWEN A. LAMONT AND RICHARD H. THALER

1. INTRODUCTION

There are two important implications of the efficient market hypothesis. The first is that it is not easy to earn excess returns. The second is that prices are "correct" in the sense that prices reflect fundamental value. This latter implication is, in many ways, more important than the first. Do asset markets offer rational signals to the economy about where to invest real resources? If some firms have stock prices that are far from intrinsic value, then those firms will attract too much or too little capital. While important, this aspect of the efficient market hypothesis is difficult to test because intrinsic values are unobservable. That is why tests of relative valuation, for example, using closed-end funds, are important. The fact that closed-end funds often trade at substantial discounts or premia makes one wonder whether other assets may also be mispriced.

The most basic test of relative valuation is the law of one price: the same asset cannot trade simultaneously at different prices. The law of one price is usually thought to hold nearly exactly in financial markets, where transactions costs are small and competition is fierce. Indeed, the law of one price is in many ways the central precept in financial economics. Our goal in this chapter is to investigate violations of the law of one price, cases in which prices are almost certainly wrong in the sense that they are far from the frictionless price. Although the number of cases we examine is small, the violations of the law of one price are large.

We thank John Cochrane, Douglas Diamond, Merle Erickson, Lou Harrison, J. B. Heaton, Ravi Jagannathan, Arvind Krishnamurthy, Mark Mitchell, Todd Pulvino, Tuomo Vuolteenaho, an anonymous referee for the *Journal of Political Economy*, and seminar participants at the American Finance Association, Harvard Business School, the National Bureau of Economic Research Asset Pricing meeting, and the University of Chicago finance lunch for helpful comments. We thank Joe Cornell and Mark Minichiello of Spin-off Advisors for data and helpful discussions. We thank Frank Fang Yu for excellent research assistance. Lamont gratefully acknowledges support from the Alfred P. Sloan Foundation, the Center for Research in Security Prices at the University of Chicago Graduate School of Business, the National Science Foundation, the Investment Analyst Society of Chicago, and the Association for Investment Management and Research.

The driver of the law of one price in financial markets is arbitrage, defined as the simultaneous buying and selling of the same security for two different prices. The profits from such arbitrage trades give arbitrageurs the incentive to eliminate any violations of the law of one price. Arbitrage is the basis of much of modern financial theory, including the Modigliani-Miller capital structure propositions, the Black-Scholes option pricing formula, and the arbitrage pricing theory.

Do arbitrage trades actually enforce the law of one price? This empirical question is easier to answer than the more general question of whether prices reflect fundamental value. Tests of this more general implication of market efficiency force the investigator to take a stance on defining fundamental value. Fama (1991, p. 1575) describes this difficulty as the "joint-hypothesis" problem: "market efficiency per se is not testable. It must be tested jointly with some model of equilibrium, an asset-pricing model." In contrast, one does not need an asset-pricing model to know that identical assets should have identical prices.

The same difficulty that economists face in trying to test whether asset prices generally reflect intrinsic value is also faced by real-world arbitrageurs looking for mispriced securities. For example, suppose that security A appears to be overpriced relative to security B. Perhaps A is a glamorous growth stock, say a technology stock, and B is a boring value stock, say an oil stock. An arbitrageur could short A and buy B. Unfortunately, this strategy is exposed to "bad-model" risk, another name for the joint-hypothesis problem. Perhaps the arbitrageur has neglected differences in liquidity, risk, or taxes, differences that are properly reflected in the existing prices. In this case, the trade is unlikely to earn excess returns. Researchers have not been able to settle, for example, whether value stocks are too cheap relative to growth stocks (as argued by De Bondt and Thaler 1985, and Lakonishok, Shleifer, and Vishny 1994) or just more risky (as favored by Fama and French 1993).

Another, second, risk for the arbitrageur is fundamental risk. An arbitrageur who shorts technology companies and buys oil companies runs the risk that peace breaks out in the Middle East, causing the price of oil to plummet. In this case, perhaps the original judgment that oil stocks were cheap was correct but the bet loses money ex post.

In contrast, if A and B have identical cash flows but different prices, the arbitrageur eliminates fundamental risk. If securities A and B have other similar features, for example, similar liquidity, then bad-model risk is minimized as well. Violations of the law of one price are easier for economists to see and safer for arbitrageurs to correct. For example, suppose that A is a portfolio of stocks and B is a closed-end fund that owns A. If B has a lower price than A, then (when issues such as fund expenses are ignored) the arbitrageur can buy B, short A, and hope to make a profit if the prices converge. Unfortunately, this strategy is exposed to a third sort of risk, noise trader risk. An arbitrageur that buys the fund and shorts the underlying shares runs the risk that the discount may widen as investor sentiment shifts. This risk can be either systematic (all closed-end fund discounts widen) or idiosyncratic (Lee, Shleifer, and Thaler 1991). Since there is no guarantee that A and B will converge in price, the strategy is risky.

Noise trader risk can be eliminated in the long run in situations in which A and B are certain to converge in finite time. For example, suppose that at time T the closed-end fund B will liquidate, and all holders of B will receive a cash settlement equal to the net asset value of the portfolio, that is, A. We know that the prices of A and B will be identical at time T. Noise trader risk still exists in the intermediate period between now and T, but not over the long run. The terminal date eliminates other concerns as well; for example, liquidity is not an issue for investors holding until time T. In this case, with no fundamental risk, bad-model risk, or noise trader risk, there still is another problem that can cause the prices of A and B to be different: transactions costs (including trading costs and holding costs).

Both market efficiency and the law of one price are affected by transactions costs. If transactions costs are not zero, then arbitrageurs are prevented from forcing price all the way to fundamental value, and the same security can have different prices. In this case, then, Fama (1991, p. 1575) describes an efficient market as one in which "deviations from the extreme version of the efficiency hypothesis are within information and trading costs." An example is a market in which it is impossible to short a stock, equivalent to infinite transactions costs for short sales. In this market, a stock could be massively overpriced, yet since there is no way for arbitrageurs to make money, the market is still efficient in the sense that there is no money left on the table. Still, this is market efficiency with very wrong prices.

In this chapter we investigate apparent violations of the law of one price in which there are few risk issues involved, but transactions costs involved with short-selling play an important role in limiting arbitrage. We study equity carve-outs in which the parent has stated its intention to spin-off its remaining shares. A notable example is Palm and 3Com. Palm, which makes hand-held computers, was owned by 3Com, a profitable company selling computer network systems and services. On March 2, 2000, 3Com sold a fraction of its stake in Palm to the general public via an initial public offering (IPO) for Palm. In this transaction, called an equity carve-out, 3Com retained ownership of 95 percent of the shares. 3Com announced that, pending an expected approval by the Internal Revenue Service (IRS), it would eventually spin off its remaining shares of Palm to 3Com's shareholders before the end of the year. 3Com shareholders would receive about 1.5 shares of Palm for every share of 3Com that they owned.

This event put in play two ways in which an investor could buy Palm. The investor could buy (say) 150 shares of Palm directly or 100 shares of

3Com, thereby acquiring a claim to 150 shares of Palm plus a portion of 3Com's other assets. Since the price of 3Com's shares can never be less than zero (equity values are never negative), here the law of one price establishes a simple inequality: the price of 3Com must be at least 1.5 times the price of Palm. Since 3Com held more than $10 a share in cash and securities in addition to its other profitable business assets, one might expect 3Com's price to be well above 1.5 times the price of Palm.

The day before the Palm IPO, 3Com closed at $104.13 per share. After the first day of trading, Palm closed at $95.06 a share, implying that the price of 3Com should have jumped to at least $145 (with the precise ratio of 1.525). Instead, 3Com fell to $81.81. The "stub value" of 3Com (the implied value of 3Com's non-Palm assets and businesses) was −$63. In other words, the stock market was saying that the value of 3Com's non-Palm business was −$22 billion! The "information costs" mentioned by Fama (1991) are small in this case, since the mispricing took place in a widely publicized IPO that attracted frenzied attention. The nature of the mispricing was so simple that even the dimmest of market participants and financial journalists were able to grasp it. On the day after the issue, the mispricing was widely discussed, including in two articles in *The Wall Street Journal* and one in the *New York Times*, yet the mispricing persisted for months.

This is a gross violation of the law of one price, and one for which most of the risks identified above do not apply. An arbitrageur who buys 100 shares of 3Com and shorts 150 shares of Palm is essentially buying the 3Com stub for −$63. If things go as planned, in less than a year this value must be at least zero. We do not need to agree on a model of asset pricing to agree on the proposition that one share of 3Com should be worth at least 1.5 shares of Palm. Noise trader risk is minimized because there is a terminal date at which the shares will be distributed. When the distribution occurs, the 3Com stub cannot have a negative price. Fundamental risks about the value of Palm are completely hedged. The only remaining problem is costly arbitrage. Still, investors were willing to pay over $2.5 billion (based on the number of Palm shares issued) to buy expensive shares of Palm rather than buy the cheap Palm shares embedded in 3Com and get 3Com thrown in.

We do not claim that this mispricing creates exploitable arbitrage opportunities. To the contrary, we document the precise market friction that allows prices to be wrong, namely shorting costs. These costs arise when short sales are either very expensive or simply impossible. Although shorting costs are necessary in order for mispricing to occur, they are of course not sufficient. Shorting costs can explain why a rational arbitrageur fails to short the overpriced security, but not why anyone buys the overpriced security. To explain that, one needs investors who are (in our specific case) irrational, woefully uninformed, endowed with strange preferences, or for some other reason willing to hold overpriced assets. We shall refer to these conditions collectively as "irrational," but they could be anything that causes a downward-sloping demand curve for specific stocks (despite the presence of cheaper and nearly identical substitutes).[1] Thus two things, trading costs and irrational investors, are necessary for mispricing. Trading costs, by limiting arbitrage, create an environment in which simple supply and demand intuition is useful in explaining asset prices. In our case, the demand for certain shares by irrational investors was too large relative to the ability of the market to supply these shares via short sales, creating a price that was too high.

We investigate this question using all the cases we could find that share the key elements of the Palm-3Com situation, namely a carve-out with an announced intention to spin off the new issue in the near future. By limiting ourselves to these cases (as opposed to the much larger category of all carve-outs), we are able to minimize the risks that the spin-off never takes place and thus reduce the risk inherent in the arbitrage trade.

We start in section 2 by describing carve-outs and spin-offs, showing how we construct the sample and describing its main features. In section 3 we document high apparent returns that are implicit in market prices, describe relevant risks, and ask whether the high returns can plausibly be explained by risk. In section 4 we describe the short-sale constraints that allow mispricing to persist. We document another notable departure from the law of one price, the violation of put-call parity, and explain how this departure is consistent with short-sale constraints. In section 5 we ask why stubs become negative, look at IPO day returns on parents and issues, and show the characteristics of investors in parents and issues.

2. Sample of Carve-outs

We examine carve-outs followed by spin-offs. An equity carve-out, also known as a partial public offering, is defined as an IPO for shares (typically a minority stake) in a subsidiary company. In an equity carve-out, a subsidiary firm raises money by selling shares to the public and then typically giving some or all of the proceeds to its parent. A spin-off occurs when the parent firm gives remaining shares in the subsidiary to the parent's shareholders; no money changes hands.

---

[1] We use the term "irrational" for lack of a better word, but without wishing to engage in any deep philosophical debate about rationality. If someone buys a stock or bets on a horse because he or she likes the name and, in so doing, forgoes some financial benefit, we shall call that irrational, regardless of whether the utility derived from owning the asset with this name is large enough to compensate for the forgone financial advantage of owning a close substitute with a less desirable name. Since our chapter concerns financial markets, it seems reasonable to equate nonpecuniary with irrational.

We study a sample of equity carve-outs in which the parent firm explicitly states its intention to immediately spin off its remaining ownership in the subsidiary. We study this sample of firms since in this case negative stubs appear to present a trading opportunity with fairly clear timing. In contrast, Cornell and Liu (2001), Schill and Zhou (2001), and Mitchell, Pulvino, and Stafford (2002) look at negative stub situations generally, not necessarily involving an explicit intention to spin-off. Our focus on cases with a terminal date allows us to ignore some issues they discuss such as agency costs (the possibility that the parent firm may waste the cash generated by the subsidiary).

Spin-offs can be tax-free both to the parent firm and to its shareholders. In order to be tax-free, spin-offs need to comply with Internal Revenue Code Section 355, which requires that the parent (prior to the spin-off) owns at least 80 percent of the subsidiary. Thus if a firm plans a carve-out followed by a tax-free spin-off, it is necessary to carve-out less than 20 percent of the subsidiary.

There are several reasons why a firm might carve-out before spinning-off. First, the parent firm might want to raise capital for itself (Allen and McConnell 1998). Second, the parent might wish to raise capital for the subsidiary to use. Third, the parent might want to establish a dispersed base of shareholders in the subsidiary for strategic reasons related to corporate control (Zingales 1995). Fourth, a standard explanation is that the parent might want to establish an orderly market for the new issue by selling a small piece first (Cornell 1998). According to this explanation, the parent avoids flooding the market with a large number of new shares in a full spin-off, and the IPO gives an incentive for investment banks to market and support the new issue. Raising capital via a carve-out of the subsidiary, rather than an equity issue for the parent stock, is especially attractive if the firm believes that the parent stock is underpriced or the subsidiary will be overpriced, as in Nanda (1991) and Slovin, Sushka, and Ferraro (1995).

A. The Sample

We start building our sample by obtaining from Securities Data Corporation a list of all carve-outs in which the parent retains at least 80 percent of the subsidiary. Its list contains 155 such carve-outs from April 1985 to May 2000. To this list we added one issue (PFSWeb) that appears to have been miscoded by Securities Data and four issues occurring after May 2000. Using the Securities and Exchange Commission's (SEC's) Edgar database, we then searched registration form S-1 for explicit statements by the parent firm that it intended to distribute promptly the remaining shares to the shareholders. We discarded all firms for which we were unable to find a definitive statement that the parents intended to distribute all their shares. A typical statement, from Palm's registration, is that "3Com currently plans to complete its divestiture of Palm approximately six months following this offering by distributing all of the shares of Palm common stock owned by 3Com to the holders of 3Com's common stock." The statements often mentioned IRS approval as a precondition of distribution; the specified time frame for the distribution was usually six to twelve months.

We searched registrations starting in 1995, although since Edgar's database was incomplete prior to May 6, 1996, we were unable to find all firms before then. As it happens, we find no firms in 1995 that satisfied our requirements, so the final sample contains 18 issues from April 1996 to August 2000. This sample, shown in table 4.1, consists of every carve-out of less than 20 percent of subsidiary shares in which the parent declared its intention to distribute the remaining shares.

B. Constructing Stubs

We define the stub value using the ratio of subsidiary shares to be given to parent shareholders at the distribution date. The ratio is the parent's holdings of the subsidiary divided by the outstanding number of shares of the parent on the record date of the distribution. Unfortunately, this ratio is not known with certainty on the issue date because the number of parent shares outstanding can fluctuate, for example, because of the conversion of convertible debt or the exercise of options owned by insiders.

Let the parent stock have a date 0 price per share of P_0^P and the subsidiary stock P_0^S. Let x be the ratio of subsidiary shares that are given to parent shareholders at the distribution date. A negative stub means that $S_0 = P_0^P - xP_0^S < 0$. We can also express the stub as a fraction of the parent, which we do with a lowercase s:

$$ s_0 = \frac{P_0^P - xP_0^S}{P_0^P} = \frac{S_0}{P_0^P}. $$

Thus to calculate stub values, we have to estimate the expected ratio at each point in time. We did this in two stages. First, we simply used the naive ratio of the parent holdings in the subsidiary divided by the current parent shares outstanding, using Center for Research in Security Prices (CRSP) data on shares outstanding. Since the various contingencies generally raise the number of shares of the parent, this naive ratio likely overstates the actual ratio and thus makes the calculated stub more negative. Second, after examining the pattern of stubs in the eighteen cases, we more carefully studied the cases of potential negative stubs.

We concentrate on negative stubs in order to consider only cases of clear violations of the law of one price. Of course, there may be mispricing in other situations, but in such cases there is no uncontroversial proof

TABLE 4.1
Sample of Carve-outs

Issue Date	Parent	Subsidiary	Distribution Date	Negative Stub?
4/3/96	AT&T	Lucent Technologies	09/30/96	No
8/21/96	Tridex	TransAct Technologies	03/31/97	Marginal
11/13/96	Santa Fe Energy Resources	Monterey Resources	07/25/97	No
3/6/97	Odetics	ATL Products	10/31/97	Marginal
8/12/98	Cincinnati Bell	Convergys	12/31/98	No
12/3/98	Creative Computers	UBID	06/07/99	Yes
2/4/99	General Motors	Delphi Automotive Systems	05/28/99	No
8/10/99	Viacom	Blockbuster	Canceled	No
11/17/99	Hewlett-Packard	Agilent Technologies	06/02/00	No
11/17/99	HNC Software	Retek	09/29/00	Yes
12/1/99	Daisytek	PFSWeb	07/06/00	Yes
12/15/99	Metamor Worldwide	Xpedior	Canceled	Yes
3/1/00	3Com	Palm	07/27/00	Yes
4/3/00	Cabot Corp.	Cabot Microelectronics	09/29/00	No
6/26/00	Methode Electronics	Stratos Lightwave	4/28/01	Yes
6/26/00	Deluxe	Efunds	12/11/00	No
7/10/00	Eaton	Axcelis Technologies	12/29/00	No
8/9/00	Sea Containers	Orient Express Hotels		Marginal

Note. List of 18 equity carve-outs, 1995–2000, in which the parent stated its intention to distribute to its shareholders its remaining shares in the subsidiary. Issue date is the pricing date for the IPO, occurring one day prior to the first day of trade. Distribution date is the date on which the spin-off is completed, occurring some time after the record date for the distribution.

of mispricing. So negative stubs should be considered the extreme cases of unambiguous mispricing. For the potential negative stubs, we gathered information that was available in real time to construct the estimated ratio. In all but one case the uncertainty about the final ratio appears to be small.[2]

Of our eighteen firms, nine clearly had positive stubs. We classify three stubs as marginally negative. These were cases in which we observed small negative stubs on one or two days only or the correct ratio is sometimes unclear because of changing numbers of shares. For these cases we think that a reasonable person would not be convinced that the stub was negative given all available information. None of the three marginal cases involves a negative stub at or near the IPO date.

We identify six cases of unambiguously negative stubs: UBID, Retek, PF-SWeb, Xpedior, Palm, and Stratos Lightwave.[3] All six are technology stocks. UBID is an online auction firm. Retek produces business-to-business inventory software. PFSWeb provides transactions management services for e-commerce. Xpedior is an e-business consulting firm. Stratos Lightwave is an optical networking firm. Both the six parents and the six subsidiaries trade on NASDAQ.

As shown in table 4.2, for the six cases with negative stubs, four were negative at closing prices on the first day of trading, and the other two were negative by two days after. For five of the cases, the stub was negative for at least two months, with a maximum of 187 trading days for Stratos. For one case, Xpedior, the stub was negative for only two days before turning positive again. Xpedior's minimum stub also had a fairly small magnitude of only −19 percent of the parent company's value, unlike the other five, which had minimum stubs of −39 to −137 percent of the parent's value. Thus Xpedior is a much weaker case in terms of the persistence and magnitude of the mispricing.

Table 4.2 shows the magnitude of the mispricing in a variety of ways. Perhaps the most relevant is the market value of the shares trading in the subsidiary. This number (which uses the number of publicly trading shares, not the number of outstanding shares) is at its peak, $2.5 billion, for Palm, meaning that investors worth $2.5 billion thought it was better to own Palm than to own 3Com.

---

[2] In one case, Retek, there appears to have been substantial uncertainty about the final ratio since the parent's number of shares was somewhat volatile. Retek's parent ultimately decided to accelerate the vesting of the options held by insiders.

[3] In these six cases, we calculated the estimated distribution ratio (prior to the actual distribution ratio announcement) as follows. For UBID and Retek, we used the ratio from the CRSP shares outstanding. For Palm and Stratos, we always used the ratios provided by Spin-off Advisors. For PFSWeb, we used the ratio provided by Spin-off Advisors until March 2000 and then used the CRSP shares. For Xpedior, we used the ratio provided by the company web page (in real time).

TABLE 4.2

Stub Values and Market Values between IPO and Distribution

	Min Stub, S_p $ per Parent Share	Min Stub, S_p Fraction of Parent	Max Market Value of Issue ($ Millions)	Trading Days			
				First Negative	Next First Positive	Last Negative	Distribution Announcement
Creative/UBID	-74.81	-1.37	342	1	114	113	113
HNC/Retek	-49.01	-.56	594	2	50	178	181
Daisytek/PFSWeb	-13.72	-.63	157	1	82	81	131
Metamor/Xpedior	-5.26	-.19	315	3	5	92	67
3Com/Palm	-63.16	-.77	2,514	1	48	47	47
Methode/Stratos	-20.95	-.39	499	1	133	146	187

Note. The stub value in dollars per share is $S_t = P_t^p - xP_t^s$. The stub value as a fraction of parent value is $S_t = (P_t^p - xP_t^s)/P_t^p = S_t/P_t^p$. The first day of trading is day 1. Min stub is that between IPO and distribution. Max market value of issue is the maximum price times the number of shares issued (not outstanding) during the interval between first negative and next first positive. First negative is the first trading day with a negative stub. Next first positive is the subsequent day on which prices imply a positive stub. Last negative is the last day on which a negative stub occurs. All calculations are based on closing prices. For Metamor/Xpedior, day 67 is the day on which the takeover of parent Metamor is announced.

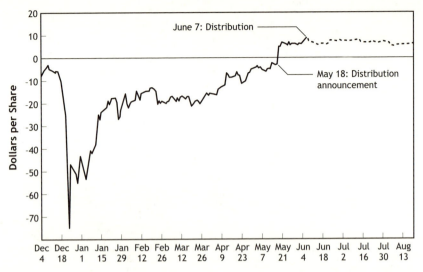

Figure 4.1. Creative Computers/UBID stub, December 4, 1998–August 24, 1999.

C. *Time Pattern of Negative Stubs*

Figures 4.1–4.4 show the time series of stub values for the six cases of negative stubs. Except in figure 4.2, the solid line shows the stub prior to distribution and the dashed line shows the parent share price after the distribution. Several patterns are apparent. First, stubs start negative and gradually get closer to zero, eventually becoming positive. Second, the announcement of

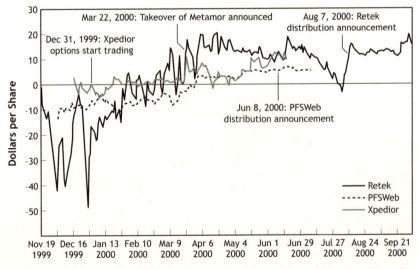

Figure 4.2. Stub values for HNC/Retek, Daiseytek/PFSWeb, and Metamor/Expedior.

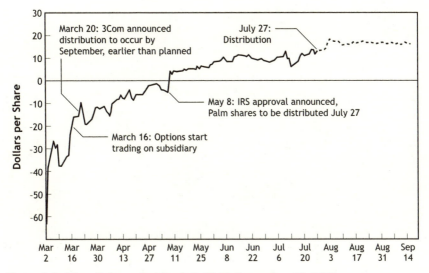

Figure 4.3. 3Com/Palm stub, March 2, 2000–September 18, 2000.

IRS approval and the consequent announcement of a distribution date (occurring on the same day) cause the stub to go from negative to positive in two cases, UBID and Palm. Thus in these cases the market is acting as though there is significant news on these days.[4]

In one case, Xpedior, the distribution never occurred. On March 22, 2000, the parent company Metamor announced that another firm was acquiring it. Xpedior's stub rises markedly on this day. However, one could argue that on and after this date, Xpedior's stub has little meaning since the distribution is presumably canceled. On the announcement day, although not explicitly canceling the spin-off, the acquirer failed to confirm the spinoff and instead announced that it had gained control of Xpedior and was investing additional money in it.

The picture is one of predictable idiosyncratic movement in stubs. Stubs start off negative and then get positive. This pattern is repeated over time and does not appear to reflect systematic exposure to some common factor, but rather idiosyncratic developments.

We draw two conclusions from the analysis so far. First, we are able to identify six cases of clearly negative stubs. We do not think that the proportion of negative stubs, one-third of the cases we study, is particularly significant. As we stressed above, a negative stub indicates a gross case of mispricing. Even a single case would raise important questions about market

---

[4] In one case, Retek, the stub has less of a trend. Because of the uncertainty about the ultimate distribution ratio, Retek's true stub is not totally clear in July 2000. The reaction of the stub to the distribution announcement has a different meaning for Retek since the announcement contains important quantitative information. The announced ratio was 1.24, whereas 10 days earlier an analyst report contains an estimate of 1.40.

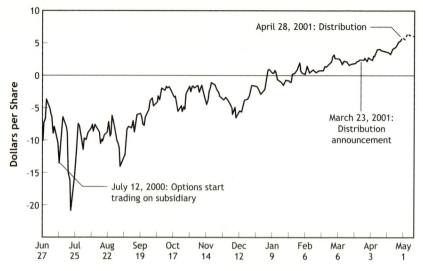

Figure 4.4. Methode/Stratos stub, June 27, 2000–May 7, 2001.

efficiency. The fact that we find six such cases indicates that the highly publicized Palm example was not unique.[5]

Second, all the cases we study show a similar time pattern of returns
whereby the stub becomes less negative over time and eventually becomes
positive. This suggests that market forces act to mitigate the mispricing, but
slowly. We return to this slow adjustment, which reflects the difficulty of
shorting due to the sluggish functioning of the market for lending stocks, in
section 4.

3. Risk and Return on Stubs

In this section, we investigate the returns to an investment strategy of buying
the parent and shorting the subsidiary. We find that this strategy produces

---

[5] It is hard to say whether the ratio of one-third overestimates or underestimates the preva-
lence of mispricing. On the one hand, perhaps firms tend to do carve-outs when they think
that their subsidiaries are overpriced, in which case the eighteen firms are not a representative
sample (firms should issue equity when that equity is overpriced, as argued by Stein [1996]).
Further, it could be that 1998–2000 was a time in which mispricing was prevalent, but in most
years mispricing is rare. Ritter and Welch (2002) show that this period was one with extraordinary IPO first-day returns, and Ofek and Richardson (2001) show that Internet-related IPOs
had especially high first-day returns in this period. On the other hand, mispricing could occur
more than one-third of the time. We show that only six of the eighteen have negative stubs.
Perhaps the other twelve have stubs that are too low or too high. So in that sense, perhaps
one-third is a lower bound for relative mispricing.

high returns with low (and largely idiosyncratic) risk. However, we caution readers not to rush out to form hedge funds to exploit this phenomenon; as we show in the next section, the high returns we find on paper are probably not achievable in practice because of the difficulty of shorting the subsidiary (although we are aware of individual investors who did make money on these situations). Thus the question we ask is whether the investment strategy would have produced profits if it could have been implemented.

This investment strategy is related to several controversies in finance: value, IPOs, and the diversification discount. First, it is a value strategy of buying cheap stocks and shorting expensive stocks. Second, it is a strategy that shorts IPOs. Ritter (1991) documents that IPOs tend to have low subsequent returns, but the statistical soundness of this finding has been the subject of a vigorous debate summarized in Fama (1998) and Loughran and Ritter (2000). In a subset of the IPO debate, Vijh (1999) finds that carve-out stocks do not have low subsequent returns. Third, it is a strategy that buys firms with a large diversification discount. Lamont and Polk (2001) show that the diversification discount partially reflects subsequent returns on diversified firms, so that the diversification discount does not reflect only agency concerns such as wasteful managers. In the case of our firms, it seems unambiguous that mispricing drives the subsequent pattern of returns, so that we have a clear example in which the value/IPO/diversification effect is due to mispricing.

A. Returns on Stub Positions

The following analysis ignores dividends and assumes that the distribution takes place with a fixed distribution ratio at time T. First, since the stub must go from negative to positive by date T, it must be the case that $R_T^P > R_T^S$, where R_T^P and R_T^S are the returns on the parent and subsidiary between date 0 and date T. Thus if an investor buys the parent and shorts an equal dollar amount of the subsidiary, she gets a positive return of $R_T^P - R_T^S$. In a frictionless market in which the investor gets access to short-sale proceeds, this strategy is a zero cost or self-financing strategy. For this strategy, the exact distribution ratio x is not important, as long as one knows that the stub is negative initially. On paper, this strategy is an arbitrage opportunity, since it has zero cost and generates strictly positive cash flow in the future.

Assuming that the distribution takes place with known ratio x, one can construct a position that is a pure bet on the stub. This second strategy eliminates the effect of fluctuations in subsidiary value and again guarantees strictly positive returns. It buys one share of the parent, shorts x shares on the subsidiary, and (again with access to the short-sale proceeds ignored) invests the resulting $-S_0$ dollars of cash in the initial period at the risk-free rate of R_F. Again, this strategy is theoretically self-financing and puts equal amounts into the long portfolio (consisting of riskless assets and the parent) and the short portfolio (consisting of the subsidiary). One can express the returns on this strategy as

$$\frac{1}{1-s_0} R_T^P + \frac{-s_0}{1-s_0} R_T^F - R_T^S.$$

Table 4.3 shows returns from the strategy of buying the parent and shorting the subsidiary at the closing price on the first day on which the stub is negative. We examine two holding periods: holding until one day after the announcement date and holding until one day before the distribution date. For the purposes of table 4.3, we use the takeover announcement for Xpedior's announcement date and the takeover consummation as Xpedior's distribution date. Table 4.3 shows that parents had returns that were 30 percent higher than subsidiaries holding until the announcement date and 33 percent higher holding until the distribution date. This difference was statistically significant. From this evidence alone, one cannot say whether the subsidiary is overvalued or the parent is undervalued. Later, we show evidence from options markets implying that it is the subsidiary that is overpriced.

B. Traditional Measures of Risk

Table 4.4 uses monthly calendar time portfolio returns reflecting a strategy of buying parents and shorting subsidiaries. On the last trading day of the month, if the subsidiary has a negative stub on that day, we buy the parent and short the subsidiary. We maintain this position until the last day of the month prior to the distribution date. We calculate equal-weighted returns on the portfolio holdings on this strategy. The strategy holds one to three paired positions each month, for the twenty-one months of returns from January 1999 to May 1999 (UBID) and December 1999 to March 2001 (the other four subsidiaries; the strategy does not take a position in Xpedior).

Over this period, the simple strategy of buying parents and shorting subsidiaries in equal dollar amounts has a monthly return that averages 10 percent per *month* (significantly different from zero) with a standard deviation of 14 percent per month, producing a monthly Sharpe ratio of 0.67 per month. The hedged strategy that takes a pure bet on the stub has a slightly higher Sharpe ratio of 0.70 a month. Over the same period, the average market excess return (value-weighted New York Stock Exchange/American Stock Exchange/NASDAQ return from CRSP minus Treasury bill returns from Ibbotson Associates) was negative. From July 1927 to March 2001 the market had a Sharpe ratio of 0.12. Thus stub strategies have risk-return trade-offs more than four times more favorable than the market's.

TABLE 4.3

Total Returns from First Negative Stub to Announcement/Distribution Days

	First Negative Stub	Announcement Day Plus One				Distribution Day Minus One			
		Stub	R_T^p	R_T^S	$R_T^p - R_T^S$	Stub	R_T^p	R_T^S	$R_T^p - R_T^S$
Creative/UBID	−8.09	5.17	.49	.00	.49	6.32	.25	−.22	.47
HNC/Retek	−8.04	14.94	−.19	−.34	.15	17.80	.23	.09	.13
Daisytek/PFSWeb	−13.72	5.64	−.48	−.84	.36	5.39	−.59	−.90	.31
Metamor/Xpedior	−3.65	7.75	.15	−.22	.37	9.89	−.06	−.48	.41
3Com/Palm	−63.16	4.09	−.41	−.69	.28	13.43	−.17	−.61	.44
Methode/Stratos	−10.06	2.42	−.59	−.72	.13	5.79	−.59	−.78	.20
Average	−17.78	6.67	−.17	−.47	.30	9.77	−.16	−.48	.33
	(−1.94)	(3.70)	(−1.02)	(−3.46)	(5.21)	(4.79)	(−1.03)	(−3.20)	(5.78)
Average excluding Xpedior	−20.61	6.45	−.24	−.52	.28	9.75	−.18	−.48	.31
	(−1.93)	(2.94)	(−1.23)	(−3.36)	(4.18)	(3.90)	(−.95)	(−2.62)	(4.69)

Note. Returns are total simple returns from the day of the first negative stub to either the day after the announcement day or the day prior to the distribution day. For Xpedior, we count the announcement day as the day on which Xpedior's parent announces that it is being acquired, and the distribution day as the day Xpedior's parent ceases trading, t-statistics of averages are in parentheses.

Table 4.4 shows estimates of a capital asset pricing model (CAPM) equation. Although the strategy has a positive and significant market beta (so that subsidiaries have more market risk than parents), α is a huge 10 percent per month for the simple strategy and 9 percent for the hedged strategy. The t-statistic on α formally tests the hypothesis that the stub trading strategy can be used to produce a higher Sharpe ratio than the market. Even using these highly undiversified portfolios with only 21 monthly observations, we are able to resoundingly reject the hypothesis that α is zero. Using the three-factor model of Fama and French (1993) does not change the conclusion.

TABLE 4.4
CAPM and Three-Factor Regression for Monthly Trading Strategies

	Simple Strategy		Hedged Strategy	
	(1)	(2)	(3)	(4)
α	.10	.10	.09	.09
	(.03)	(.03)	(.03)	(.03)
RMRF	1.22	1.41	.89	1.06
	(.53)	(.60)	(.47)	(.53)
HML		.46		.42
		(.45)		(.40)
SMB		.47		.43
		(.63)		(.56)
R^2	.22	.27	.16	.21

Note. Monthly regressions of strategy returns on factors. Calculations use closing prices. The strategy takes a position on the last day of the month if the stub is negative on that day and holds until the last day of the month prior to the distribution month. In all five cases, the position is initiated at the end of the first month of trading. Since Metamor/Xpedior does not have a negative stub at the end of the month, it is not included in this strategy. Equal-weighted returns are on from one to three paired positions per month. The simple strategy is $R_T^P - R_T^S$. The hedged strategy is

$$\frac{1}{1-s_0} R_T^P + \frac{-s_0}{1-s_0} R_T^F - R_T^S,$$

where R_T^P is the monthly return from the parent stock and R_T^S is the monthly return from the subsidiary stock: $S_0 = (P_0^P - x P_0^S)/P_0^P$ is the stub value as a percentage of the parent stock price, as of the last day of the first month of trading. RMRF is the CRSP value-weighted market return minus Ibbotson Treasury bill return. HML and SMB are the value and size factors from Fama and French (1993) and come from the web page of Kenneth French. HML is the returns on stocks with high book to market ratios minus the returns on stocks with low book to market ratios. SMB is the return on small-cap stocks minus the returns on big-cap stocks. The number of observations is 21 months. Standard errors are in parentheses.

C. *Risks Specific to Stubs*

Since our sample is so small, it is useful to discuss some events that did not occur but might be expected to occur in a larger sample. Events that might have a negative impact on arbitrage investors include canceling the spin-off or changing the distribution ratio by lowering the number of subsidiary shares that each parent shareholder receives. If the expected ratio changes, then the stub can go from negative to positive without any change in prices.

Cancelation of the distribution can occur for several reasons. First, if the firm does not receive IRS approval, the spin-off is not tax-free and will probably be canceled. Our impression is that IRS rejection is a low-probability event. Second, the firm might change its mind and cancel the spin-off even if the IRS does approve. Although the parents in our sample stated their intention to distribute their ownership, this statement is not legally binding. An example that occurred in our larger sample of eighteen carve-outs is Blockbuster. The parent, Viacom, stated in an SEC filing four months after the carve-out that it would wait until Blockbuster's share price was higher before completing the separation. In this example, Viacom's decision is not much of a negative event for the stub strategy of shorting the subsidiary, since the distribution is canceled only in the state of the world in which the subsidiary price remains low. Nevertheless, it is always possible for a canceled spin-off to cause the trading strategy to reap negative returns.

Another reason a distribution can be canceled is a takeover by a third party or shareholder pressure. We have already discussed the case of Xpedior, whose parent was acquired. As shown in table 4.3, this acquisition did not prevent the stub strategy from earning high returns. Another example from our sample is PFSWeb. Prior to the carve-out the parent firm received an unsolicited takeover bid that was conditional on canceling the spin-off, and later a large shareholder in the parent publicly objected to the spin-off and threatened legal action. Despite these events, the carve-out and distribution took place as planned.

These examples highlight the fact that the trading strategy is not riskless. It is worth noting, however, that many of these unpredictable events seem likely to benefit strategies that buy parent shares and short subsidiary shares. Takeover of the parent company (with the usual takeover premia), shareholder pressure to increase value to parent shareholders, or cancelation of the distribution due to low prices of the subsidiary all are positive for the strategy.

Since returns are high and the risks seem both quite low and almost entirely idiosyncratic, it appears that these subsidiaries are overpriced relative to the parent shares. However, with only six pairs of firms and only twenty-one months of returns, this evidence is not conclusive. It is possible that there was some negative event capable of generating large losses to the arbitrage strategy that just did not come up during the period we studied. To address these concerns we shall turn to the options market for additional evidence on mispricing.

4. Short-Sale Constraints and the Persistence of Mispricing

The previous section argued that the negative stub situations created very attractive investment opportunities. Why, then, didn't rational arbitrageurs step in to correct the mispricing by buying the parent and shorting the subsidiary? There are many types of reasons that in general might prevent rational investors from correcting mispricing. These reasons include fundamental risk, noise trader risk, liquidity risk, institutional or regulatory restrictions, and tax concerns. Shleifer and Vishny (1997) discuss idiosyncratic risk and agency problems in delegated portfolio management (see also Pontiff 1996). In the cases we study, the principal idiosyncratic risk is the possibility that the distribution will not take place, and consistent with this idea, when the distribution date is announced, the stub values sometimes go from negative to positive. This pattern is consistent with arbitrageurs who are reluctant to take on substantial idiosyncratic risk.

In many situations, noise trader risk, institutional restrictions, and so forth might cause assets to be mispriced. In our specific case, however, these issues appear to be minimal, and the chief impediment to arbitrage is short-sale constraint. First, shorting can be simply impossible. Second, when shorting is possible, it can have large costs.

A. Description of the Shorting Process

The market for shorting stock is not simply the mirror image of buying stocks long, for various legal and institutional reasons. To be able to sell a stock short, one must borrow it; and because the market for borrowing shares is not a centralized market, borrowing can be difficult or impossible for many equities. In order to borrow shares, an investor needs to find an institution or individual willing to lend shares. Financial institutions, such as mutual funds, trusts, or asset managers, typically do much of this lending. These lenders receive a fee in the form of interest payments generated by the short-sale proceeds, minus any interest rebate that the lenders return to the borrowers. Stocks that are held primarily by retail investors, stocks with low market capitalization, and illiquid stocks can be more difficult to short.

Being simply unable to short is particularly likely for individual retail investors, although there is extensive anecdotal evidence of institutional investors unable to short the overpriced subsidiaries. Regulations and procedures administered by the SEC, the Federal Reserve, the various stock exchanges, and individual brokerage firms can mechanically impede short-selling, especially immediately after the IPO. In some cases, firms ask their stockholders not to lend their stock, to prevent short sellers from driving down the price. In the specific case of Palm, *The Wall Street Journal* reported that "it may be possible to short sometime next week. . . . The brokerage firms and institutional investors that control much of Palm's stock generally agree not to immediately lend the stock to short sellers until sometime after the IPO date" (March 6, 2000, p. C15).

For institutions that are able to find shares to borrow, the cost of shorting is reflected in the interest rate rebate they receive on the short-sale proceeds. This rebate acts as a price that equilibrates supply and demand in the securities lending market. The rebate can be negative, meaning that institutions that sell short have to make a daily payment to the lender for the right to borrow the stock (instead of receiving a daily payment from the lender as interest payments on the short-sale proceeds). This rebate apparently only partially equilibrates supply and demand, because the securities lending market is not a centralized market with a "market-clearing" price. Instead, rebates reflect individual deals struck among security owners and those wishing to short, and these actors must find each other. This search may be costly and time-consuming (Duffie 1996 suggests that the securities lending market could be described by a search model).

B. Shorting Costs and Overpricing

Short-sale constraints have long been recognized as crucial to the workings of efficient markets. Diamond and Verrecchia (1987) describe a model with some informed traders, other uninformed but rational traders, and possible restrictions on shorting. In their model, although short-sale constraints impede the transmission of private information, short-sale constraints do not cause any stocks to be overpriced. Uninformed agents rationally take into account short-sale constraints and set prices realizing that negative opinion may not be reflected in trading.

With irrational traders, however, short-sale constraints can cause some stocks to become overpriced. With short-sale constraints, rational arbitrageurs can refrain only from buying overpriced stocks, and if there are enough irrational traders, stocks can be overpriced (see, e.g., Miller 1977, Russell and Thaler 1985, and Chen, Hong, and Stein 2002). A variety of evidence is consistent with such overpricing. Figlewski and Webb (1993) and Dechow et al. (2001) show that stocks with high short interest have low subsequent returns. Jones and Lamont (2002) show that stocks that are expensive to short or enter the lending market have high valuations and low subsequent returns.

Miller (1977) describes how short-sale constraints can cause prices to reflect only the views of optimistic investors. In describing the types of stocks likely to be overpriced because of divergence of opinion, he presciently lists many of the characteristics of our sample: IPOs with short operating history and exciting new products. He discusses how short-sale constraints might explain the diversification discount; our firms are extreme examples of such discounts.

One potentially confusing aspect of short sales is that the cost for those borrowing the stock is income for those lending the stock. Thus it is not quite accurate to say that only an irrational investor would buy an overpriced stock. A rational investor might be willing to buy an overpriced stock if he can derive sufficient income from lending it to short-sellers. On the basis of this fact, one might be tempted to conclude that the situation we observe is therefore "rational," since rational investors are willing to buy the subsidiaries. Along these lines, one could argue that the observed returns for Palm, for example, are not a "real" return since the true return should include the income from lending (reflecting the convenience yield or dividend from securities lending) and that the "marginal" investor sets the traded price to embody all income generated by the shares.

Such an interpretation would be a mistake. It is important to recognize that irrationality, or at least some nonstandard phenomena causing downward-sloping demand curves for stocks, is a crucial element to any explanation of the facts we are studying. Consider the following example. A firm, consisting of $100 in cash, issues 100 shares. The firm will liquidate tomorrow, and each share will pay a liquidating dividend of $1.00. These shares are issued and sold by auction to investor I, who buys all 100 shares directly from the firm. Investor I mistakenly believes that the shares will pay out $2.01 tomorrow and "wins" the auction with a bid of $2.00 per share. It is clear in this example that investor I has overpaid for the shares and that $2.00 is a "real price."

Now suppose that two other investors, Y and Z, enter the market. Investor Y buys all 100 shares from the firm for $2.00 and lends them to Z. Investor Z pays Y a fee of $1.00 for each share lent and sells the shares to I for $2.00. Now in this example, Y and Z are both acting rationally. However, there is no sense in which Y and Z are the "marginal" investors that set prices. Investors Y and Z would be just as happy with a price of $200 per share (and a corresponding loan fee of $199). It is the willingness of investor I to overpay that sets the price of the shares. The price of $2.00 is a real price, and the firm should rationally respond to the mispricing by issuing more shares. The fact that Y and Z are intervening actors between the firm and the owner is irrelevant in this example.

The number of shares not lent out must equal the number of shares outstanding; it is always true that *someone* has to own the shares issued by the firm; not all owners can lend their shares. If the firm issues 100 shares, exactly 100 shares have to be owned by someone who is not lending them out. Thus it is not an empirical issue whether the owners of Palm lent out their shares or not, but rather a simple identity: $2.5 billion worth of shares were owned by investors who were not receiving any lending income from their shares.

More generally, in any situation in which the shorting market is imperfect and some investors have a downward-sloping demand curve for a particular security, equilibrium prices depend on supply and demand. For example, Duffie (1996) and Krishnamurthy (2002) study the market for Treasury bonds. At some times, the price of on-the-run Treasury bonds is particularly high relative to off-the-run bonds, perhaps reflecting liquidity concerns. At these times, the cost of shorting reflects these price differences, so that it is not necessarily profitable to short the expensive bond and buy the cheap one, and it might well be rational to buy the expensive bond in order to reap the lending income. These price movements reflect the existence of a demand curve for on-the-run securities. In a frictionless market, arbitrageurs would be able to supply bonds to meet this demand for on-the-run securities. Similarly, in our example, if investor Z was able to manufacture new shares, he might be able to satiate investor I.

C. Evidence on Short Sales

Given the obvious nature of the mispricing in the cases of negative stubs and the publicity associated with some of the cases such as Palm, it is not surprising that many investors were interested in selling the subsidiaries short. Table 4.5 shows the level of short interest for parents and subsidiaries. Short interest is much higher in subsidiaries than in parents, consistent with

TABLE 4.5
Percentage Short Interest

	First Month		Second Month: Subsidiary	Peak: Subsidiary
	Parent	*Subsidiary*		
Creative/UBID	4.2	8.5	54.7	70.9
HNC/Retek	7.5	19.8	37.4	53.4
Daisytek/PFSWeb	1.6	17.7	48.6	63.7
Metamor/Xpedior	4.9	17.2	24.6	26.8
3Com/Palm	2.6	19.4	44.9	147.6
Methode/Stratos	1.5	31.8	50.3	114.7
Average	3.7	19.1	43.4	79.5
Difference from previous column		15.3	24.3	36.1
t-statistic		4.4	4.5	2.3

Note. Short interest calculated as a percentage of parent shares outstanding or subsidiary shares trading. The level of short interest comes from the National Association of Securities Dealers and occurs on or prior to the fifteenth calendar day of the month. The shares outstanding of the parent are taken from CRSP, and the shares issued in the IPO are taken from company SEC filings. First month is the first observed short interest after the IPO, and second month is one month later. Peak is the highest level between the IPO date and the distribution date.

the idea that the subsidiaries are overpriced. For parents, we report short interest divided by total shares outstanding. For subsidiaries, we report short interest divided by total shares sold to the public in the IPO, since these shares are the only ones trading in the market.

Table 4.5 shows that on the first reporting date after the IPO, the parents had an average of 3.7 percent of their shares shorted. The subsidiaries had a significantly larger short interest of 19.1 percent. A month later, on the second reporting date, 43.4 percent of subsidiary shares were shorted. This dramatic increase over time could be produced by some combination of two factors. First, it may take a while for investors to become aware of the mispricing and decide to try to exploit it. Second, and more plausibly, the short-sale market works sluggishly. Only shares that are held by institutions willing to lend them are available for interested short-sellers, and it takes time for lendable shares to find their way to the market for shorting.

Table 4.5 also shows the peak level of short interest for subsidiaries, for the time between the IPO and the distribution date. At the peak, short sales are 79.5 percent of total shares trading, and for Palm the level is an amazing 147.6 percent. More than all the floating shares had been sold short. This is possible if shares are borrowed and then sold short to an investor who then permits the shares to be borrowed again. Again, the multiplier-type process takes time to operate because of frictions in the securities lending market. This peak level of short interest for Palm was reached on July 14, 2000, two weeks before the announced distribution, at a time when the stub was positive but rising.

Figures 4.5 and 4.6 show short interest (expressed as a percentage of total shares issued) and stub value (expressed in dollars per parent company stock price) for Palm and Stratos over the relevant period. The figures show that as the supply of shares available grows via short sales, the stub value gets more positive. One might interpret this pattern as roughly tracing out the demand curve for the overpriced subsidiary. As the supply of shares grows via short sales, we move down the demand curve of irrational investors and the subsidiary price falls relative to the parent.

Although quantity data in the shorting market are readily available, price data are not. We do not know precisely what the cost of shorting the overpriced subsidiaries was. We do have scattered evidence for four of the six subsidiaries. D'Avolio (2002) reports maximum borrowing costs of 50 percent (in annual terms) for Stratos Lightwave in December 2000, 35 percent for Palm in July 2000, and 10 percent each for PFSWeb in June 2000 and Retek in September 2000.[6]

Given these high lending fees, it might seem surprising that it took so long for owners to offer their shares to the lending market. This apparent

---

[6] With the exception of Stratos Lightwave (which has a distribution date occurring after D'Avolio's sample ends), all these dates are on or near the distribution date.

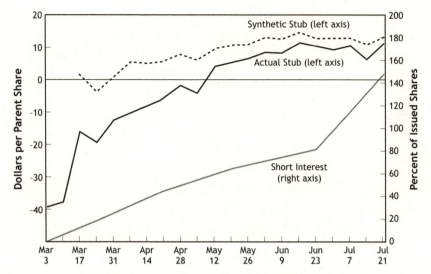

Figure 4.5. 3Com/Palm: actual stub, synthetic stub, and short interest, March 3, 2000–July 21, 2000.

money left on the table reflects the dysfunctional nature of the securities lending market. The system is just not set up to facilitate lending of shares held primarily in retail accounts. Further, most of the outstanding shares in the subsidiaries were held by parents, and there are several reasons why parents do not lend out their subsidiary shares. First, it is typically the case

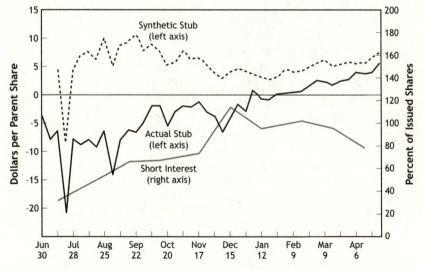

Figure 4.6. Methode/Stratos: actual stub, synthetic stub, and short interest, June 3, 2000–April 27, 2001.

that the shares owned by parents are not registered prior to the actual distribution to the shareholders and therefore cannot be publicly traded. Second, lending shares might breach the fiduciary duties that parent directors owe to the parent or subsidiary. Third, lending shares could jeopardize the ability to do a spin-off tax-free by calling into question the "independent business purpose" of the spin-off, or by reducing the parent's control below important tax thresholds.

We next look at options markets to get more complete quantitative evidence on just how expensive it is to sell short.

D. Short-selling Constraints: Evidence from Options

Options can facilitate shorting, both because options can be a cheaper way of obtaining a short position and because options allow short-sale-constrained investors to trade with other investors who have better access to shorting. Figlewski and Webb (1993) show that optionable stocks have higher short interest. Sorescu (2000) finds that in the period from 1981 to 1995, the introduction of options for a specific stock caused its price to fall, consistent with the idea that options allow negative information to become impounded into the stock price.[7]

In a frictionless market, one expects to observe put-call parity. It should hold exactly (within trading costs) for European options and approximately for American options. One way of expressing put-call parity is to say that synthetic shares (constructed using options plus borrowing and lending) should have the same price as actual shares, plus or minus trading costs such as the bid/ask spread. This equality is just another application of the law of one price. A weaker condition than put-call parity, which should always hold for non-dividend-paying American options, is the following inequality: the call price minus the put price is greater than the stock price minus the exercise price. For options that are at-the-money (so that the option's exercise price is equal to the current price of the stock), this inequality says that call prices should be greater than put prices.

For our six cases with negative stubs, three had exchange-traded American options within the relevant time frame: Xpedior, Palm, and Stratos. We used weekly share prices and weekly options prices, as of 4:00 P.M. eastern time on Friday.

Table 4.6 shows an example from the first week of trading in Palm's options (occurring more than two weeks after the IPO) using options that are closest to being at-the-money. Options on Palm display massive violations of put-call parity and violate the weaker inequality as well. Instead of observing at-the-money call prices that are greater than put prices, we find

---

[7] This effect was present in our sample, since in the three cases with negative stubs, when exchange-traded options were introduced, all three had sizable increases in the stub value. In all three cases, the subsidiary fell on the day on which options started trading.

TABLE 4.6
Palm Options on March 17, 2000

A. Options Prices

	Call		Put		Synthetic Short	Percentage Deviation	Synthetic Long	Percentage Deviation
	Bid	Ask	Bid	Ask				
May 55	5.75	7.25	10.625	12.625	47.55	−14	51.05	−8
August 55	9.25	10.75	17.25	19.25	43.57	−21	47.07	−15
November 55	10	11.5	21.625	23.625	39.12	−29	42.62	−23

B. Other Prices

LIBOR:
   3-month   6.21
   6-month   6.41
Stock prices:
   Palm   55.25
   3Com   69

Note. May options expire May 20, 2000; August options expire August 19, 2000; and November options expire November 18, 2000. A synthetic short position buys a put (at the ask price), sells a call (at the bid price), and borrows the present value of the strike price. A synthetic long position sells a put (at the bid price), buys a call (at the ask price), and lends the present value of the strike price. We discount May cash flows by three-month LIBOR and August and November cash flows by six-month LIBOR. Source of options price data: Chicago Board Options Exchange. Source of LIBOR: Datastream

that puts were about twice as expensive as calls. We also calculate the implied price of synthetic securities. For example, on March 17, one can create a synthetic short position in Palm by buying a November put (at the ask price), writing a November call (at the bid price), and borrowing dollars. Both the synthetic short and the actual short position, if held until November, give the same payoff of the negative of the price of Palm in November. These calculations are done using the assumption that one can borrow from March to November at the six-month London Interbank offer rate (LIBOR). On March 16 the price of the synthetic short was about $39.12, far below the actual trading price of Palm of $55.25. This constellation of prices is a significant violation of the law of one price since the synthetic security is worth 29 percent less than the actual security. May and August options also showed substantial, though smaller, violations of put-call parity.

The synthetic shorts at different horizons in table 4.6 can be used to calculate the implied holding cost of borrowing Palm's shares. For an investor who is indifferent to shorting actual Palm shares from March until May and creating a synthetic short, the holding costs must be 14 percent over two months, or about 119 percent at an annual rate. For an investor planning to short for eight months, until November, the holding costs must be 29 percent, or 147 percent at an annual rate. Thus the options prices suggest either that shorting Palm was incredibly expensive or that there was a large excess demand for borrowing Palm shares, a demand that the market could not meet for some institutional reasons.

Since the evidence from D'Avolio (2002) indicates a much lower, 35 percent, shorting cost for Palm during this period, it is clear that there must be other risks and costs associated with shorting Palm. First, there is the cost of actually finding shares to borrow. Second, as discussed in Liu and Longstaff (2000) and Mitchell et al. (2002), short-sellers are required to post additional collateral if the price of Palm rises. Third, as discussed in Mitchell et al., there is "buy-in" risk, the fact that the Palm lender has the right to recall his loan at any time. If the Palm lender decides to sell his shares after they have risen in price, the short-sellers may be forced to close their position at a loss if they are unable to find other shares to borrow. Fourth, even if the loan is not recalled, the cost of shorting could increase if the rebate changes.

We now have three different market estimates of Palm's value: the embedded value reflected in 3Com's share price, the value reflected in options prices, and the actual share price. The options market and the shareholders in 3Com seemed to agree: Palm was worth far less than its market price. The direction of the deviation from the law of one price is consistent with the difficulty of shorting Palm. To profit from the difference between the synthetic security and the underlying security, one would need to short Palm and buy the synthetic long. The price of the synthetic short reflects the high demand for borrowing Palm stock and the low supply. Similarly, Figlewski and Webb (1993) find that, in general, stocks with high short interest have puts that are more expensive relative to calls (although they look at implied volatilities instead of put-call parity).

Again, although the prices here are consistent with very high shorting costs, one can turn the inequality around and ask why anyone would ever buy Palm (without lending it). On March 17 one can create a synthetic long Palm by buying a call and selling a put, and this synthetic long is 23 percent cheaper than buying an actual share of Palm and holding it until November.[8] Arguments about the risk that the planned spin-off may not occur are irrelevant to the synthetic long constructed using options. Why are investors who buy Palm shares directly willing to pay much more than they could pay using the options market? One plausible explanation is that the type of investor buying Palm is ignorant about the options market and unaware of the cheaper alternative.[9]

---

[8] Of course, the put-call parity formula holds only for stocks paying no dividends. One benefit of owning Palm is that it yields a "dividend" from lending it out to short-sellers. As before, however, someone is holding all the Palm stock without lending it out; this owner would be better off owning the synthetic short.

[9] In the model of Duffie, Garleanu, and Pedersen (2001), all investors seek to lend the stock out in order to reap lending income. Since the securities lending market works sluggishly, although everyone is trying to lend, not all succeed, and at any one time 100 percent of the

One can use the synthetic short price of Palm to create a synthetic stub value. On March 17, 2000, the actual stub value for Palm was −$16.26 per · share. The synthetic stub for Palm, constructed using the synthetic short price implied in six-month, at-the-money options, was positive at $1.56. Although this value seems low (i.e., less than the cash 3Com held), it is at least positive and thus no longer so close to a pure arbitrage opportunity.

We have seen earlier that the actual stubs became less negative over time and eventually turned positive. In figure 4.5 we display the time series of the actual stubs along with the synthetic stubs for the time period up to the distribution date (constructing synthetic stubs using options that are closest to six months and at-the-money). The solid line, the actual stub, goes from strongly negative at the beginning to positive $10 a share. The dotted line, the synthetic stub, is positive in all but one week. By the distribution date, the difference between the two lines is close to zero, roughly consistent with put-call parity. The pattern shows that options prices adjust to virtually eliminate profitable trading opportunities. Put differently, the implied cost of shorting falls as the desirability of shorting falls.

Figure 4.6 shows the case for Stratos. The pattern is similar; again, there is a single week in which the synthetic stub is negative at the beginning, and the synthetic stub stays around $5 per share, correctly forecasting the eventual free-standing price of the parent. As the stub becomes less negative, the gap between the actual and synthetic stub narrows. Thus Stratos also supports the idea that the high cost of shorting allows the new subsidiary to be overpriced.

Our third case with exchange-traded options is Xpedior. Unfortunately, Xpedior is a marginal case, and it produces a stub that is strongly negative for only one week when options are trading. When we examine the difference between actual and synthetic prices (not shown in a figure), Xpedior does not seem to display a high cost of shorting, although we have little power since the actual stub is so marginally negative.

It is intriguing that in figures 4.5 and 4.6 there are some negative synthetic stub observations that seem to be exploitable opportunities. We can report that these opportunities truly were exploitable and reflected actual prices, since one of the authors (Lamont) traded on these opportunities and made profits. We suspect that these opportunities were quite limited in size, however, since individual equity options are illiquid, with low volume, low open interest, and high price impact. If arbitrageurs had attempted to buy a few million dollars worth of puts, it seems likely that the price of puts would have risen to eliminate profitable opportunities. However, it still remains a puzzle why arbitrageurs did not buy until the prices adjusted.

---

shares are owned by someone. It is not clear whether this explanation is quantitatively plausible in the case of Palm, since the reported lending income is substantially less than the amount necessary to make buyers indifferent between owning actual shares and synthetic shares.

In table 4.7, we regress the violation of put-call parity (the deviation of the synthetic stub) on the actual stub for Palm and Stratos. For Palm, the synthetic stub deviation moves strongly with the actual stub, and even with just nineteen weekly observations, we can reject the hypothesis that the two do not move together. The R^2 is a whopping .96, suggesting that violations of put-call parity are strongly related to apparent near-arbitrage opportunities. For Stratos, the R^2 is lower at .70, but again we can easily reject the hypothesis that the stub and the deviation of actual from synthetic are unrelated.

Are these violations of put-call parity unusual? Most empirical studies of options prices have found that put-call parity basically holds, with small or fleeting violations due perhaps to trading costs or asynchronous price data (Klemkosky and Resnick 1979, Bodurtha and Courtadon 1986). One might wonder whether put-call parity generally holds using data from our sample period and using our sources and methods. Although a thorough investigation of put-call parity for all equity options is beyond the scope of this chapter, we did do a brief check as follows. We picked a random date, October 10, 2000, and compared the synthetic short on Stratos with those of other options. Stratos options started trading on the Chicago Board Options Exchange (CBOE) on July 12, 2000. We looked at 28 other firms in which options were initially listed on the CBOE between June 11 and July 12, 2000. Most of these firms were, like Stratos, recent technology

TABLE 4.7
Regression of Synthetic Stub Deviation on Actual Stub

	Palm	Stratos
Constant	−8.15	−5.95
	(.24)	(.50)
S_t	.50	.83
	(.02)	(.08)
Observations	19	42
R^2	.96	.71

Note. The dependent variable is the deviation between the actual stub and the synthetic stub, expressed in dollars per parent share. The actual stub, S_t uses actual prices of the shares. The synthetic stub uses the actual price of parent shares and the synthetic short price of subsidiary shares. The synthetic short price is constructed by selling a six-month at-the-money call at the bid prices, buying a six-month at-the-money put at the ask prices, and borrowing the present value of the exercise price at the six-month LIBOR rate. The regression for Palm uses 19 weekly observations as of Friday March 17, 2000–July 21, 2000; the regression for Stratos uses 42 weekly observations as of Friday July 14, 2000–April 27, 2001

IPOs. We omitted firms paying dividends or firms with a stock price below $10 a share. On October 10, the stub value for Stratos was −$1.66 a share, and the synthetic short price constructed using six-month options was 24 percent below the actual price of Stratos (similar to the deviation seen for Palm in table 4.6), or $5.89 below the actual price per share. For the twenty-eight other firms, the average synthetic short price was only 3 percent below the actual price, or 87 cents per share, easily explainable with bid/ask spreads on options. The maximum deviation was 8 percent below the actual price, only a third of the deviation observed for Palm and Stratos. On the basis of this evidence, the Palm and Stratos cases appear to present unusually large violations of put-call parity.

To conclude, in the case of Palm and Stratos, we have strong evidence from options markets confirming that the new issues are overpriced, and no one should buy them (at least without lending them out, which not everyone can do in equilibrium) because cheaper alternatives are available. Although shares in the parent are not perfect substitutes for shares in the subsidiary (because of the risk of spin-off), the synthetic shares are virtually identical. Although not an exploitable arbitrage opportunity, this is a case of blatant mispricing.

5. What Causes Mispricing?

We hope to have convinced even the most jaded reader that the cases we are studying are clear violations of the law of one price. Given that arbitrage cannot correct the mispricing, why would anyone buy the overpriced security? Why are some investors willing to buy shares in Palm when there are cheaper alternatives available in the market, either by buying the parent or by buying Palm synthetically in the options market? In this section we investigate this question, first by asking a simple question: Who buys the expensive subsidiary shares, and how long do they hold them? We then look at IPO day returns for evidence on how these investors affect prices of the parent.

A. Investor Characteristics

Columns 1 and 2 of table 4.8 display volume data for both parents and subsidiaries in our six cases with negative stubs. We show turnover for the first twenty days of trading, defined as average daily volume divided by shares outstanding (for parents) or by total shares sold to the public (for the IPO). The turnover measure does not include the first day of trading itself. All twelve stocks trade on NASDAQ. Since NASDAQ is a dealer market, reported volume includes dealer trades, and the turnover caused by trades between actual investors is approximately half the turnover reported in table 4.8.

TABLE 4.8
Volume, Liquidity, and Institutional Ownership

	Turnover		Bid/Ask Spread		Institutional Ownership	
	Parent (1)	Subsidiary (2)	Parent (3)	Subsidiary (4)	Parent (5)	Subsidiary (6)
Creative/UBID	23.98	106.47	.69	.93	17.71	10.38
HNC/Retek	3.68	22.19	.32	.26	96.38	72.28
Daisytek/PFSWeb	2.42	25.53	.62	.81	71.88	69.95
Metamor/Xpedior	2.13	11.79	.42	.49	53.06	35.96
3Com/Palm	4.54	19.18	.09	.14	52.22	46.01
Methode/Stratos	2.63	41.67	.42	.20	69.47	36.63
Average	6.56	37.80	.43	.47	60.12	45.20
Difference, parent vs. subsidiary	31.24		.04		−14.92	
t-statistic	2.83		.62		−3.06	

Note. Turnover is daily volume as a percentage of parent shares outstanding or subsidiary shares trading. Subsidiary shares trading are shares sold to the public in the IPO. Volume is average daily volume from the first 20 trading days after the IPO date (not including the first day of trading). The shares outstanding of the parent are taken from CRSP, and the shares issued in the IPO are taken from company SEC filings. Bid/ask spread is the average percentage of prices from the first 20 trading days after the IPO date (not including the first day of trading). Institutional ownership, from 13F filings to the SEC (via Securities Data Corp.), pertains to the first quarterly filing after the IPO. Institutional ownership refers to a percentage of parent shares outstanding or subsidiary shares trading.

The first thing to note is that subsidiaries have turnover that is more than five times that of parent turnover, with 37.8 percent of all tradable shares turning over *per day*. Higher turnover means that subsidiary shareholders have lower holding periods, and thus shorter horizons, compared to parent shareholders. Nondealer shareholders of UBID, for example, had an average horizon of two trading days, since turnover was more than 100 percent (implying 50 percent turnover, with dealer trades excluded).

These turnover figures suggest that the subsidiaries may have been more liquid than the parents. If investors value liquidity, then more liquid securities should have higher value and should have higher turnover. To investigate this possibility, columns 3 and 4 of table 4.8 report bid/ask spreads as a percentage of price for the first twenty days of trading. Contrary to the hypothesis of greater liquidity, there is no significant difference in bid/ask spread for the parents and subsidiaries.

Another interpretation of high volume is that it is consistent with the greater fool theory, where investors buy the subsidiary knowing that it is overpriced but hoping it will rise even higher. If they are holding the stock for only a few days, they might not care that they can obtain a cheaper version with identical payoff six months from now (see also Cochrane 2002). Formalizations of this idea include Harrison and Kreps (1978) and De Long et al. (1990). Harrison and Kreps have a model in which agents have different beliefs and act rationally conditional on these beliefs, but short-sale constraints mean that only optimistic investors hold the stock. The model has the remarkable property that stock prices can be above the valuations of the most optimistic investors. In some cases, all investors agree that the stock is overpriced, yet some are still willing to hold it. The reason is that they all think they are following a dynamic strategy that allows them to cash out when the stock gets really overpriced. An essential part of this story is the dynamic trading strategy generating high volume and low holding periods.

Columns 5 and 6 of table 4.8 also show institutional ownership for parents and subsidiaries using data from quarterly 13F filings, reflecting holdings by institutional investment managers having equity assets under management of $100 million or more. In the first quarter after the IPO, institutional ownership is 15 percent higher for parents than for subsidiaries (this difference is understated because of the heavy short interest in subsidiaries).[10]

One potential explanation for the mispricing involves restrictions on what institutions are allowed to hold. For example, Froot and Dabora (chapter 3, this volume) show that Royal Dutch and Shell (two stocks representing the same firm) seem mispriced relative to each other. In recent years, the stock that is part of the S&P 500 (Royal Dutch) trades at a premium to the stock that is not (Shell), possibly reflecting the fact that index funds are forced to buy the more expensive stock and cannot substitute the cheaper one. Similarly, one money manager told us (discussing stub situations in general) that although he was well aware that a particular subsidiary was overpriced relative to the parent, he could not buy the cheaper parent instead of the subsidiary because he ran a growth fund, and the cheaper stock was, by definition, value! However, table 4.8 suggests that such institutional explanations are unlikely to explain the overpricing since most owners are individuals.

The information in table 4.8 also helps explain why the supply of lendable shares to short was so sluggish. First, high turnover impedes securities lending because when a share lender sells his shares, the share borrower is obliged to return the shares and must find a new lender. Second, shares held by individual investors are less likely to be lent than shares held by institutions.

---

[10] We report institutional ownership as a percentage of parent shares outstanding or subsidiary shares trading. For example, Palm sold 26.5 million shares in the IPO on March 2, 2000, had 5.1 million shares in short interest as of March 15, and had institutional ownership of 12.1 million shares at the end of March. Although 26.5 million shares were issued, 31.6 million shares were owned by somebody, thanks to short-sellers who borrowed shares and sold them. Thus institutions held 46 percent of the shares issued, but only 38 percent of all the ownable shares.

In summary, table 4.8 shows that subsidiaries had very high turnover but not high liquidity and had low institutional ownership. This evidence is perfectly consistent with the view that irrational or ignorant investors drove up the price of the subsidiary shares and limits to arbitrage prevented rational investors from correcting this mispricing. We next turn to evidence from IPO day returns for additional evidence.

B. IPO Day Returns

Hand and Skantz (1998), looking at carve-outs generally, provide evidence that irrational investors can affect carve-out pricing. As documented in Schipper and Smith (1986) and Allen and McConnell (1998), when announcing the carve-out, parents earn excess announcement returns of around 2 percent. Hand and Skantz show that on the IPO date itself, parents have excess returns of –2 percent. One explanation is that optimistic investors who desire to hold the subsidiary drive up the price of the parent on the announcement days and then dump the parent in favor of the subsidiary on the IPO day.

Table 4.9 looks at evidence for segmentation in our sample from IPO day returns. It compares IPO day returns for the 14 subsidiaries that had positive stubs on the IPO date and the four subsidiaries with negative stubs (for Xpedior and Retek the stubs became negative after only a few days of trading). Table 4.9 shows that subsidiaries resulting in negative stubs had much higher IPO returns than other subsidiaries, where the returns are offer price to closing price for the new subsidiary. This difference is unsurprising since one way to get negative stubs is to have a high price of the subsidiary.

Another way to get a negative stub is to have a low price of the parent. Table 4.9 also shows that the prices of parents in negative stub situations fell 14 percent from the day before the IPO to the close on the IPO day. For the fourteen cases with positive stubs on the IPO date, the parents fell an average of 1 percent. The differences between the positive stub and negative stub IPOs are large and statistically significant for both parent returns and subsidiary returns (the statistical significance does not change if one categorizes Xpedior and Retek, which had negative stubs in the next few days, in the second group).

The large decline in parent prices in negative stub situations is surprising since the parents own so much of the new issue. One might think that when the subsidiary does unexpectedly well on the issue date, the parent would benefit as the value of its holdings increases. For example, prior to the issue, Palm's underwriters had originally estimated the offering price to be $14–$16 per share. After gauging investor demand, they increased the estimated offering price to $30–$32. Finally, the night before the offer, they chose $38 as the final issuing price. On the first day of trading, Palm immediately went to $145 and later rose to as high as $165, before ending the day

TABLE 4.9
IPO Day Returns for Entire Carve-out Sample

	Subsidiary			Parent		
	Offer Price	Closing Price	Percentage Change	Pre-IPO Price	Closing Price	Percentage Change
HP/Agilent	30.00	42.75	43	78.00	94.31	21
Odetics/ATL	11.00	11.88	8	19.63	18.25	−7
Eaton/Axcelis	22.00	23.94	9	69.50	69.50	0
Viacom/ Blockbuster	15.00	15.00	0	40.56	39.94	−2
Cabot Corp/ Cabot Micro	20.00	24.88	24	29.50	28.00	−5
Cincinnati Bell/Convergys	15.00	16.63	11	29.75	28.69	−4
GM/Delphi	17.00	18.63	10	87.06	85.94	−1
Deluxe/Efunds	13.00	12.00	−8	23.88	23.31	−2
AT&T/Lucent	27.00	30.63	13	64.13	62.88	−2
Santa Fe/ Monterey	14.50	16.50	14	14.75	15.00	2
Sea Containers/ Orient Express	19.00	19.75	4	28.13	26.25	−7
HNC/Retek	15.00	32.56	117	61.00	60.88	0
Tridex/TransAct	8.50	8.75	3	10.44	10.63	2
Metamor/Xpedior	19.00	26.00	37	33.19	29.00	−13
Average for 14 subsidiaries with positive stub on first day			20			−1
3Com/Palm	38.00	95.06	150	104.13	81.81	−21
Daisytek/PFSWeb	17.00	44.13	160	22.63	21.94	−3
Methode/Stratos	21.00	34.13	63	43.94	41.88	−5
Creative/UBID	15.00	48.00	220	35.25	26.25	−26
Average for four subsidiaries with negative stub on first day			148			−14
t-statistic for difference in means, 14 carve-outs vs. four carve-outs			5.69			2.61

Note. Daily closing prices are taken from CRSP. Pre-IPO price is the price of the parent on the day previous to the IPO.

at \$95.06 a share. Thus the very high subsidiary return seems likely to have been a surprise, making the drop in the price of 3Com that day mystifying.[11]

These patterns are all consistent with irrational investors. Prior to the IPO, irrational optimists who desire to own Palm have to hold 3Com instead. 3Com trades in the optimistic segment of the market. Once the IPO occurs, these optimists buy Palm directly (ignoring the cheaper alternative of holding 3Com). 3Com now trades in the more rational segment of the market, and its price falls to the rational price.

6. CONCLUSION

One of us used to have a colleague who, when teaching the basic finance course to impressionable young first-year master of business administration students, would shout the name of a well-known game show as a key conclusion of efficient markets: *The Price Is Right*! He would offer little empirical support for this claim, but could rest assured that it was a claim that was hard to disprove. The trick to testing the "price is right" hypothesis is to find unambiguous relative price comparisons, such as closed-end funds.

The negative stubs in this paper are in a similar category, though the mispricing appears to be even more blatant. In contrast to closed-end funds, where arguments about agency costs by the fund managers, tax liabilities, and bad estimates of net asset value can cloud the picture, in this case any investor who can multiply by 1.5 should be able to tell that Palm is overpriced relative to 3Com. The evidence from options markets shows that these stocks were unambiguously overpriced, and it is difficult to explain why in equilibrium anyone would own these shares. The mispricing persisted because of the sluggish functioning of the shorting market.

There are two key findings of this chapter that need to be understood as a package. First, we observe gross violations of the law of one price. Second, they do *not* present exploitable arbitrage opportunities because of the costs of shorting the subsidiary. In other words, the no free lunch component of the efficient market hypothesis is intact, but the price equals intrinsic value component takes another beating.

Still, it is possible to argue that we have only six cases here that collectively represent a tiny portion of the U.S. equity market. Maybe everything else is just fine. Why should we be concerned? Put another way, are these cases of blatant mispricing the tip of a much bigger iceberg or the entire iceberg? In one respect, our overpriced stocks are clearly different from most

---

[11] More generally, Bergstresser and Karlan (2000) examine cross-corporate equity holdings similar to the ones considered here (but without the terminal date) and find that parent firm stock prices underreact to changes in the value of their holdings. Similarly, closed-end funds trading in the United States but holding foreign securities have prices that do not always react properly to foreign market movements (see Klibanoff, Lamont, and Wizman 1998).

stocks. They were difficult or expensive to borrow because the supply of lendable shares did not quickly respond to the mispricing. In contrast, most stocks and particularly large-cap stocks are easy to borrow. Reed (2001) and D'Avolio (2002) show that few stocks are expensive to short, and Figlewski and Webb (1993) report that average short interest as a percentage of outstanding shares is only 0.2 percent. Although Ofek and Richardson (2001) report that Internet stocks had higher average short interest and were more expensive to short than non-Internet stocks in the period we study, the average difference in cost was only 1 percent per year. So perhaps it is only the rare cases in which shorting is very expensive that lead to mispricing. That is the rosy interpretation of our findings.

There is another interpretation, however, that is less rosy but more plausible. We think that a sensible reading of our evidence should cast doubt on the claim that market prices reflect rational valuations because the cases we have studied should be ones that are particularly easy for the market to get right. Suppose we consider the possibility that Internet stocks were priced much too high between 1998 and 2000. The standard efficient markets reaction to such claims is to say that this cannot happen. If irrational investors bid up prices too high, arbitrageurs will step in to sell the shares short and, in so doing, will drive the prices back down to rational valuations. The lesson to be learned from this chapter is that arbitrage does not always enforce rational pricing. In the case of Palm, arbitrageurs faced little risk but could not find enough shares of Palm to satiate the demands of irrational investors. We have identified cases in which arbitrageurs are *unable* to arbitrage relative mispricing. More generally, there can be cases of mispricing in which arbitrageurs are *unwilling* to establish positions because of fundamental risk or noise trader risk. Many investors thought that Internet stocks were overpriced during the mania, but only a small minority were willing to take a short position, and these short-sellers were not enough to drive prices down to rational valuations. Further, many institutions either are not permitted to sell short or simply choose not to do so for various reasons. Almazan et al. (2001) find that only about 30 percent of mutual funds are allowed to sell short, and only 2 percent actually do sell short.

Limits of arbitrage can create market segmentation. If irrational investors are willing to buy Palm at an unrealistically high price and rational but risk-averse investors are unwilling or unable to sell enough shares short, then two inconsistent prices can coexist. The same argument can apply to any apparent mispricing, from closed-end fund discounts and premia to differences in returns between value stocks and growth stocks. The traditional view is that a stock with a low expected return must have low risk. The examples given here suggest an alternative possibility, namely that the investors who buy apparently expensive stocks are just making a mistake.

The conclusion we draw is that there is one law of economics that does still hold: the law of supply and demand. Prices are set so that the number of shares demanded equals the number of shares supplied. In the case of Palm, the supply of shares could not rise to meet demand because of the sluggish response of lendable shares to short. Similarly, if optimists are willing to bid up the shares of some faddish stocks and not enough courageous investors are willing to meet that demand by selling short, then optimists will set the price.

References

Allen, Jeffrey W., and John J. McConnell, 1998, Equity Carve-outs and Managerial Discretion. *Journal of Finance* 53, 163–86.

Almazan, Andres, Keith C. Brown, Murray Carlson, and David A. Chapman, 2001, Why Constrain Your Mutual Fund Manager?, Manuscript, University of Texas.

Bergstresser, Daniel, and Dean Karlan, 2000, The Market Valuation of Cross-Corporate Equity Holdings. Manuscript, MIT.

Bodurtha, James N., Jr., and Georges R. Courtadon, 1986, Efficiency Tests of the Foreign Currency Options Market. *Journal of Finance* 41, 151–62.

Chen, Joseph, Harrison Hong, and Jeremy C. Stein, 2002, Breadth of Ownership and Stock Returns. *J. Financial Econ.* 66, 171–205.

Cochrane, John H., 2002, Stocks as Money: Convenience Yield and the Tech-Stock Bubble. Manuscript, Univ. Chicago, Grad. School Bus.

Cornell, Bradford, and Qiao Liu, 2001, The Parent Company Puzzle: When Is the Whole Worth Less than One of the Parts?, *J. Corp. Finance* 7, 341–66.

Cornell, Joseph W., 1998, *Spin-off to Pay-off: An Analytical Guide to Investing in Corporate Divestitures*. McGraw-Hill.

D'Avolio, Gene, 2002, The Market for Borrowing Stock, *J. Financial Econ.* 66, 271–306.

De Bondt, Werner F., and Richard H. Thaler, 1985, Does the Stock Market Overreact? *Journal of Finance* 40, 793–805.

Dechow, Patricia M., Amy P. Hutton, Lisa Meulbroek, and Richard G. Sloan, 2001, Short-Sellers, Fundamental Analysis, and Stock Returns, *J. Financial Econ.* 61, 77–106.

De Long, J. Bradford, Andrei Shleifer, Lawrence H. Summers, and Robert J. Waldmann, 1990, Positive Feedback Investment Strategies and Destabilizing Rational Speculation. *Journal of Finance* 45, 379–95.

Diamond, Douglas W., and Robert E. Verrecchia, 1987, Constraints on Short-Selling and Asset Price Adjustment to Private Information. *J. Financial Econ.* 18, 277–311.

Duffie, Darrell, Special Repo Rates, 1996, *Journal of Finance* 51, 493–526.

Duffie, Darrell, Nicolai Garleanu, and Lasse Heje Pedersen, 2001, Securities Lending, Shorting, and Pricing. Manuscript, Stanford Univ., Grad. School Bus.

Fama, Eugene F., 1991, Efficient Capital Markets: II. *Journal of Finance* 46, 1575–1617.

———, Market Efficiency, Long-Term Returns, and Behavioral Finance, 1998, *J. Financial Econ.* 49, 283–306.

Fama, Eugene F., and Kenneth R. French, 1993, Common Risk Factors in the Returns on Stocks and Bonds, *J. Financial Econ.* 33, 3–56.

Figlewski, Stephen, and Gwendolyn P. Webb, 1993, Options, Short Sales, and Market Completeness. *Journal of Finance* 48, 761–77.

Hand, John R. M., and Terrance R. Skantz, 1998, Noise Traders in Event Studies? The Case of Equity Carve-outs. Manuscript, Univ. North Carolina.

Harrison, J. Michael, and David M. Kreps, 1978, Speculative Investor Behavior in a Stock Market with Heterogeneous Expectations. *Q.J.E.* 92, 323–36.

Jones, Charles M., and Owen A. Lamont, 2002, Short-Sale Constraints and Stock Returns. *J. Financial Econ.* 66, 207–39.

Klemkosky, Robert C., and Bruce G. Resnick, 1979, Put-Call Parity and Market Efficiency. *Journal of Finance* 34, 1141–55.

Klibanoff, Peter, Owen Lamont, and Thierry A. Wizman, 1998, Investor Reaction to Salient News in Closed-End Country Funds, *Journal of Finance* 53, 673–99.

Krishnamurthy, Arvind, 2002, The Bond/Old-Bond Spread. *J. Financial Econ.* 66, 463–506.

Lakonishok, Josef, Andrei Shleifer, and Robert W. Vishny, 1994, Contrarian Investment, Extrapolation, and Risk. *Journal of Finance* 49, 1541–78.

Lamont, Owen A., and Christopher Polk, 2001, The Diversification Discount: Cash Flows versus Returns, *Journal of Finance* 56, 1693–1721.

Lee, Charles M. C., Andrei Shleifer, and Richard H. Thaler, 1991, Investor Sentiment and the Closed-End Fund Puzzle. *Journal of Finance* 46, 75–109.

Liu, Jun, and Francis A. Longstaff, 2000, Losing Money on Arbitrages. Manuscript. Univ. California, Los Angeles.

Loughran, Tim, and Jay R. Ritter, 2000, Uniformly Least Powerful Tests of Market Efficiency, *J. Financial Econ.* 55, 361–89.

Miller, Edward M., 1977, Risk, Uncertainty, and Divergence of Opinion, *Journal of Finance* 32, 1151–68.

Mitchell, Mark, Todd Pulvino, and Erik Stafford, 2002, Limited Arbitrage in Equity Markets. *Journal of Finance* 57, 551–84.

Nanda, Vikram, 1991, On the Good News about Equity Carve-outs, *Journal of Finance* 46, 1717–37.

Ofek, Eli, and Matthew Richardson, 2001, Dotcom Mania: A Survey of Market Efficiency in the Internet Section. Manuscript, New York Univ.

Pontiff, Jeffrey, 1996, Costly Arbitrage: Evidence from Closed-End Funds. *Q.J.E.* 111, 1135–51.

Reed, Adam, 2001, Costly Short-Selling and Stock Price Adjustment to Earnings Announcements, Manuscript, Univ. North Carolina.

Ritter, Jay R., 1991, The Long-Run Performance of Initial Public Offerings, *Journal of Finance* 46, 3–27.

Ritter, Jay R., and Ivo Welch, 2002, A Review of IPO Activity, Pricing, and Allocations. *Journal of Finance* 57, 1795–1828.

Russell, Thomas, and Richard Thaler, 1985, The Relevance of Quasi Rationality in Competitive Markets. *A.E.R.* 75, 1071–82.

Schill, Michael J., and Chungsheng Zhou, 2001, Pricing an Emerging Industry: Evidence from Internet Subsidiary Carve-outs. *Financial Management* 30, 5–33.

Schipper, Katherine, and Abbie Smith, 1986, A Comparison of Equity Carve-outs and Seasoned Equity Offerings: Share Price Effects and Corporate Restructuring, *J. Financial Econ.* 15, 153–86.

Shleifer, Andrei, and Robert W. Vishny, 1997, The Limits of Arbitrage, *Journal of Finance* 52, 35–55.

Slovin, Myron B., Marie E. Sushka, and Steven R. Ferraro, 1995, A Comparison of the Information Conveyed by Equity Carve-outs, Spin-offs, and Asset Sell-offs. *J. Financial Econ.* 37, 89–104.

Sorescu, Sorin M., 2000, The Effect of Options on Stock Prices: 1973 to 1995, *Journal of Finance* 55, 487–514.

Stein, Jeremy C., Rational Capital Budgeting in an Irrational World, 1996, *J. Bus.* 69, 429–55.

Vijh, Anand M., Long-Term Returns from Equity Carveouts, 1999, *J. Financial Econ.* 51, 273–308.

Zingales, Luigi, 1995, Insider Ownership and the Decision to Go Public, *Rev. Econ. Studies* 62, 425–48.

PART II

Stock Returns and the Equity Premium

Chapter 5

VALUATION RATIOS AND THE LONG-RUN STOCK

MARKET OUTLOOK: AN UPDATE

JOHN Y. CAMPBELL AND ROBERT J. SHILLER

WHEN STOCK MARKET valuation ratios are at extreme levels by historical standards, as dividend/price and price/earnings ratios have been for some years in the United States, one naturally wonders what this means for the stock market outlook. It seems reasonable to suspect that prices are not likely ever to drift too far from their normal levels relative to indicators of fundamental value, such as dividends or earnings. Thus it seems natural to give at least some weight to the simple mean-reversion theory that when stock prices are very high relative to these indicators, as they have been recently, prices will eventually fall in the future to bring the ratios back to more normal historical levels. The idea that they should do so seems intuitive and basic. Metaphorically, when one is mountaineering, one can enjoy the exhilarating view from high up on a mountain, and may look forward to the possibility of discovering a way up to a much higher level. But one will reflect that, realistically, at a random date years from now, one will probably be back down at ground level.

On December 3, 1996, we testified before the Federal Reserve Board that, despite all the evidence that stock returns are hard to forecast in the short-run, this simple theory of mean reversion is basically right and does indeed imply a poor long-run stock market outlook. We amplified our testimony and published it in 1998, continuing to assert our pessimistic long-run scenario.[1]

The stock market did not immediately move to encourage faith in our theory. Since our testimony, the stock market, as measured by the real

This chapter was written at the beginning of 2001 and circulated as NBER Working Paper 8221. It is based on our joint testimony before the Board of Governors of the Federal Reserve System, December 3, 1996, on material circulated in Shiller (1996), and on Campbell and Shiller (1998). We acknowledge the able research assistance of Elena Ranguelova and Daniel Waldman, help with data from Robert J. Gordon, and the helpful comments of Paul Samuelson. For this volume, we have updated references but have made no substantive changes to NBER Working Paper 8221.

[1] Over this interval we also published related papers, Campbell (1999) and Shiller (1999), and wrote two books, Campbell and Viceira (2002) and Shiller (2000), that expand on our views.

(inflation-corrected) S&P Composite Index, has increased by 80 percent above its value when we testified, and 30 percent above its value when we published.

Despite these developments, we believe that our original testimony and article are even more relevant today. Valuation ratios moved up in the year 2000 to levels that were absolutely unprecedented, and are still nearly as high as of this writing at the beginning of 2001. Even allowing for the possibility that the economy and financial markets have undergone some structural changes, these ratios imply a stronger case for a poor stock market outlook than has ever seen before. To underscore this conviction, we present here an extended version of our 1998 paper, with data updated to 2000.

1. HISTORICAL BEHAVIOR OF VALUATION RATIOS

We should first understand what the stability of a valuation ratio itself implies about mean reversion. If we accept the premise for the moment that valuation ratios will continue to fluctuate within their historical ranges in the future, and neither move permanently outside nor get stuck at one extreme of their historical ranges, then when a valuation ratio is at an extreme level either the numerator or the denominator of the ratio must move in a direction that restores the ratio to a more normal level. *Something* must be forecastable based on the ratio, either the numerator or the denominator. For example, high prices relative to dividends—a low dividend/price ratio—must forecast some combination of unusual increases in dividends and declines (or at least unusually slow growth) in prices.

The conventional random-walk theory of the stock market is that stock price changes are not predictable, so that neither the dividend/price ratio nor any other valuation ratio has any ability to forecast movements in stock prices. But then, if the random-walk theory is not to imply that the dividend/price ratio will move beyond its historical range or get stuck forever at the current extreme, it requires that the dividend/price ratio predicts future growth in dividends.[2]

---

[2] The random-walk theory is a special case of the efficient-markets theory of stock prices. In general, the efficient-markets theory allows the equilibrium rate of return required by investors to vary over time (see, for example, Campbell and Cochrane 1999). The random-walk theory assumes that this required rate of return is constant. We are in fact oversimplifying the random-walk theory in this essay, because the theory actually says that stock *returns*, not prices, should be unforecastable. Since the dividend/price ratio is itself a component of the stock return, the random-walk theory says that a lower dividend/price ratio should be associated with slightly more rapid price growth to offset the lower dividend component of return. In other words, the theory says that prices should move in a direction that drives the dividend/price ratio away from its historical average; dividends must do more than all the adjustment necessary to bring the ratio back to its historical average. However, the difference between return and price change is small and in practice forecasts of returns and forecasts of price changes are very similar. See our

Does the dividend/price ratio forecast future dividend movements as required by the random-walk theory, or does it instead forecast future movements in stock prices? We answer this question using a long-run annual U.S. data set that extends today's S&P 500 Index back in time to 1872.[3] The answer is given by the pair of scatterplots shown in figure 5.1. Each scatterplot has the dividend/price ratio, measured as the previous year's dividend divided by the January stock price, on the horizontal axis. (The horizontal axis scale is logarithmic but the axis is labeled in levels for ease of reference.) Over this period the historical mean value for the dividend/price ratio was 4.65 percent.

In the top part of the figure the vertical axis is the growth rate of real dividends (measured logarithmically as the change in the natural log of real dividends) over a time interval sufficient to bring the dividend/price ratio back to its historical mean of 4.65 percent. More precisely, we measure the dividend growth rate from the year preceding the year shown until the year before the dividend/price ratio again crossed 4.65 percent. Because dividends enter the dividend/price ratio with a one-year lag, this is the appropriate way to measure growth in dividends from the base level embodied in a given year's dividend/price ratio to the level that prevailed when the dividend/price ratio next crossed its historical mean.[4]

Since 1872, the dividend/price ratio has crossed its mean value twenty-nine times, with intervals between crossings ranging from one year to twenty years (the twenty-year interval being between 1955 and 1975). Selected years are indicated on the scatter diagram by two-digit numbers; a * after a number denotes a nineteenth-century date. The last year shown is 1983, since this is the last year that was followed by the dividend/price ratio crossing its mean. (The ratio has been below its mean ever since.) A regression line is fit through these data points, and a vertical line is drawn to indicate the dividend/price ratio at the start of the year 2000. The implied forecast for dividend growth is the horizontal dashed line marked where the vertical line intersects the regression line.

(1988a) paper for a careful analysis of dividend forecasts within the context of a log-linearized mathematical representation of the efficient-markets theory, or Campbell, Lo, and MacKinlay (1997), chapter 7, for a recent textbook exposition.

[3] The data in this chapter use the January S&P Composite stock price for each year since 1872, while earnings and dividends are for the entire previous year. Data before 1926 are based on Cowles (1939). The price index used to deflate nominal values to real values is the producer price index. See Shiller (1989) for a description of these data.

[4] The time intervals required to bring the dividend/price ratio back to its mean typically exceed one year, so the dividend growth rate for any particular year can affect several successive observations. This overlapping of successive time intervals implies that the different points in the scatterplot are not statistically independent. There are, however, twenty-nine nonoverlapping time intervals in our sample, so the data are not insubstantial. Statistical tests of the significance of analogous relations with fixed horizons, taking account of the overlapping intervals, are reported in Campbell and Shiller (1988b, 1989).

It is obvious from the top part of figure 5.1 that the dividend/price ratio has done a poor job as a forecaster of future dividend growth to the date when the ratio is again borne back to its mean value. The regression line is nearly horizontal, implying that the forecast for future dividend growth is almost the same regardless of the dividend/price ratio. The R^2 statistic for the regression is 0.25 percent, indicating that only one-quarter of one percent of the variation of dividend growth is explained by the initial dividend/price ratio.

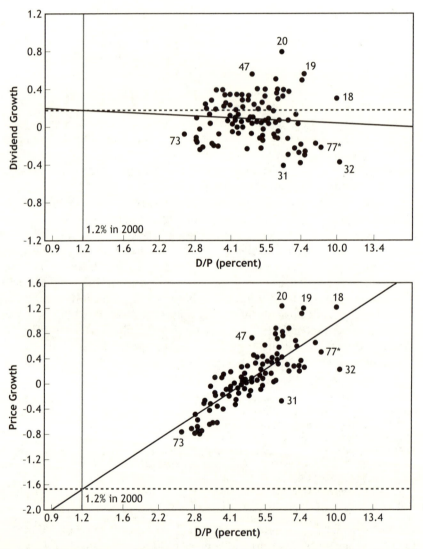

Figure 5.1. Dividend growth till the next time D/P crosses its mean. Price growth till the next time D/P crosses its mean.

It must follow, therefore, that the dividend/price ratio forecasts movements in its denominator, the stock price, and that it is the stock price that has moved to restore the ratio to its mean value. In the lower part of figure 5.1 the vertical axis shows the growth rate of real stock prices (measured logarithmically as the change in log real stock prices) between the year shown and the next year when the dividend/price ratio crossed its mean value. The scatterplot shows a strong tendency for the dividend/price ratio to predict future price changes. The regression line has a strongly positive slope, and the R^2 statistic for the regression is 63 percent. We have answered our question: It is the denominator of the dividend/price ratio that brings the ratio back to its mean, not the numerator.

At the start of 2000, the dividend/price ratio was only 1.2 percent, well to the left of any points shown in the figure. The lower part of figure 5.1 shows that on previous occasions when the dividend/price ratio has been below 3.4 percent, the stock market has *always* declined in real terms over the interval to the next crossing of the mean dividend/price ratio; real declines in stock prices have *always* played a role in restoring such extreme low dividend/price ratios to the mean. The fitted value of the regression line for 2000 indicates that the next time that the dividend/price ratio is back to its mean, the log real value of the stock market will be more than 1.6 lower than it is today. Translating into percentage terms, this says that the stock market will lose more than three-quarters of its real value! Can we take such a forecast seriously? What modifications should we make to such a forecast?

Fixed-Horizon Forecasts from the Dividend/Price Ratio

Figure 5.1 shows the powerful ability of the dividend/price ratio to predict price movements to the date at which the dividend/price ratio next crosses its mean. We looked at the figure to see what it is that restores the ratio to its mean: the numerator or the denominator. But, the problem with these forecasts is that we do not know when the dividend/price ratio will next cross its mean; historically this has ranged from one to twenty years. We now show scatterplots like figure 5.1, but where the vertical axis is changed to show growth rates of dividends and prices over a fixed horizon. The horizon is one year in figure 5.2, and ten years in figure 5.3. We should expect to see a worse fit than in figure 5.1, of course, since with these figures we do not measure dividend and price growth rates over intervals when the ratio returned to its mean value.

The upper part of figure 5.2 shows that over one year, the dividend/price ratio does forecast dividend growth with the negative sign predicted by the efficient-markets theory. Years in which January stock prices are high, relative to last year's dividends, tend to be years in which this year's dividends are high relative to last year's dividends. The dividend/price ratio is able to explain 13 percent of the annual variation in dividend growth.

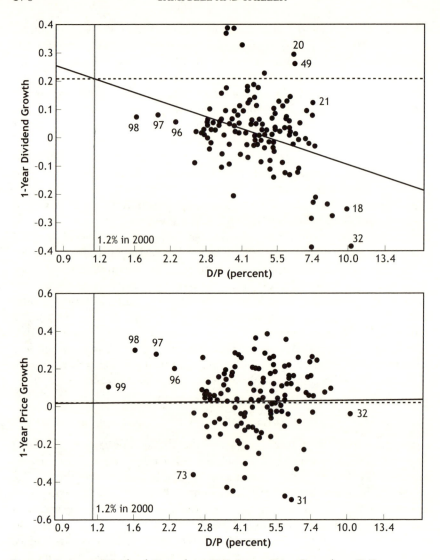

Figure 5.2. 1-year Dividend Growth vs. D/P. 1-year Price Growth vs. D/P.

Such short-horizon forecasting power should not be surprising; dividends are fairly predictable over a few quarters, and the January stock price is measured well after most of last year's dividends have been paid, at a time when it may be relatively easy for market participants to anticipate the level of dividends during the coming year.

The lower part of figure 5.2 shows that the dividend/price ratio has little forecasting power for stock price changes over the next year. Prices do have a very slight tendency to fall in years when they are initially high relative to dividends, but this relationship explains less than 1 percent of the annual variance of stock prices. The short-run noise in stock prices swamps the predictable variation that was visible in figure 5.1.[5]

In figure 5.3, however, where the horizon is ten years rather than one year, many of the patterns of figure 5.1 become apparent again. Just as in figure 5.1, there is only a very weak relation between the dividend/price ratio and subsequent ten-year dividend growth. In fact the relation in figure 5.3 is even less consistent with the efficient-markets theory than the relation in figure 5.1, because the figure 5.3 relation is positive, implying that dividends tend to move in the wrong direction to restore the dividend/price ratio to its historical average level. Just as in figure 5.1, there is a substantial positive relation between the dividend/price ratio and subsequent ten-year price growth. The R^2 statistics are a trivial 1 percent for dividend growth but 9 percent for price growth.

The unusual recent behavior of the stock market is visible in the bottom panels of both figures 5.2 and 5.3. In figure 5.2, the low dividend/price ratios and large price increases of the years from 1995 through 1999 are visible as five points at the top left of the figure. In figure 5.3, price increases during the 1990s have a somewhat smaller effect but are visible in three points for the years 1988, 1989, and 1990 at the top left of the figure.

Given the low value for the dividend/price ratio at the start of 2000, the regression in the bottom panel of figure 5.3 implies a decline of 0.6 in the log real stock price over the next ten years. This corresponds to a 55 percent loss of real value.[6]

Alternative Valuation Ratios

The dividend/price ratio is a widely used valuation ratio, but it has the disadvantage that its behavior can be affected by shifts in corporate financial policy, a point we discuss later in the paper. Accordingly it is worthwhile to explore alternative measures of the level of stock prices.

Figure 5.4 illustrates some key valuation ratios in our long-run annual U.S. data set. The top left panel of the figure shows the price/earnings ratio,

[5] Campbell, Lo, and MacKinlay (1997), chapter 7, explains in more formal terms how R^2 statistics can rise with the length of the horizon over which returns are measured.

[6] As we mentioned in footnote 2, stock returns differ from stock price changes because they include the direct contribution of dividends. Figure 5.3 implies an unusually poor year-2000 outlook for stock returns, for three reasons. First, dividends are initially low relative to prices. Second, the top part of figure 5.3 shows that dividends are predicted to grow slowly over the next ten years. Third, the bottom part of the figure shows that real prices are predicted to fall over the next ten years. A scatterplot with ten-year real stock returns on the vertical axis looks much like the bottom part of figure 5.3, but with a better fit (an R^2 statistic of 16 percent rather than 9 percent). The cumulative continuously compounded ten-year return forecast implied by the January 2000 dividend/price ratio is −44 percent.

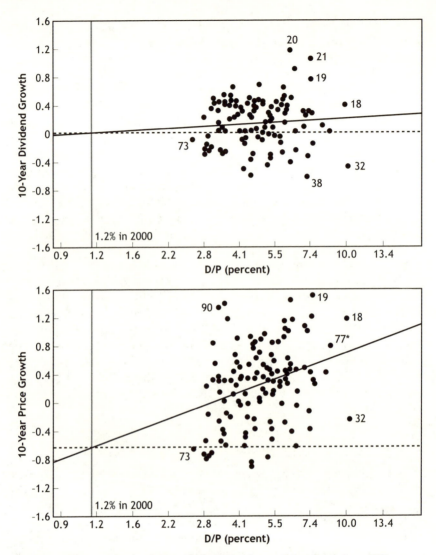

Figure 5.3. 10-year Dividend Growth vs. D/P. 10-year Price Growth vs. D/P.

calculated using the January stock price in each year divided by the level of earnings from the previous year. The bottom left panel shows the dividend/price ratio, calculated using the dividends from the previous year divided by the January stock price. These ratios are not adjusted to express them in real terms, because it is assumed that the same general price index applies to the earnings or dividend series and the stock price series.

Figure 5.4 illustrates the fact that price/earnings ratios have normally moved in a range from 8 to about 20, with a mean of 14.5 and occasional spikes down as far as 6 or up as high as 26. At the beginning of 2000, the

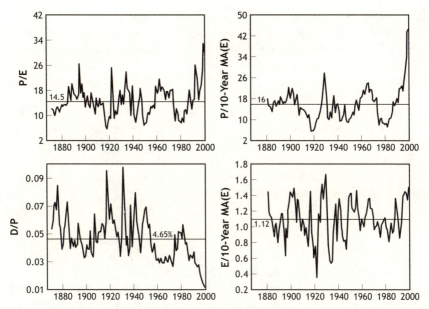

Figure 5.4. S&P Composite Stock data, January values 1872–1997.

price/earnings ratio was high, at 29.6, but not at a record level. Dividend/price ratios have normally moved in a range from 3 percent to about 7 percent, with a mean of 4.65 percent and occasional movements up to almost 10 percent. Very recently the dividend/price ratio has fallen to a record low of 1.2 percent, well below the historical range.

Since stock price increases drive up price/earnings ratios and drive down dividend/price ratios, it is not surprising that the two series in figure 5.4 generally move opposite to one another. There are, however, various spikes in the price/earnings ratio that do not show up in the dividend/price ratio. These spikes occur when recessions temporarily depress corporate earnings. Since we use previous-year earnings to calculate price/earnings ratios, depressed earnings in 1921, 1933, and 1991, for example, show up in our price/earnings series in 1922, 1934, and 1992.

A clearer picture of stock market variation emerges if one averages earnings over several years. Benjamin Graham and David Dodd, in their now famous 1934 textbook *Security Analysis*, said that for purposes of examining valuation ratios, one should use an average of earnings of "not less than five years, preferably seven or ten years" (p. 452). Following their advice we smooth earnings by taking an average of real earnings over the past ten years.[7] The top right panel of figure 5.4 shows the ratio of the January real

---

[7] We first looked at smoothed real earnings in our (1988b) paper. There we averaged log real earnings rather than levels of real earnings (that is, we used a geometric rather than an arithmetic average), but this makes little difference to the results. We also compared ten-year and thirty-year moving averages of earnings, and found that they have similar properties.

stock price to smoothed real earnings from the previous year. This price/smoothed-earnings ratio responds to long-run variations in the level of stock prices. It has roughly the same range of variation as the conventional price/earnings ratio, with a slightly higher mean of 16.0, but the record high of 44.9 now appears at the start of 2000. This record ratio dwarfs the previous record of 28.0, set in 1929.

The bottom right panel of figure 5.4 shows the ratio of current real earnings to smoothed real earnings. This figure shows that in 2000 real earnings have indeed grown quite well when compared to their ten-year past average, but this earnings growth is not record-breaking and there are a number of comparable experiences in history. It is price growth, not earnings growth, that has set all-time records lately.

Forecasts from the Price/smoothed-Earnings Ratio

Figures 5.5 and 5.6 have the same format as figures 5.2 and 5.3, except that the ratio of price to a ten-year moving average of real earnings appears on the horizontal axis of each scatterplot, and we look at the growth rate of the ten-year moving average of earnings rather than the growth rate of dividends. The price/smoothed-earnings ratio has little ability to predict future growth in smoothed earnings; the R^2 statistics are 1 percent over one year and 5 percent over ten years. However, the ratio is a good forecaster of ten-year growth in stock prices, with an R^2 statistic of 30 percent. The fit of this relation is substantially better than we found for the dividend/price ratio in figure 5.3.[8]

Noting that the price/smoothed-earnings ratio for January 2000 is a record 44.9, the regression illustrated in figure 5.6 is predicting a catastrophic ten-year decline in the log real stock price. We do not find this extreme forecast credible; when the independent variable has moved so far from the historically observed range, we cannot trust a linear regression line. However, this extreme forecast does, we think, suggest some real concerns that future price growth will be small or negative.

Ratios' Forecasts of Productivity

Popular commentators on the stock market often justify high valuation ratios by reference to expectations of future productivity growth, that is, future growth in output per man-hour, as if productivity were another

---

[8] The price/smoothed-earnings ratio is also a much better predictor than the conventional price/earnings ratio. The noise in annual earnings distorts the fundamental relation illustrated in figure 5.6. The superior forecasting power of the price/smoothed-earnings ratio carries over to ten-year real returns; a regression of ten-year returns on the price/smoothed-earnings ratio has an R^2 statistic of 40 percent, whereas a regression of ten-year returns on the dividend/price ratio has an R^2 statistic of only 16 percent.

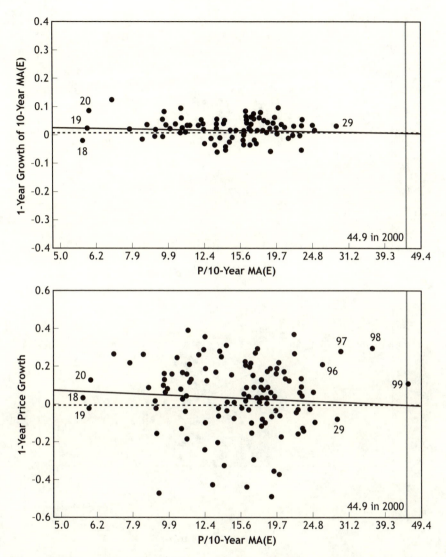

Figure 5.5. 1-year Growth of 10-year MA(E) vs. P/10-year MA(E). 1-year Price Growth vs. P/10-year MA(E).

indicator of the value of firms. They point to rapid productivity growth in the second half of the 1990s and argue that the stock market rationally anticipates a continuation, or even an acceleration, of this trend.[9] A difficulty

[9] While popular discussion normally emphasizes productivity growth in a few new economy sectors, Nordhaus (2000) shows that productivity growth rate increases in the 1990s were widespread and not narrowly focused on these sectors.

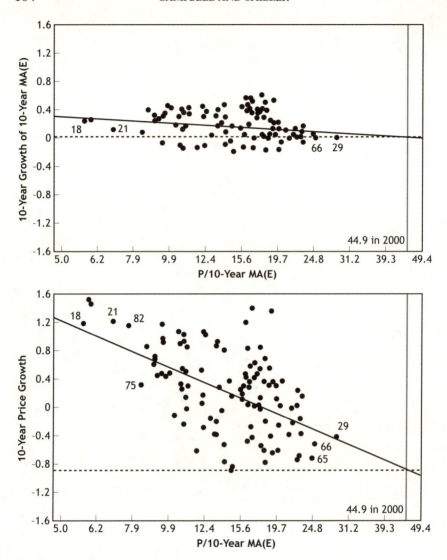

Figure 5.6.

with this line of argument is that higher output per man-hour in the future may well accrue to workers, or to the entrepreneurs who create new firms, rather than to the owners of existing firms. Nonetheless it is interesting to ask whether the stock market has historically predicted variations in productivity growth. We can extend our previous analysis by substituting productivity growth, in place of earnings growth, as the variable to be forecasted.

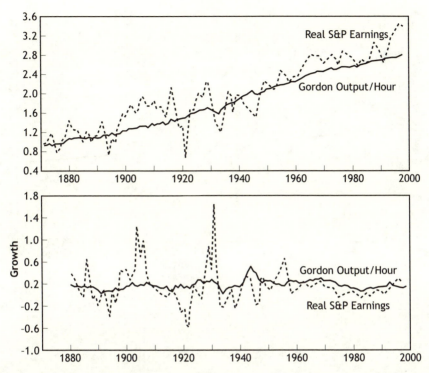

Figure 5.7. Output/hour and real earnings.

The top panel of figure 5.7 shows the log of real output per hour for the nonfarm housing private economy, along with the same log real earnings series we plotted in figure 5.4.[10] Note that productivity has virtually the same growth rate as real S&P earnings, but productivity has much less volatility, it more nearly hugs a trend line. The bottom panel of figure 5.7 shows ten-year growth rates of output per hour and real earnings. There are some short-run comovements in the two series, probably reflecting the short-run effects of recessions on both profits and productivity.

Figure 5.8 is a scatter diagram with the ratio of price to smoothed ten-year earnings on the horizontal axis, and the subsequent ten-year growth in productivity on the vertical axis. We see that the price/smoothed-earnings ratio has virtually no ability to predict future productivity growth. A scatter with the conventional price/earnings ratio on the horizontal axis, not shown here, is even less successful. These results do not support the view that movements in stock prices reflect rational forecasts of future productivity growth.

[10] Robert J. Gordon (2000, figure 3, p. 66) supplied the productivity series. His multifactor productivity is fairly similar in appearance to the output per hour series used here.

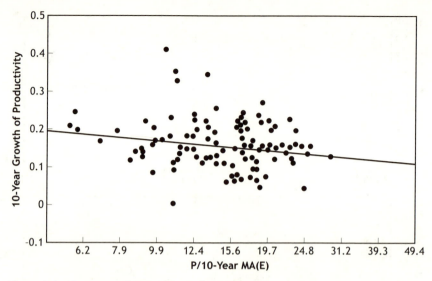

Figure 5.8. 10-year productivity growth vs. P/10-year MA(E).

2. Is the Twenty-first Century a New Era?

Over the past century the American economy has been transformed in many fundamental ways. Agriculture gave way to industry, and industry has given way to services as the economy's leading sector. Automobiles and airplanes have revolutionized transport, while radio, television, and now the Internet have transformed communication. Massive corporations emerged to exploit the economies of mass production, but these are now being replaced by smaller, more flexible organizations that can exploit information technology more effectively.

These changes have affected the financial sector just as deeply as any other part of the economy. Yet certain aspects of financial market behavior have remained remarkably stable throughout the tumult of the twentieth century. We have seen that stock market valuation ratios have moved up and down within a fairly well-defined range, without strong trends or sudden breaks.

Despite the historical stability of valuation ratios, some market observers question whether historical patterns offer a reliable guide to the future. Various arguments are put forward to justify the notion that financial markets are entering a "new era." Some of these arguments have to do with corporate financial policy, while others concern investor behavior or the structure of the U.S. economy. We now briefly review some of these arguments.

Repurchases and the Dividend/Price Ratio

Dividends represent cash paid to ongoing shareholders, and this makes dividends appealing indicators of fundamental value. In fact, over very long holding periods the return to shareholders is dominated by dividends, because the end-of-holding-period stock price becomes trivially small when it is discounted from the end to the beginning of a long holding period.

Nonetheless, an important criticism of the dividend/price ratio is that it can be affected by corporate financial policy. As a tax-favored alternative to paying dividends, companies can repurchase their stock. Repurchases transfer cash to those shareholders who sell their stock, and benefit ongoing shareholders because future dividend payments will be divided among fewer shares. If a corporation permanently diverts funds from dividends to a repurchase program, it reduces current dividends but begins an ongoing reduction in the number of shares and thus increases the long-run growth rate of dividends per share. This in turn can permanently lower the dividend/price ratio, driving it outside its normal historical range. Many commentators have argued that repurchases, not excessive stock prices, are responsible for record low dividend/price ratios in the late 1990s.

One way to adjust the dividend/price ratio for shifts in corporate financial policy is to add net repurchases (dollars spent on repurchases less dollars received from new issues) to dividends. Cole, Helwege, and Laster (1996) did this for S&P 500 firms over the period 1975–1996, and found that dividend/price ratios should be adjusted upwards significantly during the mid-1980s and the mid-1990s, for example by 0.8 percent in 1996. This approach assumes that both repurchases and issues of shares take place at market value, so that dollars spent and received correspond directly to shares repurchased and issued. In practice, however, many companies issue shares below market value as part of their employee stock option incentive plans. Liang and Sharpe (1999) correct for this in a study of the largest 144 firms in the S&P 500; they find that the dividend/price ratio for those firms should be adjusted upwards by 1.39 percent in 1997 (a number that they argue is not sustainable in the long run) and 0.75 percent in 1998.

A glance at figure 5.4 shows that an adjustment of this magnitude brings the dividend/price ratio back closer to the bottom of its normal historical range, but does not bring it anywhere close to the middle of the normal range. For this reason, and because repurchase programs do not affect price/earnings ratios, corporate financial policy cannot be the only explanation of the abnormal valuation ratios observed in recent years.

Intangible Investment and the Price/Earnings Ratio

A criticism that is commonly directed against use of the conventional price/earnings ratio as an indicator of stock market valuation is that the denominator of the ratio, earnings, has become biased downward because the new economy involves substantial investments in intangibles, which are, following conventional accounting procedures, deducted from earnings as current expenses. For example, it is a hallmark of many companies in the new economy that they plan to attract a large volume of customers but to lose money for years, hoping that the high level of activity will enable them to build an effective high-tech business organization as well as to solidify public acceptance of their product. The cost of activities that promote such intangible capital, these critics argue, should not really be deducted directly from earnings, since they are effectively long-term investments.

Hall (2000) has called such intangible capital "e-capital," and argues that there has been a great deal of investment in e-capital in the 1990s "resulting at least in part from technological progress in forming e-capital."[11] He tells a story in which the accumulation of e-capital in the 1990s explains the much higher measured price/earnings ratios as well as the higher wages paid to college graduates (who create e-capital) relative to the wages paid to those who did not graduate from college. His story is also consistent with the fact that gains in measured productivity in the late 1990s have been modest, well below the gains of the 1950s and 1960s.

McGrattan and Prescott (2001) have presented estimates of the correction that should be made to earnings in the 1990s due to investment in intangible capital in the corporate sector. They estimate the earnings correction by first estimating the return to capital in the non-corporate sector. They then assume that this estimated return, which is approximately the risk-free rate, should apply to the corporate sector as well, and thereby estimate the component of corporate earnings that cannot be attributed to measured tangible capital. They attribute this component of corporate earnings to returns to intangible capital. Their analysis implies that corporate earnings correctly measured to account for investments in intangible capital would be 27 percent higher.[12]

These new economy stories are interesting possibilities to explain the stock market, but they are just stories: no convincing justification has been given for assuming that investment in intangibles is really dramatically more important in recent years than it was in earlier years. Neither Hall nor McGrattan and Prescott show that their models fit long historical time series data. Their calibrated models explain only recent observations, and hence their fit is of little persuasiveness in judging the current valuation ratios. Hall's model would imply that most U.S. firms had negative e-capital in the period 1980–1987.[13]

---

[11] Hall "E-Capital . . ." (2000, p. 76). See also Hall (2001).

[12] See McGrattan and Prescott (2001). Their discussion surrounding their equation 17, p. 13, implies that while NIPA corporate profits in the 1990s have been 7.3 percent of gross national product, the correctly measured profits would be higher by an amount equal to 3 percent of intangible capital, which they estimate at 64.5 percent of annual GNP.

[13] Cummins (2000), p. 109.

Bond and Cummins (2000), using data on 459 individual firms over the period 1982–1998, partially measure intangible capital investment by expenditures the firms make on research and development and on marketing. They consider the effect of intangible capital on investment equations and conclude that intangible investments do not appear to justify the current high valuation in the market.[14]

The Baby Boom, Market Participation, and the Demand for Stock

Many observers suggest that there has been a secular shift in the attitudes of the investing public towards the stock market. As the baby-boom generation comes to dominate the economically and financially active population, its attitudes become more important while those of earlier generations have less and less weight. It is argued that baby boomers are more risk-tolerant (perhaps because they do not remember the extreme economic conditions of the 1930s), and that they tend to favor stocks over bonds (perhaps because they are influenced by the extremely poor performance of bonds during the inflationary 1970s). Thus valuation ratios may be extreme today because baby boomers are willing to pay high prices for stocks; the ratios may remain extreme for as long as this demographic effect persists—that is, well into the twenty-first century—and may even move further outside their historical ranges if the demographic effect strengthens.

A variant of this argument emphasizes that economists have had great difficulty in reconciling historical stock price levels with standard equilibrium asset pricing models. Mehra and Prescott (1985) pointed out that stock prices have been much lower than standard models would predict; they initiated an enormous literature on the "equity premium puzzle," but no entirely convincing explanation has been found. Perhaps the baby-boom generation is the first to realize that historical valuation ratios were a mistake, and recent stock price movements represent a correction of the mistake.[15]

Alternatively, baby boomers may benefit from institutional innovations that make it easier for less well-off people to participate in the stock market,

---

[14] Bond and Cummins (2000) find that the coefficient of Tobin's Q in the investment equation is usually not significant after including their additional intangible capital measures unless one replaces the usual Tobin's Q ratio with a ratio that has as its numerator not the actual price but the forecasted present value of future earnings. Thus, firms' behavior suggests that managers themselves do not believe the valuations for the market even after partial correction for intangible investment.

[15] Siegel (1998) presents a moderate version of this argument, while Glassman and Hassett (1999) present an extreme version, arguing that stocks should not carry any risk premium at all, and that stock prices will rise dramatically further once investors come to realize this fact. Both Siegel and Glassman–Hassett emphasize that stock returns have historically had lower risk at long horizons than at short horizons. This is a manifestation of the same mean-reversion documented in this paper, but Siegel and Glassman–Hassett do not stress the low return forecasts that are implied by mean-reversion.

and to hold diversified portfolios. Heaton and Lucas (1999) and Vissing–Jørgenson (1998) show that broader participation and cheaper diversification can drive up the demand for stock and increase stock prices. However, such effects are unlikely to explain large movements in the stock market because most wealth is now, and always has been, controlled by wealthy people who face few barriers to stock market participation and diversification.

In support of this line of thought, it has been pointed out that the dividend/price ratio shows some evidence of trend decline during the whole of the period since World War II. The appearance of long-run stability in this ratio in figure 5.4 would be much weaker if the figure began in the mid-twentieth century rather than in 1872.[16] On the other hand, long-run trends in stock market participation are not plausible candidates to explain the sharp run-up in stock prices during the late 1990s.

While it may be true that the demand for stock has increased, this does not necessarily contradict the pessimistic stock market outlook presented earlier in this chapter. The argument is that demand has driven stock prices up relative to dividends and earnings. But since the demand for stock does not change the expected paths of future dividends and earnings, higher stock prices today must depress subsequent stock returns unless demand is even stronger at the end of the holding period. Over the ten-year holding period emphasized in this chapter, there does not seem to be any good reason to expect stock demand to strengthen further from today's high levels.

Also, it may not be correct to think of investors' attitudes as shifting only slowly, in reaction to long-run demographic changes. Economic conditions may also be important. It is noticeable that stock prices tend to be high relative to indicators of fundamental value at times when the economy has been growing strongly. This tendency is visible in figure 5.4; high price/earnings and price/smoothed-earnings ratios and low dividend/price ratios are characteristic of periods, such as the 1920s, 1960s, and mid-1990s, when real earnings have been growing rapidly so that current earnings are well above smoothed earnings. If economic growth in general, or earnings growth in particular, influences investors' attitudes, then weaker economic conditions could rapidly bring prices back down to more normal levels.[17]

[16] Blanchard (1993) emphasizes the postwar declining trend in the dividend/price ratio and in various other measures of the risk premium investors demand for holding stocks. Bakshi and Chen (1994) argue that demographic effects can explain the high stock market of the 1960s and 1980s and low stock market of the 1970s, but they do not ask whether their demographic measures have explanatory power for other countries or time periods.

[17] This leaves open the question of why investors' attitudes might be affected by economic conditions. Barsky and De Long (1993) and Barberis, Shleifer, and Vishny (1998) argue that investors irrationally extrapolate recent earnings growth into the future, so that the stock market becomes overvalued when earnings growth has been strong. Campbell and Cochrane (1999) argue that investors become more risk-tolerant when the economy is strong, because their well being is determined by their consumption relative to past standards, rather than by the absolute level of consumption.

Inflation

Other observers have argued that today's high stock prices can be justified by the steady decline in inflation that has taken place since the early 1980s. These observers point out that since 1960, the dividend/price ratio has moved closely with the inflation rate and with the yield on long-term government bonds, which is closely associated with expectations of future inflation. Thus it should not be surprising to see high stock prices, given low recent inflation.

There are two weaknesses in this argument. First, the correlation between stock prices and inflation is much stronger before the mid-1990s than during the late 1990s. It is hard to explain the recent rise in the stock market by any large change in the inflation outlook.

Second, it is not clear that the association between stock prices and inflation is consistent with the efficient-markets theory that stock prices reflect future real dividends, discounted at a constant real interest rate. That is, low inflation may help to *explain* high stock prices but may not *justify* these prices as rational. Modigliani and Cohn (1979) argued over twenty years ago that the stock market irrationally discounts real dividends at nominal interest rates, undervaluing stocks when inflation is high and overvaluing them when inflation is low.[18] At that time their argument implied stock market undervaluation; today the same argument would imply overvaluation. Whether or not one accepts Modigliani and Cohn's behavioral hypothesis, it should be clear that the relation between inflation and stock prices does not necessarily contradict our pessimistic long-run forecast for stock returns.

3. INTERNATIONAL EVIDENCE

We have emphasized that in the United States data prices, rather than dividends or earnings, appear to adjust to bring abnormal valuation ratios back to historical average levels. Do other countries' stock markets behave in the same way, or is the U.S. experience anomalous?

Unfortunately very little long-term data are available for most stock markets. One standard data source is Morgan Stanley Capital International, but these data go back only to 1970 or so. To appreciate how short this sample is, note from figure 5.4 that since the early 1970s the time-series plot of the U.S. dividend/price ratio has been dominated by a single hump-shaped pattern. With under thirty years of data, it is not sensible to use a ten-year horizon, so we reduce the horizon to four years.

Figure 5.9 presents scatterplots like figures 5.2 and 5.3, but with quarterly data and a four-year horizon. The dividend/price ratio appears on the horizontal axis of each scatterplot, and four-year dividend or price growth

---

[18] Ritter and Warr (2002) have recently revisited this hypothesis.

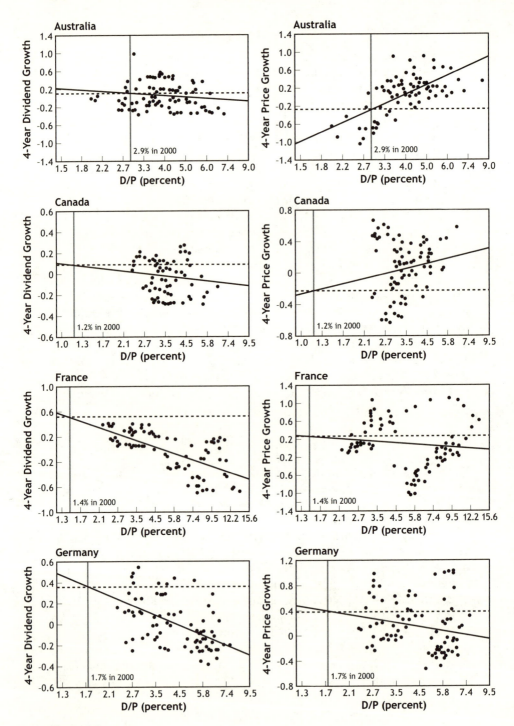

Figure 5.9

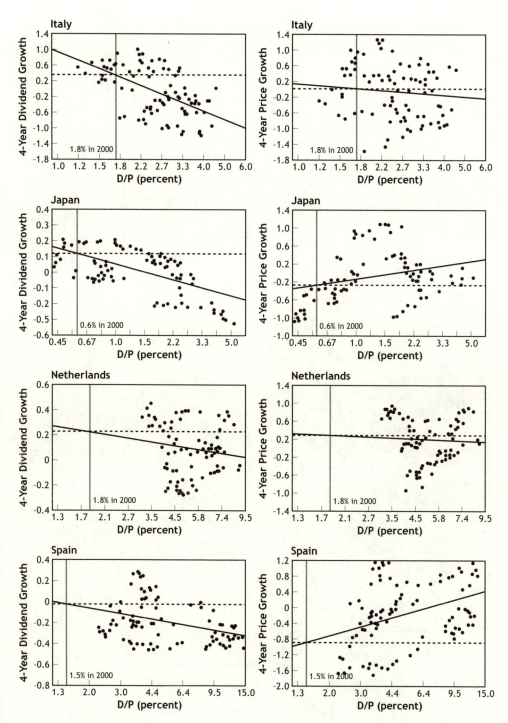

Figure 5.9 (*continued*)

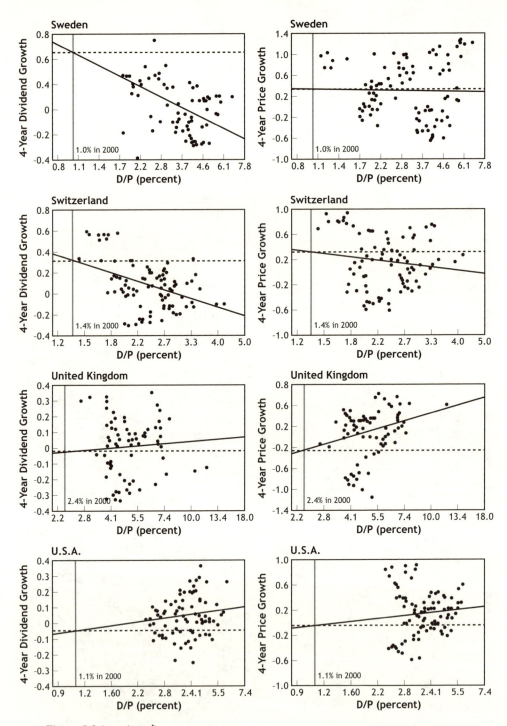

Figure 5.9 (*continued*)

appears on the vertical axis. Results are shown for twelve countries: Australia, Canada, France, Germany, Italy, Japan, the Netherlands, Spain, Sweden, Switzerland, the United Kingdom, and, for comparison, the United States.[19]

The countries in figure 5.8 fall into three main groups. The English-speaking countries—Australia, Canada, and the United Kingdom—behaved over this short sample period very much like the United States. The dividend/price ratio was positively associated with subsequent price growth, and showed little relation to subsequent dividend growth. Several Continental European countries, France, Germany, Italy, Sweden, and Switzerland, showed a very different pattern over this sample period. In these countries a high dividend/price ratio was associated with weak subsequent dividend growth, just as the efficient-markets theory would imply. There was little relation between the dividend/price ratio and subsequent price growth. Japan and Spain represent an intermediate case in which the dividend/price ratio appears to have been associated with both subsequent dividend growth ahd subsequent price growth. Finally the Netherlands show no clear relation between the dividend/price ratio and subsequent growth rates of either dividends or prices.

These recent international data provide mixed evidence. Recent price movements, often the very price movements that have made the valuation ratios so anomalous today, have a large effect on the scatterplots in figure 5.9, and this makes them somewhat hard to interpret.

4. Some Statistical Pitfalls

Some subtle statistical issues arise when one tries to draw conclusions from scatter diagrams such as those presented here. Since the observations are overlapping whenever the horizon is greater than one year (or one quarter in figure 5.9), the different points are not statistically independent of one another. We must correct for this problem in judging the statistical significance of our results. Also, valuation ratios are random rather than deterministic, and it is well known that regressions with random regressors can have biased coefficients in small samples.

Let us consider the conclusions that we drew from looking at figure 5.1. We noted that the slope of the regression line in the top part of the figure, predicting log real dividend growth over the time interval to the next crossing of the mean of the dividend/price ratio, was not substantially negative as the efficient-markets theory would predict. Were we right to conclude that real dividends do not behave in accordance with the efficient-markets theory? Or, are our regression results possibly spurious?

[19] See Campbell (1998) for a more detailed analysis of these international data.

In the 1998 version of this chapter we did a simple Monte Carlo experiment to study this issue. We constructed artificial data in which the dividend/price ratio does not forecast future price changes over any fixed horizon. In other words, we generated data that satisfied the efficient-markets prediction that the real stock price is a random walk.[20] Also, we generated the data to match several important characteristics of the actual annual U.S. data.

We began by estimating a first-order autoregressive (AR[1]) model for the log dividend/price ratio using our 125 observations for the period 1872 to 1997. We corrected the regression coefficient for small-sample bias using the Kendall correction, obtaining a coefficient of 0.81. Using a random normal number generator with the estimated standard error of the error term in the bias-corrected regression, and using a random normal starting value whose variance equals the unconditional variance for this AR(1) model, we generated 125 observations of a simulated AR(1) log dividend/price ratio. Next, we generated 125 observations of a simulated random walk for the log real stock price, using a random normal number generator with the estimated standard deviation of the actual change in the log real price. In the actual data, changes in the stock price and in the dividend/price ratio have a negative covariance; we also matched this covariance in our artificial data. Finally, we generated a log real previous-year dividend by adding the log dividend/price ratio and the log stock price.

We repeated this exercise 100,000 times. In each iteration, we used the artificial data to produce scatters and regression lines based on 125 observations like those shown in the top part of figure 5.1. We found that the average number of crossings of the mean of the dividend/price ratio was 26.5, not far from the number of twenty-nine observed with our actual data. But in 100,000 iterations we found that the slope of the regression line shown in the top part of figure 5.1 was almost always much more negative than the estimated slope with the actual data. The estimated slope in the artificial data was greater than the estimated slope with actual data (–0.04) only 0.02 percent, two hundredths of one percent, of the time. The estimated regression coefficient in these Monte Carlo iterations tended to be close to minus one, very far from the almost-zero slope coefficient represented by the line in the figure. In this respect, our Monte Carlo results are extremely different from the results with the actual data. We conclude that our result in the top part of figure 5.1 is indeed anomalous from the standpoint of the efficient-markets theory.

Next we used the change in the log real stock price as the dependent variable in the Monte Carlo experiment, so that in each iteration we estimated

---

[20] As before, we are oversimplifying the efficient-markets theory by ignoring the distinction between price changes and returns. In Campbell and Shiller (1989) we generated artificial data for a Monte Carlo study in which returns, rather than stock price changes, are unpredictable. This procedure is considerably more complicated, however, and it only makes the patterns seen in the actual data more anomalous.

the regression line shown in the bottom part of figure 5.1. In 100,000 iterations we never once obtained a regression coefficient as great as the slope coefficient of 1.25 shown in the bottom part of figure 5.1. While the average estimated slope coefficient in Monte Carlo experiments is positive, the average value is only 0.18, far below the estimated coefficient with actual data.[21]

Other Monte Carlo experiments relevant to judging the results in this paper are reported in Campbell and Shiller (1989), Goetzmann and Jorion (1993), Nelson and Kim (1993), and Kirby (1997). Nelson and Kim generate artificial data from vector autoregressions (VARs) of stock returns and dividend yields on lagged returns and yields. The artificial stock-return series are constructed to be unforecastable but correlated with innovations in dividend yields. Campbell and Shiller (1989) follow a similar approach.[22] Nelson and Kim find that ten-year regression coefficients and R^2 statistics are highly unlikely to be as large as those found in the actual data if expected stock returns are truly constant. Campbell and Shiller's results are consistent with this finding.

Goetzmann and Jorion use a different approach. They construct artificial data using randomly generated returns and historical dividends, which of course are fixed across different Monte Carlo runs. They combine these two series to get random paths for dividend yields. The problem with this methodology is that it produces nonstationary dividend yields that have no tendency to return to historical average levels. Thus Goetzmann and Jorion avoid the need for dividend yields to forecast either dividend growth or price growth; in their simulations stock prices are equally uninformative about fundamental value and about future returns. Goetzmann and Jorion also confine their attention to horizons of four years or less. Large long-horizon regression coefficients and R^2 statistics occur somewhat more often in the Goetzmann–Jorion Monte Carlo study than in the Nelson–Kim study, but the four-year results in the actual data remain quite anomalous.

Kirby (1997) uses Monte Carlo methods to further illustrate biases that can arise in conventional statistical tests of market efficiency. Kirby's results are not very relevant to our regressions, however. He uses a sample of only

[21] The Monte Carlo results for the bottom part of figure 5.1 are related to the results for the top part of the figure. If we had continuous data, so that the change in the dividend/price ratio to the next crossing of the mean was just minus the current demeaned dividend/price ratio, then the price regression coefficient for the bottom part and the dividend regression coefficient for the top part of figure 5.1 would have to differ by one. In fact our data are not continuous but are measured annually, so the change in the dividend/price ratio to the next crossing of the mean exceeds the current demeaned dividend/price ratio in absolute value, and the two regression coefficients differ by slightly more than one. It is still true, however, that if the price regression coefficient is close to one then the dividend regression coefficient must be close to zero.

[22] Campbell and Shiller use a VAR that includes dividend growth, the dividend yield, and the ratio of smoothed earnings to prices. They construct a loglinearized approximation to the stock return from the dividend growth rate and the dividend yield.

fifty-eight observations, considers return horizons only up to four years, and does not try to construct a data generating mechanism that replicates observed characteristics of the actual data.

These studies all agree that there are statistical pitfalls in evaluating long-run stock market performance. But it is striking how well the evidence for stock market predictability survives the various corrections and adjustments that have been proposed in this research.

5. CONCLUSION

We concluded in the 1998 version of this chapter that the conventional valuation ratios, the dividend/price and price/smoothed-earnings ratios, have a special significance when compared with many other statistics that might be used to forecast stock prices. In 1998 these ratios were extraordinarily bearish for the U.S. stock market. The ratios are even more so at the time of this writing in early 2001.

These valuation ratios deserve a special place among forecasting variables because we have such a long time series of data on these ratios, and because they relate stock prices to careful evaluations of the fundamental value of corporations. Earnings have been calculated and reported by U.S. corporations for over a hundred years for the express purpose of allowing us to judge intrinsic value. Dividend distribution decisions have been made by corporations for just as long with a sense that dividends should be set in such a way that they can reasonably be expected to continue.

Linear regressions of price changes and total returns on the log valuation ratios suggest substantial declines in real stock prices, and real stock returns below zero, over the next ten years. This result must of course be interpreted with caution. The valuation ratios are now so far from their historical averages that we have very little comparable historical data; our regressions extrapolate linearly from a relation between log valuation ratios and long-horizon returns that holds in historically normal times to get a prediction for the current, historically abnormal situation. It is quite possible that the true relation between log valuation ratios and long-horizon returns is non-linear, in which case linear regression forecasts might be excessively bearish. But while this point may moderate the extreme pessimism of our linear regressions, it certainly does not support optimism about the stock market outlook.

It is also possible that forecasting relations that worked in the past will cease to work now. But these ratios are not forecasting variables that were discovered yesterday, ex post. They are ex ante forecasting relations that have been continually discussed over the last century.

The very fact that ratios have moved so far outside their historical range poses a challenge however, both to the traditional view that stock prices reflect rational expectations of future cash flows, and to our view that they are substantially driven by mean reversion. Observers of either persuasion must face the fact that something extremely unusual has occurred. In this situation a broad judgment of our position in history, of the uniqueness of recent technological advances and investment patterns, and of the state of market psychology assumes more than usual importance in judging the outlook for the stock market. There is no purely statistical method to resolve finally whether the data indicate that we have entered a new era, invalidating old relations, or whether we are still in a regime where ratios will revert to old levels. In our personal judgment, while we do not expect a complete return to traditional valuation levels, we still interpret the broad variety of evidence as suggesting a poor long-term outlook for the stock market.

References

Bakshi, Gurdip S., and Zhiwu Chen, 1994, Baby Boom, Population Aging, and Capital Markets, *Journal of Business* 67, 165–202.

Barberis, Nicholas, Andrei Shleifer, and Robert Vishny, 1998, A Model of Investor Sentiment, *Journal of Financial Economics* 49, 307–43.

Barsky, Robert B., and J. Bradford De Long, 1993, Why Does the Stock Market Fluctuate?, *Quarterly Journal of Economics* 107, 291–311.

Blanchard, Olivier J., 1993, Movements in the Equity Premium, *Brookings Papers on Economic Activity* 2, 75–118.

Bond, Stephen R., and Jason G. Cummins, 2000, The Stock Market and Investment in the New Economy, *Brookings Papers on Economic Activity*, 61–108.

Campbell, John Y., 1999, Asset Prices, Consumption, and the Business Cycle, in John Taylor and Michael Woodford (eds.), *Handbook of Macroeconomics*, Vol. 1C, 1231–1303, Elsevier.

Campbell, John Y., and John H. Cochrane, 1999, By Force of Habit: A Consumption-Based Explanation of Aggregate Stock Market Behavior, *Journal of Political Economy* 107, 205–51.

Campbell, John Y., Andrew W. Lo, and A. Craig MacKinlay, 1997, *The Econometrics of Financial Markets*, Princeton University Press.

Campbell, John Y., and Robert J. Shiller, 1988a, The Dividend–Price Ratio and Expectations of Future Dividends and Discount Factors, *Review of Financial Studies* 1, 195–228.

———, 1988b, Stock Prices, Earnings, and Expected Dividends, *Journal of Finance* 43(3), 661–76.

———, 1989, The Dividend–Ratio Model and Small Sample Bias: A Monte Carlo Study, *Economics Letters* 29, 325–31.

Campbell, John Y., and Luis M. Viceira, 2002, *Strategic Asset Allocation: Portfolio Choice for Long-Term Investors*, Oxford University Press.

Cole, Kevin, Jean Helwege, and David Laster, 1996, Stock Market Valuation Indicators: Is This Time Different?, *Financial Analysts Journal*, 56–64.

Cowles, Alfred, et al., 1939, *Common Stock Indexes*, 2nd ed., Principia Press.

Cummins, Jason G., 2000, Comments and Discussion (on Hall paper), *Brookings Papers on Economic Activity*, 103–10.

Glassman, James K., and Kevin A. Hassett, 1999, *Dow 36,000: The New Strategy for Profiting from the Coming Rise in the Stock Market*, Times Books.

Goetzmann, William N., and Philippe Jorion, 1993, Testing the Predictive Power of Dividend Yields, *Journal of Finance* 48, 663–79.

Gordon, Robert J., 2000, Interpreting the One Big Wave in U.S. Long-Term Productivity Growth, National Bureau of Economic Research Working Paper No. 7552.

Graham, Benjamin, and David L. Dodd, 1934, *Security Analysis*, 1st ed., McGraw Hill.

Hall, Robert E., 2000, E-Capital: The Link between the Stock Market and the Labor Market in the 1990s, *Brookings Papers on Economic Activity*, 73–118.

———, 2001, Struggling to Understand the Stock Market, *American Economic Review*, Papers and Proceedings 91, 1–11.

Heaton, John, and Deborah Lucas, 1999, Stock Prices and Fundamentals, in Ben S. Bernanke and Julio J. Rotemberg (eds.), *NBER Macroeconomics Annual*, 213–41.

Kirby, Chris, 1997, Measuring the Predictable Variation in Stock Returns, *Review of Financial Studies* 10, 579–630.

Liang, J. Nellie, and Steven A. Sharpe, 1999, Share Repurchases and Employee Stock Options and Their Implications for S&P 500 Share Retirements and Expected Returns, unpublished paper, Board of Governors of the Federal Reserve System.

McGrattan, Ellen R., and Edward C. Prescott, 2001, Is the Stock Market Overvalued?, National Bureau of Economic Research Working Paper Series #8077, National Bureau of Economic Research, Cambridge, MA.

Mehra, Rajnish, and Edward C. Prescott, 1985, The Equity Premium: A Puzzle, *Journal of Monetary Economics* 15, 145–61.

Modigliani, Franco, and Richard A. Cohn, 1979, Inflation, Rational Valuation, and the Market, *Financial Analysts Journal*, 24–44.

Nelson, Charles R., and Myung J. Kim, 1993, Predictable Stock Returns: The Role of Small Sample Bias, *Journal of Finance* 48, 641–61.

Nordhaus, William D., 2000, Productivity Growth and the New Economy, Cowles Foundation Discussion Paper No. 1284, Cowles Foundation, Yale University.

Ritter, Jay R., and Richard S. Warr, 2002, The Decline of Inflation and the Bull Market of 1982 to 1997, *Journal of Financial and Quantitative Analysis* 37, 29–61.

Shiller, Robert J., 1989, *Market Volatility*, MIT Press.

———, 1996, Price–Earnings Ratios as Forecasters of Returns: The Stock Market Outlook in 1996, unpublished paper, Yale University, http:www.econ.yale.edu/~shiller.

———, 1999, Human Behavior and the Efficiency of the Financial System, in John Taylor and Michael Woodford (eds.), *Handbook of Macroeconomics*, Vol. 1C, 1305–40, Elsevier.

———, 2000, *Irrational Exuberance*, Princeton University Press.

Siegel, Jeremy J., 1998, *Stocks for the Long Run*, 2nd ed., McGraw-Hill.

Vissing–Jørgenson, Annette, 1998, *Limited Stock Market Participation*, PhD diss., MIT.

Chapter 6

MYOPIC LOSS AVERSION AND THE EQUITY

PREMIUM PUZZLE

SHLOMO BENARTZI AND RICHARD H. THALER

1. INTRODUCTION

There is an enormous discrepancy between the returns on stocks and fixed income securities. Since 1926 the annual real return on stocks has been about 7 percent, while the real return on treasury bills has been less than 1 percent. As demonstrated by Mehra and Prescott (1985), the combination of a high equity premium, a low risk-free rate, and smooth consumption is difficult to explain with plausible levels of investor risk aversion. Mehra and Prescott estimate that investors would have to have coefficients of relative risk aversion in excess of 30 to explain the historical equity premium, whereas previous estimates and theoretical arguments suggest that the actual figure is close to 1.0. We are left with a pair of questions: Why is the equity premium so large, or, Why is anyone willing to hold bonds?

The answer we propose in this chapter is based on two concepts from the psychology of decision making. The first concept is *loss aversion*. Loss aversion refers to the tendency for individuals to be more sensitive to reductions in their levels of well-being than to increases. The concept plays a central role in Kahneman and Tversky's (1979) descriptive theory of decision making under uncertainty, prospect theory.[1] In this model, utility is defined over gains and losses relative to some neutral reference point, such as the status quo, as opposed to wealth as in expected utility theory. This utility function has a kink at the origin, with the slope of the loss function steeper than the gain function. The ratio of these slopes at the origin is a measure

Some of this research was conducted while Thaler was a visiting scholar at the Russell Sage Foundation. He is grateful for its generous support. While there, he also had numerous helpful conversations on this topic, especially with Colin Camerer and Daniel Kahneman. Olivier Blanchard, Kenneth French, Russell Fuller, Robert Libby, Roni Michaely, Andrei Shleifer, Amos Tversky, Jean-Luc Vila, and the participants in the Russell Sage-NBER behavioral finance workshop have also provided comments. This research has also been supported by the National Science Foundation, Grant # SES-9223358.

[1] The notion that people treat gains and losses differently has a long tradition. For example, Swalm (1966) noted this phenomenon in a study of managerial decision making. See Libby and Fishburn (1977) for other early references.

of loss aversion. Empirical estimates of loss aversion are typically in the neighborhood of 2, meaning that the disutility of giving something up is twice as great as the utility of acquiring it (Tversky and Kahneman 1991, Kahneman, Knetsch, and Thaler 1990).

The second behavioral concept we employ is *mental accounting* (Kahneman and Tversky 1984, Thaler 1985). Mental accounting refers to the implicit methods individuals use to code and evaluate financial outcomes: transactions, investments, gambles, etcetera. The aspect of mental accounting that plays a particularly important role in this research is the dynamic aggregation rules people follow. Because of the presence of loss aversion, these aggregation rules are not neutral. This point can best be illustrated by example.

Consider the problem first posed by Samuelson (1963). Samuelson asked a colleague whether he would be willing to accept the following bet: a 50 percent chance to win $200 and a 50 percent chance to lose $100. The colleague turned this bet down, but announced that he was happy to accept 100 such bets. This exchange provoked Samuelson into proving a theorem showing that his colleague was irrational.[2] Of more interest here is what the colleague offered as his rationale for turning down the bet: "I won't bet because I would feel the $100 loss more than the $200 gain." This sentiment is the intuition behind the concept of loss aversion. One simple utility function that would capture this notion is the following:

$$U(x) = \begin{matrix} x & x \geq 0 \\ 2.5x & x < 0, \end{matrix} \tag{1}$$

where x is a *change* in wealth relative to the status quo. The role of mental accounting is illustrated by noting that if Samuelson's colleague had this utility function he would turn down one bet but accept two or more *as long as he did not have to watch the bet being played out*. The distribution of outcomes created by the portfolio of two bets ($400, .25; 100, .50; -$200, .25) yields positive expected utility with the hypothesized utility function, though of course simple repetitions of the single bet are unattractive if evaluated one at a time. As this example illustrates, when decision makers are loss averse, they will be more willing to take risks if they evaluate their performance (or have their performance evaluated) infrequently.

The relevance of this argument to the equity premium puzzle can be seen by considering the problem facing an investor with the utility function defined above. Suppose that the investor must choose between a risky asset that pays an expected 7 percent per year with a standard deviation of 20 percent

---

[2] Specifically, the theorem says that if someone is unwilling to accept a single play of a bet at any wealth level that could occur over the course of some number of repetitions of the bet (in this case, the relevant range is the colleague's current wealth plus $20,000 to current wealth minus $10,000) then accepting the multiple bet is inconsistent with expected utility theory.

(like stocks) and a safe asset that pays a sure 1 percent. By the same logic that applied to Samuelson's colleague, the attractiveness of the risky asset will depend on the time horizon of the investor. The longer the investor intends to hold the asset, the more attractive the risky asset will appear, so long the investment is not evaluated frequently. Put another way, two factors contribute to an investor being unwilling to bear the risks associated with holding equities, loss aversion and a short evaluation period. We refer to this combination as *myopic loss aversion*.

Can myopic loss aversion explain the equity premium puzzle? Of course, there is no way of demonstrating that one particular explanation is correct, so in this chapter we perform various tests to determine whether our hypothesis is plausible. We begin by asking what combination of loss aversion and evaluation period would be necessary to explain the historical pattern of returns. For our model of individual decision making, we use the recent updated version of prospect theory (Tversky and Kahneman 1992) for which the authors have provided parameters that can be considered as describing the representative decision maker. We then ask, how often would an investor with this set of preferences have to evaluate his portfolio in order to be indifferent between the historical distribution of returns on stocks and bonds? Although we do this several ways (with both real and nominal returns, and comparing stocks with both bonds and treasury bills), the answers we obtain are all in the neighborhood of one year, clearly a plausible result. We then take the one-year evaluation period as given and ask what asset allocation (that is, what combination of stocks and bonds) would be optimal for such an investor. Again we obtain a plausible result: close to a 50-50 split between stocks and bonds.

2. Is the Equity Premium Puzzle Real?

Before we set out to provide an answer to an alleged puzzle, we should probably review the evidence about whether there is indeed a puzzle to explain. We address the question in two ways. First, we ask whether the post-1926 time period studied by Mehra and Prescott is special. Then we review the other explanations that have been offered. As any insightful reader might guess from the fact that we have written this essay, we conclude that the puzzle is real and that the existing explanations come up short.

The robustness of the equity premium has been addressed by Siegel (1991, 1992) who examines the returns since 1802. He finds that real equity returns have been remarkably stable. For example, over the three time periods 1802–1870, 1871–1925, and 1926–1990, real compound equity returns were 5.7, 6.6, and 6.4 percent. However, returns on short-term government bonds have fallen dramatically, the figures for the same three time periods being 5.1, 3.1, and 0.5 percent. Thus, there was no equity premium in the first two-thirds of the nineteenth century (because bond returns were high), but over the last one hundred and twenty years, stocks have had a significant edge. The equity premium does not appear to be a recent phenomenon.

The advantage of investing in stocks over the period 1876 to 1990 is documented in a rather different way by MaCurdy and Shoven (1992). They look at the historical evidence from the point of view of a faculty member saving for retirement. They assume that 10 percent of the hypothetical faculty member's salary is invested each year, and ask how the faculty members would have done investing in portfolios of all stocks or all bonds over their working lifetimes. They find that faculty who had allocated all of their funds to stocks would have done better in virtually every time period, usually by a large margin. For working lifetimes of only twenty-five years, all-bond portfolios occasionally do better (e.g., for those retiring in a few years during the first half of the decades of the 1930s and 1940s) though never by more than 20 percent. In contrast, those in all-stock portfolios often do better by very large amounts. Also, all twenty-five-year careers since 1942 would have been better off in all stocks. For working lifetimes of forty years, there is not a single case in which the all-bond portfolio wins (though there is a virtual tie for those retiring in 1942), and for those retiring in the late 1950s and early 1960s, stock accumulators would have more than seven times more than bond accumulators. MaCurdy and Shoven conclude from their analysis that people must be "confused about the relative safety of different investments over long horizons" (p. 12).

Could the large equity premium be consistent with rational expected utility maximization models of economic behavior? Mehra and Prescott's contribution was to show that risk aversion alone is unlikely to yield a satisfactory answer. They found that people would have to have a coefficient of relative risk aversion over 30 to explain the historical pattern of returns. In interpreting this number, it is useful to remember that a logarithmic function has a coefficient of relative risk aversion of 1.0. Also, Mankiw and Zeldes (1991) provide the following useful calculation. Suppose that an individual is offered a gamble with a 50 percent chance of consumption of $100,000 and a 50 percent chance of consumption of $50,000. A person with a coefficient of relative risk aversion of 30 would be indifferent between this gamble and a certain consumption of $51,209. Few people can be this afraid of risk.

Previous efforts to provide alternative explanations for the puzzle have been, at most, only partly successful. For example, Reitz (1988) argued that the equity premium might be the rational response to a time-varying risk of economic catastrophe. While this explanation has the advantage of being untestable, it does not seem plausible. (See Mehra and Prescott's [1988] reply.) First of all, the data since 1926 do contain the crash of 1929, so the catastrophe in question must be of much greater magnitude than that. Second, the hypothetical catastrophe must affect stocks and not bonds.

For example, a bout of hyperinflation would presumably hurt bonds more than stocks.

Another line of research has aimed at relaxing the link between the coefficient of relative risk aversion and the elasticity of intertemporal substitution, which are inverses of each other in the standard discounted expected utility framework. For example, Weil (1989) introduces Kreps-Porteus non-expected utility preferences, but finds that the equity premium puzzle simply becomes transformed into a "risk-free rate puzzle." That is, the puzzle is no longer why are stock returns so high, but rather why are T-Bill rates so low. Epstein and Zin (1990) also adopt a nonexpected utility framework using Yaari's (1987) "dual" theory of choice. Yaari's theory shares some features with the version of prospect theory that we employ below (namely a rank-dependent approach to probability weights) but does not have loss aversion or short horizons, the two key components of our explanation. Epstein and Zin find that their model can only explain about one-third of the observed equity premium. Similarly, Mankiw and Zeldes (1991) investigate whether the homogeneity assumptions necessary to aggregate across consumers could be the source of the puzzle. They point out that a minority of Americans hold stock, and their consumption patterns differ from non-stockholders. However, they conclude that while these differences can explain a part of the equity premium, a significant puzzle remains.

An alternative type of explanation is suggested by Constantinides (1990). He proposes a habit-formation model in which the utility of consumption is assumed to depend on past levels of consumption. Specifically, consumers are assumed to be averse to reductions in their level of consumption. Constantinides shows that this type of model can explain the equity premium puzzle. However, Ferson and Constantinides (1991) find that while the habit-formation specification improves the ability of the model to explain the intertemporal dynamics of returns, it does not help the model explain the differences in average returns across assets.

While Constantinides is on the right track in stressing an asymmetry between gains and losses, we feel that his model does not quite capture the right behavioral intuitions. The problem is that the link between stock returns and consumption is quite tenuous. The vast majority of Americans hold no stocks outside their pension wealth. Furthermore, most pensions are of the defined benefit variety, meaning that a fall in stock prices is inconsequential to the pension beneficiaries. Indeed, most of the stock market is owned by three groups of investors: pension funds, endowments, and very wealthy individuals. It is hard to see why the habit-formation model should apply to these investors.[3]

---

[3] We stress the word "should" in the previous sentence. Firms may adopt accounting rules with regard to their pension wealth that create a sensitivity to short-run fluctuations in pension fund assets, and foundations may have spending rules that produce a similar effect. An investigation of this issue is presented below.

3. Prospect Theory and Loss Aversion

The problem with the habit-formation explanation is the stress it places on consumption. The way we incorporate Constantinides's intuition about behavior into preferences is to assume that investors have preferences over returns, per se, rather than over the consumption profile that the returns help provide. Specifically, we use Kahneman and Tversky's (1979, 1992) prospect theory in which utility is defined over gains and losses (i.e., returns) rather than levels of wealth. Specifically, they propose a value function of the following form:

$$v(x) = \begin{cases} x^\alpha & \text{if } x \geq 0 \\ -\lambda(-x)^\beta & \text{if } x < 0, \end{cases} \tag{2}$$

where λ is the coefficient of loss aversion.[4] They have estimated α and β to be 0.88 and λ to be 2.25. Notice that the notion of loss aversion captures the same intuition that Constantinides used, namely that reductions are painful.[5]

The "prospective utility" of a gamble, G, which pays off x_i with probability p_i is given by

$$V(G) = \sum \pi_i v(x_i), \tag{3}$$

where π_i is the decision weight associated assigned to outcome i. In the original version of prospect theory (Kahneman and Tversky 1979), π_i is a simple nonlinear transform of p_i. In the cumulative version of the theory (Tversky and Kahneman 1992), as in other rank-dependent models, one transforms cumulative rather than individual probabilities. Consequently, the decision weight π_i depends on the cumulative distribution of the gamble, not only on p_i. More specifically, let w denote the nonlinear transform of the cumulative distribution of G, let P_i be the probability of obtaining an outcome that is at least as good as x_i, and let P_i^* be the probability of obtaining an outcome that is strictly better than x_i. Then the decision weight attached to x_i is $\pi i = w(P_i) - w(P_i^*)$. (This procedure is applied separately for gains and losses.)

Tversky and Kahneman have suggested the following one-parameter approximation:

$$w(p) = \frac{p^\gamma}{(p^\gamma + (1-p)^\gamma)^{1/\gamma}} \tag{4}$$

---

[4] Note that since x is a change it is measured as the difference in wealth with respect to the last time wealth was measured, so the status quo is moving over time.

[5] This value of λ is consistent with other measures of loss aversion estimated in very different contexts. For example, Kahneman, Knetsch, and Thaler (1990) (KKT) investigate the importance of loss aversion in a purely deterministic context. In one experiment half of a group

and estimated γ to be 0.61 in the domain of gains and 0.69 in the domain of losses.

As discussed in the introduction, the use of prospect theory must be accompanied by a specification of frequency that returns are evaluated. We refer to the length of time over which an investor aggregates returns as the *evaluation period*. This is not, in any way, to be confused with the planning horizon of the investor. A young investor, for example, might be saving for retirement thirty years off in the future, but nevertheless experience the utility associated with the gains and losses of his investment every quarter when he opens a letter from his mutual fund. In this case his horizon is thirty years but his evaluation period is three months.

That said, in terms of the model an investor with an evaluation period of one year behaves very much *as if* he had a planning horizon of one year. To see this, compare two investors. Mr. X receives a bonus every year on January 1st and invests the money to spend on a Christmas vacation the following year. Both his planning horizon and evaluation period are one year. Ms. Y has received a bonus and wishes to invest it toward her retirement thirty years away. She evaluates her portfolio annually. Thus, she has a planning horizon of thirty years but a one-year evaluation period. Though X and Y have rather different problems, in terms of the model they will behave approximately the same way. The reason for this is that in prospect theory, the carriers of utility are assumed to be changes in wealth, or returns, and the effect of the level of wealth is assumed to be second order. Therefore, every year Y will solve her asset allocation problem by choosing the portfolio that maximizes her prospective utility one year away, just as X does.[6] In this sense, when we estimate the evaluation period of investors below, we are also estimating their implicit time horizons.

Of course, in a model with loss aversion, the more often an investor evaluates his portfolio, or the shorter his horizon, the less attractive he will find a high mean, high risk investment such as stocks. This is in contrast to the well-known results of Merton (1969) and Samuelson (1969). They investigate the following question. Suppose that an investor has to choose between stocks and bonds over some fixed horizon of length T. How should the allocation change as the horizon increases? There is a strong intuition that a rational risk-averse investor would decrease the proportion of his assets in

---

of Cornell students are given a Cornell insignia coffee mug, while the other half of the subjects are not given a mug. Then, markets are conducted for the mugs in which mug owners can sell their mug while the nonowners can buy one. KKT found that the reservation prices for two groups were significantly different. Specifically, the median reservation price of the sellers was roughly 2.5 times the median reservation price of the buyers.

[6] An important potential qualification is if recent gains or losses influence subsequent decisions. For example, Thaler and Johnson (1990) find evidence for a "house money effect." Namely, people who have just won some money exhibit less loss aversion toward gambles that do not risk their entire recent winnings.

stocks as he nears retirement and T approaches zero. The intuition comes from the notion that when T is large, the probability that the return on stocks will exceed the return on bonds approaches 1.0, while over short horizons there can be substantial shortfalls from stock investments. However, Merton and Samuelson show that this intuition is wrong. Specifically, they prove that as long as the returns on stocks and bonds are a random walk,[7] a risk-averse investor with utility function that displays constant relative risk in aversion (e.g., a logarithmic or power function) should choose the same allocation for any time horizon. An investor who wants mostly stocks in his portfolio at age thirty-five should still want the same allocation at age sixty-four. Without questioning the normative validity of Merton and Samuelson's conclusions, we offer a model that can reveal why most investors find this result extremely counterintuitive.

4. How Often Are Portfolios Evaluated?

Mehra and Prescott asked the question, How risk averse would the representative investor have to be to explain the historical equity premium? We ask a different question. If investors have prospect theory preferences, how often would they have to evaluate their portfolios to explain the equity premium? We pose the question two ways. First, What evaluation period would make investors indifferent between holding all their assets in stocks or bonds? We then take this evaluation period and ask a question with more theoretical justification. For an investor with this evaluation period, what combination of stocks and bonds would maximize prospective utility?

We use simulations to answer both questions. The method is to draw samples from the historical (1926–1990) monthly returns on stocks, bonds, and treasury bills provided by CRSP. For the first exercise we then compute the prospective utility of holding stocks, bonds, and T-Bills for evaluation periods starting at one month and then increasing one month at a time.

The simulations are conducted as follows. First, distributions of returns are generated for various time horizons by drawing 100,000 n-month returns (with replacement) from the CRSP time series.[8] The returns are then

[7] If stock returns are instead mean reverting, then the intuitive result that stocks are more attractive to investors with long horizons holds.

[8] Our method, by construction, removes any serial correlation in asset price returns. Since some research does find mean reversion in stock prices over long horizons, some readers have worried about whether our results are affected by this. This should not be a concern. The time horizons we investigate in the simulations are relatively short (in the neighborhood of one year) and at short horizons there is only trivial mean reversion. For example, Fama and French (1988) regress returns on the value weighted index in year t on returns in year $t - 1$ and estimate the slope coefficient to be -0.03. The fact that there is substantial mean reversion at longer horizons (the same coefficient at three years is -0.25) only underscores the puzzle of the equity premium since mean reversion reduces the risk to a long-term investor.

ranked, from best to worst, and the return is computed at twenty intervals along the cumulative distribution.[9] (This is done to accommodate the cumulative or rank-dependent formulation of prospect theory.) Using these data, it is possible to compute the prospective utility of the given asset for the specified holding period.

We have done this simulation four different ways. The CRSP stock index is compared both with treasury bill returns and with five-year bond returns, and these comparisons are done both in real and nominal terms. While we have done all four simulations for the sake of completeness, and to give the reader the opportunity to examine the robustness of the method, we feel that the most weight should be assigned to the comparison between stocks and bonds in nominal terms. We prefer bonds to T-Bills because we think that for long-term investors these are the closest substitutes. We prefer nominal to real for two reasons. First, returns are usually reported in nominal dollars. Even when inflation-adjusted returns are calculated, it is the nominal returns that are given prominence in most annual reports. Therefore, in a descriptive model, nominal returns should be the assumed units of account. Second, the simulations reveal that if investors were thinking in real dollars they would not be willing to hold treasury bills over any evaluation period as they always yield negative prospective utility.[10]

The results for the stock and bond comparisons are presented in figure 6.1, Panels A and B. The lines show the prospective value of the portfolio at different evaluation periods. The point where the curves cross is the evaluation period at which stocks and bonds are equally attractive. For nominal returns, the equilibrium evaluation period is about thirteen months, while for real returns it is between ten and eleven months.[11]

How should these results be interpreted? Obviously, there is no single evaluation period that applies to every investor. Indeed, even a single investor may employ a combination of evaluation periods, with casual evaluations every quarter, a more serious evaluation annually, and evaluations associated with long-term planning every few years. Nevertheless, if one had to pick a single most plausible length for the evaluation period, one year might well be it. Individual investors file taxes annually, receive their most comprehensive reports from their brokers, mutual funds, and retirement accounts once a year, and institutional investors also take the annual

---

[9] We have also tried dividing the outcomes into 100 intervals instead of 20, and the results are substantially the same.

[10] This suggests a solution to the "risk-free rate puzzle" employing a combination of framing and money illusion. In nominal terms, treasury bills offer the illusion of a sure gain that is very attractive to prospect theory investors, while in real terms treasury bills offer a combination of barely positive mean returns and a substantial risk of a loss—not an attractive combination.

[11] The equilibrium evaluation period between stocks and T-Bills is about one month less in both real and nominal dollars.

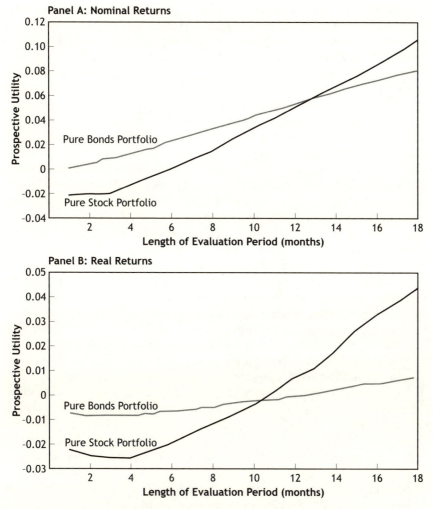

Figure 6.1. Prospective utility as function of the evaluation period.

reports most seriously. As a possible evaluation period, one year is at least highly plausible.

There are two reasonable questions to ask about these results. Which aspects of prospect theory drive the results, and how sensitive are the results to alternative specifications? The answer to the first question is that loss aversion is the main determinant of the outcomes. The specific functional forms of the value function and weighting functions are not critical. For example, if the weighting function is replaced by actual probabilities, the evaluation period for which bonds have the same prospective utility as stocks falls from eleven–twelve months to ten months. Similarly, if actual probabilities are used and the value function is replaced by a piecewise linear form with a loss aversion factor of 2.25 (that is, $v(x) = x$, $x \geq 0$, $v(x) = 2.25\ x$, $x < 0$), then the equilibrium evaluation period is eight months. With this model (piecewise linear value function and linear probabilities) a twelve-month evaluation period is consistent with a loss aversion factor of 2.77.

The previous results can be criticized on the grounds that investors form portfolios rather than choose between all bonds or all stocks. Therefore, we perform a second simulation exercise that is grounded in an underlying optimization problem. We use this as a reliability check on the previous results. Suppose that an investor is maximizing prospective utility with a one-year horizon. What mix of stocks and bonds would be optimal? We investigate this question as follows. We compute the prospective utility of each portfolio mix between 100 percent bonds and 100 percent stocks, in 10 percent increments. The results are shown in figure 6.2, using nominal returns. (Again, the results for real returns are similar.) As the figure shows, portfolios between about 30 percent and 55 percent stocks all yield approximately the same prospective value. Once again, this result is roughly consistent with observed behavior. For example, Greenwich Associates reports that institutions (primarily pensions funds and endowments) invest, on average, 47 percent of the assets on bonds and 53 percent in stocks. For individuals, consider the participants in TIAA-CREF, the defined contribution retirement plan at many universities, and the largest of its kind in the United States. The most frequent allocation between CREF (stocks) and TIAA (mostly bonds) is 50-50, with the average allocation to stocks below 50 percent.[12]

5. Myopia and the Magnitude of the Equity Premium

According to our theory, the equity premium is produced by a combination of loss aversion and frequent evaluations. Loss aversion plays the role of risk aversion in standard models, and can be considered a fact of life (or, perhaps, a fact of preferences). In contrast, the frequency of evaluations is a

---

[12] See MaCurdy and Shoven (1992) for illustrative data. It is interesting to note that average allocation of new contributions is now and has always been more than half in TIAA, but the size of the two funds is now about equal because of the higher growth rate of CREF. As Samuelson and Zeckhauser (1988) report, the typical TIAA-CREF participant makes one asset allocation decision and never changes it. This does not seem consistent with any coherent optimization. Consider a contributor who has been dividing funds equally between TIAA and CREF, and now has two-thirds of his assets in CREF because of higher growth. If he likes the 2:1 ratio of stocks to bonds consistent with his asset holdings, why not change the flow of new funds? But if a 50-50 allocation is optimal, then why not switch some of the existing CREF holdings into TIAA (which can be done costlessly)?

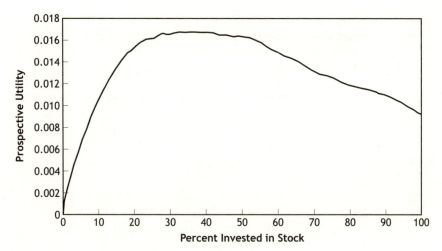

Figure 6.2. Prospective utility as function of asset allocation (one-year evaluation period).

policy choice that presumably could be altered, at least in principle. Furthermore, as the charts in figure 6.1 show, stocks become more attractive as the evaluation period increases. This observation leads to the natural question: By how much would the equilibrium equity premium fall if the evaluation period increased?

Figure 6.3 shows the results of an analysis of this issue using real returns on stocks, and the real returns on five-year bonds as the comparison asset. With the parameters we have been using, the actual equity premium in our

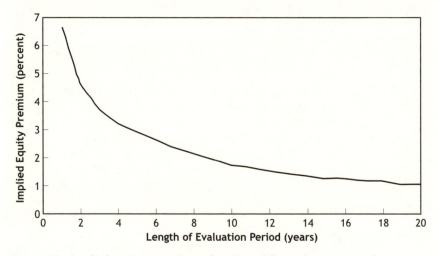

Figure 6.3. Implied equity premium as function of the evaluation period.

data (6.5 percent per year) is consistent with an evaluation period of one year. If the evaluation period were two years, the equity premium would fall to 4.65 percent. For five, ten, and twenty-year evaluation periods, the corresponding figures are 3.0 percent, 2.0 percent, and 1.4 percent. One way to think about these results is that for someone with a twenty-year investment horizon, the psychic costs of evaluating the portfolio annually are 5.1 percent per year! That is, someone with a twenty-year horizon would be indifferent between stocks and bonds if the equity premium were only 1.4 percent, and the remaining 5.1 percent is potential rents payable to those who are able to resist the temptation to count their money often. In a sense, 5.1 percent is the price of excessive vigilance.[13]

6. Do Organizations Display Myopic Loss Aversion?

There is a possible objection to our explanation in that it has been based on a model of *individual* decision making, while the bulk of the assets we are concerned with are held by organizations, in particular pension funds and endowments. This is a reasonable concern, and our response should help indicate the way we interpret our explanation.

As we stressed above, the key components of our explanation are loss aversion and frequent evaluations. While we have used a specific parameterization of cumulative prospect theory in our simulation tests, we did so because we felt that it provided a helpful discipline. We did not allow ourselves the luxury of selecting the parameters that would fit the data best. That said, it remains true that almost any model with loss aversion and frequent evaluations will go a long way toward explaining the equity premium puzzle, so the right question to ask about organizations is whether they display these traits.

A. Pension Funds

Consider first the important case of defined benefit pension funds. In this, this most common type of pension plan, the firm promises each vested worker a pension benefit that is typically a function of final salary and years of service. For these plans, the firm, not the employees, is the residual claimant. If the assets in the plan earn a high return, the firm can make smaller contributions to the fund in future years, whereas if the assets do not earn a high enough return, the firm's contribution rate will have to increase to satisfy funding regulations.

---

[13] Blanchard (1993) has recently argued that the equity premium has fallen. If so, then our interpretation of his result would be that the length of the average evaluation period has increased.

Although asset allocations vary across firms, a common allocation is about 60 percent stocks and 40 percent bonds and treasury bills. Given the historical equity premium, and the fact that pension funds have essentially an infinite time horizon, it is a bit puzzling why pension funds do not invest a higher proportion in stocks.[14] We argue that myopic loss aversion offers an explanation. In this context the myopic loss aversion is produced by an agency problem.

While the pension *fund* is indeed likely to exist as long as the company remains in business (barring a plan termination), the pension fund *manager* (often the corporate treasurer, chief financial officer [CFO], or staff member who reports to the CFO) does not expect to be in this job forever. He or she will have to make regular reports on the funding level of the pension plan and the returns on the funds assets. This short horizon creates a conflict of interest between the pension fund manager and the stockholders.[15] This view appears to be shared by two prominent Wall Street advisors. In Leibowitz and Langetieg (1989) the authors make numerous calculations regarding the long-term results of various asset allocation decisions. They conclude as follows:

> If we limit our choice to "stocks" and "bonds" as represented by the S&P 500 and the BIG Index, then under virtually any reasonable set of assumptions, stocks will almost surely outperform bonds as the investment horizon is extended to infinity. Unfortunately, most of us do not have an infinite period of time to work out near term losses. Most investors and investment managers set personal investment goals that must be achieved in time frames of 3 to 5 years." (p. 14)

Also, when discussing simulation results for twenty-year horizons under so-called favorable assumptions (e.g., that the historic equity premium and mean reversion in equity returns will continue) they offer the following remarks. "[Our analysis] shows that, under 'favorable' assumptions, the stock/bond [return] ratio will exceed 100% most of the time. *However, for investors who must account for near term losses, these long-run results may*

---

[14] See Black (1980) for a different point of view. He argues that pension funds should be invested entirely in bonds because of a tax arbitrage opportunity. However, his position rests on the efficient market premise that there is no equity premium puzzle; that is, the return on stocks is just enough to compensate for the risk.

[15] The importance of short horizons in financial contexts is stressed by Shleifer and Vishny (1990). For a good description of the agency problems in defined-benefit pension plans see Lakonishok, Shleifer, and Vishny (1992). Our agency explanation of myopic loss aversion is very much in the same spirit of the one they offer to explain a different puzzle: why the portion of the pension fund that *is* invested in equities is invested so poorly. The equity component of pension plans systematically underperforms market benchmarks such as the S&P 500. Although pension fund managers eschew index funds, they often inadvertently achieve an inferior version of an index fund by diversifying across money managers who employ different styles. The portfolio of money managers is worse on two counts: lower performance and higher fees.

have little significance" (p. 15, emphasis added). In other words, agency costs produce myopic loss aversion.[16]

B. Foundation and University Endowments

Another important group of institutional investors is endowment funds held by universities and foundations. Once again, an even split between stocks and bonds is common, although the endowment funds are explicitly treated as perpetuities. In this case, however, there appear to be two causes for the myopic loss aversion. First, there are agency problems similar to those for pension plans. Consider a foundation with 50 percent of its assets invested in stocks. Suppose that the president of the foundation wanted to increase the allocation to 100 percent, arguing that with an infinite horizon, stocks are almost certain to outperform bonds. Again the president will face the problem that his horizon is distinctly finite *as are the horizons of his board members*. In fact, there is really no one who represents the interests of the foundation's potential beneficiaries in the twenty-second century. This is an agency problem without a principal!

An equally important source of myopic loss aversion comes from the spending rules used by most universities and foundations. A typical rule specifies that the organization can spend x percent of an n-year moving average of the value of the endowment, where n is typically five or less.[17] Although the purpose of such moving averages is to smooth out the impact of stock market fluctuations, a sudden drop or a long bear market can have a pronounced effect on spending. The institution is forced to choose between the competing goals of maximizing the present value of spending over an infinite horizon, and maintaining a steady operating budget. The fact that stocks have outperformed bonds over every twenty-year period in history is cold comfort after a decade of zero nominal returns, an experience most institutions still remember.

There is an important difference between universities (and operating foundations) and individuals saving for retirement. For an individual saving for retirement, it can be argued that the only thing she should care about is the size of the annuity that can be purchased at retirement, that is, terminal wealth. Transitory fluctuations impose only psychic costs. For universities and operating foundations, however, there is both a psychic cost to seeing the value of the endowment fall and the very real cost of cutting back programs if there is a cash flow reduction for a period of years. This in no way diminishes the force of the myopic loss aversion explanation for the equity premium. If anything, the argument is strengthened by the exis-

---

[16] Of course, many observers have accused American firms of myopia. The pension asset allocation decision may be a useful domain for measuring firms' horizons.

[17] Foundations also have minimum spending rules that they have to obey to retain their tax-free status.

tence of economic factors contributing to loss aversion. Nevertheless, institutions could probably do better at structuring their spending rules to facilitate a higher exposure to risky assets.

7. CONCLUSIONS

The equity premium *is* a puzzle within the standard expected utility-maximizing paradigm. As Mehra and Prescott forcefully argue, it seems impossible to reconcile the high rates of return on stocks with the very low risk-free rate. How can investors be extremely unwilling to accept variations in returns, as the equity premium implies, and yet be willing to delay consumption to earn a measly 1 percent per year? Our solution to the puzzle is to combine a high sensitivity to losses with a prudent tendency to frequently monitor one's wealth. The former tendency shifts the domain of the utility function from consumption to returns, and the latter makes people demand a large premium to accept return variability. In our model investors are unwilling to accept return variability even if the short-run returns have no effect on consumption.

In their reply to Reitz, Mehra, and Prescott (1988) offer the following guidelines for what they think would constitute a solution to the equity premium puzzle.

> Perhaps the introduction of some other preference structure will do the job. . . . For such efforts to be successful, though, they must convince the profession that the proposed alternative preference structure is more useful than the now-standard one for organizing and interpreting not only these observations on average asset returns, but also other observations in growth theory, business cycle theory, labor market behavior, and so on. (p. 134)

While prospect theory has not yet been applied in all the contexts Mehra and Prescott cite, it has been extensively tested and supported in the study of decision making under uncertainty, and loss aversion appears to offer promise as a component of an explanation for unemployment[18] and for understanding the outcomes in many legal contexts.[19] For this reason, we believe that myopic loss aversion deserves consideration as a possible solution to Mehra and Prescott's fascinating puzzle.

---

[18] For example, Kahneman, Knetsch, and Thaler (1988) find that perceptions of fairness in labor market contexts are strongly influenced by whether actions are framed as imposing losses or reducing gains.

[19] See Hovenkamp (1991).

Appendix: Experimental Tests

In our paper on myopic loss aversion reproduced here, we used the concept to try to "explain" the equity premium puzzle. We did so by estimating the evaluation period that would make investors indifferent between stocks and bonds. The answer was one year. In that paper, we did not actually "test" our explanation other than by asking whether this evaluation period seemed plausible. Since this paper has been published, researchers have offered several experimental tests of myopic loss aversion, which we summarize in this appendix.

Thaler et al. (1997) explored the separate effects of myopia and loss aversion in a setting that allows for learning. In particular, they asked eighty undergraduate students to allocate an endowment between a generic stock fund and a generic bond fund. The two funds, however, were unlabeled, and the subjects had to learn about the risk and return profiles of the funds through a simulated twenty-five-years of experience. The experiment included four conditions, and the subjects were randomly assigned to one of the conditions. In the "monthly" condition, the subjects made two hundred investment decisions, each corresponding to (approximately) a one-month period. In the "yearly condition," the subjects made twenty-five annual decisions, and in the "five-yearly" condition, they made five decisions. There was also another condition, where losses were eliminated by introducing a high level of inflation. However, the specific rate of inflation was unknown to the subjects, so they were induced to think in nominal terms. Hereafter, we refer to this condition as the "inflated monthly" condition, since it was based on the monthly data. At the end of the twenty-five-years of learning experience, the subjects made a final allocation decision for the following fifty years.

The results are consistent with myopic behavior. In particular, as the aggregation period lengthens, so does the allocation to stocks. The final allocations to stocks in the monthly, yearly, and five-yearly conditions are 40.9 percent, 69.6 percent, and 66.2 percent, respectively. The small difference between the yearly and five-yearly allocations is in the wrong direction and could be attributed to the limited learning opportunities in the five-yearly condition (five trials). The results are also consistent with loss aversion. The final allocation to stocks in the inflated monthly condition is 72.4 percent, versus 40.9 percent in the noninflated monthly condition.

Gneezy and Potters (1997) provided additional tests showing that the thought of what the aggregate data looks like could by itself reduce myopic behavior. In particular, they presented eighty-three undergraduate students with a sequence of three independent lotteries. Each of the lotteries had a probability of two-thirds to lose the amount invested, and a probability of one-third to win two and half times the amount invested. The subjects were provided an endowment, and they had to decide how much to invest in the above lottery. Half of the subjects played twelve individual rounds, whereas the other half played them in blocks of three. Those playing in blocks of three were provided feedback at the end of the third, sixth, ninth, and twelve rounds. The feedback included a side-by-side display of the three individual outcomes, though the sum of the three amounts was not displayed. Again, the results are consistent with myopic loss aversion. Those playing the bets in blocks of three took more risk, and as a result, earned higher returns. The difference in allocations to the lottery varied between 10 and 20 percent, depending on the specific rounds.

We have also conducted several experiments on myopic loss aversion (Benartzi and Thaler 1999). In one of our tests, we gave thirty-nine undergraduate students a choice between a certain amount and multiple plays of a gamble. The subjects were presented with three gambles that had different payoffs if played once, but virtually the same distribution of final payoffs if played repeatedly. The specific gambles are displayed below and the certain amount was $3. Whereas a single play of the first gamble entails a loss fifty times greater than that of the third gamble, the final distribution of payoffs at the end of the multiple plays are virtually the same for the three gambles.

1. 90% chance to win $0.10
   10% chance to lose $0.50
      Played 150 times.

2. 50% chance to win $0.25
   50% chance to lose $0.15
      Played 120 times.

3. 10% chance to win $0.75
   90% chance to lose $0.01
      Played 90 times.

Traditional economic analysis predicts that the attractiveness of the three gambles is approximately the same, because they all have the same distribution of final payoffs. Myopic loss aversion, however, predicts that the characteristics of the single play of the gambles make a difference. In particular, myopic loss aversion predicts that the potential loss of the single play has an important role in decision making. The results are consistent with myopic loss aversion. Only 49 percent of the subjects preferred the first gamble to the certain amount, in which they faced a potential loss of $0.50 on each trial. In comparison, 64 percent and 75 percent preferred the second and third gambles to the certain amount, where the potential loss per trial was $0.15 and a penny, respectively. We should highlight that loss aversion by itself cannot explain the results, since the distribution of final payoffs is virtually the same for the three gambles. It is actually the combination of loss aversion and myopia that describes the observed behavior.

The subjects were also presented with the explicit distribution of final outcomes that the three gambles entail. Once the subjects viewed the distribution of final outcomes, virtually all of them (95%) preferred the gamble to the certain amount. Hence, the subjects found the gambles much more attractive when the data was aggregated on their behalf. This result suggests that, left alone, the subjects overestimated the likelihood of losing money. We tested this hypothesis directly, by asking subjects to estimate the probability of losing money after all the one hundred and fifty trials of the first gamble were completed. The average (median) answer was 0.237 (0.150), whereas the correct answer is 0.003. The gross overstatement of the chances to lose money is consistent with myopic loss aversion. However, it is in complete contrast to what Samuelson called "the fallacy of large numbers." We elaborate on this issue and discuss new experimental data below.

As you might recall, Samuelson offered his colleague the following bet: heads you win $200, tails you lose $100. Samuelson's colleague rejected a single play of the bet, but expressed a desire to play it 100 times. Samuelson proved that this combination of responses is inconsistent, and accused his colleague of the fallacy of large numbers. Specifically, Samuelson argued that his colleague did not understand that the variance of final outcomes grows proportionally to the number of plays. If Samuelson's colleague was typical, then most people would prefer the series of plays to the single play. In addition, once the explicit distribution is presented, people are expected to change their mind and reject the series of bets. We found just the opposite. People tend to accept the single bet, but then reject the series of bets. Furthermore, once the explicit distribution of the series is presented, virtually everybody accepts it. We conclude that Samuelson's colleague is atypical. Most people, we believe, tend to follow the "fallacy of small numbers." Not only do they not understand that the variance of final outcomes increases proportionally to the number of plays, they often think it grows much faster than the number of plays.

We end our tests by turning to an important implication of myopic loss aversion, which relates to the worldwide trend toward investor autonomy. In the United States, for instance, people are responsible for managing their retirement funds through 401(k), among other, defined contribution saving plans. One interesting question is whether the frequency at which performance is evaluated influences investment choices. In particular, myopic loss aversion predicts that frequent reporting will accentuate the perceived risk of stocks, because the likelihood of stocks experiencing a loss in the short-term is relatively high.

To test the role of myopic loss aversion in retirement saving plans, we presented USC staff employees with the distribution of either the historical annual returns on stocks and bonds or simulated thirty-year returns on the same asset classes. The two investment choices, stocks and bonds, were un-labeled and the subjects were asked to allocate their retirement contributions between the two funds. The results are consistent with myopic loss aversion. Those viewing the annual returns allocated, on average, 41 percent to stocks, whereas those viewing the long-term returns allocated 82 percent. The difference in the median allocations was even larger: 40 percent versus 90 percent. It is quite disturbing that alternative presentation modes of the "same" data could yield dramatic differences in investment choices. The results raise difficult questions for employers and regulators about the proper frequency of performance reporting.

In this appendix, we reviewed several tests of myopic loss aversion, all of which are supportive of the concept. The evidence on myopic loss aversion is consistent with a more general phenomenon Kahneman and Lovallo (1993) labeled "narrow framing" (i.e., thinking about gambles or investments one at a time rather than aggregating them into a portfolio). Put differently, aggregation could reduce aggravation. Unfortunately, there is very little we know about the way people set their evaluation frequency, or more generally, the way people define frames. These issues are promising avenues for future research.

References

Benartzi, Shlomo, and Richard H. Thaler, 1995, Myopic Loss Aversion and the Equity Premium Puzzle, *Quarterly Journal of Economics* 110.1, 73–92.

Benartzi, Shlomo, and Richard H. Thaler, 1999, Risk Aversion or Myopia? Choices in Repeated Gambles and Retirement Investments, *Management Science* 45.3, 364–81.

Black, Fischer, 1980, The Tax Consequences of Long-Run Pension Policy, *Financial Analysts Journal* 36, 21–28.

Blanchard, Olivier, 1993, Movements in the Equity Premium, *Brookings Papers on Economic Activity*, 519–43.

Constantinides, George M., 1990, Habit Formation: A Resolution of the Equity Premium Puzzle, *Journal of Political Economy* 98, 519–43.

Epstein, L. G., and S. E. Zin, 1990, 'First Order' Risk Aversion and the Equity Premium Puzzle, *Journal of Monetary Economics* 26, 387–407.

Ferson, Wayne, and George M. Constantinides, 1991, Habit Persistence and Durability in Aggregate Consumption: Empirical Tests, *Journal of Financial Economics* 39, 199–240.

Gneezy, Uri, and an Potters, 1997, An Experiment on Risk Taking and Evaluation Periods, *Quarterly Journal of Economics* 112, 631–45.

Hovencamp, H., 1991, Legal Policy and the Endowment Effect, *Journal of Legal Studies* 20, 225–47.

Kahneman, Daniel, Jack Knetsch, and Richard H. Thaler, 1986, Fairness as a Constraint on Profit Seeking: Entitlements in the Market, *American Economic Review* 76, 728–41.

———, 1990, Experimental Tests of the Endowment Effect and the Coase Theorem, *Journal of Political Economy* 98, 1325–48.

Kahneman, Daniel, and Dan Lovallo, 1993, Timid Choices and Bold Forecasts: A Cognitive Perspective on Risk Taking, *Management Science* 39, 17–31.

Kahneman, Daniel, and Amos Tversky, 1979, Prospect Theory: An Analysis of Decision Under Risk, *Econometrica* 47, 263–91.

———, 1984, Choices Values and Frames, *American Psychologist* 39, 341–50.

Lakonishok, Josef, Andrei Shleifer, and Robert Vishny, 1992, The Structure and Performance of the Money Management Industry, *Brookings Papers: Microeconomics*, 339–91.

Leibowitz, M. L., and T. C. Langetieg, 1989, Shortfall Risks and the Asset Allocation Decision: A Simulation Analysis of Stock and Bond Risk Profiles, Salomon Brothers Research Department.

Libby, Robert, and Peter C. Fishburn, 1977, Behavioral Models of Risk Taking in Business, *Journal of Accounting Research* 15, 272–92.

MaCurdy, Thomas, and John Shoven, 1992, Accumulating Pension Wealth with Stocks and Bonds, Stanford University Working Paper.

Mankiw, N. Gregory, and S. P. Zeldes, 1991, The Consumption of Stockholders and Nonstockholders, *Journal of Financial Economics* 29, 97–112.

Mehra, R., and Edward C. Prescott, 1985, The Equity Premium Puzzle, *Journal of Monetary Economics* 15, 145–61.

———, 1988, The Equity Premium Puzzle: A Solution? *Journal of Monetary Economics* 21, 133–36.

Merton, Robert, 1969, Lifetime Portfolio Selection Under Uncertainty: The Continuous Time Case, *Review of Economics and Statistics* 51, 247–57.

Pratt, John W., and Richard J. Zeckhauser, 1987, Proper Risk Aversion, *Econometrica* 55, 143–54.

Reitz, Thomas, 1988, The Equity Risk Premium: A Solution? *Journal of Monetary Economics* 21, 117–32.

Samuelson, Paul A., 1963, Risk and Uncertainty: A Fallacy of Large Numbers, *Scientia* 98, 108–13.

———, 1969, Lifetime Portfolio Selection by Dynamic Stochastic Programming, *Review of Economics and Statistics* 51, 238–46.

Samuelson, William, and Richard J. Zeckhauser, 1988, Status Quo Bias in Decision Making, *Journal of Risk and Uncertainty* 1, 7–59.

Shleifer, Andrei, and Robert Vishny, 1990, Equilibrium Short Horizons of Investors and Firms, *American Economic Review* 80, 148–53.

Siegel, Jeremy J., 1991, The Real Rate of Interest from 1800–1990: A Study of the U. S. and U. K., Working Paper, Wharton School.

———, 1992, The Equity Premium: Stock and Bond Returns Since 1802, *Financial Analysts Journal* 48, 28–38.

Swalm, R. O., 1966, Utility Theory—Insights into Risk Taking, *Harvard Business Review* 44, 123–36.

Thaler, Richard H., 1985, Mental Accounting and Consumer Choice, *Marketing Science* 4, 199–214.

Thaler, Richard H., Amos Tversky, Daniel Kahneman, and Alan Schwartz, 1997, The Effect of Myopia and Loss Aversion on Risk Taking: An Experimental Test, *Quarterly Journal of Economics* 112, 647–61.

Thaler, Richard H., and Eric J. Johnson, 1990, Gambling with the House Money and Trying to Break Even: The Effects of Prior Outcomes on Risky Choice, *Management Science* 36, 643–60.

Tversky, Amos, and Maya Bar-Hillel, 1983, Risk: The Long Run and the Short, *Journal of Experimental Psychology: Human Learning, Memory, and Cognition* 9, 713–17.

Tversky, Amos, and Daniel Kahneman, 1991, Loss Aversion and Riskless Choice: A Reference Dependent Model, *Quarterly Journal of Economics* 107, 1039–61.

———, 1992, Advances in Prospect Theory: Cumulative Representation of Uncertainty, *Journal of Risk and Uncertainty* 5, 297–323.

Weil, Philippe, 1989, The Equity Premium Puzzle and the Risk-free Rate Puzzle, *Journal of Monetary Economics* 24, 401–21.

Yaari, M. E., 1987, The Dual Theory of Choice Under Risk, *Econometrica* 55, 95–115.

Chapter 7

PROSPECT THEORY AND ASSET PRICES

Nicholas Barberis, Ming Huang, and Tano Santos

1. Introduction

For many years now, the standard framework for thinking about aggregate stock market behavior has been the consumption-based approach. As is well known, this approach presents a number of difficulties. In its simplest form, it does not come close to capturing the stock market's high historical average return and volatility, nor the striking variation in expected stock returns over time.[1] Over the past decade researchers have used ever more sophisticated specifications for utility over consumption in an attempt to approximate the data more closely.[2] These efforts have yielded some success. However, some basic features of stock returns, such as their low correlation with consumption growth, remain hard to understand.

In this chapter we make the case for an alternative way of thinking about the aggregate stock market. Instead of trying to refine the consumption-based model further, we propose departing from it in a particular way. In the model we present below, the investor derives direct utility not only from consumption but also from changes in the value of his financial wealth. When deciding how much to invest in the stock market, he takes both types of utility into account: the objective function he maximizes includes an extra term reflecting a direct concern about financial wealth fluctuations. This contrasts with the traditional approach to asset pricing, which holds that the only thing people take into account when choosing a portfolio is the future consumption utility that their wealth will bring.

We are grateful to John Cochrane, George Constantinides, Kent Daniel, Darrell Duffie, Lars Hansen, Sendhil Mullainathan, Canice Prendergast, Andrei Shleifer, Kenneth Singleton, Richard Thaler, Stanley Zin, three anonymous referees for *The Quarterly Journal of Economics*, the editor Edward Glaeser, and participants in numerous workshops in the United States and Great Britain for helpful comments on earlier drafts.

[1] See, for example, Hansen and Singleton (1983), Mehra and Prescott (1985), and Hansen and Jagannathan (1991).

[2] Recent papers in this line of research include Abel (1990), Campbell and Cochrane (1999), Constantinides (1990), Epstein and Zin (1989, 1991), and Sundaresan (1989). Another strand of the literature emphasizes market incompleteness due to uninsurable income shocks; see, for example, Heaton and Lucas (1996) and Constantinides and Duffie (1996). Cochrane (1998) and Kocherlakota (1996) provide excellent surveys.

Our specification of this additional source of utility captures two ideas we think are important for understanding investor behavior. First, our investor is much more sensitive to reductions in his financial wealth than to increases, a feature sometimes known as *loss aversion*. Second, how loss averse the investor is, depends on his prior investment performance. After prior gains, he becomes less loss averse: the prior gains will cushion any subsequent loss, making it more bearable. Conversely, after a prior loss, he becomes more loss averse: after being burned by the initial loss, he is more sensitive to additional setbacks.

By extending the traditional asset pricing framework in this way, we find that we are able to understand many of the hitherto perplexing features of aggregate data. In particular, starting from an underlying consumption growth process with *low* variance, our model generates stock returns with a high mean, high volatility, significant predictability, and low correlation with consumption growth, while maintaining a low and stable riskless interest rate.

In essence, our story is one of changing risk aversion. After a run-up in stock prices, our agent is less risk averse because those gains will cushion any subsequent loss. After a fall in stock prices, he becomes more wary of further losses and hence more risk averse. This variation in risk aversion allows returns in our model to be much more volatile than the underlying dividends: an unusually good dividend raises prices, but this price increase also makes the investor less risk averse, driving prices still higher. We also generate predictability in returns much like that observed in the data: following a significant rise in prices, the investor is less risk averse, and subsequent returns are therefore on average lower.

The model also produces a substantial equity premium: the high volatility of returns means that stocks often perform poorly, causing our loss-averse investor considerable discomfort. As a result, a large premium is required to convince him to hold stocks.

Our framework offers a distinct alternative to consumption-based models that attempt to understand the high mean, high volatility, and significant predictability of equity returns. Campbell and Cochrane (1999) explain these empirical features using an external habit level for consumption that generates time-varying risk aversion as current consumption moves closer to or farther from habit. Although our model is also based on changing risk aversion, we generate it by introducing loss aversion over financial wealth fluctuations and allowing the degree of loss aversion to be affected by prior investment performance.

The differences between our framework and a consumption-based approach like Campbell and Cochrane (1999) are highlighted by the distinct predictions of each. In the consumption-based model, a large component of stock return volatility comes from changes in risk aversion that are ultimately driven by consumption. It is therefore inevitable that stock returns and consumption are significantly correlated, although this is not the case in the data. In our framework, changes in risk aversion are driven by past stock market movements and hence ultimately by news about dividends. Since dividends are only weakly correlated with consumption, returns in our model are also only weakly correlated with consumption.

Our approach is also related to the literature on first-order risk aversion, as introduced using recursive utility by Epstein and Zin (1990) among others. So far, this literature has not allowed for time-varying risk aversion and is therefore unable to account for the high volatility of stock returns, although this could be incorporated without difficulty. A more basic difference is that most implementations of first-order risk aversion effectively make the investor loss averse over *total* wealth fluctuations as opposed to financial wealth fluctuations, as in this essay. This distinction is important because it underlies a number of our predictions, including the low correlation between consumption growth and stock returns.

At a more fundamental level, our framework differs from the consumption-based approach in the way it defines risk. In consumption-based models, assets are only risky to the extent that their returns covary with consumption growth. In our framework, the investor cares about fluctuations in financial wealth whether or not those fluctuations are correlated with consumption growth. Since we are measuring risk differently, it is not surprising that the level of risk aversion we need to explain the data is also affected. While we do assume a substantial level of risk aversion, it is not nearly as extreme as that required in many consumption-based approaches.

The design of our model draws on two long-standing ideas in the psychology literature. The idea that people care about changes in financial wealth and that they are loss averse over these changes is a central feature of the prospect theory of Kahneman and Tversky (1979). Prospect theory is a descriptive model of decision making under risk, originally developed to help explain the numerous violations of the expected utility paradigm documented over the years.

The idea that prior outcomes may affect subsequent risk-taking behavior is supported by another strand of the psychology literature. Thaler and Johnson (1990), for example, find that when faced with sequential gambles, people are more willing to take risks if they made money on prior gambles than if they lost. They interpret these findings as revealing that losses are less painful to people if they occur after prior gains, and more painful if they follow prior losses. The result that risk aversion goes down after prior gains, confirmed in other studies, has been labeled the "house money" effect, reflecting gamblers' increased willingness to bet when ahead.

Our work is related to that of Benartzi and Thaler (1995), who examine single-period portfolio choice for an investor with prospect-type utility. They find that loss aversion makes investors reluctant to invest in stocks, even in the face of a sizable equity premium. This suggests that bringing prospect theory into a formal pricing model may help us understand the level of average returns. While our work confirms this, we find that loss aversion cannot *by itself* explain the equity premium; incorporating the effect of prior outcomes is a critical ingredient as well. To see this, we also examine a simpler model where prior outcomes are ignored and hence where the pain of a loss is the same, regardless of past history. The investor's risk aversion is then constant over time, and stock prices lose an important source of volatility. With less volatile returns and hence less risk, we are no longer able to produce a substantial equity premium.

Another set of papers, including Barberis, Shleifer, and Vishny (1998) and Daniel, Hirshleifer, and Subrahmanyam (1998), explains some empirical features of asset returns by assuming that investors exhibit irrationality when making forecasts of quantities such as cash flows. Other papers, including Hong and Stein (1999), suppose that investors are only able to process subsets of available information. Here, we take a different approach. While we do modify the investor's preferences to reflect experimental evidence about the sources of utility, the investor remains rational and dynamically consistent throughout.[3]

In section 2 we show how loss aversion over financial wealth fluctuations and the effect of prior outcomes can be introduced into an asset pricing framework. Section 3, discusses studies in the psychology literature that we draw on in specifying the model. Section 4 characterizes equilibrium asset prices and presents intuition for the results. In section 5 we investigate the model's ability to explain the aggregate data through a detailed numerical analysis. In section 6 we examine the importance of taking account of prior outcomes by analyzing a simpler model where they are ignored. Section 7 concludes.

2. INVESTOR PREFERENCES

Our starting point is the traditional consumption-based asset pricing model of Lucas (1978). There is a continuum of identical infinitely lived agents in the economy, with a total mass of one, and two assets: a risk-free asset in zero net supply, paying a gross interest rate of $R_{f,t}$ between time t and $t + 1$; and one unit of a risky asset, paying a gross return of R_{t+1} between time t and $t + 1$. In the usual way, the risky asset—stock—is a claim to a stream of perishable output represented by the dividend sequence $\{D_t\}$, where dividend growth is given by

$$\log(D_{t+1}/D_t) = g_D + \sigma_D \epsilon_{t+1}, \tag{1}$$

where $\epsilon_{t+1} \sim$ i.i.d. $N(0,1)$.

---

[3] See Shleifer (1999) for a recent treatment of irrationality in financial markets.

Up to this point, our framework is entirely standard. We depart from the usual setup in the way we model investor preferences. In particular, our agents choose a consumption level C_t and an allocation to the risky asset S_t to maximize

$$\mathrm{E}\left[\sum_{t=0}^{\infty}\left(\rho^t\,\frac{C_t^{1-\gamma}}{1-\gamma} + b_t\rho^{t+1}v(X_{t+1}, S_t, z_t)\right)\right]. \tag{2}$$

The first term in this preference specification, utility over consumption C_t, is a standard feature of asset pricing models. Although our framework does not require it, we specialize to power utility, the benchmark case studied in the literature. The parameter ρ is the time discount factor, and $\gamma > 0$ controls the curvature of utility over consumption.[4]

The second term represents utility from fluctuations in the value of financial wealth. The variable X_{t+1} is the gain or loss the agent experiences on his financial investments between time t and $t + 1$, a positive value indicating a gain and a negative value, a loss. The utility the investor receives from this gain or loss is $v(X_{t+1}, S_t, z_t)$. It is a function not only of the gain or loss X_{t+1} itself, but also of S_t, the value of the investor's risky asset holdings at time t, and a state variable z_t which measures the investor's gains or losses prior to time t as a fraction of S_t. By including S_t and z_t as arguments of v, we allow the investor's prior investment performance to affect the way subsequent losses are experienced, and hence his willingness to take risk. Finally, b_t is an exogenous scaling factor that we specify later.

The utility that comes from fluctuations in financial wealth can be interpreted in a number of different ways. We prefer to think of it as capturing feelings unrelated to consumption. After a big loss in the stock market, an investor may experience a sense of regret over his decision to invest in stocks; he may interpret his loss as a sign that he is a second-rate investor, thus dealing his ego a painful blow; and he may feel humiliation in front of friends and family when word leaks out.[5]

In summary, the preference specification in (2) recognizes that people may get direct utility from sources other than consumption, and also says that they anticipate these other sources of utility when making decisions

---

[4] For $\gamma = 1$, we replace $C_t^{1-\gamma}/(1 - \gamma)$ with $\log(C_t)$.

[5] One could potentially also interpret the second term in (2) as capturing utility over *anticipated* consumption: when an investor finds out that his wealth has gone up, he may get utility from savoring the thought of the additional future consumption that his greater wealth will bring. The difficulty with this interpretation is that it is really only an explanation of why people might get utility from fluctuations in *total* wealth. To motivate utility over financial wealth fluctuations, one would need to argue that investors track different components of their wealth separately and get utility from fluctuations in each one. It would then be natural to add to (2) a term reflecting a concern for fluctuations in the value of human capital, another major source of wealth. In fact, it turns out that doing so does not affect our results so long as the labor income process underlying human capital is exogenously specified.

today. This is a departure from traditional approaches, which hold that the only thing people think about when choosing a portfolio is the future consumption utility that their wealth will bring. While our preferences are nonstandard, this does not mean that they are irrational in any sense: it is not irrational for people to get utility from sources other than consumption, nor is it irrational for them to anticipate these feelings when making decisions.

Introducing utility over gains and losses in financial wealth raises a number of issues: (1) How does the investor measure his gains and losses X_{t+1}? (2) How does z_t track prior gains and losses? (3) How does utility v depend on the gains and losses X_{t+1}?, and (4) How does z_t change over time? Subsections A through D below tackle each of these questions in turn. Finally, subsection E discusses the scaling factor b_t.

A. Measuring Gains and Losses

The gains and losses in our model refer to changes in the value of the investor's *financial wealth*, even if this is only one component of his overall wealth. For simplicity, we go one step further. Even though there are two financial assets, we suppose that the investor cares only about fluctuations in the value of the risky asset.[6]

Next, we need to specify the horizon over which gains and losses are measured. Put differently, How often does the agent seriously evaluate his investment performance? We follow the suggestion of Benartzi and Thaler (1995) that the most natural evaluation period is a year. As they point out, we file taxes once a year and receive our most comprehensive mutual fund reports once a year; moreover, institutional investors scrutinize their money managers' performance most carefully on an annual basis. Since this is an important assumption, we will investigate its impact on our results later in the chapter.

Our investor therefore monitors fluctuations in the value of his stock portfolio from year to year and gets utility from those fluctuations. To fix ideas, suppose that S_t, the time t value of the investor's holdings of the risky asset, is $100. Imagine that by time $t+1$, this value has gone up to $S_t R_{t+1} = \$120$. The exact way the investor measures this gain depends on the reference level with which $120 is compared. One possible reference level is the status quo or initial value $S_t = \$100$. The gain would then be measured as $20, or more generally as $X_{t+1} = S_t R_{t+1} - S_t$.

This is essentially our approach, but for one modification that we think is realistic: we take the reference level to be the status quo *scaled up by the*

---

[6] A simple justification for this is that since the return on the risk-free asset is known in advance, the investor does not get utility from changes in its value in the way that he does from changes in risky asset value. We also show later that for one reasonable way of measuring gains and losses, it makes no difference whether they are computed over total financial wealth or over the risky asset alone.

risk-free rate, $S_t R_{f,t}$. In our example, and with a risk-free rate of say 5 percent, this means a reference level of 105. An end-of-period risky asset value of 120 would then lead the investor to code a gain of 15, while a value of 100 would generate a loss of −5. In general terms, the investor will code a gain or loss of

$$X_{t+1} = S_t R_{t+1} - S_t R_{f,t}. \tag{3}$$

The idea here is that in an economy offering a riskless return of 5 percent, the investor is likely to be disappointed if his stock market investment returns only 4 percent. The riskless return may not be the investor's only point of comparison, although we suggest that it is a reasonable one. We will examine the sensitivity of our results to this choice later in the chapter.[7]

B. Tracking Prior Investment Outcomes

Now that we have explained how gains and losses are measured, we need to specify the utility they bring the investor. The simplest approach is to say that the utility of a gain or loss X_{t+1} is $v(X_{t+1})$, in other words, a function of the size of the gain or loss alone.

In our model, we allow the pain of a loss to depend not only on the size of the loss but also on investment performance *prior* to the loss. A loss that comes after substantial prior gains may be less painful than usual because it is cushioned by those earlier gains. Put differently, the investor may not care much about a stock market dip that follows substantial prior gains because he can still tell himself that he is "up, relative to a year ago," say.

Conversely, losses that come on the heels of substantial prior losses may be more painful than average for the investor. If he has been burned by a painful loss, he may be particularly sensitive to additional setbacks.

To capture the influence of prior outcomes, we introduce the concept of a *historical benchmark level* Z_t for the value of the risky asset.[8] We propose that when judging the recent performance of a stock, investors compare S_t, the value of their stock holdings today, with some value Z_t which represents a price that they remember the stock trading at in the past. Different investors will form this benchmark in different ways. For some investors, it may represent an average of recent stock prices. For others, it may be the

---

[7] Note that if the investor does use the risk-free rate as a reference level, it is irrelevant whether gains and losses are calculated over total financial wealth or over the risky asset alone: if B_t and S_t represent the investor's holdings of the risk-free asset and the risky asset, respectively, at time t, then $(B_t R_{f,t} + S_t R_{t+1}) - (B_t + S_t) R_{f,t}$ is the same as $S_t (R_{t+1} - R_{f,t})$.

[8] We use the term "*benchmark* level" to distinguish Z_t from the *reference* level $S_t R_{f,t}$. The reference level determines the size of the gain or loss. The benchmark level Z_t determines the magnitude of the utility received from that gain or loss, in a way that we soon make precise. While we are careful to stick to this terminology, some readers may find it helpful to think of Z_t as a secondary reference level that also affects the investor's decisions.

specific stock price at salient moments in the past, such as the end of a year. Whichever way the benchmark level is formed, the difference $S_t - Z_t$, when positive, is the investor's personal measure of how much "he is up" on his investment at time t and conversely, when negative, how much "he is down."

Introducing Z_t is helpful in modeling the influence of prior outcomes on the way subsequent gains and losses are experienced. When $S_t > Z_t$, the investor has had prior gains, making subsequent losses less painful and lowering the investor's risk aversion. Conversely, when $S_t < Z_t$, the investor has endured prior losses. Subsequent losses are more painful, and the investor is more risk averse than usual.

Since S_t and Z_t summarize how the investor perceives his past performance, a simple way of capturing the effect of prior outcomes would be to write the utility of financial wealth fluctuations as $v(X_{t+1}, S_t, Z_t)$. For modeling purposes, we find it more convenient to write it as $v(X_{t+1}, S_t, z_t)$, where $z_t = Z_t/S_t$.

C. Utility from Gains and Losses

In defining $v(X_{t+1}, S_t, z_t)$, we consider three separate cases: $z_t = 1$, where the investor has neither prior gains nor prior losses on his investments; $z_t < 1$, the case of prior gains; and $z_t > 1$, the case of prior losses.

We start with the case of $z_t = 1$. We want to model the idea that investors are much more sensitive to reductions in financial wealth than to increases, a feature sometimes known as *loss aversion*. We capture this by defining

$$v(X_{t+1}, S_t, 1) = \begin{cases} X_{t+1} \\ \lambda X_{t+1} \end{cases} \quad \text{for} \quad \begin{matrix} X_{t+1} \geq 0 \\ X_{t+1} < 0, \end{matrix} \tag{4}$$

with $\lambda > 1$. This is a piecewise linear function, shown as the line marked "$z_t = 1$" in figure 7.1. It is kinked at the origin, where the gain equals zero.

We now turn to $z_t < 1$, where the investor has accumulated prior gains in the stock market. The upper-most line in figure 7.1 shows the form of $v(X_{t+1}, S_t, z_t)$ in this case. It differs from $v(X_{t+1}, S_t, 1)$ in the way losses are penalized. Small losses are not penalized very heavily, but once the loss exceeds a certain amount, it starts being penalized at a more severe rate. The intuition is that if the investor has built up a cushion of prior gains, these gains may soften the blow of small subsequent losses, although they may not be enough to protect him against larger losses.

To understand how we formalize this intuition, an example may be helpful. Suppose that the current stock value is $S_t = \$100$, but that the investor has recently accumulated some gains on his investments. A reasonable historical benchmark level is $Z_t = \$90$, since the stock must have gone up in value recently. As discussed above, we can think of $\$90$ as the value

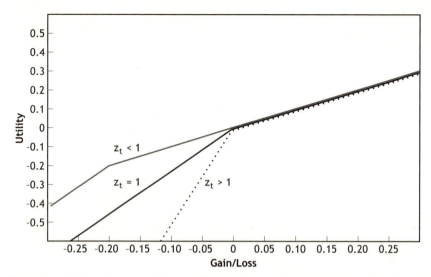

Figure 7.1. Utility of gains and losses. The top line represents the case where the investor has prior gains, the dotted line the case of prior losses, and the middle line the case where he has neither prior gains nor losses.

of the stock one year ago, which the investor still remembers. The difference $S_t - Z_t = \$10$ represents the cushion, or reserve of prior gains that the investor has built up. Suppose finally that the risk-free rate is zero.

Imagine that over the next year, the value of the stock falls from $S_t = \$100$ down to $S_t R_{t+1} = \$80$. In the case of $z_t = 1$, where the investor has no prior gains or losses, equations (3) and (4) show that we measure the pain of this loss as

$$(80 - 100)(\lambda) = -40$$

for a λ of 2.

When the investor has some prior gains, this calculation probably overstates actual discomfort. We propose a more realistic measure of the pain caused: since the first $10 drop, from $S_t = \$100$ down to $Z_t = \$90$, is completely cushioned by the $10 reserve of prior gains, we penalize it at a rate of only 1, rather than λ. The second part of the loss, from $Z_t = \$90$ down to $S_t R_{t+1} = \$80$ will be *more* painful since all prior gains have already been depleted, and we penalize it at the higher rate of λ. Using a λ of 2 again, the overall disutility of the $20 loss is

$$(90 - 100)(1) + (80 - 90)(\lambda) = (90 - 100)(1) + (80 - 90)(2) = -30,$$

or in general terms

$$(Z_t - S_t)(1) + (S_t R_{t+1} - Z_t)(\lambda) = S_t(z_t - 1)(1) + S_t(R_{t+1} - z_t)(\lambda).$$

Note that if the loss is small enough to be completely cushioned by the prior gain—in other words, if $S_t R_{t+1} > Z_t$, or equivalently, $R_{t+1} > z_t$—there is no need to break the loss up into two parts. Rather, the entire loss of $S_t R_{t+1} - S_t$ is penalized at the gentler rate of 1.

In summary, then, we give $v(X_{t+1}, S_t, z_t)$ the following form for the case of prior gains, or $z_t \leq 1$:

$$v(X_{t+1}, S_t, z_t)$$
$$= \begin{cases} S_t R_{t+1} - S_t \\ S_t(z_t - 1) + \lambda S_t(R_{t+1} - z_t) \end{cases} \text{ for } \begin{matrix} R_{t+1} \geq z_t \\ R_{t+1} < z_t. \end{matrix} \quad (5)$$

For the more relevant case of a nonzero riskless rate $R_{f,t}$, we scale both the reference level S_t and the benchmark level Z_t up by the risk-free rate, so that[9]

$$v(X_{t+1}, S_t, z_t)$$
$$= \begin{cases} S_t R_{t+1} - S_t R_{f,t} \\ S_t(z_t R_{f,t} - R_{f,t}) + \lambda S_t(R_{t+1} - z_t R_{f,t}) \end{cases} \text{ for } \begin{matrix} R_{t+1} \geq z_t R_{f,t} \\ R_{t+1} < z_t R_{f,t}. \end{matrix} \quad (6)$$

Finally, we turn to $z_t > 1$, where the investor has recently experienced losses on his investments. The form of $v(X_{t+1} S_t, z_t)$ in this case is shown as the dotted line in figure 7.1. It differs from $v(X_{t+1}, S_t, 1)$ in that losses are penalized more heavily, capturing the idea that losses that come on the heels of other losses are more painful than usual. More formally,

$$v(X_{t+1}, S_t, z_t) = \begin{cases} X_{t+1} \\ \lambda(z_t)X_{t+1} \end{cases} \text{ for } \begin{matrix} X_{t+1} \geq 0 \\ X_{t+1} < 0, \end{matrix} \quad (7)$$

where $\lambda(z_t) > \lambda$. Note that the penalty $\lambda(z_t)$ is a function of the size of prior losses, measured by z_t. In the interest of simplicity, we set

$$\lambda(z_t) = \lambda + k(z_t - 1), \quad (8)$$

where $k > 0$. The larger the prior loss, or equivalently, the larger z_t is, the more painful subsequent losses will be.

We illustrate this with another example. Suppose that the current stock value is $S_t = \$100$, and that the investor has recently experienced losses. A reasonable historical benchmark level is then $Z_t = \$110$, higher than $100 since the stock has been falling. By definition, $z_t = 1.1$. Suppose for now that $\lambda = 2$, $k = 3$, and that the risk-free rate is zero.

Imagine that over the next year, the value of the stock falls from $S_t = \$100$ down to $S_t R_{t+1} = \$90$. In the case of $z_t = 1$, where the investor

[9] Although the formula for v depends on R_{t+1} as well, we do not make the return an explicit argument of v since it can be backed out of X_{t+1} and S_t.

has no prior gains or losses, equations (3) and (4) show that we measure the pain of this loss as

$$(90 - 100)(\lambda) = (90 - 100)(2) = -20.$$

In our example, though, there has been a prior loss and $z_t = 1.1$. This means that the pain will now be

$$(90 - 100)(\lambda + 3(0.1)) = (90 - 100)(2 + 3(0.1)) = -23,$$

capturing the idea that losses are more painful after prior losses.

D. Dynamics of the Benchmark Level

To complete our description of the model, we need to discuss how the investor's cushion of prior gains changes over time. In formal terms, we have to specify how z_t moves over time, or equivalently how the historical benchmark level Z_t reacts to changes in stock value S_t. There are two ways that the value of the investor's stock holdings can change. First, it can change at time t because of an action taken by the investor: he may take out the dividend and consume it, or he may buy or sell some shares. For this type of change, we assume that Z_t changes in proportion to S_t, so that z_t remains constant. For example, suppose that the initial value of the investor's stock holdings is $S_t = \$100$ and that $Z_t = \$80$, implying that he has accumulated \$20 of prior gains. If he sells \$10 of stock for consumption purposes, bringing S_t down to \$90, we assume that Z_t falls to \$72, so that z_t remains constant at 0.8. In other words, when the investor sells stock for consumption, we assume that he uses up some of his prior gains.

The assumption that the investor's actions do not affect the evolution of z_t is reasonable for transactions of moderate size, or more precisely, for moderate deviations from a strategy in which the investor holds a fixed number of shares and consumes the dividend each period. However, larger deviations—a complete exit from the stock market, for example—might plausibly affect the way z_t evolves. In supposing that they do not, we make a strong assumption, but one that is very helpful in keeping our analysis tractable. We discuss the economic interpretation of this assumption further in section 4 when we compute equilibrium prices.

The second way stock value can change is simply through its return between time t and time $t + 1$. In this case, the only requirement we impose on Z_t is that it respond *sluggishly* to changes in the value of the risky asset. By this we mean that when the stock price moves up by a lot, the benchmark level also moves up, but by less. Conversely, if the stock price falls sharply, the benchmark level does not adjust downwards by as much.

Sluggishness turns out to be a very intuitive requirement to impose. To see this, recall that the difference $S_t - Z_t$ is the investor's measure of his reserve of prior gains. How should this quantity change as a result of a change in the level of the stock market? If the return on the stock market is particularly good, investors should feel as though they have increased their reserve of prior gains. Mathematically, this means that the benchmark level Z_t should move up less than the stock price itself, so that the cushion at time $t + 1$, namely $S_{t+1} - Z_{t+1}$, be larger than the cushion at time t, $S_t - Z_t$. Conversely, if the return on market is particularly poor, the investor should feel as though his reserves of prior gains are depleted. For this to happen, Z_t must fall less than S_t.

A simple way of modeling the sluggishness of the benchmark level Z_t is to write the dynamics of z_t as

$$z_{t+1} = z_t \frac{\overline{R}}{R_{t+1}}, \tag{9}$$

where $\overline{R}$ is a fixed parameter. This equation then says that if the return on the risky asset is particularly good, so that $R_{t+1} > \overline{R}$, the state variable $z = Z/S$ falls in value. This is consistent with the benchmark level Z_t behaving sluggishly, rising less than the stock price itself. Conversely, if the return is poor and $R_{t+1} < \overline{R}$, then z goes up. This is consistent with the benchmark level falling less than the stock price.[10]

$\overline{R}$ is not a free parameter in our model, but is determined endogenously by imposing the reasonable requirement that in equilibrium, the median value of z_t be equal to one. In other words, half the time the investor has prior gains, and the rest of the time he has prior losses. It turns out that $\overline{R}$ is typically of similar magnitude to the average stock return.

We can generalize (9) slightly to allow for varying degrees of sluggishness in the dynamics of the historical benchmark level. One way to do this is to write

$$z_{t+1} = \eta \left(z_t \frac{\overline{R}}{R_{t+1}} \right) + (1 - \eta)(1). \tag{10}$$

When $\eta = 1$, this reduces to (9), which represents a sluggish benchmark level. When $\eta = 0$, it reduces to $z_{t+1} = 1$, which means that the benchmark level Z_t tracks the stock value S_t one-for-one throughout—a very fast-moving benchmark level.

The parameter η can be given an interpretation in terms of the investor's memory: it measures how far back the investor's mind stretches when recalling past gains and losses. When η is near zero, the benchmark level Z_t is always close to the value of the stock S_t: prior gains and losses are quickly swallowed up and are not allowed to affect the investor for long. In effect, the investor has a short-term memory, recalling only the most recent prior outcomes. When η is closer to one, though, the benchmark level moves

[10] The benchmark level dynamics in (9) are one simple way of capturing sluggishness. More generally, we can assume dynamics of the form $z_{t+1} = g(z_t, R_{t+1})$, where $g(z_t, R_{t+1})$ is strictly increasing in z_t and strictly decreasing in R_{t+1}.

sluggishly, allowing past gains and losses to linger and affect the investor for a long time; in other words, the investor has a long memory.[11]

E. The Scaling Term b_t

We scale the prospect theory term in the utility function to ensure that quantities like the price/dividend ratio and risky asset risk premium remain stationary even as aggregate wealth increases over time. Without a scaling factor, this will not be the case because the second term of the objective function will come to dominate the first as aggregate wealth grows. One reasonable specification of the scaling term is

$$b_t = b_0 \overline{C}_t^{-\gamma}, \tag{11}$$

where $\overline{C}_t$ is the *aggregate* per capita consumption at time t, and hence exogenous to the investor. By using an exogenous variable, we ensure that b_t simply acts as a neutral scaling factor, without affecting the economic intuition of the previous paragraphs.

The parameter b_0 is a nonnegative constant that allows us to control the overall importance of utility from gains and losses in financial wealth relative to utility from consumption. Setting $b_0 = 0$ reduces our framework to the much studied consumption-based model with power utility.

3. Evidence from Psychology

The design of our model is influenced by some long-standing ideas from psychology. The idea that people care about changes in financial wealth and that they are loss averse over these changes is a central feature of the prospect theory of Kahneman and Tversky (1979). Prospect theory is a descriptive model of decision making under risk that was originally developed to help explain the numerous violations of the expected utility paradigm documented over the years.

While our model is influenced by the work of Kahneman and Tversky (1979), we do not attempt an exhaustive implementation of all aspects of prospect theory. Figure 7.2 shows Kahneman and Tversky's utility function over gains and losses:[12]

$$w(X) = \begin{cases} X^{0.88} \\ -2.25(-X)^{0.88} \end{cases} \quad \text{for} \quad \begin{aligned} X &\geq 0 \\ X &< 0. \end{aligned} \tag{12}$$

[11] A simple mathematical argument can be used to show that the "half-life" of the investor's memory is equal to $-0.693/\log \eta$. In other words, after this amount of time, the investor has lost half of his memory. When $\eta = 0.9$, this quantity is 6.6 years, and when $\eta = 0.8$, it equals 3.1 years.

[12] This functional form is proposed in Tversky and Kahneman (1992) and is based on experimental findings.

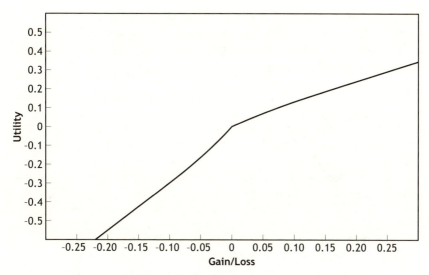

Figure 7.2. Kahneman-Tversky value function.

It is similar to $v(X_{t+1}, S_t, 1)$—the middle line in figure 7.1—but is also mildly concave over gains and convex over losses. This curvature is most relevant when choosing between prospects that involve *only* gains or between prospects that involve *only* losses.[13] For gambles that can lead to both gains and losses—such as the one-year investment in stocks that our agent is evaluating—loss aversion at the kink is far more important than the degree of curvature away from the kink. For simplicity then, we make v linear over both gains and losses.

In our framework the "prospective utility" the investor receives from gains and losses is computed by taking the expected value of v, in other words by weighting the value of gains and losses by their probabilities. As a way of understanding Allais-type violations of the expected utility paradigm, Kahneman and Tversky (1979) suggest weighting the value of gains and losses not with the probabilities themselves but with a nonlinear transformation of those probabilities. Again, for simplicity, we abstract from this feature of prospect theory, and have no reason to believe that our results are qualitatively affected by this simplification.[14]

---

[13] Indeed, it is by offering subjects gambles over *only* losses or *only* gains that Kahneman and Tversky (1979) deduce the shape of the value function. They propose concavity over gains because subjects prefer a gamble that offers $2,000 w.p. ¼, $4,000 w.p. ¼, and $0 w.p. ½ to the mean-preserving spread offering $6,000 w.p. ¼ and $0 otherwise. Preferences switch when the signs are flipped, suggesting convexity over losses.

[14] Two other assumptions inherent in our framework are worth noting. First, we assume that investors rationally forecast the loss aversion that they will feel in the future. Loewenstein, O'Donoghue, and Rabin (1999) suggest that reality is more complex in that people have trouble forecasting how they will feel about future events. A more complete model would take

The idea that prior outcomes may affect willingness to take risk is also supported by recent studies in psychology. Thaler and Johnson (1990) study risk-taking behavior in an experimental setting using a large sample of Cornell undergraduate and MBA students. They offer subjects a sequence of gambles and find that outcomes in earlier gambles affect subsequent behavior: following a gain, people appear to be more risk seeking than usual, taking on bets they would not normally accept. This result has become known as the "house money" effect, because it is reminiscent of the expression "playing with the house money" used to describe gamblers' increased willingness to bet when ahead. Thaler and Johnson argue that these results suggest that losses are less painful after prior gains, perhaps because those gains cushion the subsequent setback.

Thaler and Johnson also find that after a loss, subjects display considerable reluctance to accept risky bets. They interpret this as showing that losses are more painful than usual following prior losses.[15]

The stakes used in Thaler and Johnson (1990) are small—the dollar amounts are typically in double digits. Interestingly, Gertner (1993) obtains similar results in a study involving much larger stakes. He studies the risk-taking behavior of participants in the television game show *Card Sharks*, where contestants place bets on whether a card to be drawn at random from a deck will be higher or lower than a card currently showing. He finds that the amount bet is a strongly increasing function of the contestant's winnings up to that point in the show. Once again, this is evidence of more aggressive risk-taking behavior following substantial gains.

The evidence we have presented suggests that in the context of a sequence of gains and losses, people are less risk averse following prior gains and more risk averse after prior losses. This may initially appear puzzling to readers familiar with Kahneman and Tversky's original value function, which is concave in the region of gains and convex in the region of losses. In particular, the convexity over losses is occasionally interpreted to mean that "after a loss, people are risk seeking," contrary to Thaler and Johnson's evidence. Hidden in this interpretation, though, is a critical assumption, namely that people *integrate* or "merge" the outcomes of successive gambles. Suppose that you have just suffered a loss of $1,000, and are contemplating a gamble equally likely to win you $200 as to lose you $200. Integration of outcomes

---

this evidence into account, although we do not attempt it here. Second, we assume that investors rationally forecast future changes in the reference level $S_t R_{f,t}$. It is sometimes claimed that such rationality is inconsistent with loss aversion: if people know they are eventually going to reset their reference level after a stock market drop, why are they so averse to the loss in the first place? Levy and Wiener (1997) provide one answer, noting that changing the reference level forces the investor to confront and accept the loss, and this is the part that is painful.

[15] It is tempting to explain these results using a utility function where risk aversion decreases with wealth. However, any utility function with sufficient curvature to produce lower risk aversion after a $20 gain, regardless of initial wealth level, inevitably makes counterfactual predictions about attitudes to large-scale gambles.

means that you make the decision about whether to take the gamble by comparing the average of $w(-1200)$ and $w(-800)$ with $w(-1000)$, where w is defined in equation (12). Of course, under this assumption, convexity in the region of losses leads to risk-seeking after a loss.

The idea that people integrate the outcomes of sequential gambles, while appealingly simple, is only a hypothesis. Tversky and Kahneman (1981) themselves note that prospect theory was originally developed only for elementary, one-shot gambles and that any application to a dynamic context must await further evidence on how people think about sequences of gains and losses. A number of papers, including Thaler and Johnson (1990), have taken up this challenge, conducting experiments on whether people integrate sequential outcomes, segregate them, or do something else again. That these experiments have uncovered *increased* risk aversion after prior losses does not contradict prospect theory; it simply rejects the hypothesis that people integrate sequential gambles.[16]

Thaler and Johnson (1990) do find some situations where prior losses lead to risk-seeking behavior. These are situations where after the prior loss, the subject can take a gamble that offers a good chance of breaking even and only limited downside. In conjunction with the other evidence, this suggests that while losses after prior losses are very painful, gains that enable people with prior losses to break even are especially sweet. We have not been able to introduce this break-even effect into our framework in a tractable way. It is worth noting, though, that outside of the special situations uncovered by Thaler and Johnson, it is increased risk aversion that appears to be the norm after prior losses.

4. EQUILIBRIUM PRICES

We now derive equilibrium asset prices in an economy populated by investors with preferences of the type described in section 2. It may be helpful to summarize those preferences here. Each investor chooses consumption C_t and an allocation to the risky asset S_t to maximize

$$E\left[\sum_{t=0}^{\infty}\left(\rho^t\,\frac{C_t^{1-\gamma}}{1-\gamma}+b_0\overline{C}_t^{-\gamma}\rho^{t+1}v(X_{t+1},S_t,z_t)\right)\right],\qquad(13)$$

subject to the standard budget constraint, where

$$X_{t+1}=S_tR_{t+1}-S_tR_{f,t},\qquad(14)$$

---

[16] There is another sense in which integration of sequential outcomes is an implausible way to implement prospect theory in a multiperiod context. If investors did integrate many years of stock market gains and losses, they would essentially be valuing absolute levels of wealth, and not the *changes* in wealth that are so important to prospect theory. We thank J. B. Heaton for this observation.

and where for $z_t \leq 1$,

$$v(X_{t+1}, S_t, z_t)$$
$$= \begin{cases} S_t R_{t+1} - S_t R_{f,t} \\ S_t(z_t R_{f,t} - R_{f,t}) + \lambda S_t(R_{t+1} - z_t R_{f,t}) \end{cases} \quad \text{for} \quad \begin{array}{l} R_{t+1} \geq z_t R_{f,t} \\ R_{t+1} < z_t R_{f,t}, \end{array} \quad (15)$$

and for $z_t > 1$,

$$v(X_{t+1}, S_t, z_t) = \begin{cases} S_t R_{t+1} - S_t R_{f,t} \\ \lambda(z_t)(S_t R_{t+1} - S_t R_{f,t}) \end{cases} \quad \text{for} \quad \begin{array}{l} R_{t+1} \geq R_{f,t} \\ R_{t+1} < R_{f,t}, \end{array} \quad (16)$$

with

$$\lambda(z_t) = \lambda + k(z_t - 1). \quad (17)$$

Equations (15) and (16) are pictured in figure 7.1. Finally, the dynamics of the state variable z_t are given by

$$z_{t+1} = \eta \left(z_t \frac{\overline{R}}{R_{t+1}} \right) + (1 - \eta)(1). \quad (18)$$

We calculate the price P_t of a dividend claim—in other words, the stock price—in two different economies. The first economy, which we call "Economy I," is the one analyzed by Lucas (1978). It equates consumption and dividends so that stocks are modeled as a claim to the future consumption stream.

Due to its simplicity, the first economy is the one typically studied in the literature. However, we also calculate stock prices in a more realistic economy—"Economy II"—where consumption and dividends are modeled as separate processes. We can then allow the volatility of consumption growth and of dividend growth to be very different, as they indeed are in the data. We can think of the difference between consumption and dividends as arising from the fact that investors have other sources of income besides dividends. Equivalently, they have other forms of wealth, such as human capital, beyond their financial assets.

In our model, changes in risk aversion are caused by changes in the level of the stock market. In this respect, our approach differs from consumption-based habit formation models, where changes in risk aversion are due to changes in the level of consumption. While these are different ideas, it is not easy to illustrate their distinct implications in an economy like Economy I, where consumption and the stock market are driven by a single shock, and are hence perfectly conditionally correlated. This is why we emphasize Economy II: since consumption and dividends do not have to be equal in equilibrium, we can model them as separate processes, driven by shocks that are only imperfectly correlated. The contrast between our approach and the consumption-based framework then becomes much clearer.

In both economies, we construct a one-factor Markov equilibrium in which the risk-free rate is constant and the Markov state variable z_t determines the distribution of future stock returns. Specifically, we assume that the price/dividend ratio of the stock is a function of the state variable z_t:

$$f_t \equiv P_t/D_t = f(z_t), \tag{19}$$

and then show for each economy in turn that there is indeed an equilibrium satisfying this assumption. Given the one-factor assumption, the distribution of stock returns R_{t+1} is determined by z_t and the function $f(\cdot)$ using

$$R_{t+1} = \frac{P_{t+1} + D_{t+1}}{P_t} = \frac{1 + P_{t+1}/D_{t+1}}{P_t/D_t} \frac{D_{t+1}}{D_t} = \frac{1 + f(z_{t+1})}{f(z_t)} \frac{D_{t+1}}{D_t}. \tag{20}$$

A. Stock Prices in Economy I

In the first economy we consider, consumption and dividends are modeled as identical processes. We write the process for aggregate consumption $\overline{C}_t$ as

$$\log(\overline{C}_{t+1}/\overline{C}_t) = \log(D_{t+1}/D_t) = g_C + \sigma_C \epsilon_{t+1}, \tag{21}$$

where $\epsilon_t \sim$ i.i.d. $N(0,1)$. Note from equation (1) that the mean g_D and volatility σ_D of dividend growth are constrained to equal g_C and σ_C, respectively. Together with the one-factor Markov assumption, this means that the stock return is given by

$$R_{t+1} = \frac{1 + f(z_{t+1})}{f(z_t)} e^{g_C + \sigma_C \epsilon_{t+1}}. \tag{22}$$

Intuitively, the value of the risky asset can change because of news about consumption ϵ_{t+1} or because the price/dividend ratio f changes. Changes in f are driven by changes in z_t, which measures past gains and losses: past gains make the investor less risk averse, raising f, while past losses make him more risk averse, lowering f.

In equilibrium, and under rational expectations about stock returns and aggregate consumption levels, the agents in our economy must find it optimal to consume the dividend stream and to hold the market supply of zero units of the risk-free asset and one unit of stock at all times.[17] Proposition 1 characterizes the equilibrium.[18]

---

[17] We need to impose rational expectations about aggregate consumption because the agent's utility includes aggregate consumption as a scaling term.

[18] We assume that $\log \rho + (1 - \gamma)g_C + 0.5(1 - \gamma)^2\sigma_C^2 < 0$ so that the equilibrium is well behaved at $t = \infty$.

Proposition 1. For the preferences given in (13)–(18), there exists an equilibrium in which the gross risk-free interest rate is constant at

$$R_f = \rho^{-1} e^{\gamma g_C - \gamma^2 \sigma_C^2/2}, \tag{23}$$

and the stock's price-dividend ratio $f(\cdot)$, as a function of the state variable z_t, satisfies for all z_t:

$$1 = \rho \, E_t \left[\frac{1 + f(z_{t+1})}{f(z_t)} e^{(1-\gamma)(g_C + \sigma_C \epsilon_{t+1})} \right]$$
$$+ b_0 \rho \, E_t \left[\hat{v} \left(\frac{1 + f(z_{t+1})}{f(z_t)} e^{g_C + \sigma_C \epsilon_{t+1}}, z_t \right) \right], \tag{24}$$

where for $z_t \leq 1$,

$$\hat{v}(R_{t+1}, z_t) = \begin{cases} R_{t+1} - R_{f,t} \\ (z_t R_{f,t} - R_{f,t}) + \lambda(R_{t+1} - z_t R_{f,t}) \end{cases} \quad \text{for} \quad \begin{matrix} R_{t+1} \geq z_t R_{f,t} \\ R_{t+1} < z_t R_{f,t}, \end{matrix} \tag{25}$$

and for $z_t > 1$,

$$\hat{v}(R_{t+1}, z_t) = \begin{cases} R_{t+1} - R_{f,t} \\ \lambda(z_t)(R_{t+1} - R_{f,t}) \end{cases} \quad \text{for} \quad \begin{matrix} R_{t+1} \geq R_{f,t} \\ R_{t+1} < R_{f,t}. \end{matrix} \tag{26}$$

We prove this formally in the Appendix. At a less formal level, our results follow directly from the agent's Euler equations for optimality at equilibrium, derived using standard perturbation arguments:

$$1 = \rho R_f E_t [(\overline{C}_{t+1}/\overline{C}_t)^{-\gamma}], \tag{27}$$

$$1 = \rho E_t [R_{t+1}(\overline{C}_{t+1}/\overline{C}_t)^{-\gamma}] + b_0 \rho E_t [\hat{v}(R_{t+1}, z_t)]. \tag{28}$$

Readers may find it helpful to compare these equations with those derived from standard asset pricing models with power utility over consumption. The Euler equation for the risk-free rate is the usual one: consuming a little less today and investing the savings in the risk-free rate does not change the investor's exposure to losses on the risky asset. The first term in the Euler equation for the risky asset is also the familiar one first obtained by Mehra and Prescott (1985). However, there is now an additional term. Consuming less today and investing the proceeds in the risky asset exposes the investor to the risk of greater losses. Just how dangerous this is, is determined by the state variable z_t.

In constructing the equilibrium in proposition 1, we follow the assumption laid out in subsection 2.D, namely that buying or selling on the part of the investor does not affect the evolution of the state variable z_t. Equivalently, the investor believes that his actions will have no impact on the future evolution of z_t. As we argued earlier, this is a reasonable assumption for many actions the investor might take, but is less so in the case of a complete exit from the stock market. In essence, our assumption means that the investor does not consider using his cushion of prior gains in a strategic fashion, perhaps by waiting for the cushion to become large, exiting from the stock market so as to preserve the cushion and then reentering after a market crash when expected returns are high.[19]

B. Stock Prices in Economy II

In Economy II, consumption and dividends follow distinct processes. This allows us to model the stock for what it really is, namely a claim to the dividend stream, rather than as a claim to consumption. Formally, we assume

$$\log(\overline{C}_{t+1}/\overline{C}_t) = g_C + \sigma_C \eta_{t+1}, \tag{29}$$

and

$$\log(D_{t+1}/D_t) = g_D + \sigma_D \epsilon_{t+1}, \tag{30}$$

where

$$\begin{pmatrix} \eta_t \\ \epsilon_t \end{pmatrix} \sim \text{i.i.d.} \ N\left(\begin{pmatrix} 0 \\ 0 \end{pmatrix}, \begin{pmatrix} 1 & \omega \\ \omega & 1 \end{pmatrix} \right). \tag{31}$$

This assumption, which makes $\log \overline{C}_t/D_t$ a random walk, allows us to construct a one-factor Markov equilibrium in which the risk-free interest rate is constant and the price-dividend ratio of the stock is a function of the state variable z_t.[20] The stock return can then be written as

$$R_{t+1} = \frac{1 + f(z_{t+1})}{f(z_t)} e^{g_D + \sigma_D \epsilon_{t+1}}. \tag{32}$$

Given that the consumption and dividend processes are different, we need to complete the model specification by assuming that each agent also receives a stream of nonfinancial income $\{Y_t\}$—labor income, say. We assume

---

[19] Allowing the investor to consider such strategies does not change the qualitative nature of our results. It may affect our quantitative results depending on how one specifies the evolution of the investor's cushion of prior gains after he leaves the stock market.

[20] Another approach would model $\overline{C}_t$ and D_t as cointegrated processes, but we would then need at least one more factor to characterize equilibrium prices.

that $\{Y_t\}$ and $\{D_t\}$ form a joint Markov process whose distribution gives $\overline{C}_t \equiv D_t + Y_t$ and D_t the distributions in (29)–(31).

We construct the equilibrium through the Euler equations of optimality (27) and (28). The risk-free rate is again constant and given by (27). The one-factor Markov structures of stock prices in (19) and (32) satisfy the Euler equation (28). The next proposition characterizes this equilibrium. The Appendix gives more detailed calculations and proves that the Euler equations indeed characterize optimality.[21]

Proposition 2. In Economy II, the risk-free rate is constant at

$$R_f = \rho^{-1} e^{\gamma g_C - \gamma^2 \sigma_C^2 / 2}, \tag{33}$$

and the stock's price/dividend ratio $f(\cdot)$ is given by

$$1 = \rho e^{g_D - \gamma g_C + \gamma^2 \sigma_C^2 (1 - \omega^2)/2} \, E_t \left[\frac{1 + f(z_{t+1})}{f(z_t)} e^{(\sigma_D - \gamma \omega \sigma_C) \epsilon_{t+1}} \right]$$

$$+ b_0 \rho E_t \left[\hat{v} \left(\frac{1 + f(z_{t+1})}{f(z_t)} e^{g_D + \sigma_D \epsilon_{t+1}}, z_t \right) \right], \tag{34}$$

where $\hat{v}$ is defined in Proposition 1.

C. Model Intuition

In section 5 we solve for the price/dividend ratio numerically and use simulated data to show that our model provides a way of understanding a number of puzzling empirical features of aggregate stock returns. In particular, our model is consistent with a low volatility of consumption growth on the one hand, and a high mean and volatility of stock returns on the other, while maintaining a low and stable risk-free rate. Moreover, it generates long horizon predictability in stock returns similar to that observed in empirical studies and predicts a low correlation between consumption growth and stock returns.

It may be helpful to outline the intuition behind these results before moving to the simulations. Return volatility is a good place to start: How can our model generate returns that are more volatile than the underlying dividends? Suppose that there is a positive dividend innovation this period. This will generate a high stock return, increasing the investor's reserve of prior gains. This makes him less risk averse, since future losses will be cushioned by the prior gains, which are now larger than before. He therefore discounts

---

[21] We assume that $\log \rho - \gamma g_C + g_D + 0.5(\gamma^2 \sigma_C^2 - 2\gamma \omega \sigma_C \sigma_D + \sigma_D^2) < 0$ so that the equilibrium is well behaved at $t = \infty$.

the future dividend stream at a lower rate, giving stock prices an extra jolt upward. A similar story holds for a negative dividend innovation. It generates a low stock return, depleting prior gains or increasing prior losses. The investor is more risk averse than before, and the increase in risk aversion pushes prices still lower. The effect of all this is to make returns substantially more volatile than dividend growth.

The same mechanism also produces long horizon predictability. Put simply, since the investor's risk aversion varies over time depending on his investment performance, expected returns on the risky asset also vary. To understand this in more detail, suppose once again that there is a positive shock to dividends. This generates a high stock return, which lowers the investor's risk aversion and pushes the stock price still higher, leading to a higher price/dividend ratio. Since the investor is less risk averse, subsequent stock returns will be lower on average. Price/dividend ratios are therefore inversely related to future returns, in exactly the way that has been documented by numerous studies, including Campbell and Shiller (1988) and Fama and French (1988b).

If changing loss aversion can indeed generate volatile stock prices, then we may also be able to generate a substantial equity premium. On average, the investor is loss averse, and fears the frequent drops in the stock market. He may therefore charge a high premium in return for holding the risky asset. Earlier research provides hope that this will be the case: Benartzi and Thaler (1995) analyze one-period portfolio choice for loss-averse investors— a partial equilibrium analysis where the stock market's high historical mean and volatility are exogenous—and find that these investors are unwilling to invest much of their wealth in stocks, even in the face of the large historical premium. This suggests that loss aversion may be a useful ingredient for equilibrium models trying to understand the equity premium.

Finally, our framework also generates stock returns that are only weakly correlated with consumption, as in the data.[22] To understand this, note that in our model, stock returns are made up of two components: one due to news about dividends, and the other to a change in risk aversion caused by movements in the stock market. Both components are ultimately driven by shocks to dividends, and so in our model, the correlation between returns and consumption is very similar to the correlation between dividends and consumption—a low number. This result distinguishes our approach from consumption-based habit formation models of the stock market such as Campbell and Cochrane (1999). In those models, changes in risk aversion are caused by changes in consumption levels. This makes it inevitable that returns will be significantly correlated with consumption shocks, in contrast to what we find in the data.

---

[22] This is a feature that is unique to Economy II, which allows for a meaningful distinction between consumption and dividends.

Another well-known difficulty with consumption-based models is that attempts to make them match features of the stock market often lead to counterfactual predictions for the risk-free rate. For example, these models typically explain the equity premium with a high curvature γ of utility over consumption. However, this high γ also leads to a strong desire to smooth consumption intertemporally, generating high interest rates. Furthermore, the habit formation feature that many consumption-based models use to explain stock market volatility can also make interest rates counterfactually volatile.[23]

In our framework we use loss aversion over financial wealth fluctuations rather than a high curvature of utility over consumption to explain the equity premium. We do not therefore generate a counterfactually high interest rate. Moreover, since changes in risk aversion are driven by past stock market performance rather than by consumption, we can maintain a stable, indeed constant interest rate.

One feature that our model does share with consumption-based models like that of Campbell and Cochrane (1999) is contrarian expectations on the part of investors. Since stock prices in these models are high when investors are less risk averse, these are also times when investor require—and expect—lower returns than on average.

Durell (1999) has examined investor expectations about future stock market behavior and found evidence of extrapolative, rather than contrarian expectations. In other words, some investors appear to expect higher than average returns precisely at market peaks. Shiller (1999) presents results of a survey of investor expectations over the course of the U.S. bull market of the late 1990s. He finds no evidence of extrapolative expectations; but neither does he find evidence of contrarian expectations. It is not clear whether the samples used by Durell and Shiller are representative of the investing population, but they do suggest that the story in this chapter—or indeed the consumption-based story—may not be a complete description of the facts.

D. A Note on Aggregation

The equilibrium pricing equations in subsections 4.A and 4.B are derived under the assumption that the investors in our economy are completely homogeneous. This is certainly a strong assumption. Investors may be heterogeneous along numerous dimensions, which raises the question of whether the intuition of our model still goes through once investor heterogeneity is recognized. For any particular form of heterogeneity, we need to check that

---

[23] Campbell and Cochrane's paper (1999) is perhaps the only consumption-based model that avoids problems with the risk-free rate. A clever choice of functional form for the habit level over consumption enables them to use precautionary saving to counterbalance the strong desire to smooth consumption intertemporally.

loss aversion remains in the aggregate and, moreover, that aggregate loss aversion still varies with prior stock market movements. If these two elements are still present, our model should still be able to generate a high premium, volatility, and predictability.

One form of heterogeneity does aggregate satisfactorily: this is the case where investors have different wealth levels, but identical wealth to income ratios. We can model this by having several cohorts of investors, each cohort containing a continuum of equally wealthy investors. Since wealth is not a nontrivial state variable, all our results go through.[24]

There is reason to hope that our intuition will also survive other forms of heterogeneity. For example, it is possible that investors differ in the extent of their prior gains or losses, perhaps because they entered the stock market at different times. In other words, investors may have different z_ts.

Note that even if z_t varies across investors, each individual investor is still more sensitive to losses than to gains, and there is no reason to believe that this will be lost in the aggregate. Hence there is no reason to think that the equity premium will be much reduced in the presence of this kind of heterogeneity. Furthermore, if the stock market experiences a sustained rise, this will increase prior gains for most investors, making them less risk averse. Therefore, it is very reasonable to think that risk aversion will also fall in the aggregate. If aggregate loss aversion still varies over time, our model should still be able to generate substantial volatility and predictability.

5. NUMERICAL RESULTS AND FURTHER DISCUSSION

In this section we present price/dividend ratios $f(z_t)$ that solve equations (24) and (34). We then create a long time series of simulated data and use it to compute various moments of asset returns which can be compared with historical numbers. We do this for both economies described in section 4: Economy I, where stocks are modeled as a claim to the consumption stream; and the more realistic Economy II where stocks are a claim to dividends, which are no longer the same as consumption.

A. Parameter Values

Table 7.1 summarizes our choice of parameter values for Economy I. For g_C and σ_C, the mean and standard deviation of log consumption growth, we follow Cecchetti, Lam, and Mark (1990) who obtain $g_C = 1.84$ percent and $\sigma_C = 3.79$ percent from a time series of annual data from 1889 to 1985.

---

[24] The only subtlety is that since aggregate consumption $\bar{C}_t$ enters preferences, we need to assume that people use the average consumption of a reference group of people with identical wealth to set C_t, rather than average consumption in the economy as a whole.

TABLE 7.1
Parameter Values for Economy I

Parameter	
g_C	1.84%
σ_C	3.79%
γ	1.0
ρ	0.98
λ	2.25
k	(range)
b_0	(range)
η	0.9

These numbers are very similar to those used by Mehra and Prescott (1985) and Constantinides (1990).

The investor's preference parameters are γ, ρ, λ, k, and b_0. We choose the curvature γ of utility over consumption and the time discount factor ρ so as to produce a sensibly low value for the risk-free rate. Given the values of g_C and σ_C, Eq. (23) shows that $\gamma = 1.0$ and $\rho = 0.98$ bring the risk-free interest rate close to $R_f - 1 = 3.86$ percent.

The value of λ determines how keenly losses are felt relative to gains in the case where the investor has no prior gains or losses. This is the case that is most frequently studied in the experimental literature: Tversky and Kahneman (1992) estimate $\lambda = 2.25$ by offering subjects isolated gambles, and we use this value.

The parameter k determines how much more painful losses are when they come on the heels of other losses. It is an important determinant of the investor's *average* degree of loss aversion over time. In the results that we present, we pick k in two different ways. Our first approach is to choose k so as to make the investor's average loss aversion close to 2.25, where average loss aversion is computed in a way that we make precise in the Appendix. After prior gains, the investor does not fear losses very much, so his effective loss aversion is less than 2.25; after prior losses, he is all the more sensitive to additional losses, so his effective loss aversion is higher than 2.25, to a degree governed by k. We find that choosing $k = 3$ keeps average loss aversion close to 2.25. To understand what a k of 3 means, suppose that the state variable z_t is initially equal to 1, and that the stock market then experiences a sharp fall of 10 percent. From equation (10) with $\eta = 1$, this means that z_t increases by approximately 0.1, to 1.1. From (8), any additional losses will now penalized at $2.25 + 3(0.1) = 2.55$, a slightly more severe penalty.

Our second approach to picking k is to go to the data for guidance: we simply look for values of k that bring the predicted equity premium close to its empirical value.

The parameter b_0 determines the relative importance of the prospect utility term in the investor's preferences. We do not have strong priors about what constitutes a reasonable value for b_0 and so present results for a range of values.[25]

The two final parameters, η and $\overline{R}$, arise in the definition of the state variable dynamics. $\overline{R}$ is not a parameter we have any control over: it is completely determined by the other parameters *and* the requirement that the equilibrium median value of z_t be equal to one. The variable η controls the persistence of z_t and hence also the persistence of the price/dividend ratio. We find that an η of 0.9 brings the autocorrelation of the price/dividend ratio that we generate close to its empirical value.

B. Methodology

Before presenting our results, we briefly describe the way they were obtained. The identical technique is used for both Economy I and II, so we describe it only for the case of Economy I. The difficulty in solving equation (24) comes from the fact that z_{t+1} is a function of both ϵ_{t+1} and $f(\cdot)$. In economic terms, our state variable is endogenous: it tracks prior gains and losses, which depend on past returns, themselves endogenous. Equation (24) is therefore self-referential and needs to be solved in conjunction with

$$z_{t+1} = \eta \left(z_t \frac{\overline{R}}{R_{t+1}} \right) + (1 - \eta)(1), \qquad (35)$$

and

$$R_{t+1} = \frac{1 + f(z_{t+1})}{f(z_t)} e^{g_C + \sigma_C \epsilon_{t+1}}. \qquad (36)$$

We use the following technique. We start out by guessing a solution to (24), $f^{(0)}$ say. We then construct a function $h^{(0)}$ so that $z_{t+1} = h^{(0)}(z_t, \epsilon_{t+1})$ solves equations (35) and (36) for this $f = f^{(0)}$. The function $h^{(0)}$ determines the distribution of z_{t+1} conditional on z_t.

Given the function $h^{(0)}$, we get a new candidate solution $f^{(1)}$ through the following recursion:

$$1 = \rho E_t \left[\frac{1 + f^{(i)}(z_{t+1})}{f^{(i+1)}(z_t)} e^{(1-\gamma)(g_C + \sigma_C \epsilon_{t+1})} \right. $$
$$\left. + b_0 \rho E_t \left[\hat{v} \left(\frac{1 + f^{(i)}(z_{t+1})}{f^{(i+1)}(z_t)} e^{g_C + \sigma_C \epsilon_{t+1}}, z_t \right) \right], \forall z_t. \qquad (37)$$

---

[25] One way to think about b_0 is to compare the disutility of losing a dollar in the stock market with the disutility of having to consume a dollar less. When computed at equilibrium, the ratio of these two quantities equals $b_0 \rho \lambda$. By plugging numbers into this expression, we can see how b_0 controls the relative importance of consumption utility and nonconsumption utility.

With $f^{(1)}$ in hand, we can calculate a new $h = h^{(1)}$ that solves equations (35) and (36) for $f = f^{(1)}$. This $h^{(1)}$ gives us a new candidate $f = f^{(2)}$ from (37). We continue this process until convergence occurs: $f^{(i)} \rightarrow f$, and $h^{(i)} \rightarrow h$.

C. Stock Prices in Economy I

Figure 7.3 presents price/dividend ratios $f(z_t)$ that solve equation (24) for three different values of b_0: 0.7, 2, and 100, and with k fixed at 3. Note that $f(z_t)$ is a decreasing function of z_t in all cases. The intuition for this is straightforward: a low value of z_t means that recent returns on the asset have been high, giving the investor a reserve of prior gains. These gains cushion subsequent losses, making the investor less risk averse. He therefore discounts future dividends at a lower rate, raising the price/dividend ratio. Conversely, a high value of z_t means that the investor has recently experienced a spate of painful losses; he is now especially sensitive to further losses, which makes him more risk averse and leads to lower price/dividend ratios.

Figure 7.3 by itself does not tell us the range of price/dividend ratios we are likely to see in equilibrium. For that, we need to know the equilibrium distribution of the state variable z_t. Figure 7.4 shows this distribution for

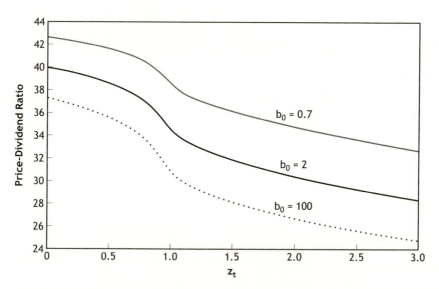

Figure 7.3. Price-dividend ratios in Economy I. The price-dividend ratios are plotted against z_t, which measures prior gains and losses: a low z_t indicates prior gains. The parameter b_0 controls how much the investor cares about financial wealth fluctuations. We fix the parameter k at 3, bringing average loss aversion close to 2.25 in all cases.

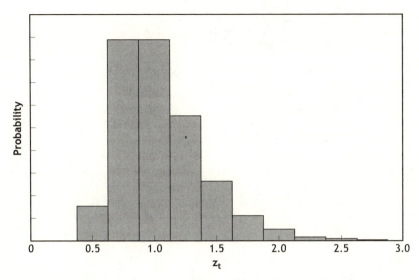

Figure 7.4. Distribution of the state variable z_t. The distribution is based on Economy I with $b_0 = 2$ and $k = 3$.

one case that we will consider in more detail later: $b_0 = 2$, $k = 3$. To obtain it, we draw a long time series $\{\epsilon_t\}_{t=1}^{50,000}$ of 50,000 independent draws from the standard normal distribution and starting with $z_0 = 1$, use the function $z_{t+1} = h(z_t, \epsilon_{t+1})$ described in subsection V.B to generate a time series for z_t. Note from the graph that the average z_t is close to one, and this is no accident. The value of $\overline{R}$ in equation (10) is chosen precisely to make the median value of z_t as close to one as possible.

As we generate the time series for z_t period by period, we also compute the returns along the way using equation (20). We now present sample moments computed from these simulated returns. The time series is long enough that sample moments should serve as good approximations to population moments.

Table 7.2 presents the important moments of stock returns for different values of b_0 and k. In the top panel, we vary b_0 and set k to 3, which keeps average loss aversion over time close to 2.25. At one extreme we have $b_0 = 0$, the classic case considered by Mehra and Prescott (1985). As we push b_0 up, the asset return moments eventually reach a limit that is well approximated with a b_0 of 100. The table also reports the investor's average loss aversion, calculated in the way described in the Appendix.

Note that as we raise b_0 while keeping k fixed, the equity premium goes up. There are two forces at work here. As b_0 gets larger, prior outcomes affect the investor more, causing his risk aversion to vary more, and hence generating more volatile stock returns. Moreover, as b_0 grows, loss aversion becomes a more important feature of the investor's preferences, pushing up

TABLE 7.2
Asset Returns in Economy I

	$b_0 = 0$	$b_0 = 0.7$ $k = 3$	$b_0 = 2$ $k = 3$	$b_0 = 100$ $k = 3$	Empirical Value
Log risk-free rate	3.79	3.79	3.79	3.79	0.58
Log excess stock return					
Mean	0.07	0.63	0.88	1.26	6.03
Standard deviation	3.79	4.77	5.17	5.62	20.02
Sharpe ratio	0.02	0.13	0.17	0.22	0.3
Average loss aversion		2.25	2.25	2.25	

	$b_0 = 0.7$ $k = 150$	$b_0 = 2$ $k = 100$	$b_0 = 100$ $k = 50$
Log risk-free rate	3.79	3.79	3.79
Log excess stock return			
Mean	3.50	3.66	3.28
Standard deviation	10.43	10.22	9.35
Sharpe ratio	0.34	0.36	0.35
Average loss aversion	10.7	7.5	4.4

Moments of asset returns are expressed as annual percentages. Empirical values are based on Treasury Bill and NYSE data from 1926–1995. The parameter b_0 controls how much the investor cares about financial wealth fluctuations, while k controls the increase in loss aversion after a prior loss.

the Sharpe ratio. The higher volatility and higher Sharpe ratio combine to raise the equity premium.

Although the results in table 7.2 are encouraging from a qualitative standpoint, the magnitudes are not impressive. Changes in risk aversion do give returns a volatility higher than the 3.79 percent volatility assumed for dividend growth, but this effect is not nearly large enough to match historical volatility. Since the investor does not observe any particularly large market crashes, he does not charge a particularly high equity premium either. The highest equity premium we can possibly generate for this value of k is 1.28 percent.

The bottom panel of table 7.2 shows that we can come closer to matching the historical equity premium by increasing the value of k. Since the investor is now extremely loss averse in some states of the world, average loss aversion also climbs steeply. Note, however, that return volatility here is still far too low.

An unrealistic feature of Economy I is that consumption and dividends are constrained to follow the same process. This means that we are modeling stocks as a claim to a very smooth consumption stream, rather than as what they really are, namely a claim to a far more volatile dividend stream. We therefore turn to Economy II which allows us to relax this constraint.

D. Stock Prices in Economy II

We now calculate stock prices in a more general economy where consumption and dividends are modeled as distinct processes. Table 7.3 presents our choice of parameters in this economy. To make comparison easier, we also show the parameters used for Economy I alongside.

Allowing consumption and dividends to follow different processes introduces three new parameters: g_D, the mean dividend growth rate; σ_D, the volatility of dividend growth; and ω, the correlation of shocks to dividend growth and consumption growth. For simplicity, we set $g_D = g_C = 0.0184$. Using NYSE data from 1926–1995 from CRSP, we find $\sigma_D = 0.12$. Campbell (2000) estimates ω in a time series of U.S. data spanning the past century, and based on his results, we set $\omega = 0.15$. As the table shows, we keep all other parameters fixed at the values discussed in subsection 5.A.

Figure 7.5 presents price/dividend ratios that solve equation (34) for three different values of b_0: 0.7, 2, and 100, with k fixed at 3. Unconditional moments of stock returns are shown in table 7.4 for various values of b_0 and k. The top panel keeps k fixed at 3, bringing the average degree of loss aversion close to 2.25. A quick comparison with table 7.2 shows that separating consumption and dividends improves the results significantly. The volatility of returns is now much higher than what we obtained in Economy I because dividend growth volatility is now 12 percent rather than just 3.79 percent. The equity premium is also much higher: the investor now sees far more severe downturns in the stock market and charges a much larger premium as compensation.

TABLE 7.3
Parameter Values for Economy II

Parameter	Economy II	Economy I
g_C	1.84%	1.84%
g_D	1.84%	—
σ_C	3.79%	3.79%
σ_D	12.0%	—
ω	0.15	—
γ	1.0	1.0
ρ	0.98	0.98
λ	2.25	2.25
k	(range)	(range)
b_0	(range)	(range)
η	0.9	0.9

The parameter values used for Economy I and shown in table 7.1 are repeated here for ease of comparison.

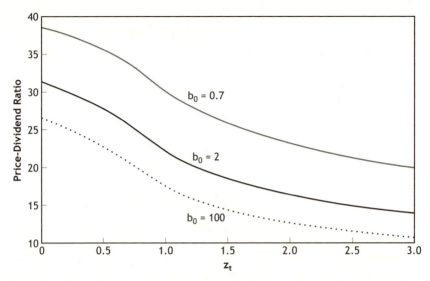

Figure 7.5. Price-dividend ratios in Economy II. The price-dividend ratios are plotted against z_t, which measures prior gains and losses: a low z_t indicates prior gains. The parameter b_0 controls how much the investor cares about financial wealth fluctuations. We fix the parameter k at 3, bringing average loss aversion close to 2.25 in all cases.

Modeling consumption and dividends separately also leads to higher re-turn volatility in consumption-based models such as that of Campbell and Cochrane (1999). However, the fact that the equity premium goes up is unique to our model: as Campbell and Cochrane demonstrate, separating consumption and dividends has no *effect* on the equity premium in a consumption-based model. The reason is that in a consumption-based model, the canonical measure of a stock's risk is its covariance with con-sumption growth. By separating consumption and dividends, the volatility of stock returns goes up, but the correlation of stock returns with consump-tion goes down, since dividends are poorly correlated with consumption. Overall, the covariance with consumption remains unaffected, and the eq-uity premium remains as hard to explain as before.

The investor in our model cares not only about consumption but also about fluctuations in the value of his investments. An increase in dividend volatility makes stocks more volatile, scaring the investor into charging a higher equity premium. It is true that stocks are now less correlated with consumption, but this does not matter in our model, since the investor cares about fluctuations in the stock market per se, not merely about how those fluctuations covary with consumption growth.

Table 7.4 confirms that stock returns are only weakly correlated with con-sumption growth in our model. As discussed earlier, this prediction is unique to our framework: since consumption-based models ascribe a significant

TABLE 7.4
Asset Prices and Returns in Economy II

	$b_0 = 0$	$b_0 = 0.7$ $k = 3$	$b_0 = 2$ $k = 3$	$b_0 = 100$ $k = 3$	Empirical Value
Log risk-free rate	3.79	3.79	3.79	3.79	0.58
Log excess stock return					
Mean	−0.65	1.3	2.62	3.68	6.03
Standard deviation	12.0	17.39	20.87	20.47	20.02
Sharpe ratio	−0.05	0.07	0.13	0.18	0.3
Correlation w/consumption growth	0.15	0.15	0.15	0.15	0.1
Price-dividend ratio					
Mean	76.6	29.8	22.1	17.5	25.5
Standard deviation	0	2.9	2.7	2.4	7.1
Average loss aversion		2.25	2.25	2.25	

	$b_0 = 0.7$ $k = 20$	$b_0 = 2$ $k = 10$	$b_0 = 100$ $k = 8$
Log risk-free rate	3.79	3.79	3.79
Log excess stock return			
Mean	5.17	5.02	5.88
Standard deviation	25.85	23.84	24.04
Sharpe ratio	0.2	0.21	0.24
Correlation w/consumption growth	0.15	0.15	0.15
Price-dividend ratio			
Mean	14.0	14.6	12.7
Standard deviation	2.6	2.5	2.2
Average loss aversion	5.8	3.5	3.2

Moments of asset returns are expressed as annual percentages. Empirical values are based on Treasury Bill and NYSE data from 1926–1995. The parameter b_0 controls how much the investor cares about financial wealth fluctuations, while k controls the increase in loss aversion after a prior loss.

fraction of price volatility to changes in consumption, stock returns are inevitably highly correlated with consumption growth.

We also report the mean and standard deviation of the simulated price/dividend ratio. It is striking that while we *are* successful at matching the volatility of returns, we significantly underpredict the volatility of the price/dividend ratio. To understand how this can be, it is helpful to consider the following approximate relationship, derived by Campbell, Lo, and MacKinlay (1997) with the help of a log-linear approximation:[26]

$$r_{t+1} \approx A + \log f_{t+1} - \log f_t + \sigma_D \epsilon_{t+1}.$$

[26] More specifically, this follows from equation 7.1.19 in chapter 7 of the book.

In words, up to a constant A, the log return r_{t+1} is approximately equal to the change in the log price/dividend ratio plus the innovation to dividend growth $\sigma_D \epsilon_{t+1}$. This gives

$$\text{var}(r_{t+1}) \approx \text{var}\left(\log\frac{f_{t+1}}{f_t}\right) + \sigma_D^2 + 2\,\text{cov}\left(\log\frac{f_{t+1}}{f_t}, \sigma_D\epsilon_{t+1}\right).$$

Our simulated price/dividend ratio is not sufficiently volatile, making $\text{var}(\log(f_{t+1}/f_t))$ too low in our model relative to what it is in the data. The reason we are still able to match the volatility of returns $\text{var}(r_{t+1})$ is that $\text{cov}(\log(f_{t+1}/f_t), \sigma_D\epsilon_{t+1})$ is too *high* in our model relative to what it is in the data: in our framework, changes in price/dividend ratios are perfectly conditionally correlated with dividend shocks.

Since our model relies on only one factor to generate movement in the price/dividend ratio, it is not surprising that we underpredict its volatility. In a more realistic model, other factors will also affect the price/dividend ratio: consumption relative to habit is one possible factor suggested by the habit formation literature. Adding such factors will increase the volatility of the price/dividend ratio and decrease its correlation with dividend shocks, improving the model's fit with the data. It is worth emphasizing, though, that a *purely* consumption-based approach will not fare well, since it will predict that changes in price/dividend ratios are perfectly conditionally correlated with consumption shocks, and that returns are highly correlated with consumption. A model that merges habit formation over consumption with a direct concern about financial wealth fluctuations may be much more fruitful.

The bottom panel in table 7.4 shows that we can significantly improve our results by increasing k, which increases investors' loss aversion after prior losses. In Economy I, we had to make the investor extraordinarily loss averse in some states of the world to even come close to matching the equity premium. Interestingly, the increases in k we need now are much more modest. For $b_0 = 2$, for example, a k of 10 is enough to give a premium of 5.02 percent and a volatility of 23.84 percent; note also that this corresponds to an average loss aversion of only 3.5; this is not a small level of risk aversion, but neither is it extreme.

Figure 7.6 presents some additional results of interest. The left panel plots the conditional expected stock return as a function of z_t, obtained by numerically integrating the return equation (32) over the conditional distribution of z_{t+1} given by $z_{t+1} = h(z_t, \epsilon_{t+1})$. The value of b_0 here is 2 and k is 3. The conditional expected return is an increasing function of the state variable. Low values of z_t mean that the investor has accumulated prior gains that will cushion future losses. He is therefore less risk averse, leading to a lower expected return in equilibrium. The dashed line shows the level of the constant risk-free rate for comparison.

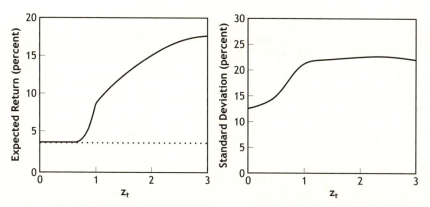

Figure 7.6. Conditional moments of stock returns. The conditional stock return mean and volatility are plotted against z_t, which measures prior gains and losses: a low z_t, indicates prior gains. The results are for Economy II with $b_0 = 2$ and $k = 3$. The dotted line in the left-hand panel indicates the level of the risk-free rate.

The right panel in figure 7.6 graphs the conditional volatility of returns as a function of the state variable. Since much of the return volatility in our model is generated by changing risk aversion, the conditional volatility in any state depends on how sensitive the investor's risk aversion in that state is to dividend shocks. Empirically, volatility has been found to be higher after market crashes than booms, which in our context would mean an upward sloping conditional volatility curve. For much of the range of the state variable, this is exactly what we find. However, this result is sensitive to how we make the degree of loss aversion depend on prior outcomes, so we do not attach too much weight to it.

Table 7.5 presents autocorrelations of log returns and of the price/dividend ratio. As expected, our model produces negatively autocorrelated returns at all lags: high prices lower risk aversion and lead to lower returns on average. These negative autocorrelations imply long horizon mean reversion of the kind documented by Poterba and Summers (1988) and Fama and French (1988a). Moreover, the price/dividend ratio is highly autocorrelated in our model, closely matching its actual behavior.

Since the investor's risk aversion changes over time, expected returns also vary, and hence returns are predictable. To demonstrate this, we use our simulated data to run regressions of cumulative log returns over a j-year horizon on the lagged dividend/price ratio for $j = 1, 2, 3$, and 4:

$$r_{t+1} + r_{t+2} + \cdots + r_{t+j} = \alpha_j + \beta_j (D_t/P_t) + \epsilon_{j,t}. \qquad (38)$$

where r_t is the log return. Table 7.6 presents the slope coefficients β_j and $R^2(j)$ obtained from our simulated data alongside the empirical values. Note that our simulated results capture the main features of the empirical findings, including an R^2 that increases with the return horizon.

TABLE 7.5

Autocorrelations of Log Returns and Price-Dividend Ratios in Economy II

	$b_0 = 2$ $k = 3$	$b_0 = 2$ $k = 10$	Empirical Value
corr(r_t, r_{t-j})			
$j = 1$	−0.07	−0.12	0.07
$j = 2$	−0.05	−0.09	−0.17
$j = 3$	−0.04	−0.06	−0.05
$j = 4$	−0.04	−0.04	−0.11
$j = 5$	−0.02	−0.03	−0.04
corr($(P/D)_t, (P/D)_{t-j}$)			
$j = 1$	0.81	0.72	0.70
$j = 2$	0.66	0.52	0.50
$j = 3$	0.53	0.38	0.45
$j = 4$	0.43	0.28	0.43
$j = 5$	0.35	0.20	0.40

Empirical values are based on NYSE data from 1926–1995.

E. Sensitivity Analysis

We now analyze the sensitivity of our results to various parameters of interest. For each parameter that we vary, the other parameters are kept fixed at the values given in table 7.3.

Table 7.7 shows the effect of varying k, which governs how much loss aversion goes up after prior losses. Raising k has a large effect on the equity premium since it raises average loss aversion. It also raises volatility somewhat because a higher k means more rapid *changes* in risk aversion.

TABLE 7.6

Return Predictability Regressions in Economy II

$\beta_j, R^2(j)$	$b_0 = 2$ $k = 3$	$b_0 = 2$ $k = 10$	Empirical Value
β_1	4.6	4.4	4.2
β_2	8.3	7.5	8.7
β_3	11.6	9.7	12.1
β_4	13.7	11.5	15.9
$R^2(1)$	2%	6%	7%
$R^2(2)$	4%	10%	16%
$R^2(3)$	5%	12%	22%
$R^2(4)$	6%	14%	30%

Coefficients and R^2 in regressions of j-year cumulative log returns on the lagged dividend-price ratio, $r_{t+1} + r_{t+2} + \cdots + r_{t+j} = \alpha_j + \beta_j(D_t/P_t) + \epsilon_{j,t}$. Empirical values are based on annual NYSE data from 1926–1995.

TABLE 7.7
Sensitivity of Asset Returns to k

	$k = 3$	$k = 5$	$k = 10$	Empirical Value
Log excess stock return				
Mean	2.62	3.15	5.02	6.03
Standard deviation	20.87	20.93	23.84	20.02
Sharpe ratio	0.13	0.15	0.21	0.3
Average loss aversion	2.25	2.6	3.5	

The parameter k controls how much loss aversion increases after a prior loss. Moments of asset returns are expressed as annual percentages. The results are for Economy II with $b_0 = 2$; other parameters are fixed at the values in table 7.3.

Throughout our analysis we have fixed λ at 2.25 since many independent experimental studies have estimated it at around this level. Table 7.8 shows how the results change as we vary λ. An increase in λ raises the equity premium because average loss aversion is now higher.

Table 7.9 examines the effect of varying η. This parameter determines how far into the future the investor will be affected by a substantial gain or loss this year. The primary effect of η is on volatility: if η is high, a loss this year will make the investor more loss averse for many years to come, leading him to discount cash flows at a higher rate many years into the future, and causing a more dramatic price drop today. More directly, η affects the persistence of the state variable and hence the autocorrelation of the price/dividend ratio.

So far in our analysis, we have taken the length of the period over which the investor evaluates gains and losses to be one year. Table 7.10 analyzes the effect of changing this. It shows that the length of the evaluation period mainly affects the equity premium: if the investor evaluates more frequently, he is more likely to experience losses, and since he is averse to losses, he will charge a higher premium.

TABLE 7.8
Sensitivity of Asset Returns to λ

	$\lambda = 1.5$	$\lambda = 2.25$	$\lambda = 3$	Empirical Value
Log excess stock return				
Mean	3.8	5.02	5.6	6.03
Standard deviation	25.68	23.84	23.21	20.02
Sharpe ratio	0.15	0.21	0.24	0.3
Average loss aversion	3.2	3.5	3.9	

The parameter λ controls the investor's loss aversion. Moments of asset returns are expressed as annual percentages. The results are for Economy II with $b_0 = 2$ and $k = 10$; other parameters are fixed at the values in table 7.3.

TABLE 7.9
Sensitivity of Asset Returns to η

	$\eta = 1$	$\eta = 0.9$	$\eta = 0.8$	Empirical Value
Log excess stock return				
Mean	7.68	5.02	3.91	6.03
Standard deviation	34.54	23.84	19.12	20.02
Sharpe ratio	0.22	0.21	0.2	0.3
Autocorrelation of price/				
dividend ratio	0.81	0.72	0.65	0.7
Average loss aversion	4.5	3.5	3.0	

The parameter η governs how long-lasting the effects of prior gains and losses are. Moments of asset returns are expressed as annual percentages. The results are for Economy II with $b_0 = 2$ and $k = 10$; other parameters are fixed at the values in table 7.3.

As described in section 2, we suppose that the investor uses the risk-free rate as a reference level when calculating gains and losses. Table 7.11 studies the sensitivity of our results to that assumption. Given the parameter values in table 7.3, the risk-free rate is $R_f - 1 = 3.86$ percent. The table shows the effect of using a reference level that is one or two percentage points lower than this. Note that the equity premium falls as we use a lower reference level: a lower reference point means that the investor is less likely to code stock market movements as losses, and hence less inclined to charge a high premium for holding stocks.

6. The Importance of Prior Outcomes

The model in section 2 makes use of both loss aversion and the effect of prior outcomes to match asset prices. The reader may wonder whether both these

TABLE 7.10
Sensitivity of Asset Returns to the Evaluation Period

	6 months	1 year	2 years	Empirical Value
Log excess stock return				
Mean	7.63	5.02	2.85	6.03
Standard deviation	27.78	23.84	20.15	20.02
Sharpe ratio	0.27	0.21	0.14	0.3
Average loss aversion	3.5	3.5	3.6	

The evaluation period is the length of time over which the investor measures his gains and losses. Moments of asset returns are expressed as annual percentages. The results are for Economy II with $b_0 = 2$ and $k = 10$; other parameters are fixed at the values in table 7.3.

TABLE 7.11
Sensitivity of Asset Returns to the Reference Level

	0%	−1%	−2%	*Empirical Value*
Log excess stock return				
Mean	5.02	4.11	3.43	6.03
Standard deviation	23.84	24.25	25.20	20.02
Sharpe ratio	0.21	0.17	0.14	0.3
Average loss aversion	3.5	3.5	3.7	

A "0%" reference level means that the investor compares the stock return with the risk-free rate when measuring gains and losses. "−1%" means a reference level one percent lower than the risk-free rate. Moments of asset returns are expressed as annual percentages. The results are for Economy II with $b_0 = 2$ and $k = 10$; other parameters are fixed at the values in table 7.3.

ingredients are truly necessary. After all, Benartzi and Thaler (1995) show that a loss-averse investor is very reluctant to allocate much of his portfolio to stocks even when faced with the large historical equity premium. This suggests that perhaps an equilibrium model with loss aversion *alone* would be enough to understand the data. Is it really necessary to incorporate the effect of prior outcomes?

We answer this by examining the predictions of a version of the model of section 2 which ignores the effect of prior outcomes. In particular, we make the utility v of a gain or loss a function of the gain or loss X_{t+1} *alone*, and remove the dependence on the state variable z_t. In this model, the degree of loss aversion is the same in all circumstances, regardless of the investor's prior investment performance.

More formally, the investor chooses consumption C_t and an allocation to the risky asset S_t to maximize

$$E\left[\sum_{t=0}^{\infty}\left(\rho^t \frac{C_t^{1-\gamma}}{1-\gamma} + b_t \rho^{t+1} v(X_{t+1})\right)\right], \qquad (39)$$

subject to the standard budget constraint, where

$$X_{t+1} = S_t R_{t+1} - S_t R_{f,t}, \qquad (40)$$

and

$$v(X_{t+1}) = \begin{cases} X_{t+1} \\ \lambda X_{t+1} \end{cases} \quad \text{for} \quad \begin{array}{l} X_{t+1} \geq 0 \\ X_{t+1} < 0. \end{array} \qquad (41)$$

The next proposition presents the equations that govern equilibrium prices in an economy like Economy II where consumption and dividends are separated out. We show that there is an equilibrium in which the risk-free rate and the stock's price/dividend ratio are both constant and stock returns are i.i.d.

Proposition 3. For the preferences given by (39)–(41), there exists an equilibrium in which the gross risk-free interest rate is constant at

$$R_f = \rho^{-1} e^{\gamma g_C - \gamma^2 \sigma_C^2/2}, \tag{42}$$

and the stock's price/dividend ratio, f_t, is constant at f and given by

$$
\begin{aligned}
1 = \rho e^{g_D - \gamma g_C + \gamma^2 \sigma_C^2 (1-\omega^2)/2} \frac{1+f}{f} \, \mathrm{E}_t[e^{(\sigma_D - \gamma\omega\sigma_C)\epsilon_{t+1}}] \\
+ b_0 \rho \, \mathrm{E}_t\left[\hat{v}\left(\frac{1+f}{f} e^{g_D + \sigma_D \epsilon_{t+1}} \right) \right],
\end{aligned} \tag{43}
$$

where

$$
\hat{v}(R_{t+1}) = \begin{cases} R_{t+1} - R_{f,t} \\ \lambda(R_{t+1} - R_{f,t}) \end{cases} \quad \text{for} \quad \begin{matrix} R_{t+1} \geq R_{f,t} \\ R_{t+1} < R_{f,t}. \end{matrix} \tag{44}
$$

That returns are i.i.d. is a direct consequence of the fact that the price/dividend ratio is constant. To see this, note that the stock return is related to the stock's price/dividend ratio, denoted by $f_t \equiv P_t/D_t$, as follows:

$$R_{t+1} = \frac{P_{t+1} + D_{t+1}}{P_t} = \frac{1 + P_{t+1}/D_{t+1}}{P_t/D_t} \frac{D_{t+1}}{D_t} = \frac{1+f_{t+1}}{f_t} \frac{D_{t+1}}{D_t}. \tag{45}$$

Given the assumption that the dividend growth is i.i.d. (see [1]), a constant price/dividend ratio $f_t = f$ implies that stock returns are i.i.d.

Table 7.12 summarizes our choices of parameter values. Many of the parameters of the earlier model now no longer play a role. The parameters that remain are g_C, g_D, σ_C, σ_D, γ, ρ, γ, and b_0, and we assign them exactly the same values as those chosen earlier. For comparison, we list the earlier parameters alongside.

Figure 7.7 presents the implied values of the price/dividend ratio and equity premium for different values of b_0 and table 7.13 reports unconditional moments of returns. By comparing the results in table 7.13 with those in the bottom panel of table 7.4, we can isolate the impact of prior outcomes.

Our results suggest that a model which relies on loss aversion alone cannot provide a complete description of aggregate stock market behavior.

TABLE 7.12
Parameter Values for a Model Where Prior Outcomes Have No Effect

Parameter	Section 6	Subsection 5.D
g_C	1.84%	1.84%
g_D	1.84%	1.84%
σ_C	3.79%	3.79%
σ_D	12.0%	12.0%
γ	1.0	1.0
ρ	0.98	0.98
λ	2.25	2.25
k	—	(range)
b_0	(range)	(range)
η	—	0.9

Parameter values used for Economy II in subsection 5.D are presented alongside for comparison.

The fundamental weakness of such a model comes in explaining volatility: the standard deviations of returns in table 7.13 are much lower than both the empirical value and the values in table 7.4. The reason for this failure is straightforward. Since

$$R_{t+1} = \frac{P_{t+1} + D_{t+1}}{P_t} = \frac{1 + f_{t+1}}{f_t} \frac{D_{t+1}}{D_t} = \frac{1 + f}{f} e^{g_D + \sigma_D \epsilon_{t+1}}, \qquad (46)$$

the volatility of log returns in this model is equal to the volatility of log dividend growth, namely 12 percent. This problem is not unique to the model

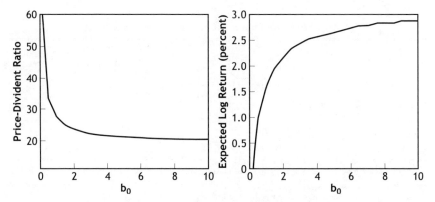

Figure 7.7. Stock prices and returns when prior outcomes have no effect. The price-dividend ratio and the equity premium are plotted against b_0, which controls how much the investor cares about financial wealth fluctuations.

of this section, but is shared by all consumption-based models with constant discount rates.[27]

The unrealistically low stock return volatility generated by the model also hampers its ability to explain the equity premium: the average stock returns in table 7.13 are considerably lower than the empirical value. Intuitively, even though our investor is loss averse, the stock market fluctuations are not large enough to scare him into demanding a high equity premium as compensation. More generally, our results show that loss aversion can be helpful in understanding the equity premium, but only in conjunction with a mechanism that makes stock returns more volatile than underlying cash flows. In our model, this mechanism is a changing degree of loss aversion, but it could also be based on changing perceptions of risk, or excessive extrapolation of cash flows into the future.

7. CONCLUSION

In this chapter we study asset prices in an economy where investors derive direct utility not only from consumption but also from fluctuations in the value of their financial wealth. They are loss averse over these fluctuations and how loss averse they are, depends on their prior investment performance.

Our main finding is that in such an economy, asset prices exhibit phenomena very similar to what has been observed in historical data. In particular, stock returns have a high mean, are excessively volatile, and are significantly predictable in the time series. They are also only weakly correlated with consumption growth.

The analysis in this chapter raises a number of questions for further investigation. For the sake of simplicity, we have studied an economy containing

TABLE 7.13
Asset Returns When Prior Outcomes Have No Effect

	$b_0 = 0$	$b_0 = 0.7$	$b_0 = 2$	$b_0 = 100$	Empirical Value
Log risk-free rate	3.79	3.79	3.79	3.79	0.58
Log excess stock return					
Mean	−0.65	1.30	2.17	2.88	6.03
Standard deviation	12.0	12.0	12.0	12.0	20.02
Sharpe ratio	−0.05	0.11	0.18	0.24	0.3

Moments of asset returns are expressed as annual percentages. Empirical values are based on Treasury Bill and NYSE data from 1926–1995. The parameter b_0 controls how much the investor cares about financial wealth fluctuations.

[27] This category includes papers that use first-order risk-aversion, such as Epstein and Zin (1990). See Campbell (2000) for a discussion of this issue.

a single risky asset. In a more realistic economy with many risky assets, it is not immediately clear what investors are loss averse about: do they feel loss averse over changes in the value of individual securities that they own, or only over portfolio fluctuations? In essence, this is a question about how people summarize and think about their investment performance, or about how they do their "mental accounting," in the language of psychology. How mental accounting affects asset prices is as yet an unexplored topic.

Another question that may warrant further study asks to what extent our preferences can explain not only financial data but also experimental evidence on attitudes to risky gambles. In order to explain the high equity premium, consumption-based models typically assume a high curvature of utility over consumption. As is well-known, this high curvature is consistent with attitudes to small-scale gambles, but unfortunately also predicts that people will reject extremely attractive large-scale gambles.[28] In our model, we do not use a high curvature of utility of consumption, and the loss aversion we assume is not far from that estimated from experimental evidence. This offers the intriguing possibility that preferences of the kind studied here may be able to reconcile attitudes to both large- and small-scale gambles with the empirical facts about stock returns.

[28] See, for example, Epstein and Zin (1990) and Kandel and Stambaugh (1991).

Appendix

Proof of Proposition 1. Proposition 1 is a special case of Proposition 2 with $Y_t = 0$ and $C_t = D_t$ for all t.

Proof of Proposition 2. We first show that if the risk-free interest rate is given by (33) and stock returns are determined by (18), (19), (32), and (34), then the strategy of consuming $C_t = \overline{C}_t = D_t + Y_t$ and holding the market supply of financial securities indeed satisfies the Euler equations of optimality (27) and (28). We then show that these Euler equations are necessary and sufficient conditions for optimality.

Given (29), the interest rate R_f in (33) satisfies the Euler equation (27). For Euler equation (28), note that z_{t+1} is determined only by z_t and ϵ_{t+1} through (18) and (32), so we have

$$
\begin{aligned}
\mathrm{E}_t\left[R_{t+1}\left(\frac{\overline{C}_{t+1}}{\overline{C}_t}\right)^{-\gamma}\right] &= \mathrm{E}_t\left[\frac{1+f(z_{t+1})}{f(z_t)}e^{g_D + \sigma_D\epsilon_{t+1}}e^{-\gamma(g_C + \sigma_C\eta_{t+1})}\right] \\
&= e^{g_D - \gamma g_C}\mathrm{E}_t\left[\mathrm{E}_t[e^{-\gamma\sigma_C\eta_{t+1}}|\epsilon_{t+1}]e^{\sigma_D\epsilon_{t+1}}\frac{1+f(z_{t+1})}{f(z_t)}\right] \\
&= e^{g_D - \gamma g_C + \gamma^2\sigma_c^2(1-\omega^2)/2}\mathrm{E}_t\left[\frac{1+f(z_{t+1})}{f(z_t)}e^{(\sigma_D - \gamma\omega\sigma_C)\epsilon_{t+1}}\right].
\end{aligned}
$$

Applying this, we find that the strategy of consuming $\overline{C}_t$ and holding the market securities indeed satisfies Euler equation (28).

Euler equations are necessary conditions for optimality. To prove that they are sufficient conditions as well, we apply a method used by Duffie and Skiadas [1994] and Constantinides and Duffie [1996].

To simplify notation, let $u_t(C_t) = \rho^t C_t^{1-\gamma}/(1-\gamma)$ and $\overline{b}_t = \rho^{t+1}b_t$. Assume that the strategy (C^*, S^*) satisfies the Euler equations,

$$
u_t'(C_t^*) = R_f\, \mathrm{E}_t[u_{t+1}'(C_{t+1}^*)], \tag{47}
$$

$$
u_t'(C_t^*) = \mathrm{E}_t[R_{t+1}u_{t+1}'(C_{t+1}^*)] + \overline{b}_t\mathrm{E}_t[\hat{v}(R_{t+1}, z_t)]. \tag{48}
$$

Consider any alternative strategy $(C^* + \delta C, S^* + \delta S)$ that satisfies the budget constraint

$$
\delta W_{t+1} = (\delta W_t - \delta C_t)R_f + \delta S_t(R_{t+1} - R_f). \tag{49}
$$

The increase in expected utility from using the alternative strategy is

$$E\left[\sum_{t=0}^{\infty}[u_t(C_t^* + \delta C_t) - u_t(C^*) + \overline{b}_t \delta S_t \hat{v}(R_{t+1}, z_t)]\right] \tag{50}$$

$$\leq \Delta(\delta C, \delta S) \equiv E\left[\sum_{t=0}^{\infty}[u_t'(C_t^*)\delta C_t + \overline{b}_t \delta S_t \hat{v}(R_{t+1}, z_t)]\right], \tag{51}$$

where we have made use of the concavity of $u_t(\cdot)$ and the linearity of the prospect utility term with respect to S_t. It is therefore enough to show that $\Delta(\delta C, \delta S) = 0$ under budget constraint (49).

Multiplying $u_{t+1}'(C_{t+1}^*)$ with (49) and applying Euler equations (47) and (48), we have

$$E_t[u_t'(C_t^*)\delta C_t + \overline{b}_t \delta S_t \hat{v}(R_{t+1}, z_t)] \tag{52}$$
$$= u_t'(C_t^*)\delta W_t - E_t[u_{t+1}'(C_{t+1}^*)\delta W_{t+1}].$$

Summing up (52) for all t and taking expectations, we have

$$\Delta(\delta C, \delta S) = u_0(C_0^*)\delta W_0 - \lim_{T\to\infty} E[u_T'(C_T^*)\delta W_T].$$

The budget constraint implies that $\delta W_0 = 0$. By requiring feasible strategies to use bounded units of financial securities, and with a unit of the risk-free security priced at one, we can show that the limiting term also goes to zero if our model parameters satisfy $\log \rho - \gamma g_C + g_D + 0.5(\gamma^2\sigma_C^2 - 2\gamma\omega\sigma_C\sigma_D + \sigma_D^2) < 0$, a condition which we already noted in footnote 21.[29] So $\Delta(\delta C, \delta S) = 0$ for any feasible alternative to (C^*, S^*).

We have thus shown that any other budget feasible strategy cannot increase utility. The Euler equations are therefore necessary and sufficient conditions of optimality.

Proof of Proposition 3. This is a special case of Proposition 1 with $\eta = 0$ and $z_t = 1$ for all t, which is in turn a special case of Proposition 2, proved above.

Computation of Average Loss Aversion. Many of the tables present the investor's average loss aversion over time. There is only one difficulty in computing this quantity: when $z_t < 1$—in other words, when the investor has prior gains—part of any subsequent loss is penalized at a rate of one, and part of it is penalized at a rate of 2.25. Therefore, it is not obvious what single number should be used to describe the investor's loss aversion

---

[29] The proof of this last step is available upon request.

in this case. When $z_t \geq 1$, there is no such problem because losses are penalized at a single rate: 2.25 for $z_t = 1$, and higher than 2.25 for $z_t > 1$.

We adopt the following technique for dealing with the case of $z_t \leq 1$: we take the loss aversion component of the investor's utility, namely

$$v(X_{t+1}, S_t, z_t) = \begin{cases} S_t R_{t+1} - S_t R_{f,t} & R_{t+1} \geq z_t R_{f,t} \\ S_t(z_t R_{f,t} - R_{f,t}) + \lambda S_t(R_{t+1} - z_t R_{f,t}) & R_{t+1} < z_t R_{f,t}, \end{cases} \text{ for}$$

and for $S_t = 1$ and a risk-free rate of $R_{f,t} = 3.86$ percent, we compute $E(v)$, the expected loss aversion when the excess stock return is distributed as

$$\log R_{t+1} - \log R_f \sim N(0.06, 0.2^2),$$

a good approximation to the historical distribution of the excess stock return. We then compute the quantity $\bar{\lambda}$ for which an investor with utility function

$$\bar{v}(X_{t+1}, S_t) = \begin{cases} S_t(R_{t+1} - R_{f,t}) & R_{t+1} \geq R_{f,t} \\ \bar{\lambda} S_t(R_{t+1} - R_{f,t}) & R_{t+1} < R_{f,t} \end{cases} \text{ for}$$

would have exactly the same expected loss aversion for this distribution of the excess stock return, again with $S_t = 1$. This $\bar{\lambda}$ is our measure of the investor's effective loss aversion for any particular $z_t < 1$.

REFERENCES

Abel, Andrew, 1990, Asset Prices under Habit Formation and Catching up with the Joneses, *American Economic Review*, 80, 38–42.

Barberis, Nicholas, Andrei Shleifer, and Robert Vishny, 1998, A Model of Investor Sentiment, *Journal of Financial Economics*, 49, 307–43.

Benartzi, Shlomo, and Richard Thaler, 1995, Myopic Loss Aversion and the Equity Premium Puzzle, *Quarterly Journal of Economics*, 110, 73–92.

Campbell, John Y., 2000, Asset Prices, Consumption and the Business Cycle, in *Handbook of Macroeconomics*, John Taylor and Michael Woodford (eds.), North-Holland.

Campbell, John Y., and John H. Cochrane, 1999, By Force of Habit: A Consumption-Based Explanation of Aggregate Stock Market Behavior, *Journal of Political Economy*, 107, 205–51.

Campbell, John Y., Andrew W. Lo, and A. Craig MacKinlay, 1997, *The Econometrics of Financial Markets*, Princeton University Press.

Campbell, John Y., and Robert Shiller, 1988, Stock Prices, Earnings, and Expected Dividends, *Journal of Finance*, 43, 661–76.

Cecchetti, Stephen, Pok-sang Lam, and Nelson Mark, 1990, Mean Reversion in Equilibrium Asset Prices, *American Economic Review*, 80, 398–418.

Cochrane, John H., 1998, Where Is the Market Going: Uncertain Facts and Novel Theories, Federal Reserve Bank of Chicago Discussion Paper.

Constantinides, George, 1990, Habit Formation: A Resolution of the Equity Premium Puzzle, *Journal of Political Economy*, 98, 531–52.

Constantinides, George, and Darrell Duffie, 1996, Asset Pricing with Heterogeneous Consumers, *Journal of Political Economy*, 104, 219–40.

Daniel, Kent, David Hirshleifer, and Avanidhar Subrahmanyam, 1998, Investor Psychology and Security Market Under- and Over-reactions, *Journal of Finance*, 53, 1839–85.

Duffie, Darrell, and Costis Skiadas, 1994, Continuous-Time Security Pricing: A Utility Gradient Approach, *Journal of Mathematical Economics*, 23, 107–31.

Durell, Alan, 1999, Consumer Confidence and Stock Market Returns, Working Paper, Harvard University.

Epstein, Larry G., and Stanley E. Zin, 1989, Substitution, Risk Aversion, and the Temporal Behavior of Asset Returns: A Theoretical Framework, *Econometrica*, 57, 937–68.

———, 1990, First-Order Risk Aversion and the Equity Premium Puzzle, *Journal of Monetary Economics*, 26, 387–407.

———, 1991, Substitution, Risk Aversion, and the Temporal Behavior of Consumption Growth and Asset Returns II: An Empirical Analysis, *Journal of Political Economy*, 99, 263–86.

Fama, Eugene, and Kenneth French, 1988a, Permanent and Temporary Components of Stock Prices, *Journal of Political Economy*, 96, 246–73.

———, 1988b, Dividend Yields and Expected Stock Returns, *Journal of Financial Economics*, 22, 3–25.

Gertner, Robert, 1993, Game Shows and Economic Behavior: Risk Taking on 'Card Sharks,' *Quarterly Journal of Economics*, 151, 507–21.

Hansen, Lars P., and Ravi Jagannathan, 1991, Restrictions on Intertemporal Marginal Rates of Substitutions Implied by Asset Returns, *Journal of Political Economy*, 99, 225–62.

Hansen, Lars P., and Kenneth Singleton, 1983, Stochastic Consumption, Risk Aversion and the Temporal Behavior of Asset Returns, *Journal of Political Economy*, 91, 249–65.

Heaton, John, and Deborah Lucas, 1996, Evaluating the Effects of Incomplete Markets on Risk Sharing and Asset Pricing, *Journal of Political Economy*, 104, 668–712.

Hong, Harrison, and Jeremy Stein, 1999, A Unified Theory of Underreaction, Momentum Trading and Overreaction in Asset Markets, *Journal of Finance*, 54, 2143–84.

Kahneman, Daniel, and Amos Tversky, 1979, Prospect Theory: An Analysis of Decision under Risk, *Econometrica*, 37, 263–91.

Kandel, Shmuel, and Robert Stambaugh, 1991, Asset Returns and Intertemporal Preferences, *Journal of Monetary Economics*, 27, 39–71.

Kocherlakota, Narayana, 1996, The Equity Premium: It's Still a Puzzle, *Journal of Economic Literature*, 34, 42–71.

Levy, Haim, and Zvi Wiener, 1997, Prospect Theory and Utility Theory: Temporary and Permanent Attitudes toward Risk, Working Paper, Hebrew University of Jerusalem.

Loewenstein, George, Ted O'Donoghue, and Matthew Rabin, 1999, Projection Bias in Predicting Future Utility, Working Paper, Carnegie Mellon University.

Lucas, Robert, 1978, Asset Prices in an Exchange Economy, *Econometrica*, 46, 1419–1446.

Mehra, Rajnish, and Edward Prescott, 1985, The Equity Premium Puzzle, *Journal of Monetary Economics*, 15, 145–61.

Poterba, James, and Lawrence Summers, 1988, Mean-Reversion in Stock Returns: Evidence and Implications, *Journal of Financial Economics*, 22, 27–60.

Shiller, Robert, 1999, Measuring Bubble Expectations and Investor Confidence, Working Paper, Yale University.

Shleifer, Andrei, 1999, *Inefficient Markets: An Introduction to Behavioral Finance*, Oxford University Press.

Sundaresan, Suresh, 1989, Intertemporally Dependent Preferences and the Volatility of Consumption and Wealth, *Review of Financial Studies*, 2, 73–88.

Thaler, Richard H., and Eric J. Johnson, 1990, Gambling with the House Money and Trying to Break Even: The Effects of Prior Outcomes on Risky Choice, *Management Science*, 36, 643–60.

Tversky, Amos, and Daniel Kahneman, 1981, The Framing of Decisions and the Psychology of Choice, *Science*, 211, 453–58.

Tversky, Amos, and Daniel Kahneman, 1992, Advances in Prospect Theory: Cumulative Representation of Uncertainty, *Journal of Risk and Uncertainty*, 5, 297–323.

PART III

Empirical Studies of Overreaction and Underreaction

Chapter 8

CONTRARIAN INVESTMENT,

EXTRAPOLATION, AND RISK

Josef Lakonishok, Andrei Shleifer,
and Robert W. Vishny

For many years, scholars and investment professionals have argued that value strategies outperform the market (Graham and Dodd 1934, and Dreman 1977). These value strategies call for buying stocks that have low prices relative to earnings, dividends, historical prices, book assets, or other measures of value. In recent years, value strategies have attracted academic attention as well. Basu (1977), Jaffe, Keim, and Westerfield (1989), Chan, Hamao, and Lakonishok (1991), and Fama and French (1992) show that stocks with high earnings/price ratios earn higher returns. De Bondt and Thaler (1985, 1987) argue that extreme losers outperform the market over the subsequent several years. Despite considerable criticism (Chan 1988, and Ball and Kothari 1989), their analysis has generally stood up to the tests (Chopra, Lakonishok, and Ritter 1992). Rosenberg, Reid, and Lanstein (1984) show that stocks with high book relative to market values of equity outperform the market. Further work (Chan, Hamao, and Lakonishok 1991, and Fama and French 1992) has both extended and refined these results. Finally, Chan, Hamao, and Lakonishok (1991) show that a high ratio of cash flow to price also predicts higher returns. Interestingly, many of these results have been obtained for both the United States and

We are indebted to Gil Beebower, Fischer Black, Stephen Brown, K. C. Chan, Louis Chan, Eugene Fama, Kenneth French, Bob Haugen, Jay Ritter, René Stulz, and two anonymous referees of *The Journal of Finance* for helpful comments and to Han Qu for outstanding research assistance. This work has been presented at the Berkeley Program in Finance, University of California (Berkeley), the Center for Research in Securities Prices Conference, the University of Chicago, the University of Illinois, the Massachusetts Institute of Technology, the National Bureau of Economic Research (Asset Pricing and Behavioral Finance Groups), New York University, Pensions and Investments Conference, the Institute for Quantitative Research in Finance (United States and Europe), Society of Quantitative Analysts, Stanford University, the University of Toronto, and Tel Aviv University. The research was supported by the National Science Foundation, Bradley Foundation, Russell Sage Foundation, the National Bureau of Economic Research Asset Management Research Advisory Group, and the National Center for Supercomputing Applications, University of Illinois.

Japan. Certain types of value strategies, then, appear to have beaten the market.

While there is some agreement that value strategies have produced superior returns, the interpretation of why they have done so is more controversial. Value strategies might produce higher returns because they are *contrarian* to "naive"[1] strategies followed by other investors. These naive strategies might range from extrapolating past earnings growth too far into the future, to assuming a trend in stock prices, to overreacting to good or bad news, or to simply equating a good investment with a well-run company irrespective of price. Regardless of the reason, some investors tend to get overly excited about stocks that have done very well in the past and buy them up, so that these "glamour" stocks become overpriced. Similarly, they overreact to stocks that have done very badly, oversell them, and these out-of-favor "value" stocks become underpriced. Contrarian investors bet against such naive investors. Because contrarian strategies invest disproportionately in stocks that are underpriced and underinvest in stocks that are overpriced, they outperform the market (see De Bondt and Thaler 1985, and Haugen 1994).

An alternative explanation of why value strategies have produced superior returns, argued most forcefully by Fama and French (1992), is that they are *fundamentally riskier*. That is, investors in value stocks, such as high book-to-market stocks, tend to bear higher fundamental risk of some sort, and their higher average returns are simply compensation for this risk. This argument is also used by critics of De Bondt and Thaler (Chan 1988, and Ball and Kothari 1989) to dismiss their overreaction story. Whether value strategies have produced higher returns because they are contrarian to naive strategies or because they are fundamentally riskier remains an open question.

In this chapter, we try to shed further light on the two potential explanations for why value strategies work. We do so along two dimensions. First, we examine more closely the predictions of the contrarian model. In particular, one natural version of the contrarian model argues that the overpriced *glamour stocks* are those that, first, have performed well in the past, and second, are expected by the market to perform well in the future. Similarly, the underpriced out-of-favor or *value stocks* are those that have performed poorly in the past and are expected to continue to perform poorly. Value strategies that bet against those investors who extrapolate past performance too far into the future produce superior returns. In principle, this version of the contrarian model is testable because past performance and expectation of future performance are two distinct and separately measurable characteristics of glamour and value. In this chapter, past performance

---

[1] What we call "naive strategies" are also sometimes referred to as "popular models" (Shiller 1984) and "noise" (Black 1986).

is measured using information on past growth in sales, earnings, and cash flow, and expected performance is measured by multiples of price to current earnings and cash flow.

We examine the most obvious implication of the contrarian model, namely that value stocks outperform glamour stocks. We start with simple one-variable classifications of glamour and value stocks that rely in most cases on measures of either past growth or expected future growth. We then move on to classifications in which glamour and value are defined using both past growth and expected future growth. In addition, we compare past, expected, and future growth rates of glamour and value stocks. Our version of the contrarian model predicts that differences in expected future growth rates are linked to past growth and overestimate actual future growth differences between glamour and value firms. We find that a wide range of value strategies have produced higher returns, and that the pattern of past, expected, and actual future growth rates is consistent with the contrarian model.

The second question we ask is whether value stocks are indeed fundamentally riskier than glamour stocks. To be fundamentally riskier, value stocks must underperform glamour stocks with some frequency, and particularly in the states of the world when the marginal utility of wealth is high. This view of risk motivates our tests. We look at the frequency of superior (and inferior) performance of value strategies, as well as at their performance in bad states of the world, such as extreme down markets and economic recessions. We also look at the betas and standard deviations of value and glamour strategies. We find little, if any, support for the view that value strategies are fundamentally riskier.

Our results raise the obvious question of how the higher expected returns on value strategies could have continued if such strategies are not fundamentally riskier? We present some possible explanations that rely both on behavioral strategies favored by individual investors and on agency problems plaguing institutional investors.

The next section of the article briefly discusses our methodology. Section 2 examines a variety of simple classification schemes for glamour and value stocks based on the book-to-market ratio, the cash flow-to-price ratio, the earnings-to-price ratio, and past growth in sales. Section 2 shows that all of these simple value strategies have produced superior returns and is what motivates our subsequent use of combinations of measures of past and expected growth. Section 3 then examines the performance of value strategies that are defined using both past growth and current multiples. These two-dimensional value strategies outperform glamour strategies by approximately 10 to 11 percent per year. Moreover, the superior performance of value stocks relative to glamour stocks persists when we restrict our attention to the largest 50 percent or largest 20 percent of stocks by market capitalization. Section 4 provides evidence that contrarian strategies work because they exploit expectational errors implicit in stock prices. Specifically, the differences in expected growth rates between glamour and value stocks implicit in their relative valuation multiples significantly overestimate actual future growth rate differences. Section 5 examines risk characteristics of value strategies and provides evidence that, over longer horizons, value strategies have outperformed glamour strategies quite consistently and have done particularly well in "bad" states of the world. This evidence provides no support for the hypothesis that value strategies are fundamentally riskier. Finally, section 6 attempts to interpret our findings.

1. METHODOLOGY

The sample period covered in this study is from the end of April 1963 to the end of April 1990. Some of our formation strategies require five years of past accounting data. Consequently, we look at portfolios formed every year starting at the end of April 1968.[2] We examine subsequent performance and other characteristics of these portfolios for up to five years after formation using returns data from the Center for Research in Security Prices (CRSP) and accounting data from COMPUSTAT (including the research file). The universe of stocks is the New York Stock Exchange (NYSE) and the American Stock Exchange (AMEX).

A key question about this sample is whether results for stock returns are contaminated by significant look-ahead or survivorship bias (Banz and Breen 1986, and Kothari, Shanken, and Sloan 1992). The potentially most serious bias is due to COMPUSTAT's major expansion of its database in 1978, which increased its coverage from 2,700 NYSE/AMEX firms and large National Association of Securities Dealers Automated Quotation (NASDAQ) firms to about 6,000 firms. Up to five years of data were added retroactively for many of these firms. As Kothari, Shanken, and Sloan (1992) point out, this raises the prospect of a look-ahead bias. Particularly among the firms that start out small or low priced, only those that perform well are added to the database. Hence, as one goes to lower and lower market valuation firms on COMPUSTAT, one finds that the population is increasingly selected from firms having good five-year past performance records. This could potentially explain the positive association between low initial valuation and future returns. The potential bias toward high returns among low valuation firms is driven by data for the first five or so years that the firm appears on COMPUSTAT.

Our results potentially suffer from the same bias. However, our methodology differs from those in other recent studies in ways that should mitigate this bias. First, many of the strategies we focus on require five years of past

---

[2] We form portfolios in April to ensure that the previous year's accounting numbers were available at the time of formation.

data to classify firms before we start measuring returns. This means that we do not use returns for the first five years that the firm appears on COMPU-STAT to evaluate our strategies. But these first five years of returns is where the look-ahead bias in returns is found. Second, we study only NYSE and AMEX firms. The major expansion of COMPUSTAT largely involved adding (successful) NASDAQ firms. Finally, we also report results for the largest 50 percent of firms on the NYSE and AMEX. The selection bias is less serious among these larger firms (La Porta 1993).

Within each of our portfolios, we weight equally all the stocks and compute returns using an annual buy-and-hold strategy for years +1, +2, . . . , +5 relative to the time of formation. If a stock disappears from CRSP during a year, its return is replaced until the end of the year with the return on a corresponding size decile portfolio. At the end of each year, the portfolio is rebalanced and each surviving stock gets the same weight.

For most of our results, we present size-adjusted returns as well as raw returns. To adjust portfolio returns for size, we first identify, for every stock in the sample, its market capitalization decile at the end of the previous year. We then construct a size benchmark return for each portfolio as follows. For each stock in the portfolio, replace its return in each year with an annual buy-and-hold return on an equally weighted portfolio of all stocks in its size decile for that year. Then equally weight these returns across all stocks in the original portfolio. The annual size-adjusted return on the original portfolio is then computed as the return on that portfolio minus the return on that year's size benchmark portfolio.

In addition to returns for the various portfolios, we compute growth rates and multiples for accounting measures such as sales, earnings, and cash flow. All accounting variables are taken from COMPUSTAT. Earnings are measured before extraordinary items, and cash flow is defined as earnings plus depreciation.

Let us illustrate our procedure for computing growth rates using the case of earnings growth from year −4 to year −3 relative to portfolio formation. We consider the portfolio that invests $1 in each stock at the end of year −4. This fixes the proportion of each firm owned at 1/(market capitalization), where market capitalization is calculated at the end of year −4. We then calculate the earnings per dollar invested that are generated by this portfolio in each of years −4 and −3 as follows. For each stock in the portfolio, we multiply total firm earnings by the proportion of the firm owned. We then sum these numbers across all stocks in the portfolio for that year and divide by the number of stocks in the portfolio. Computing growth rates from these numbers is complicated by the fact that the earnings (and cash flows) are negative for some entire portfolios for some years.[3] This makes it impossible to compute the average earnings growth rate from period −4 to

---

[3] Obviously, there is no such problem for sales. However, for symmetry we use the same methodology to compute growth rates of sales, earnings, and cash flow.

period −3 as the average of the (−4, −3) growth rates across all 22 formation periods since, for some formation periods, the base year −4 earnings is negative. Even without the negative earnings years, these year-to-year growth rates are highly volatile because the base year's earnings were sometimes very close to zero. This makes year-by-year averaging of growth rates unreliable. To deal with these problems, we average year −4 and year −3 portfolio earnings across all twenty-two formation periods *before* computing growth rates. Hence, the earnings growth rate from year −4 to year −3 is computed as $(AE_{(-3)} - AE_{(-4)})/AE_{(-4)}$ where $AE_{(-3)}$ and $AE_{(-4)}$ are just the averages across all formation periods of the portfolio earnings in years −3 and −4. In this fashion, we compute the growth rate in earnings, cash flow, and sales for each portfolio and for each year prior and postformation.

Finally, we compute several accounting ratios, such as cash flow-to-price and earnings-to-price. These ratios are also used to sort individual stocks into portfolios. For these classifications, we consider only stocks with positive ratios of cash flow-to-price or earnings-to-price because negative ratios cannot be interpreted in terms of expected growth rates.[4] For purposes other than classifying individual stocks into portfolios, these ratios are computed for the entire equally weighted portfolios (and then averaged across all formation periods) without eliminating individual stocks in the portfolio that have negative values for the variable. For example, we compute the cash flow-to-price ratio for each stock and then take the average over all stocks in the portfolio. This gives us the cash flow per $1 invested in the portfolio where each stock receives the same dollar investment.

2. SIMPLE GLAMOUR AND VALUE STRATEGIES

Table 8.1, Panel A presents the returns on a strategy that has received a lot of attention recently (Fama and French 1992), namely the book-to-market strategy. We divide the universe of stocks annually into book-to-market (B/M) deciles, where book value is taken from COMPUSTAT for the end of the previous fiscal year, and market value is taken from CRSP as the market

---

[4] While we would ultimately like to say something about the future returns of firms with negative earnings, not including them here should not be viewed as a source of bias. As long as our strategy is feasible, in the sense that it constructs portfolios based on characteristics that were observable at the time of portfolio formation (see our discussion on look-ahead biases), the estimated differences in returns should be viewed as an unbiased measures of actual return differences *between subsets of films that are all part of the set of firms with positive earnings*. While a strategy that incorporates the negative earnings firms may produce different returns, this is quite a different strategy from the one that we are studying. In our regression in table 8.4, we do include firms with negative earnings or cash flow by separately including a dummy variable for negative earnings or cash flow along with the actual E/P ratio or C/P ratio if the numerator is positive.

value of equity at portfolio formation time. In general, we focus on long-horizon returns (of up to five years) on various strategies. The reason for looking at such long horizons is that we are interested in performance of alternative investment strategies over horizons suitable for long-term investors. Moreover, we assume annual buy and hold periods in contrast to monthly buy and hold periods assumed in most previous studies. Because of various market microstructure issues as well as execution costs, our procedure produces returns that are closer to those that investors can actually capture. We defer statistical testing of return differences across value and glamour portfolios to table 8.6 where year-by-year return differences are reported starting in April 1968 and ending in April 1990.

In Panel A of table 8.1, we present the returns for years 1 through 5 after the formation (R_1 through R_5), the average annual five-year return (AR), the cumulative five-year return (CR_5), and the size-adjusted average annual five-year return (SAAR). The numbers presented are the averages across all formation periods in the sample. The results confirm and extend the results established by Rosenberg, Reid, and Lanstein (1984), Chan, Hamao, and Lakonishok (1991), and Fama and French (1992). On average over the postformation years, the low B/M (glamour) stocks have an average annual return of 9.3 percent and the high B/M (value) stocks have an average annual return of 19.8 percent, for a difference of 10.5 percent per year. If portfolios are held with the limited rebalancing described above, then cumulatively value stocks outperform glamour stocks by 90 percent over years 1 through 5. Adjusting for size reduces the estimated return differences between value and glamour stocks somewhat, but the differences are still quite large. The size-adjusted average annual return is −4.3 percent for glamour stocks and 3.5 percent for value stocks, for a difference of 7.8 percent.

The natural question is: what is the B/M ratio really capturing? Unfortunately, many different factors are reflected in this ratio. A low B/M may describe a company with a lot of intangible assets, such as research and development (R & D) capital, that are not reflected in the accounting book value because R & D is expensed. A low B/M can also describe a company with attractive growth opportunities that do not enter the computation of book value but do enter the market price. Also, a natural resource company, such as an oil producer without good growth opportunities but with high temporary profits, might have a low B/M after an increase in oil prices. A stock whose risk is low and future cash flows are discounted at a low rate would have a low B/M as well. Finally, a low B/M may describe an overvalued glamour stock. The point here is simple: although the returns to the B/M strategy are impressive, B/M is not a "clean" variable uniquely associated with economically interpretable characteristics of the firms.

Arguably, the most important of such economically interpretable characteristics are the market's expectations of future growth and the past growth of these firms. To proxy for expected growth, we use ratios of various

TABLE 8.1
Returns for Decile Portfolios Based on One-Dimensional Classifications by Various Measures of Value

At the end of each April between 1968 and 1989, 10-decile portfolios are formed in ascending order based on B/M, C/P, E/P, and GS. B/M is the ratio of book value of equity to market value of equity; C/P is the ratio of cash flow to market value of equity; E/P is the ratio of earnings to market value of equity, and GS refers to preformation 5-year average growth rate of sales. The returns presented in the table are averages over all formation periods. R_t is the average return in year t after formation, $t = 1, \ldots, 5$. AR is the average annual size-adjusted return over 5 postformation years. CR$_5$ is the compounded 5-year return assuming annual rebalancing. SAAR is the average annual size-adjusted return computed over 5 postformation years. The glamour portfolio refers to the decile portfolio containing stocks ranking lowest on B/M, C/P, or E/P, or highest on GS. The value portfolio refers to the decile portfolio containing stocks ranking highest on B/M, C/P, or E/P, or lowest on GS.

| | Glamour | | | | | | | | | Value |
	1	2	3	4	5	6	7	8	9	10
					Panel A: B/M					
R_1	0.110	0.117	0.135	0.123	0.131	0.154	0.154	0.170	0.183	0.173
R_2	0.079	0.107	0.140	0.145	0.153	0.156	0.169	0.164	0.182	0.188
R_3	0.107	0.132	0.155	0.167	0.165	0.172	0.191	0.207	0.196	0.204
R_4	0.081	0.133	0.136	0.160	0.170	0.169	0.188	0.204	0.213	0.207
R_5	0.088	0.137	0.163	0.175	0.171	0.176	0.216	0.201	0.206	0.215
AR	0.093	0.125	0.146	0.154	0.158	0.166	0.184	0.189	0.196	0.198
CR$_6$	0.560	0.802	0.973	1.045	1.082	1.152	1.320	1.375	1.449	1.462
SAAR	-0.043	-0.020	-0.003	0.004	0.006	0.012	0.024	0.028	0.033	0.035
					Panel B: C/P					
R_1	0.084	0.124	0.140	0.140	0.153	0.148	0.157	0.178	0.183	0.183
R_2	0.067	0.108	0.126	0.153	0.156	0.170	0.177	0.180	0.183	0.190
R_3	0.096	0.133	0.153	0.172	0.170	0.191	0.191	0.202	0.193	0.204

	1	2	3	4	5	6	7	8	9	10
R_4	0.098	0.111	0.146	0.159	0.166	0.172	0.182	0.192	0.223	0.218
R_5	0.108	0.134	0.161	0.162	0.187	0.177	0.191	0.209	0.212	0.208
AR	0.091	0.122	0.145	0.157	0.166	0.171	0.180	0.192	0.199	0.201
CR_5	0.543	0.779	0.969	1.074	1.158	1.206	1.283	1.406	1.476	1.494
SAAR	−0.049	−0.025	−0.006	0.005	0.013	0.019	0.025	0.034	0.037	0.039

Panel C: E/P

	1	2	3	4	5	6	7	8	9	10
R_1	0.123	0.125	0.140	0.130	0.135	0.156	0.170	0.180	0.193	0.162
R_2	0.101	0.113	0.124	0.143	0.167	0.164	0.180	0.185	0.183	0.174
R_3	0.118	0.138	0.157	0.171	0.171	0.191	0.198	0.188	0.188	0.195
R_4	0.111	0.124	0.145	0.151	0.157	0.159	0.198	0.199	0.205	0.214
R_5	0.119	0.129	0.151	0.167	0.171	0.168	0.196	0.201	0.211	0.207
AR	0.114	0.126	0.143	0.152	0.160	0.167	0.188	0.191	0.196	0.190
CR_5	0.717	0.808	0.953	1.031	1.102	1.168	1.370	1.393	1.446	1.388
SAAR	−0.035	−0.024	−0.009	−0.001	0.005	0.013	0.026	0.026	0.029	0.019

Panel D: GS

	Value									Glamour
	1	2	3	4	5	6	7	8	9	10
R_1	0.187	0.183	0.164	0.169	0.162	0.157	0.159	0.164	0.142	0.114
R_2	0.181	0.180	0.186	0.169	0.166	0.162	0.152	0.157	0.147	0.131
R_3	0.204	0.206	0.194	0.186	0.181	0.180	0.168	0.178	0.157	0.138
R_4	0.205	0.193	0.201	0.190	0.181	0.174	0.160	0.153	0.167	0.126
R_5	0.197	0.213	0.194	0.199	0.168	0.184	0.185	0.168	0.163	0.125
AR	0.195	0.195	0.188	0.183	0.171	0.171	0.165	0.164	0.155	0.127
CR_5	1.434	1.435	1.364	1.314	1.205	1.206	1.144	1.136	1.057	0.818
SAAR	0.022	0.027	0.025	0.024	0.015	0.015	0.008	0.008	0.000	−0.024

measures of profitability to price, so that firms with lower ratios have *higher* expected growth. The idea behind this is Gordon's formula, which states that $P = D(+1)/(r - g)$, where $D(+1)$ is next period's dividend, P is the current stock price, r is the required rate of return on the stock, and g is the expected growth rate of dividends (Gordon and Shapiro 1956). A similar formula applies to cash flow and earnings. For example, to get an expression in terms of cash flow, we write $D(+1) = \rho C(+1)$, where $C(+1)$ is next period's cash flow and ρ, the payout ratio, is the constant fraction of cash flow paid out as dividends. We can then write $P = \rho C(+1)/(r - g)$ where the growth rate g for dividends is also the growth rate for cash flow on the assumption that dividends are proportional to cash flow. A similar formula would apply to earnings but with a different payout ratio. According to these expressions, *holding discount rates and payout ratios constant*,[5] a high cash flow-to-price (C/P) firm has a low expected growth rate of cash flow, while a low C/P firm has a high expected growth rate of cash flow, and similarly for the ratio of earnings-to-price (E/P).[6] While the assumption of a constant growth rate for dividends and strict proportionality between cash flow (or earnings) and dividends are restrictive, the intuition behind Gordon's formula is quite general. Differences in C/P or E/P ratios across stocks should proxy for differences in expected growth rates.[7]

Panel B of table 8.1 presents the results of sorting on the ratio of C/P. High C/P stocks are identified with value stocks because their growth rate of cash flow is expected to be low or, alternatively, their prices are low per dollar of cash flow. Conversely, low C/P stocks are glamour stocks. On average, over the five postformation years, first-decile C/P stocks have a return of 9.1 percent per annum, whereas the tenth-decile C/P stocks have an average return of 20.1 percent per annum, for a difference of 11 percent. The five-year cumulative returns are 54.3 percent and 149.4 percent, respectively, for a difference of 95.1 percent. On a size-adjusted basis, the difference in returns is 8.8 percent per annum. Sorting on C/P thus appears to produce somewhat bigger differences in returns than sorting on B/M ratios. This is consistent with the idea that measuring the market's expectations of future growth more directly gives rise to better value strategies.[8]

Another popular multiple, studied by Basu (1977), is the E/P. Table 8.1, Panel C presents our results for E/P. On average, over the five postformation years, first-decile E/P stocks have an average annual return of 11.4 percent

[5] In section 5, we compare risk characteristics, and hence appropriate discount rates, of the various portfolios.

[6] An alternative approach is to use analysts' forecasts to proxy for expectations of future growth. This approach is used by La Porta (1993).

[7] We use current cash flow and earnings rather than one-period-ahead numbers because we require our investment strategies to be functions of observable variables only.

[8] La Porta (1993) shows that contrarian strategies based directly on analysts' forecasts of future growth can produce even larger returns than those based on financial ratios.

and tenth-decile E/P stocks have an average annual return of 19.0 percent, for a difference of 7.6 percent. On a size-adjusted basis, the difference in returns is 5.4 percent per annum. Low E/P stocks underperform high E/P stocks by a fairly wide margin, although the difference is not as large as that between extreme B/M or C/P deciles. One possible reason for this is that stocks with temporarily depressed earnings are lumped together with well-performing glamour stocks in the high expected growth/low E/P category. These stocks with depressed earnings do not experience the same degree of poor future stock performance as the glamour stocks, perhaps because they are less overpriced by the market.

An alternative way to operationalize the notions of glamour and value is to classify stocks based on past growth rather than by expectations of future growth. We measure past growth by growth in sales (GS) since sales is less volatile than either cash flow or earnings, particularly for stocks in the extreme portfolios that we are most interested in. Specifically, for each company for each of years $-1, -2, \ldots, -5$ prior to formation, we calculate the GS in that year. Then, for each year, we rank all firms by GS for that year. We then compute each firm's weighted average rank, giving the weight of five to its growth rank in year -1, the weight of four to its growth rank in year -2, etcetera. Finally, we form deciles based on each stock's weighted average sales growth rank. This procedure is a crude way to both pick out stocks with consistently high past GS, and to give greater weight to more recent sales growth in ranking stocks.[9]

Table 8.1, Panel D presents the results for the GS strategy. On average, over the five postformation years, the portfolio of firms in the lowest decile of past sales growth earns an average return of 19.5 percent per annum and the portfolio of firms in the highest decile earns an average return of 12.7 percent per annum. On a size-adjusted basis the average annual abnormal returns are 2.2 percent for the low GS strategy and -2.4 percent for the high GS strategy. These magnitudes are not as dramatic as those for the B/M and C/P strategies, nevertheless the spread in returns is sizeable.

In this section, we have largely confirmed and extended the results of others. A wide variety of simple value strategies based on classification of firms by a single fundamental variable produce very large returns over the twenty-two-year period April 1968 to April 1990. In contrast to previous work, our strategies involve classifying firms based on fundamentals and then buying and holding for five years. In the next section, we explore more sophisticated two-dimensional versions of these strategies that are designed to correct some of the misclassification of firms inherent in a one-variable approach. For example, low E/P stocks, which are supposedly glamour stocks, include many stocks with temporarily depressed earnings that are

---

[9] We have also tried a procedure in which we equally weight the ranks for all five years of past sales growth and obtain very similar results.

expected to recover. The two-dimensional strategies of the next section are formulated with an eye toward more directly exploiting the possible mistakes made by naive investors.

3. ANATOMY OF A CONTRARIAN STRATEGY

A. *Performance of Contrarian Strategies*

Much psychological evidence indicates that individuals form their predictions of the future without a full appreciation of mean reversion. That is, individuals tend to base their expectations on past data for the individual case they are considering without properly weighting data on what psychologists call the "base rate," or the class average. Kahneman and Tversky (1982, p. 417) explain:

> One of the basic principles of statistical prediction, which is also one of the least intuitive, is that the extremeness of predictions must be moderated by considerations of predictability. . . . Predictions are allowed to match impressions only in the case of perfect predictability. In intermediate situations, which are of course the most common, the prediction should be regressive; that is, it should fall between the class average and the value that best represents one's impression of the case at hand. The lower the predictability the closer the prediction should be to the class average. Intuitive predictions are typically nonregressive: people often make extreme predictions on the basis of information whose reliability and predictive validity are known to be low.

To exploit this flaw of intuitive forecasts, contrarian investors should sell stocks with high past growth as well as high expected future growth and buy stocks with low past growth as well as low expected future growth. Prices of these stocks are most likely to reflect the failure of investors to impose mean reversion on growth forecasts. Accordingly, we define a glamour stock to be a stock with high growth in the past and high expected future growth. A value stock must have had low growth in the past and be expected by the market to continue growing slowly. In this section, we continue to use high ratios of C/P (E/P) as a proxy for a low expected growth rate.

Table 8.2, Panel A presents the results for the strategy that sorts on both GS and C/P. Since we are sorting on two variables, sorting stocks into deciles on each variable is impractical. Accordingly, we independently sort stocks into three groups—(1) bottom 30 percent, (2) middle 40 percent, and (3) top 30 percent—by GS and by C/P, and then take intersections resulting from the two classifications. Because the classifications are done independently, extreme glamour (high GS, low C/P) and value portfolios (low GS, high C/P) contain greater than average numbers of stocks, since GS and C/P are negatively correlated.

TABLE 8.2

Returns for Portfolios Based on Two-dimensional Classifications by Various Measures of Value

At the end of each April between 1968 and 1989, 9 groups of stocks are formed. The stocks are independently sorted in ascending order into 3 groups ((1) bottom 30 percent, (2) middle 40 percent, and (3) top 30 percent) based on each of two variables. The sorts are for 5 pairs of variables: C/P and GS, B/M and GS, E/P and GS, E/P and B/M, and B/M and C/P. C/P is the ratio of cash flow to market value of equity; B/M is the ratio of book value of equity to market value of equity; E/P is the ratio of earnings to market value of equity; and GS refers to preformation 5-year average growth rate of sales. The returns presented in the table are averages over all formation periods. R_t is the average return in year t after formation, $t = 1, \ldots, 5$. AR is the average annual return over 5 postformation years. CR_5 is the compounded 5-year return assuming annual rebalancing. SAAR is the average annual size-adjusted return computed over 5 postformation years. Depending on the two variables being used for classification, the value portfolio either refers to the portfolio containing stocks ranked in the top group (3) on both variables from among C/P, E/P, or B/M, or else the portfolio containing stocks ranking in the top group on one of those variables and in the bottom group (1) on GS. The glamour portfolio contains stocks with precisely the opposite set of rankings.

Panel A: C/P and GS

	Glamour						Value		
C/P	1	1	1	2	2	2	3	3	3
GS	1	2	3	1	2	3	1	2	3
R_1	0.157	0.131	0.113	0.181	0.156	0.139	0.215	0.202	0.137
R_2	0.147	0.120	0.100	0.191	0.165	0.167	0.213	0.188	0.165
R_3	0.165	0.140	0.121	0.197	0.190	0.165	0.227	0.195	0.172
R_4	0.164	0.124	0.114	0.198	0.169	0.166	0.231	0.204	0.177
R_5	0.179	0.135	0.121	0.200	0.173	0.151	0.218	0.216	0.184
AR	0.162	0.130	0.114	0.193	0.171	0.157	0.221	0.201	0.167
CR_5	1.122	0.843	0.712	1.419	1.200	1.076	1.711	1.497	1.163
SAAR	−0.006	−0.020	−0.033	0.030	0.014	0.003	0.054	0.036	0.008

TABLE 8.2 (cont.)

Panel B: E/P and GS

E/P	Glamour						Value		
GS	1	1	1	2	2	2	3	3	3
	1	2	3	1	2	3	1	2	3
R_1	0.184	0.148	0.118	0.188	0.153	0.139	0.224	0.205	0.174
R_2	0.167	0.134	0.100	0.204	0.174	0.154	0.214	0.187	0.190
R_3	0.185	0.153	0.119	0.222	0.189	0.169	0.221	0.198	0.189
R_4	0.190	0.138	0.103	0.205	0.175	0.160	0.232	0.217	0.188
R_5	0.189	0.163	0.104	0.201	0.180	0.157	0.215	0.210	0.199
AR	0.183	0.147	0.109	0.204	0.174	0.156	0.221	0.203	0.188
CR_5	1.315	0.986	0.674	1.533	1.230	1.063	1.716	1.523	1.365
SAAR	0.005	-0.011	-0.037	0.033	0.013	0.002	0.040	0.034	0.017

Panel C: B/M and GS

B/M	Glamour						Value		
GS	1	1	1	2	2	2	3	3	3
	1	2	3	1	2	3	1	2	3
R_1	0.147	0.141	0.132	0.160	0.159	0.121	0.204	0.185	0.135
R_2	0.127	0.138	0.127	0.175	0.166	0.150	0.200	0.172	0.163
R_3	0.149	0.149	0.137	0.190	0.186	0.152	0.221	0.192	0.182
R_4	0.147	0.130	0.130	0.191	0.176	0.154	0.222	0.190	0.195
R_5	0.158	0.140	0.124	0.203	0.180	0.165	0.216	0.211	0.164
AR	0.146	0.140	0.130	0.184	0.173	0.148	0.212	0.190	0.168
CR_5	0.974	0.925	0.842	1.325	1.224	0.996	1.618	1.387	1.171
SAAR	-0.009	-0.012	-0.021	0.022	0.015	-0.009	0.039	0.030	0.017

Panel D: E/P and B/M

	Glamour								Value
E/P	1	1	1	2	2	2	3	3	3
B/M	1	2	3	1	2	3	1	2	3
R_1	0.116	0.118	0.186	0.142	0.143	0.174	0.135	0.174	0.189
R_2	0.086	0.120	0.194	0.146	0.163	0.192	0.173	0.178	0.185
R_3	0.114	0.154	0.201	0.157	0.184	0.220	0.177	0.178	0.204
R_4	0.093	0.151	0.218	0.150	0.166	0.193	0.188	0.200	0.214
R_5	0.093	0.188	0.218	0.168	0.169	0.209	0.241	0.205	0.204
AR	0.100	0.146	0.203	0.152	0.165	0.198	0.183	0.187	0.199
CR_5	0.613	0.976	1.521	1.032	1.146	1.464	1.311	1.354	1.479
SAAR	-0.039	-0.009	0.022	0.002	0.009	0.033	0.003	0.023	0.030

Panel E: B/M and C/P

	Glamour								Value
B/M	1	1	1	2	2	2	3	3	3
C/P	1	2	3	1	2	3	1	2	3
R_1	0.111	0.153	0.141	0.101	0.144	0.171	0.170	0.161	0.194
R_2	0.085	0.164	0.172	0.111	0.160	0.181	0.174	0.173	0.189
R_3	0.111	0.172	0.179	0.147	0.177	0.191	0.192	0.206	0.207
R_4	0.101	0.153	0.187	0.155	0.168	0.200	0.177	0.195	0.219
R_5	0.108	0.162	0.250	0.184	0.178	0.208	0.233	0.201	0.209
AR	0.103	0.161	0.186	0.139	0.165	0.190	0.189	0.187	0.203
CR_5	0.633	1.108	1.339	0.917	1.148	1.387	1.378	1.355	1.524
SAAR	-0.037	0.007	0.018	-0.021	0.011	0.026	0.006	0.020	0.037

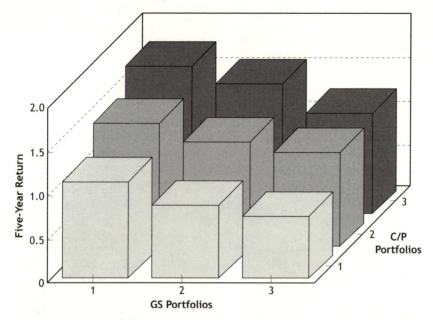

Figure 8.1. Compounded 5-year return for portfolios formed on the basis of C/P and GS. At the end of each April between 1968 and 1989, 9 groups of stocks are formed. The stocks are independently sorted in ascending order into 3 groups ((1) bottom 30 percent, (2) middle 40 percent, and (3) top 30 percent) based on each of two variables: cash flow-to-price (C/P) and growth-in-sales (GS). Returns presented are compounded 5-year postformation returns assuming annual rebalancing for these 9 portfolios.

In an average postformation year in this sample, the glamour portfolio had a return of 11.4 percent, and the value portfolio had a return of 22.1 percent, for a difference of 10.7 percent per year. Over the five postformation years, the cumulative difference in returns is 100 percent. On a size-adjusted basis, the difference in returns is 8.7 percent per year. As figure 8.1 illustrates, both C/P and GS contribute a great deal of explanatory power in these bivariate classifications. For example, low C/P stocks with low past sales growth, which we don't define as glamour stocks, have an average annual future return of 16.2 percent, but low C/P stocks with a high past sales growth, which we do define as glamour stocks, have an average annual future return of only 11.4 percent.

Table 8.2, Panel B presents the return results for a classification scheme using both past GS and the E/P ratio. The average annual difference in returns over the five-year period between the two extreme portfolios is 11.2 percent per year, which cumulatively amounts to 104.2 percent over five years. As with C/P and GS, the (E/P, GS) strategy produces substantially higher returns than either the E/P or the GS strategy alone. For example, among firms with the lowest E/P ratios, the average annual future return varies from 10.9 percent for firms with the highest past sales growth to 18.3 percent for those with the lowest past sales growth. Even more so than for C/P, using an E/P strategy seems to require differentiating between the stocks with depressed earnings expected to recover and the true glamour firms.[10] Once this finer classification scheme is used, the two-dimensional strategy based on E/P generates returns as high as those produced by the two-dimensional strategy based on C/P.

Table 8.2, Panel C presents results for portfolios classified by B/M and GS. The results show that GS has significant explanatory power for returns even after sorting by B/M. For example, within the set of firms whose B/M ratios are the highest, the average difference in returns between the low sales growth and high sales growth subgroups is over 4 percent per year (21.2 versus 16.8 percent). A similar result holds for the other two groups sorted by B/M. Note that these results do not appear to be driven by the role of the superimposed GS classification in creating a more precise partition of the firms by B/M. The B/M ratios across GS subgroups are not very different.

Panels D and E of table 8.2 present results for (B/M, E/P) and (B/M, C/P), respectively. Once again, the results confirm the usefulness of more precise classification schemes. For example, among firms with the lowest C/P ratios, future returns vary substantially according to B/M ratios. Future returns vary from 10.3 percent per year for the true glamour firms, to 18.6 percent per year for firms with low ratios of C/P but high B/M ratios. Most likely, the B/M ratio adds information here because it proxies for past growth, which is useful in conjunction with a measure of expected future growth.

The results of this subsection can be summarized and interpreted as follows. First, two-dimensional value strategies, in which firms are independently classified into three subgroups according to each of two fundamental variables, produce returns on the order of 10 to 11 percent per year higher than those on similarly constructed glamour strategies over the April 1968 to April 1990 period. Second, the results suggest that value strategies based jointly on past performance and expected future performance produce higher returns than more ad hoc strategies such as that based exclusively on the B/M ratio.

B. Do These Results Apply As Well to Large Stocks?

Even though we have shown that the superior returns to value strategies persist even after adjusting for size, the returns on such strategies might still

---

[10] This probably results from the greater year-to-year percentage swings for earnings than for cash flows.

be driven by the smaller stocks. Larger firms are of greater interest for implementable trading strategies, especially for institutional investors. Larger firms are also more closely monitored, and hence might be more efficiently priced. Finally, the look-ahead and survivorship biases discussed by Banz and Breen (1986) and Kothari, Shanken, and Sloan (1992) should be less important for the larger stocks.

Table 8.3 presents a summary version of table 8.2 for the subsample consisting of the largest 50 percent of our NYSE/AMEX firms. The results are similar to those obtained for the whole sample. For example, using the (C/P, GS) classification scheme, the difference in average annual size-adjusted returns between the value and glamour portfolios is 8.7 percent, exactly the same as for the entire sample. Using the (E/P, GS) classification scheme, this difference is 8.3 percent per year, compared to 7.7 percent per year for the entire sample. Raw return differences between value and glamour portfolios are slightly lower for the large-firm subsample because the extra return to value firms from their smaller average size is not present in that subsample. Value and glamour firms are essentially the same size in the large firm subsample. We have also done the analysis for the largest 20 percent of the stocks, which effectively mimics the S&P 500, and get a very similar spread of returns between glamour and value stocks. The conclusion is clear: our results apply to the largest stocks as well.

C. Regression Analysis

Previous analysis has identified a variety of variables that can define glamour and value portfolios. In this section, we ask which of these variables are significant in a multiple regression. Table 8.4 presents the results of regressions of raw returns for each stock on the characteristics of stocks that we have identified. Recall that in our analysis we have twenty-two portfolio formation periods. We run regressions separately for each postformation year, starting with +1 and ending with +5. Thus, for postformation year +1, we run twenty-two separate cross-sectional regressions in which the dependent variable is the annual return on stock i and the independent variables are characteristics of stock i observed at the beginning of the year. Then, using the Fama-MacBeth (1973) procedure, the coefficients for these twenty-two cross-sectional regressions are averaged and the t-statistics are computed. We applied the same procedure for years +2, +3, +4, and +5 after the formation. The results presented in table 8.4 are for the year +1.

We use the ratios of C/P and of E/P in the regression analysis. However, for some stocks these ratios are negative, and hence cannot be plausibly interpreted as expected growth rates. We deal with this problem in the same way as Fama and French (1992). Specifically, we define variables C/P+ and E/P+, which are equal to zero when C/P and E/P are negative, and are equal to C/P and E/P when they are positive. We also include in the regressions

TABLE 8.3
Returns for Portfolios Based on Two-Dimensional Classifications for the Largest 50 Percent of Stocks

At the end of each April between 1968 and 1989, 9 subgroups of the largest 50 percent of stocks by market capitalization are formed. The stocks are independently sorted in ascending order into 3 groups ((1) bottom 30 percent, (2) middle 40 percent, and (3) top 30 percent) based on each of two variables. The sorts are for 5 pairs of variables: C/P and GS, B/M and GS, E/P and GS, E/P and B/M, and C/P. C/P is the ratio of cash flow to market value of equity; B/M is the ratio of book value of equity to market value of equity; E/P is the ratio of earnings to market value of equity; and GS refers to preformation 5-year average growth rate of sales. The returns presented in the table are averages over all formation periods. AR is the average annual return over 5 postformation periods. CR_5 is the compounded 5-year return assuming annual rebalancing. SAAR is the average annual size-adjusted abnormal return computed over 5 postformation years. Depending on the two variables being used for classification, the value portfolio either refers to the portfolio containing stocks ranked in the top group (3) on both variables from among C/P, E/P, or B/M, or else the portfolio containing stocks ranking in the top group on one of those variables and in the bottom group (1) on GS. The glamour portfolio contains stocks with precisely the opposite set of rankings.

Panel A: C/P and GS

	Glamour						Value		
C/P	1	1	1	2	2	2	3	3	3
GS	1	2	3	1	2	3	1	2	3
AR	0.159	0.125	0.106	0.178	0.161	0.153	0.184	0.174	0.141
CR_5	1.094	0.799	0.654	1.270	1.106	1.040	1.328	1.226	0.934
SAAR	0.001	-0.020	-0.039	0.030	0.010	0.001	0.048	0.021	-0.010

Panel B: E/P and GS

	Glamour						Value		
E/P	1	1	1	2	2	2	3	3	3
GS	1	2	3	1	2	3	1	2	3
AR	0.168	0.136	0.103	0.182	0.163	0.148	0.186	0.181	0.163
CR_5	1.176	0.894	0.631	1.307	1.126	0.997	1.344	1.301	1.124
SAAR	0.012	-0.011	-0.037	0.034	0.012	-0.002	0.046	0.031	0.007

Table 8.3 (cont.)

Panel C: B/M and GS

	Glamour						Value		
B/M	1	1	1	2	2	2	3	3	3
GS	1	2	3	1	2	3	1	2	3
AR	0.149	0.140	0.124	0.176	0.158	0.131	0.186	0.172	0.153
CR_5	1.001	0.922	0.793	1.248	1.080	0.849	1.347	1.211	1.039
SAAR	0.000	-0.008	-0.025	0.027	0.006	-0.020	0.043	0.022	0.005

Panel D: E/P and B/M

	Glamour						Value		
E/P	1	1	1	2	2	2	3	3	3
B/M	1	2	3	1	2	3	1	2	3
AR	0.104	0.146	0.185	0.156	0.155	0.178	0.184	0.170	0.175
CR_5	0.636	0.979	1.335	1.063	1.054	1.265	1.318	1.190	1.244
SAAR	-0.035	0.000	0.028	0.006	0.006	0.037	0.014	0.021	0.031

Panel E: B/M and C/P

	Glamour						Value		
B/M	1	1	1	2	2	2	3	3	3
C/P	1	2	3	1	2	3	1	2	3
AR	0.109	0.166	0.148	0.139	0.157	0.168	0.182	0.173	0.178
CR_5	0.675	1.152	0.991	0.909	1.074	1.175	1.301	1.222	1.264
SAAR	-0.031	0.015	-0.007	-0.011	0.010	0.019	0.028	0.029	0.037

TABLE 8.4
Regression of Returns on Characteristics for All Firms

At the end of each April between 1968 and 1989, we compute for every firm in the sample the 1-year holding-period return starting at the end of April. We then run 22 cross-sectional regressions with these returns for each formation period as dependent variables. The independent variables are (1) GS, the preformation 5-year weighted average rank of sales growth; (2) B/M, the ratio of end of previous year's book value of equity to market value of equity; (3) SIZE, the end of April natural logarithm of market value of equity (in millions); (4) E/P+, equal to E/P—the ratio of previous year's earnings to end-of-April market value of equity—if E/P is positive—and to zero if E/P is negative; (5) DE/P, equal to 1 if E/P is negative, and zero if E/P is positive; (6) C/P+, equal to C/P—the ratio of previous-year's cash flow to end-of-April market value of equity—if C/P is positive—and zero if C/P is negative; (7) DC/P, equal to 1 if C/P is negative, and zero if C/P is positive. The reported coefficients are averages over the 22 formation periods. The reported t-statistics are based on the time-series variation of the 22 coefficients.

	Int.	GS	B/M	SIZE	E/P+	DE/P	C/P+	DC/P
Mean	0.180	−0.061						
t-statistic	3.251	−2.200						
Mean	0.108		0.039					
t-statistic	2.167		2.132					
Mean	0.185			−0.009				
t-statistic	2.140			−1.095				
Mean	0.110				0.526			
t-statistic	2.029				2.541			
Mean	0.099						0.356	
t-statistic	1.873						4.240	
Mean	0.129	−0.058	0.006				0.301	−0.029
t-statistic	2.584	−2.832	0.330				3.697	−1.222
Mean	0.143		0.009	−0.009			0.280	−0.032
t-statistic	1.562		0.565	−1.148			4.223	−1.625
Mean	0.169	−0.044	0.000	−0.009			0.296	−0.036
t-statistic	1.947	−2.125	0.005	−1.062			4.553	−1.625
Mean	0.172	−0.051	0.016	−0.009	0.394	−0.032		
t-statistic	1.961	−2.527	1.036	−1.065	2.008	−1.940		

dummy variables, called DC/P and DE/P, which take the value of 1 when C/P or E/P are negative, respectively, and zero otherwise. This approach enables us to treat observations with negative E/P and C/P differently from observations with positive E/P and C/P.

The first result emerging from table 8.4 is that, taken separately, each of GS, B/M, E/P, and C/P, although not *SIZE*, have statistically significant predictive power for returns. These results are in line with Fama and French (1992), although on a stand-alone basis C/P, and not B/M is the most significant variable. When we use the dependent variables in combination, the weakness of B/M relative to C/P, E/P, and GS begins to emerge, and its coefficient drops significantly. For example, when GS, C/P, and B/M are included in the same regression, the first two are significant, but B/M is not. In fact, the coefficient on B/M is essentially zero. Similarly, when GS, E/P, and B/M are included in the same regression, E/P and GS are significant, but B/M is not. The variables that stand out in the multiple regressions are GS and C/P.

4. A TEST OF THE EXTRAPOLATION MODEL

So far we have shown that strategies contrarian to extrapolation earn high abnormal returns relative to the market and to extrapolation strategies. We have not, however, provided any direct evidence that excessive extrapolation and expectational errors are indeed what characterizes glamour and value stocks.[11] In this section, we provide such evidence. The essence of extrapolation is that investors are excessively optimistic about glamour stocks and excessively pessimistic about value stocks because they tie their expectations of future growth to past growth. But if investors make mistakes, these mistakes can presumably be detected in the data. A direct test of extrapolation, then, is to look directly at *actual* future growth rates and compare them to *past* growth rates and to *expected* growth rates as implied by the multiples.

Table 8.5 presents some descriptive characteristics for our glamour and value portfolios regarding their valuation multiples, past growth rates, and future growth rates. Panel A reveals that the value portfolios had much higher ratios of fundamentals to price.[12] We interpret these ratios in terms of lower expected growth rates for value stocks. Panel B shows that, using

---

[11] In their study of contrarian strategies based on past stock returns, De Bondt and Thaler (1987) provide some evidence for the expectational errors view.

[12] The one exception is for the E/P ratio using the B/M classification scheme. Apparently, because of the large number of stocks with temporarily depressed earnings in the highest B/M decile, the E/P ratio for this group is extremely low. This result goes away when looking at the top two deciles together or when looking at the top decile within the largest 50 percent of our firms.

TABLE 8.5
Fundamental Variables, Past Performance, and Future
Performance of Glamour and Value Stocks

Panel 1: At the end of each April between 1968 and 1989, 10-decile portfolios are formed based on the ratio of end-of-previous-year's book value of equity to end-of-April market value of equity. Numbers are presented for the first (lowest B/M) and tenth (highest B/M) deciles. These portfolios are denoted Glamour and Value, respectively.

Panel 2: At the end of each April between 1968 and 1989, 9 groups of stocks are formed. The stocks are independently sorted in ascending order into 3 groups ((1) bottom 30 percent, (2) middle 40 percent, (3) top 30 percent) based on C/P, the ratio of cash flow to market value of equity, and GS, the preformation 5-year weighted average sales growth rank. Numbers are presented for $(C/P_1, GS_3)$, the bottom 30 percent by C/P and the top 30 percent by GS, and for $(C/P_3, GS_1)$ the top 30 percent by C/P and the bottom 30 percent by GS. These portfolios are denoted Glamour and Value, respectively.

All numbers in the table are averages over all formation periods.

E/P, C/P, S/P, D/P, B/M, and SIZE, defined below, use the end-of-April market value of equity and preformation year accounting numbers. E/P is the ratio of earnings to market value of equity. S/P is the ratio of sales to market value of equity. D/P is the ratio of dividends to market value of equity. B/M is the ratio of book value to market value of equity. SIZE is the total dollar value of equity (in millions). $AEG_{(i,j)}$ is the geometric average growth rate of earnings for the portfolio from year i to year j. $ACG_{(i,j)}$ and $ASG_{(i,j)}$ are defined analogously for cash flow and sales, respectively. $RETURN_{(-3,0)}$ is the cumulative stock return on the portfolio over the 3 years prior to formation.

	Panel 1		Panel 2	
	Glamour B/M_1	Value B/M_{10}	Glamour $C/P_1, GS_3$	Value $C/P_3, GS_1$
Panel A: Fundamental Variables				
E/P	0.029	0.004	0.054	0.114
C/P	0.059	0.172	0.080	0.279
S/P	0.993	6.849	1.115	5.279
D/P	0.012	0.032	0.014	0.039
B/M	0.225	1.998	0.385	1.414
SIZE	663	120	681	390
Panel B: Past Performance—Growth Rates and Past Returns				
$AEG_{(-5,0)}$	0.309	−0.274	0.142	0.082
$ACG_{(-5,0)}$	0.217	−0.013	0.210	0.078
$ASG_{(-5,0)}$	0.091	0.030	0.112	0.013
$RETURN_{(-2,0)}$	1.455	−0.119	1.390	0.225

TABLE 8.5 *(cont.)*

Panel C: Future Performance				
$AEG_{(0,5)}$	0.050	0.436	0.089	0.086
$ACG_{(0,5)}$	0.127	0.070	0.112	0.052
$ASG_{(0,5)}$	0.062	0.020	0.100	0.037
$AEG_{(2,5)}$	0.070	0.215	0.084	0.147
$ACG_{(2,5)}$	0.086	0.111	0.095	0.088
$ASG_{(2,5)}$	0.059	0.023	0.082	0.038

several measures of past growth, including earnings, cash flow, sales, and stock return, glamour stocks grew substantially faster than value stocks over the five years before portfolio formation. Finally, Panel C shows that over the five postformation years the relative growth of fundamentals for glamour stocks was much less impressive. Indeed, over years +2 to +5 relative to formation the growth rates of fundamentals for the value portfolio were often higher. This deterioration of relative growth rates of glamour stocks compared to past relative growth and expected future relative growth is explored more systematically below.

To interpret differences in financial ratios such as C/P and E/P in terms of expected growth rates, we come back to Gordon's formula (Gordon and Shapiro 1956). Recall that for cash flow, this formula can be rewritten as $\rho C(+1)/P = r - g$, where $C(+1)$ is one period ahead cash flow, P is the current stock price, r is the required rate of return on the stock, g is the expected growth rate of cash flow, and ρ, the payout ratio for cash flows, is the constant fraction of cash flows received as dividends. An identical formula applies for earnings, under the assumption that dividends are also some fixed fraction of earnings. Taken literally, these formulas imply that, holding discount rates and payout ratios constant, we can directly calculate differences in expected growth rates based on differences in C/P or E/P ratios. Because the assumptions behind these simple formulas are restrictive (e.g., constant growth rates, strict proportionality of dividends, cash flows and earnings, identical payout ratios across stocks, etc.), we do not calculate exact estimates of differences in expected growth rates between value and glamour portfolios. Instead, we choose to analyze differences in past growth, valuation multiples and future growth rates in a way that is more robust with respect to departures from these assumptions. However, the idea behind this analysis is the same. We ask whether the large differences in C/P and E/P ratios between value and glamour stocks can be justified by differences in future growth rates.

We start with the data for portfolios classified according to (C/P, GS). As we know already, the past growth of glamour stocks by any measure was much faster than that of value stocks. For example, over the five years before portfolio formation, the annual growth rate of cash flow for the glamour portfolio was 21.0 percent compared to 7.8 percent for the value portfolio. The difference in cash flow multiples between the value and glamour port-folios suggests that the market was expecting these growth differences to persist for many years. A dollar invested in the value portfolio was a claim to 27.9 cents in a current cash flow while a dollar invested in the glamour portfolio was a claim to only 8 cents of current cash flow. Ignoring any dif-ferences in required rates of return (this possibility is examined in section 5), these large differences in C/P would have to be justified either by big dif-ferences in payout ratios between value and glamour firms or else by an ex-pectation of very different growth rates over a long period of time. A quick look at the respective dividend yields on the value and glamour portfolios suggests that the difference was not due to differences in payout ratios. A dollar invested in the value portfolio was a claim to 3.9 cents in current dividends, while a dollar invested in the glamour portfolio brought in only 1.4 cents in dividends. These differ by roughly the same factor of 3 as for C/P. While the cash flow payout ratios were slightly higher for glamour stocks (0.175 versus 0.140),[13] this does not account for most of the differ-ence in C/P.

Under the assumption that payout ratios and discount rates were ap-proximately equal, at some future date the expected cash flows per current dollar invested must have been higher for the glamour portfolio than for the value portfolio. Accordingly, we can ask how many years it would take for the cash flows per dollar invested in the glamour portfolio (0.080) to equal the cash flows of the value portfolio (0.279), assuming that the differ-ences in past cash flow growth rates persisted (i.e., 21.0 versus 7.8 percent). The answer turns out to be approximately eleven years. If we do the same calculations using D/P ratios to take account of differences in payout ratios, it would have taken approximately nine years for dividends per dollar in-vested in the glamour portfolio (currently 0.014) to catch up to those of the value portfolio (currently 0.039), assuming that past growth rate differ-ences persisted. Note that this equality is on a flow basis not on a present-value basis. Equality on a present-value basis would require an even longer time period over which glamour firms should experience superior growth.

We can now compare these implied growth expectations to the actual cash flow growth experienced by the glamour and value portfolios. Over the first five years after formation, the cash flows of the glamour portfolio grew by 11.2 percent per year versus 5.2 percent for the value portfolio. Hence, cash flow per dollar invested grew from 0.080 initially to 0.136 at the end of year 5, while for the value portfolio cash flow per dollar invested grew from 0.279 to 0.360, still leaving a large gap in cash flow returns between the two portfolios in year 5. More importantly, the superior postformation

---

[13] We estimate these payout ratios by dividing D/P by C/P.

growth is driven almost entirely by higher growth in the first one to two postformation years. From year +2 to +5 postformation, the annual cash flow growth rates were 9.5 and 8.8 percent for glamour and value, respectively. While the market correctly anticipated higher growth in the very short-term, the persistence of these higher growth rates seems to have been grossly overestimated.[14] If growth rates after year 5 were comparable to growth rates observed over years +2 to +5, then, after ten years, cash flows per dollar on the glamour portfolio would be only 0.214 compared to 0.549 for value. These data are consistent with the idea that the market was too optimistic about the future growth of glamour firms relative to value firms.

A similar conclusion emerges from an analysis of earnings numbers. Over the five years before portfolio formation, the growth rate of earnings per dollar invested for the glamour portfolio was 14.2 percent versus 8.2 percent for the value portfolio. At formation, the E/P ratio for glamour was 0.054 compared to 0.114 for value. This difference in E/P ratios does not appear to be driven by differences in earnings payout ratios since the payout ratio for value was actually somewhat higher than for glamour (0.34 versus 0.26). Once again, we can examine the postformation growth rates to see whether higher postformation growth for glamour could justify its lower initial E/P ratio. Here the numbers are even more dramatic than for cash flow. Over the five postformation years, cumulative growth in earnings per dollar of initial investment was almost identical for the two portfolios. Earnings growth averaged 8.9 percent per year for glamour versus 8.6 percent per year for value. While growth in the first one to two years was higher for glamour, this was reversed over the following nine years. If investors expected the superior growth of glamour firms to persist (as suggested by the differences in E/P ratios), the data indicate that they significantly overestimated future growth rate differences between glamour and value stocks.

Analogous results for portfolios classified according to B/M are also presented in table 8.5. We focus only on the numbers for cash flow because the E/P ratios for the extreme decile portfolios are so low as to make an expected growth computation somewhat questionable. For example, the E/P ratio for decile 10 (value) was only 0.004, indicating a high proportion of firms with temporarily depressed earnings. Because cash flows are less volatile and less often negative, the C/P ratios are much better behaved. For the glamour portfolio (B/M$_1$), C/P was equal to 0.059 versus 0.172 for the value portfolio (B/M$_{10}$). These numbers are quite similar to those for the (C/P, GS) portfolios.

Presumably, this difference in C/P reflects, at least in part, the market's expectation that the superior growth of glamour firms would continue.

[14] The result that growth rates of earnings are highly mean reverting is not new. Little (1962) shows this quite clearly in his pathbreaking article.

Over the previous five years cash flow for the glamour portfolio had grown at 21.7 percent per year while cash flow growth for the value portfolio had been −1.3 percent per year. Estimated cash flow payout ratios for glamour and value firms were quite similar (0.203 and 0.186, respectively). Hence, differential payout ratios alone could not justify much of the difference in C/P ratios.

Postformation cash flow numbers indicate that glamour stocks indeed outgrew value stocks over the five years after formation, but that this is due to much higher growth at the beginning of the postformation period. In the last three years of the postformation period, cash flows for the value port-folio actually grew faster (11.1 percent per year versus 8.6 percent per year). In sum, at the end of five years cash flow per initial dollar invested rose from 0.059 to 0.107 for the glamour portfolio and from 0.172 to 0.241 for the value portfolio. If cash flow growth rates over years +2 to +5 postformation were any indication of growth rates after year 5, the cash flow return on glamour stocks did not get any closer to that for value stocks. These results mirror those for the (C/P, GS) classification. They are consistent with the view that the superior postformation return on value stocks are explained by upward revisions in expectations about the relative growth rates of value versus glamour stocks.

Contrary to the assertions of Fama and French (1993, section 5), the market was likely to learn about its mistake only slowly over time since its expectation of higher relative growth for individual glamour firms was often confirmed in the short-run but then disconfirmed only in the longer run. Hence, we do not necessarily expect to see a clear spike in returns or E/P ratios. In this respect, the motivation behind the contrarian strategies explored in this article is quite different from that for the strategies ex-plored by Jegadeesh and Titman (1993), Bernard and Thomas (1989), and Givoly and Lakonishok (1979). The momentum-based strategies of those articles rely on the market's short-term failure to recognize a trend. In con-trast, the superior returns to value strategies documented here seem to be driven by the market's unwarranted belief in the continuation of a long-term trend and its gradual abandonment of that belief.

In summary, the evidence in table 8.5 is consistent with the extrapolation model. Glamour stocks have historically grown fast in sales, earnings, and cash flow relative to value stocks. According to most of our measures, the market expected the superior growth of glamour firms to continue for many years. In the very short run, the expectations of continued superior growth of glamour stocks were on average born out. However, beyond the first couple years, growth rates of glamour stocks and value stocks were es-sentially the same. The evidence suggests that forecasts were tied to past growth rates and were too optimistic for glamour stocks relative to value stocks. This is precisely what the extrapolation model would predict. In this respect, the evidence in table 8.5 goes beyond the customary evidence on returns in that it shows a relationship between the past, the forecasted, and the actual future growth rates that is largely consistent with the predictions of the extrapolation model.

5. ARE CONTRARIAN STRATEGIES RISKIER?

Two alternative theories have been proposed to explain why value strategies have produced higher returns in the past. The first theory says that they have done so because they exploit the mistakes of naive investors. The previous section showed that investors appear to be extrapolating the past too far into the future, even though the future does not warrant such extrapolation. The second explanation of the superior returns to value strategies is that they expose investors to greater systematic risk. In this section, we examine this explanation directly.

Value stocks would be fundamentally riskier than glamour stocks if, first, they underperform glamour stocks in some states of the world, and second, those are on average "bad" states, in which the marginal utility of wealth is high, making value stocks unattractive to risk-averse investors. This simple theory motivates our empirical approach.

To begin, we look at the consistency of performance of the value and glamour strategies over time and ask how often value underperforms glamour. We then check whether the times when value underperforms are recessions, times of severe market declines, or otherwise "bad" states of the world in which the marginal utility of consumption is high. These tests do not provide much support for the view that value strategies are fundamentally riskier. Finally, we look at some traditional measures of risk, such as beta and the standard deviation of returns, to compare value and glamour strategies.

Table 8.6 and figure 8.2 present the year-by-year performance of the value strategy *relative* to the glamour strategy over the April 1968 to April 1990 period. We consider differences in cumulative returns between deciles (9, 10) and (1, 2) for C/P and B/M, and between groups (3, 1) and (1, 3) for (C/P, GS) over one-, three-, and five-year holding horizons starting each year in the sample (1968, 1969, etc.). The arithmetic mean across years for each horizon is reported at the bottom of each column along with t-statistics for the test of the hypothesis that the difference in returns between value and glamour portfolios is equal to zero. Standard errors for t-tests involving overlapping three- and five-year horizons are computed using the method of Hansen-Hodrick (1980), assuming annual $MA_{(2)}$ and $MA_{(4)}$ processes, respectively.

The results show that value strategies have consistently outperformed glamour strategies. Using a one-year horizon, value outperformed glamour in 17 out of 22 years using C/P to classify stocks, in 19 out of 22 years

TABLE 8.6
Year-by-Year Returns: Value–Glamour

Panel 1: At the end of each April between 1968 and 1989, 10-decile portfolios are formed based on the ratio of previous-year's cash flow to end-of-April market-value of equity (C/P). For each portfolio, 1-, 3-, and 5-year holding-period returns are computed. For each formation period, Panel 1 reports the difference in the 1-, 3-, and 5-year return between the 2 highest C/P (value) and 2 lowest C/P (glamour) portfolios.

Panel 2: At the end of each April between 1968 and 1989, 9 groups of stocks are formed as follows. All stocks are independently sorted into 3 groups ((1) bottom 30 percent, (2) middle 40 percent, and (3) top 30 percent) by the ratio of previous-year's cash flow to end-of-April market-value of equity (C/P) and by the preformation 5-year weighted average rank-of-sales growth (GS). The 9 portfolios are intersections resulting from these 2 independent classifications. For each portfolio, 1-, 3-, and 5-year holding period returns are computed. For each formation period, Panel 2 reports the difference in the 1-, 3-, and 5-year return between the lowest GS, highest C/P (value) and the highest GS, lowest C/P (glamour) portfolios.

Panel 3: At the end of each April between 1968 and 1989, 10-decile portfolios are formed based on the ratio of the end-of-previous-year's book value of equity to end-of-April market value of equity (B/M). For each portfolio, 1-, 3-, and 5-year-holding-period returns are computed. For each formation period, Panel 3 reports the difference in the 1-, 3-, and 5-year return between the highest B/M (value) and lowest B/M (glamour) decile portfolios.

The last two rows respectively report the arithmetic mean across periods and the t-statistic for the test of the hypothesis that the difference in returns between value and glamour is equal to zero. These t-statistics are based on standard errors computed according to Hansen and Hodrick (1980).

| | Panel 1 | | | Panel 2 | | | Panel 3 | | |
| | (C/P:9,10 – 1,2) | | | (C/P-GS:3,1 – 1,3) | | | (B/M:9,10 – 1,2) | | |
	1-Year	3-Year	5-Year	1-Year	3-Year	5-Year	1-Year	3-Year	5-Year
1968	0.022	0.287	0.474	0.144	0.153	0.267	0.098	0.201	0.344
1969	0.123	0.195	0.410	0.065	−0.143	0.283	0.074	0.070	0.303
1970	0.135	0.246	0.428	0.002	0.160	0.356	0.023	0.032	0.279
1971	−0.078	0.231	0.478	−0.144	0.196	0.531	−0.108	0.156	0.463
1972	0.155	0.319	0.693	0.134	0.362	0.932	0.098	0.328	0.784

TABLE 8.6 (cont.)

	Panel 1 (C/P:9, 10 − 1, 2)			Panel 2 (C/P-GS:3, 1 − 1, 3)			Panel 3 (B/M:9, 10 − 1, 2)		
	1-Year	3-Year	5-Year	1-Year	3-Year	5-Year	1-Year	3-Year	5-Year
1973	0.021	0.382	0.846	0.152	0.702	1.416	0.042	0.450	0.925
1974	−0.007	0.496	1.343	0.069	0.650	1.597	0.050	0.642	1.726
1975	0.262	0.816	1.310	0.379	1.115	1.229	0.418	1.034	1.182
1976	0.174	0.673	1.468	0.217	0.715	1.235	0.132	0.727	0.993
1977	0.193	0.247	0.764	0.219	0.149	0.844	0.195	0.181	0.614
1978	0.048	−0.106	0.272	0.039	−0.072	0.581	0.037	−0.264	0.286
1979	−0.168	−0.102	0.274	−0.176	0.098	0.757	−0.207	−0.123	0.569
1980	0.039	0.745	1.225	0.110	1.246	2.000	−0.034	1.066	1.676
1981	0.203	0.650	1.584	0.236	0.940	2.134	0.185	0.810	1.955
1982	−0.032	0.338	1.253	0.118	0.539	1.886	0.240	0.589	1.477
1983	0.204	0.332	0.851	0.252	0.578	1.470	0.221	0.256	0.648
1984	0.192	0.552	0.888	0.052	0.641	1.092	0.043	0.324	0.640
1985	0.014	0.322	0.576	−0.032	0.531	0.708	−0.007	0.237	0.299
1986	0.108	0.339		0.196	0.427		0.051	0.149	
1987	0.093	0.170		0.111	0.290		0.078	0.015	
1988	0.092			0.089			−0.037		
1989	−0.063			0.010			−0.207		
Average	0.079	0.357	0.841	0.102	0.464	1.073	0.063	0.344	0.842
t-statistic	3.379	6.164	7.630	3.746	4.524	5.939	2.076	3.475	7.104

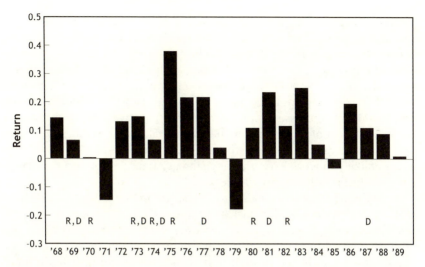

Figure 8.2. Year-by-year returns: Value minus glamour. At the end of each April between 1968 and 1989, 9 groups of stocks are formed. The stocks are independently sorted in ascending order into 3 groups (1) bottom 30 percent, (2) middle 40 percent, and (3) top 30 percent based on each of two variables: cash flow-to-price (C/P) and growth-in-sales (GS). The value portfolio consists of those stocks in the highest C/P groups and the lowest GS group. The glamour portfolio consists of those stocks in the lowest C/P group and the highest GS group. The numbers presented are annual buy-and-hold returns for the value portfolio minus returns for the glamour portfolio. Annual buy-and-hold returns are calculated beginning at the end of April for the given year. R indicates NBER recession years, and D indicates years in which the CRSP equally weighted index declined in nominal terms.

using C/P and GS, and in 17 out of 22 years using the B/M ratio. As we move to longer horizons, the consistency of performance of the value strategy relative to the glamour strategy increases. For all three classification schemes, the value portfolio outperforms the glamour portfolio over every five-year horizon in the sample period.

These numbers pose a stiff challenge to any risk-based explanation for the higher returns on value stocks. Consider the (C/P, GS) classification. Over a three-year horizon, the value strategy underperformed the glamour strategy in only two instances. In those instances, the magnitude of the value strategy's underperformance was small relative to its mean outperformance of 46.4 percent. Over any five-year horizon in the sample, the value strategy was a sure winner. Even for a one-year horizon, the downside of this strategy was fairly low. To explain these numbers with a multifactor risk model would require that the relatively few instances of underperformance of the value portfolio are tightly associated with very bad states of the world as defined by some payoff relevant factor. Put another way, the covariance between the negative realizations of the value minus glamour return and this payoff-relevant factor should be high and the risk-premium associated with that factor should also be quite high.

While it is difficult to reject a risk-based explanation that relies on an unspecified multifactor model, we can examine a set of important payoff-relevant factors that are likely to be associated with large risk premia. If, after examining the association between the negative relative returns to value and this set of factors, we are unable to make sense of the higher average returns on value strategies, we can conclude that a risk-based explanation is unlikely to work except by appealing to large risk premia on factors that are a priori of lesser payoff relevance.

In examining the payoff relevant factors, we do not restrict ourselves to tightly parameterized models such as the Sharpe-Lintner model or the consumption Capital Asset Pricing Model (using consumption data) which are too likely to lead to rejection of risk-based explanations. For example, we do not assume that beta is the appropriate measure of exposure to the market factor. Instead, we proceed nonparametrically and examine the performance of value strategies in extreme down markets. Moreover, we allow for the possibility that the distribution of stock returns does not provide a complete characterization of good and bad states of the world. Barro (1990) and others find that, while the stock market is useful in predicting economic aggregates such as GNP growth, the R^2 is only around 0.4 in the post war subperiod.

Some evidence on the performance of value and glamour strategies in bad states of the world can be gleaned from table 8.6 and figure 8.2. According to the National Bureau of Economic Research, there were four recessions during our sample period: a mild one from December 1969 to November 1970, a very deep one from November 1973 to March 1975, and also significant ones from January 1980 to July 1980 and July 1981 to November 1982. An examination of table 8.6 shows that the value strategy did about the same or somewhat better than glamour just before and during the 1970 recession, did much better around the severe recession of 1973 to 1975, did somewhat worse in 1979 to 1980, and did significantly better in 1981 to 1982.[15] It is implausible to conclude from this that value strategies did particularly badly in recessions, when the marginal utility of consumption is especially high.

A second approach is to compare the performance of value and glamour portfolios in the worst months for the stock market as a whole. Table 8.7, Panel 1 presents the performance of our portfolios in each of four states of the world; the twenty-five worst stock return months in the sample based on the equally weighted index, the remaining eighty-eight negative months

---

[15] Recall that returns are computed starting at the end of April of the year listed through April of the following year.

TABLE 8.7

Performance of Portfolios in Best and Worst Times

Panel 1: All months in the sample are divided into 25 worst stock return months based on the equally weighted index (W_{25}), the remaining 88 negative months other than the 25 worst (N_{88}), the 122 positive months other than the 25 best (P_{122}), and the 25 best months (B_{25}) in the sample.

Panel 1A: At the end of each April between 1968 and 1989, 9 groups of stocks are formed as follows. All stocks are independently sorted into 3 groups ((1) bottom 340 percent, (2) middle 40 percent, and (3) top 30 percent) by the ratio of previous year's cash flow to end-of-April market value of equity (CP) and by the preformation 5-year weighted average rank of sales growth (GS). The 9 portfolios are intersections resulting from these 2 independent classifications. For each portfolio (changing every April), Panel 1A presents its average return over the W_{25}, N_{88}, P_{122}, and B_{25} months.

Panel 1B: At the end of each April between 1968 and 1989, 10-decile portfolios are formed based on the ratio of end-of-previous year's book value of equity to end-of-April market value of equity (B/M). For each portfolio (changing every April), Panel 1B presents its average return over the W_{25}, N_{88}, P_{122}, and B_{25} months.

Panel 2A and 2B have the same structure, but the states are defined in terms of the best and worst quarters for GNP growth. All quarters in the sample are divided into 4 sets: 10 quarters of the lowest real GNP growth during the sample period, 34 next lowest real GNP growth quarters, 34 next worst growth quarters, and 10 highest real GNP growth quarters.

In Panel 2A, the value portfolio contains stocks ranking in the bottom group on C/P and in the bottom group on GS. The Glamour portfolio contains stocks ranking in the top group on C/P and in the top group on GS. In Panel 2B, the Value portfolio contains stocks ranking in the bottom two deciles on B/M. The Glamour portfolio contains stocks ranking in the top two deciles on B/M. The right-most column contains the t-statistic for testing the hypothesis that the difference in returns between the Value and Glamour portfolios is equal to zero.

Panel 1A

Panel 1: Portfolio Returns across Best and Worst Stock Market Months

C/P GS	Glamour					Value				Index	Value-Glamour (1,3 – 3,1)	t-Statistic
	1 1	1 2	1 3	2 1	2 2	2 3	3 1	3 2	3 3			
W_{25}	-0.114	-0.103	-0.103	-0.090	-0.091	-0.100	-0.086	-0.080	-0.105	-0.102	0.018	3.040
N_{88}	-0.023	-0.025	-0.029	-0.016	-0.020	-0.025	-0.015	-0.016	-0.022	-0.023	0.014	4.511
P_{122}	0.039	0.039	0.038	0.040	0.038	0.039	0.040	0.038	0.038	0.037	0.002	0.759
B_{25}	0.131	0.111	0.110	0.110	0.104	0.115	0.124	0.113	0.124	0.121	0.014	1.021

Table 8.7 (cont.)

Panel 1B

B/M	Glamour								Value		Index	Value-Glamour (9,10−1,2)	t-Statistic
	1	2	3	4	5	6	7	8	9	10			
W_{25}	−0.112	−0.110	−0.104	−0.100	−0.097	−0.091	−0.093	−0.092	−0.098	−0.102	−0.102	0.011	1.802
N_{88}	−0.029	−0.028	−0.026	−0.025	−0.023	−0.020	−0.021	−0.020	−0.018	−0.022	−0.023	0.008	2.988
P_{122}	0.038	0.040	0.039	0.037	0.036	0.037	0.038	0.037	0.038	0.039	0.037	−0.001	−0.168
B_{25}	0.114	0.114	0.119	0.113	0.112	0.113	0.117	0.126	0.133	0.148	0.121	0.026	1.729

Panel 2: Portfolio Returns across Best and Worst GNP Growth Quarters

Panel 2A

C/P GS	Glamour				Value				Value		GNP	Value-Glamour (1,3 -3,1)	t-Statistic
	1 1	1 2	1 3	2 1	2 2	2 3	3 1	3 2	3 3				
Worst 10	0.032	0.014	−0.009	0.037	0.016	0.013	0.041	0.020	0.008	−0.017	0.050	2.485
Next worst 34	0.021	0.010	0.011	0.018	0.014	0.011	0.027	0.023	0.012	0.000	0.016	1.473
Next best 34	0.026	0.029	0.026	0.040	0.033	0.029	0.046	0.046	0.034	0.012	0.020	2.176
Best 10	0.122	0.107	0.103	0.140	0.123	0.123	0.139	0.133	0.136	0.031	0.036	1.786

Panel 2B

B/M	Glamour								Value		GNP	Value-Glamour (9,10 -1,2)	t-Statistic
	1	2	3	4	5	6	7	8	9	10			
Worst 10	−0.004	0.001	0.012	0.018	0.009	0.016	0.017	0.028	0.021	0.015	−0.017	0.020	0.983
Next worst 34	0.011	0.008	0.011	0.009	0.008	0.010	0.010	0.016	0.017	0.012	0.000	0.005	0.494
Next best 34	0.022	0.028	0.027	0.025	0.030	0.035	0.036	0.035	0.041	0.039	0.012	0.015	1.555
Best 10	0.092	0.102	0.118	0.117	0.117	0.135	0.132	0.141	0.145	0.151	0.031	0.051	2.685

other than the twenty-five worst, the one hundred and twenty-two positive months other than the twenty-five best, and the twenty-five best months in the sample. The average difference in returns between value and glamour portfolios for each state is also reported along with t-statistics for the test that the difference of returns is equal to zero. The results in this table are fairly clear. Using both the B/M and (C/P, GS) classification schemes, the value portfolio outperformed the glamour portfolio in the market's worst twenty-five months. For example, using the (C/P, GS) classification, the value portfolio lost an average of 8.6 percent of its value in the worst twenty-five months, whereas the glamour portfolio lost 10.3 percent of its value. Similarly, using both classification schemes, the value portfolio on average outperformed the glamour portfolio and the index in the next worst eighty-eight months in which the index declined. Using the (C/P, GS) classification, the value portfolio lost 1.5 percent in these months when the index experiences a mild decline, compared to 2.9 percent for the glamour portfolio and 2.3 percent for the index itself. So the value strategy did better when the market fell. The value strategy performed most closely to the glamour strategy in the one hundred and twenty-two positive months other than the best twenty-five. In the very best months, the value strategy substantially outperformed the glamour strategy and the index, but not by as much as it does when the market fell sharply. Some care should be taken in interpreting these mean differences for the positive market return months, however, given the low t-statistics. Overall, the value strategy performed somewhat better than the glamour strategy in all states and significantly better in some states. If anything, the superior performance of the value strategy was skewed toward negative market return months rather than positive market return months. The evidence in table 8.7, Panel 1 thus indicates that the value strategy did not expose investors to greater downside risk.

Table 8.7, Panel 2 provides numbers analogous to those in Panel 1 except now the states of the world are realizations of real GNP growth.[16] The data are quarterly, so that we have eighty-eight quarters in the sample. These quarters are classified into four states of the world; the worst ten quarters, the next worst thirty-four quarters, the best ten quarters, and the next best thirty-four quarters. The quarterly returns on the various glamour and value portfolios are then matched up with the changes in real GNP for one quarter ahead, since evidence indicates that the stock market leads GNP by approximately one quarter. Average quarterly returns for each portfolio are then computed for each state.

The results in Panel 2 mirror the basic conclusions from Panel 1; namely, the value strategy has not been fundamentally riskier than the glamour

---

[16] In an earlier draft of this article we included results using the change in the unemployment rate. The results are quite similar to those for GNP growth.

strategy. For both classification schemes, the value strategy performed at least as well as the glamour strategy *in each of the 4 states* and substantially better in most states. Unlike the results in Panel 1, there was some tendency for the relative returns on value to be higher in good states than in bad states, especially for extreme good states. Roughly speaking, value stocks could be described as having higher up-market betas and lower down-market betas than glamour stocks with respect to economic conditions. Importantly, while the value strategy did disproportionately well in extreme good times, its performance in extreme bad times was also quite impressive. Performance in extreme bad states is often the last refuge of those claiming that a high return strategy *must* be riskier, even when conventional measures of risk such as beta and standard deviation do not show it. The evidence indicates some positive relation between relative performance of the value strategy and measures of prosperity, but there are no significant traces of a conventional asset pricing equilibrium in which the higher returns on the value strategy are compensation for higher systematic risk.

Finally, for completeness, table 8.8 presents some more traditional risk measures for portfolios using our classification schemes. These risk measures are calculated using annual measurement intervals over the postformation period, because of the problems associated with use of preformation period data (Ball and Kothari 1989). For each of our portfolios, we have twenty-two annual observations on its return in the year following the formation, and hence can compute the standard deviation of returns. We also have corresponding returns on the value-weighted CRSP index and the risk-free asset, and hence can calculate a beta for each portfolio.

First, the betas of value portfolios with respect to the value-weighted index tend to be about 0.1 higher than the betas of the glamour portfolios. As we have seen earlier, the high betas probably come from value stocks having higher "up-market" betas,[17] and that, if anything, the superior performance of the value strategy occurs disproportionally during "bad" realizations of the stock market. Even if one takes a very strong pro-beta position, the difference in betas of 0.1 can explain a difference in returns of only up to 1 percent per year (assuming a market risk premium of 8 percent per year) and surely not the 10 to 11 percent difference in returns that we find.

Table 8.8 also presents average annual standard deviations of the various portfolio returns. The results show that value portfolios have somewhat higher standard deviations of returns than glamour portfolios. Using the (C/P, GS) classification, the value portfolio has an average standard deviation of returns of 24.1 percent relative to 21.6 percent for the glamour portfolio. Three remarks about these numbers are in order. First, we have

---

[17] De Bondt and Thaler (1987) obtain a similar result for their contrarian strategy based on buying stocks with low past returns.

TABLE 8.8
Traditional Risk Measures for Portfolios

For each portfolio described below, we compute, using 22 year-after-the-formation returns as observations, its beta with respect to the value-weighted index. Using the 22 formation periods, we also compute the standard deviation of returns and the standard deviation of size-adjusted returns in the year after formation.

Panel 1: At the end of each April between 1968 and 1989, 10-decile portfolios are formed based on the ratio of previous-year's cash flow to end-of-April market value of equity (C/P). For each decile portfolio, Panel 1 presents its beta, standard deviation of returns, and standard deviation of size-adjusted returns defined above.

Panel 2: At the end of each April between 1968 and 1989, 9 groups of stocks are formed as follows. All stocks are independently sorted into 3 groups ((1) bottom 30 percent, (2) middle 40 percent, and (3) top 30 percent) by the ratio of previous-year's cash flow to end-of-April market value of equity (C/P) and by the preformation 5-year weighted-average rank of sales growth (GS). The 9 portfolios are intersections resulting from these 2 independent classifications. For each group of stocks, Panel 2 presents its beta, standard deviation of returns, and standard deviation of size-adjusted returns defined above.

Panel 3: At the end of each April between 1968 and 1989, 10-decile portfolios are formed based on the ratio of end-of-previous year's book value of equity to end-of-April market value of equity (B/M). For each decile portfolio, Panel 3 presents its beta, standard deviation of returns, and standard deviation of size-adjusted returns defined above.

Panel 1

C/P	1	2	3	4	5	6	7	8	9	10	Equally Weighted Index
β	1.268	1.293	1.321	1.333	1.318	1.237	1.182	1.247	1.224	1.384	1.304
Standard deviation	0.224	0.227	0.239	0.237	0.232	0.221	0.212	0.223	0.224	0.252	0.250
Standard deviation of size-adjusted return	0.037	0.044	0.049	0.036	0.033	0.034	0.042	0.036	0.048	0.058	—

TABLE 8.8 (cont.)

Panel 2

C/P	1	2	3	1	2	3	1	2	3	Equally Weighted Index
GS	3	3	3	2	2	2	1	1	1	
β	1.249	1.296	1.293	1.239	1.184	1.214	1.330	1.258	1.322	1.304
Standard deviation	0.216	0.232	0.241	0.215	0.207	0.213	0.242	0.224	0.241	0.250
Standard deviation of size-adjusted return	0.061	0.040	0.066	0.049	0.033	0.047	0.066	0.047	0.065	—

Panel 3

B/M	1	2	3	4	5	6	7	8	9	10	Equally Weighted Index
β	1.248	1.268	1.337	1.268	1.252	1.214	1.267	1.275	1.299	1.443	1.304
Standard deviation	0.223	0.223	0.236	0.225	0.221	0.214	0.225	0.233	0.248	0.276	0.250
Standard deviation of size-adjusted return	0.076	0.050	0.040	0.035	0.031	0.040	0.035	0.043	0.046	0.071	—

already shown that, because of its much higher mean return, the value strategy's higher standard deviation does not translate into greater downside risk. Second, the higher standard deviation of value stocks appears to be due largely to their smaller average size, since the standard deviation of size-adjusted returns is virtually the same for value and glamour portfolios. But the results in table 8.3 suggest that, by focusing on larger value stocks, investors could still get most of the extra return from value stocks without this higher standard deviation. The extra return on a portfolio of large value stocks cannot therefore be explained by appealing to its higher standard deviation. Finally, the difference in standard deviation of returns between value and glamour portfolios (24.1 versus 21.6 percent per year) is quite small in comparison to the difference in average return (10 percent per year). For example, over the 1926 to 1988 period the extra return on the S&P 500 over T-Bills was approximately 8 percent per year, while the average standard deviation on the S&P 500 was 21 percent compared to 3 percent for T-Bills. In comparison to the reward-to-risk ratio for stocks vis-à-vis T-Bills, the reward-to-risk ratio for investing in value stocks is extremely high. A risk model based on differences in standard deviation cannot explain the superior returns on value stocks.

6. Summary and Interpretation of the Findings

The results in this chapter establish (in varying degrees of detail) three propositions. First, a variety of investment strategies that involve buying out-of-favor (value) stocks have outperformed glamour strategies over the April 1968 to April 1990 period. Second, a likely reason that these value strategies have worked so well relative to the glamour strategies is the fact that the actual future growth rates of earnings, cash flow, etcetera of glamour stocks relative to value stocks turned out to be much lower than they were in the past, or as the multiples on those stocks indicate the market expected them to be. That is, market participants appear to have consistently overestimated future growth rates of glamour stocks relative to value stocks. Third, using conventional approaches to fundamental risk, value strategies appear to be no riskier than glamour strategies. Reward for bearing fundamental risk does not seem to explain higher average returns on value stocks than on glamour stocks.

While one can never reject the "metaphysical" version of the risk story, in which securities that earn higher returns must *by definition* be fundamentally riskier, the weight of evidence suggests a more straightforward model. In this model, out-of-favor (or value) stocks have been underpriced relative to their risk and return characteristics, and investing in them has indeed earned abnormal returns.

This conclusion raises the obvious question: How can the 10 to 11 percent per year in extra returns on value stocks over glamour stocks have persisted for so long? One possible explanation is that investors simply did not know about them. This explanation has some plausibility in that quantitative portfolio selection and evaluation are relatively recent activities. Most investors might not have been able, until recently, to perform the analysis done in this chapter. Of course, advocacy of value strategies is decades old, going back at least to Graham and Dodd (1934). But such advocacy is usually not accompanied by defensible statistical work and hence might not be entirely persuasive, especially since many other strategies are advocated as well.

Another possible explanation is that we have engaged in data snooping (Lo and MacKinlay 1990) and have merely identified an ex post pattern in the data. Clearly, these data have been mined in the sense that others have looked at much of these same data before us. On the other hand, we think there is good reason to believe that the cross-sectional return differences reported here reflect an important economic regularity rather than sampling error. First, similar findings on the superior returns of value strategies have been obtained for several different time series. Davis (1994) finds similar results on a subsample of large U.S. firms over the period 1931 to 1960. Chan, Hamao and Lakonishok (1991) find similar results for Japan. Capaul, Rowley, and Sharpe (1993) find similar results for France, Germany, Switzerland, and the United Kingdom, as well as for the United States and Japan.

Second, we have documented more than just a cross-sectional pattern of returns. The evidence suggests a systematic pattern of expectational errors on the part of investors that is capable of explaining the differential stock returns across value and glamour stocks. Investor expectations of future growth appear to have been excessively tied to past growth despite the fact that future growth rates are highly mean reverting. In particular, investors expected glamour firms to continue growing faster than value firms, but they were systematically disappointed. La Porta (1993) shows that a similar pattern of expectational errors and returns on value strategies obtains when growth expectations are measured by analysts' five-year earnings growth forecasts rather than by financial ratios such as E/P or C/P. The evidence on expectational errors supports the view that the cross-sectional differences in returns reflect a genuine economic phenomenon.

We conjecture that the results in this chapter can best be explained by the preference of both individual and institutional investors for glamour strategies and by their avoidance of value strategies. Below we suggest some reasons for this preference that might potentially explain the observed returns anomaly.

Individual investors might focus on glamour strategies for a variety of reasons. First, they may make judgment errors and extrapolate past growth rates of glamour stocks, such as Walmart or Microsoft, even when such growth rates are highly unlikely to persist in the future. Putting excessive weight on recent past history, as opposed to a rational prior, is a common judgment error in psychological experiments and not just in the stock market. Alternatively, individuals might just equate well-run firms with good investments, regardless of price. After all, how can you lose money on Microsoft or Walmart? Indeed, brokers typically recommend "good" companies with "steady" earnings and dividend growth.

Presumably, institutional investors should be somewhat more free from judgment biases and excitement about "good companies" than individuals, and so should flock to value strategies.[18] But institutional investors may have reasons of their own for gravitating toward glamour stocks. Lakonishok, Shleifer, and Vishny (1992b) focus on the agency context of institutional money management. Institutions might prefer glamour stocks because they appear to be "prudent" investments, and hence are easy to justify to sponsors. Glamour stocks have done well in the past and are unlikely to become financially distressed in the near future, as opposed to value stocks, which have previously done poorly and are more likely to run into financial problems. Many institutions actually screen out stocks of financially distressed firms, many of which are value stocks, from the universe of stocks they pick. Indeed, sponsors may mistakenly believe glamour stocks to be safer than value stocks, even though, as we have seen, a portfolio of value stocks is no more risky. The strategy of investing in glamour stocks, while appearing "prudent," is not prudent at all in that it earns a lower expected return and is not fundamentally less risky. Nonetheless, the career concerns of money managers and employees of their institutional clients may cause money managers to tilt towards "glamour" stocks.

Another important factor is that most investors have shorter time horizons than are required for value strategies to consistently pay off (De Long et al. 1990, and Shleifer and Vishny 1990). Many individuals look for stocks that will earn them high abnormal returns within a few months, rather than 4 percent per year over the next five years. Institutional money managers often have even shorter time horizons. They often cannot afford to underperform the index or their peers for any nontrivial period of time, for if they do, their sponsors will withdraw the funds. A value strategy that takes three to five years to pay off but may underperform the market in the meantime (i.e., have a large tracking error) might simply be too risky for money managers from the viewpoint of career concerns, especially if the strategy itself is more difficult to justify to sponsors. If a money manager fears getting fired before a value strategy pays off, he will avoid using such a strategy. Importantly, while tracking error can explain why a money manager would not want too strong a tilt toward *either* value or growth, it does

[18] According to Dreman (1977), professional money managers are also quite likely to suffer from these biases.

not explain why he would not tilt slightly toward value given its apparently superior risk/return profile. Hence, these horizon and tracking error issues *can* explain why money managers do not more aggressively "arbitrage" the differences in returns across value and glamour stocks, but they *cannot* explain why such differences are there in the first place. In our view, such return differences are ultimately explained by the tendency of investors to make judgmental errors and perhaps also by a tendency for institutional investors to actively tilt toward glamour to make their lives easier.

Are the anomalous excess returns on value stocks likely to persist? It is possible that over time more investors will become convinced of the value of being a contrarian with a long horizon and the returns to value strategies will fall. Perhaps the recent move into disciplined quantitative investment strategies, evaluated based only on performance and not on individual stock picks, will increase the demand for value stocks and reduce the agency problems that result in picking glamour stocks. Such sea changes rarely occur overnight, however. The time-series and cross-country evidence support the idea that the behavioral and institutional factors underlying the higher returns to value stocks have been pervasive and enduring features of equity markets.

Perhaps the most interesting implication of the conjecture that institutional investors gravitate toward glamour stocks is that this may explain their inferior performance. In an earlier article, we focused on the striking underperformance of pension fund money managers relative to the market index (Lakonishok, Shleifer, and Vishny 1992b). The large difference in returns on glamour and value stocks can, at least in principle, explain why money managers have underperformed the market by over 100 basis points per year before accounting for management fees. By looking at the actual portfolios of institutional money managers, one can find out whether they have been overinvested in glamour stocks and underinvested in value stocks. We plan to do that in a follow-up article.

References

Ball, R., and S. Kothari, 1989, Non-stationary expected returns: Implications for tests of market efficiency and serial correlation of returns, *Journal of Financial Economics* 25, 51–74.

Banz, R., and W. Breen, 1986, Sample dependent results using accounting and market data: Some evidence, *Journal of Finance* 41, 779–93.

Barro, R., 1990, The stock market and investment, *Review of Financial Studies* 3, 115–31.

Basu, S., 1977, Investment performance of common stocks in relation to their price earnings ratios: A test of the efficient market hypothesis, *Journal of Finance* 32, 663–82.

Bernard, V., and J. Thomas, 1989, Post-earnings announcement drift: Delayed price response or risk premium, *Journal of Accounting Research* 27 (Supplement), 1–36.

Black, F., 1986, Noise, *Journal of Finance* 41, 529–43.

Brown, S., W. Goetzmann, and S. Ross, 1993, Survivorship bias in autocorrelation and long-term memory studies, Mimeo, New York University, Columbia University and Yale University, September.

Capaul, C., I. Rowley, and W. Sharpe, 1993, International value and growth stock returns, *Financial Analysts Journal*, January/February, 27–36.

Chan, K., 1988, On the contrarian investment strategy, *Journal of Business* 61, 147–63.

Chan, L., Y. Hamao, and J. Lakonishok, 1991, Fundamentals and stock returns in Japan, *Journal of Finance* 46, 1739–64.

Chopra, N., J. Lakonishok, and J. Ritter, 1992, Measuring abnormal performance: Do stocks overreact?, *Journal of Financial Economics* 31, 235–68.

Davis, James, 1994, The cross-section of realized stock returns: The pre-COMPUSTAT evidence, *Journal of Finance* 49, 1579–93.

De Bondt, W., and R. Thaler, 1985, Does the stock market overreact?, *Journal of Finance* 40, 793–805.

———, 1987, Further evidence on investor overreaction and stock market seasonality, *Journal of Finance* 42, 557–81.

De Long, J. B., A. Shleifer, L. Summers, and R. Waldmann, 1990, Noise trader risk in financial markets, *Journal of Political Economy* 98, 703–38.

Dreman, D., 1977, *Psychology and the Stock Market: Why the Pros Go Wrong and How to Profit*, Warner Books.

Fama, E., and K. French, 1992, The cross-section of expected stock returns, *Journal of Finance* 46, 427–66.

———, 1993, Size and book-to-market factors in earnings and returns, Mimeo, University of Chicago.

Fama, E., and J. MacBeth, 1973, Risk, return and equilibrium: Empirical tests, *Journal of Political Economy* 81, 607–36.

Givoly, D., and J. Lakonishok, 1979, The information content of financial analysts' forecasts of earnings: Some evidence on semi-strong inefficiency, *Journal of Accounting and Economics* 1, 165–85.

Gordon, M., and E. Shapiro, 1956, Capital equipment analysis: the required rate of profit, *Management Science* 3, 102–10.

Graham, B., and D. Dodd, 1934, *Security Analysis*, McGraw-Hill.

Hansen, L. P., and R. Hodrick, 1980, Forward exchange rates as optimal predictors of future spot rates; An econometric analysis, *Journal of Political Economy* 88, 829–53.

Haugen, R., 1994, *The New Finance: The Case Against Efficient Markets*, Prentice-Hall.

Jaffe, J., D. B. Keim, and R. Westerfield, 1989, Earnings yields, market values, and stock returns, *Journal of Finance* 44, 135–48.

Jegadeesh, N., and S. Titman, 1993, Returns to buying winners and selling losers: Implications for market efficiency, *Journal of Finance* 48, 65–92.

Kahneman, D., and A. Tversky, 1982, Intuitive prediction: Biases and corrective procedures, in D. Kahneman, P. Slovic, and A. Tversky (eds.), *Judgment under Uncertainty: Heuristics and Biases*, Cambridge University Press.

Kothari, S. P., J. Shanken, and R. Sloan, 1992, Another look at the cross-section of expected stock returns, mimeo, University of Rochester.

La Porta, R., 1993, Expectations and the cross-section of stock returns, mimeo, Harvard University.

Lakonishok, J., A. Shleifer, R. Thaler, and R. Vishny, 1991, Window dressing by pension fund managers, *American Economic Review Papers and Proceedings* 81, 227–31.

Lakonishok, J. A. Shleifer, and R. Vishny, 1992a, The impact of institutional trading on stock prices, *Journal of Financial Economics* 32, 23–43.

———, 1992b, The structure and performance of the money management industry, *Brookings Papers on Economic Activity: Microeconomics*, 339–91.

Little, I. M. D., 1962, Higgledy piggledy growth, *Bulletin of the Oxford University Institute of Economics and Statistics* 24, November.

Lo, A., and C. MacKinlay, 1990, Data-snooping biases in tests of financial asset pricing models, *Review of Financial Studies* 3, 431–67.

Rosenberg, B., K. Reid, and R. Lanstein, 1984, Persuasive evidence of market inefficiency, *Journal of Portfolio Management* 11, 9–17.

Shiller, R., 1984, Stock prices and social dynamics, *Brookings Papers on Economic Activity*, 457–98.

Shleifer, A., and R. Vishny, 1990, Equilibrium short horizons of investors and firms, *American Economic Review Papers and Proceedings* 80, 148–53.

Chapter 9

EVIDENCE ON THE CHARACTERISTICS OF CROSS-
SECTIONAL VARIATION IN STOCK RETURNS

Kent Daniel and Sheridan Titman

THERE IS NOW CONSIDERABLE evidence that the cross-sectional pattern of stock returns can be explained by characteristics such as size, leverage, past returns, dividend-yield, earnings-to-price ratios, and book-to-market ratios.[1] Fama and French (1992, 1996) examine all of these variables simultaneously and conclude that, with the exception of the momentum strategy described by Jegadeesh and Titman (1993), the cross-sectional variation in expected returns can be explained by only two of these characteristics, size and book-to-market (B/M), Beta, the traditional Capital Asset Pricing Model (CAPM) measure of risk, explains almost none of the cross-sectional dispersion in expected returns once size is taken into account.[2]

There is considerable disagreement about the reason for the high discount rate assigned to small and high B/M firms. The traditional explanation for these observations, exposited by Fama and French (1993, 1996), is that the higher returns are compensation for higher systematic risk. Fama and French (1993) suggest that B/M and size are proxies for distress and that distressed firms may be more sensitive to certain business cycle

We thank participants of seminars at Dartmouth, Harvard Business School, MIT, Northwestern, UCLA, University of Chicago, University of Illinois Urbana-Champaign, University of Michigan, University of Southern California, University of Tokyo, Wharton, the February 1995 NBER Behavioral Finance Workshop, the Pacific Capital Markets, Asia Pacific Finance Association and American Finance Association conferences, and Jonathan Berk, Mark Carhart, Randy Cohen, Douglas Diamond, Vijay Fafat, Wayne Ferson, Kenneth French, Narasimhan Jegadeesh, Steven Kaplan, Mark Kritzman, Josef Lakonishok, Craig MacKinlay, Alan Marcus, Chris Polk, Richard Roll, Robert Vishny, and especially Eugene Fama for helpful discussions, comments, and suggestions. We also wish to thank the editor, René Stulz, of *The Journal of Finance*, and an anonymous referee for their thoughtful suggestions. Daniel thanks the Center for Research in Security Prices (CRSP) at the University of Chicago for research support. Titman gratefully acknowledges research support from the John L. Collins, S. J. Chair in International Finance. We are, of course, responsible for any errors.

[1] The size anomaly was documented by Banz (1981) and Keim (1983), leverage by Bhandari (1988), the past returns effect by DeBondt and Thaler (1985) and Jegadeesh and Titman (1993), the earnings-to-price ratio by Basu (1983), the book-to-market effect by Stattman (1980) and Rosenberg, Reid, and Lanstein (1985).

[2] See also Jegadeesh (1992).

factors, like changes in credit conditions, than firms that are financially less vulnerable. In addition, the duration of high growth firms' earnings should be somewhat longer than the duration of the earnings of low growth firms; therefore, term structure shifts should affect the two groups of firms differently.

In contrast, Lakonishok, Shleifer, and Vishny (1994) (LSV) suggest that the high returns associated with high B/M (or *value*) stocks are generated by investors who incorrectly extrapolate the past earnings growth rates of firms. They suggest that investors are overly optimistic about firms that have done well in the past and are overly pessimistic about those that have done poorly. LSV also suggest that low B/M (or *growth*) stocks are more glamorous than value stocks and may thus attract naive investors who push up prices and lower the expected returns of these securities.[3]

Fama and French (1993) provide several tests that suggest a firm's B/M ratio and size are in fact proxies for the firm's loading on priced risk factors. First, they show that the prices of high B/M and small size stocks tend to move up and down together in a way that is suggestive of a common risk factor. Secondly, they find that the loadings on zero cost factor portfolios formed based on size (a small capitalization portfolio minus large capitalization portfolio they call SMB) and B/M ratios (a high B/M portfolio minus a low B/M portfolio they call HML) along with a value-weighted market portfolio (Mkt) explain the excess returns of a full set of B/M and size-sorted portfolios.[4]

While LSV do not dispute the possibility that there may be priced factors associated with value (or growth) stocks, they argue that the return premia associated with these factor portfolios are simply too large and their covariances with macro factors are just too low (and in some cases negative) to be considered compensation for systematic risk.[5] LSV present compelling

[3] There is also a third potential explanation: Kothari, Shanken, and Sloan (1995) suggest that selection-bias problems in the construction of B/M portfolios could be another cause of the premium. However, recent work by Chan, Jegadeesh, and Lakonishok (1995) shows that the selection biases are not large. Further, Cohen and Polk (1995a) construct portfolios in a way that completely eliminates the COMPUSTAT selection bias and find similar evidence. Finally, Davis (1994) forms B/M sorted portfolios free of selection bias in the 1940 to 1963 period (out-of-sample relative to the Fama and French 1963–1992 sample period) and finds a B/M effect similar in magnitude to that found by Fama and French (1992).

[4] As further evidence, Fama and French (1993) show that Mkt, HML, and SMB portfolios formed from one-half of the CRSP sample of stocks can explain the returns of portfolios formed with stocks form the other half. In addition, Fama and French (1995) show that the same return factors are present in a firm's earnings, and Cohen and Polk (1995a) show that portfolios formed based on individual firm's covariances with the SMB and HML factor exhibit the same premia as do the original size and B/M sorted portfolios.

[5] MacKinlay (1995) makes a similar argument: He calculates the statistical distribution of the ex-ante Sharpe-ratio of the mean-variance efficient portfolio from the returns of the Fama and French (1993) portfolios, and concludes that the likely value of the Sharpe-ratio obtainable is "too-high" to be explained within the context of efficient market theory.

evidence to support their claim; however, their results are not inconsistent with multifactor models, such as Merton (1973) and Ross (1976), which allow for priced factors that are orthogonal to the overall market return. An explanation for these return anomalies, based for example on Merton, would require that we find a priced factor that is orthogonal to the market, yet affects future investment opportunities.

While we would expect that it would be very difficult to verify that the returns associated with size and B/M portfolios do indeed satisfy the above condition, it is likely to be equally difficult to verify that the returns do not satisfy this condition. To show that these returns are not a factor in the Merton sense requires that we show that the factor *cannot* explain the component of consumption growth that is orthogonal to the market return. Given the difficulties associated with linking observed risk premia on the overall market to macro variables like aggregate consumption, this could be difficult to demonstrate.

In summary, the existing literature does not directly dispute the supposition that the return premia of high B/M and small size stocks can be explained by a factor model; rather, the debate centers on whether the factors can possibly represent economically relevant aggregate risk. In contrast, this chapter addresses the more fundamental question of whether the return patterns of characteristic-sorted portfolios are really consistent with a factor model at all. Specifically, we ask: (1) whether there really are pervasive factors that are directly associated with size and B/M; and (2) whether there are risk premia associated with these factors. In other words, we directly test whether the high returns of high B/M and small size stocks can be attributed to their factor loadings.

Our results indicate that: (1) there is no discernible separate risk factor associated with high or low B/M (characteristic) firms, and (2) there is no return premium associated with any of the three factors identified by Fama and French (1993), suggesting that the high returns related to these portfolios cannot be viewed as compensation for factor risk. To elaborate, we find that although high B/M stocks do covary strongly with other high B/M stocks, the covariances do not result from there being particular risks associated with distress, but rather reflect the fact that high B/M firms tend to have similar properties; for example, they might be in related lines of businesses, in the same industries, or from the same regions. Specifically, we find that while high B/M stocks do indeed covary with one another, their covariances were equally strong *before* the firms became distressed. To determine whether characteristics or covariances determine expected returns we investigate whether portfolios with similar characteristics, but different loadings on the Fama and French (1993) factors, have different returns. We find that the answer is no. Once we control for firm characteristics, expected returns do not appear to be positively related to the loadings on the market, HML, or SMB factors.

Our results are disturbing in that, like Fama and French (1992), they suggest that traditional measures of risk do not determine expected returns. In equilibrium asset pricing models the covariance structure of returns determine expected returns. Yet we find that variables that reliably predict the future covariance structure do not predict future returns. Our results indicate that high B/M stocks and stocks with low capitalizations have high average returns whether or not they have the return patterns (i.e., covariances) of other high B/M and small stocks. Similarly, after controlling for size and B/M ratios, a common share that "acts like" a bond (i.e., has a low market beta) has the same expected return as other common shares with high market betas.

The article is organized as follows: In section 1 we reexamine the return characteristics of portfolios of stocks sorted on size and B/M, paying particular attention to seasonalities in these returns, something that is important in our later analysis. In section 2 we present a simple, purely descriptive, return-generating model that provides some structure to our discussion of the empirical evidence presented in sections 3 and 4. The model also provides some insights about why the Fama and French (1993) tests might fail to reject the factor pricing model when the model is incorrect, and why a factor analysis test, like the tests presented in Roll (1994), might falsely reject a factor pricing model. In section 3 we present evidence on one feature of this model, that there is no additional factor risk associated with high B/M firms. Then in section 4 we perform a set of empirical tests on another implication of our descriptive model, showing that, after controlling for firm characteristics, estimated factor loadings do not explain returns. Section 5 concludes the article.

1. A SUMMARY OF THE RETURN PATTERNS OF SIZE AND BOOK-TO-MARKET SORTED PORTFOLIOS

In this section we reexamine the return patterns of size and B/M sorted portfolios. What we show is that there are important interactions between the size and B/M effects and that the return patterns are different in January and non-January months. As we later discuss, both of these observations play important roles in our research design.

Panel A of table 9.1 presents the mean excess returns for the twenty-five size/book-to-market sorted portfolios from Fama and French (1993), over the period 63:07 to 93:12.[6] These portfolios are based on unconditional sorts using New York Stock Exchange (NYSE) breakpoints. Therefore, for example, the small/low B/M portfolio is that set of firms included on NYSE/Amex or Nasdaq that have B/M ratios in the range of the lowest quintile of NYSE

---

[6] We wish to thank Eugene Fama and Kenneth French for supplying the portfolio returns. The construction of these portfolios is described in detail in Fama and French (1993).

TABLE 9.1

Monthly Mean Excess Returns (in Percent) of Size and
Book-to-Market Sorted Portfolios (63:07–93:12)

We first rank all NYSE firms by their book-to-market at the end of year $t-1$ and their market capitalization (ME) at the end of June of year t. We form quintile break-points for book-to-market and ME based on these rankings. Starting in July of year t, we then place all NYSE/Amex and Nasdaq stocks into the five book-to-market groups and the five size groups based on these breakpoints. The firms remain in these portfolios from the beginning of July of year t the end of June of year $t+1$.

Panel A presents the average of the monthly value weighted returns for each of these portfolios, net of the one month T-Bill return from the CRSP RISKFREE file. Panel B presents the average returns for January only, and Panel C presents the average return, excluding the returns in January.

	Low		Book-to-Market		High
			Panel A: All Months		
Small	0.371	0.748	0.848	0.961	1.131
	0.445	0.743	0.917	0.904	1.113
Size	0.468	0.743	0.734	0.867	1.051
	0.502	0.416	0.627	0.804	1.080
Big	0.371	0.412	0.358	0.608	0.718
			Panel B: Januarys Only		
Small	6.344	6.091	6.254	6.827	8.087
	3.141	4.456	4.522	4.914	6.474
Size	2.397	3.374	3.495	3.993	5.183
	1.416	1.955	2.460	3.515	5.111
Big	0.481	1.224	1.205	2.663	4.043
			Panel C: Non-Januarys Only		
Small	−0.162	0.271	0.365	0.438	0.510
	0.204	0.412	0.595	0.545	0.635
Size	0.296	0.509	0.488	0.588	0.682
	0.420	0.278	0.463	0.562	0.720
Big	0.361	0.340	0.283	0.424	0.421

firms and market equity in the lowest quintile of NYSE firms. All returns presented here are of value-weighted portfolios that are rebalanced annually, and consequently the results should not be driven by bid-ask bounce.[7]

Panel A illustrates the magnitude of the return differential across the portfolios. First, we see that the difference in returns between the high B/M

[7] It is important to note that these premia may seem small, particularly across size quintiles, relative to results presented in other studies. This is because of the value-weighting and the use of NYSE breakpoints.

quintiles and the low B/M quintiles of the same size were more than 50 basis points (bp) per month over this period (except for the very largest firms, where the difference is only 34 bp per month).[8] Across size quintiles, the premia for the smallest quintile of firms over the largest is 30–50 bp per month, except for the low B/M quintile where they are equal.

An analysis of these returns suggests that after controlling for B/M there is more of a large firm rather than a small firm anomaly. Although the returns are almost monotonic in size, there are no significant differences in the returns of the small and medium size firms within any of the B/M groupings. However, the largest quintile of firms do have significantly lower returns than the rest, with this being especially true for the high B/M stocks.[9] One implication of this is that a simple linear or log-linear regression of returns on capitalization and B/M ratios will not adequately characterize observed stock returns. There are important interaction effects that would be ignored in such a specification. For this reason, we will continue our strategy of examining the return patterns of various characteristic-sorted portfolios.

It is also possible that a factor structure could be artificially induced because of a common January seasonal. For this reason, we separately analyze the returns of the size and B/M sorted portfolios in January and non-January months. Panels B and C of table 9.1 give the mean returns of the same twenty-five Fama and French portfolios, only now separated into January and non-January months. This table shows that the size effect is almost exclusively a January phenomenon and that the B/M phenomenon occurs mainly in January for the larger firms, while the medium size and smaller high B/M firms exhibit about a 3 percent return premium in January and another 3 percent premium over the other eleven months. For the largest quintile of firms, high B/M stocks exhibit the same 3 percent January premium over the returns of low B/M stocks; however, for these stocks, the difference between the high and low B/M portfolio returns has been negative in the other eleven months.[10]

2. A Model of the Return Generating Process

In this section we present three models that clarify the motivation for our empirical tests. These should be viewed as purely descriptive models that

---

[8] Interestingly, we also find that the market-betas for both small and large high B/M stocks are lower than for the corresponding low B/M stocks.

[9] The contrast between this and what has typically been found in other studies is due to our use of value-weighted portfolios. The very smallest firms do have larger returns, but these firms are not heavily weighted in these portfolios.

[10] Davis (1994) finds similar results. We note also that this is consistent with DeBondt and Thaler (1985), although they look at past returns rather than B/M ratios.

provide a concrete framework for describing some of the opposing views described in the introduction. The first model, which we consider our null hypothesis, is consistent with the views described by Fama and French (1993, 1994, 1996) where there exists a "distress" factor with a positive risk premium. The second model represents an alternative hypothesis in which the factor structure is stable over time, and expected returns are determined by a firm's loading on factors with time varying return premia. In the third model, firm characteristics rather than factor loadings determine expected returns. Extant empirical evidence is consistent with all three models, but in sections 3 and 4 we will present empirical evidence that is inconsistent with all but the characteristic-based model.

In addition to motivating our own research design, the models presented in this section illustrate some possible pitfalls associated with past studies that examine whether loadings on factor portfolios explain the returns on characteristic-based portfolios. First, we argue that empirical studies that form benchmarks based on principal components or any other form of factor analysis may falsely reject a linear factor pricing model which in fact properly prices all assets. These arguments apply to the recent study by Roll (1994), which shows that factor loadings from a principal components analysis fail to explain the B/M effect, as well as to earlier tests of the arbitrage pricing theory that used factor analysis.[11] In addition, we argue that research designs that use the returns of characteristic-based portfolios as independent variables may fail to reject a factor pricing model when the model is in fact incorrect. Such designs include Fama and French (1993), as well as Chan, Chen, and Hsieh (1985), Jagannathan and Wang (1996) and Chan and Chen (1991).

A. Model 1: The Null Hypothesis

Our null hypothesis is that returns are generated by the following factor structure:

$$\tilde{r}_{i,t} = E_{t-1}[\tilde{r}_{i,t}] + \sum_{j=1}^{J} \beta_{i,j}\,\tilde{f}_{j,t} + \theta_{i,t-1}\tilde{f}_{D,t} + \tilde{\varepsilon}_{i,t} \qquad \varepsilon_{i,t} \sim \mathcal{N}(0, \sigma_{ei}^2), \quad f_{j,t} \sim \mathcal{N}(0, 1)$$

$$(1)$$

where $\beta_{i,j}$ is the time-invariant loading of firm i on factor j and $\tilde{f}_{j,t}$ is the return on factor j at time t. In addition, in this equation we separate out $\theta_{i,t-1}$, firm i's loading on the distress factor, and $\tilde{f}_{D,t}$, the return on the distress

---

[11] These would include articles by Lehmann and Modest (1988) and Connor and Korajczyk (1988) that use size-sorted portfolios as independent variables, but form factors based on individual firm returns.

factor at time t. In this factor pricing model, expected returns are a linear function of all factor loadings:

$$E_{t-1}[\tilde{r}_{i,t}] = r_{f,t} + \sum_{j=1}^{J} \beta_{i,j}\lambda_j + \theta_{i,t-1}\lambda_D \qquad (2)$$

Here, the B/M ratio of the firm proxies for $\theta_{i,t-1}$, the loading on the distress factor. The premium associated with this distress factor, λ_D, is positive, meaning that firms that load on this distress factor (that is, high B/M firms) earn a positive risk premium.

It is also important to note that $\theta_{i,t-1}$ varies over time as firms move in and out of distress. This means that an experiment in which one estimates the factors using a purely statistical factor analysis, and then determines whether the premia of the high B/M portfolio can be explained by the loadings on these factors, would give invalid results: since there is no group of firms that continually loads on the distress factor, the factor cannot be extracted with a purely statistical factor analysis.[12]

B. Model 2: A Model with Time Varying Factor Risk Premia

Our first alternative hypothesis is a model in which there is no separate distress factor and in which the covariance matrix of returns is stable over time. This means that factor loadings do not change as firms become distressed. However, since distressed firms on average have high loadings on factors that have had negative realizations in the past, it appears as if a distress factor exists. For example, following a string of negative realizations on the oil factor, a portfolio of high B/M firms will contain a large number of oil stocks. As econometricians, we would identify movements in the oil factor at this point as movements in the distress factor, when in fact they are movements in the "distressed" oil factor.

In Model 2, a factor's risk premium increases following a string of negative factor realizations. Since many of the firms in the high B/M portfolio load on the distressed factor, the high B/M portfolio will have higher expected returns. In the example from the last paragraph, a portfolio of high B/M firms would earn a high return because it contains many oil firms that load on the "distressed" oil factor, which now has a high return premium.

More formally, we assume that a time-invariant, J-factor model describes the variance-covariance matrix of returns.

$$\tilde{r}_{i,t} = E_{t-1}[\tilde{r}_{i,t}] + \sum_{j=1}^{J} \beta_{i,j}\tilde{f}_{j,t} + \tilde{\varepsilon}_{i,t} \qquad \varepsilon_{i,t} \sim \mathcal{N}(0, \sigma_{ei}^2), \quad f_{j,t} \sim \mathcal{N}(0, 1)$$

---

[12] However, if there were changing weight portfolios of distressed firms included as returns in the principal components stage, it would be possible to properly extract the distress factor.

The difference between this equation and equation (1) is that there is no separate distress factor $\tilde{f}_D$. Furthermore, we assume that the remaining β's in this model are constant over time, so that the covariance structure does not change as firms move in and out of distress. Again, the factor structure describes expected returns:

$$E_{t-1}[\tilde{r}_{i,t}] = r_{f,t} + \sum_{j=1}^{J} \beta_{i,j}\lambda_{j,t-1} \tag{3}$$

Now, however, unlike in Eq. (2), the risk premia on the J factors vary through time. Also, the changes in the premia are negatively correlated with the past performance of the firms loading on this factor. This means that when a factor experiences negative realizations, the firms that load on the factor become distressed (their B/M ratios increase) and their expected returns increase because the λ associated with this factor increases.

Finally, we again assume that there is an observable variable $\theta_{i,t}$ (i.e., the B/M ratio). θ obeys a slowly mean-reverting process and the innovations in θ are negatively correlated with past returns (so that distressed firms have high θ's). This means that, across firms, θ should be correlated with the factor loading on the currently distressed factor. Therefore, if a portfolio of the stocks of high θ firms is assembled, the stocks are likely to be those that have high loadings on factors with (currently) high λ's. In other words, the high θ portfolio is successfully timing the factors. This characterization is similar to that proposed by Jagannathan and Wang (1996), who suggest that small firms have high average returns because they have high betas on the market when the expected return on the market is high.[13]

C. Model 3: A Characteristic-Based Pricing Model

In contrast to the factor pricing models presented in subsections A and B, the characteristic-based model presented in this section assumes that high B/M stocks realize a return premium that is unrelated to the underlying covariance structure. This model is thus inconsistent with Merton (1973) or Ross (1976) in that it permits asymptotic arbitrage.

As in Model 2, covariances are stationary over time and can be described by a factor structure.[14] Specifically, we again assume that a time-invariant,

[13] However, the setting here is slightly different: In the Jagannathan and Wang (1996) setting, the loadings of the individual (small) firms on the market factor change through time, while in the model presented here, factor loadings are constant but the composition of the high B/M firms changes over time.

[14] Although we focus on the relation between B/M ratios and returns in this section, the analysis also applies to the relation between size and returns.

approximate J-factor structure describes the variance-covariance matrix of returns.

$$\tilde{r}_{i,t} = E_{t-1}[\tilde{r}_{i,t}] + \sum_{j=1}^{J} \beta_{i,j}\tilde{f}_{j,t} + \tilde{\varepsilon}_{i,t} \quad \varepsilon_{i,t} \sim \mathcal{N}(0, \sigma_{ei}^2), \quad f_{j,t} \sim \mathcal{N}(0, 1). \quad (4)$$

However, in contrast to the previous models, factor loadings do not describe expected returns. Instead, we assume expected returns are a function of the observable, slowly varying firm attribute $\tilde{\theta}_{i,t}$:

$$E_{t-1}[\tilde{r}_{i,t}] = a + b_1 \cdot \tilde{\theta}_{i,t-1}. \quad (5)$$

As in Model 2, the innovations in θ are negatively correlated with the returns on the stock, but θ is not directly related to the loadings on the distressed factors. What is unique about Model 3 is that firms exist that load on the distressed factors but which are not themselves distressed, and therefore have a low θ and commensurately low return (and vice-versa). If Model 3 is true, then following a string of negative shocks to the oil factor there may be some stocks that, despite their high loadings on the oil factor, are still not distressed. Model 2 suggests that these firms should still earn the distress premium, because they behave like other distressed firms. In contrast, Model 3 suggests their returns behavior does not matter: if they are not distressed they will not earn the premium. Note also that Model 3 implies that a clever investor can earn the B/M return premium without loading on any common factors.

D. Empirical Implications of the Models

The empirical evidence in Fama and French (1993) can be summarized with two empirical facts: (1) the stocks in the high B/M portfolio strongly covary with one another; and (2) high B/M stocks have high returns. The conclusion conventionally drawn from this evidence is that the firms in the high B/M portfolio are all loading on a factor that has a high premium; this is indeed the intuition suggested by the first two models.

Models 2 and 3 illustrate why this conclusion need not follow from the evidence. It is true that since the distressed firms covary with one another, on average these firms must load on the same factor, which we can call the distressed factor. Of course, a firm will become distressed when a factor on which it loads has a strong negative realization. Using Bayesian reasoning, it therefore follows that firms that are distressed will, on average, load on the same factor. In both Model 2 and 3 (the characteristic-based model), this is why distressed firms covary with one another, not because of the presence of a separate distress factor. One way to discriminate between Model 1 and Models 2 and 3 is to see whether the return standard deviation of a portfolio of stocks increases if they all simultaneously become distressed. If the factor structure is stable and there is no separate distress factor (that is, if Model 1 is false), then the return standard deviation should stay approximately constant.

Model 3 also indicates these existing empirical observations do not necessarily imply that returns are determined by factor loadings. In the characteristic-based model, the high returns are earned by *all* distressed firms, whether they load on the distressed factor or not. Some firms may have become distressed by virtue of bad realizations on an idiosyncratic term rather than on a common factor. Models 1 and 2 predict that such firms should not exhibit a premium; however, if the characteristic-based model is correct, they should.

In tests where the test portfolio returns are constructed from characteristic sorted portfolios (as in Fama and French 1993), the factor will *appear* to be associated with a high premium: since the average firm in the distressed portfolio does load on this factor, a strong correlation will be found between distressed factor loadings and return premia. Hence, to discriminate between the models, a test method must be used that separates out the firms that are high B/M, but that do not behave like high B/M firms. This is what our test in section 4 does.

The stability of the covariance matrix turns out to be quite important for testing the pricing aspect of the characteristics-based model. If the factor structure is reasonably stable, we can use past factor loadings to predict future loadings and determine whether it is characteristics or factor loadings that determine returns. However, if the covariance matrix is unstable, it will be difficult to determine how firms will behave in the future, and consequently to find, for example, value firms that behave more like growth firms.

3. THE COVARIATION OF STOCKS WITH SIMILAR CHARACTERISTICS

The characteristics-pricing model described in subsection C differs from our null hypothesis as presented in subsection A in two important ways. First, the characteristics model has no "distress" factor; the common variation in high B/M stocks arises because stocks with similar factor loadings are likely to become distressed at the same time. Second, the model specifies that average returns are determined by characteristics like B/M and size rather than factor loadings.

The first aspect of the model is important because the common variation among value and growth stocks has been interpreted as evidence of a distress factor. This is based on the following reasoning: if you randomly select 1,000 stocks and go long a dollar in each of these, and randomly select 1,000 stocks and go short a dollar in each of these, the resulting portfolio will effectively net out the various sources of factor risk, and you should end up with a portfolio with an extremely small return variance. Assuming that the residual standard deviation of the individual stocks is roughly 10 percent per month, then the standard deviation of this random portfolio's returns would be about 0.25 percent per month. Instead, the HML portfolio has a standard deviation of about 2.5 percent per month indicating that the portfolio is subject to considerable factor risk. Fama and French (1993) interpret this evidence in the following way: "Portfolios constructed to mimic risk factors related to size and BE/ME capture strong common variation in returns, no matter what else is in the time series regression. This is evidence that size and book-to-market equity indeed proxy for sensitivity to common risk factors in stock returns."

In contrast, the characteristics model assumes that this common variation arises because the HML portfolio consists of "similar" firms that have similar factor loadings *whether or not they are distressed*. In other words, the return generating model is assumed to be reasonably stable, but firms with similar factor loadings are expected to be distressed at the same time.

A. The Portfolio Returns

In this section we examine how the risk characteristics of stocks change in the years leading up to their inclusion in the various characteristic portfolios. If Model 1 provides a good characterization of the data, then on average, the covariances between the stocks should be higher when they are in the high B/M portfolio than when they are not. However, under the specifications in Models 2 and 3, covariances are constant over time.

Following Fama and French (1993), we form six portfolios based on the intersection of the three book-to-market categories (*High, Medium* and *Low*) and two size categories (*Small* and *Big*). These portfolios are designated LS, MS, HS, LB, MB, and HB. In addition we form the two zero-investment portfolios *HML* (High-Minus-Low) and *SMB* (Small-Minus-Big), which Fama and French use to capture the B/M and size effect.[15] We then calculate the *preformation* and *postformation* return standard deviations, in each of the five years before and five years after the formation date, of hypothetical portfolios that have constant portfolio weights equal to the formation date weights of the eight portfolios described above.[16]

---

[15] SMB portfolio returns are defined to be $r_{SMB} = (r_{HS} + r_{MS} + r_{LS} - r_{HB} - r_{MB} - r_{LB})/3$, and the HML returns are defined as $r_{HML} = (r_{HB} + r_{HS} - r_{LB} - r_{LS})/2$. Also, the value-weighted portfolio Mkt is formed and it contains all of the firms in these portfolios, plus the otherwise excluded firms with B/M values of less than zero.

[16] Note that this gives us slightly different returns over the period July:t through June: $(t + 1)$ than for the standard HML portfolio; we are holding the weights constant here, so we are not generating buy-and-hold returns. Elsewhere in the article we calculate true buy-and-hold returns.

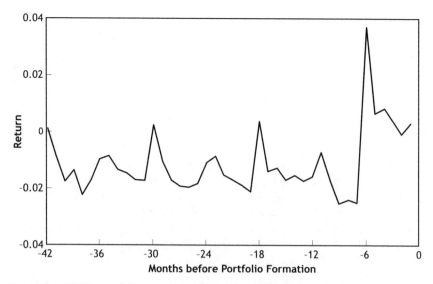

Figure 9.1. HML portfolio pre-formation returns. We first rank all NYSE firms by their book-to-market ratio at the end of year $t-1$ and their market capitalization (ME) at the end of June of year t, as described in the Appendix. We form 30 percent and 70 percent breakpoints for book-to-market and a 50 percent breakpoint for ME based on these rankings. Starting in July of year t, we then place all NYSE/AMEX and NASDAQ stocks into the three book-to-market groups (High, Medium, and Low) and two size categories (Small and Big) based on these breakpoints. The HML portfolio returns are then defined to be $r_{HML} = (r_{HB} + r_{HS} - r_{LB} - r_{LS})/2$. For this figure, we calculate the returns of the HML portfolio in each of forty-two months prior to the formation date. This is done for each of the formation dates from June 1963 through June 1993, and then the *preformation* returns are averaged to obtain the returns plotted presented in the figure. The portfolio weights used in calculating the *preformation* returns for each of the HB, HS, LB, and LS portfolios are the market values of the firms on the last trading day of June of year t, divided by the sum of these market values for the portfolio.

Before looking at pre- and postformation date standard deviations we will examine the average returns of stocks included in the HML portfolios prior to the formation date. We calculate these average preformation returns for the entire set of formation dates from June 1963 through June 1993, and plot these in figure 9.1. This figure shows that the preformation returns of the HML portfolio are strongly negative, supporting the contention of Fama and French that high B/M firms are distressed and that low B/M firms have performed well in the past. Another important feature of this plot is the larger average returns experienced in every January of the preformation period. Every preformation (average) return outside of January is negative and every average January return is positive. Note also that there is a large "step" in the returns in January of the formation year. This is because the portfolios are formed based on the B/M ratios at the end of the preceding year, as described earlier.

To determine how covariances change in the pre- and postformation period, we examine the pre- and postformation return *standard deviations* of the eight portfolios. One difficulty with this analysis is that a considerable fraction of the firms in the HML portfolio are not traded five years before or five years after the portfolio formation date. For example, about half of the small growth stocks (L/S portfolio) do not have CRSP or COMPUSTAT data five years prior to their inclusion in the portfolio. Similarly, about 25 percent of the H/S firms do not have data five years subsequent to their inclusion. Therefore, to generate this table, we have also imposed the additional requirement that, for a firm to be included in the analysis, it must have returns reported on CRSP in June:$(t - 5)$ for the Backward Looking Analysis (where June:t is the formation date), and at June:$(t + 5)$ for the forward looking analysis. Without this restriction, the formation-year 5 and −5 portfolios would contain a substantially smaller number of firms than the lag 0 portfolios.[17]

These standard deviations are presented in table 9.2. First, consider the leftmost column in Panel A, labeled with formation-year 5. The numbers in this column are the excess return standard deviations for the portfolio formed based on the characteristics five years in the future. For example, the portfolio's composition between July 1963 and June 1964 is based on firm sizes at the end of June 1968 and B/M ratios at the end of December of 1967.

Because of data restrictions we investigate only the 63:07 to 89:06 period for the "Backward Looking" portfolios: reforming the formation-year 5 portfolio in 89:07 would require stock prices for June of 1994, which we do not currently have access to. For the "Forward Looking" Analysis in the right side of the table we use the sample period from/through 68:07 to 93:12 because B/M ratios are not available before December 1962. We calculate the standard deviations of each of these fifty-four series (six lagged years times nine portfolios) for each lag and tabulate these in Panel A of table 9.2. We see that the difference in the lags ±5 and lag 0 standard deviations is close to zero for all series except the HML, for which the standard deviations increase from 2.2 to 2.5. However, part of the increase in standard deviation for the HML portfolio arises because it exhibits a large January seasonal, as we saw in figure 9.1. In Panel B of table 9.2 we perform the same standard deviation calculation, only we now exclude all Januarys from the sample. There is still a slight increase in standard deviation

---

[17] We also generated the table without imposing this requirement. The results do not change materially.

TABLE 9.2

Pre-Formation Monthly Return Standard Deviations of Portfolios

This table presents pre-formation characteristics of the set of size and book-to-market portfolios. Six portfolios are formed based on unconditional sorts on book-to-market (B/M) (High, Medium, and Low) and size (Small and Big). Mkt, SMB, HML portfolios are also formed (Fama and French (1993) using 30 percent and 70 percent breakpoints for book-to-market and a 50 percent breakpoint for size). For this table, we also impose the additional requirement the CRSP report a valid return for the firm five years (prior to/after) to the formation for the (forward/backward) looking analysis. The formation year 0 returns consists of returns from July of year t through June of year $t + 1$ for value-weighted portfolios reformed each year at the end of June of year t, based on the B/M at the end of year $t - 1$ and the market value in June of t. These returns are approximately equivalent to those presented in Fama and French (1993). For formation years (FY) other than zero, the portfolio time series of returns consists again of the returns from July of year t through June of year $t + 1$, but are now formed based on the B/M at the end of year $t - 1 + FY$ and the market value in the June of $t + FY$. The portfolio weights in these calculations are based on the market value in June of $t + FY$.

Panel A presents the simple time-series standard deviations of each of these portfolios. For the backward looking portfolios, for each of the six lags, the return time series is from 63:07 to 89:06. For the forward-looking portfolios, the time period is 68:07–93:12. Panel B also presents the time-series standard deviations the portfolios, but here the January returns are excluded from each of the time series.

	Formation Year											
Size/BM Portfolio	Backward Looking						Forward Looking					
	5	4	3	2	1	0	0	−1	−2	−3	−4	−5
	Panel A: Standard Deviations											
L/S	7.01	6.94	6.95	6.97	6.74	6.61	6.56	6.60	6.70	6.62	6.57	6.41
M/S	5.73	5.77	5.74	5.67	5.61	5.55	5.25	5.36	5.46	5.45	5.43	5.42
H/S	5.74	5.73	5.69	5.70	5.97	5.67	5.25	5.18	5.38	5.48	5.47	5.40
L/B	4.89	4.92	4.84	4.88	4.91	4.82	4.61	4.66	4.79	4.83	4.81	4.79
M/B	4.42	4.40	4.47	4.49	4.47	4.37	4.16	4.27	4.37	4.46	4.48	4.42
H/B	4.61	4.68	4.59	4.58	4.77	4.55	4.23	4.23	4.27	4.34	4.37	4.46
Mkt	5.13	5.13	5.09	5.07	5.05	4.96	4.74	4.80	4.92	4.94	4.93	4.88
SMB	3.04	3.02	2.96	2.88	2.78	2.80	2.63	2.68	2.76	2.79	2.78	2.75
HML	2.20	2.29	2.53	2.88	3.30	2.55	2.51	2.28	2.12	2.13	2.20	2.21
	Panel B: Standard Deviations–Januarys Excluded											
L/S	6.63	6.54	6.60	6.66	6.59	6.31	6.22	6.15	6.20	6.17	6.06	5.90
M/S	5.32	5.37	5.33	5.28	5.27	5.16	4.84	4.92	5.03	5.00	5.01	5.01
H/S	5.30	5.26	5.13	5.09	5.21	5.11	4.63	4.67	4.91	5.03	5.07	4.99
L/B	4.83	4.85	4.76	4.77	4.82	4.73	4.46	4.48	4.58	4.62	4.62	4.61
M/B	4.33	4.30	4.34	4.37	4.27	4.21	3.90	4.08	4.17	4.27	4.25	4.21
H/B	4.42	4.45	4.33	4.27	4.32	4.27	3.88	3.87	4.05	4.14	4.23	4.27
Mkt	4.89	4.87	4.82	4.79	4.76	4.68	4.40	4.45	4.59	4.62	4.62	4.57
SMB	2.74	2.71	2.66	2.60	2.62	2.56	2.39	2.41	2.47	2.54	2.54	2.52
HML	2.20	2.31	2.46	2.76	2.92	2.45	2.38	2.24	2.09	2.09	2.15	2.18

in moving from formation-year 5 to 0, (and a decrease in moving from formation-year −5 to 0) but this increase is only about 10 percent.[18]

In summary, the reason that high B/M stocks exhibit strong common variation is not because they load on a separate distress factor. If this were the case, this common variation would disappear when we look prior to and after the time when these firms are most distressed. We instead find that the common variation is present both five years before and after these firms are in the distress/growth portfolio. This suggests that the common variation is always present for the set of H and L firms, and is not a result of loading on a separate factor that is present only when they are in a distress/growth phase.[19]

4. Cross-Sectional Tests of the Factor Model

If a factor pricing model is correct, then a high B/M stock with a low B/M factor loading should have a low average return. In contrast, if prices are based on characteristics rather than on factor loadings, then a high B/M stock should have a high expected return regardless of its loading. This section presents tests of the two factor pricing models (Models 1 and 2) against the characteristic-based alternative (Model 3).

As discussed in section D, discriminating between these models requires portfolios that exhibit low correlation between their factor loadings and their characteristics (e.g., high B/M ratios but low loadings on the HML factor). In order to construct such portfolios we first form portfolios based on characteristics (size and B/M), and then sort each of these into subportfolios based on the firms preformation factor loadings. In this respect, our analysis is very similar to the analysis in Fama and French (1992) and Jegadeesh (1992) who construct portfolios that exhibit independent variation in size and beta. As in these articles, we then analyze whether the returns for the subportfolios vary with the factor loading, as Models 1 and 2 predict they should.

---

[18] We note that the HML portfolio returns exhibit high standard deviations at −1 and −2 years. Recall that these portfolios are formed based on ex-post information that they will (on-average) experience large positive (for the H portfolios) or negative returns (for the L portfolios) in formation-years 1 and 2. Perhaps this contributes to the high standard deviations. Notice that there is no such effect for the formation-year −1 and −2 portfolios, which are formed based on ex-ante information.

[19] We consider the possibility that the returns standard deviations change very little because the B/M ratios of the six portfolios change very little. However, we calculate the average B/M ratio for the six portfolios in the table, and show that they do change significantly (these data are available upon request). In addition, we regress the time series of returns in panel A of table 9.2 on the three Fama/French factor-mimicking portfolios. For the HML portfolio, the β_{HML} coefficient falls substantially in moving from 0 lags to either +5 or −5. The coefficient is 0.46 for formation year 5, and 0.36 for formation year −5, versus a coefficient of approximately 1 at lag 0. This demonstrates that the high standard deviation of the lead or lagged HML portfolio returns cannot be attributed to comovement with the current set of value/growth firms.

A. *Construction of the Test Portfolios*

We first rank all NYSE firms by their B/M ratios at the end of year $t - 1$ and their market capitalizations (ME) at the end of June of year t, as described in the appendix. We form 33.3 percent and 66.6 percent break-points for B/M and ME based on these rankings. Starting in July of year t, we then place all NYSE/AMEX and NASDAQ stocks into the three B/M groups and the three size groups based on these breakpoints. The firms remain in these portfolios from July of year t to June of year $t + 1$.

The stocks in each of these nine portfolios are then placed into smaller portfolios, based on the stocks' expected future HML factor loading, using information that is ex-ante observable. The resulting sets of portfolios consist of stocks with approximately the same size and B/M ratios, but with different loadings on the B/M factor HML. These portfolios allow us to examine the extent to which average returns are generated by the factor loadings rather than the characteristics.

We use the stocks' *preformation* factor loadings as instruments for their future expected loadings. To estimate these, we regress each stock's returns on three *preformation* factor portfolios (described in the next paragraph) for the period −42 to −7 relative to the portfolio formation date. We did not use the month −6 to 0 observations to estimate these loadings because the factor portfolios are formed based on stock prices existing six months previously. This is illustrated in figure 9.1. From this plot, it can be seen that returns are very negative up to $t = -6$, when the B/M ratios are calculated. However, the portfolio returns are large between $t = -6$ and $t = -1$. This "step function" in the return pattern would add noise to our factor loading estimates, so we exclude it from our estimation period.

The factor portfolios used to calculate the *preformation* factor loadings differ from the Fama and French factor portfolios in an important respect. The Fama and French factor portfolio weights change every year as firm size and B/M change. What we do is take the portfolio weights of the Fama and French factor portfolios at the end of June of year t and apply these constant weights to returns from date −42 to −7 to calculate the returns of constant weight factor portfolios, as described in section A. Based on our hypothesis that the covariance matrix is stationary over time, factor loadings calculated from factor portfolios constructed in this way should provide much better predictions of the future covariance of firms with the HML factor. As our evidence in the last section indicates, covariances between stocks entering the high B/M portfolio seem relatively stable.[20]

---

[20] As further evidence on this point, we also construct portfolios by sorting stocks based on their covariances with past HML returns. The dispersion in *postformation* factor loadings across portfolios formed in this way was substantially smaller than the dispersion in ex-post factor loadings of portfolios constructed in the manner described above.

Based on these ex-ante estimates of the factor loadings we then equally divide each of the nine B/M and size sorted portfolios into five value-weighted portfolios. Unfortunately, several of the forty-five portfolios formed in this way have as few as one stock in them for the years between 1963 and 1973. As a result, we must restrict our time-series tests to the 1973–1993 period where the number of stocks in each portfolio is almost always above ten.

B. Empirical Results

Table 9.3 presents the mean excess returns for the forty-five portfolios described in the previous section. As we move from columns 1 to 5 in this table we are moving from portfolios with low ex-ante loadings on the HML factor to portfolios with high loadings. The table reveals no discernible relation between factor loadings and returns for the portfolios of smaller stocks, but a relatively weak positive relation between the factor loadings and returns for the portfolios comprised of larger stocks; however, the difference between the average returns of first and fifth factor loading portfolios is only 0.07 percent per month. Moreover, it is possible that this weak positive relation occurs because, in sorting on the HML factor loading, we are picking up variation in the B/M ratio within the relatively broad categories.

We examine this possibility in table 9.4, which provides the average book to market ratios and sizes of each of the forty-five portfolios. The average B/M ratios and sizes reported for each portfolio are calculated relative to the median NYSE firm at each formation date. What we find is that across factor-loading portfolios, within any book-to-market/size grouping, there is some covariation between the average B/M ratio and the HML factor loading. And indeed, this pattern is strongest for the large firm ($Sz = 3$) portfolios, which is also where we see the strongest positive relation between factor loadings and returns.[21] This factor/characteristic covariation will decrease the power of our test to reject the factor model (Model 1) in favor of the characteristics model (Model 3); however, we will see later that the test is still adequately powerful to reject the null hypothesis.

The lack of a relation between the loadings and the returns could potentially reflect the fact that *preformation* betas are weak predictors of future (or *postformation*) loadings. However, the results reported in table 9.5 indicate that our method does in fact achieve considerable dispersion in the

---

[21] Mean size is roughly constant across the factor loading portfolios. The only regular pattern is that the more extreme factor loading portfolios (portfolios 1 and 5) tend to be slightly smaller. This is probably because smaller stocks have higher return standard deviations, and therefore the $\hat{\beta}$s calculated for these firms are likely to be more extreme than for the larger firms.

TABLE 9.3

Mean Excess Monthly Returns (in Percentage) of the 45 Portfolios Formed on the Basis of Size, Book-to-Market, and Predicted HML Factor Loadings

We first rank all NYSE firms by their book-to-market at the end of year $t-1$ and their market capitalization (ME) at the end of June of year t. We form 33.3 percent and 66.7 percent breakpoints for book-to-market and ME based on these rankings. Starting in July of year t, we then place all NYSE/AMEX and NASDAQ stocks into the three book-to-market groups and the three size groups based on these breakpoints. The firms remain in these portfolios from the beginning of July of year t the end of June of year $t+1$. Each of the individual firms in these nine portfolios is then further sorted into one of five subportfolios based on their β_{HML} coefficients in the regression:

$$\tilde{R}_{i,j,k} - R_f = \alpha + \beta_{\text{HML}} \cdot \tilde{R}_{\text{HML}} + \beta_{\text{SMB}} \cdot \tilde{R}_{\text{SMB}} + \beta_{\text{Mkt}} \cdot (\tilde{R}_{\text{Mkt}} - R_f).$$

The regression is run between 42 months and 6 months prior to the formation date (June of year t), as is described in Section A. The value-weighted returns for each of these portfolios are then calculated for each month between July 1973 and December 1993. The formation process results in portfolios which are buy-and-hold, and which are rebalanced at the end of June of each year.

This table presents the mean excess returns of the 45 portfolios formed on the basis of size (Sz), book-to-market (B/M) and the estimated factor loadings on the HML portfolio, for the period from July 1973 through December of 1993. Each of the five columns provides the monthly excess returns of portfolios of stocks that are ranked in a particular quintile with respect to the HML factor loading (with column 1 being the lowest and column 5 being the highest). The firm size and book-to-market rankings of the stocks in each of the portfolios are specified in the 9 rows. For example, the top left entry in the table (0.202) is the mean excess return of a value-weighted portfolio of the stocks that have the smallest size, the lowest book-to-market, and the lowest expected loading on the HML factor.

Char Port		Factor Loading Portfolio				
B/M	SZ	1	2	3	4	5
1	1	0.202	0.833	0.902	0.731	0.504
1	2	0.711	0.607	0.776	0.872	0.710
1	3	0.148	0.287	0.396	0.400	0.830
2	1	1.036	0.964	1.014	1.162	0.862
2	2	0.847	0.957	0.997	0.873	0.724
2	3	0.645	0.497	0.615	0.572	0.718
3	1	1.211	1.112	1.174	1.265	0.994
3	2	1.122	1.166	1.168	1.080	0.955
3	3	0.736	0.933	0.571	0.843	0.961
Average		0.740	0.817	0.846	0.866	0.806

336   DANIEL AND TITMAN

TABLE 9.4
Average Book-to-Market and Size of Test Portfolios

Portfolios are formed based on size (SZ), book-to-market (B/M), and preformation
HML factor loadings. At each yearly formation date, the average size and book-to-
market for each portfolio is then calculated, using value weighting:

$$\overline{SZ}_t = \frac{1}{\Sigma_i \, \text{ME}_{i,t}} \sum_i \text{ME}_{i,t}^2 \qquad \overline{BM}_t = \frac{1}{\Sigma_i \, \text{ME}_{i,t} \, \Sigma_i \, \text{BM}_{i,t} \cdot \text{ME}_{i,t}}.$$

Then, at each point, $\overline{SZ}_t$ and $\overline{BM}_t$ are divided by the median market equity (ME)
and median book-to-market for NYSE firms at that point in time. The two time se-
ries are then averaged to get the numbers that are presented in the table below.

Char Port		Factor Loading Portfolio				
B/M	SZ	1	2	3	4	5
		Panel A: Book-to-Market Relative to Median				
1	1	0.415	0.466	0.492	0.501	0.440
1	2	0.404	0.453	0.487	0.501	0.505
1	3	0.360	0.399	0.457	0.507	0.542
2	1	0.980	0.991	1.013	1.017	1.011
2	2	0.963	0.996	1.003	1.013	1.021
2	3	0.949	0.975	0.998	1.027	1.025
3	1	1.908	1.841	1.876	1.941	2.242
3	2	1.624	1.725	1.708	1.732	1.890
3	3	1.568	1.563	1.554	1.638	1.747
Average		1.019	1.045	1.065	1.097	1.158
		Panel B: Market Equity Relative to Median				
1	1	0.239	0.262	0.255	0.251	0.212
1	2	1.178	1.235	1.280	1.239	1.240
1	3	34.716	42.269	55.325	30.111	24.842
2	1	0.226	0.248	0.265	0.264	0.239
2	2	1.194	1.171	1.197	1.205	1.204
2	3	23.951	41.405	27.428	25.675	21.163
3	1	0.173	0.207	0.227	0.237	0.205
3	2	1.146	1.187	1.215	1.217	1.191
3	3	10.615	27.661	21.152	11.626	15.288
Average		8.160	12.849	12.038	7.981	7.287

TABLE 9.5

Portfolios Sorted by Characteristics and Predicted HML Factor Loadings

Portfolios are formed based on size (SZ), book-to-market (B/M), and preformation HML factor loadings. This table presents each of the coefficients estimates and t-statistics from the following time-series regression of these portfolio returns on the excess-Market, SMB, and HML portfolio returns:

$$\tilde{R}_{ss,bm,fl} - R_f = \alpha + \beta_{HML} \cdot \tilde{R}_{HML} + \beta_{SMB} \cdot \tilde{R}_{SMB} + \beta_{Mkt} \cdot (\tilde{R}_{Mkt} - R_f).$$

Char Port		Factor Loading Portfolio					Factor Loading Portfolio				
B/M	SZ	1	2	3	4	5	1	2	3	4	5
				$\hat{\alpha}$					$t(\hat{\alpha})$		
1	1	-0.58	0.14	0.06	-0.17	-0.67	-3.97	1.04	0.48	-1.34	-4.00
1	2	0.16	0.05	0.13	0.16	-0.08	0.94	0.47	1.12	1.33	-0.63
1	3	0.02	0.05	0.06	-0.06	0.28	0.15	0.42	0.50	-0.55	2.26
2	1	0.13	0.08	0.06	0.21	-0.31	1.05	0.87	0.73	2.13	-2.31
2	2	0.03	0.20	0.22	0.01	-0.31	0.24	1.71	2.05	0.14	-2.66
2	3	0.19	-0.08	0.05	-0.10	-0.07	1.13	-0.50	0.35	-0.67	-0.46
3	1	0.08	0.05	0.10	0.01	-0.47	0.70	0.55	1.06	0.10	-3.27
3	2	0.17	0.22	0.25	0.05	-0.31	1.25	1.67	1.94	0.36	-1.63
3	3	-0.01	0.16	-0.23	-0.12	-0.18	-0.04	1.13	-1.45	-0.74	-0.90
Average		0.02	0.10	0.08	0.00	-0.24	0.16	0.82	0.75	0.08	-1.51
				$\hat{\beta}_{HML}$					$t(\hat{\beta}_{HML})$		
1	1	-0.40	-0.38	-0.11	-0.04	0.25	-7.09	-7.09	-2.32	-0.84	3.91
1	2	-0.60	-0.32	-0.18	-0.05	0.05	-9.13	-7.15	-3.98	-1.02	1.01
1	3	-0.70	-0.44	-0.22	-0.11	-0.02	-12.85	-9.85	-4.72	-2.48	-0.44
2	1	0.02	0.19	0.32	0.35	0.48	0.39	5.51	9.69	9.06	9.13
2	2	0.17	0.23	0.28	0.36	0.49	3.23	5.14	6.59	8.67	10.98
2	3	0.03	0.24	0.22	0.31	0.49	0.50	3.90	4.03	5.53	8.40
3	1	0.42	0.50	0.57	0.75	0.91	9.74	13.00	16.26	19.74	16.11
3	2	0.40	0.58	0.56	0.72	0.82	7.32	11.40	11.07	13.91	11.26
3	3	0.45	0.56	0.67	0.81	1.00	6.69	10.03	10.91	12.81	12.90
Average		-0.02	0.13	0.23	0.34	0.50	-0.13	2.77	5.28	7.26	8.14
				$\hat{\beta}_{SMB}$					$t(\hat{\beta}_{SMS})$		
1	1	1.23	1.07	1.07	1.18	1.39	23.27	21.29	24.34	26.33	22.97
1	2	0.81	0.55	0.62	0.55	0.61	13.06	13.04	14.93	12.78	14.18
1	3	-0.14	-0.17	-0.16	-0.08	0.04	-2.84	-4.16	-3.59	-1.88	0.83
2	1	1.19	0.95	0.94	0.89	1.15	27.05	29.40	30.56	24.74	23.63
2	2	0.54	0.45	0.44	0.47	0.72	10.99	10.87	11.09	12.10	17.112
2	3	-0.22	-0.25	-0.15	-0.10	-0.07	-3.63	-4.39	-3.02	-1.96	-1.21
3	1	1.24	1.01	0.95	1.04	1.25	30.74	27.73	28.97	29.27	23.67
3	2	0.61	0.43	0.37	0.43	0.69	12.08	9.09	7.86	8.80	10.17
3	3	-0.06	-0.15	-0.17	0.05	0.10	-1.02	-2.90	-3.04	0.82	1.35
Average		0.58	0.43	0.43	0.49	0.65	12.19	11.11	12.01	12.33	12.52

TABLE 9.5 (cont.)

Char Port		Factor Loading Portfolio					Factor Loading Portfolio				
B/M	SZ	1	2	3	4	5	1	2	3	4	5
		$\hat{\beta}_{\text{Mkt}}$					$t(\hat{\beta}_{\text{Mkt}})$				
1	1	1.12	1.03	1.07	1.04	1.15	33.32	32.30	38.04	36.38	29.66
1	2	1.14	1.03	1.03	1.07	1.08	28.90	38.38	38.90	39.26	39.07
1	3	0.99	0.98	0.95	1.04	1.04	30.72	36.77	33.61	38.47	36.39
2	1	0.99	0.93	0.95	0.95	1.08	35.45	45.11	48.49	41.54	34.84
2	2	1.06	0.96	0.94	1.01	1.06	33.42	35.91	37.40	41.19	39.56
2	3	0.97	1.02	0.96	1.04	1.07	25.56	28.22	29.97	31.22	30.42
3	1	1.01	0.92	0.94	1.05	1.17	39.10	39.96	45.23	46.16	34.94
3	2	1.05	0.99	0.98	1.02	1.20	32.59	32.78	32.32	32.82	27.74
3	3	1.02	1.03	0.99	1.03	1.15	25.81	31.25	26.97	27.20	24.96
Average		1.04	0.99	0.98	1.03	1.11	31.65	35.63	36.77	37.14	33.06

postformation factor loadings. In table 9.5, we report the results of regressing the *postformation* excess returns for each of the forty-five portfolios on an intercept and on the returns of the zero-investment Mkt, HML, and SMB portfolios.

We see in table 9.5 that the HML coefficients are clearly different for the different B/M groups, as they should be: we know that, unconditionally, B/M ratios and HML loadings should be highly correlated. But the important thing for us is that *within a book-to-market/size grouping*, the sort on the *preformation* HML factor loadings produces a monotonic ordering of the *postformation* factor loadings. Moreover, there appears to be a highly significant difference between the loadings of the low and high factor-loading portfolios, something we shall verify shortly.[22]

We are especially interested in the estimated intercepts. Models 1 and 2 predict that the regression intercepts (αs) should be zero, while Model 3 suggests that the mean returns of the portfolios should depend only on characteristics (size and B/M), and should be independent of variation in the factor loadings. Hence, Model 3 also predicts that the αs of the low factor-loading portfolios should be positive and that those of the high factor-loading portfolios should be negative. The αs reported in table 9.5 indicate that this is generally the case. Only one of the nine high loading portfolios (see column 5) has a positive α and only two of the low loading portfolios (see column 1) has a negative α. Furthermore, the average α for factor loading portfolio 1 is 0.02 percent per month, and for factor loading

[22] We note that the dispersion in *preformation* factor-loadings is considerably greater. This is because the *preformation* factor loading dispersion is due to both measurement error effects and the actual variation in factor-loadings. The *postformation* dispersion results almost exclusively from true variation in the loadings.

portfolio 5 it is −0.24 percent/month. The difference is −0.26 percent/month. Recall that table 9.3 shows that the difference in average returns for these portfolios is only 0.07 percent per month.

In table 9.6 we formally test whether the αs associated with the high and low factor loadings are significantly different from each other. To do this we calculate the returns to portfolios which, for each of the nine B/M and

TABLE 9.6
Regression Results for the Characteristic-Balanced Portfolios

This table presents each of the coefficients and t-statistics from the following time-series regression of the zero-investment portfolio returns, described below, on the excess-Market, SMB and HML portfolio returns:

$$\tilde{R}_{i,j,k} - R_f = \alpha + \beta_{\text{Mkt}} \cdot (\tilde{R}_{\text{Mkt}} - R_f) + \beta_{\text{HML}} \cdot \tilde{R}_{\text{HML}} + \beta_{\text{SMB}} \cdot \tilde{R}_{\text{SMB}}.$$

The regressions are over the period July 1973 to December 1993.

The left hand side portfolios are formed based on size (SZ), book-to-market (B/M), and preformation HML factor loadings, and their returns are calculated as follows. From the resulting forty-five returns series, a zero-investment returns series is generated from each of the nine size and book-to-market categories. These portfolios are formed, in each category, by subtracting the sum of the returns on the 4th and 5th quintile factor-loading portfolios from the sum of the returns on 1st and 2nd factor-loading portfolios.

The first nine rows of the table present the t-statistics for the characteristic-balanced portfolio that has a long position in the low expected factor loading portfolios and a short position in the high expected factor loading portfolios that have the same size and book-to-market rankings. The bottom row of the table provides the coefficient estimates as well as the t-statistics for this regression for a combined portfolio that consists of an equally-weighted combination of the above nine zero-investment portfolios.

Chart Port		Char-Balanced Portfolio: t-Statistics				
B/M	SZ	$\hat{\alpha}$	$\hat{\beta}_{\text{Mkt}}$	$\hat{\beta}_{\text{SMB}}$	$\hat{\beta}_{\text{HML}}$	R^2
1	1	1.43	−0.43	−2.69	−9.21	31.48
1	2	0.50	0.18	1.98	−8.99	31.48
1	3	−0.48	−1.62	−2.52	−8.57	27.11
2	1	1.37	−2.02	1.31	−7.13	18.43
2	2	2.12	−0.99	−2.07	−4.69	10.96
2	3	0.79	−1.41	−2.34	−3.96	9.11
3	1	2.53	−5.30	−0.48	−8.00	23.36
3	2	2.01	−2.30	−0.63	−4.52	8.58
3	3	1.08	−1.30	−2.36	−4.98	12.39
Combined portfolio		0.354	−0.110	−0.134	−0.724	41.61
		(2.30)	(−3.10)	(−2.40)	(−12.31)	

size groupings, invests one dollar in each of the factor-loading portfolios 1 and 2 and sells one dollar of each of factor-loading portfolios 4 and 5. We call these "characteristic-balanced" portfolios, since both the long and short positions in the portfolios are constructed to have approximately equal B/M ratios and capitalizations. The t-statistics of the intercept and the three regression coefficients for each of these nine portfolios are shown in the table. In the last row of the table, we combine the nine zero cost portfolios to form one zero cost characteristic-balanced portfolio.[23] We present both the coefficients and the t-statistics for this portfolio.

The characteristic-based model predicts that the average return from these zero cost characteristic-balanced portfolios should be indistinguishable from zero. In addition, the characteristic-based model predicts that the estimated intercept from a regression of the returns of these zero cost portfolios on the Fama and French factor portfolios should be positive. In contrast, the factor pricing models described in Models 1 and 2 predict that the average returns should differ from zero, but that the intercept from the factor model should be indistinguishable from zero.

The results reported in table 9.6 reveals that all but one of the αs from the time-series regressions of the nine individual characteristic-balanced portfolio returns on the factor returns are positive, and three of the nine have t-statistics above two. Furthermore, the intercept for the regression of the returns of the combined characteristic-balanced portfolio on the factor portfolios, given in the last row of the table, is large (0.354 percent per month or over 4 percent per year) and is statistically different from zero.[24] In contrast, the mean return of this portfolio is only -0.116 percent per month (t-statistic of -0.60), which is only one-third of the size of the factor model intercept, and is insignificantly different from zero. These results are consistent with the characteristic-based pricing model and are inconsistent with the factor pricing models (Models 1 and 2).

C. Sorting by Other Factor Loadings

This section presents similar tests that allow us to determine whether the SMB and Mkt *factors* are priced, after controlling for size and B/M *characteristics*. First, we construct a set of portfolios in the manner described in the last section, except that now we sort the nine portfolios into quintiles based on the preformation SMB factor loadings, rather than on the HML factor leadings. The upper panels of table 9.7 present the intercepts, the

---

[23] We also construct portfolios by investing one dollar in portfolio 1 and selling one dollar of portfolio 5 and obtain very similar results.

[24] The intercept, α, is the return of a portfolio that has βs of zero on all three factors, and which is constructed by buying one dollar of the combined portfolio and selling quantities of the zero-investment factor-mimicking portfolios (Mkt, SMB, and HML) that are equal to the regression coefficients shown at the bottom of table 9.6.

TABLE 9.7
Time-Series Regressions—Predicted SMB Factor Loading-Sorted Portfolios

The upper two panels present the intercepts and r_{SMB} coefficient estimates and t-statistics from the following multivariate time-series regression:

$$\tilde{R}_{ss,bm,fl} - R_f = \alpha + \beta_{\text{HML}} \cdot \tilde{R}_{\text{HML}} + \beta_{\text{SMB}} \cdot \tilde{R}_{\text{SMB}} + \beta_{\text{Mkt}} \cdot (\tilde{R}_{\text{Mkt}} - R_f).$$

The coefficient estimates for β_{HML} and β_{Mkt} are not presented here.

The left hand side portfolios are formed based on size (SZ), book-to-market (B/M) and preformation SMB factor loadings, with the exception that the factor loadings used to form the portfolios are the SMB factor loadings (rather than the HML factor loadings).

The lower left panel gives the mean monthly returns (in %) for the 45 portfolios, and the lower right the t-statistics for the regressions of the characteristic-balanced portfolios on the factors. The bottom row of the lower right panel gives the coefficients and t-statistics (in parenthesis) for the regression of the combined characteristic-balanced portfolio on the factors.

Char Port		$\hat{\alpha}$					$t(\hat{\alpha})$				
B/M	SZ	1	2	3	4	5	1	2	3	4	5
1	1	−0.28	−0.01	−0.06	−0.10	−0.65	−1.94	−0.06	−0.44	−0.75	−3.58
1	2	0.07	0.20	0.13	0.01	0.01	0.57	1.79	1.10	0.08	0.03
1	3	0.25	0.06	0.01	−0.08	0.05	2.40	0.55	0.06	−0.67	0.38
2	1	0.16	0.07	0.06	−0.05	0.06	1.38	0.73	0.69	−0.48	0.37
2	2	0.11	−0.10	0.06	0.12	−0.05	0.84	−0.87	0.54	1.05	−0.38
2	3	0.08	0.01	−0.16	0.10	−0.03	0.50	0.08	−1.04	0.88	−0.27
3	1	0.02	0.11	−0.06	−0.13	−0.11	0.21	1.14	−0.63	−1.14	−0.75
3	2	0.19	0.23	−0.12	−0.01	0.15	1.20	1.79	−0.91	−0.07	0.75
3	3	0.23	−0.10	−0.16	−0.38	0.08	1.29	−0.67	−1.09	−2.58	0.45
Average		0.09	0.05	−0.03	−0.06	−0.05	0.72	0.50	−0.19	−0.41	−0.33

Char Port		$\hat{\beta}_{\text{SMB}}$					$t(\hat{\beta}_{\text{SMB}})$				
B/M	SZ	1	2	3	4	5	1	2	3	4	5
1	1	1.01	1.06	1.18	1.20	1.45	19.14	24.93	26.04	25.18	21.96
1	2	0.49	0.54	0.59	0.71	0.84	11.33	13.21	13.38	15.00	15.40
1	3	−0.29	−0.11	−0.11	−0.03	0.15	−7.81	−2.58	−2.50	−0.69	2.89
2	1	0.84	0.85	0.91	1.17	1.57	20.58	26.15	26.53	29.86	28.18
2	2	0.25	0.45	0.47	0.67	0.86	5.29	10.74	12.01	16.38	18.15
2	3	−0.38	−0.26	−0.14	0.06	0.25	−6.38	−5.46	−2.54	1.44	5.44
3	1	0.89	0.93	1.06	1.23	1.49	21.34	26.51	30.70	28.70	27.07
3	2	0.12	0.34	0.57	0.65	0.91	2.05	7.43	11.53	12.56	12.96
3	3	−0.33	−0.11	0.05	0.00	0.20	−5.27	−2.04	0.87	0.01	3.21
Average		0.29	0.41	0.51	0.63	0.86	6.70	10.99	12.89	14.27	15.03

TABLE 9.7 (*cont.*)

Char Port		Mean Returns					Char-Balanced Portfolio: t-Statistics				
B/M	SZ	1	2	3	4	5	$\hat{\alpha}$	$\hat{\beta}_{Mkt}$	$\hat{\beta}_{SMB}$	$\hat{\beta}_{HML}$	R^2
1	1	0.52	0.80	0.79	0.75	0.38	1.76	−3.85	−6.15	0.75	25.84
1	2	0.64	0.84	0.81	0.65	0.75	0.96	−3.37	−5.47	2.10	24.16
1	3	0.49	0.38	0.30	0.35	0.46	1.21	−3.82	−5.12	0.13	20.98
2	1	1.09	0.93	1.03	0.94	1.22	0.86	−5.51	−11.72	2.82	52.98
2	2	0.85	0.69	0.87	1.00	1.01	−0.22	−5.74	−8.56	0.53	40.82
2	3	0.57	0.54	0.42	0.80	0.86	0.08	−4.23	−8.19	−1.56	33.03
3	1	1.13	1.23	1.14	1.15	1.27	1.43	−6.15	−9.29	0.78	44.85
3	2	1.01	1.23	0.96	1.09	1.29	0.76	−4.81	−8.25	2.11	39.09
3	3	0.84	0.72	0.77	0.69	1.08	1.15	−6.02	−4.80	−2.13	26.41
Avg/coef		0.79	0.82	0.79	0.82	0.92	0.258	−0.331	−0.790	0.057	
(*t* stat)							(1.68)	(−9.25)	(−14.10)	(0.96)	

coefficients on the SMB factor, and the associated *t*-statistics, for the regressions of these nine portfolios on the three factors, and the lower-left panel of the table gives the mean returns of the portfolios. It can be seen in the SMB betas that our sorting method is picking up dispersion in the SMB factor loadings within the size-sorted portfolios.

The lower-right panel of table 9.7 provides the *t*-statistics for the regression of the nine characteristic-balanced portfolio returns on the three factors. Again, the characteristic-balanced portfolio returns are the differences in returns between the two lowest factor-loading portfolios (in columns 1 and 2 of the upper panels) and the two highest factor loading portfolios (in columns 4 and 5), that is, the return on a zero-cost portfolio where the long and short components have similar characteristics. First, the column giving the *t*-statistic on the intercept on the SMB factor shows that there is substantial negative loading on the SMB portfolios. Second, the characteristic-based model suggests that the intercepts should be positive, and indeed all but one of them are, although the *t*-statistics are not large. The last row of the last panel, headed "single portfolio," gives the coefficients and *t*-statistics for the regression of the sum of the characteristic-balanced portfolio returns on the three factors. Although the coefficient is large in magnitude, representing an excess return of more than 3 percent per year, it is only marginally significant.

The analysis presented in table 9.8 is the same, only now we sort on the *Mkt* loadings. Again, the *t*-statistics for the characteristic-balanced portfolios indicate that the factor model is rejected in favor of the characteristic-based model. Also, since the mean return of the combined characteristic-balanced portfolio is 0.10 percent per month (*t-statistic* of 0.3),[25] the data do not

---

[25] In the lower-left panel of 9.8, this is the sum of the sum of the average returns in columns 1 and 2 minus the sum of columns 4 and 5.

TABLE 9.8

Time-Series Regressions—Predicted Mkt Factor Loading-Sorted Portfolios

The upper two panels present the intercepts, r_{Mkt} coefficient estimates, and t-statistics from the following multivariate time-series regression:

$$\tilde{R}_{ss,bm,fl} - R_f = \alpha + \beta_{\text{HML}} \cdot \tilde{R}_{\text{HML}} + \beta_{\text{SMB}} \cdot \tilde{R}_{\text{SMB}} + \beta_{\text{Mkt}} \cdot (\tilde{R}_{\text{Mkt}} - R_f).$$

The coefficient estimates for β_{HML} and β_{SMB} are not presented here.

The left-hand-side portfolios are formed based on size (SZ), book-to-market (BM) and preformation Mkt factor loadings, with the exception that the factor loading used to sort the portfolios is the Mkt factor loading (rather than the HML factor loading).

The lower left panel gives the mean monthly returns (in %) for the 45 portfolios, and the lower right the t-statistics for the regressions of the characteristic-balanced portfolios on the factors. The bottom row of the lower right panel gives the coefficients and t-statistics (in parenthesis) for the regression of the combined characteristic-balanced portfolio on the factors.

Char Port		$\hat{\alpha}$					$t(\hat{\alpha})$				
B/M	SZ	1	2	3	4	5	1	2	3	4	5
1	1	−0.22	−0.11	−0.07	−0.16	−0.39	−1.30	−0.89	−0.54	−1.22	−2.46
1	2	0.31	0.26	0.08	−0.10	−0.17	2.76	2.42	0.64	−0.72	−1.17
1	3	0.31	0.07	0.05	0.00	−0.30	2.40	0.66	0.42	0.03	−2.16
2	1	−0.02	0.16	0.25	−0.06	−0.08	−0.19	1.64	2.30	−0.69	−0.60
2	2	0.16	0.09	−0.02	−0.01	−0.01	1.22	0.82	−0.14	−0.10	−0.10
2	3	0.04	−0.03	−0.01	0.01	−0.21	0.24	−0.18	−0.07	0.04	−1.23
3	1	0.25	0.07	0.09	−0.05	−0.36	1.77	0.69	1.05	−0.50	−3.63
3	2	0.21	0.39	−0.06	0.19	−0.31	1.18	2.65	−0.43	1.36	−1.57
3	3	0.08	−0.11	0.05	−0.06	−0.25	0.38	−0.66	0.32	−0.39	−1.45
Average		0.12	0.09	0.04	−0.03	−0.23	0.94	0.79	0.39	−0.24	−1.60

Char Port		$\hat{\beta}_{\text{Mkt}}$					$t(\hat{\beta}_{\text{Mkt}})$				
B/M	SZ	1	2	3	4	5	1	2	3	4	5
1	1	1.00	0.96	1.07	1.11	1.20	25.90	32.58	38.44	36.26	32.20
1	2	0.95	0.98	1.07	1.16	1.20	36.16	39.08	35.77	34.41	35.14
1	3	0.90	0.95	1.00	1.07	1.16	30.51	38.71	36.38	40.47	35.94
2	1	0.79	0.87	0.94	1.04	1.19	27.77	37.87	37.78	47.48	39.26
2	2	0.81	0.91	0.99	1.07	1.23	26.48	34.61	40.70	42.46	34.61
2	3	0.82	0.91	1.05	1.15	1.21	21.27	25.42	27.76	35.02	30.03
3	1	0.84	0.85	0.97	1.08	1.26	25.44	34.55	46.30	45.87	54.38
3	2	0.84	0.94	1.04	1.13	1.30	20.44	27.72	32.63	35.62	28.09
3	3	0.84	0.94	1.09	1.19	1.20	18.06	25.15	28.39	33.62	30.59
Average		0.87	0.92	1.02	1.11	1.22	25.78	32.85	36.02	39.02	35.58

TABLE 9.8 *(cont.)*

Char Port		Mean Returns:					Char-Balanced Portfolio: t-Statistics				
B/M	SZ	1	2	3	4	5	$\hat{\alpha}$	$\hat{\beta}_{Mkt}$	$\hat{\beta}_{SMB}$	β_{HML}	R^2
1	1	0.69	0.73	0.81	0.63	0.49	0.73	−4.86	−0.14	4.19	24.61
1	2	0.91	0.86	0.70	0.67	0.52	2.98	−6.56	−3.74	1.43	30.54
1	3	0.54	0.31	0.39	0.35	0.22	2.20	−5.36	−5.46	−0.16	27.78
2	1	0.80	1.04	1.16	0.98	1.07	1.11	−9.76	−7.41	0.87	51.41
2	2	0.88	0.86	0.84	0.87	0.98	0.91	−8.22	−5.24	1.63	41.88
2	3	0.59	0.46	0.59	0.71	0.58	0.56	−7.16	−3.60	0.47	30.88
3	1	1.33	1.13	1.23	1.20	1.03	2.87	−10.89	−5.53	−0.03	49.85
3	2	1.06	1.36	0.95	1.31	0.84	1.66	−6.40	−4.95	1.53	33.44
3	3	0.77	0.73	0.89	1.00	0.74	0.60	−5.72	−4.63	0.59	27.70
Avg/coef		0.84	0.83	0.84	0.86	0.72	0.474	−0.540	−0.540	0.150	
(*t*-stat)							(2.19)	(−10.78)	(−6.87)	(1.78)	

provide evidence against Model 3, and in support of the factor model. Strikingly, the mean return of this portfolio is positive, even though the portfolio's market beta is −0.54. Here we again find that the characteristic matters and not the factor loading. In other words a stock earns the "stock" premium even if its return pattern is similar to that of a bond (i.e., it has a low β_{Mkt}).

These results are similar to the results reported by Fama and French (1992) and Jegadeesh (1992), who show that, after controlling for size, there is a slightly negative relationship with beta.[26] We also see from the last row of the table that the three-factor model is rejected for this portfolio with a *t*-statistic of 2.2.

D. Factor Loadings, Characteristics, Turnover, and Past Returns

The fact that there are stocks with similar capitalizations and B/M ratios but very different factor loadings deserves further analysis. We do not find this surprising, given that firms in very different industries can be similar along these two dimensions. However, we would like to know if these differences in factor loadings are significantly related to either trading volume or returns in the recent past, since there is evidence suggesting that momentum (Jegadeesh and Titman 1993) and liquidity (Amihud and Mendelson 1986) can be important predictors of stock returns.

One possibility is that the low factor-loading stocks are the less liquid stocks. (Perhaps, the factor loadings of the less liquid stocks are underestimated because their returns lag the returns of the more liquid stocks in the

---

[26] Bear in mind, though, that we are looking at the market coefficient in a multiple regression, whereas the two cited articles use a univariate regression.

factor portfolios.) If this were the case, and if in addition there was a liquidity premium, then one might expect that the lower expected returns associated with having a lower factor loading would be offset by the return premia associated with illiquidity.

Similarly, we might expect that the low factor-loading stocks are those that did very poorly over the previous year and just recently entered the high B/M portfolio. However, this would bias our tests toward supporting the factor model, since the momentum effect would lower the returns of these low loading stocks. In order to bias our results against the factor model, the past years' returns of the stocks must be negatively related to the factor loading.

To explore these possibilities, we calculate the average turnover and the average return over the twelve preformation months for each of the forty-five portfolios. These are tabulated in tables 9.9 and 9.10. The findings reported in these tables suggests that our lack of support for a factor model is

TABLE 9.9

Average Turnover for Portfolios Sorted by Size, B/M, and HML Loading

Portfolios are formed based on size (SZ), book-to-market (B/M), and preformation HML factor loadings. The numbers presented are the average turnover for each of the portfolios, for the period 1973:07–1993:12, where turnover is defined as the trading volume (VOL) for the month (as reported by Center for Research in Security Prices (CRSP)) divided by the number of shares (NS) outstanding at the beginning of the month, times 1000. The averages are value-weighted and ME is market equity, so turnover in month t is defined as

$$\text{Turnover}_t = \frac{1}{\Sigma_t \, \text{ME}_{i,t}} \sum_i \left(\frac{\text{VOL}_{i,t}}{\text{NS}_{i,t}} \right) \cdot \text{ME}_{i,t}.$$

Char Port		Factor Loading Portfolio				
B/M	SZ	1	2	3	4	5
1	1	75.6	66.1	60.3	60.1	58.7
1	2	96.6	61.8	50.6	47.4	56.3
1	3	52.7	39.3	37.9	41.1	45.8
2	1	61.9	43.7	40.2	40.2	46.2
2	2	62.3	42.5	38.4	39.9	42.8
2	3	44.6	39.3	37.6	38.7	39.9
3	1	49.1	38.6	38.2	42.0	45.4
3	2	56.2	43.1	44.7	44.2	51.6
3	3	49.0	41.5	38.8	45.9	44.5
Average		60.89	46.21	42.97	44.39	47.91

TABLE 9.10
Mean Past 12-Month Return of Test Portfolios

Portfolios are formed based on size, book-to-market and preformation HML factor loadings. At each yearly formation date, the average past 12-month return for each portfolio was calculated using value weighting:

$$\bar{r}_{i-r1,t-r2} = \frac{1}{\Sigma_i \, ME_{i,t}} \sum_i ME_{i,t} \cdot r_{i,t-11,t}.$$

The last column is the difference between the factor-loading portfolios 5 and 1.

Char Port		Factor Loading Portfolio					
B/M	SZ	1	2	3	4	5	5–1
1	1	1.74	1.83	1.79	1.77	1.50	−0.24
1	2	2.59	2.15	1.79	1.88	1.93	−0.66
1	3	1.88	1.62	1.41	1.40	1.52	−0.36
2	1	1.25	1.31	1.17	1.15	1.24	−0.02
2	2	1.30	1.17	1.12	1.26	1.37	0.06
2	3	1.09	1.26	1.03	1.08	1.25	0.17
3	1	0.87	0.96	0.90	0.84	0.61	−0.26
3	2	0.97	1.01	0.96	1.04	0.89	−0.08
3	3	0.85	1.02	1.23	1.14	1.09	0.24
Average		1.39	1.37	1.27	1.28	1.27	−0.13

not due to either momentum or liquidity. Indeed, the portfolios with the lowest factor loadings seem to have the highest turnover, suggesting that if liquidity does have an effect on returns, it would bias our results toward finding a relation between factor loadings and returns. In addition, there does not seem to be any noticeable relation between past returns and factor loadings.

5. CONCLUSIONS

The analysis in this chapter demonstrates two things: First, we show that there is no evidence of a separate distress factor. Most of the comovement of high B/M stocks is not due to distressed stocks being exposed to a unique "distress" factor, but rather, because stocks with similar factor sensitivities tend to become distressed at the same time. Second, our evidence suggests that it is characteristics rather than factor loadings that determine expected returns. We show that factor loadings do not explain the high returns associated with small and high B/M stocks beyond the extent to which they act as proxies for these characteristics. Further, our results show that, with equities, the market beta has no explanatory power for returns even after controlling for size and B/M ratios. Although our analysis focused on the factor portfolios suggested by Fama and French (1993), we conjecture that factor loadings measured with respect to the various macro factors used by Chan, Chen, and Hsieh (1985), Chen, Roll, and Ross (1986), and Jagannathan and Wang (1996) will also fail to explain stock returns once characteristics are taken into account. These papers explain the returns of size and/or B/M-sorted portfolios and are thus subject to our criticism of the Fama and French (1993) analysis.

Some of our colleagues have argued that although we have shown that the Fama and French factors are inefficient, we have not refuted the more general claim that the size and B/M effects can be explained by a factor model.[27] This argument is based on the idea that the HML portfolio contains noise as well as factor risk. If this is true and if the B/M ratio is a very good proxy for the priced factor loading, then β_{HML} may provide almost no additional information on the true factor loading, after controlling for the B/M ratio. Under these assumptions, in sorting on factor loading as we do in table 9.5, we are picking out variation in the measured β_{HML}s that is not associated with variation in the priced factor loading, and hence we cannot expect returns to vary with β_{HML}.

While we certainly cannot rule out the possibility that a factor model can explain this data, we still find this argument unconvincing for several reasons. First, the argument suggests that if the models are estimated with less noisy factors, we are less likely to reject the factor model. However, more recent evidence suggest that this is not the case. Cohen and Polk (1995b) and Frankel and Lee (1995) show that refined measures of the B/M characteristic have considerably more ability to predict future returns than the standard B/M ratio. More importantly, Cohen and Polk show that when they replicate our cross-sectional test (in table 9.5) with their more efficient industry-adjusted HML factor,[28] they find that the factor model is still rejected in favor of our characteristics model.[29]

In addition, if the excess returns of distressed stocks do arise because of their sensitivity to an unobserved factor, it must be the case that the unobserved factor portfolios have significantly higher Sharpe ratios than not

[27] We thank Kenneth French for bringing this possibility to our attention.

[28] "More efficient" here means that it has a higher Sharpe ratio.

[29] Specifically, Cohen and Polk (1995b) calculate *adjusted* B/M ratios based on the ratio of individual firm's ratio to the long-run average B/M ratio for the industry the firm is in. They construct an HML portfolio based on this measure and find that it has a considerably higher Sharpe-ratio than the Fama and French (1993) HML portfolio (and is therefore more efficient). They redo the tests presented here with the more efficient portfolios and find that the factor model is still rejected in favor of the characteristic-based model.

only the Fama and French portfolios but also the more efficient portfolios of Cohen and Polk, and Frankel and Lee. In other words, the payoff associated with bearing the risks associated with these distressed factors must be significantly greater than the payoff from holding the size and B/M factor portfolios. MacKinlay (1995) suggests that the Sharpe ratio achievable using the three Fama and French (1993) factor portfolios is already "too large" to be explained by efficient market theories; in order to explain the returns of the portfolios in table 9.5 we would require factor portfolios that would generate still higher Sharpe ratios.

If expected returns are indeed based on characteristics rather than risk, the implications for portfolio analysis, performance evaluation, and corporate finance are striking. As we have already discussed, our results suggest that portfolios can be constructed that earn the B/M premium without loading heavily on common factors. This means that higher Sharpe ratios are achievable than was indicated by previous studies. In terms of performance evaluation, our results suggest that comparing the evaluated returns to matched samples formed on the basis of capitalization, B/M, and probably also past returns (to account for the Jegadeesh and Titman [1993] momentum effect) would be preferred to using the intercepts from regressions on factor portfolios. A recent example of the matched sample approach is Ikenberry, Lakonishok, and Vermaelen (1995). We are substantially more tentative about the implications of our results for corporate finance. It should be noted, however, that the characteristics model is inconsistent with the Modigliani and Miller (1958) theorem, so if we do want to take the characteristic-based pricing model seriously, we will have to rethink most of what we know about corporate finance.

However, before beginning to consider the implications of these results, it is worthwhile to consider why it might be that characteristics are the determinants of returns rather than risk. Lakonishok, Shleifer, and Vishny (1994) suggest a behavioral explanation: that investors may incorrectly extrapolate past growth rates. Lakonishok, Shleifer, and Vishny (1992) suggest an agency explanation: that investment fund managers might be aware of the expected returns associated with value stocks, but nonetheless prefer growth stocks because these are easier to justify to sponsors. Liquidity-based explanations may also be plausible, since volume tends to be related to size and past returns, but the evidence in table 9.9 suggests that the relationship between B/M and turnover is relatively weak.

Another possibility is that investors consistently held priors that size and B/M ratios were proxies for systematic risk and, as a result, attached higher discount rates to stocks with these characteristics. For example, they may have believed that stocks with these characteristics would be more sensitive to aggregate economic or credit conditions, beliefs that many financial economists shared. With the benefit of hindsight we can now say that B/M ratios do not seem to be particularly good proxies for systematic risk of this sort. However, we think it is quite plausible that investors in the 1960s and 1970s, with limited ability to access and manipulate the returns/accounting data used in this study, would incorrectly hold such beliefs. If this is the case, then the patterns we have observed in the data should not be repeated in the future.

Construction of the Portfolios

The construction of the B/M and size portfolios follows Fama and French (1993). Using the merged CRSP/COMPUSTAT files maintained by CRSP we form portfolios of common shares based on the ratio of the book equity to market equity (B/M) and on market equity (ME). Book equity is defined to be stockholder's equity plus any deferred taxes and any investment tax credit, minus the value of any preferred stock, all from COMPUSTAT. To determine the value of preferred stock we use redemption value if this is available, otherwise we use liquidating value if it is available, and if not we use carrying value. In calculating B/M, we use the book equity from any point in year $t - 1$, and the market equity on the last trading day in year $t - 1$, where the market equity, from CRSP, is defined as the number of shares outstanding times the share price. The ME used in forming the size portfolios is the market equity on the last trading day of June of year t. We only include firms in our analysis that have been listed on COMPUSTAT for at least two years and that have prices available on CRSP in both December of $t - 1$ and June of year t. The B/M ratios, and MEs of the firms thus determined are then used to form the portfolios from July of t through June of year $t + 1$. As discussed in Fama and French (1993), the end of June is used as the portfolio formation date because the annual report containing the book-equity value for the preceding year is virtually certain to be public information by that time.

To form our portfolios, we first exclude from the sample all firms with B/M values of less than zero. We take all NYSE stocks in the sample and rank them on their B/M and size as described above. Based on these rankings, we calculate breakpoints for B/M and size. For the analysis in section 3, we follow Fama and French (1993) and use 30 percent and 70 percent breakpoints for B/M and a 50 percent breakpoint for size. To form the nine book-to-market/size portfolios we use in section 4, we use $33\frac{1}{3}$ percent and $66\frac{2}{3}$ percent breakpoints for both size and B/M.

Note that since these breakpoints are based only on NYSE firms, we have considerable variation in the number of firms in each of the nine portfolios formed in this way. For example, since there are many more small firms on NASDAQ and AMEX, the number of firms in the small firm portfolios is much larger than the number of firms in the large firm portfolios.

References

Amihud, Yakov, and Haim Mendelson, 1986, Asset pricing and the bid-ask spread, *Journal of Financial Economics* 17, 223–49.

Banz, Rolf W., 1981, The relationship between return and the market value of common stocks, *Journal of Financial and Quantitative Analysis* 14, 421–41.

Basu, S., 1983, The relationship between earnings yield, market value, and return for NYSE common stocks. *Journal of Financial Economics* 12, 126–56.

Bhandari, Laxmi C., 1988, Debt/equity ratios and expected common stock returns: Empirical evidence, *Journal of Finance* 43, 507–28.

Chan, K. C., and Nai-Fu Chen, 1991, Structural and return characteristics of small and large firms, *Journal of Finance* 46, 1467–84.

Chan, K. C., Nai-fu Chen, and David A. Hsieh, 1985, An exploratory investigation of the firm size effect, *Journal of Financial Economics* 14, 451–71.

Chan, Louis K. C., Narasimhan Jegadeesh, and Josef Lakonishok, 1995, Issues in evaluating the performance of value versus glamour stocks: Selection bias, risk adjustment and data snooping, *Journal of Financial Economics* 38, 269–96.

Chen, Nai-Fu, Richard Roll, and Stephen A. Ross, 1986, Economic forces and the stock market, *Journal of Business* 59, 383–403.

Cohen, Randolph B., and Christopher K. Polk, 1995a, COMPUSTAT selection bias in tests of the Sharpe-Litner-Black CPAM, Working Paper, University of Chicago.

———, 1995b, An investigation of the impact of industry factors in asset-pricing tests, Working Paper, University of Chicago.

Connor, Gregory, and Robert A. Korajczyk, 1988, Risk and return in an equilibrium apt: Application of a new test methodology, *Journal of Financial Economics* 21, 255–89.

Davis, James L., 1994, The cross-section of realized stock returns: The pre-COMPUSTAT evidence, *Journal of Finance* 50, 1579–93.

DeBondt, Werner F., and Richard H. Thaler, 1985, Does the stock market overreact?, *Journal of Finance* 40, 793–808.

Fama, Eugene F., and Kenneth R. French, 1992, The cross-section of expected stock returns, *Journal of Finance* 47, 427–65.

———, 1993, Common risk factors in the returns on stocks and bonds, *Journal of Financial Economics* 33, 3–56.

———, 1994, Industry costs of equity, Working Paper, University of Chicago.

———, 1995, Size and book-to-market factors in earnings and returns, *Journal of Finance* 50, 131–56.

———, 1996, Multifactor explanations of asset pricing anomalies, *Journal of Finance* 51, 55–84.

Frankel, Richard, and Charles Lee, 1995, Accounting valuation, market expectation, and the book-to-market effect, Working Paper, University of Michigan.

Ikenberry, David, Josef Lakonishok, and Theo Vermaelen, 1995, Market underreaction to open market share repurchases, *Journal of Financial Economics* 39, 181–208.

Jagannathan, Ravi, and Zhenyu Wang, 1996, The CAPM is alive and well, *Journal of Finance* 51.

Jegadeesh, Narasimhan, 1992, Does market risk really explain the size effect? *Journal of Financial and Quantitative Analysis* 27, 337–51.

Jegadeesh, Narasimhan, and Sheridan Titman, 1993, Returns to buying winners and selling losers: Implications for stock market efficiency, *Journal of Finance* 48, 65–91.

Keim, Donald B., 1983, Size related anomalies and stock return seasonality: Further evidence, *Journal of Financial Economics* 12, 13–32.

Kothari, S. P., Jay Shanken, and Richard Sloan, 1995, Another look at the cross-section of expected returns, *Journal of Finance* 50, 185–224.

Lakonishok, Josef, Andrei Shleifer, and Robert W. Vishny, 1992, The structure and performance of the money management industry, *Brookings Papers on Economic Activity: Microeconomics*, 339–91.

———, 1994, Contrarian investment, extrapolation, and risk, *Journal of Finance* 49, 1541–78.

Lehmann, Bruce, and David Modest, 1988, Empirical foundations of the arbitrage pricing theory, *Journal of Financial Economics* 21, 213–54.

MacKinlay, A. Craig, 1995, Multifactor models do not explain deviations from the CAPM. *Journal of Financial Economics* 38, 3–28.

Merton, Robert C., 1973, An intertemporal capital asset pricing model, *Econometrica* 41, 867–87.

Modigliani, Franco, and Merton Miller, 1958, The cost of capital, corporation finance, and the theory of investment, *American Economic Review* 53, 261–97.

Roll, Richard W., 1994, Style return differentials: Illusions, risk premia, or investment opportunities?, Working Paper, UCLA.

Rosenberg, Barr, Kenneth Reid, and Ronald Lanstein, 1985, Persuasive evidence of market inefficiency, *Journal of Portfolio Management* 11, 9–17.

Ross, Stephen A., 1976, The arbitrage theory of capital asset pricing, *Journal of Economic Theory* 13, 341–60.

Stattman, Dennis, 1980, Book values and stock returns, *The Chicago MBA: A Journal of Selected Papers* 4, 25–45.

Chapter 10

MOMENTUM

Narasimhan Jegadeesh and Sheridan Titman

A GROWING BODY of literature documents evidence of stock return predictability based on a variety of firm-specific variables. Among these anomalies, the price momentum effect is probably the most difficult to explain within the context of the traditional risk-based asset pricing paradigm. For example, Jegadeesh and Titman (1993) show that stocks that perform the best (worst) over a three- to twelve-month period tend to continue to perform well (poorly) over the subsequent three to twelve months. The best performers appear to be less risky than the worst performers. Therefore, standard risk adjustments tend to increase rather than decrease the return spread between past winners and past losers. Moreover, as we show in figure 10.1, the returns of a zero cost portfolio with a long position in past winners and a short position in past losers makes money in every five-year period since 1940. It is difficult to develop a risk-based theory to explain the evidence that the past winners almost always outperform past losers.

Practitioners in the money management industry are aware of the momentum effect and it appears that they at least screen stocks based on price momentum. For example, Grinblatt, Titman, and Wermers (1995) and Chan, Jegadeesh, and Wermers (2000) find that mutual funds tend to buy past winners and sell past losers. Also, Womack (1996) and Jegadeesh, Kim, Krische, and Lee (2003), among others, report that analysts generally recommend high-momentum stocks more favorably than low-momentum stocks. However, despite the popularity of momentum strategies in the investment community and its visibility in the academic community, there is no evidence of the effect disappearing. Jegadeesh and Titman (2001) show that momentum strategies are profitable in the nineties as well, which is a period subsequent to the sample period in Jegadeesh and Titman (1993).

The momentum strategies are also profitable outside the United States. For example, Rouwenhorst (1998) reports that the momentum strategies examined by Jegadeesh and Titman (1993) for the U.S. market are also profitable in the European markets. Indeed, Japan is the only large developed stock market that does not exhibit momentum (see, Chui, Titman, and Wei 2000). Momentum strategies implemented on samples consisting of stocks

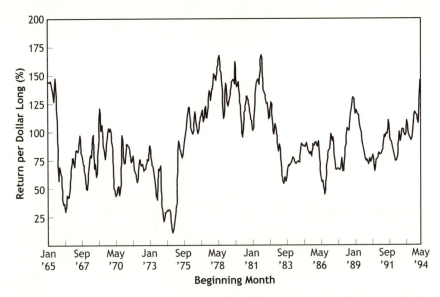

Figure 10.1. This figure presents the cumulative five-year returns for a strategy that buys the decile of stocks that earned the highest returns over the previous six-months and sells the decile of stocks that earned the lowest returns over the previous six-months. The holding period is six months. The figure presents the cumulative returns starting from the month on the x-axis.

from a number of less developed stock markets also exhibit momentum, (see Rouwenhorst 1999, and Chui, Titman, and Wei 2000), although the momentum strategies are not always profitable within individual countries. In addition, recent papers by Chan, Hameed, and Tong (2000), and Bhojraj and Swaminathan (2003) find that international stock market indexes also exhibit momentum.

This chapter presents a review of the evidence on momentum strategies and the hypotheses that have been proposed to explain the momentum effect. Section 1 provides a brief summary of the evidence on price momentum. Section 2 discusses the potential sources of momentum profits. Section 3 briefly describes some of the behavioral explanations for the momentum effect. These behavioral explanations have implications for the long horizon returns of momentum portfolios, as well as for cross-sectional differences in momentum profits. Section 4 and section 5 review the empirical evidence in the context of these predictions. Section 6 summarizes the literature on earnings momentum and the relation between earnings and price momentum, and section 7 provides our conclusions.

1. THE MOMENTUM EVIDENCE

If stock prices either overreact or underreact to information, then profitable trading strategies that select stocks based on their past returns will exist. In an influential paper, DeBondt and Thaler (1985) examine the returns earned by contrarian strategies that buy past losers and sell past winners. Specifically, they consider strategies with formation periods (the period over which the past returns are measured) and holding periods of between one and five years and find that in most cases, contrarian portfolios earned significantly positive returns.[1] Jegadeesh (1990) and Lehmann (1990) examine the performance of trading strategies based on one-week to one-month returns and find that these short horizon strategies yield contrarian profits over the next one week to one month. These studies of very long-term and very short-term reversals generally led to the conclusion that stock prices overreact to information.

Jegadeesh and Titman (1993) (JT) examine the performance of trading strategies with formation and holding periods between three and twelve months. Their strategy selects stocks on the basis of returns over the past J months and holds them for K months, where J and K vary from three to twelve months. JT construct their J-month/K-month strategy as follows: At the beginning of each month t, they rank securities in ascending order on the basis of their returns in the past J months. Based on these rankings, they form ten portfolios that equally weight the stocks in each decile. The portfolios formed with the stocks in the highest and lowest return deciles are the "winner" and "loser" portfolios, respectively. The momentum strategies buy the winner portfolios and sell the loser portfolios.

JT examine the performance of momentum strategies using stocks traded on the NYSE and AMEX during the 1965 to 1989 period. Table 10.1 reports the average returns earned by different buy and sell portfolios as well as the zero-cost, winners minus losers portfolios. All zero-cost portfolios here earn positive returns. The table also presents the returns for a second set of strategies that skip a week between the portfolio formation period and holding period. By skipping a week, these strategies avoid some of the bid-ask spread, price pressure, and lagged reaction effects that underlie the evidence of short horizon return reversals in Jegadeesh (1990) and Lehmann (1990).

All returns on the zero-cost portfolios are statistically significant except for the three-month/three-month strategy that does not skip a week. The

[1] The evidence in DeBondt and Thaler (1985) indicates that for a one-year formation period and a one-year holding period, past winners earn higher returns than past losers. Since DeBondt and Thaler primarily focus on longer-term contrarian strategies, they provide no further discussion or analysis of the momentum effect that is apparent over the one-year horizon.

TABLE 10.1
Momentum Portfolio Returns

This table forms momentum portfolios based on past J-month returns and holds them for K months. The stocks are ranked in ascending order on the basis of J-month lagged returns, and an equally weighted portfolio of stocks in the highest past return decile is the *buy* portfolio, and an equally weighted portfolio of stocks in the lowest past return decile is the *sell* portfolio. This table presents the average monthly returns (in percentages) of these portfolios. The momentum portfolios in panel A are formed immediately after the lagged returns are measured for the purpose of portfolio formation. The momentum portfolios in panel B are formed one week after the lagged returns used for forming these portfolios are measured. The t-statistics are reported in parentheses. The sample period is January 1965 to December 1989.

J		Panel A				Panel B			
	$K=$	3	6	9	12	3	6	9	12
3	Sell	1.08	0.91	0.92	0.87	0.83	0.79	0.84	0.83
		(2.16)	(1.87)	(1.92)	(1.87)	(1.67)	(1.64)	(1.77)	(1.79)
3	Buy	1.40	1.49	1.52	1.56	1.56	1.58	1.58	1.60
		(3.57)	(3.78)	(3.83)	(3.89)	(3.95)	(3.98)	(3.96)	(3.98)
3	Buy-Sell	0.32	0.58	0.61	0.69	0.73	0.78	0.74	0.77
		(1.10)	(2.29)	(2.69)	(3.53)	(2.61)	(3.16)	(3.36)	(4.00)
6	Sell	0.87	0.79	0.72	0.80	0.66	0.68	0.67	0.76
		(1.67)	(1.56)	(1.48)	(1.66)	(1.28)	(1.35)	(1.38)	(1.58)
6	Buy	1.71	1.74	1.74	1.66	1.79	1.78	1.75	1.66
		(4.28)	(4.33)	(4.31)	(4.13)	(4.47)	(4.41)	(4.32)	(4.13)
6	Buy-Sell	0.84	0.95	1.02	0.86	1.14	1.10	1.08	0.90
		(2.44)	(3.07)	(3.76)	(3.36)	(3.37)	(3.61)	(4.01)	(3.54)

9	Sell	0.77 (1.47)	0.65 (1.29)	0.71 (1.43)	0.82 (1.66)	0.58 (1.13)	0.58 (1.15)	0.66 (1.34)	0.78 (1.59)
9	Buy	1.86 (4.56)	1.86 (4.53)	1.76 (4.30)	1.64 (4.03)	1.93 (4.72)	1.88 (4.56)	1.76 (4.30)	1.64 (4.04)
9	Buy-Sell	1.09 (3.03)	1.21 (3.78)	1.05 (3.47)	0.82 (2.89)	1.35 (3.85)	1.30 (4.09)	1.09 (3.67)	0.85 (3.04)
12	Sell	0.60 (1.17)	0.65 (1.29)	0.75 (1.48)	0.87 (1.74)	0.48 (0.93)	0.58 (1.15)	0.70 (1.40)	0.85 (1.71)
12	Buy	1.92 (4.63)	1.79 (4.36)	1.68 (4.10)	1.55 (3.81)	1.96 (4.73)	1.79 (4.36)	1.67 (4.09)	1.54 (3.79)
12	Buy-Sell	1.31 (3.74)	1.14 (3.40)	0.93 (2.95)	0.68 (2.25)	1.49 (4.28)	1.21 (3.65)	0.96 (3.09)	0.69 (2.31)

Source: Jegadeesh and Titman (1993).

most successful zero-cost strategy selects stocks based on their returns over
the previous twelve months and then holds the portfolio for three months.
This strategy yields 1.31 percent per month when there is no time lag between the portfolio formation period and the holding period (see panel A).
The six-month formation period produces returns of about 1 percent per
month regardless of the holding period.

A. Evidence around the World

Momentum strategies are profitable not only in the United States, but also
in many major markets throughout the world. For example, Rouwenhorst
(1998) replicates JT for 12 European countries and finds very similar results. Table 10.2 presents his findings. The six-month/six-month strategy
return is 1.16 percent per month with European stocks, compared with .95
percent for the U.S. market. Although Rouwenhorst's sample period is
shorter than JT's, his *t*-statistics are larger. Therefore, the volatility of momentum strategies is lower in Europe than in the United States.

A more recent study by Griffin, Ji, and Martin (2003) examines momentum strategies in forty countries from around the world. This paper finds
that the momentum strategies are profitable in North America, Europe,
and Latin America, but they are not significantly profitable in Asia. An
earlier paper by Chui, Titman, and Wei (2000) also finds that the momentum profits in Japan and the other Asian countries are not reliably greater
than zero.

B. Seasonality

Momentum strategies exhibit an interesting pattern of seasonality in January. Table 10.3 presents the returns for the six-month/six-month momentum
strategy within and outside January, which we reproduce from Jegadeesh
and Titman (2001). The basic strategy in this chapter is the same as that in
JT, although the samples are slightly different. Jegadeesh and Titman
(2001) cover the 1965 to 1998 sample period, and include Nasdaq stocks
while JT consider only NYSE and AMEX listed stocks. However, Jegadeesh
and Titman (2001) exclude stocks with low liquidity by screening out
stocks priced less than $5 and stocks in the smallest market cap decile,
based on NYSE size decile cut off.

The momentum strategy loses in January, but earns positive returns in
every calendar month outside of January. The January return is −1.55 percent and the non-January return is 1.48 percent per month.[2] Earlier studies

[2] JT report that the momentum strategy earns −6.86 percent in January. The negative return in Jegadeesh and Titman (2001) is smaller because they exclude the smallest firms, which
account for much of the January return reversals.

TABLE 10.2

Momentum Portfolio Returns: European Evidence

At the end of each month all stocks are ranked in ascending order based on previous J-month performance. The stocks in the bottom decile (lowest previous performance) are assigned to the Loser portfolio, those in the top decile to the Winner portfolio. The portfolios are initially equally weighted and held for K months. The table gives the average monthly buy-and-hold returns on those portfolios for the period 1980 to 1995. In Panel A the portfolios are formed immediately after ranking, in Panel B the portfolio formation occurs one month after the ranking takes place. The t-stat is the average return divided by its standard error. The sample consists of monthly total returns in local currency for 2,190 firms in twelve European countries (Austria, Belgium, Denmark, France, Germany, Italy, The Netherlands, Norway, Spain, Sweden, Switzerland, and the United Kingdom) and consists of between 60 and 90 percent of each country's market capitalization.

J		Panel A				Panel B			
	$K=$	3	6	9	12	3	6	9	12
3	Loser	1.16	1.04	1.08	1.09	0.77	0.87	0.94	1.05
	Winner	1.87	1.92	1.90	1.91	1.85	1.91	1.90	1.84
	Winner-Loser	0.70	0.88	0.82	0.82	1.09	1.05	0.95	0.79
	t-stat	(2.59)	(3.86)	(4.08)	(4.56)	(4.29)	(4.74)	(4.99)	(4.64)
6	Loser	0.95	0.90	0.92	1.04	0.72	0.76	0.88	1.06
	Winner	2.08	2.06	2.04	1.95	2.04	2.05	2.00	1.87
	Winner-Loser	1.13	1.16	1.12	0.91	1.31	1.28	1.12	0.81
	t-stat	(3.60)	(4.02)	(4.35)	(3.94)	(4.27)	(4.59)	(4.50)	(3.62)
9	Loser	0.88	0.83	0.97	1.11	0.64	0.77	0.95	1.14
	Winner	2.12	2.13	2.04	1.93	2.09	2.07	1.97	1.84
	Winner-Loser	1.24	1.29	1.07	0.82	1.45	1.30	1.02	0.70
	t-stat	(3.71)	(4.19)	(3.78)	(3.19)	(4.50)	(4.36)	(3.77)	(2.83)
12	Loser	0.84	0.94	1.08	1.21	0.77	0.93	1.10	1.25
	Winner	2.19	2.09	1.97	1.85	2.08	1.98	1.88	1.76
	Winner-Loser	1.35	1.15	0.89	0.64	1.31	1.05	0.78	0.51
	t-stat	(3.97)	(3.66)	(3.07)	(2.40)	(4.03)	(3.48)	(2.80)	(1.98)

Source: Rouwenhorst (1998).

TABLE 10.3
Momentum Portfolio Returns in January and Outside January

This table presents the average monthly momentum portfolio returns. The sample includes all stocks traded on the NYSE, AMEX, or NASDAQ excluding stocks priced less than $5 at the beginning of the holding period and stocks in smallest market cap decile (NYSE size decile cut off). The momentum portfolios are formed based on past six-month returns and held for six months. P1 is the equal-weighted portfolio of ten percent of the stocks with the highest past six-month returns and P10 is the equal-weighted portfolio of the ten percent of the stocks with the lowest past six-month returns. The sample period is January 1965 to December 1998.

	P1	P10	P1 – P10	t-statistic	Percent Positive
Jan	3.40	4.95	−1.55	−1.87	29
Feb–Dec	1.49	0.01	1.48	7.89	69
All	1.65	0.42	1.23	6.46	66

Source: Jegadeesh and Titman (2001).

have found a January seasonality for other anomalies such as the size effect (see Keim, 1983) and long-horizon return reversals (DeBondt and Thaler, 1985). In fact, these anomalies are almost entirely concentrated in January, and are insignificant outside January. In marked contrast, the momentum effect is entirely a non-January phenomenon and January returns hurt the momentum strategy.

2. POTENTIAL SOURCES OF MOMENTUM PROFITS

A natural interpretation of the fact that past winner and losers continue the trend is that stock prices underreact to information. For example, suppose a firm releases good news but the stock prices only react partially to the news. Then, stock prices would rise during the news release but will continue to rise even after the news becomes public, as the market fully adjusts to the new information. Therefore, underreaction is one possible source of momentum profits. However, this is not the only possible reason why past winners outperform past losers. Another possible reason is that past winners may be riskier than past losers, and the difference between winner and loser portfolio returns could simply be compensation for risk. Also, if the premiums for bearing certain types of risk vary across time in a serially correlated fashion, momentum strategies will be profitable. We can use the following single-factor model to formally examine the contribution of these sources of momentum profits:[3]

$$r_{it} = \mu_i + b_i f_t + e_{it},$$
$$E(f_t) = 0$$
$$E(e_{it}) = 0 \tag{1}$$
$$Cov(e_{it}, f_t) = 0, \quad \forall i$$
$$Cov(e_{it}, e_{jt-1}) = 0, \quad \forall i \neq j$$

where μ_i is the unconditional expected return on security i, r_{it} is the return on security i, f_t is the unexpected return on a factor-mimicking portfolio, e_{it} is the firm-specific component of return at time t, and b_i is the factor sensitivity of security i.

The superior performance of momentum strategies implies that stocks that generate higher than average returns in one period also generate higher than average returns in the period that follows. In other words, these results imply that:

$$E(r_{it} - \bar{r}_t | r_{it-1} - \bar{r}_{t-1} > 0) > 0$$

and

$$E(r_{it} - \bar{r}_t | r_{it-1} - \bar{r}_{t-1} < 0) < 0,$$

where a bar above a variable denotes its cross-sectional average.

Therefore,

$$E\{(r_{it} - \bar{r}_t)(r_{it-1} - \bar{r}_{t-1})\} > 0. \tag{2}$$

The cross-sectional covariance in (2) turns out to equal the expected profits to a trading strategy that weights stocks by the difference between the past returns of the respective stocks and the equally weighted index. Specifically, the portfolio weight for stock i in month t for this strategy is:

$$w_i = r_{i,t-1} - \bar{r}_{t-1}.$$

This weighted relative strength strategy (WRSS) is closely related to the strategy in table 10.1 and it has a correlation of .95 with the returns on P1–P10. While the equally weighted decile portfolios are used in most empirical tests, the closely related WRSS provides a tractable framework for examining analytically the sources of momentum profits and evaluating the relative importance of each of these sources.

---

[3] The model we discuss here is from JT. Similar models have also been used by Lo and MacKinlay (1990) and Jegadeesh (1990) to understand the sources of short-horizon contrarian profits.

Given the one-factor model defined in (1), the WRSS profits given in (2) can be decomposed into the following three terms:

$$E\left(\sum_{i=1}^{N} w_i r_{it}\right) = \sigma_\mu^2 + \sigma_b^2 Cov(f_t, f_{t-1}) + \frac{1}{N}\sum_{i=1}^{N} Cov(e_{it}, e_{it-1}),\qquad(3)$$

Where N in the number of stocks and σ_μ^2 and σ_b^2 are the cross-sectional variances of expected returns and factor sensitivities, respectively.

In this decomposition, the three terms on the right-hand side correspond to the three potential sources of momentum profits that we discussed earlier. The first term here is the cross-sectional dispersion in expected returns. Intuitively, since realized returns contain a component related to expected returns, securities that experience relatively high returns in one period can be expected to earn higher than average returns in the following period. The second term is related to the potential to time the factor. If factor portfolio returns are positively serially correlated, large factor realizations in one period will be followed by higher than average factor realizations in the next period. The momentum strategy tends to pick stocks with high factor sensitivities following periods of large factor realizations, and hence it will benefit from the higher expected future factor realizations. The last term in the above expression is the average serial covariance of the idiosyncratic components of security returns. This term would be positive if stock prices underreact to firm-specific information.

To assess whether the existence of momentum profits imply market inefficiency, it is important to identify the sources of the profits. If the profits are due to either the first or the second term in Eq. (3), they may be attributed to compensation for bearing systematic risk and need not be an indication of market inefficiency. However, if the profitability of the momentum strategies were due to the third term, then the results would suggest market inefficiency.

A. Cross-sectional Differences in Expected Returns

Several papers examine whether the cross-sectional differences in returns across the momentum portfolios can be explained by differences in risk under specific asset pricing models. JT adjust for risk using the CAPM, and Fama and French (1996), Grundy and Martin (2001), and Jegadeesh and Titman (2001) adjust for risk using the Fama-French three-factor model.

Table 10.4 presents the size decile ranks and Fama and French factor sensitivities of the momentum portfolios. This table assigns size decile ranks based on the NYSE size decile cutoffs, where size rank of 1 is the smallest decile and size rank 10 is the largest decile. Both winners and losers tend to

TABLE 10.4
Momentum Portfolio Characteristics

This table reports the characteristics of momentum portfolios. The sample includes all stocks traded on the NYSE, AMEX, or NASDAQ excluding stocks priced less than $5 at the beginning of the holding period and stocks in smallest market cap decile (NYSE size cut off). P1 is the equal-weighted portfolio of ten percent of the stocks with the highest past six-month returns, P2 is the equal-weighted portfolio of the ten percent of the stocks with the next highest past six-month returns and so on. Average size decile rank is the average rank of the market capitalization of equity (based on NYSE size decile cut offs) of the stocks in each portfolio at the beginning of the holding period. FF factor sensitivities are the slope coefficients in the Fama-French three-factor model time-series regressions. "Market" is the market factor, "SMB" is the size factor and "HML" is the book-to-market factor. The sample period is January 1965 to December 1998.

| | *Average Size Decile Rank* | *FF Factor Sensitivities* | | |
		Market	*SMB*	*HML*
P1	4.81	1.08	0.41	−0.24
P2	5.32	1.03	0.23	0.00
P3	5.49	1.00	0.19	0.08
P4	5.51	0.99	0.17	0.14
P5	5.49	0.99	0.17	0.17
P6	5.41	0.99	0.19	0.19
P7	5.36	0.99	0.22	0.19
P8	5.26	1.01	0.24	0.16
P9	5.09	1.04	0.30	0.11
P10	4.56	1.12	0.55	−0.02
P1–P10	0.25	−0.04	−0.13	−0.22

Source: Jegadeesh and Titman (2001).

be smaller than the average stock in the sample because smaller firms have more volatile returns, and are thus more likely to be in the extreme return sorted portfolios. The average size rank for the winner portfolio is larger than that for the loser portfolio.

The factor sensitivities in table 10.4 indicate that the market betas for winners and losers are virtually the same. However, the losers are somewhat more sensitive to the SMB and HML factors. The factor sensitivities to the SMB factor are .55 and .41, and to the HML factor are −.24, and −.02 for the losers and winners, respectively.

The relative sensitivities of the extreme momentum portfolios to the SMB and HML factors reflect the intuitive relation between past returns, and firm size and B/M ratios. The winners increase in market capitalization over the ranking period and hence tend to be larger firms, and also have

TABLE 10.5
CAPM and Fama-French Alphas

This table reports the risk-adjusted returns of momentum portfolios. The sample comprises all stocks traded on the NYSE, AMEX, or NASDAQ excluding stocks priced less than $5 at the beginning of the holding period and stocks in smallest market cap decile (NYSE size decile cut off). P1 is the equal-weighted portfolio of ten percent of the stocks with the highest past six-month returns, P2 is the equal-weighted portfolio of the ten percent of the stocks with the next highest past six-month returns and so on. This table reports the intercepts from the market model regression (CAPM Alpha) and Fama-French three-factor regression (FF Alpha). The sample period is January 1965 to December 1998. The *t*-statistics are reported in parentheses.

	CAPM Alpha	FF Alpha
P1	0.46	0.50
	(3.03)	(4.68)
P2	0.29	0.22
	(2.86)	(3.51)
P3	0.21	0.10
	(2.53)	(2.31)
P4	0.15	0.02
	(1.92)	(.41)
P5	0.13	−0.02
	(1.70)	(−.43)
P6	0.10	−0.06
	(1.22)	(−1.37)
P7	0.07	−0.09
	(.75)	(−1.70)
P8	−0.02	−0.16
	(−.19)	(−2.50)
P9	−0.21	−0.33
	(−1.69)	(−4.01)
P10	−0.79	−0.85
	(−4.59)	(−7.54)
P1 − P10	1.24	1.36
	(6.50)	(−7.04)

Source: Jegadeesh and Titman (2001).

lower B/M ratios than the losers. Therefore, the SMB and HML sensitivities of losers are larger than that for the winners. Overall, the results in table 10.4 indicate that the losers are riskier than the winners since they are more sensitive to all three Fama-French factors.

Table 10.5 reports the momentum portfolio alphas that Jegadeesh and Titman (2001) estimate by regressing the monthly momentum returns (less the risk-free rate except for the zero investment P1–P10 portfolio) on the monthly returns of both the value-weighted index less the risk-free rate (CAPM alpha) and the three Fama-French factors (Fama-French alpha). The CAPM alpha for the winner minus loser portfolio is about the same as the raw return difference since both winners and losers have about the same betas. The Fama-French alpha is 1.36 percent, which is larger than the corresponding raw return of 1.23 percent that Jegadeesh and Titman (2001) report. This difference arises because the losers are more sensitive to the Fama-French factors.

The results here indicate that the cross-sectional differences in expected returns under the CAPM or the Fama-French three-factor model cannot account for the momentum profits. Of course, it is possible that these models omit some priced factors and hence provide inadequate adjustments for differences in risk. To circumvent the need for specifying an equilibrium asset pricing model to determine the benchmarks, Conrad and Kaul (1998) assume that unconditional returns are constant, and use the sample mean of realized returns of each stock (including the ranking period returns) as their measure of the stock's expected return. Then, they use the decomposition in Eq. (3) to examine the contribution of cross-sectional differences in expected returns (the first term on the right-hand side) to momentum profits. They find that the cross-sectional variance of sample mean returns is close to the momentum profits for the WRSS. This finding leads them to conclude erroneously that the observed momentum profits can be entirely explained by cross-sectional differences in expected returns rather than any "time-series patterns in stock returns."

Jegadeesh and Titman (2002), however, point out that while sample mean is an unbiased estimate of unconditional expected return, the cross-sectional variance of sample mean is not an unbiased estimate of the variance of true expected returns. Since sample means contain both expected and unexpected components of returns, variance of sample mean is the sum of the variances of these components. Consequently, the variance of sample mean overstates the dispersion in true expected returns, and therefore, the Conrad and Kaul approach overestimates the contribution the first term on the right-hand side in (3).

Jegadeesh and Titman (2002) address this bias in detail and suggest a few alternatives to avoid the bias. In one of their tests, they use the sample average returns outside the ranking and holding periods to obtain unbiased estimates of unconditional expected returns during the holding period. They find that with this estimate, cross-sectional differences in expected holding-period returns explain virtually none of the momentum profits.[4] Their additional tests also confirm this conclusion.

---

[4] Also see Grundy and Martin (2001).

B. Serial Covariance of Factor Returns

JT examine whether the serial covariance of factor returns, the second term in the decomposition given by Eq. (3), can explain momentum profits. Under model (1), the serial covariance of an equally weighted portfolio of a large number of stocks is:[5]

$$\text{cov}(\bar{r}_t, \bar{r}_{t-1}) = \bar{b}_i^2 \text{Cov}(f_t, f_{t-1}). \qquad (4)$$

If the serial covariance of factor returns were to contribute to momentum profits, then the factor realizations should be positively serially correlated (see Eq. [3]). Although the underlying factor is unobservable, Eq. (4) indicates that the serial covariance of the equally weighted market index will have the same sign as that of the common factor. JT examine this implication, and find that the serial covariance of six-month returns of the equally weighted index is negative (−0.0028). Since the momentum strategy can only benefit from positive serial covariance in factor returns, the finding here indicates that the factor return serial covariance does not contribute to momentum profits.

C. Lead-lag Effects and Momentum Profits

In addition to the three sources in Eq. (3), momentum profits can also potentially arise if stock prices react to common factors with some delay. Intuitively, if stock prices react with a delay to common information, investors will be able to anticipate future price movements based on current factor realizations and devise profitable trading strategies. In some situations such delayed reactions will result in profitable contrarian strategies and in some other situations, it will result in profitable momentum strategies. To see this, consider the following return generating process:

$$r_{it} = \mu_i + \beta_{0,i} f_t + \beta_{1,i} f_{t-1} + e_{it} \qquad (5)$$

where $\beta_{0,i}$ and $\beta_{1,i}$ are sensitivities to contemporaneous and lagged factor realizations. Several papers, including Lo and MacKinlay (1990), JT, Jegadeesh and Titman (1995), and Brennan, Jegadeesh, and Swaminathan (1993) use this delayed-reaction model to characterize stock return dynamics. If stock i partly reacts to the factor with a lag then $\beta_{1,i} > 0$, and if it overreacts to contemporaneous factor realizations and this overreaction is corrected in the subsequent period then $\beta_{1,i} < 0$. Empirically, $\beta_{1,i} > 0$ when the value-weighted market index is used as the common factor (see Jegadeesh and Titman 1995), and therefore stocks seem to underreact to this factor.

---

[5] The contribution of the serial covariances of e_{it} to the serial covariance of the equally weighted index becomes arbitrarily small as the number of stocks in the index becomes arbitrarily large.

The WRSS profits under this model is:

$$\mathrm{E}\left(\sum_{i=1}^{N} w_i r_{i,t}\right) = \sigma_\mu^2 + \delta\sigma_f^2, \tag{6}$$

where,

$$\delta \equiv \frac{1}{N}\sum_{i=1}^{N} (\beta_{0,i} - \overline{\beta}_{0,i})(\beta_{1,i} - \overline{\beta}_{1,i}), \tag{7}$$

and, $\overline{\beta}_0$ and $\overline{\beta}_1$ are the cross-sectional averages of $\beta_{0,i}$ and $\beta_{1,i}$, respectively.

Eq. (6) indicates that the delayed reaction would generate positive momentum profits when $\delta > 0$. Intuitively, δ is greater than zero if firms with large contemporaneous betas also exhibit large lagged betas. Here, the contemporaneous betas are less dispersed than the sum of contemporaneous and lagged betas. When $\delta > 0$, stock prices tend to move too closely together. In other words, if the market moves up, the prices of high beta stocks will increase more than that of low beta stocks, but not by as much as they would if the market fully responds to factor realizations contemporaneously. Hence, the higher beta stocks have higher returns in the subsequent period as well due to delayed reactions. Since momentum strategies tend to buy high beta stocks following a market increase, they will profit from the delayed response in the following period.

When lead-lag effects are generated in this way, large factor realizations will be followed by large delayed reactions, and hence the profit in any period will depend on the magnitude of factor realizations in the previous period. Formally, JT show that the expected WRSS profits conditional on the past factor portfolio return:

$$\mathrm{E}\left(\sum_{i=1}^{N} w_i r_{i,t}\,\big|\,f_{t-1}\right) = \sigma_\mu^2 + \delta f_{t-1}^2, \tag{8}$$

Eq. (8) implies that if the lead-lag effect contributes to momentum profits, then the magnitude of the profits should be positively related to the squared factor portfolio return in the previous period.

To investigate the importance of this source, JT estimate the following regression using the value-weighted index as a proxy for the factor portfolio:

$$r_{pt,6} = \alpha_p + \theta_p r_{mt,-6}^2 + u_{it},$$

where $r_{pt,6}$ is the WRSS profits and $r_{mt,-6}$ is the demeaned return on the value-weighted index in months $t - 6$ through $t - 1$. Their estimates of θ_p and the corresponding autocorrelation-consistent t-statistic over the 1965 to 1989 sample period are -1.77 and -3.56, respectively. The significantly negative slope coefficient indicates that the momentum profits are lower following large factor realizations. Therefore, the marketwide lead-lag effect does not contribute to the momentum profits.

D. Industry Momentum

The results we discuss in the last section clearly indicate that the common factor in a single factor model with the market index as the common factor cannot explain momentum profits. Therefore, momentum profits are due to the predictability of the nonmarket component of returns. While the idiosyncratic component of returns is the only nonmarket component in a single factor model, it is possible that momentum is related to other common factors in a multifactor setting. For example, if we introduce industry factors, serial covariance of industry returns, rather than the serial covariance of firm-specific component of returns, may account for the momentum profits.

Moskowitz and Grinblatt (1999) evaluate momentum in industry returns. They form value-weighted industry portfolios and rank stocks based on past industry returns. They find that high momentum industries outperform low momentum industries in the six months after portfolio formation. To assess the extent to which industry momentum contributes to overall momentum profits, they examine the performance of a "random industry" strategy. Specifically, they replace the firms in the winner and loser industries with other firms that are not in these industries, but have the same ranking period returns as the firms that they replace. The random industry portfolios have similar levels of past returns as the winner and loser industry portfolios. However, Moskowitz and Grinblatt find that their random industry momentum strategy earns close to zero returns. Primarily based on this evidence, they conclude that the momentum strategy profits from industry momentum, and not from firm specific momentum.

Grundy and Martin (2001) reexamine the importance of industry momentum. They replicate Moskowitz and Grinblatt and find that for a six-month ranking period and a contiguous six-month holding period, the actual industry strategy earns a significantly positive return of .78 percent per month, while the random industry strategy earns zero returns (see table 10.6, panel A). Additionally, Grundy and Martin consider a strategy that skips a month between the ranking period and holding period in order to avoid potential biases due to bid-ask spreads. When industry portfolios are formed in this manner, the momentum strategy does not yield significant profits either for the actual industry strategy or for the simulated industry strategy. In comparison, the momentum strategy with individual stocks earns a significantly positive profit of .79 percent per month.

Recall from table 10.1 that the momentum strategy with individual stocks is more profitable when the ranking period and holding period are

TABLE 10.6

Real and Random Industry Momentum Strategies

Each month t, all NYSE and AMEX stocks are assigned to 1 of 20 industry portfolio, I, which are ranked according to the criterion $\sum_{\tau=t-7}^{t-2} r_{I\tau}$, where $r_{I\tau}$ is the month θ return on industry I. The real industry momentum strategy then designates winners and losers as the top and bottom three industries from this ranking. Portfolios are formed monthly. The sample period is July 1963 through July 1995 (385 months). The random industry momentum strategy maintains the portfolio weights within each winner and loser industry for month t, but each stock j in a winner or loser portfolio is replaced by the stock ranking one place higher than stock j when all NYSE and AMEX stocks i are ranked based on their ranking period returns. The strategy for individual stocks ranks stocks based on their returns over the ranking periods and the top ten percent are assigned to the winner portfolio and bottom ten percent are assigned to the loser portfolio. Panel B presents the results for ranking period $t − 6$ through $t − 1$.

	Real Industry Strategy			Random Industry Strategy			Individual Stocks		
	Overall	January	NonJan	Overall	January	NonJan	Overall	January	NonJan
Panel A: Month t portfolios formed based on returns over months $t − 6$ to $t − 1$									
Value-weighted portfolios									
Mean (%)	0.47	−0.34	0.55	0.00	−1.31	0.12	—	—	—
t-statistic	(2.27)	(−0.38)	(2.57)	(0.00)	(−1.33)	(0.68)			
Equal-weighted portfolios									
Mean (%)	0.78	−0.42	0.89	−0.01	−1.45	0.12			
t-statistic	(4.30)	(−0.49)	(4.92)	(−0.10)	(−3.26)	(1.39)			
Panel B: Month t portfolios formed based on returns over months $t − 7$ to $t − 2$									
Value-weighted portfolios									
Mean (%)	0.16	−0.90	0.26	−0.01	−2.37	0.21	—	—	
t-statistic	(0.79)	(−1.03)	(1.23)	(−0.03)	(−2.61)	(1.25)			
Equal-weighted portfolios									
Mean (%)	0.37	−1.24	0.52	0.07	−1.65	0.22	0.76	−7.79	1.54
t-statistic	(2.09)	(−1.47)	(2.92)	(0.71)	(−3.66)	(2.40)	(2.39)	(−3.82)	(6.04)

Source: Grundy and Martin (2001).

not contiguous than when they are contiguous. When the holding period and the ranking period are contiguous, the profits to the momentum strategy are attenuated by the negative serial correlation in returns induced by bid-ask spreads, and by short horizon return reversals. Grundy and Martin note that stocks in the random industry portfolio tend to be smaller than the stocks in the real industry portfolio, and hence it is likely that the returns to the random industry strategy are more adversely affected by the bid-ask bounce. Also, a strategy that selects stocks based on their industry returns would tend to suffer less from reversals due to bid-ask bounce than a strategy that selects stocks based on their own returns.

In the case of industry momentum however, the profits entirely disappear for the six-month ranking period when the ranking period and the holding period are not contiguous. Therefore, industry momentum seems to benefit from positive first-order serial correlation in industry returns while individual stock momentum is hurt by short-horizon return reversals. These results indicate that the momentum strategies most commonly used in the literature clearly benefit from the predictability of firm specific returns, although they may also benefit from industry momentum.

A recent paper by Lewellen (2002) also finds that industry portfolios generate significant momentum profits. Lewellyn, however, concludes that industry momentum is driven primarily by a lead-lag effect within industry. Specifically, his evidence suggests that industry portfolio returns tend to move too much together. In addition, he finds that size and B/M portfolios also exhibit momentum. The overall evidence suggests that neither industry momentum nor firm-specific momentum subsume one another, but they are both important.

3. BEHAVIORAL MODELS

As we mentioned in the introduction, it is very difficult to explain observed momentum profits with a risk-based model. Therefore, researchers have turned to behavioral models to explain this phenomenon. Since these models are described in greater detail elsewhere in this book, we will provide only a brief description of them in order to motivate some of the more recent empirical work on momentum.

Most of these models assume that the momentum-effect is caused by serial correlations of individual stock returns, which as we discussed above, appears to be consistent with the evidence. However, they differ as to whether the serial correlation is caused by underreaction or delayed overreaction. If the serial correlation is caused by underreaction, then we expect to see the positive abnormal returns during the holding period followed by normal returns in the subsequent period. However, if the abnormal returns are caused by delayed overreaction, then we expect that the abnormal momentum returns in the holding period will be followed by negative returns since the delayed overreaction must be subsequently reversed. Hence, these behavioral models suggest that we should examine the long-term profitability of momentum strategies to understand whether momentum is driven by underreaction or by delayed overreaction.

Delong, Shleifer, Summers, and Waldman (1990) were among the first to formally model how irrational portfolio strategies could affect asset prices. In particular, they argue that investors tend to follow "positive feedback trading strategies" (investment strategies that buy past winners and sell past losers). They show that such investor behavior will cause market prices to deviate from fundamental values in the short run and give rise to a momentum effect. As prices revert to fundamentals, long-horizon returns exhibit reversals. To a large extent, the subsequent literature presents behavioral models that formalize how various behavioral biases can lead investors to follow positive feedback strategies.

Barberis, Shleifer, and Vishny (1998) discuss how a "conservatism bias" might lead investors to underreact to information, giving rise to momentum profits. The conservatism bias, identified in experiments by Edwards (1968), suggests that investors tend to underweight new information when they update their priors. If investors act in this way, prices are slow to incorporate new information, but once prices fully incorporate information, there is no further predictability in stock returns.

Additionally, Barberis et al. assume that investors also suffer from a "representative heuristic" bias, which gives rise to delayed overreaction. The representative heuristic bias, as Tversky and Kahneman (1974) originally describe, is the tendency of individuals to identify "an uncertain event, or a sample, by the degree to which it is similar to the parent population." In the context of stock prices, Barberis et al. argue that this bias leads investors to mistakenly conclude that firms that exhibit consistently extraordinary earnings growths will continue to experience similar extraordinary growth in the future. They argue that although the conservatism bias in isolation leads to underreaction, this bias in conjunction with the representative heuristic can lead to prices overshooting their fundamental values in the short run and return reversals in the long run.[6]

Daniel, Hirshleifer, and Subramanyam (1998), and Hong and Stein (1999) propose alternative models that are also consistent with short-term momentum and long-term reversals. Daniel et al. argue that the behavior of informed traders can be characterized by a "self-attribution" bias. In their model, investors observe positive signals about a set of stocks, some of

---

[6] The time horizon over which various biases come into play in the Barberis et al. (and in other behavioral models) is unspecified. One could argue that the six-month ranking period used in this paper may not be long enough for delayed overreaction due to the representative heuristic effect. In such an event we would only observe underreaction due to the conservatism bias.

which perform well after the signal is received. Because of their cognitive biases, the informed traders attribute the performance of ex-post winners to their stock selection skills and that of the ex-post losers to bad luck. As a result, these investors become overconfident about their ability to pick winners and thereby overestimate the precision of their signals for these stocks. Based on their increased confidence in their signals, they push up the prices of the winners above their fundamental values. The delayed overreaction in this model leads to momentum profits that are eventually reversed as prices revert to their fundamentals.

Hong and Stein (1999) do not directly appeal to any behavioral biases on the part of investors but they consider two groups of investors who trade based on different sets of information. The informed investors, or the "news watchers" in their model, obtain signals about future cash flows but ignore information in the past history of prices. The other investors in their model trade based on a limited history of prices and, in addition, do not observe the signal about the fundamentals that is available to the news watchers. The information obtained by the informed investors is transmitted with a delay and hence is only partially incorporated in the prices when first revealed to the market. This part of the model contributes to underreaction, resulting in momentum profits. The technical traders extrapolate based on past prices and tend to push prices of past winners above their fundamental values. Return reversals obtain when prices eventually revert to their fundamentals. Both groups of investors in this model act rationally in updating their expectations conditional on their information sets, but return predictability obtains due to the fact that each group uses only partial information in updating its expectations.

4. Long-Horizon Returns of Momentum Portfolios

As we discussed earlier, the momentum-effect is consistent with both investors underreacting to information, as well as with investors overreacting to past information with a delay, perhaps due to positive feedback trading. The positive feedback effect, which is consistent with some of the behavioral models described in section 3, implies that the momentum portfolio should generate negative returns in the periods following the holding periods considered in previous sections.

JT, and Jegadeesh and Titman (2001) examine the long-horizon performance of momentum strategies to examine whether the evidence suggests returns reversals in the post-holding periods. We reproduce figure 10.2 from Jegadeesh and Titman (2001), which presents the cumulative momentum profits over a sixty-month post-formation period. Over the 1965 to 1998 sample period, the results reveal a dramatic reversal of returns in the second through fifth years. Cumulative momentum profit increases

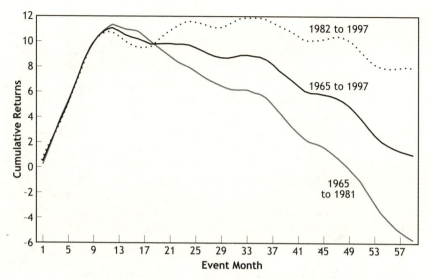

Figure 10.2. This figure presents cumulative momentum portfolio returns with a sample of stocks traded on the NYSE, AMEX or NASDAQ. The sample comprises all stocks that are larger than the smallest NYSE market cap decile at the beginning of the event period. Stocks priced less that $5 at the beginning of each event month are excluded from the sample. See Table 10.1 for a description of momentum portfolio construction. *Source*: Jegadeesh and Titman (2001a).

monotonically until it reaches 12.17 percent at the end of month 12. From month 13 to month 60 the momentum profits are on average negative. By the end of month 60 the cumulative momentum profit declines to −.44 percent. Most of the reversals are observed four to five years after portfolio formation.

The robustness of long-horizon return reversals can be evaluated by examining the performance of momentum portfolios in two separate time periods, the 1965 to 1981 and 1982 to 1998 subperiods. In addition to being the halfway point, 1981 represents somewhat of a break point for the Fama and French factor returns. The Fama-French SMB and HML factors have higher returns in the pre-1981 period than in the post-1981 period. The average SMB and HML factors returns in the pre-1981 period are .53 percent and .48 percent per month and in the post-1981 period are −.18 percent and .33 percent per month, respectively. Since the momentum portfolios have significant exposures to these factors (see table 10.4), the factor related reversals would be larger in the pre-1981 period than in the post-1981 period.

The evidence indicates that the momentum strategy is significantly profitable in the first twelve months following the formation date both of these subperiods, and the profits are of a similar magnitude. The returns in the post-holding periods, however, are quite different in the two subperiods. In the 1965 to 1981 subperiod, the cumulative momentum profit declines from 12.10 percent at the end of month 12 to 5.25 percent at the end of month 36 and then declines further to -6.29 percent at the end of month 60. Therefore, the evidence in this subperiod supports the behavioral models that suggest that positive feedback traders generate momentum. In the 1982 to 1998 subperiod the cumulative profit decreases insignificantly from 12.24 percent, at the end of month 12, to 6.68 percent at the end of month 36 and then stays at about the same level for the next twenty-four months. The evidence in the second subperiod, however, does not support the behavioral models. Overall, positive momentum returns are sometimes associated with post-holding period reversals but sometimes not. Therefore, the long-horizon performance of the momentum portfolio does not provide strong support for the behavioral models.

5. Cross-Sectional Determinants of Momentum

The insights provided by the behavioral models also suggest that stocks with different characteristics should exhibit different degrees of momentum. For example, to the extent that the momentum-effect is due to inefficient stock price reaction to firm specific information, it is likely to be related to various proxies for the quality and type of information that is generated about the firm; the relative amounts of information disclosed publicly and being generated privately; and to the cost associated with arbitraging away the momentum profits.

The empirical evidence suggests that each of these factors is important. For example, JT and a number of more recent papers find that there is greater momentum for smaller firms. A recent working paper by Lesmond, Schill, and Zhou (2001) reports that the most important cross-sectional predictor of the momentum-effect is the price level of the stock. Both firm size and price levels are correlated with transaction costs. Hence, the evidence in these papers suggests that differences in the momentum-effect across stocks is likely to be at least partly due to differences in transaction costs.

Hong, Lim, and Stein (2000) find that even after controlling for size, firms that are followed by fewer stock analysts exhibit greater momentum. Table 10.7, which reproduces a table from Hong, Lim, and Stein (2000), shows that the returns associated with a momentum strategy implemented on stocks with relatively low analyst coverage are fairly large.

Since there is less public information about stocks with low analyst coverage, information about the companies may be incorporated into their stock prices more slowly. Therefore this finding is consistent with the Hong and Stein (1999) prediction that slow dissemination of public information

TABLE 10.7

Monthly Returns for Portfolios Based on Price Momentum and Analyst Coverage

This table includes only stocks above the NYSE/AMEX 20th percentile. The momentum portfolios are formed based on six-month lagged raw returns and held for 6 months. The stocks are ranked in ascending order on the basis of six-month lagged returns. Portfolio P1 is an equally-weighted portfolio of stocks in the worst performing 30%, portfolio P2 includes the middle 40% and portfolio P3 includes the best performing 30%. This table reports the average monthly returns (in percentages) of these portfolios and portfolios formed using an independent sort on Model 1 analyst coverage residuals of log size and a NASDAQ dummy (see cited paper). The least covered firms are in Sub1, the medium covered firms in Sub2, the most covered firms in Sub3. Mean (median) size is in millions, and the t-statistics are in parentheses.

			Residual Coverage Class		
Past	All Stocks	Low:Sub1	Medium:Sub2	High:Sub3	Sub1–Sub3
P1	0.62	0.27	0.67	0.97	−0.70
	(1.54)	(0.66)	(1.70)	(2.31)	(−5.16)
P2	1.37	1.26	1.40	1.44	−0.18
	(4.40)	(4.20)	(4.58)	(4.29)	(−2.11)
P3	1.56	1.40	1.58	1.69	−0.28
	(4.35)	(3.95)	(4.52)	(4.45)	(−2.80)
P3 – P1	0.94	1.13	0.92	0.72	0.42
	(4.89)	(5.46)	(4.64)	(3.74)	(3.50)
Mean Size		962	986	455	
Median Size		103	200	180	
Mean Analyst		1.5	6.7	9.7	
Median Analyst		0.1	3.5	7.6	

Source: Hong, Lim, and Stein (2000).

increases momentum profits. However, this result is also consistent with the overconfidence hypothesis. Since there is less public information available about the low analyst coverage stocks, one might expect relatively more private information to be produced for these stocks. Daniel, Hirshleifer, and Subrahmanyam (1998) suggest that overconfidence will be stronger when there is more active collection of private information.

Daniel and Titman (1999) find that momentum profits are significantly larger when the strategy is implemented with growth (low B/M) stocks than with value (high B/M) stocks. Table 10.8, which we reproduce from Daniel and Titman, shows that the momentum profits are not reliably different from zero when implemented on stocks with the highest B/M ratios. The growth stocks are perhaps harder to evaluate than value stocks. Psychologists report that individuals tend to be more overconfident about their ability

TABLE 10.8

Returns of Book-to-Market and Momentum Sorted Portfolios

For this table all listed common stocks from the NYSE, AMEX, and NASDAQ are sorted into three quintile groupings based on market capitalization, book-to-market ratio and prior-year return. Panel A presents the average monthly returns (in percentages) of 25 prior-year return/book-to-market sorted portfolios over the 1963:07–1997:12 period. These 25 portfolios are formed by equally weighting the five corresponding size-sorted portfolios. Panel B examines similar strategies that exclude the largest and smallest quintile stocks.

	Low		B/M		High	H–L	t-stat
	Panel A: Raw Returns, All Quintiles						
Low	0.45	0.71	1.07	1.17	1.39	0.94	(5.27)
	0.73	0.98	1.14	1.29	1.46	0.73	(4.75)
Past	0.92	1.06	1.17	1.30	1.37	0.45	(2.73)
returns							
	1.04	1.14	1.16	1.36	1.40	0.36	(1.93)
High	1.21	1.42	1.37	1.51	1.49	0.23	(1.45)
H–L	0.75	0.71	0.30	0.35	0.11	HH–LL	
t-stat	(3.84)	(4.03)	(1.87)	(2.18)	(0.59)	1.04	(5.66)
	Panel B: Raw Returns, Quintiles 2–4 only						
	Low		B/M		High	H–L	t-stat
Low	0.55	0.65	1.06	1.16	1.53	0.98	(5.02)
	0.69	0.97	1.16	1.17	1.51	0.82	(4.63)
Past	0.90	1.03	1.12	1.33	1.42	0.52	(2.74)
returns							
	1.00	1.10	1.15	1.40	1.43	0.43	(1.99)
High	1.34	1.50	1.41	1.52	1.61	0.27	(1.11)
H–L	0.79	0.85	0.34	0.36	0.08	HH–LL	
t-stat	(3.33)	(4.26)	(1.96)	(2.13)	(0.42)	1.06	(5.02)

Source: Daniel and Titman (1999).

to do more ambiguous tasks. So, the evidence that the momentum effect is stronger for growth stocks is consistent with the overconfidence hypothesis.

Lee and Swaminathan (2000) examine the relation between momentum profits and turnover, and find that momentum is higher for stocks with greater turnover. Table 10.9, which presents some of the results from their paper, shows that momentum profits are almost three times as large for stocks with the highest turnover than for stocks with the lowest turnover. This finding is somewhat surprising when viewed from the transaction cost

TABLE 10.9

Monthly Returns for Portfolios Based on Price Momentum and Trading Volume

This table presents average monthly returns from portfolio strategies based on an independent two-way sort based on past returns and past average daily turnover for the 1964 to 1995 time period. At the beginning of each month all available stocks in the NYSE/AMEX are sorted independently based on past 6 month returns and divided into 10 portfolios. R1 represents the *loser* portfolio and R10 represents the *winner* portfolio. The stocks are then independently sorted based on average daily volume over the past 6 months and divided into three portfolios, where turnover is used as a proxy of trading volume. V1 represents the lowest trading volume portfolio and V3 represents the highest trading volume portfolio. The stocks at the intersection of the two sorts are grouped together to form portfolios based on past returns and past trading volume. Monthly returns are computed as an equal-weighted average of returns from strategies initiated at the beginning of this month and past months. The numbers in parentheses are simple *t*-statistics.

	V1	V2	V3	V3 – V1
R1	1.12	0.67	0.09	−1.04
	(2.74)	(1.61)	(0.20)	(−5.19)
R10	1.67	1.78	1.55	−0.12
	(5.30)	(5.41)	(4.16)	(−0.67)
R10 – R1	0.54	1.11	1.46	0.91
	(2.07)	(4.46)	(5.93)	(4.61)

Source: Lee and Swaminathan (2000).

perspective. Stocks with higher turnover can be traded more easily and hence should have lower transactions costs. Also, analysts following and institutional ownership are larger for high turnover stocks than for low turnover stocks, and hence we would expect investors to be less overconfident for these stocks.

One potential explanation for their findings may be that there are larger differences of opinion about higher turnover stocks, and larger differences of opinion may arise from difficulties in evaluating the fundamental values of these stocks. Hence, the Daniel and Titman explanation for why growth stocks exhibit greater momentum may also apply to high-turnover stocks. Another explanation is that turnover is related to the amount of attention that a stock attracts. Therefore, high-turnover stocks may be more exposed to positive feedback trading strategies proposed by Delong, Shleifer, Summers, and Waldman (1990).

The evidence that we review in this section indicates that momentum profits are larger for low analyst coverage stocks than for high analyst coverage stocks, larger for growth stocks than for value stocks, and larger for high-turnover stocks than for low-turnover stocks. The behavioral models provide

a basis for understanding the cross-sectional differences in momentum profits. However, these cross-sectional differences can be explained by multiple
behavioral biases that underlie these models. Therefore, it is hard to use these
findings to assess which particular behavioral bias gives rise to momentum
profits. Very likely, all biases play some role.

6. Earnings Momentum

The results so far have focused on the profitability of momentum strategies
based on past returns. Naturally, returns are driven by changes in underlying stock fundamentals. Stock returns tend to be high, for example, when
earnings growth exceeds expectations and when consensus forecasts of future earnings are revised upward. An extensive literature examines return
predictability based on momentum in past earnings and momentum in expectations of future earnings as proxied by revisions in analyst forecasts.
This section selectively reviews the evidence from the earnings momentum
literature and presents the interaction between earnings momentum and
price momentum.

A partial list of papers that investigate the relation between past earnings
momentum and futures returns includes: Jones and Litzenberger (1970),
Latane and Jones (1979), Foster, Ohlsen, and Shevlin (1984), Bernard and
Thomas (1989), and Chan, Jegadeesh, and Lakonishok (1996). These papers typically measure earnings momentum using a measure of standardized unexpected earnings (SUE). SUE is defined as:

$$ \text{SUE} = \frac{\text{Quarterly earnings} - \text{Expected quarterly earnings}}{\text{Standard deviation of quarterly earnings growth}}. $$

These papers use different variations of time-series models to determine
earnings expectations. Typically, the papers assume that quarterly earnings
follow a seasonal random walk with drift, but they differ in their assumptions about earnings growth. Specifically, Jones and Litzenberger (1976)
and Latane and Jones (1979) assume that quarterly earnings grow at a constant rate, Foster et al. (1984), and Bernard and Thomas (1989) model
quarterly earnings growth as an AR(1) process, and Chan et al. (1996) assume zero expected growth in quarterly earnings.

Among these statistical models for quarterly earnings growth, the AR(1)
model is the most realistic specification since it captures the mean reversion
in earnings growth.[7] However, the robustness of the results across different
papers indicates that the accuracy of the model used to specify expected

---

[7] See Foster et al. (1984) for an evaluation of the relative accuracy of various statistical
models to capture the time-series properties of quarterly earnings.

TABLE 10.10

Returns for Portfolios Formed Based on Standardized Unexpected Earnings (SUE).

This table presents the returns of extreme SUE portfolios reported in various papers. SUE is defined as.

$$SUE = \frac{\text{Quarterly earnings} - \text{Expected quarterly earnings}}{\text{Standard deviation of quarterly earnings}}.$$

The High and Low SUE portfolios in Latane and Jones (1969) are comprise stocks with SUE greater than 2 and less than −2 respectively. The High and Low SUE portfolios in Bernard and Thomas (1989) and Chan, Jegadeesh, and Lakonishok (1996) comprise the decile of stocks with the highest and lowest SUE respectively. Latane and Jones, and Bernard and Thomas report abnormal returns and Chan et al. report raw returns.

				Returns		
Paper	Sample Period	Holding Period	Sample	High SUE	Low SUE	Difference
Latane and Jones (1979)	1974–1977	6 months	All Firms	3.1	−4.2	7.3
Bernard and Thomas (1989)	1974–1986	120 days	Small	2.6	−5.4	8.0
			Medium	2.3	−4.8	7.1
			Large	2.0	−2.1	4.1
Chan Jegadeesh and Lakonishok (1996)	1973–1993	6 months	All Firms	11.9	5.1	6.8
		12 months	All Firms	21.3	13.8	7.5

earnings growth is not particularly important for the purpose of measuring unexpected earnings to predict returns.

Table 10.10 summarizes the returns on portfolios formed based on SUE. Latane and Jones examine the profitability of SUE strategies over the 1974 to 1977 sample period and find that the difference in returns between the extreme SUE portfolios is about 7.3 percent over a six-month period. The extreme portfolios in Latane and Jones comprise stocks with SUE greater than 2 for the high SUE portfolio and less than −2 for the low SUE portfolio. With this classification, roughly 15 percent of the stocks in the sample are allocated to each extreme portfolio. Bernard and Thomas (1989) report similar levels of return differences across the extreme SUE deciles for the small and medium firms. For the large firms, the return difference between the extreme decile portfolios is 4.1 percent.

Chan et al. (1996) find a six-month return difference of 7.5 percent between the extreme SUE portfolios over the 1973 to 1993 sample period. The return difference over a twelve-month holding period is 7.5 percent,

TABLE 10.11

Returns for Portfolios Formed Based on Analyst Forecast Revisions

This table presents the returns for portfolios formed based on analyst forecast revisions. The Up revision portfolio in Givoly and Lakonishok comprises stocks with analyst forecast revision greater than 5% and the Down revision portfolio comprises stocks with analyst forecast revision less than −5%. The Up and Down revision portfolios in Stickel (1991) comprise five percent of the stocks with the highest and lowest analyst forecast revisions. The top panel for Stickel presents results based on forecast revisions by individual analysts and the bottom panel presents results based on consensus earnings forecast revisions. Chan, Jegadeesh, and Lakonishok rank stocks based on a six-month moving average of the ratio of analyst forecast revision to stock price. The Up and Down revision portfolios in Stickel (1991) comprise decile of stocks with the highest and lowest analyst forecast revisions. Givoly and Lakonishok, and Stickel report abnormal returns and Chan et al. report raw returns.

| | | | | Returns | | |
| | | | | Up | Down | |
Paper	Sample Period	Sample	Holding Period	Revisions	Revisions	Difference
Givoly and Lakonishok (1979)	1967– 1974	49 Firms from S&P Earnings Forecaster	2 months	2.70	−1.00	3.70
Stickel (1991)	1981– 1985	NYSE/AMEX stocks on Zachs	125 days	2.99	−4.08	7.07
				2.83	−3.53	6.36
Chan, Jegadeesh and Lakonishok (1996)	1973– 1993	NYSE/AMEX/ NASDAQ stocks on IBES	6 months	12.30	4.60	7.70
			12 months	22.90	13.20	8.70

which is only marginally higher that the return difference for the first six months. Therefore, compared with the price momentum strategy, the superior performance of the SUE-based strategy is relatively short-lived.

A partial review of the literature on the revision of analyst earnings forecasts is summarized in table 10.11. A study by Givoly and Lakonishok (1979), which examines a sample of sixty-seven firms from 1967 to 1974, considers earnings forecast data from Standard and Poors Earnings forecaster. They form Up and Down revision portfolios that comprise stocks where the earnings forecast is revised upward or downward by 5 percent. They find that the Up revision portfolio earns about 3.1 percent higher returns than the down portfolio. Stickel (1991) examines a sample of New York and American stock exchange firms that are included in the Zacks

Investment Research database over the 1981 to 1984 sample period. He considers various measures of Up and Down revisions based on both individual analyst's forecast revisions and consensus forecast revisions. Stickel's Up and Down revision portfolios comprise 5 percent of stocks with the highest and lowest forecast revisions. He finds that the Up minus Down revision portfolio earns 7.07 percent using consensus forecast revisions, and 6.36 percent using individual analyst's forecast revisions.

Chan, Jegadeesh, and Lakonishok (1996) use the sample of firms covered by I/B/E/S over the 1977 to 1993 sample period. They define forecast revision as a six-month moving average of the ratio of consensus earnings forecast revision to the stock price. The Up and Down revision portfolios in Chan et al. comprise the decile of stocks with the largest and smallest forecast revisions, respectively. Chan et al. find that the Up minus Down revision portfolio earns 7.7 percent six months after portfolio formation, and 8.7 percent after twelve months. The profitability of analyst forecast revision strategy is also relatively short-lived, which is similar to the SUE strategy.

The collective evidence in the literature indicates that the analyst forecast revision strategy is remarkably robust. The profitability of this strategy is not sensitive to the specific definition of forecast revisions, nor is it sensitive to the data source for analyst forecasts. Also, both the SUE strategy and the forecast revision strategy continue to be profitable although the original evidence was published over twenty years ago.

A. Relation between Earnings and Return Momentum Strategies

Chan et al. (1996) present a detailed analysis of the interactions among various momentum strategies and this subsection closely follows that paper. As they point out, it is possible that a price momentum strategy is profitable mainly because price momentum and earnings momentum are correlated, and earnings momentum may be the dominant source of return predictability. Alternatively, strategies based on price momentum and earnings momentum may be profitable because they exploit market underreaction to different pieces of information. For instance, earnings momentum strategies may exploit underreaction to information about the short-term prospects of companies that will ultimately be manifested in near-term earnings. Price momentum strategies may exploit slow reaction to a broader set of value-relevant information, including the long-term prospects of companies that are not fully captured by near-term earnings forecasts or past earnings growth. If both these explanations were true, then a strategy based on past returns and on earnings momentum in combination should lead to higher profits than either strategy individually.

Chan et al. (1996) present the correlation between price and earnings momentum variables, and their results are reproduced in table 10.12. Not

TABLE 10.12
Correlations among Prior Six-month Return and
Earnings Momentum Variables

This table presents the correlations among stock return over the prior six months (R6), standardized
unexpected earnings (the change in the most recent
past quarterly earnings per share from its value four
quarters ago), scaled by the standard deviation of
unexpected earnings over the past eight quarters
(SUE), and a moving average of the past six months'
revisions in IBES median analyst earnings forecasts
relative to beginning-of-month stock price (REV6).

	R6	SUE	REV6
R6	1.00		
SUE	0.29	1.00	
REV6	0.29	0.44	1.00

Source: Chan, Jegadeesh, and Lakonishok, 1996.

surprisingly, the price momentum and earnings momentum measures are
positively correlated with one another. The highest correlation (0.44) obtains for the two earnings momentum variables. The correlations of past
six-month returns with standardized unexpected earnings and with analyst
forecast revisions indicate that past earnings surprises and revisions of expectations about the following year's earnings are about equal. The less
than perfect correlations suggest, however, that the different momentum
variables do not reflect the same information. Rather, they capture different
aspects of improvement or deterioration in a company's performance.

B. Two-way Analysis

Earnings and return momentum strategies are individually useful for predicting stock returns six to twelve months in the future. Because these variables tend to move together, it is possible that the findings may reflect not
three separate effects but different manifestations of a single effect. For example, if earnings momentum, as reflected by SUE, is the direct source of
return predictability, then it should subsume the predictive ability of the
other variables. However, if each of these momentum variables contains
different pieces of information about future returns then each variable
should exhibit incremental predictive ability.

    Chan et al. (1996, 2000) address this issue with predictability tests
based on two-way classifications. At the beginning of each month, they sort
stocks on the basis of their past six-month returns and assign them to one
of three equal-sized portfolios. Independently, they sort stocks into three

equal-sized portfolios on the basis of SUE and analyst forecast revisions. Each stock, therefore, falls into one of nine portfolios for each two-way sort.

Panel A of table 10.13 reports the results when portfolios are based on rankings by past six-month returns and SUE. The most important observation is that past six-month returns and SUE predict returns in the subsequent period. In particular, the two-way sort generates large differences in returns between stocks jointly ranked highest and stocks jointly ranked lowest. For example, the highest ranked portfolio outperforms the lowest ranked portfolio by 8.1 percent in the first six months and 11.5 percent in the first year.

Each variable (R6 and SUE) contributes some incremental predictive power for future returns. In Panel A, when prior returns are held fixed, stocks with high SUEs earned 4.3 percent more, on average, than stocks with low SUEs in the first six months following portfolio formation. In comparison, the returns on stocks with high and low past prior returns but similar levels of SUE differ on average by only 3.1 percent. In the first six months, the marginal contribution of SUE is larger than that of past returns. When the returns over the first year after portfolio formation are considered, however, a different picture emerges. The marginal contribution of SUE is only 3.8 percent, compared with a contribution of 7 percent for past returns.

A similar picture emerges from the two-way classification by past six-month returns and analyst forecast revisions (Panel B of table 10.13). The marginal contribution of analyst revisions in the first six months is 3.8 percent, compared with 4.5 percent for past returns. Although the marginal contribution of analyst revisions remains at about the same level twelve months after portfolio formation, the marginal contribution of past returns increases to 9.2 percent.

It is possible that SUE and analyst earnings forecast revisions capture the same information. For instance, Stickel (1989), and Ivković and Jegadeesh (2004) find that analyst revision of earnings forecasts is concentrated around earnings announcements. Since forecast revisions tend to be in the same direction as the surprises in quarterly earnings announcements, it is important to examine whether these analyst forecast revisions and SUE capture the same effect. Chan et al. address this issue and table 10.13, Panel C presents their results, indicating that both SUE and analyst forecast revisions make individual contributions to return predictability, and their level of contribution is about the same. The marginal contribution of SUE is 3.4 percent and 3.7 percent for six and twelve months, respectively, after portfolio formation. The corresponding contributions of analyst revisions are 3.2 percent and 4.3 percent.

Overall, none of the momentum variables here subsumes any of the others. Instead, they each exploit underreaction to different pieces of information. The results, however, indicate that the component of superior performance associated with earnings variables is more short-lived than the component associated with prior returns.

TABLE 10.13

Returns for Portfolios Classified Based on Past Return Momentum and Earnings Momentum: Two-way Classification

This table presents the six-month and twelve-month returns for portfolios formed based on stock returns over the prior six months, standardized unexpected earnings (the change in the most recent past quarterly earnings per share from its value four quarters ago), scaled by the standard deviation of unexpected earnings over the past eight quarters, and a moving average of the past six months' revisions in IBES median analyst earnings forecasts relative to beginning-of-month stock price prior six-month returns. This table first ranks stocks independently based on each of these variables independently. The equal-weighted portfolios are formed with stocks in the intersection of the tertile ranks of two variables at a time.

Panel A: Standardized unexpected earnings and prior 6-month return

Standardized unexpected earnings	1(Low)	2	3	1	2	3	1	2	3(High)
Prior 6-month return	1(Low)	1	1	2	2	2	3	3	3(High)
First six months	5.5	9.4	8.5	7.6	10.6	11.3	7.4	11.8	13.6
First year	14.2	19.0	15.7	18.3	22.4	21.6	19.0	25.3	25.7

Panel B: Revision in analyst forecasts and prior 6-month return

Revision in analyst forecasts	1(Low)	2	3	1	2	3	1	2	3(High)
Prior 6-month return	1(Low)	1	1	2	2	2	3	3	3(High)
First six months	4.2	6.3	8.5	7.7	8.8	11.2	9.3	10.3	13.0
First year	11.3	13.4	15.2	18.0	18.6	21.4	21.4	21.5	24.6

Panel C: Revision in analyst forecasts and standardized unexpected earnings

Revision in analyst forecasts	1(Low)	2	3	1	2	3	1	2	3(High)
Standardized unexpected earnings	1(Low)	1	1	2	2	2	3	3	3(High)
First six months	5.1	6.5	9.3	8.4	9.3	11.1	9.3	9.6	12.1
First year	13.7	15.3	19.0	18.4	19.6	22.4	18.5	18.7	22.0

Source: Chan, Jegadeesh, and Lakonishok, 1996.

Chan et al. propose a potential explanation for the relative longevity of the predictive component of the different types of information. The earnings momentum strategies are based on the performance of near-term income—the surprises in quarterly earnings or changes in analysts' forecasts of earnings for the current fiscal year. In contrast, when stocks are ranked on the basis of high or low prior returns, the extreme portfolios comprise stocks for which the market made large revisions in its expectations for the company's future outlook. The stocks in the highest-ranked portfolio in the return momentum strategy rose in price by roughly 70 percent, on average, and the stocks in the lowest-ranked portfolio fell in price by about 30 percent, on average, over the ranking period. Changes of this magnitude are unlikely to have arisen solely from quarter-to-quarter news in earnings. Chan et al. report that the corresponding past six-month returns of the portfolio ranked highest (lowest) by analyst revisions is about 25 (−7 percent). Because the reappraisal of market beliefs for the price momentum portfolios is larger, and given that the market's adjustment is not immediate, it is not surprising that the spread in future returns is larger for the price momentum strategy.

7. Conclusion

Underlying the efficient market hypothesis is the notion that if any predictable patterns exist in returns, investors will quickly act to exploit them, until the source of predictability is eliminated. However, this does not seem to be the case for either past returns or earnings-based momentum strategies. Both strategies have been well-known and were well-publicized by at least the early 1990s, but both continue to generate profits.

The momentum-effect is quite pervasive and it is unlikely that it can be explained by risk. The momentum strategies have generated consistently positive returns for at least the past sixty years in the United States, including the 1990s, a period that was not included in the original momentum tests. Momentum profits have also been found in most major developed markets throughout the world. The only notable exception is Japan, where there is very weak and statistically insignificant evidence of momentum.

We would argue that the momentum-effect represents perhaps the strongest evidence against the efficient markets hypothesis. For this reason it has attracted substantial research. At this point, we have a number of interesting facts to explain it as well as several possible theoretical explanations. However, financial economists are far from reaching a consensus on what generates momentum profits, making this an interesting area for future research.

REFERENCES

Barberis, Nicholas, Andrei Shleifer, and Robert Vishny, 1998, A model of investor sentiment, *Journal of Financial Economics* 49, 307–43.

Bernard, Victor L., and Jacob K. Thomas, 1989, Post-earnings-announcement drift: delayed price response or risk premium? *Journal of Accounting Research* 27, 1–36.

Bhojraj, Sanjeev, and Bhaskaran Swaminathan, 2003, Macromomentum: Returns predictability in international equity indices, *Journal of Business*, forthcoming.

Brennan, Michael J., Narasimhan Jegadeesh, and Bhaskaran Swaminathan, 1993, Investment analysis and the adjustment of stock prices to common information, *Review of Financial Studies* 6, 799–824.

Chan, K., A. Hameed, and W. Tong, 2000, Profitability of momentum strategies in international equity markets, *Journal of Financial and Quantitative Analysis* 35, 153–72.

Chan, Louis K. C., Narasimhan Jegadeesh, and Josef Lakonishok, 1996, Momentum strategies, *Journal of Finance* 51, 1681–1713.

Chen, Hsiu-Lang, Narasimhan Jegadeesh, and Russ Wermers, 2000, The value of active mutual fund management: An examination of the stockholdings and trades of fund managers, *Journal of Financial and Quantitative Analysis* 35, 343–68.

Chui, Andy, Sheridan Titman, and K. C. John Wei, 2000, Momentum, ownership structure, and financial crises: An analysis of Asian stock markets, Working Paper, University of Texas at Austin.

Conrad, Jennifer, and Gautam Kaul, 1998, An anatomy of trading strategies, *Review of Financial Studies* 11, 489–519.

Daniel, Kent, David Hirshleifer, and Avanidhar Subrahmanyam, 1998, Investor psychology and security market under- and overreactions, *Journal of Finance* 53, 1839–86.

Daniel, Kent, and Sheridan Titman, 1999, Market efficiency in an irrational world, *Financial Analyst Journal*, 55, 28–40.

DeBondt, Werner F. M., and Richard H. Thaler, 1985, Does the stock market over-react?, *Journal of Finance* 40, 793–805.

DeLong, J. Bradford, Andrei Shleifer, Lawrence H. Summers, and Robert J. Waldmann, 1990, Positive feedback investment strategies and destabilizing rational speculation, *Journal of Finance* 45, 379–95.

Edwards, W., 1968, Conservatism in human information processing, in B. Kleimutz, (ed.), *Representation of Human Judgement,* Wiley.

Fama, Eugene, and Kenneth French, 1996, Multifactor explanations of asset pricing anomalies, *Journal of Financial Economics* 51, 55–84.

Foster, George, Chris Olsen, and Terry Shevlin, 1984, Earnings releases, anomalies, and the behavior of security returns, *The Accounting Review* 59, 574–603.

Givoly, Dan, and Josef Lakonishok, 1979, The information content of financial analysts' forecasts of earnings: Some evidence on semi-strong inefficiency, *Journal of Accounting and Economics* 1, 165–85.

Griffin, John, Susan Ji, and Spencer Martin, 2003, Momentum investing and business cycle risk: Evidence from pole to pole, *Journal of Finance*, 2515–47.

Grinblatt, Mark, and Sheridan Titman, 1989, Mutual fund performance: An analysis of quarterly portfolio holdings, *Journal of Business* 62, 394–415.

Grinblatt, Mark, Sheridan Titman, and Russ Wermers, 1995, Momentum investment strategies, portfolio performance, and herding: A study of mutual fund behavior, *American Economic Review*, 1088–1105.

Grundy, Bruce D., and Spencer J. Martin, 2001, Understanding the nature of risks and the sources of rewards to momentum investing, *Review of Financial Studies* 14, 29–78.

Hong, Harrison, and Jeremy Stein, 1999, A unified theory of underreaction, momentum trading and overreaction in asset markets, *Journal of Finance* 54, 2143–84.

Hong, Harrison, Terence Lim, and Jeremy C. Stein, 2000, Bad news travels slowly: Size, analyst coverage, and the profitability of momentum strategies, *Journal of Finance* 55, 265–95.

Ivković, Zoran and Narasimhan Jegadeesh, 2004, The timing and value of forecast and recommendation revisions, *Journal of Financial Economics*, 433–63.

Jegadeesh, Narasimhan, 1990, Evidence of predictable behavior of security returns, *Journal of Finance* 45, 881–98.

Jegadeesh, Narasimhan, and Sheridan Titman, 1993, Returns to buying winners and selling losers: Implications for stock market efficiency, *Journal of Finance* 48, 65–91.

———, 1995, Overreaction, delayed reaction and contrarian profits, *Review of Financial Studies* 8, 973–93.

———, 2001, Profitability of momentum strategies: An evaluation of alternative explanations, *Journal of Finance* 56, 699–720.

———, 2002, Cross-sectional and time-series determinants of momentum returns, *Review of Financial Studies*, 143–57.

Jegadeesh, Narasimhan, Joonghyuk Kim, Susan Krische, and Charles Lee, 2004, Analyzing the analysts: When do recommendations add value? *Journal of Finance*, 1082–1124.

Jones, Charles P., and Robert H. Litzenberger, 1970, Quarterly earnings reports and intermediate stock price trends, *Journal of Finance* 25, 143–48.

Keim, Donald, 1983, Size-realted anomalies and stock market seasonality, *Journal of Financial Economics* 12, 13–32.

Latane, Henry A., and Charles P. Jones, 1979, Standardized unexpected earnings— 1971–1977, *Journal of Finance* 34, 717–24.

Lewellen, Jonathan, 2002, Momentum and autocorrelation in stock returns, *Review of Financial Studies* 15, 533–63.

Lee, Charles, and Bhaskaran Swaminathan, 2000, Price momentum and trading volume, *Journal of Finance* 55, 1217–69.

Lehmann, Bruce, 1990, Fads, martingales and market efficiency, *Quarterly Journal of Economics* 105, 1–28.

Lesmond, David A., Michael J. Schill, and Chunsheng Zhou, 2001, The illusory nature of momentum profits, Working Paper, Tulane.

Lo, Andrew, and A. Craig MacKinlay, 1990, When are contrarian profits due to stock market overreaction? *Review of Financial Studies* 3, 175–208.

Moskowitz, Tobias J., and Grinblatt, Mark, 1999, Does industry explain momentum? *Journal of Finance* 54, 1249–90.

Rouwenhorst, K. Geert, 1998, International momentum strategies, *Journal of Finance* 53, 267–84.

Stickel, Scott E., 1989, The timing of and incentives for annual earnings forecasts near interim earnings announcements, *Journal of Accounting and Economics*, 275–92.

———, 1991, Common stock returns surrounding earnings forecast revisions: More puzzling evidence, *Accounting Review*, 402–16.

Tversky, Amos, and Daniel Kahneman, 1974, Judgement under uncertainty: Heuristics and biases, *Science* 185, 1124–31.

Womack, Kent L., 1996, Do brokerage analysts' recommendations have investment value? *Journal of Finance*, 137–67.

Chapter 11

MARKET EFFICIENCY AND BIASES
IN BROKERAGE RECOMMENDATIONS

RONI MICHAELY AND KENT L. WOMACK

INTRODUCTION

The study of decision making by security analysts, specifically the decisions by sell-side analysts to issue buy, sell, or hold recommendations on stocks, provides evidence on some of the most fundamental questions in finance.[1] Among these are, Can analysts identify future winners and losers? If so, how quickly do prices incorporate the information value of these recommendations? Do investors' profits from these recommendations exceed transaction costs? Can analysts intentionally manipulate stock prices even temporarily from their equilibrium values? And perhaps most importantly, What does the evidence about analyst recommendations say about the efficiency of financial markets?

If markets are efficient, one presumes that market participants are not able to consistently forecast future out- and under-performers. Analyst recommendations offer one of the purest tests of whether investment "skill" exists. Security analysts are usually industry specialists, typically covering between five and twenty-five stocks. They regularly keep a portion of the stocks they follow on their "buy list" and maintain a quasi-numerical rating of all stocks within their followed universe. A significant aspect of their job is to update this relative valuation information on the stocks they follow and transmit this information to their customers. It seems clear that this level of specialization qualifies them as "informed investors" in the Grossman (1976) sense if indeed informed (non-insider) investors exist. Thus, there is a reason to believe that analysts' efforts to become informed may lead to the corresponding superior performance of the stocks they recommend. In equilibrium, with analysts competing with each other, the marginal cost of gathering and obtaining this information should be equal to its marginal benefit, or the rent analysts (or their firms) receive. Those rents

We would like to thank Leslie Boni for her valuable comments.

[1] "Sell-side analysts" are securities analysts employed by banks and brokerage firms. "Buy-side analysts" are those employed by institutional investment firms, such as pension funds, mutual funds, and insurance companies.

may be a function of the success of their recommendations, although there may be other benefits too.

The evidence is overwhelming that analysts' announcements of changes in recommendations have significant market impacts, affecting the prices of individual stocks not just immediately but for weeks after the announcement. Controlling for the market and industry in various ways, research shows that investors can earn abnormal profits (before transactions costs) by transacting at the time of recommendation changes.[2]

Most, if not all, empirical research finds that on average, the market reacts favorably to a positive change in recommendation and has a negative reaction to a drop in recommendation. These market reactions to brokers' announcements of changes in the level of recommendations are quite substantial. For example, Womack (1996) reports that the average return in the three-day period surrounding changes to "buy," "strong buy" or "added to the recommended list" was 3 percent. This compares to new "sell" recommendations where the average reaction is even larger, at about −4.5 percent.

Investors transact vigorously in response to recommendation upgrades or downgrades whether or not they are coincidental with other corporate news. Thus, they have important *perceived* information content. Figure 11.1 shows that for a typical recommendation upgrade from a top-fifteen brokerage firm, trading volume approximately doubles, relative to an average day's volume. For recommendation downgrades (e.g., from "buy" to "hold"), the volume on average triples.

If the only significant empirical results were in the short event window when analysts make valuation upgrades and downgrades, one might (and probably should) conclude that the market is quite efficient in reacting to the new brokerage information. However, the evidence is compelling that stock prices of recommended companies continue to drift in the direction recommended by analysts for one to several months after the recommendation change announcement. Womack (1996), and Boni and Womack (2002c), for example, find that for new buy recommendations, the one-month excess return beginning on the third day after the recommendation is more than 1.5 percent, with further drift being insignificant after six to eight weeks.

Market reactions to *removals* of buy recommendations are also quite significant. The initial excess returns are about −3 percent, and the subsequent six-month period return ranges from −2 to −5 percent. In other words, markets, on average, respond more in the short run and prices drift for a longer period after negative reports.

While the frequency of outright sell recommendations is low, their value to investors, like that of "buy" removals, is even greater than for initiations

---

[2] It is as yet an unresolved question what an optimal trading strategy is for using brokerage information and determining how much of these excess returns are "given back" in transactions costs.

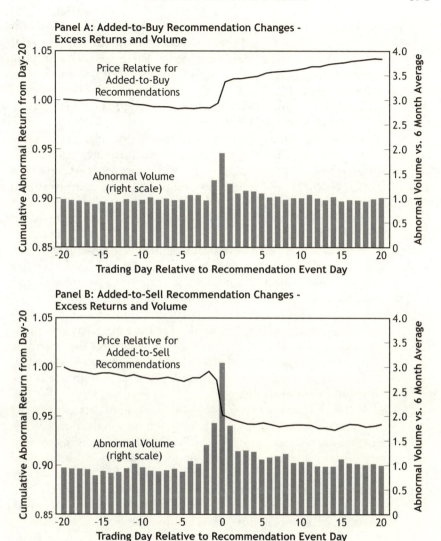

Figure 11.1 *Source*: Womack, Kent L. 1996. Do Brokerage Analysts' Recommendations Have Investment Value? *The Journal of Finance* L1 (no.1):137–67.

of "buy." The initial reaction by the market to the news of a new sell recommendation is, on average, large and negative. Depending on the benchmark used, stocks given "sell" ratings by analysts average a decline of 3 to 4 percent in the three-day window around the announcement. Even more significant, however, is the post-event decline. Depending on the benchmark used, stocks with new sell recommendations declined an additional 4 to 7 percent on average over the six-month period after the event.

There is also clear evidence that analysts are optimistically biased: the buy-to-sell recommendations ratio was about 10 or 20-to-1 in the early 1990s and became even larger later in the 1990s. There is evidence that analyst's recommendations are overly optimistic in general (Rajan and Servaes 1997, and Barber et al. 2001) and in particular when the brokerage house they work for has investment baking relations with the firm they recommend (Michaely and Womack, 1999).

Not only do sell-side analysts, through their recommendations, attempt to predict and influence relative stock price movements in individual stocks and industries, but also they are important contributors to the underwriting arm of their investment banks. In many cases they help the investment bankers secure new business through their knowledge of the target firm's industry and their reputation as a key opinion leader and valuation expert for the industry.

We also observe that errors in analysts' judgments are systematically biased, particularly when their judgments are challenged by conflicting agency and incentive problems like selling and underwriting relationships.

In this chapter, we will assess the informational inputs and outputs of analysts, drawing the conclusion that the recommendations that analysts provide investors have modest investment value, at least in the short-term of several weeks or months after the recommendations are out (not counting for transaction costs). The accumulated evidence also makes it clear that sell-side analyst recommendations are biased, and that investors may not recognize the full extent of the bias.

The rest of this chapter is organized as follows. Section 1 starts with several stylized facts about the stocks they tend to follow and then reviews the literature on the short- and long-term market reaction to analysts' recommendations. Section 2 is devoted to the literature on analysts' biases, and section 3 concludes. Appendix A contains a description of the sell-side research environment, analysts' incentives that are important to understanding how the market interpret their recommendations and why they may have an incentive to issue biased recommendations.

1. Do Analysts' Recommendations Provide Investment Value?

A. Cross-sectional Characteristics of Recommended Stocks

What are the characteristics of stocks that analysts follow and recommend? First, there is a large capitalization bias in the stocks followed and recommended by sell-side analysts. Using size decile cutoffs on the NYSE/AMEX CRSP files, Womack reports that 57 percent of recommendations by the top fourteen brokers are on stocks in the top two capitalization deciles while only 1 percent of recommendations are on stocks in the bottom two size deciles. This is to be expected if analysts are producing research that caters to larger investors' needs, since investors by definition own larger holdings in large cap stocks and also because institutional investors face severe trading costs and constraints in smaller stocks and thus would be less likely to own them.

Jegadeesh et al. (2002) document that analysts tend to prefer growth stocks with glamour characteristics. Specifically, stocks with high positive price momentum, high volume, greater past sales growth, and higher expected long-term earnings growth rates are given more positive recommendations by analysts. Thus ironically, analysts typically favor growth firms that are over-valued according to traditional valuation metrics. Even more importantly, they show that the most valuable recommendations ex post are those with positive changes in the recommendation consensus level combined with favorable quantitative characterstics (i.e., value stocks and positive momentum stocks).

Welch (2000) shows that analysts' recommendations are influenced by the recommendations of previous analysts. In effect, analysts "herd" on short-lived information in the most recent analysts' recommendation revisions. Presumably, it is not surprising that in stocks where there might be a twenty- to thirty-analyst following, that analysts' opinions would be positively correlated.

B. Recommendations Research in the 1980s and Earlier

The fundamental question of whether "experts" can beat the market has attracted much attention from very early on. Alfred Cowles, a pioneering economist at Yale, wrote a study in 1933 titled, "Can Stock Market Forecasters Forecast?" In it, Cowles documents that twenty fire insurance companies and sixteen financial services attempted to "forecast the course of individual stock prices" during the time period January 1928 to July 1932. His conclusion was that the recommendations of most analysts did not produce abnormal returns. Naturally, we know with hindsight that this was a particularly difficult period in the stock market that included the great crash of 1929 and that, at that time, there was not a good understanding of benchmarking investments relative to risk incurred. Hence, it may be that Cowles's computations showing underperformance by the "experts" were incorrect and misstated the risks of recommended stocks relative to the simple benchmark of the market index that he used.

After Cowles, the research on analysts' recommendations in academic outlets was essentially nonexistent until the 1960s and 1970s. In those decades, several papers attempted to quantify the value of tips or recommendations given by analysts or other sources. Colker (1963) tried to measure the "success" of recommendations in the *Wall Street Journal* "Market Views—ANALYSIS" section from 1960 and 1961 using the SP425 as a market benchmark. He found that those recommendations slightly outperformed the market but concluded, "either the state of the art does not permit professional securities dealers to translate their financial acumen into an impressive degree of prophecy, or their best projections do not become public knowledge."

Logue and Tuttle (1973) examined the recommendations of six major brokerage firms in 1970 and 1971 using *The Wall Street Transcript*, which at that time was a comprehensive source. They found that "brokerage house recommendations did not lead to the kind of superior investment performance that one might have expected given the cost of obtaining such recommendations." Interestingly, they did find that "sell" advice was more valuable in that those stocks underperformed the market significantly after three and six months. This is a common theme that we discuss further.

Bidwell (1977) used a beta-adjusted benchmark on the recommendations of eleven brokerage firms, and found that using recommendations produced no superior investment results. Groth et al. (1979) analyzed the complete set of recommendations by one firm from 1964 to 1970 and found, interestingly, that there was much more excess return *prior* to a positive recommendation than after one.

Yet, until the 1980s, it was difficult for researchers to test the essential idea in a systematic and unbiased way. First, without comprehensive databases, finding representative samples that were not biased by survivorship or availability biases was difficult. Second, the issue of the appropriate benchmarking of stocks relative to their fundamental risks was being rapidly developed through the decade of the 1990s, so that, even if the samples were legitimate and unbiased, it was hard to know whether tests failing to reject the null hypothesis of market efficiency were bona fide results or failures to benchmark appropriately.

Two significant papers on analysts' recommendations stand out as noteworthy in the decade of the 1980s. Dimson and Marsh (1984) gathered through a U.K. investment manager a substantial dataset of unpublished stock return forecasts made by the major U.K. brokerage houses. One of the benefits of this study was the lack of ex post selection bias because the decision to undertake the research was made before the data were collected and analyzed. They collected 4,187 one-year forecasts on 206 U.K. stocks made in 1980–1981 by thirty-five brokers. The analysis was not an event study per se but a measurement of the correlation between forecast return and actual return. Dimson and Marsh's findings suggest that analysts were able to distinguish winners from losers, albeit with some amount of overconfidence. The forecast returns of quintiles were −10, −1, 3, 8, and 18 percent while the actual returns were −3.6, 1, 4.4, and 4.5 percent. Hence, brokers, while directionally correct, had a tendency to exaggerate in the sense that high forecasts tended to be overestimates and low forecasts tended to be underestimates.

Elton, Gruber, and Grossman (1986) examined an extensive database comprising 720 analysts at thirty-three brokerage firms from 1981 to 1983. They chose to focus predominately on larger capitalization stocks by eliminating stocks where there were not at least three analysts following the company. The data were sell-side analysts' end-of-the-month ratings on a 1 to 5 scale. Not surprisingly, 48 percent of the ratings were buys (1s or 2s) while only 2 percent were sells (5s). Approximately 11 percent of ratings changed each month.

The important analysis in Elton et al. focused on changes each month to a new rating from a lower ("upgrades") or a higher ("downgrades") one. Upgrades, especially to the most favorable category ("1"), resulted in significant (beta-adjusted) excess returns of 3.43 percent in the month of the announcement plus the next two. Downgrades (to "5" or "sell") resulted in negative excess returns of –2.26 percent. While the analysis of Elton, Gruber, and Grossman is large and beta-adjusted, a potential weakness of the work is its use of calendar-month returns. If markets respond rapidly to new information, it is not clear from looking at monthly returns what the actual response to the recommendation change is, and what other relevant information, like earnings releases, might have occurred in the same month. By not using daily returns, the power of the tests to determine the response to the information in recommendation changes (as opposed to other information) was diluted.

C. New Dimensions in Analyzing Recommendations in the 1990s and Beyond

Using more comprehensive databases and careful empirical analysis, Stickel (1995) and Womack (1996) were able to provide new insights about the sell-side recommendations environment. The benefits of these newer studies in the 1990s were several fold.

First, the analyses identified more precisely the dates of the recommendation changes and used daily returns to increase the precision of the results. The earlier comprehensive papers, by Elton, Gruber, and Grossman (1986), and Dimson and Marsh (1984), used calendar-month return data. Monthly data obscured the precise market response to brokerage information versus other contaminating information releases. Another benefit of the 1990s studies was the combining of other information into the event studies, for example, including earnings release dates and cross-sectional characteristics of the firms and analysts making the recommendations.

Stickel (1995) used a large database of about 17,000 recommendation changes from 1988 to 1991. His database, supplied by Zacks Investment Research, obtained recommendation changes by attempting to collect recommendation information from the various brokerage firms. The weakness of that database in that particular time frame (1988 to 1991) was that the precise day of the recommendation change was not always well identified. It appears that often the dates identified as changes in Zacks were a few days to a week or more after the actual informative announcement. In an environment in which full information is impounded into stock prices over approximately four to twelve weeks, an error of a week or more in reporting the "date" of the recommendation change can cause several improper inferences. The approach taken by Womack (1996) to correct the dating problem was to search a different real-time database, First Call, for all "comments" by the fourteen most prominent U.S. brokers and then to scan using key-word searches to identify all recommendation *changes* to and from "buy" and "sell." In that way, he specifically identified the date and time of brokerage announcements. Earlier studies (for example, Bjerring, Lakonishok, and Vermaelen 1983), were tainted by ex post selection bias, where the data source (a broker) agreed after the fact to allow its data to be analyzed. One of First Call's advantages was that there was no possibility of hindsight bias since data were captured in real time each day as the brokerage firms submitted it. The potential weaknesses of Womack's approach were: (1) that the database he collected was several times smaller than Stickel's (1,600 vs. 17,000 recommendation changes), (2) his time series was about half as long as that of Stickel (eighteen months for most of the sample), and (3) he focused on the largest fourteen firms that potentially had larger responses to their new information than smaller brokers.

Correspondingly, the benefits of Womack's approach were: (1) precision in identification of the correct dates of changes in recommendations, and (2) higher confidence that the information events analyzed were available to and regularly used by professional investment managers (since most prominent investment managers would have brokerage relationships with most or all of the fourteen brokers analyzed). Finally, newer techniques of benchmarking using Fama-French factors and industry-adjusted returns were used by Womack and later papers to adjust more appropriately for risk and allow a more thorough analysis of the return characteristics of stocks recommended.

Womack (1996) reported that the average return in the three-day period surrounding changes to "buy," "strong buy," or "added to the recommended list" was over 3 percent. A stock that was added to the "sell" category experienced, on average, a price drop of 4.5 percent. Perhaps more importantly, Womack reports a positive price drift for one to two months after positive changes in recommendations, and negative price drifts after downgrades in recommendations. Using size-adjusted, industry-adjusted, and the Fama-French three-factor models, he found that for new buy recommendations, the one-month excess return (beginning on the third day after the recommendation is made) is more than 2 percent. Boni and Womack (2002c) replicate his findings with data from 1996 to 2001 and find upgrade "drift" closer to 1.5 percent. Obviously, these numbers are *averages* across many recommendations and do not reflect any one actual recommendation. Individual stock returns (even excess returns) are quite volatile: the average one-month post-event return has a standard deviation of about 8 percent. Therefore, if these returns repeat in future periods, to implement an excess return trading strategy would require a portfolio approach. A randomly chosen recommended stock has about a 40 percent chance of *underperforming* its benchmarks over the post-event one- or three-month periods.

The long-term drift after sell recommendations was negative and highly significant. The average decline was somewhere between 4 to 9 percent (depending on the benchmark used) over the six-month period after the recommendation was made.

Womack (1996) makes two additional observations. First, the post-event excess returns are not mean-reverting. That is, the market appears to move in the direction predicted by the analysts, and this does not appear to be temporary price pressure that corrects after a few weeks or months. Second, Womack goes on to decompose the excess returns into industry and stock-specific portions. He finds that pessimistic recommendations (added-to-sell and removed-from-buy types) are aided by significant industry underperformance in the post-event period. The results suggest that the positive post-event excess returns following new buy recommendations, however, are not primarily an industry effect but rather stock specific abnormal returns.

Barber, Lehavy, McNichols, and Trueman (2001) provide evidence on the profitability of analyst recommendations using specific strategies and imputed transactions costs. Whereas the Stickel and Womack papers primarily analyze event-time returns, Barber et al. focus on a calendar-time perspective. Specifically, they analyze whether changes in the consensus rating (the average across all analysts following a particular stock) provide returns that are sufficient to justify the transaction costs to capture those returns.

The main finding of the paper is that, controlling for Fama-French and momentum factors, the most highly recommended stocks earn a positive alpha of over 4 percent per year while the least favorably recommended stocks earn a negative alpha of almost 5 percent per year. As in Womack (1996), the results are most pronounced for small firms.

However, Barber et al. show that these returns are very time sensitive. For investors who react after two weeks (as opposed to daily), the excess returns are about half as large and not reliably different from zero. Naturally, when one attempts to trade on the information content of recommendations, transaction costs should also be accounted for. Barber et al. suggest that very frequent rebalancing (and the associated high transactions cost) is crucial to capturing the excess returns. They claim that under the assumption of daily rebalancing of the buy and sell portfolios, the turnover would be in excess of 400 percent annually. Less frequent rebalancing leads to lower turnover but also lower excess returns. Their conclusion is that the semi strong form of market efficiency is probably not violated by analysts' information. In essence, the study supports the implications of the earlier studies that the market significantly responds to analyst information, but that the value of that information to investors decays rapidly over four to six weeks for buy recommendations and somewhat longer for sell recommendations. Whether portfolio strategies based on analysts' recommendations can outperform their benchmark after transaction costs is still an open question.[3]

In the past several years (particularly since 1997) many brokerage houses issued price target forecasts in addition to recommendations. Target prices are available for about 90 percent of firms, in terms of market value. These are prices research analysts project those firms to have a year out. A natural question is whether those target prices provide information over and above recommendations. In a recent paper, Brav and Lehavy (2002) address this issue. Using recommendations and target prices data from 1997 to 1999, they document a significant market reaction to changes in target prices. For the group of stocks with the largest change in target price (relative to current price), they document a price reaction of around 2 percent. For those with a negative revision in the target price, the market reaction is negative but the magnitude is a lower, though both are significant.

Consistent with prior studies, Brav and Lehavy document a positive price drift of around 3 percent for the six-month period following recommendation upgrades. Perhaps more interestingly, they show that price drifts are almost twice as high when stocks receive both an upgrade and are in the category of "most favorable (target) price revision." Thus price targets have information content beyond what is contained in recommendations. The excess positive price drift associated with favorable price revision placement suggests that the market fails to recognize the full value of this information.

Another related question is whether the speed of adjustment to analysts' comments and recommendations depend on the type of audience and distribution method. Presumably, if recommendations are disseminated through mass media, such as newspapers or television, their price impact should be more immediate. Barber and Loeffler (1993) examine the impact of analysts' recommendations as they appeared in the Dartboard column in *The Wall Street Journal*. On the publication day, they find a significant price impact of over 4 percent for the pro's picks, and no price impact for the Dartboard stocks. Likewise, the trading volume for the pro's picks is highly significant

---

[3] The sensitivity to the time period is best illustrated by the following example: During the year 2000 the stocks least favorably recommended by analysts earned an annualized market-adjusted return of 48.66 percent while the stocks most highly recommended fell 31.20 percent, a return difference of almost 80 percentage points. As Barber et al. (2002) concludes: "the year 2000 was a disaster," (See Barber et al. 2002 for a more detailed description.)

(80 percent above normal trading volume), but no abnormal trading for the Dartboard's picks. Barber and Loeffler also report that after twenty-five days, some of the abnormal return reverses itself, but that at least a portion of the impact is still visible even a month after the recommendation. The Dartboard column, which ran in *The Wall Street Journal* for fourteen years and ended in 2000, pitted a randomly chosen group of stocks against individual picks of experts for 142 six-month contests. All in all, the pros came out ahead, with a semi-annual average return of 10.2 percent. The darts managed just a 3.5 percent six-month gain, on average, over the same period, while the Dow industrials posted an average rise of 5.6 percent. The pros beat the Dow in 53 percent of the contests. Despite the obvious biases (e.g., pros tend to chose riskier portfolios), this evidence seems to suggest that there is some value in investment research, though it is not clear whether investors can devise a trading strategy that can capitalize on it, after accounting for transaction costs.

Busse and Green (2002) examine the impact of analysts' views about individual stocks that are broadcast when the market is open on CNBC *Morning Call* and *Midday Call* segments. They find that stocks discussed experience a positive statistically and economically significant price impact beginning seconds after the stock is first mentioned that lasts approximately one minute. The response to negative reports is more gradual, lasting fifteen minutes, perhaps due to the higher costs of short-selling. Overall, the price response pattern is similar to the pattern of abnormal performance in work on traditional analyst recommendations, such as Womack (1996), only measured in minutes instead of days or months.

D. Research about Non-Brokerage Recommendations

Empirical research often tends to be constrained by the availability of data. Before the 1990s, it was difficult to assemble a brokerage database that was not tainted with single firm, hindsight, or lookback biases.[4] Therefore, not surprisingly, other easier-to-access data sources were used to examine issues similar to brokerage recommendations.

Value Line was the world's largest published advisory service in the 1970s and 1980s. It provided a convenient source of data in that it ranked 1,700 stocks on a "1" (most attractive) to "5" (least attractive) with possible ranking changes occurring each week. A study by Black (1973) indicated significant positive abnormal performance of stocks ranked 1 and 2 and negative abnormal performance of stocks ranked 4 and 5. The results were very significant and appeared to be a convincing violation of semi-strong-form efficiency. Copeland and Mayers (1982) re-analyzed a longer

---

[4] Bjerring, Lakonishok, and Vermaelen (1983) illustrates one example of a single brokerage firm's attempt to beat the market.

time series of Value Line data and came to the same conclusion, albeit with lesser economic significance. They find, depending on the market model benchmark used, a roughly 1.5 percent outperformance for 1s and 3 percent underperformance for 5s over a six-month time horizon after ranking changes. Over a one-year time frame, stocks ranked 1 outperformed stocks ranked 5 by 6.8 percent. Stickel (1985) re-examined the Value Line results in short-run event studies, and observed that while there were modest returns available to investors in the first few days after the "announcement" date, the ranking upgrades and downgrades were a response to large stock price movements previous to the change dates. He also showed, not surprisingly, that smaller market capitalization companies responded more vigorously to the ranking changes. In fact, abnormal returns in approximately the top quartile were not necessarily above transaction costs necessary to earn the returns. Stickel reports that stocks with significant abnormal returns at the event day continue to move over a multiple-day period, but he does not concentrate on this issue.

The weakness of the Value Line studies is that while it is not a brokerage firm per se, its ranking scheme is a singular process. Should it be generalized? Might there be even better processes? In the 1990s, as other (especially on-line) databases have become available, research effort expended toward Value Line has waned.

2. The Trouble with Sell-side Analysts: Biases in Recommendations

A. The Sell-side Environment: The Many Hats of Brokerage Analysts

Investment banks traditionally have had three main sources of income: (1) corporate financing, issuance of securities, and merger advisory services; (2) brokerage commissions; and (3) proprietary trading. These three income sources may create conflicts of interest within the bank and with its clients. A firm's proprietary trading activities, for example, can conflict with its fiduciary responsibility to obtain "best execution" for clients. One of the potentially more acute conflicts of interest occurs between a bank's corporate finance arm and its brokerage operation. The corporate finance division of the bank is responsible primarily for completing transactions such as initial public offerings (IPOs), seasoned equity offerings, and mergers for new and current clients. The brokerage operation and its equity research department, on the other hand, are motivated to maximize commissions by providing timely, high quality—and presumably unbiased—information to their clients. These two objectives may conflict.

Many reports in the financial press also suggest that conflicts of interest in the investment banking industry may be important issues and have a potentially significant effect on the analyst's job environment and recommendations. For example, according to a story appeared in *The Wall Street Journal* on July 13, 1995, Paine Webber allegedly forced one of its top analysts to start covering Ivax Corp., a stock that it had taken public and sold to its clients. According to the story, the "stock was reeling and needed to be covered." In another story, on February 1, 1996, *The Wall Street Journal* reported that the attitude of the investment bank analysts toward AT&T was a major factor in AT&T's choice of the lead underwriter of the Lucent Technologies IPO.

One source of conflict lies in the compensation structure for equity research analysts. It was common for a significant portion of the research analyst's compensation to be determined by the analyst's "helpfulness" to the corporate finance professionals and their financing efforts (see, for example, *The Wall Street Journal*, June 19, 1997: "All Star Analysts 1997 Survey."). At the same time, analysts' external reputations depend at least partially on the quality of their recommendations. And, this external reputation is the other significant factor in their compensation.

When analysts issue opinions and recommendations about firms that have business dealings with their corporate finance divisions, this conflict may result in recommendations and opinions that are positively biased. A Morgan Stanley internal memo (*The Wall Street Journal*, July 14, 1992), for example, indicated that the company would take a dim view of an analyst's negative report on one of its clients: "Our objective . . . is to adopt a policy, fully understood by the entire firm, including the Research Department, that we do not make negative or controversial comments about our clients as a matter of sound business practice." Another possible outcome of this conflict of interest is pressure on analysts to follow specific companies. There is implicit pressure on analysts to issue and maintain positive recommendations on a firm that is either an investment banking client or a potential client.

Thus, the working environment and the pay structure of analysts lead to several distortions (relative to a perfect world without conflicts of interest). First, analysts may be encouraged to cover some firms that they would not cover otherwise. In the same vein, they would also be encouraged not to issue negative opinions about firms. Issuing negative recommendations is also likely to reduce their access to information from the company, and at the same time may negatively affect the ability of their investment banking firm to do business with that company in the future. The outcome of these pressures is the optimism bias. This optimism bias is an outcome of conflict of interest between the principal (the investing public) and the agents (the investment bank in general and analysts in particular).

This optimism bias manifests itself in analysts' reluctance to issue sell recommendations. We observed a ratio of 20 buy recommendations to 1 sell recommendation throughout the 1980s, and an even higher ratio in the

1990s. It may also manifest itself in generally overly optimistic forecasts of earnings, recommendations, and price targets. There are substantially more "buy" recommendations than "unattractive" or "sell" recommendations. Barber et al. (2001) reports that 53 percent of recommendations are in the "buy" and "strong buy" categories in the larger period from 1985 to 1996. Only 3 percent of recommendations recorded by Zacks in the same period are coded "sell." The positive bias appears to keep getting worse. In the more recent period of 1996 to 2001, Boni and Womack (2002c) find about two-thirds of recommendations in the "buy" and "strong buy," while only 1 percent are "sells."

In an important study, Chan, Karceski, and Lakonishok (2003) examine the difference between analysts' forecasts of earnings' growth rates and realized growth rates. They report evidence of rampant optimism bias by analysts. For example, over the period 1982 to 1998, the median of the distribution of IBES growth *forecasts* is about 14.5 percent while the median *realized* five-year growth rate is about 9 percent. This result is even more pronounced for those stocks with "high" past earnings' growth: the median growth forecast is 22.4 percent, much higher than their median realized growth rate, which is only 9.5 percent.

Rajan and Servaes (1997) examine analysts' optimism bias and its potential effect on the market in the context of IPOs. They find that analysts at the time of the IPO systematically overestimate the future earnings of these firms. They also find that the extent of this overoptimism increases as the length of the forecast period increases. The result is that analysts are overly optimistic in general and even more overly optimistic about the firm's long-term prospects. Rajan and Servaes also compare the optimism to stock price performance. They find that firms with the highest projected growth significantly underperform their benchmarks. Firms with the lowest growth prospect significantly outperform their benchmark. This is an important finding, as it indicates that investors tend to believe inflated forecasts and act on them.[5]

Another way to examine the potential bias in analysts' recommendations is through their forecast of price targets. Brav, Lehavy and Michaely (2002) compared the consensus price target estimate of sell-side analysts to the forecast of price target of the Value Line service, an independent research provider. During the years 1997 to 2001, after controlling for risk factors, the sell-side analyst consensus was on average 14 percent higher than that of Value Line. This evidence suggests that the bias not only exists, but that it may be more acute for sell-side analysts than for independent analysts.

Optimism may be particularly acute during periods when corporations are selecting banks to assist them with borrowing, mergers and acquisitions,

---

[5] Many other papers, in different settings, also document the optimism bias in analysts' forecasts. See for example, Dugar and Nathan (1995), and McNichols and O'Brien (1997).

and seasoned offerings. Under these circumstances, analysts whose firms are bidding for a corporation's financing business have greater incentives to paint a positive picture.

Another explanation, which has its roots in heuristics and cognitive biases, exists for this optimism. It is possible that analysts genuinely believe that the firms they underwrite are better than other firms. In fact, history (or research) is not likely to change their priors. They strongly believe in their recommendations.

B. Underwriting Conflicts of Interest and Resulting Biases

Conflicts between the desire of corporate finance to complete transactions and the need of brokerage analysts to protect and enhance their reputations are likely to be particularly acute when corporate transactions generate significant fees for investment banks. The IPO process is a case in point. First, this market is a lucrative one for the investment banking industry: the average fees are 7 percent. Moreover, recent SEC investigations allege that laddering and commission kickback arrangements make this 7 percent conservative.[6]

Second, implicit in the underwriter-issuer relationship is the underwriter's intention to follow the newly issued security in the aftermarket: that is, to provide (presumably positive) analyst coverage. This coverage is important to most new firms because they are not known in the marketplace, and they believe that their value will be enhanced when investors, especially institutional investors, hear about them. For example, Galant (1992), and Krigman, Shaw, and Womack (1999) report surveys of CEOs and CFOs doing IPOs in the 1990s. About 75 percent of these decision makers indicated that the quality of the research department and the reputation of the underwriter's security analyst in their industry were key factors in choosing a lead underwriter. Hence, a well-known analyst who follows a potential new client's industry represents an important marketing tool for the underwriters.

Finally, positive recommendations after an IPO may enhance the likelihood that the underwriter will be chosen to lead the firm's next security offering. Consequently, there is substantial pressure on analysts to produce positive reports on clients. The potential conflict of interest between a research analyst's fiduciary responsibility to investing clients and the analyst's responsibility to corporate finance clients suggests several implications. First, underwriter analysts may issue recommendations that are more optimistic than recommendations made by nonunderwriter competitors. Second, these analysts may be compelled to issue more positive recommendations

---

[6] *The Wall Street Journal*, "NASD proposes tougher rules on IPO abuses—Agency would bar brokers from allocating hot issues to curry favor with clients," July 29, 2002, p. A1.

(than nonunderwriter analysts) on firms that have traded poorly in the IPO aftermarket, since these are exactly the firms that need a "booster shot" (a positive recommendation when the stock is falling). The implication is that rational market participants should, at the time of a recommendation, discount underwriters' recommendations compared to those of nonunderwriters.

Michaely and Womack (1999) test these implications in the context of analysts' recommendations during the first year firms have gone public. Consistent with the notion of some potential bias, they find that in the month after the quiet period (a time when no recommendations are allowed) lead underwriter analysts issue 50 percent more buy recommendations on the IPO than do analysts from less affiliated firms.

Their results are shown in table 11.1 and in figure 11.2. The first thing to note is that indeed, the market reacts differently to recommendation announcements by underwriters and nonunderwriters. Both are greeted positively by the market (2.7 percent and 4.4 percent return respectively), but those recommended by nonunderwriter analysts are received more positively by the market. The market seems to recognize, at least to some extent, the potential bias and self-interest in underwriters' recommendations. If investors are *fully* aware of the bias, however, we should expect no difference in the long-term performance of those stocks recommended by their own underwriters' analysts and those that are recommended by independent analysts.

In the year following recommendations, the firms recommended by underwriter analysts underperformed the nonunderwriter analysts' recommendations by a wide margin of 18.4 percent. This difference in abnormal performance is statistically significant. The strategy of buying stocks recommended by the underwriters' analysts yields a negative abnormal return of 5.3 percent. Their conclusion was that underwriters' analysts recommendations are biased and the market does not understand the full extent of the bias.

If underwriters attempt to boost stock prices of firms they have taken public, the time to administer a booster shot is when it is really needed—when a firm's stock price is depressed. Indeed, as can be seen in figure 11.2 and table 11.1, the abnormal price performance of companies prior to buy recommendations is significantly different for underwriters and nonunderwriters. Returns of firms with underwriter recommendations declined, on average, 1.6 percent in the thirty trading days prior to the buy recommendation, while firms receiving nonunderwriter buy recommendations increased 4.1 percent over the same period, a significant difference (t-statistic = 2.36). Sixty percent of the firms recommended by their own underwriters experienced negative price movement in the thirty days before the recommendation announcement, compared with only 34 percent of the firms recommended by independent sources.

Michaely and Womack also analyze the performance of IPO stocks, depending on whether they are recommended by only the underwriter, by

TABLE 11.1.
Excess Returns before, at, and after Analyst Buy Recommendations
Differentiated by Underwriting Relationship

Excess returns (size-adjusted mean and median buy-and-hold returns) are calculated for periods before, at, and after the added-to-buy recommendation event date given on *First Call* for the 214 observations in our sample. Size adjustment is calculated by subtracting the buy-and-hold return from the appropriate value-weighted CRSP decile. We define "by underwriter" as recommendations made by equity research analysts of the lead manager of the IPO and "by non-underwriter" as recommendations made by other brokerage firm analysts. "Days after IPO date" is the number of days after the initial IPO date until the added-to-buy recommendation. T-statistics are calculated using the cross-sectional variance in the excess returns and assume independence. The Z-statistic from the Wilcoxon rank-sum test compares the distributions of the underwriter and non-underwriter recommendations non-parametrically.

Added-to-Buy Recommendations	All Buy Recs N = 214	By Underwriter N = 112	By Non-Underwriter N = 102	T-Statistic/ Z-Statistic of the Difference U vs. Non-U
Excess Return, prior 30 days				
Mean	1.2%	−1.6%	4.1%	2.36*
Median	0.7%	−1.5%	3.5%	2.71*
Excess Return, 3-day Event				
Mean	3.5%	2.7%	4.4%	1.55
Median	2.5%	2.2%	2.8%	1.15
Days after IPO date, Mean	83	66	102	2.60*
Days after IPO date, Median	50	47	63	3.48*
Excess Return, Event + 3 mos.				
Mean	7.8%	3.6%	12.5%	2.43*
Median	6.3%	3.3%	8.0%	2.44*
Excess Return, Event + 6 mos.				
Mean	8.2%	3.2%	13.8%	1.69
Median	5.7%	3.9%	7.8%	1.58
Excess Return, Event + 12 mos.				
Mean	3.5%	−5.3%	13.1%	2.29*
Median	−5.1%	−11.6%	3.5%	2.71*

*Significant at 0.05 level.

Source: Michaely, Roni, Womack, 1999. Conflict of Interest and the Credibility of Underwriter Analyst Recommendations. *The Review of Financial Studies* Special 1999, 12 (4): 653–86.

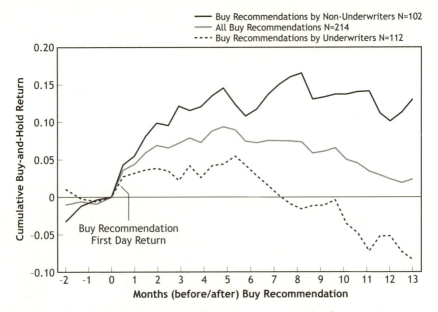

Figure 11.2. Cumulative mean size-adjusted event return for firms receiving new buy recommendations within one year of their IPO, conditional upon the source of recommendation. *Source*: Roni, Michaely, and Kent L. Womack. 1999. Conflict of Interest and the Credibility of Underwriter Analyst Recommendations. *The Review of Financial Studies* Special 1999, 12 (4):653–86.

nonunderwriters, or by both. Excess returns from the first day of trading are calculated contingent on the source of the recommendation. The IPOs in the sample are categorized into five groups by source using information available from First Call. Four of these are analyzed in figure 11.3. First, there are 191 firms for which there are no recommendations available on First Call within one year of the IPO date. Second, there are sixty-three firms with recommendations made only by their lead underwriters. Third, there are forty-one firms with recommendations made by both underwriters and nonunderwriters. Finally, there are forty-four firms with recommendations made only by nonunderwriters. The fifth group, omitted from the figure, is the fifty-two firms with only non-buy recommendations.

For each group shown, initial (first-day) returns average around +10.5 percent. Within six months after the IPO, however, a distinct difference among the groups becomes evident. The IPOs recommended only by their own underwriter had increased by 7.7 percentage points (to an 18.1 percent excess return, including the first day), while the group recommended only by nonunderwriters averaged an additional excess return of 18.6 percentage points (to 28.9 percent). The difference in performance between the two groups is even larger one and two years later. The mean excess return

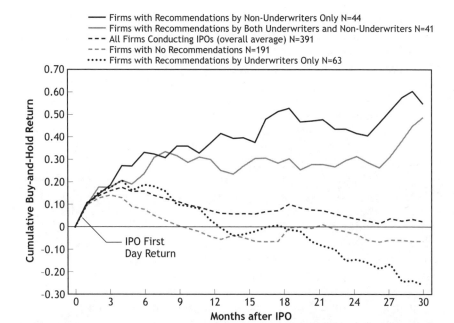

Figure 11.3. Cumulative mean buy-and-hold size-adjusted return for companies conducting IPO in 1990–1991 conditional upon source of brokerage recommendations. Cumulative return begins at the IPO price. *Source*: Roni, Michaely, Kent L. Womack. 1999. Conflict of Interest and the Credibility of Underwriter Analyst Recommendations. *The Review of Financial Studies* Special 1999, 12 (4):653–86.

for the IPOs recommended by underwriters is −18.1 percent after two years, compared with a mean excess return of +45 percent for the IPOs recommended by nonunderwriters.

These results demonstrated that underwriter recommendations, on average, underperform those of nonunderwriters. They reveal that the best indicator for long-term performance of an IPO is not whether the underwriter recommends, but what the more unaffiliated sources say. Stocks recommended by nonunderwriter analysts do well in the long run, with or without the underwriter analyst's blessing, and similarly stocks not recommended by nonunderwriter analysts do poorly.

As we discussed earlier, this bias may have its roots in an investment bank's agency relationship with the IPO firm from which it receives sizable underwriting fees. Alternatively, it may be a result of some cognitive behavior of analysts. That is, it is possible that underwriter analysts genuinely believe that the firms they underwrite are better than the firms underwritten by other investment banks and history (or research) is unlikely to change their priors. This reasoning is a direct outcome of what Kahneman and Lovallo (1993) label "the inside view."

According to this theory, analysts view IPOs underwritten by their firms in a uniquely narrow frame (much like parents who see their children as special). They are unable to accept the statistical reality that many of their IPOs will turn out to be average or below average. Unaffiliated analysts take the "outside view," developing their judgment about the quality of an IPO by considering *all* IPOs probabilistically in comparable situations. Thus, they frame the problem more broadly and more accurately.[7]

Michaely and Womack conducted a survey of investment professionals to determine respondent *perceptions* of the cause for the bias. The survey pool consisted of MBA recipients with at least four years' work experience in either the investment banking or investment management industry. When survey participants were asked to choose between the conflict of interest explanation and the selection bias explanation, they overwhelmingly chose conflict of interest. In fact, 100 percent of investment managers (buy-side respondents) believed the conflict of interest story best explains the documented bias. Moreover, only three of thirteen investment-banking professionals, or 23 percent, chose the benign winner's curse explanation.

Evidence of bias by underwriter analysts around other events, such as seasoned equity offerings (SEOs), is not as dramatic. Lin and McNichols (1997) report that recommendation classifications are more positive for underwriters' recommendations. Dugar and Nathan (1995) find, despite the fact that affiliated analysts are more optimistic, that their earnings forecasts "are, on average, as accurate as those of non-investment banker analysts." More recently, however, Dechow, Hutton, and Sloan (2000) conclude that the earnings estimates of underwriters' analysts are significantly more optimistic than those of unaffiliated analysts, and that stocks are most overpriced when they are covered by affiliated underwriters.

Overall, if market participants are informed and rational, and can incorporate information and can understand incentives, then this bias in analysts' recommendations is benign. The market should simply discount biased recommendations accordingly. But the empirical results of Michaely and Womack show that the market does not respond appropriately, at least in the short run, and does not recognize the full extent of the bias.

---

[7] A related cognitive bias is the "anchoring bias." The underwriter analysts establish or anchor their views and opinions during the due diligence phase, long before the firm goes public. This anchoring bias explains not only why they recommend stocks that have dropped in price (51 percent of underwriter analyst recommendations are for firms that experienced a price depreciation of more than 20 percent from the offering day), but also why they do not always recommend stocks that rise in price when nonaffiliated analysts do. Their priors are presumably fixed and do not change, whatever the market says and does. They are too anchored to change their views. This anchoring idea is consistent with the underwriter firm giving an implicit recommendation at the offering price. In essence: "If I sold this IPO to you at $18, it sure better be attractive at $14," but, since "I sold it to you at $18 and it is now $28, I'm 'off the hook' and don't need to recommend it." Presumably, unaffiliated analysts are less anchored by the offering price and are more willing to recommend high-momentum new issues.

3. Conclusions

Sell-side analysts have come under fire from investors, politicians, and regulators in 2001 and 2002 for their perceived power in influencing investors' decisions and stock prices. The broad claim has been that analysts have been manipulative and insincere, recommending stocks not necessarily because they expect them to be out-performers, but rather because doing so will increase the investment banking or trading profits of their firms, their compensation, and even their own personal investments. Largely motivated by angry investors reeling from technology stock losses, Congress held hearings titled "Analyzing the Analysts" in the summer of 2001. By early 2002, analysts again made front-page news, accused of contributing to massive losses experienced by Enron investors. Fifteen of seventeen analysts covering Enron were still recommending the company's stock as a "buy" or "strong buy" just six weeks before its bankruptcy filing.[8] The analysts' employers, the largest banks and brokerage houses, had received hundreds of millions of dollars in fees for lending, underwriting, merger and acquisition advice, and trading.[9] In the spring of 2002, Merrill Lynch settled with the state of New York, agreeing to pay $100 million in fines and change some research practices after analysts' private emails, trashing the stocks of some companies they touted publicly, were disclosed.[10] In the aftermath, several reforms have been proposed and enacted that may help to safeguard against some potential abuses. It is premature to opine on the effect of these reforms, but many investment professionals believe that some of these reforms will be beneficial in enhancing the integrity of the markets.[11]

What is the role of security analysts in the capital markets? It seems clear that analysts are, in economic terms, first and foremost marketing agents for their employers, most of which are hybrid brokerage/investment banks. Their raison d'etre is to increase the revenues and profits of their employers. Thus, their reports and recommendations are designed to increase brokerage commissions and generate investment banking fees.

However, investors, regulators, and politicians have expected from and given analysts a larger role as unbiased advisors to the public on the valuation of marketable securities. In fact they implicitly expect analysts to have a fiduciary responsibility toward the investing public (despite the fact that

[8] *The Wall Street Journal*, "Most Analysts Remained Plugged in to Enron," October 26, 2001, p. C1.

[9] *The Wall Street Journal*, "How the Street Greased Enron's Money Engine," January 14, 2002, p. C1.

[10] *The Wall Street Journal*, "Merrill Lynch to Pay Big Fine, Increase Oversight of Analysts— New York Attorney General Wins $100 Million Penalty; Emails Exposed Research," May 22, 2002, p. A1.

[11] See Boni and Womack (2002a) for a further discussion of the developments that led to passage of new NASD Rule 2711 and amendments to NYSE Rule 472 on analyst research.

analysts are not in a fiduciary relation with the investing public). The assumption these parties make, naturally, is that analysts' advice is unbiased and valuable to investors and the markets as a whole. The hope is that security analysts will be the market's financial "watchdogs," keeping managements honest and focused through their criticism as well as their praise. If analysts are producers of valuable information, then they will strengthen the integrity and efficiency of the securities market.

As part of their marking efforts, investment banks and analysts claim that their views are unbiased. For example, Morgan Stanley's response to the accusation that the corporate finance division "put pressure on the firm's research analysts to influence their view of the stock" (*The Wall Street Journal*, July 14, 1992) is exactly along these lines. Morgan Stanley argued that customers of its equity research report recommendations are too sophisticated to accept research influenced by investment banking pressure, and thus there is no reason for the corporate finance division to exert any pressure on research analysts.

What does the empirical evidence tell us about these issues? On average, the value of analysts as information gatherers *is* modestly justified, since their pronouncements move stock prices to new price equilibria that are not mean reverting. It is reasonable to say, therefore, that analysts do make the market more efficiently priced. But as we also point out, their pronouncements and advice are not unbiased. Their projections are overly optimistic and they issue many more buy than sell recommendations, at least partially as part of their marketing efforts. The corporate finance arm of the bank, corporate issuers and, to a lesser extent, institutional investors prefer to hear positive analysis rather than negative. As Ken Lay, former chairman of now bankrupt Enron so blatantly put it in criticizing Merrill's Enron analyst who had maintained the unattractive "hold" recommendation on his firm (as reported in *The Wall Street Journal*), "We are for our friends." Later, when that analyst was replaced with another who upgraded his Enron recommendation, Merrill landed substantial investment banking business from the company.[12]

If investors are aware of this marketing bias and discount it appropriately, then, to some extent, no harm is done: Analysts gather information, issue recommendations (albeit biased) and investors, recognizing the bias, discount their recommendations, especially when banking relationships exist. But the empirical evidence suggests that investors do not recognize the full extent of the bias: despite the fact that the long-term performance after positive recommendations by conflicted analysts is negative, the immediate market reaction is positive. At least some investors cannot separate bias from valuable information content.

---

[12] *The Wall Street Journal*, "Merrill Defends Ties to Enron Before Congress—Yet a Veteran Analyst's Perspective On the Firms' Dealings Shows Pressures From Major Clients," July 31, 2002, p. C1.

This "mistake" has at least two real economic consequences: First it damages the integrity of the market in that some (private) investors feel that they are not privileged to the same information others had. Institutional investors may know when a buy recommendation means a buy and when it does not. But individual investors potentially do not. Second, and even more important from a policy perspective, the gap between investors' perspectives of the role of analysts and what they really do may erode investors' confidence in the integrity of financial markets with the end result that capital is scarcer and cost of capital is increased for those firms that can raise capital.

Presently, in 2002, there is considerable foment among politicians, regulators, and, investors to increase the disclosure by analysts and their firms about the affiliations they have with the firm being recommended. Almost surely, this is a good thing, and it would appear to be an important research agenda to analyze which reforms are most valuable. The solutions to these problems are not trivial. The first and most obvious step that has been adopted is to force analysts to explicitly and prominently state their connections to the firms they recommend. Just as the Surgeon General forces the tobacco companies to label cigarettes as posing a danger to health, the NASDAQ or the SEC has asked analysts to display in their reports, and in public appearances, the nature of their personal and the corporate relationships to the firms they recommend. The recent increased disclosures give investors the some tools they need to "debias" analysts' potentially optimistic or misleading reports.

Since many of the abuses are related to IPO firms, as part of an effort "to reassure investors and build investor confidence," the NASDAQ is proposing new rules that would bar any association between IPO allocations and future business with the investment bank that serves as the underwriter that would result in excessive compensation.[13]

A more significant change in the industry structure is a separation of investment banking from research, suggested for example by New York State Attorney General Spitzer.[14] Given the current structure of the industry, it is not clear that there is a demand (i.e., clients that are willing to pay) for independent equity research: Investment banks claim that institutional and especially private investors do not pay the full cost of investment research through their trading commissions. Recall that brokerage research is a bundled good, meaning that investors do not pay "hard" dollars for it, they instead pay for the research through trading commissions and taking investment banking

---

[13] *The Wall Street Journal*, "NASD proposes tougher rules on IPO abuses—Agency would bar brokers from allocating hot issues to curry favor with clients," July 29, 2002, p. A1. The proposed rule states that it "would prohibit the allocation if IPO shares in exchange for excessive compensation relative to the services provided by the underwriter."

[14] *The Wall Street Journal*, "Merrill Lynch Will Negotiate With Spitzer," April 15, 2002, p. C1.

deals. Institutional investors pay about 4 to 5 cents per share, and trading costs are said to be at least half of that per share. Thus the marginal revenue available to help pay for investment research departments is one to two cents per share, far lower than the cost of the research being produced. Thus, the investment banking subsidizes research departments by paying more than 50 percent of the direct costs of analysts' salaries and other research costs. Currently, there is no convincing evidence that investors are willing to pay for independent research. It is possible that regulatory intervention could force such a market and make it viable, but it is also possible that the unintended impact would be less information gathering and less price transparency.

The literature on security analysts in general and on analysts' recommendations in particular show that behavioral biases matter. Biases affect analysts' choices and recommendations, and even more importantly, biases affect how investors interpret those recommendations. Potentially the most valuable outcome of the current rulemaking and proceedings is to make investors more aware of the potential biases in analysts' pronouncements, since it is unlikely any time soon that most market participants will choose to pay the full cost of (possibly) unbiased investment research.

APPENDIX A: THE SELL-SIDE RESEARCH ENVIRONMENT

A. THE MECHANICS OF DELIVERY OF SELL-SIDE RECOMMENDATIONS TO CUSTOMERS

Brokerage analysts ("sell-side" analysts) distribute reports such as "buy recommendations" to investors.[15] These provide external ("buy-side") customers with information and insights into particular companies they follow. Most analysts focus on a specific industry, although some are generalists, covering multiple industries or stocks that do not easily fit into industry groupings.

The analyst's specific information dissemination tasks can be categorized as (1) gathering new information on the industry or individual stock from customers, suppliers, and firm managers; (2) analyzing these data and forming earnings estimates and recommendations; and (3) presenting recommendations and financial models to buy-side customers in presentations and written reports.

The analyst's dissemination of information to investment customers occurs in three different time circumstances: urgent, timely, and routine. The result is the "information merchandise" that is transmitted to customers on a given day. An urgent communication may be made following a surprising quarterly earnings announcement or some type of other corporate announcement while the market is open for trading. In this case, the analyst immediately notifies the salespeople at the brokerage firm, who in turn call customers who they believe might care (and potentially transact) on the basis of the change. Once the sales force is notified, the analyst may directly call, fax, or send email to the firm's largest customers if the analyst knows of their interest in the particular stock.

Less urgent but timely information is usually disseminated through a morning research conference call. Such conference calls are held at most brokerage firms about two hours before the stock market opens for trading in New York. Analysts and portfolio strategists speak about, interpret, and possibly change opinions on firms or sectors they follow. Both institutional and retail salespeople at the brokerage firm listen to this call, take notes, and ask questions.

After the call, and usually before the market opens, the salespeople will call and update their larger or transaction-oriented customers (professional

---

[15] Recommendations are not the only informational output analysts provide for investing clients; in fact, they are only one of the products of an extensive analysis that includes building pro forma valuation models, forecasting future earnings, cash flows and price targets. Hence, even though this chapter will not review the literature on earnings estimate projections by analysts in depth, that function and its literature precede and share common themes with the research on recommendations discussed here.

buy-side traders and portfolio managers) with the important news and recommendation changes of the day. The news from the morning call is dupli-
cated in written notes, and released for distribution to internal and external
sources such as First Call. Important institutional clients may receive fac-
simile transmissions of the highlights of the morning call from many different brokerage firms.

Thus, the "daily news" from all brokerage firms is available to most buy-
side customers, usually well before the opening of the market at 9:30 AM.
The information is sometimes retransmitted via the Dow Jones News Service, Reuters, CNNfn, or other news sources when the price response in the
market is significant.

The importance and timeliness of the "daily news" varies widely. One
type of announcement is a change of opinion by an analyst on a stock. New
"buy" recommendations are usually scrutinized by a research oversight
committee or the legal department of the brokerage firm before release.
Thus, a new added-to-buy recommendation may have been in the planning
stage for several days or weeks before an announcement. Sudden changes
in recommendations (especially, removals of "buy" recommendations) may
occur in response to new and significant information about the company.
Womack (1996) shows that new recommendation changes, particularly
"added to the buy list" and "removed from the buy list," create significant
price and volume changes in the market. For example, on the day that a
new buy recommendation is issued, the target stock typically appreciates 2
percent or more, and its trading volume doubles.

For routine news or reports, most of the items are compiled in written reports and mailed to customers. At some firms, a printed report is dated several days after the brokerage firm first disseminates the news. Thus, smaller
customers of the brokerage firm who are not called immediately may not
learn of the earnings estimate or recommendation changes until they receive the mailed report.

More extensive research reports, whether an industry or a company
analysis, are often written over several weeks or months. Given the length
of time necessary to prepare an extensive report, the content is typically less
urgent and transaction-oriented. These analyst reports are primarily delivered to customers by mail or the Internet, and less often cause significant
price and volume reactions.

B. Sell-side Security Analysts' Compensation, Incentives, and Biases

An important aspect of the recommendation environment is sell-side security analysts' compensation, since a significant portion of it is based on
their ability to generate revenue through service to the corporate finance
arm of the investment bank.

At most brokerage firms, analyst compensation is based on two major factors. The first is the analyst's perceived (external) reputation. The annual *Institutional Investor* All-American Research Teams poll is perhaps the most significant external influence driving analyst compensation (see Stickel, 1992). All-American rankings are based on a questionnaire asking over 750 money managers and institutions to rank analysts in several categories: stock picking, earnings estimates, written reports, and overall service. Note that only the first two criteria are directly related to accurate forecasts and recommendations.

The top analysts in each industry are ranked as first-, second-, or third-place winners or (sometimes several) runner-ups. Directors of equity research at brokerage firms refer to these results when they set compensation levels for analysts. Polls indicate that analysts' being "up to date" is of paramount importance. The timely production of earnings estimates, buy and sell opinions, and written reports on companies followed are also key factors. Polls also indicate that initiation of timely calls on relevant information is a valuable characteristic in a successful (and hence, well-compensated) analyst.

An analyst's ability to generate revenues and profits is a very significant factor in his or her compensation. An analyst's most measurable profit contribution comes from involvement in underwriting and merger deals. Articles in the popular financial press describe the competition for deal-making analysts as intense. Analysts who help to attract underwriting for clients have in the past received a portion of the fees or, more likely, bonuses that are several times those of analysts without underwriting contributions. The distinction between vice president and managing director (or, partner) for analysts at the largest investment banks has been highly correlated with contributions to underwriting fees (see Galant 1992, for example). Despite recent reforms designed to eliminate or moderate compensation for analysts directly tied to investment banking fees, Boni and Womack (2002a) suggest that it will be quite difficult to devise a compensation scheme where the implicit incentive to report more positively on more highly profitable investment banking transactions will be subverted.[16] The reality is that commissions from trading do not cover the cost of research departments completely. Some estimates put the subsidy from investment banking toward research department costs at higher than 50 percent.

Another potential source of revenues, commissions generated by transactions in the stock of the companies the analyst follows, may also be a factor in the analyst's compensation. It is difficult, however, to define an analyst's precise contribution to trading volume. There are many other factors, including the trading "presence" of the investment bank that affect it. Moreover,

---

[16] Several brokerage houses, such as Merrill Lynch, recently announced that in the future, their analysts' compensation would be independent of their contribution to the revenue stream of the investment banking division.

customers regularly use the ideas of one firm's analysts, but transact through another firm. For institutional customers, this is the rule rather than the exception. In the short run, institutional "buy-side" customers seek out the most attractive bids and offers independently of analysts' research helpfulness. Over a quarter or a year, the allocation of commission dollars among brokerage firms is more closely tied to research value-added, but it is important to emphasize that a brokerage firm putting out a new research recommendation will not typically garner even a majority of the immediate transaction volume in the stock it recommends.

References

Amir, Eli, and Baruch Lev, and Theodore Sougiannis, 1999, What Value Analysts?, Working Paper.

Barber, Brad M., Douglas Loeffler, 1993, The "Dartboard" Column: Second-Hand Information and Price Pressure, *Journal of Financial and Quantitative Analysis* 28, 273–84.

Barber, Brad, Reuven Lehavy, Maureen McNichols, and Brett Trueman, 2001, Can Investors Profit from the Prophets? Security Analyst Recommendations and Stock Returns. *The Journal of Finance* 61(2): 531–63.

————2002, Prophets And Losses: Reassessing the Returns To Analysts' Stock Recommendations, forthcoming, *Financial Analysts Journal*.

Beneish, Messod D., 1991, Stock Prices and the Dissemination of Analysts' Recommendations. *Journal of Business* 64, 393–416.

Bidwell, Clinton M. III., 1977, How Good is Institutional Brokerage Research? *Journal of Portfolio Management*, 26–31.

Bjerring, James H., Josef Lakonishok, and Theo Vermaelen, 1983, Stock Prices and Financial Analysts' Recommendations, *Journal of Finance* 38, 187–204.

Black, Fischer, 1973, Yes, Virginia, There Is Hope: Tests of the Value Line Ranking System, *Financial Analysts Journal* 29, 10–14.

Boni, Leslie, and Kent L. Womack, 2002a, Wall Street's Credibility Problem: Misaligned Incentives and Dubious Fixes?, Brookings-Wharton Papers on Financial Services, edited by Robert Litan and Richard Herring, 93–130.

————. 2002b, Solving the Sell-Side Research Problem: Insights from Buy-Side Professionals, Dartmouth College Working Paper.

————. 2002c, Industries, Analysts, and Price Momentum, Dartmouth College Working Paper.

Brav, Alon and Reuven Lehavy, 2002, An Empirical Analysis of Analysts' Target Prices: Short-Term Informativeness and Long-Term Dynamics. *Journal of Finance*.

Brav, Alon, Reuven Lehavy, and Roni Michaely, 2002, Expected returns and asset pricing" Working Paper, Cornell University.

Busse, Jeffrey A., T. Clifton Green, 2002, Market efficiency in real time, *Journal of Financial Economics* 65(3).

Chan, Louis K. C., Jason Karceski, and Josef Lakonishok, 2003, The Level and Persistence of Growth Rates, *Journal of Finance*. 58, 643–84.

Chung, Kee H., 2000, Marketing of Stocks by Brokerage Firms: The Role of Financial Analysts. *Financial Management*, summer, 35–54.

Colker, S. S., 1963, An Analysis of Security Recommendations by Brokerage Houses, *The Quarterly Review of Economics and Business*, 19–28.

Copeland Thomas E., David Mayers, 1982, The Value Line Enigma (1965–1978), *Journal of Financial Economics* 10, 289–321.

Cowles, Alfred III, Can Stock Market Forecasters Forecast?, *Econometrica* 1 (3): 309–24.

Davies, Peter Lloyd, Michael Canes, 1978, Stock Prices and the Publication of Second-Hand Information. *Journal of Business* 51 (1): 43–56.

Dechow, Patricia, Amy Hutton, W. Richard Sloan, 2000, The relation between affiliated analyst's long-term earnings forecasts and stock price performance following equity offerings, *Contemporary Accounting Research,* 17.

Desai, Hemang, Bing Liang, Ajai K. Singh, 2000, Do All-Stars Shine? An Evaluation of Analysts' Recommendations, *Financial Analysts Journal* 56, 20–29.

Diefenbach, R. E. 1972. How Good Is Institutional Brokerage Research? *Financial Analysts Journal* January–February, 54–60.

Dimson, Elroy, and Paul Marsh, 1984, An Analysis of Brokers' and Analysts' Unpublished Forecasts of UK Stock Returns, *Journal of Finance* 39, 1257–92.

Dimson, Elroy, and Paulo Fraletti, 1986, Brokers' Recommendations: The Value of a Telephone Tip, *The Economic Journal* 96, 139–60.

Dugar, Amitabh, and Siva Nathan, 1995, The Effect of Investment Banking Relationships on Financial Analysts' Earnings Forecasts and Investment Recommendations, *Contemporary Accounting Research*, 12, 131–60.

Elton, Edwin, Martin J. Gruber, and Seth Grossman, 1986, Discrete Expectational Data and Portfolio Performance, *Journal of Finance* 90(3), 699–714.

Finger Catherine A., Wayne R. Landsman, 2003, In What Do Analysts' Stock Recommendations Really Mean? *Review of Accounting and Finance* 2, 65–85.

Galant, Debbie, 1992, Going public, *Institutional Investors*, April, 127–29.

Graham John, and Campbell Harvey, 1996, Market Timing Ability and Volatility Implied in Investment Newsletters' Asset Allocation Recommendations, *Journal of Financial Economics* 42, 397–421.

Grossman Sanford, 1976, On the Efficiency of Competitive Stock Markets Where Trades Have Diverse Information, *Journal of Finance* 31, 573–85.

Groth, John C., Wilbur G. Lewellen, Gary G. Schlarbaum, and Ronald C. Lease, 1979, An Analysis of Brokerage House Securities Recommendations, *Financial Analysts Journal* January-February, 32–40.

Hemang Desai, Prem C. Jain, 1995, An Analysis of the Recommendations of the "Superstar" Money Managers at Barron's Annual Roundtable, *The Journal of Finance* 1 (4), 1257–73.

Ho, Michael J., Robert S. Harris, 2000, "Brokerage Analysts' Rationale for Investment Recommendations: Market Responses to Different Types of Information." *Journal of Financial Research* 23 (4), 449–468.

Hong, Harrison, Jeffrey D. Kubik. August, 2000, Measuring the Career Concerns of Secuiryt Analysts: Job Separations, Stock Coverage Assignments and Brokerage House Status. Working Paper.

Jegadeesh, Narasimhan, Joonghyuk Kim, Susan D. Krische, and Charles M. C. Lee, 2004, Analyzing the analysts: When do recommendations add value? *Journal of Finance* 59, 1083–1124.

Juergens, Jennifer L., 1999, How Do Stock Markets Process Analysts' Recommendations? An Intra-daily Analysis, Working Paper, Arizona State University.

Kahneman, Daniel and Don Lovallo, 1993, Timid choices and bold forecasts: A cognitive perspective on risk taking, *Management Science*, 39, 17–31.

Krigman, Laurie, Wayne Shaw, and Kent L. Womack, 1999, Why Do Firms Switch Underwriters?, *Journal of Financial Economics*.

Liang, Bing, 1999, Price Pressure: Evidence from the "Dartboard Column," *Journal of Business* 72 (1), 119–34.

Lin, Hsiou-wei, 1998, Underwriting Relationships and Analysts' Earnings Forecasts and Investment Recommendations, *Journal of Accounting and Economics* 25(1), 101–27.

Liu, Pu, Stanley D. Smith, and Azmat A. Syed, 1990, Stock Price Reactions to The Wall Street Journal's Securities Recommendations, *Journal of Financial and Quantitative Analysis* 25, 399–410.

Logue, Dennis E., and Donald L. Tuttle, 1973, Brokerage House Investment Advice, *Financial Review*, 38–54.

McNichols, Maureen and Patricia O'Brien, 1997, Self-selection and analyst coverage, *Journal of Accounting* Research (supp) 35, 167–99.

Michaely, Roni, Kent L. Womack, 1999, Conflict of Interest and the Credibility of Underwriter Analyst Recommendations, *The Review of Financial Studies*, 12 (4), 653–86.

Rajan, Raghuram, and Henri Servaes, 1997, Analyst following of initial public offerings, *Journal of Finance* 52(2), 507–29.

Stanley, Kenneth L, Wilbur G. Lewellen, and Gary G. Schlarbaum, 1981, Further Evidence on the Value of Professional Investment Research, *Journal of Financial Research* 4, 1–9.

Stickel, Scott E., 1985, The Effect of Value Line Investment Survey Rank Changes on Common Stock Prices, *Journal of Financial Economics* 14, 121–43.

———. 1995, The Anatomy of the Performance of Buy and Sell Recommendations, *Financial Analysts Journal* 1995, 25–39.

Welch, Ivo, 2000. Herding among security analysts. *Journal of Financial Economics* 58, 369–96.

Womack, Kent L., 1996, Do Brokerage Analysts' Recommendations Have Investment Value? *The Journal of Finance* 51 (1), 137–67.

PART IV

Theories of Overreaction
and Underreaction

Chapter 12

A MODEL OF INVESTOR SENTIMENT

Nicholas Barberis, Andrei Shleifer, and Robert W. Vishny

1. Introduction

Recent empirical research in finance has identified two families of pervasive regularities: underreaction and overreaction. The underreaction evidence shows that over horizons of perhaps 1–12 months, security prices underreact to news.[1] As a consequence, news is incorporated only slowly into prices, which tend to exhibit positive autocorrelations over these horizons. A related way to make this point is to say that current good news has power in predicting positive returns in the future. The overreaction evidence shows that over longer horizons of perhaps 3–5 years, security prices overreact to consistent patterns of news pointing in the same direction. That is, securities that have had a long record of good news tend to become overpriced and have low average returns afterwards.[2] Put differently, securities with strings of good performance, however measured, receive extremely high valuations, and these valuations, on average, return to the mean.[3]

The evidence presents a challenge to the efficient markets theory because it suggests that in a variety of markets sophisticated investors can earn superior returns by taking advantage of underreaction and overreaction without bearing extra risk. The most notable recent attempt to explain the evidence from the efficient markets viewpoint is Fama and French (1996).

We are grateful to the NSF for financial support, and to Oliver Blanchard, Alon Brav, John Campbell (a referee for the *Journal of Financial Economics*), John Cochrane, Edward Glaeser, J. B. Heaton, Danny Kahneman, David Laibson, Owen Lamont, Drazen Prelec, Jay Ritter (a referee), Ken Singleton, Dick Thaler, an anonymous referee, and the editor, Bill Schwert, for comments.

[1] Some of the work in this area, discussed in more detail in section 2, includes Cutler et al. (1991), Bernard and Thomas (1989), Jegadeesh and Titman (1993), and Chan et al. (1997).

[2] Some of the work in this area, discussed in more detail in Section 2, includes Cutler et al. (1991), De Bondt and Thaler (1985), Chopra et al. (1992), Fama and French (1992), Lakonishok et al. (1994), and La Porta (1996).

[3] There is also some evidence of nonzero return autocorrelations at very short horizons such as a day (Lehmann, 1990). We do not believe that it is essential for a behavioral model to confront this evidence because it can be plausibly explained by market microstructure considerations, such as the fluctuation of recorded prices between the bid and the ask.

The authors believe that their three-factor model can account for the over-reaction evidence, but not for the continuation of short-term returns (underreaction). This evidence also presents a challenge to behavioral finance theory because early models do not successfully explain the facts.[4] The challenge is to explain how investors might form beliefs that lead to both underreaction and overreaction.

In this chapter, we propose a parsimonious model of investor sentiment—of how investors form beliefs—that is consistent with the available statistical evidence. The model is also consistent with experimental evidence on both the failures of individual judgment under uncertainty and the trading patterns of investors in experimental situations. In particular, our specification is consistent with the results of Tversky and Kahneman (1974) on the important behavioral heuristic known as representativeness, or the tendency of experimental subjects to view events as typical or representative of some specific class and to ignore the laws of probability in the process. In the stock market, for example, investors might classify some stocks as growth stocks based on a history of consistent earnings growth, ignoring the likelihood that there are very few companies that just keep growing. Our model also relates to another phenomenon documented in psychology, namely conservatism, defined as the slow updating of models in the face of new evidence (Edwards 1968). The underreaction evidence in particular is consistent with conservatism.

Our model is that of one investor and one asset. This investor should be viewed as one whose beliefs reflect "consensus forecasts" even when different investors hold different expectations. The beliefs of this representative investor affect prices and returns.

We do not explain in the model why arbitrage fails to eliminate the mispricing. For the purposes of this chapter, we rely on earlier work showing why deviations from efficient prices can persist (De Long et al. 1990a, Shleifer and Vishny 1997). According to this work, an important reason why arbitrage is limited is that movements in investor sentiment are in part unpredictable, and therefore arbitrageurs betting against mispricing run the risk, at least in the short run, that investor sentiment becomes more extreme and prices move even further away from fundamental value. As a consequence of such "noise trader risk," arbitrage positions can lose money in the short run. When arbitrageurs are risk-averse, leveraged, or manage other people's money and run the risk of losing funds under management when performance is poor, the risk of deepening mispricing reduces the size of the positions they take. Hence, arbitrage fails to eliminate the mispricing

---

[4] The model of De Long et al. (1990a) generates negative autocorrelation in returns, and that of De Long et al. (1990b) generates positive autocorrelation. Cutler et al. (1991) combine elements of the two De Long et al. models in an attempt to explain some of the autocorrelation evidence. These models focus exclusively on prices and hence do not confront the crucial earnings evidence discussed in section 2.

completely and investor sentiment affects security prices in equilibrium. In the model below, investor sentiment is indeed in part unpredictable, and therefore, if arbitrageurs were introduced into the model, arbitrage would be limited.[5]

While these earlier papers argue that mispricing can persist, they say little about the nature of the mispricing that might be observed. For that, we need a model of how people form expectations. The current work provides one such model.

In our model, the earnings of the asset follow a random walk. However, the investor does not know that. Rather, he believes that the behavior of a given firm's earnings moves between two "states" or "regimes." In the first state, earnings are mean-reverting. In the second state, they trend, that is, are likely to rise further after an increase. The transition probabilities between the two regimes, as well as the statistical properties of the earnings process in each one of them, are fixed in the investor's mind. In particular, in any given period, the firm's earnings are more likely to stay in a given regime than to switch. Each period, the investor observes earnings, and uses this information to update his beliefs about which state he is in. In his updating, the investor is Bayesian, although his model of the earnings process is inaccurate. Specifically, when a positive earnings surprise is followed by another positive surprise, the investor raises the likelihood that he is in the trending regime, whereas when a positive surprise is followed by a negative surprise, the investor raises the likelihood that he is in the mean-reverting regime. We solve this model and show that, for a plausible range of parameter values, it generates the empirical predictions observed in the data.

Daniel et al. (1998) also construct a model of investor sentiment aimed at reconciling the empirical findings of overreaction and underreaction. They, too, use concepts from psychology to support their framework, although the underpinnings of their model are overconfidence and self-attribution, which are not the same as the psychological ideas we use. It is quite possible that both the phenomena that they describe, and those driving our model, play a role in generating the empirical evidence.

Section 2 summarizes the empirical findings that we try to explain. Section 3 discusses the psychological evidence that motivates our approach. Section 4 presents the model. Section 5 solves it and outlines its implications for the data. Section 6 concludes.

---

[5] The empirical implications of our model are derived from the assumptions about investor psychology or sentiment, rather than from those about the behavior of arbitrageurs. Other models in behavioral finance yield empirical implications that follow from limited arbitrage alone, without specific assumptions about the form of investor sentiment. For example, limited arbitrage in closed-end funds predicts average underpricing of such funds regardless of the exact form of investor sentiment that these funds are subject to (see De Long et al. 1990a; Lee et al. 1991).

2. The Evidence

In this section, we summarize the statistical evidence of underreaction and overreaction in security returns. We devote only minor attention to the behavior of aggregate stock and bond returns because these data generally do not provide enough information to reject the hypothesis of efficient markets. Most of the anomalous evidence that our model tries to explain comes from the cross-section of stock returns. Much of this evidence is from the United States, although some recent research has found similar patterns in other markets.

2.1. Statistical Evidence of Underreaction

Before presenting the empirical findings, we first explain what we mean by underreaction to news announcements. Suppose that in each time period, the investor hears news about a particular company. We denote the news he hears in period t as z_t. This news can be either good or bad, that is, $z_t = G$ or $z_t = B$. By underreaction we mean that the average return on the company's stock in the period following an announcement of good news is *higher* than the average return in the period following bad news:

$$E(r_{t+1}|z_t = G) > E(r_{t+1}|z_t = B).$$

In other words, the stock underreacts to the good news, a mistake that is corrected in the following period, giving a higher return at that time. In this chapter, the good news consists of an earnings announcement that is higher than expected although, as we discuss below, there is considerable evidence of underreaction to other types of news as well.

Empirical analysis of aggregate time series has produced some evidence of underreaction. Cutler et al. (1991) examine autocorrelations in excess returns on various indexes over different horizons. They look at returns on stocks, bonds, and foreign exchange in different markets over the period 1960 to 1988 and generally, though not uniformly, find positive autocorrelations in excess index returns over horizons of between one month and one year. For example, the average one-month autocorrelation in excess stock returns across the world is around 0.1 (and is also around 0.1 in the United States alone), and that in excess bond returns is around 0.2 (and around zero in the United States). Many of these autocorrelations are statistically significant. This autocorrelation evidence is consistent with the underreaction hypothesis, which states that stock prices incorporate information slowly, leading to trends in returns over short horizons.

More convincing support for the underreaction hypothesis comes from the studies of the cross-section of stock returns in the United States, which look at the actual news events as well as the predictability of returns. Bernard

(1992) surveys one class of such studies, which deals with the underreaction of stock prices to announcements of company earnings.

The findings of these studies are roughly as follows. Suppose we sort stocks into groups (say deciles) based on how much of a surprise is contained in their earnings announcement. One naive way to measure an earnings surprise is to look at standardized unexpected earnings (SUE), defined as the difference between a company's earnings in a given quarter and its earnings during the quarter a year before, scaled by the standard deviation of the company's earnings. Another way to measure an earnings surprise is by the stock price reaction to an earnings announcement. A general (and unsurprising) finding is that stocks with positive earnings surprises also earn relatively high returns in the period prior to the earnings announcement, as information about earnings is incorporated into prices. A much more surprising finding is that stocks with higher earnings surprises also earn higher returns in the period after portfolio formation: the market underreacts to the earnings announcement in revising a company's stock price. For example, over the sixty trading days *after* portfolio formation, stocks with the highest SUE earn a cumulative risk-adjusted return that is 4.2 percent higher than the return on stocks with the lowest SUE (see Bernard 1992). Thus, stale information, namely the SUE or the past earnings announcement return, has predictive power for future risk-adjusted returns. Or, put differently, information about earnings is only slowly incorporated into stock prices.

Bernard also summarizes some evidence on the actual properties of the time series of earnings, and provides an interpretation for his findings. The relevant series is changes in a company's earnings in a given quarter relative to the same calendar quarter in the previous year. Over the period 1974 to 1986, using a sample of 2,626 firms, Bernard and Thomas (1990) find that these series exhibit an autocorrelation of about 0.34 at a lag of one quarter, 0.19 at two quarters, 0.06 at three quarters, and -0.24 at four quarters. That is, earnings changes exhibit a slight trend at one-, two-, and three-quarter horizons and a slight reversal after a year. In interpreting the evidence, Bernard conjectures that market participants do not recognize the positive autocorrelations in earnings changes, and in fact believe that earnings follow a random walk. This belief causes them to underreact to earnings announcements. Our model in section 3 uses a related idea for generating underreaction: We suppose that earnings follow a random walk but that investors typically assume that earnings are mean-reverting. The key idea that generates underreaction, which Bernard's and our analyses share, is that investors typically (but not always) believe that earnings are more stationary than they really are. As we show below, this idea has firm foundations in psychology.

Further evidence of underreaction comes from Jegadeesh and Titman (1993), who examine a cross-section of U.S. stock returns and find reliable evidence that over a six-month horizon, stock returns are positively auto-correlated. Similarly to the earnings drift evidence, they interpret their finding of the "momentum" in stock returns as pointing to underreaction to information and slow incorporation of information into prices.[6] More recent work by Rouwenhorst (1997) documents the presence of momentum in international equity markets. Chan et al. (1997) integrate the earnings drift evidence with the momentum evidence. They use three measures of earnings surprise: SUE, stock price reaction to the earnings announcement, and changes in analysts' forecasts of earnings. The authors find that all these measures, as well as the past return, help predict subsequent stock returns at horizons of six months and one year. That is, stocks with a positive earnings surprise, as well as stocks with high past returns, tend to subsequently outperform stocks with a negative earnings surprise and poor returns. Like the other authors, Chan, Jegadeesh, and Lakonishok conclude that investors underreact to news and incorporate information into prices slowly.

In addition to the evidence of stock price underreaction to earnings announcements and the related evidence of momentum in stock prices, there is also a body of closely related evidence on stock price drift following many other announcements and events. For example, Ikenberry et al. (1995) find that stock prices rise on the announcement of share repurchases but then continue to drift in the same direction over the next few years. Michaely et al. (1995) find similar evidence of drift following dividend initiations and omissions, while Ikenberry et al. (1996) document such a drift following stock splits. Finally, Loughran and Ritter (1995), and Spiess and Affleck-Graves (1995) find evidence of a drift following seasoned equity offerings. Daniel et al. (1998) and Fama (1998) summarize a large number of event studies showing this type of underreaction to news events, which a theory of investor sentiment should presumably come to grips with.

2.2. Statistical Evidence of Overreaction

Analogous to the definition of underreaction at the start of the previous subsection, we now define overreaction as occurring when the average return following not one but a series of announcements of good news is *lower* than the average return following a series of bad news announcements. Using the same notation as before,

$$E(r_{t+1}|z_t = G, z_{t-1} = G, \ldots, z_{t-j} = G)$$
$$< E(r_{t+1}|z_t = B, z_{t-1} = B, \ldots, z_{t-j} = B),$$

where j is at least one and probably rather higher. The idea here is simply that after a series of announcements of good news, the investor becomes overly optimistic that future news announcements will also be good and

---

[6] Early evidence on momentum is also contained in De Bondt and Thaler (1985).

hence overreacts, sending the stock price to unduly high levels. Subsequent news announcements are likely to contradict his optimism, leading to lower returns.

Empirical studies of predictability of aggregate index returns over long horizons are extremely numerous. Early papers include Fama and French (1988), and Poterba and Summers (1988); Cutler et al. (1991) examine some of this evidence for a variety of markets. The thrust of the evidence is that, over horizons of three–five years, there is a relatively slight negative autocorrelation in stock returns in many markets. Moreover, over similar horizons, some measures of stock valuation, such as the dividend yield, have predictive power for returns in a similar direction: a low dividend yield or high past return tend to predict a low subsequent return (Campbell and Shiller 1988).

As before, the more convincing evidence comes from the cross-section of stock returns. In an early important paper, De Bondt and Thaler (1985) discover from looking at U.S. data dating back to 1933 that portfolios of stocks with extremely poor returns over the previous five years dramatically outperform portfolios of stocks with extremely high returns, even after making the standard risk adjustments. De Bondt and Thaler's findings are corroborated by later work (e.g., Chopra et al. 1992). In the case of earnings, Zarowin (1989) finds that firms that have had a sequence of bad earnings realizations subsequently outperform firms with a sequence of good earnings. This evidence suggests that stocks with a consistent record of good news, and hence extremely high past returns, are overvalued, and that an investor can therefore earn abnormal returns by betting against this overreaction to consistent patterns of news. Similarly, stocks with a consistent record of bad news become undervalued and subsequently earn superior returns.

Subsequent work has changed the focus from past returns to other measures of valuation, such as the ratio of market value to book value of assets (De Bondt and Thaler 1987, Fama and French 1992), market value to cash flow (Lakonishok et al. 1994), and other accounting measures. All this evidence points in the same direction. Stocks with very high valuations relative to their assets or earnings (glamour stocks), which tend to be stocks of companies with extremely high earnings growth over the previous several years, earn relatively low risk-adjusted returns in the future, whereas stocks with low valuations (value stocks) earn relatively high returns. For example, Lakonishok et al. find spreads of 8–10 percent per year between returns of the extreme value and glamour deciles. Again, this evidence points to overreaction to a prolonged record of extreme performance, whether good or bad: the prices of stocks with such extreme performance tend to be too extreme relative to what these stocks are worth and relative to what the subsequent returns actually deliver. Recent research extends the evidence on value stocks to other markets, including those in Europe, Japan, and emerging markets (Fama and French 1998, Haugen and Baker 1996).

The economic interpretation of this evidence has proved more controversial, since some authors, particularly Fama and French (1992, 1996), argue that glamour stocks are in fact less risky, and value stocks more risky, once risk is properly measured. In a direct attempt to distinguish risk and overreaction, La Porta (1996) sorts stocks on the basis of long-term growth rate forecasts made by professional analysts, and finds evidence that analysts are excessively bullish about the stocks they are most optimistic about and excessively bearish about the stocks they are most pessimistic about. In particular, stocks with the highest growth forecasts earn much lower future returns than stocks with the lowest growth forecasts. Moreover, on average, stocks with high growth forecasts earn negative returns when they subsequently announce earnings and stocks with low growth forecasts earn high returns. All this evidence points to overreaction not just by analysts but more importantly in prices as well: in an efficient market, stocks with optimistic growth forecasts should not earn low returns.

Finally, La Porta et al. (1997) find direct evidence of overreaction in glamour and value stocks defined using accounting variables. Specifically, glamour stocks earn negative returns on the days of their future earnings announcements, and value stocks earn positive returns. The market learns when earnings are announced that its valuations have been too extreme.

In sum, the cross-sectional overreaction evidence, like the cross-sectional underreaction evidence, presents rather reliable regularities. These regularities taken in their entirety are difficult to reconcile with the efficient markets hypothesis. More important for this work, the two regularities challenge behavioral finance to provide a model of how investors form beliefs that can account for the empirical evidence.

3. SOME PSYCHOLOGICAL EVIDENCE

The model we present below is motivated by two important phenomena documented by psychologists: *conservatism* and the *representativeness heuristic*. In this subsection, we briefly describe this psychological evidence as well as a recent attempt to integrate it (Griffin and Tversky 1992).

Several psychologists, including Edwards (1968), have identified a phenomenon known as conservatism. Conservatism states that individuals are slow to change their beliefs in the face of new evidence. Edwards benchmarks a subject's reaction to new evidence against that of an idealized rational Bayesian in experiments in which the true normative value of a piece of evidence is well defined. In his experiments, individuals update their posteriors in the right direction, but *by too little* in magnitude relative to the rational Bayesian benchmark. This finding of conservatism is actually more pronounced the more objectively useful is the new evidence. In Edwards's own words: "It turns out that opinion change is very orderly, and usually proportional to numbers calculated from the Bayes Theorem—but it is insufficient in amount. A conventional first approximation to the data would say that it takes anywhere from two to five observations to do one observation's worth of work in inducing a subject to change his opinions" (p. 359).

Conservatism is extremely suggestive of the underreaction evidence described above. Individuals subject to conservatism might disregard the full information content of an earnings (or some other public) announcement, perhaps because they believe that this number contains a large temporary component, and still cling at least partially to their prior estimates of earnings. As a consequence, they might adjust their valuation of shares only partially in response to the announcement. Edwards would describe such behavior in Bayesian terms as a failure to properly aggregate the information in the new earnings number with investors' own prior information to form a new posterior earnings estimate. In particular, individuals tend to underweight useful statistical evidence relative to the less useful evidence used to form their priors. Alternatively, they might be characterized as being overconfident about their prior information.

A second important phenomenon documented by psychologists is the representativeness heuristic (Tversky and Kahneman 1974): "A person who follows this heuristic evaluates the probability of an uncertain event, or a sample, by the degree to which it is (1) similar in its essential properties to the parent population, and, (2) reflects the salient features of the process by which it is generated" (p. 33). For example, if a detailed description of an individual's personality matches up well with the subject's experiences with people of a particular profession, the subject tends to significantly overestimate the actual probability that the given individual belongs to that profession. In overweighting the representative description, the subject underweights the statistical base-rate evidence of the small fraction of the population belonging to that profession.

An important manifestation of the representativeness heuristic, discussed in detail by Tversky and Kahneman, is that people think they see patterns in truly random sequences. This aspect of the representativeness heuristic is suggestive of the overreaction evidence described above. When a company has a consistent history of earnings growth over several years, accompanied as it may be by salient and enthusiastic descriptions of its products and management, investors might conclude that the past history is representative of an underlying earnings growth potential. While a consistent pattern of high growth may be nothing more than a random draw for a few lucky firms, investors see "order among chaos" and infer from the in-sample growth path that the firm belongs to a small and distinct population of firms whose earnings just keep growing. As a consequence, investors using the representativeness heuristic might disregard the reality that a history of high earnings growth is unlikely to repeat itself; they will overvalue the company, and be disappointed in the future when the forecasted earnings growth fails to materialize. This, of course, is what overreaction is all about.

In a recent study, Griffin and Tversky (1992) attempt to reconcile conservatism with representativeness. In their framework, people update their beliefs based on the "strength" and the "weight" of new evidence. Strength refers to such aspects of the evidence as salience and extremity, whereas weight refers to statistical informativeness, such as sample size.[7] According to Griffin and Tversky, in revising their forecasts, people focus *too much* on the strength of the evidence, and *too little* on its weight, relative to a rational Bayesian. In the Griffin–Tversky framework, conservatism like that documented by Edwards would occur in the face of evidence that has high weight but low strength: People are unimpressed by the low strength and react mildly to the evidence, even though its weight calls for a larger reaction. On the other hand, when the evidence has high strength but low weight, overreaction occurs in a manner consistent with representativeness. Indeed, representativeness can be thought of as excessive attention to the strength of particularly salient evidence, in spite of its relatively low weight.

In the context at hand, Griffin and Tversky's theory suggests that individuals might underweight the information contained in isolated quarterly earnings announcements, since a single earnings number seems like a weakly informative blip exhibiting no particular pattern or strength on its own. In doing so, they ignore the substantial *weight* that the latest earnings news has for forecasting the level of earnings, particularly when earnings are close to a random walk. At the same time, individuals might overweight consistent multiyear patterns of noticeably high or low earnings growth. Such data can be very salient, or have high strength, yet their weight in forecasting earnings growth rates can be quite low.

Unfortunately, the psychological evidence does not tell us quantitatively what kind of information is strong and salient (and hence is overreacted to) and what kind of information is low in weight (and hence is underreacted to). For example, it does not tell us how long a sequence of earnings increases is required for its strength to cause significant overpricing. Nor does the evidence tell us the magnitude of the reaction (relative to a true Bayesian) to information that has high strength and weight, or low strength and weight. For these reasons, it would be inappropriate for us to say that our model is derived from the psychological evidence, as opposed to just being motivated by it.

There are also some stock trading experiments that are consistent with the psychological evidence as well as with the model presented below. Andreassen and Kraus (1990) show subjects (who are university undergraduates

---

[7] To illustrate these concepts, Griffin and Tversky use the example of a recommendation letter. The "strength" of the letter refers to how positive and warm its content is; "weight" on the other hand, measures the credibility and stature of the letter-writer.

untrained in finance) a time series of stock prices and ask them to trade at the prevailing price. After the subjects trade, the next realization of price appears, and they can trade again. Trades do not affect prices: subjects trade with a time series rather than with each other. Stock prices are rescaled real stock prices taken from the financial press, and sometimes modified by the introduction of trends.

Andreassen and Kraus's basic findings are as follows. Subjects generally "track prices," that is, sell when prices rise and buy when prices fall, even when the series they are offered is a random walk. This is the fairly universal mode of behavior, which is consistent with underreaction to news in markets. However, when subjects are given a series of data with an ostensible trend, they reduce tracking, that is, they trade less in response to price movements. It is not clear from Andreassen and Kraus's results whether subjects actually switch from bucking trends to chasing them, although their findings certainly suggest it.

De Bondt (1993) nicely complements Andreassen and Kraus's findings. Using a combination of classroom experiments and investor surveys, De Bondt finds strong evidence that people extrapolate past trends. In one case, he asks subjects to forecast future stock price levels after showing them past stock prices over unnamed periods. He also analyzes a sample of regular forecasts of the Dow Jones Index from a survey of members of the American Association of Individual Investors. In both cases, the forecasted change in price level is higher following a series of previous price increases than following price decreases, suggesting that investors indeed chase trends once they think they see them.

4. A MODEL OF INVESTOR SENTIMENT

4.1. Informal Description of the Model

The model we present in this section attempts to capture the empirical evidence summarized in section 2 using the ideas from psychology discussed in section 3. We consider a model with a representative, risk-neutral investor with discount rate δ. We can think of this investor's beliefs as reflecting the "consensus," even if different investors have different beliefs. There is only one security, which pays out 100 percent of its earnings as dividends; in this context, the equilibrium price of the security is equal to the net present value of future earnings, as forecasted by the representative investor. In contrast to models with heterogeneous agents, there is no information in prices over and above the information already contained in earnings.

Given the assumptions of risk-neutrality and a constant discount rate, returns are unpredictable if the investor knows the correct process followed by the earnings stream, a fact first established by Samuelson (1965). If our model is to generate the kind of predictability in returns documented in the empirical studies discussed in section 2, the investor must be using the wrong model to form expectations.

We suppose that the earnings stream follows a random walk. This assumption is not entirely accurate, as we discussed above, since earnings growth rates at one- to three-quarter horizons are slightly positively autocorrelated (Bernard and Thomas 1990). We make our assumption for concreteness, and it is not at all essential for generating the results. What is essential is that investors sometimes believe that earnings are more stationary than they really are—the idea stressed by Bernard and captured within our model below. This relative misperception is the key to underreaction.

The investor in our model does not realize that earnings follow a random walk. He thinks that the world moves between two "states" or "regimes" and that there is a different model governing earnings in each regime. When the world is in regime 1, Model 1 determines earnings; in regime 2, it is Model 2 that determines them. Neither of the two models is a random walk. Rather, under Model 1, earnings are mean-reverting; in Model 2, they trend. For simplicity, we specify these models as Markov processes: that is, in each model the change in earnings in period t depends only on the change in earnings in period $t - 1$. The only difference between the two models lies in the transition probabilities. Under Model 1, earnings shocks are likely to be reversed in the following period, so that a positive shock to earnings is more likely to be followed in the next period by a negative shock than by another positive shock. Under Model 2, shocks are more likely to be followed by another shock of the same sign.

The idea that the investor believes that the world is governed by one of the two incorrect models is a crude way of capturing the psychological phenomena of the previous section. Model 1 generates effects identical to those predicted by conservatism. An investor using Model 1 to forecast earnings reacts too little to an individual earnings announcement, as would an investor exhibiting conservatism. From the perspective of Griffin and Tversky (1992), there is insufficient reaction to individual earnings announcements because they are low in strength. In fact, these announcements have extremely high weight when earnings follow a random walk, but investors are insensitive to this aspect of the evidence.

In contrast, the investor who believes in Model 2 behaves as if he is subject to the representativeness heuristic. After a string of positive or negative earnings changes, the investor uses Model 2 to forecast future earnings, extrapolating past performance too far into the future. This captures the way that representativeness might lead investors to associate past earnings growth too strongly with future earnings growth. In the language of Griffin and Tversky, investors overreact to the information in a string of positive or negative earnings changes since it is of high strength; they ignore the fact that it has low weight when earnings simply follow a random walk.

The investor also believes that there is an underlying regime-switching process that determines which regime the world is in at any time. We specify this underlying process as a Markov process as well, so that whether the current regime is Model 1 or Model 2 depends only on what the regime was last period. We focus attention on cases in which regime switches are relatively rare. That is, if Model 1 determines the change in earnings in period t, it is likely that it determines earnings in period $t + 1$ also. The same applies to Model 2. With some small probability, though, the regime changes, and the other model begins generating earnings. For reasons that will become apparent, we often require the regime-switching probabilities to be such that the investor thinks that the world is in the mean-reverting regime of Model 1 more often than he believes it to be in the trending regime of Model 2.

The transition probabilities associated with Models 1 and 2 and with the underlying regime-switching process are fixed in the investor's mind. In order to value the security, the investor needs to forecast future earnings. To do this, he uses the earnings stream he has observed to update his beliefs about which regime is generating earnings. Once this is done, he uses the regime-switching model to forecast future earnings. The investor updates in a Bayesian fashion even though his model of earnings is incorrect. For instance, if he observes two consecutive earnings shocks of the same sign, he believes more strongly that he is in the trending earnings regime of Model 2. If the earnings shock this period is of the opposite sign to last period's earnings shock, he puts more weight on Model 1, the mean-reverting regime.

Our model differs from more typical models of learning. In our framework, the investor never changes the model he is using to forecast earnings, but rather uses the same regime-switching model, with the same regimes and transition probabilities throughout. Even after observing a very long stream of earnings data, he does not change his model to something more like a random walk, the true earnings process. His only task is to figure out which of the two regimes of his model is currently generating earnings. This is the only sense in which he is learning from the data.[8]

We now provide some preliminary intuition for how investor behavior of the kind described above, coupled with the true random walk process for earnings, can generate the empirical phenomena discussed in section 2. In particular, we show how our framework can lead to both underreaction to earnings announcements and long-run overreaction.

In our model, a natural way of capturing overreaction is to say that the average realized return following a string of positive shocks to earnings is lower than the average realized return following a string of negative shocks to earnings. Indeed, after our investor sees a series of positive earnings shocks, he

---

[8] From a mathematical perspective, the investor would eventually learn the true random walk model for earnings if it were included in the support of his prior; from the viewpoint of psychology, though, there is much evidence that people learn *slowly* and find it difficult to shake off pervasive biases such as conservatism and representativeness.

puts a high probability on the event that Model 2 is generating current earnings. Since he believes regime switches to be rare, this means that Model 2 is also likely to generate earnings in the next period. The investor therefore expects the shock to earnings next period to be positive again. Earnings, however, follow a random walk: next period's earnings are equally likely to go up or down. If they go up, the return will not be large, as the investor is expecting exactly that, namely a rise in earnings. If they fall, however, the return is large and negative as the investor is taken by surprise by the negative announcement.[9] The average realized return after a string of positive shocks is therefore negative; symmetrically, the average return after a string of negative earnings shocks is positive. The difference between the average returns in the two cases is negative, consistent with the empirically observed overreaction.

Now we turn to underreaction. Following our discussion in section 2, we can think of underreaction as the fact that the average realized return following a positive shock to earnings is greater than the average realized return following a negative shock to earnings. Underreaction obtains in our model as long as the investor places more weight on Model 1 than on Model 2, on average. Consider the realized return following a positive earnings shock. Since, by assumption, the investor on average believes Model 1, he on average believes that this positive earnings shock will be partly reversed in the next period. In reality, however, a positive shock is as likely to be followed by a positive as by a negative shock. If the shock is negative, the realized return is not large, since this is the earnings realization that was expected by the investor. If the shock is positive, the realized return is large and positive, since this shock is unexpected. Similarly, the average realized return following a negative earnings shock is negative, and hence the difference in the average realized returns is indeed positive, consistent with the evidence of post-earnings announcement drift and short-term momentum.

The empirical studies discussed in section 2 indicate that underreaction may be a broader phenomenon than simply the delayed reaction to earnings documented by Bernard and Thomas (1989). Although our model is formulated in terms of earnings news, delayed reaction to announcements about dividends and share repurchases can be understood just as easily in our framework. In the same way that the investor displays conservatism when adjusting his beliefs in the face of a new earnings announcement, so he may also underweight the information in the announcement of a dividend cut or a share repurchase.

The mechanism for expectation formation that we propose here is related to that used by Barsky and De Long (1993) in an attempt to explain Shiller's (1981) finding of excess volatility in the price/dividend ratio. They

---

[9] A referee for the *Journal of Financial Economics* has pointed out to us that this is exactly the empirical finding of Dreman and Berry (1995). They find that glamour stocks earn small positive event returns on positive earnings surprises and large negative event returns on negative earnings surprises. The converse holds for value stocks.

suppose that investors view the growth rate of dividends as a parameter that is not only unknown but also changing over time. The optimal estimate of the parameter closely resembles a distributed lag on past one-period dividend growth rates, with declining weights. If dividends rise steadily over several periods, the investor's estimate of the current dividend growth rate also rises, leading him to forecast higher dividends in the future as well. Analogously, in our model, a series of positive shocks to earnings leads the investor to raise the probability that earnings changes are currently being generated by the trending regime 2, leading him to make more bullish predictions for future earnings.

4.2. A Formal Model

We now present a mathematical model of the investor behavior described above, and in section 5, we check that the intuition can be formalized. Suppose that earnings at time t are $N_t = N_{t-1} + y_t$, where y_t is the shock to earnings at time t, which can take one of two values, $+y$ or $-y$. Assume that all earnings are paid out as dividends. The investor believes that the value of y_t is determined by one of two models, Model 1 or Model 2, depending on the "state" or "regime" of the economy. Models 1 and 2 have the same structure: they are both Markov processes, in the sense that the value taken by y_t depends only on the value taken by y_{t-1}. The essential difference between the two processes lies in the transition probabilities. To be precise, the transition matrices for the two models are:

Model 1	$y_{t+1} = y$	$y_{t+1} = -y$	Model 2	$y_{t+1} = y$	$y_{t+1} = -y$
$y_t = y$	π_L	$1 - \pi_L$	$y_t = y$	π_H	$1 - \pi_H$
$y_t = -y$	$1 - \pi_L$	π_L	$y_t = -y$	$1 - \pi_H$	π_H

The key is that π_L is small and π_H is large. We shall think of π_L as falling between zero and 0.5, with π_H falling between 0.5 and one. In other words, under Model 1 a positive shock is likely to be reversed; under Model 2, a positive shock is more likely to be followed by another positive shock.

The investor is convinced that he knows the parameters π_L and π_H; he is also sure that he is right about the underlying process controlling the switching from one regime to another, or equivalently from Models 1 to 2. It, too, is Markov, so that the state of the world today depends only on the state of the world in the previous period. The transition matrix is

	$s_{t+1} = 1$	$s_{t+1} = 2$
$s_t = 1$	$1 - \lambda_1$	λ_1
$s_t = 2$	λ_2	$1 - \lambda_2$

The state of the world at time t is written s_t. If $s_t = 1$, we are in the first regime and the earnings shock in period t, y_t, is generated by Model 1;

similarly if $s_t = 2$, we are in the second regime and the earnings shock is generated by Model 2. The parameters λ_1 and λ_2 determine the probabilities of transition from one state to another. We focus particularly on small λ_1 and λ_2, which means that transitions from one state to another occur rarely. In particular, we assume that $\lambda_1 + \lambda_2 < 1$. We also think of λ_1 as being smaller than λ_2. Since the unconditional probability of being in state 1 is $\lambda_2/(\lambda_1 + \lambda_2)$, this implies that the investor thinks of Model 1 as being more likely than Model 2, on average. Our results do not depend, however, on λ_1 being smaller than λ_2. The effects that we document can also obtain if $\lambda_1 > \lambda_2$.

In order to value the security, the investor needs to forecast earnings into the future. Since the model he is using dictates that earnings at any time are generated by one of two regimes, the investor sees his task as trying to understand which of the two regimes is currently governing earnings. He observes earnings each period and uses that information to make as good a guess as possible about which regime he is in. In particular, at time t, having observed the earnings shock y_t, he calculates q_t, the probability that y_t was generated by Model 1, using the new data to update his estimate from the previous period, q_{t-1}. Formally, $q_t = \Pr(s_t = 1 | y_t, y_{t-1}, q_{t-1})$. We suppose that the updating follows Bayes Rule, so that

$$q_{t+1} = $$
$$\frac{((1-\lambda_1)q_t + \lambda_2(1-q_t))Pr(y_{t+1}|s_{t+1} = 1, y_t)}{((1-\lambda_1)q_t + \lambda_2(1-q_t))Pr(y_{t+1}|s_{t+1} = 1, y_t) + (\lambda_1 q_1 + (1-\lambda_2)(1-q_t))Pr(y_{t+1}|s_{t+1} = 2, y_t)}.$$

In particular, if the shock to earnings in period $t + 1$, y_{t+1}, is the same as the shock in period t, y_t, the investor updates q_{t+1} from q_t using

$$q_{t+1} = \frac{((1-\lambda_1)q_t + \lambda_2(1-q_t))\pi_L}{((1-\lambda_1)q_t + \lambda_2(1-q_t))\pi_L + (\lambda_1 q_t + (1-\lambda_2)(1-q_t))\pi_H},$$

and we show in the appendix that in this case, $q_{t+1} < q_t$. In other words, the investor puts more weight on Model 2 if he sees two consecutive shocks of the same sign. Similarly, if the shock in period $t + 1$ has the opposite sign to that in period t,

$$q_{t+1} = \frac{((1-\lambda_1)q_t + \lambda_2(1-q_t))(1-\pi_L)}{((1-\lambda_1)q_t + \lambda_2(1-q_t))(1-\pi_L) + (\lambda_1 q_t + (1-\lambda_2)(1-q_t))(1-\pi_H)},$$

and in this case, $q_{t+1} > q_t$ and the weight on Model 1 increases.

To aid intuition about how the model works, we present a simple example shown in table 12.1. Suppose that in period 0, the shock to earnings y_0 is positive and the probability assigned to Model 1 by the investor, that is, q_0, is 0.5. For a randomly generated earnings stream over the next 20 periods, the table below presents the investor's belief q_t that the time t shock to earnings is generated by Model 1. The particular parameter values chosen

TABLE 12.1

t	y_t	q_t	t	y_t	q_t
0	y	0.50			
1	$-y$	0.80	11	y	0.74
2	y	0.90	12	y	0.56
3	$-y$	0.93	13	y	0.44
4	y	0.94	14	y	0.36
5	y	0.74	15	$-y$	0.74
6	$-y$	0.89	16	y	0.89
7	$-y$	0.69	17	y	0.69
8	y	0.87	18	$-y$	0.87
9	$-y$	0.92	19	y	0.92
10	y	0.94	20	y	0.72

here are $\pi_L = \frac{1}{3} < \frac{3}{4} = \pi_H$, and $\lambda_1 = 0.1 < 0.3 = \lambda_2$. Note again that the earnings stream is generated using the true process for earnings, a random walk.

In periods 0–4, positive shocks to earnings alternate with negative shocks. Since Model 1 stipulates that earnings shocks are likely to be reversed in the following period, we observe an increase in q_t, the probability that Model 1 is generating the earnings shock at time t, rising to a high of 0.94 in period 4. From periods 10 to 14, we observe five successive positive shocks; since this is behavior typical of that specified by Model 2, q_t falls through period 14 to a low of 0.36. One feature that is evident in the above example is that q_t rises if the earnings shock in period t has the opposite sign from that in period $t-1$ and falls if the shock in period t has the same sign as that in period $t-1$.

5. MODEL SOLUTION AND EMPIRICAL IMPLICATIONS

5.1. Basic Results

We now analyze the implications of our model for prices. Since our model has a representative agent, the price of the security is simply the value of the security as perceived by the investor. In other words

$$P_t = E_t \left\{ \frac{N_{t+1}}{1+\delta} + \frac{N_{t+2}}{(1+\delta)^2} + \cdots \right\}.$$

Note that the expectations in this expression are the expectations of the investor who does not realize that the true process for earnings is a random walk. Indeed, if the investor did realize this, the series above would be simple enough to evaluate since under a random walk, $E_t(N_{t+j}) = N_t$, and price equals N_t/δ. In our model, price deviates from this correct value because the investor does not use the random walk model to forecast earnings, but rather some combination of Models 1 and 2, neither of which is a random walk. The following proposition, proved in the appendix, summarizes the behavior of prices in this context, and shows that they depend on the state variables in a particularly simple way.

Proposition 1. If the investor believes that earnings are generated by the regime-switching model described in section 4, then prices satisfy

$$P_t = \frac{N_t}{\delta} + y_t(p_1 - p_2 q_t),$$

where p_1 and p_2 are constants that depend on π_L, π_H, λ_1, and λ_2. The full expressions for p_1 and p_2 are given in the appendix.[10]

The formula for P_t has a very simple interpretation. The first term, N_t/δ, is the price that would obtain if the investor used the true random walk process to forecast earnings. The second term, $y_t(p_1 - p_2 q_t)$, gives the deviation of price from this fundamental value. Later in this section we look at the range of values of π_L, π_H, λ_1, and λ_2 that allow the price function in Proposition 1 to exhibit both underreaction and overreaction to earnings news. In fact, Proposition 2 below gives sufficient conditions on p_1 and p_2 to ensure that this is the case. For the next few paragraphs, in the run-up to Proposition 2, we forsake mathematical rigor in order to build intuition for those conditions.

First, note that if the price function P_t is to exhibit underreaction to earnings news, on average, then p_1 cannot be too large in relation to p_2. Suppose the latest earnings shock y_t is a positive one. Underreaction means that, on average, the stock price does not react sufficiently to this shock, leaving the price below fundamental value. This means that, on average, $y(p_1 - p_2 q_t)$, the deviation from fundamental value, must be negative. If q_{avg} denotes an average value of q_t, this implies that we must have $p_1 < p_2 q_{avg}$. This is the sense in which p_1 cannot be too large in relation to p_2.

On the other hand, if P_t is also to display overreaction to sequences of similar earnings news, then p_1 cannot be too small in relation to p_2. Suppose that the investor has just observed a series of good earnings shocks. Overreaction would require that price now be above fundamental value. Moreover, we know that after a series of shocks of the same sign, q_t is normally low, indicating a low weight on Model 1 and a high weight on Model 2. If we write q_{low} to represent a typical low value of q_t, overreaction then requires that $y(p_1 - p_2 q_{low})$ be positive, or that $p_1 > p_2 q_{low}$. This is the sense in which p_1 cannot be too small in relation to p_2. Putting the two conditions together, we obtain

$$p_2 q_{low} < p_1 < p_2 q_{avg}.$$

---

[10] It is difficult to prove general results about p_1 and p_2, although numerical computations show that p_1 and p_2 are both positive over most of the range of values of π_L, π_H, λ_1, and λ_2 we are interested in.

In Proposition 2, we provide sufficient conditions on p_1 and p_2 for prices to exhibit both underreaction and overreaction, and their form is very similar to what we have just obtained. In fact, the argument in Proposition 2 is essentially the one we have just made, although some effort is required to make the reasoning rigorous.

Before stating the proposition, we repeat the definitions of overreaction and underreaction that were presented in section 2. Overreaction can be thought of as meaning that the expected return following a sufficiently large number of positive shocks should be lower than the expected return following the same number of successive negative shocks. In other words, there exists some number $J \geq 1$, such that for all $j \geq J$,

$$E_t(P_{t+1} - P_t | y_t = y_{t-1} = \cdots = y_{t-j} = y)$$
$$-E_t(P_{t+1} - P_t | y_t = y_{t-1} = \cdots = y_{t-j} = -y) < 0.$$

Underreaction means that the expected return following a positive shock should exceed the expected return following a negative shock. In other words,

$$E_t(P_{t+1} - P_t | y_t = +y) - E_t(P_{t+1} - P_t | y_t = -y) > 0.$$

Proposition 2 below provides sufficient conditions on π_L, π_H, λ_1, and λ_2 for these two inequalities to hold.[11]

Proposition 2. If the underlying parameters π_L, π_H, λ_1, and λ_2 satisfy

$$\underline{k} p_2 < p_1 < \overline{k} p_2,$$

$$p_2 \geq 0,$$

then the price function in Proposition 1 exhibits both underreaction and overreaction to earnings; $\underline{k}$ and $\overline{k}$ are positive constants that depend on π_L, π_H, λ_1, and λ_2 (the full expressions are given in the Appendix).

We now examine the range of values of the fundamental parameters π_H, π_L, λ_1, and λ_2 for which the sufficient conditions for both underreaction and overreaction are satisfied. Since the conditions in Proposition 2 are somewhat involved, we evaluate them numerically for a large range of values of the four underlying parameters. Figure 12.1 illustrates one such exercise. We

---

[11] For the purposes of Proposition 2, we have made two simplifications in our mathematical formulation of under- and overreaction. First, we examine the absolute price change $P_{t+1} - P_t$ rather than the return. Second, the good news is presumed here to be the event $y_t = +y$, i.e., a positive change in earnings, rather than better-than-expected earnings. Since the expected change in earnings $E_t(y_{t+1})$ always lies between $-y$ and $+y$, a positive earnings change is in fact a positive surprise. Therefore, the results are qualitatively the same in the two cases. In the simulations in section 5.2, we calculate returns in the usual way, and condition on earnings surprises as well as raw earnings changes.

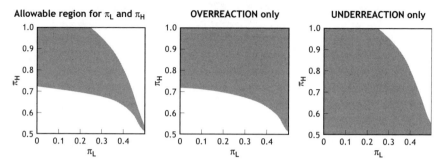

Figure 12.1. Shaded area in graph at left marks the $[\pi_L, \pi_H]$ pairs which satisfy the sufficient conditions for both underreaction and overreaction, when $\lambda_1 = 0.1$ and $\lambda_2 = 0.3$. Graph in middle (at right) shows the $[\pi_L, \pi_H]$ pairs that satisfy the condition for overreaction (underreaction) only. π_L (π_H) is the probability, in the mean-reverting (trending) regime, that next period's earnings shock will be of the same sign as last period's earnings shock. λ_1 and λ_2 govern the transition probabilities between regimes.

start by fixing $\lambda_1 = 0.1$ and $\lambda_2 = 0.3$. These numbers are small to ensure that regime switches do not occur very often and $\lambda_2 > \lambda_1$ to represent the investor's belief that the world is in the Model 1 regime more often than in the Model 2 regime.

Now that λ_1 and λ_2 have been fixed, we want to know the range of values of π_L and π_H for which the conditions for underreaction and overreaction both hold. Given the way the model is set up, π_L and π_H are restricted to the ranges $0 < \pi_L < 0.5$ and $0.5 < \pi_H < 1$. We evaluate the conditions in Proposition 2 for pairs of (π_L, π_H) where π_L ranges from zero to 0.5 at intervals of 0.01 and π_H ranges from 0.5 to one, again at intervals of 0.01.

The graph at the left of figure 12.1 marks with shading all the pairs for which the sufficient conditions hold. We see that underreaction and overreaction hold for a wide range of values. On the other hand, it is not a trivial result: There are many parameter values for which at least one of the two phenomena does not hold.

The graph shows that the sufficient conditions do not hold if both π_L and π_H are near the high end of their feasible ranges, or if both π_L and π_H are near the low end of their ranges. The reason for this is the following. Suppose both π_L and π_H are high. This means that whatever the regime, the investor believes that shocks are relatively likely to be followed by another shock of the same sign. The consequence of this is that overreaction certainly obtains, although underreaction might not. Following a positive shock, the investor on average expects another positive shock and since the true process is a random walk, returns are negative, on average. Hence the average return following a positive shock is lower than that following a negative shock, which is a characterization of overreaction rather than of underreaction.

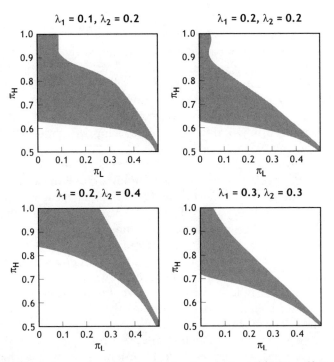

Figure 12.2. Shaded area shows the $[\pi_L, \pi_H]$ pairs which satisfy the sufficient conditions for both underreaction and overreaction for a variety of different values of λ_1 and λ_2. π_L (π_H) is the probability, in the mean-reverting (trending) regime, that next period's earnings shock will be of the same sign as last period's earnings shock. λ_1 and λ_2 govern the transition probabilities between regimes.

On the other hand, if π_L and π_H are both at the low end, the investor believes that shocks are relatively likely to be reversed, regardless of the regime: this leads to underreaction, but overreaction might not hold.

To confirm this intuition, we also show in figure 12.1 the ranges of (π_L, π_H) pairs for which only underreaction or only overreaction holds. The graph in the middle shows the parameter values for which only overreaction obtains, while the graph to its right shows the values for which only underreaction holds. The intersection of the two regions is the original one shown in the graph at left. These figures confirm the intuition that if π_L and π_H are on the high side, overreaction obtains, but underreaction might not.

Figure 12.2 presents ranges of (π_L, π_H) pairs that generate both underreaction and overreaction for a number of other values of λ_1 and λ_2. In all cases, there are nontrivial ranges of (π_L, π_H) pairs for which the sufficient conditions hold.

5.2. Some Simulation Experiments

One way of evaluating our framework is to try to replicate the empirical findings of the papers discussed in section 2 using artificial data sets of earnings and prices simulated from our model. First, we fix parameter values, setting the regime-switching parameters to $\lambda_1 = 0.1$ and $\lambda_2 = 0.3$. To guide our choice of π_L and π_H, we refer to figure 12.1. Setting $\pi_L = \frac{1}{3}$ and $\pi_H = \frac{3}{4}$ places us firmly in the region for which prices should exhibit both underreaction and overreaction.

Our aim is to simulate earnings, prices, and returns for a large number of firms over time. Accordingly, we choose an initial level of earnings N_1 and use the true random walk model to simulate 2000 independent earnings sequences, each one starting at N_1. Each sequence represents a different firm and contains six earnings realizations. We think of a period in our model as corresponding roughly to a year, so that our simulated data set covers six years. For the parameter values chosen, we can then apply the formula derived in section 5.1 to calculate prices and returns.

One feature of the random walk model we use for earnings is that it imposes a constant volatility for the earnings shock y_t, rather than making this volatility proportional to the level of earnings N_t. While this makes our model tractable enough to calculate the price function in closed form, it also allows earnings, and hence prices, to turn negative. In our simulations, we choose the absolute value of the earnings change y to be small relative to the initial earnings level N_1 so as to avoid generating negative earnings. Since this choice has the effect of reducing the volatility of returns in our simulated samples, we pay more attention to the *sign* of the numbers we present than to their absolute magnitudes.

This aspect of our model also motivates us to set the sample length at a relatively short six years. For any given initial level of earnings, the longer the sample length, the greater is the chance of earnings turning negative in the sample. We therefore choose the shortest sample that still allows us to condition on earnings and price histories of the length typical in empirical analyses.

A natural starting point is to use the simulated data to calculate returns following particular realizations of earnings. For each n-year period in the sample, where n can range from one to four, we form two portfolios. One portfolio consists of all the firms with positive earnings changes in each of the n years, and the other of all the firms with negative earnings changes in each of the n years. We calculate the difference between the returns on these two portfolios in the year after formation. We repeat this procedure for all the n-year periods in the sample and calculate the time series mean of the difference in the two portfolio returns, which we call $r_+^n - r_-^n$.

TABLE 12.2

Earnings Sort	
$r_+^1 - r_-^1$	0.0391
$r_+^2 - r_-^2$	0.0131
$r_+^3 - r_-^3$	−0.0072
$r_+^4 - r_-^4$	−0.0309

The calculation of $r_+^n - r_-^n$ for the case of $n = 1$ essentially replicates the empirical analysis in studies such as that of Bernard and Thomas (1989). This quantity should therefore be positive, matching our definition of underreaction to news. Furthermore, to match our definition of overreaction, we need the average return in periods following a long series of consecutive positive earnings shocks to be *lower* than the average return following a similarly long series of negative shocks. Therefore, we hope to see $r_+^n - r_-^n$ *decline* as n grows, or as we condition on a progressively longer string of earnings shocks of the same sign, indicating a transition from underreaction to overreaction. Table 12.2 reports the results.

The results display the pattern we expect. The average return following a positive earnings shock is greater than the average return following a negative shock, consistent with underreaction. As the number of shocks of the same sign increases, the difference in average returns turns negative, consistent with overreaction.

While the magnitudes of the numbers in the table are quite reasonable, their absolute values are smaller than those found in the empirical literature. This is a direct consequence of the low volatility of earnings changes that we impose to prevent earnings from turning negative in our simulations. Moreover, we report only point estimates and do not try to address the issue of statistical significance. Doing so would require more structure than we have imposed so far, such as assumptions about the cross-sectional covariance properties of earnings changes.

An alternative computation to the one reported in the table above would condition not on raw earnings but on the size of the surprise in the earnings announcement, measured relative to the investor's forecast. We have tried this calculation as well, and obtained very similar results.

Some of the studies discussed in section 2, such as Jegadeesh and Titman (1993), and De Bondt and Thaler (1985), calculate returns conditional not on previous earnings realizations but on previous realizations of returns. We now attempt to replicate these studies.

For each n-year period in our simulated sample, where n again ranges from one to four, we group the 2,000 firms into deciles based on their cumulative

TABLE 12.3

Returns Sort	
$r_W^1 - r_L^1$	0.0280
$r_W^2 - r_L^2$	0.0102
$r_W^3 - r_L^3$	−0.0094
$r_W^4 - r_L^4$	−0.0181

return over the n years, and compute the difference between the return of the best- and the worst-performing deciles for the year after portfolio formation. We repeat this for all the n-year periods in our sample, and compute the time series mean of the difference in the two portfolio returns, $r_W^n - r_L^n$.

We hope to find that $r_W^n - r_L^n$ decreases with n, with $r_W^1 - r_L^1$ positive just as in Jegadeesh and Titman and $r_W^4 - r_L^4$ negative as in De Bondt and Thaler. The results, shown in table 12.3, are precisely these.

Finally, we can also use our simulated data to try to replicate one more widely reported empirical finding, namely the predictive power of earnings/price (E/P) ratios for the cross-section of returns. Each year, we group the 2000 stocks into deciles based on their E/P ratio and compute the difference between the return on the highest E/P decile and the return on the lowest E/P decile in the year after formation. We repeat this for each of the years in our sample and compute the time series mean of the difference in the two portfolio returns, which we call $r_{E/P}^{hi} - r_{E/P}^{lo}$. We find this statistic to be large and positive, matching the empirical fact:

E/P sort	
$r_{E/P}^{hi} - r_{E/P}^{lo}$	0.0435

Note that this difference in average returns cannot be the result of a risk premium, since in our model the representative investor is assumed to be risk neutral.

5.3. The Event Studies Revisited

We have already discussed the direct relationship between the concept of conservatism, the specification of regime 1 in our model, and the pervasive evidence of underreaction in event studies. We believe that regime 1 is consistent with the almost universal finding across different information events that stock prices tend to drift in the same direction as the event announcement return for a period of six months to five years, with the length of the time period dependent on the type of event.

An important question is whether our full model, and not just regime 1, is consistent with all of the event study evidence. Michaely et al. (1995) find that stock prices of dividend-cutting firms decline on the announcement of the cut but then continue falling for some time afterwards. This finding is consistent with our regime 1 in that it involves underreaction to the new and useful information contained in the cut. But we also know that dividend cuts generally occur after a string of bad earnings news. Hence, if a long string of bad earnings news pushes investors towards believing in regime 2, another piece of bad news such as a dividend cut would perhaps cause an overreaction rather than an underreaction in our model.[12]

While this certainly is one interpretation of our model, an alternative way of thinking about dividend announcements is consistent with both our model and the evidence. Specifically, our model only predicts an overreaction when the new information is part of a long string of similar numbers, such as earnings or sales figures. An isolated information event such as a dividend cut, an insider sale of stock, or a primary stock issue by the firm does not constitute part of the string, even though it could superficially be classified as good news or bad news like the earnings numbers that preceded it. Investors need not simply classify all information events, whatever their nature, as either good or bad news and then claim to see a trend on this basis. Instead, they may form forecasts of earnings or sales using the time series for those variables and extrapolate past trends too far into the future. Under this interpretation, our model is consistent with an overreaction to a long string of bad earnings news and the underweighting of informative bad news of a different type which arrives shortly afterwards.

A related empirical finding is that even for extreme growth stocks that have had several consecutive years of positive earnings news, there is underreaction to quarterly earnings surprises. Our model cannot account for this evidence since it would predict overreaction in this case. To explain this evidence, our model needs to be extended. One possible way to extend the model is to allow investors to estimate the level and the growth rate of earnings separately. Indeed, in reality, investors might use annual earnings numbers over five to seven years to estimate the growth rate but higher frequency quarterly earnings announcements (perhaps combined with other information) to estimate earnings levels. Suppose, for example, that earnings have been growing rapidly over five years, so that an investor using the representativeness heuristic makes an overly optimistic forecast of the future growth rate. Suppose then that a very positive earnings number is announced. Holding the estimated long-run growth rate of earnings constant,

---

[12] Another study that presents a similar puzzle is by Ikenberry et al. (1996). They find that the positive price reaction to the announcement of a stock split is followed by a substantial drift in the same direction over the next few years. However, the split is also often preceded by a persistent run-up in the stock price, suggesting an overreaction that should ultimately be reversed.

investors might still underreact to the quarterly earnings announcement given the high weight this number has for predicting the *level* of earnings when earnings follow a random walk. That is, if such a model is contructed, it can predict underreaction to earnings news in glamour stocks. Such a model could therefore account for more of the available evidence than our simple model.

6. CONCLUSION

We have presented a parsimonious model of investor sentiment, or of how investors form expectations of future earnings. The model we propose is motivated by a variety of psychological evidence, and in particular by the idea of Griffin and Tversky (1992) that, in making forecasts, people pay too much attention to the strength of the evidence they are presented with and too little attention to its statistical weight. We have supposed that corporate announcements such as those of earnings represent information that is of low strength but significant statistical weight. This assumption has yielded the prediction that stock prices underreact to earnings announcements and similar events. We have further assumed that consistent patterns of news, such as series of good earnings announcements, represent information that is of high strength and low weight. This assumption has yielded a prediction that stock prices overreact to consistent patterns of good or bad news.

Our chapter makes reasonable, and empirically supportable, assumptions about the strength and weight of different pieces of evidence and derives empirical implications from these assumptions. However, to push this research further, it is important to develop an priori way of classifying events by their strength and weight, and to make further predictions based on such a classification. The Griffin and Tversky theory predicts most importantly that, holding the weight of information constant, news with more strength would generate a bigger reaction from investors. If news can be classified on a priori grounds, this prediction is testable.

Specifically, the theory predicts that, holding the weight of information constant, one-time strong news events should generate an overreaction. We have not discussed any evidence bearing on this prediction in this work. However, there does appear to be some evidence consistent with this prediction. For example, stock prices bounced back strongly in the few weeks after the crash of 1987. One interpretation of the crash is that investors overreacted to the news of panic selling by other investors even though there was little fundamental news about security values. Thus the crash was a high-strength, low-weight news event which, according to the theory, should have caused an overreaction. Stein (1989) relatedly finds that long-term option prices overreact to innovations in volatility, another potentially high-strength, low-weight event, since volatility tends to be highly mean-reverting. And Klibanoff et al. (1998) find that the price of a closed-end country fund reacts more strongly to news about its fundamentals when the country whose stocks the fund holds appears on the front page of the newspaper. That is, increasing the strength of the news, holding the weight constant, increases the price reaction. All these are bits of information consistent with the broader implications of the theory. A real test, however, must await a better and more objective way of estimating the strength of news announcements.

APPENDIX A

Proposition 1. If the investor believes that earnings are generated by the regime-switching model described in section 4, then prices satisfy

$$P_t = \frac{N_t}{\delta} + y_t(p_1 - p_2 q_t),$$

where p_1 and p_2 are given by the following expressions:

$$p_1 = \frac{1}{\delta}(\gamma_0'(1+\delta)[I(1+\delta) - Q]^{-1}Q\gamma_1),$$

$$p_2 = -\frac{1}{\delta}(\gamma_0'(1+\delta)[I(1+\delta) - Q]^{-1}Q\gamma_2),$$

where

$$\gamma_0' = (1,-1,1,-1),$$
$$\gamma_1' = (0,0,1,0),$$
$$\gamma_2' = (1,0,-1,0),$$

$$Q = \begin{pmatrix} (1-\lambda_1)\pi_L & (1-\lambda_1)(1-\pi_L) & \lambda_2\pi_L & \lambda_2(1-\pi_L) \\ (1-\lambda_1)(1-\pi_L) & (1-\lambda_1)\pi_L & \lambda_2(1-\pi_L) & \lambda_2\pi_L \\ \lambda_1\pi_H & \lambda_1(1-\pi_H) & (1-\lambda_2)\pi_H & (1-\lambda_2)(1-\pi_H) \\ \lambda_1(1-\pi_H) & \lambda_1\pi_H & (1-\lambda_2)(1-\pi_H) & (1-\lambda_2)\pi_H \end{pmatrix}.$$

Proof of Proposition 1: The price will simply equal the value as gauged by the uninformed investors which we can calculate from the present value formula:

$$P_t = E_t \left\{ \frac{N_{t+1}}{1+\delta} + \frac{N_{t+2}}{(1+\delta)^2} + \cdots \right\}.$$

Since

$$E_t(N_{t+1}) = N_t + E_t(y_{t+1}),$$
$$E_t(N_{t+2}) = N_t + E_t(y_{t+1}) + E_t(y_{t+2}), \text{ and so on,}$$

we have

$$P_t = \frac{1}{\delta}\left\{ N_t + E_t(y_{t+1}) + \frac{E_t(y_{t+2})}{1+\delta} + \frac{E_t(y_{t+3})}{(1+\delta)^2} + \cdots \right\}.$$

So the key is to calculate $E_t(y_{t+j})$. Define

$$q^{t+j} = (q_1^{t+j}, q_2^{t+j}, q_3^{t+j}, q_4^{t+j})',$$

where

$$q_1^{t+j} = \Pr(s_{t+j} = 1, y_{t+j} = y_t | \Phi_t),$$
$$q_2^{t+j} = \Pr(s_{t+j} = 1, y_{t+j} = -y_t | \Phi_t),$$
$$q_3^{t+j} = \Pr(s_{t+j} = 2, y_{t+j} = y_t | \Phi_t),$$
$$q_4^{t+j} = \Pr(s_{t+j} = 2, y_{t+j} = -y_t | \Phi_t),$$

where Φ_t is the investor's information set at time t consisting of the observed earnings series $(y_0, y_1, \ldots, y_t)$, which can be summarized as (y_t, q_t).

Note that

$$\Pr(y_{t+j} = y_t | \Phi_t) = q_1^{t+j} + q_3^{t+j} = \bar{\gamma}' q^{t+j}$$
$$\bar{\gamma}' = (1, 0, 1, 0).$$

The key insight is that

$$q^{t+j} = Q q^{t+j-1},$$

where Q is the transpose of the transition matrix for the states (s_{t+j}, y_{t+j}), i.e.,

$Q' =$

	(1)	(2)	(3)	(4)
(1)	$(1-\lambda_1)\pi_L$	$(1-\lambda_1)(1-\pi_L)$	$\lambda_1\pi_H$	$\lambda_1(1-\pi_H)$
(2)	$(1-\lambda_1)(1-\pi_L)$	$(1-\lambda_1)\pi_L$	$\lambda_1(1-\pi_H)$	$\lambda_1\pi_H$
(3)	$\lambda_2\pi_L$	$\lambda_2(1-\pi_L)$	$(1-\lambda_2)\pi_H$	$(1-\lambda_2)(1-\pi_H)$
(4)	$\lambda_2(1-\pi_L)$	$\lambda_2\pi_L$	$(1-\lambda_2)(1-\pi_H)$	$(1-\lambda_2)\pi_H$

where, for example,

$$\Pr(s_{t+j} = 2, y_{t+j} = y_t | s_{t+j-1} = 1, y_{t+j-1} = y_t) = \lambda_1\pi_H.$$

Therefore,

$$q^{t+j} = Q'q^t = Q'^j \begin{pmatrix} q_t \\ 0 \\ 1-q_t \\ 0 \end{pmatrix}.$$

(Note the distinction between q_t and q^t). Hence,

$$\Pr(y_{t+j} = y_t | \Phi_t) = \bar{\gamma}' Q^j q^t$$

and

$$E_t(y_{t+j} | \Phi_t) = y_t (\bar{\gamma}' Q^j q^t) + (-y_t)(\underline{\gamma}' Q^j q^t)$$

$$\gamma' = (0, 1, 0, 1).$$

Substituting this into the original formula for price gives

$$p_1 = \frac{1}{\delta} (\gamma_0'(1 + \delta)[I(1 + \delta) - Q]^{-1} Q \gamma_1),$$

$$p_2 = -\frac{1}{\delta} (\gamma_0'(1 + \delta)[I(1 + \delta) - Q]^{-1} Q \gamma_2),$$

$$\gamma_0' = (1, -1, 1, -1),$$

$$\gamma_1' = (0, 0, 1, 0),$$

$$\gamma_2' = (1, 0, -1, 0).$$

Proposition 2. Suppose the underlying parameters π_L, π_H, λ_1, and λ_2 satisfy

$$\underline{k} p_2 < p_1 < \bar{k} p_2,$$

$$p_2 \geq 0,$$

where

$$\underline{k} = \underline{q} + \tfrac{1}{2} \bar{\Delta}(\underline{q}),$$

$$\bar{k} = \bar{q}^e + \tfrac{1}{2} (c_1 + c_2 q_*),$$

$$c_1 = \frac{\bar{\Delta}(\underline{q})\bar{q} - \underline{\Delta}(\bar{q})\underline{q}}{\bar{q} - \underline{q}},$$

$$c_2 = \frac{\underline{\Delta}(\bar{q}) - \bar{\Delta}(\underline{q})}{\bar{q} - \underline{q}},$$

$$q_* = \begin{cases} \bar{q}^e & \text{if} \quad c_2 < 0, \\ \underline{q}^e & \text{if} \quad c_2 \geq 0, \end{cases}$$

where $\underline{q}^e$ and $\bar{q}^e$ are bounds on the unconditional mean of the random variable q_t. Then the conditions for both underreaction and overreaction given in section 5.1. are satisfied. (Functions and variables not yet introduced will be defined in the proof.)

Proof of Proposition 2: Before we enter the main argument of the proof, we present a short discussion of the behavior of q_t, the probability assigned by the investor at time t to being in regime 1. Suppose that the earnings shock at time $t + 1$ is of the opposite sign to the shock in period t. Let the function $\bar{\Delta}(q_t)$ denote the increase in the probability assigned to being in regime 1, that is,

$$\bar{\Delta}(q) = q_{t+1} - q_t \big|_{y_{t+1} = -y_t,\ q_t = q}$$

$$= \frac{((1 - \lambda_1)q + \lambda_2(1 - q))(1 - \pi_L)}{((1 - \lambda_1)q + \lambda_2(1 - q))(1 - \pi_L) + ((\lambda_1 q + (1 - \lambda_2)(1 - q))(1 - \pi_H)} - q.$$

Similarly, the function $\underline{\Delta}(q)$ measures the size of the fall in q_t if the period $t + 1$ earnings shock should be the same sign as that in period t, as follows:

$$\underline{\Delta}(q) = q_t - q_{t+1} \big|_{y_{t+1} = y_t,\ q_t = q}$$

$$= q - \frac{((1 - \lambda_1)q + \lambda_2(1 - q))\pi_L}{((1 - \lambda_1)q + \lambda_2(1 - q))\pi_L + ((\lambda_1 q + (1 - \lambda_2)(1 - q))\pi_H}.$$

By checking the sign of the second derivative, it is easy to see that both $\bar{\Delta}(q)$ and $\underline{\Delta}(q)$ are concave. More important, though, is the sign of these functions over the interval $[0, 1]$. Under the conditions $\pi_L < \pi_H$ and $\lambda_1 + \lambda_2 < 1$, it is not hard to show that $\bar{\Delta}(q) \geq 0$ over an interval $[0, \bar{q}]$, and that $\underline{\Delta}(q) \geq 0$ over $[\underline{q}, 1]$, where $\underline{q}$ and $\bar{q}$ satisfy $0 < \underline{q} < \bar{q} < 1$.

The implication of this is that over the range $[\underline{q}, \bar{q}]$, the following is true: if the time t earnings shock has the same sign as the time $t + 1$ earnings shock, then $q_{t+1} < q_t$, or the probability assigned to regime 2 rises. If the shocks are of different signs, however, then $q_{t+1} > q_t$, and regime 1 will be seen as more likely.

Note that if $q_t \in [\underline{q}, \bar{q}]$, then $q_\tau \in [\underline{q}, \bar{q}]$ for $\forall \tau > t$. In other words, the investor's belief will always remain within this interval. If the investor sees a very long series of earnings shocks, all of which have the same sign, q_t will fall every period, tending towards a limit of $\underline{q}$. From the updating formulas, this means that $\underline{q}$ satisfies

$$\underline{q} = \frac{((1 - \lambda_1)\underline{q} + \lambda_2(1 - \underline{q}))\pi_L}{((1 - \lambda_1)\underline{q} + \lambda_2(1 - \underline{q}))\pi_L + (\lambda_1 \underline{q} + (1 - \lambda_2)(1 - \underline{q}))\pi_H}.$$

Similarly, suppose that positive shocks alternate with negative ones for a long period of time. In this situation, q_t will rise every period, tending to the upper limit $\bar{q}$, which satisfies

$$\bar{q} = \frac{((1 - \lambda_1)\bar{q} + \lambda_2(1 - \bar{q}))(1 - \pi_L)}{((1 - \lambda_1)\bar{q} + \lambda_2(1 - \bar{q}))(1 - \pi_L) + (\lambda_1 \bar{q} + (1 - \lambda_2)(1 - \bar{q}))(1 - \pi_H)}.$$

In the case of the parameters used for the table in section 4.2., $q = 0.28$ and $\bar{q} = 0.95$.

There is no loss of generality in restricting the support of q_t to the interval $[\underline{q}, \bar{q}]$. Certainly, an investor can have prior beliefs that lie outside this interval, but with probability one, q_t will eventually belong to this interval, and will then stay within the interval forever.

We are now ready to begin the main argument of the proof. Underreaction means that the expected return following a positive shock should exceed the expected return following a negative shock. In other words,

$$E_t(P_{t+1} - P_t | y_t = +y) - E_t(P_{t+1} - P_t | y_t = -y) > 0.$$

Overreaction means that the expected return following a series of positive shocks is smaller than the expected return following a series of negative shocks. In other words, there exists some number $J \geq 1$, such that for all $j \geq J$,

$$E_t(P_{t+1} - P_t | y_t = y_{t-1} = \cdots = y_{t-j} = y)$$
$$-E_t(P_{t+1} - P_t | y_t = y_{t-1} = \cdots = y_{t-j} = -y) < 0.$$

Proposition 2 provides sufficient conditions on p_1 and p_2 so that these two inequalities hold. A useful function for the purposes of our analysis is

$$f(q) = E_t(P_{t+1} - P_t | y_t = +y, q_t = q) - E_t(P_{t+1} - P_t | y_t = -y, q_t = q).$$

The function $f(q)$ is the difference between the expected return following a positive shock and that following a negative shock, where we also condition on q_t equaling a specific value q. It is simple enough to write down an explicit expression for this function. Since

$$P_{t+1} - P_t = \frac{y_{t+1}}{\delta} + (y_{t+1} - y_t)(p_1 - p_2 q_t) - y_t p_2 (q_{t+1} - q_t)$$
$$- (y_{t+1} - y_t)p_2(q_{t+1} - q_t),$$

we find

$$E_t(P_{t+1} - P_t | y_t = +y, q_t = q) = \frac{1}{2}\left(\frac{y}{\delta} + yp_2 \underline{\Delta}(q)\right)$$
$$+ \frac{1}{2}\left(-\frac{y}{\delta} - 2y(p_1 - p_2 q) - yp_2 \bar{\Delta}(q) + 2yp_2 \bar{\Delta}(q)\right)$$
$$= y(p_2 q - p_1) + \tfrac{1}{2} yp_2 (\bar{\Delta}(q) + \underline{\Delta}(q))$$

Further, it is easily checked that

$$E_t(P_{t+1} - P_t | y_t = +y, q_t = q) = -E_t(P_{t+1} - P_t | y_t = -y, q_t = q)$$

and hence that

$$f(q) = 2y(p_2 q - p_1) + yp_2(\bar{\Delta}(q) + \underline{\Delta}(q)).$$

First, we show that a sufficient condition for overreaction is $f(\underline{q}) < 0$. If this condition holds, it implies

$$E_t(P_{t+1} - P_t | y_t = +y, q_t = \underline{q}) < E_t(P_{t+1} - P_t | y_t = -y, q_t = \underline{q}).$$

Now as $j \to \infty$,

$$E_t(P_{t+1} - P_t | y_t = y_{t-1} = \cdots = y_{t-j} = y) \to E_t(P_{t+1} - P_t | y_t = +y, q_t = \underline{q})$$

and

$$E_t(P_{t+1} - P_t | y_t = y_{t-1} = \cdots = y_{t-j} = -y)$$
$$\to E_t(P_{t+1} - P_t | y_t = -y, q_t = \underline{q}).$$

Therefore, for $\forall j \geq J$ sufficiently large, it must be true that

$$E_t(P_{t+1} - P_t | y_t = y_{t-1} = \cdots = y_{t-j} = y)$$
$$< E_t(P_{t+1} - P_t | y_t = y_{t-1} = \cdots = y_{t-j} = -y),$$

which is nothing other than our original definition of overreaction.

Rewriting the condition $f(\underline{q}) < 0$ as

$$2y(p_2\underline{q} - p_1) + yp_2(\bar{\Delta}(\underline{q}) + \underline{\Delta}(\underline{q})) < 0,$$

we obtain

$$p_1 > p_2\left(\underline{q} + \frac{\bar{\Delta}(\underline{q})}{2}\right) \tag{A.1}$$

which is one of the sufficient conditions given in the proposition.

We now turn to a sufficient condition for underreaction. The definition of underreaction can also be succinctly stated in terms of $f(q)$ as

$$E_q(f(q)) > 0,$$

where E_q denotes an expectation taken over the unconditional distribution of q. Rewriting this, we obtain:

$$2yp_2 E(q) - 2yp_1 + yp_2 E_q(\bar{\Delta}(q) + \underline{\Delta}(q)) > 0,$$

and hence,

$$p_1 < p_2\left(E(q) + \frac{E_q(\bar{\Delta}(q) + \underline{\Delta}(q))}{2}\right). \tag{A.2}$$

Unfortunately, we are not yet finished because we do not have closed form formulas for the expectations in this expression. To provide sufficient conditions, we need to bound these quantities. In the remainder of the proof, we construct a number $\bar{k}$ where

$$\bar{k} < E(q) + \frac{E_q(\overline{\Delta}(q) + \underline{\Delta}(q))}{2}.$$

This makes $p_1 < p_2\bar{k}$ a sufficient condition for (A.2). Of course, this assumes that $p_2 \geq 0$, and so we impose this as an additional constraint to be satisfied. In practice, we find that for the ranges of π_L, π_H, λ_1, and λ_2 allowed by the model, p_2 is always positive. However, we do not attempt a proof of this.

The first step in bounding the expression $E(q) + \frac{1}{2}E_q(\overline{\Delta}(q) + \underline{\Delta}(q))$ is to bound $E(q)$. To do this, note that

$$
\begin{aligned}
E(q_t) = E(q_{t+1}) &= E_{q_t}(E(q_{t+1}|q_t)) \\
&= E_{q_t}(\tfrac{1}{2}(q_t + \overline{\Delta}(q_t)) + \tfrac{1}{2}(q_t - \underline{\Delta}(q_t))) \\
&= E_q(g(q)).
\end{aligned}
$$

Consider the function $g(q)$ defined on $[\underline{q}, \bar{q}]$. The idea is to bound this function above and below over this interval by straight lines, parallel to the line passing through the endpoints of $g(q)$, namely $(\underline{q}, g(\underline{q}))$ and $(\bar{q}, g(\bar{q}))$. In other words, suppose that we bound $g(q)$ above by $\bar{g}(q) = a + bq$. The slope of this line is

$$b = \frac{g(\bar{q}) - g(\underline{q})}{\bar{q} - \underline{q}} = \frac{(\bar{q} - \underline{q}) - \frac{1}{2}(\underline{\Delta}(\bar{q}) + \overline{\Delta}(\underline{q}))}{\bar{q} - \underline{q}} < 1,$$

and a will be such that

$$\inf_{q \in [\underline{q}, \bar{q}]}(a + bq - g(q)) = 0.$$

Given that

$$E_q(g(q) - q) = 0,$$

we must have

$$E_q(\bar{g}(q) - q) \geq 0$$

or

$$E(a + bq - q) \geq 0$$

$$E(q) \leq \frac{a}{1 - b},$$

since $b < 1$. This gives us an upper bound on $E(q)$, which we will call $\overline{q}^e$. A similar argument produces a lower bound $\underline{q}_e$.

The final step before completing the argument is to note that since $\overline{\Delta}(q)$ and $\underline{\Delta}(q)$ are both concave, $\overline{\Delta}(q) + \underline{\Delta}(q)$ is also concave, so that

$$(\overline{\Delta} + \underline{\Delta})(q) > \left(\frac{q - \underline{q}}{\overline{q} - \underline{q}}\right)\underline{\Delta}(\overline{q}) + \left(\frac{\overline{q} - q}{\overline{q} - \underline{q}}\right)\overline{\Delta}(\underline{q}),$$

$$= c_1 + c_2 q$$

where

$$c_1 = \frac{\underline{\Delta}(q)\overline{q} - \underline{\Delta}(\overline{q})\underline{q}}{\overline{q} - \underline{q}},$$

$$c_2 = \frac{\underline{\Delta}(\overline{q}) - \overline{\Delta}(\underline{q})}{\overline{q} - \underline{q}}.$$

Therefore,

$$E(q) + \tfrac{1}{2}E(\overline{\Delta}(q) + \underline{\Delta}(q)) \geq \underline{q}^e + \tfrac{1}{2}E(c_1 + c_2 q) \geq \underline{q}^e + \tfrac{1}{2}(c_1 + c_2 q_*),$$

where

$$q_* = \begin{cases} \overline{q}^e & \text{if} \quad c_2 < 0, \\ \underline{q}^e & \text{if} \quad c_2 \geq 0. \end{cases}$$

This completes the proof of the proposition.

References

Andreassen, P., S. Kraus, 1990. Judgmental extrapolation and the salience of change, *Journal of Forecasting* 9, 347–72.

Barsky, R., J.B. De Long, 1993. Why does the stock market fluctuate?, *Quarterly Journal of Economics* 108, 291–311.

Bernard, V., 1992. Stock price reactions to earnings announcements, In Thaler, R. (ed.), *Advances in Behavioral Finance*, Russell Sage Foundation, 303–40.

Bernard, V., J. Thomas, 1989. Post-earnings announcement drift: delayed price response or risk premium? Journal of Accounting Research, (Suppl.) 27, 1–36.

———, 1990, Evidence that stock prices do not fully reflect the implications of current earnings for future earnings, *Journal of Accounting and Economics* 13, 305–41.

Campbell, J. Y., R. Shiller, 1988, Stock prices, earnings, and expected dividends, *Journal of Finance* 43, 661–76.

Chan, L., N. Jegadeesh, J. Lakonishok, 1997, Momentum strategies. *Journal of Finance* 51, 1681–1713.

Chopra, N., J. Lakonishok, J. Ritter, 1992, Measuring abnormal performance: do stocks overreact? *Journal of Financial Economics* 31, 235–68.

Cutler, D., J. Poterba, L. Summers, 1991, Speculative dynamics, *Review of Economic Studies* 58, 529–46.

Daniel, K., D. Hirshleifer, A. Subrahmanyam, 1998, A theory of overconfidence, self-attribution, and security market under- and over-reactions, *Journal of Finance* 53.

De Bondt, W., 1993, Betting on trends: intuitive forecasts of financial risk and return, *International Journal of Forecasting* 9, 355–71.

De Bondt, W., R. Thaler, 1985, Does the stock market overreact?, *Journal of Finance* 40, 793–808.

———, 1987, Further evidence of investor overreaction and stock market seasonality, *Journal of Finance* 42, 557–81.

De Long, J. B., A. Shleifer, L. Summers, R. Waldmann, 1990a, Noise trader risk in financial markets. *Journal of Political Economy* 98, 703–38.

———, 1990b, Positive feedback investment strategies and destabilizing rational speculation, *Journal of Finance* 45, 375–95.

Dreman, D., M. Berry, 1995, Overreaction, underreaction, and the low-P/E effect, *Financial Analysts Journal* 51, 21–30.

Edwards, W., 1968, Conservatism in human information processing, in B. Kleinmutz, (ed.), *Formal Representation of Human Judgment*. Wiley, 17–52.

Fama, E., 1998. Market efficiency, long-term returns, and behavioral finance. *Journal of Financial Economics* 49, 283–306.

Fama, E., K. French, 1988. Permanent and temporary components of stock prices. *Journal of Political Economy* 96, 246–73.

———, 1992, The cross-section of expected stock returns, *Journal of Finance* 47, 427–65.

———, 1996, Multifactor explanations of asset pricing anomalies, *Journal of Finance* 51, 55–84.

———, 1998, Value versus growth: the international evidence, *Journal of Finance* 53.

Griffin, D., A. Tversky, 1992, The weighing of evidence and the determinants of confidence. *Cognitive Psychology* 24, 411–35.

Haugen, R., N. Baker, 1996, Commonality in the determinants of expected stock returns. *Journal of Financial Economics* 41, 401–39.

Ikenberry, D., J. Lakonishok, T. Vermaelen, 1995, Market underreaction to open market share repurchases. *Journal of Financial Economics* 39, 181–208.

Ikenberry, D., G. Rankine, E. Stice, 1996, What do stock splits really signal? *Journal of Financial and Quantitative Analysis* 31, 357–75.

Jegadeesh, N., S. Titman, 1993, Returns to buying winners and selling losers: implications for stock market efficiency. *Journal of Finance* 48, 65–91.

Klibanoff, P., O. Lamont, T. Wizman, 1998, Investor reaction to salient news in closed-end country funds. *Journal of Finance* 53, 673–700.

Lakonishok, J., A. Shleifer, R. Vishny, 1994, Contrarian investment, extrapolation, and risk. *Journal of Finance* 49, 1541–78.

La Porta, R., 1996, Expectations and the cross-section of returns, *Journal of Finance* 51, 1715–42.

La Porta, R., J. Lakonishok, A. Shleifer, R. Vishny, 1997, Good news for value stocks: further evidence on market efficiency, *Journal of Finance* 52, 859–74.

Lee, C., A. Shleifer, R. Thaler, 1991, Investor sentiment and the closed-end fund puzzle, *Journal of Finance* 46, 75–110.

Lehmann, B., 1990, Fads, martingales, and market efficiency. *Quarterly Journal of Economics* 105, 1–28.

Loughran, T., J. Ritter, 1995, The new issues puzzle, *Journal of Finance* 50, 23–51.

Michaely, R., R. Thaler, K. Womack, 1995, Price reactions to dividend initiations and omissions: overreaction or drift?, *Journal of Finance* 50, 573–608.

Poterba, J., L. Summers, 1988, Mean-reversion in stock prices: evidence and implications, *Journal of Financial Economics* 22, 27–59.

Rouwenhorst, G., 1997, International momentum strategies. *Journal of Finance* 53, 267–84.

Samuelson, P., 1965, Proof that properly anticipated prices fluctuate randomly, *Industrial Management Review* 6, 41–49.

Shiller, R., 1981, Do stock prices move too much to be justified by subsequent changes in dividends?, *American Economic Review* 71, 421–36.

Shleifer, A., R. Vishny, 1997, The limits of arbitrage. *Journal of Finance* 52, 35–55.

Spiess, K., J. Affleck-Graves, 1995, Underperformance in long-run stock returns following seasoned equity offerings, *Journal of Financial Economics* 38, 243–67.

Stein, J., 1989, Overreactions in the options market, *Journal of Finance* 44, 1011–23.

Tversky, A., D. Kahneman, 1974, Judgment under uncertainty: heuristics and biases, *Science* 185, 1124–1131.

Zarowin, P., 1989. Does the stock market overreact to corporate earnings information? *Journal of Finance* 44, 1385–1400.

Chapter 13

INVESTOR PSYCHOLOGY AND SECURITY MARKET
UNDER- AND OVERREACTION

KENT DANIEL, DAVID HIRSHLEIFER,
AND AVANIDHAR SUBRAHMANYAM

IN RECENT YEARS a body of evidence on security returns has presented a sharp challenge to the traditional view that securities are rationally priced to reflect all publicly available information. Some of the more pervasive anomalies can be classified as follows (see Hirshleifer 2001 for a summary of the relevant literature):

1. Event-based return predictability (public-event-date average stock returns of the same sign as average subsequent long-run abnormal performance)
2. Short-term momentum (positive short-term autocorrelation of stock returns, for individual stocks and the market as a whole)
3. Long-term reversal (negative autocorrelation of short-term returns separated by long lags, or "overreaction")
4. High volatility of asset prices relative to fundamentals
5. Short-run post-earnings announcement stock price "drift" in the direction indicated by the earnings surprise, but possible abnormal stock price performance in the opposite direction of long-term earnings changes.

There remains disagreement over the interpretation of the above evidence of predictability. One possibility is that these anomalies are chance

We thank two anonymous referees (*Journal of Finance*, volume LIII, Number 2, December 1918–83), the editor (René Stulz), Michael Brennan, Steve Buser, Werner DeBondt, Eugene Fama, Simon Gervais, Robert Jones, Blake LeBaron, Tim Opler, Canice Prendergast, Andrei Shleifer, Matt Spiegel, Siew Hong Teoh, and Sheridan Titman for helpful comments and discussions, Robert Noah for excellent research assistance, and participants in the National Bureau of Economic Research 1996 Asset Pricing and 1997 Behavioral Finance Meetings, the 1997 Western Finance Association Meetings, the 1997 University of Chicago Economics of Uncertainty Workshop, and finance workshops at the Securities and Exchange Commission and the following universities: University of California at Berkeley, University of California at Los Angeles, Columbia University, University of Florida, University of Houston, University of Michigan, London Business School, London School of Economics, Northwestern University, Ohio State University, Stanford University, and Washington University at St. Louis, for helpful comments. Hirshleifer thanks the Nippon Telephone and Telegraph Program of Asian Finance and Economics for financial support.

deviations to be expected under market efficiency (Fama 1998). We believe the evidence does not accord with this viewpoint because some of the return patterns are strong and regular. The size, book-to-market, and momentum effects are present both internationally and in different time periods. Also, the pattern mentioned in (1) above obtains for the great majority of event studies.

Alternatively, these patterns could represent variations in rational risk-premia. However, based on the high Sharpe ratios (relative to the market) apparently achievable with simple trading strategies (MacKinlay 1995), any asset pricing model consistent with these patterns would have to have extremely variable marginal utility across states. Campbell and Cochrane (1999) find that a utility function with extreme habit persistence is required to explain the predictable variation in market returns. To be consistent with cross-sectional predictability findings (on size, B/M, and momentum, for example), a model would presumably require even more extreme variation in marginal utilities. Also, the model would require that marginal utilities covary strongly with the returns on the size, B/M, and momentum portfolios. No such correlation is obvious in examining the data. Given this evidence, it seems reasonable to consider explanations for the observed return patterns based on imperfect rationality.

Moreover, there are important corporate financing and payout patterns which seem potentially related to market anomalies. Firms tend to issue equity (rather than debt) after rises in market value, and when the firm or industry B/M ratio is low. There are industry-specific financing and repurchase booms, perhaps designed to exploit industry-level mispricings. Transactions such as takeovers that often rely on securities financing are also prone to industry booms and quiet periods.

Although it is not obvious how the empirical securities market phenomena can be captured plausibly in a model based on perfect investor rationality, no psychological ("behavioral") theory for these phenomena has won general acceptance. Some aspects of the patterns seem contradictory, such as apparent market underreaction in some contexts and overreaction in others. While explanations have been offered for particular anomalies, we have lacked an integrated theory to explain these phenomena, and out-of-sample empirical implications to test proposed explanations.

A general criticism often raised by economists against psychological theories is that, in a given economic setting, the universe of conceivable irrational behavior patterns is essentially unrestricted. Thus, it is sometimes claimed that allowing for irrationality opens a Pandora's box of *ad hoc* stories that will have little out-of-sample predictive power. However, DeBondt and Thaler (1995) argue that a good psychological finance theory will be grounded on psychological evidence about how people actually behave. We concur, and also believe that such a theory should allow for the rational side of investor decisions. To deserve consideration a theory should be parsimonious, explain a *range* of anomalous patterns in different contexts, and generate new empirical implications. The goal of this work is to develop such a theory of security markets.

Our theory is based on investor *overconfidence*, and variations in confidence arising from *biased self-attribution*. The premise of investor overconfidence is derived from a large body of evidence from cognitive psychological experiments and surveys (summarized in section 1) which shows that individuals overestimate their own abilities in various contexts.

In financial markets, analysts and investors generate information for trading through means, such as interviewing management, verifying rumors, and analyzing financial statements, which can be executed with varying degrees of skill. If an investor overestimates his ability to generate information, or to identify the significance of existing data that others neglect, he will underestimate his forecast errors. If investors are more overconfident about signals or assessments with which they have greater personal involvement, they will tend to be overconfident about the information that they themselves have generated but not about public signals. Thus, we define an *overconfident* investor as one who overestimates the precision of his private information signal, but not of information signals publicly received by all.

We find that the overconfident informed overweigh the private signal relative to the prior, and their trading pushes the price too far in the direction of the signal. When noisy public information signals arrive, the inefficient deviation of the price is partially corrected, on average. On subsequent dates, as more public information arrives, the price, on average, moves still closer to the full-information value. Thus, a central theme of this work is that stock prices overreact to private information signals and underreact to public signals. We show that this overreaction-correction pattern is consistent with long-run negative autocorrelation in stock returns, unconditional excess volatility (unconditional volatility in excess of that which would obtain with fully rational investors), and with further implications for volatility conditional on the type of signal.

The market's tendency to over- or underreact to different types of information allows us to address the remarkable pattern that the average announcement date returns in virtually all event studies are of the same sign as the average postevent abnormal returns. Suppose that the market observes a public action taken by an informed party such as the firm at least partly in response to market mispricing. For example, a rationally managed firm may tend to buy back more of its stock when managers believe their stock is undervalued by the market. In such cases, the corporate event will reflect the manager's belief about the market valuation error, and will therefore predict future abnormal returns. In particular, repurchases, reflecting undervaluation, will predict positive abnormal returns, while equity offerings will predict the opposite. More generally, actions taken by any informed party (such as a manager or analyst) in a fashion responsive to mispricing will predict future returns. Consistent with this implication, many events studied in the empirical literature can reasonably be viewed as being responsive to mispricing, and have the abnormal return pattern discussed above. Subsection 2.B.4 offers several additional implications about the occurrence of and price patterns around corporate events and for corporate policy that are either untested or have been confirmed only on a few specific events.

The empirical psychology literature reports not just overconfidence, but that as individuals observe the outcomes of their actions, they update their confidence in their own ability in a biased manner. According to *attribution theory* (Bem 1965), individuals too strongly attribute events that confirm the validity of their actions to high ability, and events that disconfirm the action to external noise or sabotage. (This relates to the notion of cognitive dissonance, in which individuals internally suppress information that conflicts with past choices.)

If an investor trades based on a private signal, we say that a later public signal *confirms* the trade if it has the same sign (good news arrives after a buy, or bad news after a sell). We assume that when an investor receives confirming public information, his confidence rises, but disconfirming information causes confidence to fall only modestly, if at all. Thus, if an individual begins with unbiased beliefs, new public signals *on average* are viewed as confirming the private signal. This suggests that public information can trigger further overreaction to a preceding private signal. We show that such continuing overreaction causes momentum in security prices, but that such momentum is eventually reversed as further public information gradually draws the price back toward fundamentals. Thus, biased self-attribution implies short-run momentum and long-term reversals.

The dynamic analysis based on biased self-attribution can also lead to a lag-dependent response to corporate events. Cash flow or earnings surprises at first tend to reinforce confidence, causing a same-direction average stock price trend. Later reversal of overreaction can lead to an opposing stock price trend. Thus, the analysis is consistent with both short-term postannouncement stock price trends in the same same direction as earnings surprises and later reversals.

In our model, investors are quasi-rational in that they are Bayesian optimizers except for their overassessment of *valid* private information, and their biased updating of this precision. A frequent objection to models that explain price anomalies as market inefficiencies is that fully rational investors should be able to profit by trading against the mispricing. If wealth flows from quasi-rational to smart traders, eventually the smart traders may dominate price-setting. However, for several reasons, we do not find this argument to be compelling, as discussed in the conclusion.

Several other papers have modeled overconfidence in various contexts. Hirshleifer, Subrahmanyam, and Titman (1994) examined how analyst/traders who overestimate the probability that they receive information before others will tend to herd in selecting stocks to study. Kyle and Wang

(1997), Odean (1998), and Wang (1998) provide specifications of overconfidence as overestimation of information precision, but do not distinguish between private and public signals in this regard (see also Caballé and Sákovics 1996). Odean (1998) examines overconfidence about, and consequent overreaction to, a private signal. As a consequence there is excess volatility and negative return autocorrelation. Because our model assumes that investors are overconfident only about private signals, we obtain underreaction as well as overreaction effects. Furthermore, because we consider time-varying confidence, there is continuing overreaction to private signals over time. Thus, in contrast with Odean, we find forces toward positive as well as negative autocorrelation; and we argue that overconfidence can decrease volatility around public news events.[1]

Daniel, Hirshleifer, and Subrahmanyam (1998) show that our specification of overconfidence can help explain several empirical puzzles regarding cross-sectional patterns of security return predictability and investor behavior. These puzzles include the ability of price-based measures (dividend yield, earnings/price, B/M, and firm market value) to predict future stock returns, possible domination of β as a predictor of returns by price-based variables, and differences in the relative ability of different price-based measures to predict returns.

A few other recent studies have addressed both overreaction and underreaction in an integrated fashion. Shefrin (1997) discusses how base-rate underweighting can shed light on the anomalous behavior of implied volatilities in options markets. In a contemporaneous paper, Barberis, Shleifer, and Vishny (1998) offer an explanation for under- and overreactions based on a learning model in which actual earnings follow a random walk, but individuals believe that earnings follow either a steady growth trend, or else are mean-reverting. Since their focus is on learning about the time-series process of a performance measure such as earnings, they do not address the sporadic events examined in most event studies. In another recent paper, Hong and Stein (1999) examine a setting where under- and overreactions arise from the interaction of momentum traders and news watchers. Momentum traders make partial use of the information contained in recent price trends, and ignore fundamental news. Fundamental traders rationally use fundamental news but ignore prices. Our work differs in focusing on psychological evidence as a basis for assumptions about investor behavior.

The remainder of the chapter is structured as follows. Section 1 describes psychological evidence of overconfidence and self-attribution bias. Section 2 develops the basic model of overconfidence. Here, we describe the economic setting and define overconfidence. We analyze the equilibrium to derive implications about stock price reactions to public versus private news,

---

[1] A recent revision of Odean's paper offers a modified model that allows for underreaction. This is developed in a static setting with no public signals, and therefore does not address issues such as short-term versus long-term return autocorrelations, and event study anomalies.

short- versus long-term autocorrelations, and volatility. Section 3 examines time variation in overconfidence, to derive implications about the signs of short-term versus long-term return autocorrelations. Section 4 concludes by summarizing our findings, relating our analysis to the literature on exogenous noise trading, and discussing issues related to the survival of overconfident traders in financial markets.

1. Overconfidence and Biased Self-Attribution

The model we present in this chapter relies on two psychological regularities: *overconfidence* and *attribution bias*. In their summary of the microfoundations of behavioral finance, DeBondt and Thaler (1995) state that "perhaps the most robust finding in the psychology of judgment is that people are overconfident." Evidence of overconfidence has been found in several contexts. Examples include psychologists, physicians and nurses, engineers, attorneys, negotiators, entrepreneurs, managers, investment bankers, and market professionals such as security analysts and economic forecasters.[2] Further, some evidence suggests that experts tend to be more overconfident than relatively inexperienced individuals (Griffin and Tversky 1992). Psychological evidence also indicates that overconfidence is more severe for diffuse tasks (e.g., making diagnoses of illnesses) that require judgment than for mechanical tasks (e.g., solving arithmetic problems); and tasks for which delayed feedback is received, as opposed to tasks that provide immediate and conclusive outcome feedback, such as weather forecasting or horse-racing handicapping (see Einhorn 1980). Fundamental valuation of securities (forecasting *long-term* cash flows) requires judgement about open-ended issues, and feedback is noisy and deferred. We therefore focus on the implications of overconfidence for financial markets.[3]

Our theory assumes that investors view themselves as more able to value securities than they actually are, so that they underestimate their forecast error variance. This is consistent with evidence that people overestimate their own abilities, and perceive themselves more favorably than they are viewed by others.[4] Several experimental studies find that individuals underestimate

---

[2] See respectively: Oskamp (1965), Christensen-Szalanski and Bushyhead (1981), Baumann, Deber, and Thompson (1991), Kidd (1970), Wagenaar and Keren (1986), Neale and Bazerman (1990), Cooper, Woo, and Dunkelberg (1988), Russo and Schoemaker (1992), Stael von Holstein (1972), Ahlers and Lakonishok (1983), Elton, Gruber, and Gultekin (1984), Froot and Frankel (1989), DeBondt and Thaler (1990), DeBondt (1991). See Odean (1998) for a good summary of empirical research on overconfidence.

[3] Odean (1998) (section 2.D) also makes a good argument for why overconfidence should dominate in financial markets.

[4] Greenwald (1980), Svenson (1981), Cooper, Woo, and Dunkelberg (1988), and Taylor and Brown (1988).

their error variance in making predictions, and overweigh their own forecasts relative to those of others.[5]

The second aspect of our theory is biased self-attribution: the confidence of the investor in our model grows when public information is in agreement with his information, but it does not fall commensurately when public information contradicts his private information. The psychological evidence indicates that people tend to credit themselves for past success, and blame external factors for failure (Fischoff 1982, Langer and Roth 1975, Miller and Ross 1975, Taylor and Brown 1988). As Langer and Roth (1975) put it, "Heads I win, tails it's chance"; see also the discussion of DeLong, Shleifer, Summers, and Waldmann (1991).

2. The Basic Model: Constant Confidence

This section develops the model with static confidence. Section 3 considers time-varying confidence. Each member of a continuous mass of agents is overconfident in the sense that if he receives a signal, he overestimates its precision. We refer to those who receive the signal as the informed, I; and those who do not as the uninformed, U. For tractability, we assume that the informed are risk neutral, whereas the uninformed are risk averse.

Each individual is endowed with a basket containing security shares, and a risk-free numeraire that is a claim to one unit of terminal-period wealth. There are 4 dates. At date 0, individuals begin with their endowments and identical prior beliefs, and trade solely for optimal risk-transfer purposes. At date 1, Is receive a common noisy private signal about underlying security value and trade with Us.[6] At date 2, a noisy public signal arrives, and further trade occurs. At date 3, conclusive public information arrives, the security pays a liquidating dividend, and consumption occurs. All random variables are independent and normally distributed.

The risky security generates a terminal value of θ, which is assumed to be normally distributed with mean $\bar{\theta}$ and variance σ_θ^2. For most of the work we set $\bar{\theta} = 0$ without loss of generality. The private information signal received by Is at date 1 is

$$s_1 = \theta + \epsilon, \tag{1}$$

[5] See Alpert and Raiffa (1982), Fischhoff, Slovic, and Lichtenstein (1977), Batchelor and Dua (1992), and the discussions of Lichtenstein, Fischoff, and Phillips (1982), and Yates (1990).

[6] Some previous models with common private signals include Grossman and Stiglitz (1980), Admati and Pfleiderer (1988), and Hirshleifer, Subrahmanyam, and Titman (1994). If some analysts and investors use the same information sources to assess security values, and interpret them in similar ways, the error terms in their signals will be correlated. For simplicity, we assume this correlation is unity; however, similar results would obtain under imperfect (but nonzero) correlation in signal noise terms.

where $\epsilon \sim N(0, \sigma_\epsilon^2)$ (so the signal precision is $1/\sigma_\epsilon^2$). The Us correctly assess the error variance, but Is underestimate it to be $\sigma_C^2 < \sigma_\epsilon^2$. The differing beliefs about the noise variance are common knowledge to all.[7] Similarly, the date 2 public signal is

$$s_2 = \theta + \eta, \tag{2}$$

where the noise term $\eta \sim N(0, \sigma_p^2)$ is independent of θ and ϵ. Its variance σ_p^2 is correctly estimated by all investors.

Our simplifying assumption that all private information precedes all public information is not needed for the model's implications. It is essential that at least some noisy public information arrives after a private signal. The model's implications stand if, more realistically, additional public information precedes or is contemporaneous with the private signal.

Since prices are set by the risk-neutral informed traders, the formal role of the uninformed in this work is minimal. The rationale for the assumption of overconfidence is that the investor has a personal attachment to his own signal. This implies some other set of investors who do not receive the same signal. Also, similar results will hold if both groups of investors are risk averse, so that both groups influence price. We have verified this analytically in a simplified version of the model. So long as the uninformed are not risk-neutral price setters, the overconfident informed will push price away from fully rational values in the direction described here.

A. Equilibrium Prices and Trades

Since the informed traders are risk neutral, prices at each date satisfy

$$P_1 = E_C[\theta | \theta + \epsilon] \tag{3}$$

$$P_2 = E_C[\theta | \theta + \epsilon, \theta + \eta], \tag{4}$$

where the subscript C denotes the fact that the expectation operator is calculated based on the informed traders' confident beliefs. Trivially, $P_3 = \theta$. By standard properties of normal variables (Anderson 1984, chapter 2)

$$P_1 = \frac{\sigma_\theta^2}{\sigma_\theta^2 + \sigma_C^2}(\theta + \epsilon) \tag{5}$$

$$P_2 = \frac{\sigma_\theta^2(\sigma_C^2 + \sigma_p^2)}{D}\theta + \frac{\sigma_\theta^2\sigma_p^2}{D}\epsilon + \frac{\sigma_\theta^2\sigma_C^2}{D}\eta, \tag{6}$$

where $D \equiv \sigma_\theta^2(\sigma_C^2 + \sigma_p^2) + \sigma_C^2\sigma_p^2$.

---

[7] It is not crucial for the analysis that the Us correctly assess the private signal variance, only that they do not underestimate it as much as the informed do. Also, since the uninformed do not possess a signal to be overconfident about, they could alternatively be interpreted as

B. Implications for Price Behavior

This section examines the implications of static confidence for over- and underreactions to information and empirical securities returns patterns. Subsection B.1 examines price reactions to public and private information, subsection B.2 examines the implications for price-change autocorrelations, and subsection B.3 examines implications for event-studies. Subsection B.4 discusses some as-yet-untested empirical implications of the model.

B.1 OVERREACTION AND UNDERREACTION

Figure 13.1 illustrates the average price path following a positive (upper curve) or negative (lower curve) date 1 private signal (date 3' of the graph has not yet been introduced). At this point we focus on the solid lines. The upper curve, an impulse-response function, shows the expected prices conditional on a private signal of unit magnitude arriving at time 1. The thin horizontal line shows the fully rational price level.

Overconfidence in the private signal $\theta + \epsilon$ causes the date 1 stock price to *overreact* to this new information. At date 2, when noisy public information signals arrive, the inefficient deviation of the price is partially corrected, on average. The same is true on subsequent public information arrival dates. We call the part of the impulse response prior to the peak or trough the *overreaction phase*, and the later section the *correction phase*.

This overreaction and correction implies that the covariance between the date 1 price change and the date 2 price change, $\text{cov}(P_2 - P_1, P_1 - P_0)$, is negative.[8] Further, the overreaction to the private signal is partially corrected by the date 2 public signal, and fully corrected upon release of the date 3 public signal, so that $\text{cov}(P_3 - P_1, P_1 - P_0) < 0$. This price change reversal arises from the continuing correction to the date 1 overreaction. Finally, the continuing correction starting at date 2 and ending at date 3 causes price changes at the time of and subsequent to the public signal to be positively correlated, so that $\text{cov}(P_3 - P_2, P_2 - P_1) > 0$. We thus have:

Proposition 1. If investors are overconfident, then:

1. Price moves resulting from private information arrival are on average partially reversed in the long run.
2. Price moves in reaction to the arrival of public information are positively correlated with later price changes.

---

fully rational traders who trade to exploit market mispricing. Furthermore, most of the results will obtain even if investors are symmetrical both in their overconfidence and their signals. Results similar to those we derive would apply in a setting where identical overconfident individuals receive correlated private signals.

[8] See appendix A.

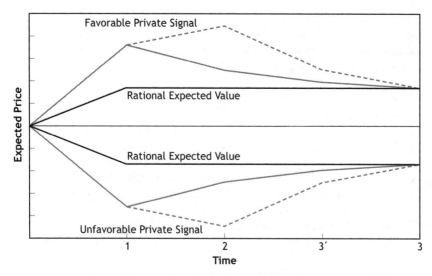

Figure 13.1. Average price as a function of time with overconfident investors. This figure shows price as a function of time for the dynamic model of section 3 with (solid line) and without (dashed line) self-attribution bias.

The pattern of correlations described in Proposition 1 is potentially testable by examining whether long-run reversals following days with public news events are smaller than reversals on days without such events. The price behavior around public announcements has implications for corporate event studies (see subsection B.3).

B.2 UNCONDITIONAL SERIAL CORRELATIONS AND VOLATILITY

Return autocorrelations in well-known studies of momentum and reversal are calculated without conditioning on the arrival of a public information signal. To calculate a return autocorrelation that does not condition on whether private versus public information has arrived, consider an experiment where the econometrician picks consecutive dates for price changes randomly (dates 1 and 2, versus dates 2 and 3). The date 2 and 3 price changes are positively correlated, but the date 1 and 2 price changes are negatively correlated. Suppose that the econometrician is equally likely to pick either pair of consecutive dates. Then the overall autocorrelation is *negative*:

Proposition 2. If investors are overconfident, price changes are unconditionally negatively autocorrelated at both short and long lags.

Thus, the constant-confidence model accords with long-run reversals (negative long-lag autocorrelations) but not with short-term momentum (positive short-lag autocorrelation). However, the short-lag autocorrelation will be positive in a setting where the extremum in the impulse response function is sufficiently smooth, because the negative autocovariance of price changes surrounding a smooth extremum will be low in absolute terms. Such a setting, based on biased self-attribution and outcome-dependent confidence, is considered in section 3.

Since overconfidence causes wider swings at date 1 away from fundamentals, it causes excess price volatility around private signals ($\text{var}(P_1 - P_0)$) as in Odean (1998). Greater overconfidence also causes relative underweighing of the public signal, which tends to reduce date 2 variance. However, the wide date 1 swings create a greater need for corrective price moves at dates 2 and 3, so that greater overconfidence can either decrease or increase the volatility around public signals ($\text{var}(P_2 - P_1)$). (Explicit expressions for the variances of this section are contained in appendix A.)

Consider again an econometrician who does not condition on the occurrence of private or public news arrival. He will calculate price change variances by placing equal weights on price changes $P_1 - P_0$, $P_2 - P_1$, and $P_3 - P_2$. The unconditional volatility is therefore just the arithmetic mean of var $(P_3 - P_2)$, $\text{var}(P_2 - P_1)$, and $\text{var}(P_1 - P_0)$. Excess volatility is the difference between the volatility with overconfidence and the volatility when $\sigma_C^2 = \sigma_\epsilon^2$.

Let the subscript R denote the volatility if all individuals were rational. We define the date t proportional excess volatility as

$$V_t^E \equiv \frac{\text{var}(P_t - P_{t-1}) - \text{var}_R(P_t - P_{t-1})}{\text{var}_R(P_t - P_{t-1})}. \tag{7}$$

Proposition 3

1. Overconfidence increases volatility around private signals, can increase or decrease volatility around public signals, and increases unconditional volatility.
2. The proportional excess volatility is greater around the private signal than around the public signal.

Thus, consistent with the findings of Odean (1998), when there are only private signals, there is a general tendency for overconfidence to create excess volatility. Excess volatility is not an automatic implication of any model with imperfect rationality. For example, if investors are *underconfident*, $\sigma_C^2 > \sigma_\epsilon^2$, then there will be *insufficient* volatility relative to the rational level. Also, in contrast with Odean, Proposition 3 implies that in samples broken down by types of news event, either excess or deficient volatility may be possible.

B.3 EVENT STUDY IMPLICATIONS

Many recent studies have investigated abnormal average return performance or "drift" following public news arrival. As mentioned in the introduction, a striking regularity in virtually all these studies is that average postevent abnormal price trends are of the same sign as the average initial event-date reaction. We now slightly generalize the model to address this event-based return predictability.

Sophisticated managers or analysts who are not overconfident are likely to undertake certain visible actions, such as repurchasing shares or making buy recommendations, selectively when a firm's shares are undervalued by the market. We will show that the nature of the stock price reaction to an event depends critically on whether or not the event is related to the date 2 mispricing by the market.

We assume that the date 2 signal is no longer public, but is instead received *privately* by the firm's manager (or other individual such as an analyst), and that this individual takes an action (the "event") that is publicly observed and fully reveals the signal. Let $P_2^C(s_2)$ be the valuation that would be placed on the security by an overconfident investor at date 2 were he to observe the signal s_2 in addition to his signal s_1. (Since we examine events that fully reveal s_2, this is in equilibrium just the postevent stock price P_2.) Let $P_2^R(s_2)$ be the comparable valuation that would be set by a fully rational investor. The date 2 *mispricing* then is defined as the difference $P_2^R(s_2) - P_2^C(s_2)$ We define different kinds of events as follows.

> **Definition 1.** An event is a random variable that depends only on the information signals s_1 and s_2. A **nonselective event** is an event that is independent of the date 2 mispricing $P_2^R(s_2) - P_2^C(s_2)$. A **selective event** is an event whose occurrence and/or magnitude depends on the date 2 mispricing.

A simple type of non-selective event is a random variable that is linearly related only to the second signal s_2.

> **Proposition 4.** If overconfident investors observe a nonselective event:
>
> 1. The true expected postannouncement abnormal price change is zero.
> 2. Conditional on the preevent return, the covariance between the announcement date and the postannouncement price change is positive: that is, $\text{cov}(P_3 - P_2, s_2 | P_1 - P_0) > 0$.

Since a non-selective event is an action that is unrelated to the pricing error at date 2, it tells us nothing about mean future price movements. Although the market underreacts to the event, it is equally likely to be underreacting downward as upward. Part 1 therefore indicates that there will be no systematic postannouncement drift following events that are unrelated to the prior market mispricing. Thus, Proposition 4 refutes the conventional interpretation of drift as being equivalent to underreaction to new information.

The lack of event-based predictive power for future returns is surprising given the positive autocorrelation of event-date and postevent price changes

(Proposition 1). However, even though the event is unrelated to the prior mispricing, the more underpriced the security, the more positive on average will be the stock price reaction to further news. Thus, a favorable event-date stock price change is associated with a positive future average trend. Clearly, then, even though the event itself does not predict future returns, the market is inefficient.

Part 2 of Proposition 4 predicts larger postevent average returns the more the nonselective event (perhaps a cash flow surprise) and the preevent stock price runup are in opposition (e.g., positive preevent runup and negative event).[9] Intuitively, holding constant the private signal (as reflected in P_1), the higher is the public signal, the more likely that the fundamental θ is high, and therefore the bigger the average shortfall of the private signal relative to the fundamental. Thus, a higher public signal is associated with a larger (more positive) postevent return.

Both parts 1 and 2 of Proposition 4 can be tested using data on specific nonselective events. These are presumably events that are not initiated by an informed party such as a manager with an incentive to take into account mispricing. Such events might include news about product demand that emanates from outside of the company (e.g., news about competitors' actions), or regulatory and legislative outcomes (e.g., FDA decisions on drugs proposed by a pharmaceutical company).

We now show that selective public events, that is, events that are correlated with preevent stock mispricing, will forecast future price changes. Consider a manager who observes P_1 (and therefore infers the private signal s_1) and receives his own signal s_2 at date 2. The manager can undertake a debt/equity exchange offering, and the attractiveness of a larger exchange depends on how high the market price is relative to fundamental value. He can condition the size of the offering on the mispricing at date 2, which he knows precisely, since he knows both s_1 and s_2. It can easily be shown that in this setting the date 2 pricing error is proportional to the expected error in the private signal, $\epsilon^* \equiv E[\epsilon|P_1, s_2]$, where the expectation is again taken with respect to rational beliefs. For tractability, we consider selective events that are linear functions of the date 2 mispricing.

When $\epsilon^* < 0$, the manager believes the market has undervalued the firm, so the firm can "profit" by exchanging debt for equity; the more undervalued the firm, the greater the size of the offering. If $\epsilon^* > 0$, an equity-for-debt swap would be preferred instead. It is easy to show that

$$E[P_3 - P_2|\epsilon^* > 0] < 0 < E[P_3 - P_2|\epsilon^* < 0]; \qquad (8)$$

that is, events taken in response to market undervaluation (e.g., repurchase) are associated with high postevent returns, and events taken in response to overvaluation (e.g., new issue) with low postevent returns.

---

[9] We thank an anonymous referee for suggesting we explore this issue.

Proposition 5. If investors are overconfident, then selective events that are initiated when the stock is undervalued (overvalued) by the market will on average be associated with positive (negative) announcement-date abnormal price changes and will on average be followed by positive (negative) postannouncement abnormal price changes.

In Proposition 4 there was underreaction to news arrival but no drift. Here, drift results from the combination of underreaction and event selection based on market mispricing. Thus, the model offers the new empirical implication that the phenomenon of abnormal postevent drift will be concentrated in events that select for market mispricing. Evidence recently brought to our attention supports this implication. Cornett, Mehran, and Tehranian (1998) find that "involuntary" issues undertaken by banks to meet capital requirements are not associated with postevent drift, whereas "voluntary" bank issues are associated with negative postevent abnormal performance. Since involuntary issues are likely to be less selective than voluntary ones, this evidence is consistent with the model.

If the announcement of an upcoming Initial Public Offering (IPO), like an Seasoned Equity Offering (SEO) announcement, reflects managers' "bad news," then Proposition 5 implies long-run underperformance following IPOs as well. Since IPO firms are private prior to the event, we have no data on the announcement-date reaction to an upcoming IPO. However, the consistent findings of negative stock price reactions to seasoned equity issue announcements, and of inferior post-IPO accounting performance (Jain and Kini 1994, Mikkelson, Partch, and Shah 1997, Teoh, Wong, and Rao 1998, Loughran and Ritter 1997), suggest that an IPO announcement is indeed on average bad news.[10] If so, the evidence that IPOs internationally exhibit long-run average underperformance for several years after the issue (Ritter 1991, and Loughran, Ritter, and Rydqvist 1994) is consistent with the model.

The event-based return predictability of Proposition 5 is not equivalent to "underreaction" to corporate events. Underreaction to public signals (as implied by overconfidence) induces positive autocorrelation of returns at the event date. However, the event realization (in contrast to the event-date return) may not predict future abnormal returns unless event size/occurrence is correlated with prior market mispricing.

We have interpreted the model in terms of firms buying or selling shares to profit from mispricing. An alternative interpretation is that a manager with favorable information ($\epsilon^* < 0$) would like to *signal* good news to the market, and chooses an action (such as a repurchase, dividend, debt for equity swap, or stock split) to reveal his information. With a continuous signal, such behavior

---

[10] The initial positive return relative to issue price, "underpricing," is *not* an announcement reaction to the news that an IPO will occur; this news is released earlier.

typically leads to full revelation, consistent with our assumption that ϵ^* is revealed to the market at the event date.[11]

Whether the model of this section is consistent with the well-known phenomenon of postearnings announcement "drift" depends on whether earnings announcements are selective events. An earnings report is favorably selective if managers report higher earnings, *ceteris paribus*, when the market undervalues their firm. A manager has an incentive to do so if he is averse to low levels of short-term stock price or personal reputation.[12] Further, managers have a great deal of discretion over earnings levels both through accounting adjustments (accruals), and by shifting the timing of actual cash flows. Accounting adjustments seem to reflect managers' inside information, as evidenced by the announcement effect of accruals on returns (distinct from the effect of cash flows); see Wilson (1986). There is extensive evidence that managers use their accounting discretion strategically to achieve their goals, such as meeting loan covenant requirements, winning proxy fights, obtaining earnings-based bonuses, and avoiding taxes; Teoh, Wong, and Rao (1998) reference about thirty such studies. If managers adjust earnings selectively, Proposition 5 can account for postearnings drift. The dynamic confidence setting of section 3 provides a distinct explanation for postearnings announcement drift that obtains even if earnings are nonselective.

Since the date 1 expected value of ϵ^* is perfectly positively correlated with P_1 (they both are linearly increasing functions of s_1), variables such as market/book or run-up $(P_1 - \bar{\theta})$ are potential measures of mispricing. As we have assumed that the size of a selective event depends on the size of the misvaluation, it follows that the size and sign of the selective event varies with the measures of mispricing. We therefore have:

Proposition 6

1. The expected size of a positive (negative) selective event is increasing (decreasing) in measures of the firm's mispricing.
2. The probability that a positive (negative) selective event will occur increases (decreases) with measures of the firm's mispricing.

We tentatively identify mispricing with variables that contain market price such as market/book ratios. The analysis then predicts that repurchases and

---

[11] The model's event study predictions also apply to events undertaken by outsiders who have information about the firm. An example is an analyst's recommendation to buy or sell shares of the firm. Thus, the analysis is consistent with evidence on stock price drift following analyst buy and sell recommendations, as discussed in Hirshleifer (2001).

[12] Either concave utility or risk of dismissal can make a manager averse to a low stock price; a rising disutility from low price is a common model assumption (see, e.g., Harris and Raviv 1985). If managers prefer a high short-term stock price but risk incurring a penalty for over-aggressive reports, then the net benefit from reporting higher earnings may be greater, *ceteris paribus*, when the stock is more undervalued.

other favorable events will tend to occur when market, industry, or firm market/book or price/earnings ratios are low, and equity issuance and other adverse selective events when such ratios are high. This is consistent with evidence that the frequency of IPOs is positively related to the market/book ratio in the company's industrial sectors (Pagano, Panetta, and Zingales 1998), and that in many countries the value and number of IPOs is positively associated with stock market levels (Loughran, Ritter, and Rydqvist 1994, Rees 1996, Ljungqvist 1997).

The analysis also implies that event-date price changes (for a given type of event) should be positively correlated with postannouncement returns. This is just underreaction, and follows under the conditions of Proposition 1.[13] Also, in the model, because the preevent price run-up maps one-to-one with market mispricing, better preevent price performance is associated with worse postevent performance (either including or excluding the event date). This follows because $\text{cov}(P_3 - P_2, P_1 - P_0) < 0$ and $\text{cov}(P_3 - P_1, P_1 - P_0) < 0$. Intuitively, mispricing arises from overreaction to private information, firms select events based on mispricing, and this causes postevent returns to be related to pre-event returns. However, the latter implication is not robust to reasonable generalization of the assumptions to allow for the possibility that public information can arrive at date 0 or 1.

Consider, for example, the case of dividend announcements. Firms that have been performing well enough to generate a lot of cash are more likely to boost dividends. Thus, a dividend increase will be associated not only with market undervaluation at date 2 (unfavorable date 1 *private* signal), but also with good past performance (favorable date 0 or 1 *public* signal). In this scenario, while the event-date and postevent mean abnormal returns are both positive, the sign of the preevent mean return will be ambiguous. We have verified formally that if the event choice (dividend) increases with both a past (date 1) public signal and the degree of market undervaluation, then the event may be associated with a positive average run-up, a positive average event date return, and a positive average postevent return.[14]

More generally, whether prior runup (or other price-related indicators such the fundamental/price ratios) is a measure of mispricing depends on whether the event in question is mainly selective for mispricing, or depends

[13] Proposition 1 is based on a nonselective news event, namely, the arrival of s_2. Even though s_2 is private information here, the result is the same because s_2 is fully revealed by the corporate action, so that P_2 is identical in all states to what it would be if s_2 were made public directly. Thus, $\text{cov}(P_3 - P_2, P_2 - P_1)$ is the same in both cases.

[14] Fama (1998) argues that our approach implies that mean pre-event abnormal returns will have the same sign as mean postevent abnormal returns, and that the evidence does not support this implication. As discussed above, event occurrence is likely to depend on past public information, in which case the model implies that average pre-event runup can have either the same or the opposite sign as average postevent abnormal returns. See Propositions 4 and 5 for model implications for event study returns that are robust with respect to pre-event public information arrival. The evidence generally supports these predictions.

heavily on past fundamental public performance measures (such as past earnings). Many events, such as dividends and stock splits, may be selective owing to a signaling motive. But events in which the firm trades against the market, such as exchange offers, repurchases, and new issues, provide an incentive to earn a trading profit. This provides an incentive to be selective above and beyond any signaling motive. Thus, runup and price/fundamental ratios should be better measures of mispricing for such market-exploitation events than for pure signaling events.

B.4 EMPIRICAL IMPLICATIONS

The model provides the following implications, which are either untested or have been tested only on a subset of possible events:

1. Average postevent returns of the same sign as average event-date returns for selective events, and zero postevent drift for nonselective events;
2. A positive correlation between initial event-date stock price reactions and postevent performance for public events;
3. A positive correlation between the size of a selective event (e.g., a repurchase or the announcement of a toehold stake) and postevent return, but no such correlation for nonselective events (e.g., news disclosed by outside sources, especially if macroeconomic or industry-wide, such as news about product demand or input prices, production processes, and regulatory events);
4. Larger postevent average returns the more the nonselective event and the pre-event stock price run-up are in opposition;
5. Greater average long-term reversal of price moves occurring on dates when there are no public news events about a firm reported in public news media than price moves occurring on public event dates;
6. Greater selective event sizes (e.g., greater repurchases) when mispricing measures (e.g., price/fundamental ratios or past run-up) are high; and,
7. Greater probability of a good news (bad news) selective event when the security is more underpriced (overpriced).

The overconfidence theory has further implications for managerial policy related to implications (6) and (7) above. We expect firms to issue securities when they believe their stocks are overvalued. If investors are overconfident, such overvaluation may be measured by recent increases in firm, industry or aggregate stock market prices, or with high price/fundamental ratios. Conversely, firms should repurchase after rundowns when the market appears to undervalue the firm. Thus, if managers act to exploit mispricing, there will be both general and industry-specific financing and repurchase booms.

The theory also suggests that when the market undervalues the firm, there should be a tilt away from dividends toward repurchase. Further, when a stock is underpriced (perhaps after run-downs or when firm or aggregate market/book ratios are low), the firm, acting in current shareholders' interests should, *ceteris paribus*, favor rights over public issues. Similarly, the firm should tilt toward debt rather than equity issues to avoid diluting current shareholders. Thus, the theory offers a possible solution to what Hovakimian, Opler, and Titman (2001) call a major puzzle from the perspective of optimal capital structure theory, that after a rise in market prices, firms tend to issue more equity rather than debt.[15]

Since these predictions seem quite intuitive, it is easy to forget that the directions would reverse in alternative models of market mispricing. For example, in a setting where the market always underreacts, firms with high recent runups or low fundamental/price ratios will, *ceteris paribus*, tend to be *undervalued*, so that (inconsistent with the evidence) we would observe repurchases rather than equity issues in such situations.

3. Outcome-dependent Confidence

The implications described so far are based on a fixed confidence level. However, psychological evidence and theory suggest that actions and resulting outcomes affect confidence; events that confirm an individual's beliefs and actions tend to boost confidence too much, while disconfirming events weaken confidence too little (see section 1). Taking into account this psychological pattern leads to implications similar to those in the static section, except that there is also short-run momentum in stock prices and event-based predictability even for nonselective events.

Consider an informed individual who initially is not overconfident, and who buys or sells a security based on his private information. A public signal *confirms* his trade if they have the same sign ("buy" and a positive signal, or "sell" and a negative signal). We assume that if the later public signal confirms his trade, the individual becomes more confident, and if it disconfirms his confidence decreases by little or remains constant. This implies that *on average*, public information can increases confidence, intensifying overreaction. The continuing overreaction leads to positive autocorrelation during the initial overreaction phase. As repeated public information arrival draws the price back toward fundamentals, the initial overreaction is gradually reversed in the long run.

The above process yields a hump-shaped impulse response function for a private signal as illustrated by the dashed lines in figure 13.1. (The date 0/1 line overlaps the solid lines showing the impulse response for the static

---

[15] However, Jung, Kim, and Stulz (1996) find that firms often depart from the pecking order (i.e., the preference of debt over equity) because of agency considerations, and that debt and equity issuers both have negative average abnormal long-run stock returns that are not statistically different from one another.

model.) The figure shows two possible date 1 prices, and the paths for expected price conditional on the date 1 move. It can be seen that with outcome-dependent confidence, there are smooth overreaction and correction phases. Pairs of returns drawn from these phases will be positively correlated, whereas the pair which straddles the extremum will be negatively correlated. The overall autocorrelation involving contiguous price changes will be positive if the extremum-straddling negative correlation is sufficiently small. However, price changes that are separated by long lags are likely to straddle the extremum of the impulse-response function, and will therefore exhibit negative autocorrelations. Thus, the pattern of momentum at short lags and reversal at long lags arises naturally from the model.

We present two models with dynamic confidence that capture this intuition. The model presented in subsection A is tractable but highly stylized. The model presented in subsection B allows us to develop more complex implications, but can only be solved by simulation.

A. The Simple Model with Outcome Dependent Confidence

We modify the basic model of section 2 as follows. We still allow for, but no longer require, initial overconfidence, so $\sigma_C^2 \leq \sigma_\epsilon^2$. For tractability, the public signal is now discrete, with $s_2 = 1$ or -1 released at date 2. We assume that the precision assessed by the investors at date 2 about their earlier private signal depends on the realization of the public signal in the following way. If

$$\text{sign}(\theta + \epsilon) = \text{sign}(s_2), \qquad (9)$$

confidence increases, so investors' assessment of noise variance decreases to $\sigma_C^2 - k$, $0 < k < \sigma_C^2$. If

$$\text{sign}(\theta + \epsilon) \neq \text{sign}(s_2), \qquad (10)$$

confidence remains constant, so noise variance is still believed to be σ_C^2.

The probability of receiving a public signal $+1$ is denoted by p. For a high value to be a favorable indicator of value, p must tend to increase with θ. However, allowing p to vary with θ creates intractable non-normalities. We therefore examine the limiting case where the signal is virtually pure noise, so that p is a constant. (Appendix C of Daniel, Hirshleifer, and Subrahmanyam [1998] provides a discrete model which derives similar results using an informative public signal.)

Given normality of all random variables, the date 1 price is

$$P_1 = E_C[\theta | \theta + \epsilon] = \frac{\sigma_\theta^2}{\sigma_\theta^2 + \sigma_C^2}(\theta + \epsilon). \qquad (11)$$

The date 0 price $P_0 = 0$, the prior mean. If sign $(\theta + \epsilon) \neq \text{sign}(s_2)$, then confidence is constant. Since the public signal is virtually uninformative, the price (virtually) does not move at date 2. However, if sign $(\theta + \epsilon) = $ sign (s_2), then the new price is calculated using the new level of the assessed variance of ϵ. This price, denoted by P_{2C}, is

$$P_{2C} = \frac{\sigma_\theta^2}{\sigma_\theta^2 + \sigma_C^2 - k}(\theta + \epsilon). \tag{12}$$

A.1 IMPLICATIONS OF THE SIMPLE MODEL

It can easily be shown that[16]

$$\text{cov}(P_2 - P_1, P_1 - P_0) > 0. \tag{13}$$

Thus, the model shows that the overreaction phase, not just the correction phase, can contribute positively to short-term momentum. As a result,

$$\text{cov}(P_3 - P_1, P_1 - P_0) < 0; \tag{14}$$

$$\text{cov}(P_3 - P_2, P_2 - P_1) < 0, \tag{15}$$

because the dates 1 and 2 overreactions must be reversed in the long-term.

Intuitively, further dates of noisy public information arrival should eventually cause the mispricing to be corrected (so long as confidence does not explode infinitely). This process causes positive autocorrelation during the correction phase, just as in the basic model of section 2. To examine this, let us add a date 3' between dates 2 and 3, where a public signal $\theta + \eta$ is released. For simplicity, we assume that overconfidence is not affected by the release of the second public signal. As in section 2, η is a zero mean, normally distributed variable with variance σ_p^2, and is independent of all other random variables. The price at date 3' when overconfidence is not revised at date 2 is given by equation (6). When overconfidence is revised at date 2, the price at date 3', denoted by $P_{3'C}$ is given by the same expression as equation (6), except that σ_C^2 is replaced by $\sigma_C^2 - k$; that is,

$$P_{3'C} = \frac{\sigma_\theta^2(\sigma_C^2 - k + \sigma_p^2)}{D}\theta + \frac{\sigma_\theta^2\sigma_p^2}{D}\epsilon + \frac{\sigma_\theta^2(\sigma_C^2 - k)}{D}\eta, \tag{16}$$

where $D \equiv \sigma_\theta^2(\sigma_C^2 - k + \sigma_p^2) + (\sigma_C^2 - k)\sigma_p^2$.

With the extra date added to the model, it is easy to show that all of the remaining single-period price change autocorrelations are negative except for $\text{cov}(P_3 - P_{3'}, P_{3'} - P_2)$, which is positive. This can be explained as follows. Date 2 is the extremum of the impulse response function (the "hump" or "trough" date after which the average correction begins). The single-period price-change single-lag autocorrelations that fall entirely within either the overreaction phase or within the correction phase are positive,

---

[16] Explicit calculations and expressions for covariances for this subsection are in presented in Appendix D of Daniel, Hirshleifer, and Subrahmanyam (1998).

while the single-period price change single-lag autocorrelation that straddles the extremum is negative.[17]

Under appropriate parameter assumptions, the negative single-lag auto-correlation surrounding the extremum will be arbitrarily close to zero. This will occur if either the extra overreaction or the start of the correction is weak (or both). The extra overreaction is small if confidence is boosted only slightly ($k > 0$ small) when an investor's trade is confirmed by public news. The initial correction is slight if the further noisy public signal is not very in-formative (σ_η^2 large). When parameter values are such that this straddling autocorrelation is not too large, it will be outweighed by the positive auto-correlations during the hearts of the overreaction or correction phases. In other words, an econometrician calculating autocorrelations uncondition-ally would find, in a large sample, a positive single-lag autocorrelation. In contrast, longer-lag pairs of price changes that straddle the extremum of the impulse response function will tend to be opposed, because a price change drawn from the overreaction phase tends to be negatively correlated with a price change drawn from the correction phase. Thus, the overconfidence theory provides a joint explanation for both short-term momentum and long-term reversals.

   Proposition 7. If investor confidence changes owing to biased self-attribution, and if overreaction or correction is sufficiently gradual, then stock price changes will exhibit unconditional short-lag posi-tive autocorrelation ("momentum") and long-lag negative autocor-relation ("reversal").

According to Jegadeesh and Titman (1993), their momentum evidence is "consistent with delayed price reactions to firm-specific information." Proposition 7 offers a very different possible interpretation, namely, that momentum occurs not because the market is slow to react to news, but be-cause the market initially overreacts to the news, and later public news trig-gers further overreaction to the initial private signal. More generally, Proposition 7 refutes the common casual equating of positive versus nega-tive autocorrelations with underreaction versus overreaction to new infor-mation. While negative autocorrelations result from overreaction in the model, positive autocorrelations also result from continuing overreaction (followed by underreaction in the correction of this error).

Evidence from the psychological literature suggests that individuals tend to be more overconfident in settings where feedback on their information or decisions is slow or inconclusive than where the feedback is clear and rapid (Einhorn 1980). Thus, mispricing should be stronger in stocks which

---

[17] Formally, $\text{cov}(P_2 - P_1, P_1 - P_0) > 0$, $\text{cov}(P_3 - P_{3'}, P_{3'} - P_2) > 0$, and $\text{cov}(P_{3'} - P_2, P_2 - P_1) < 0$. See the appendix of Daniel, Hirshleifer, and Subrahmanyam (1998).

require more judgment to evaluate, and where the feedback on this judgment is ambiguous in the short run, such as for growth stocks whose value is, on average, more strongly tied to hard to value growth options. This conjecture is consistent with recent work by Daniel and Titman (1999), which finds that the momentum effect is strong in growth stocks, but is weak or nonexistent in value stocks. This line of reasoning also suggests that momentum should be stronger for stocks that are difficult to value, such as those with high R&D expenditures or intangible assets.

B. A Dynamic Model of Outcome-dependent Confidence

We now extend this model to an arbitrary number of periods and present numerical simulations. The analysis implies patterns of security price-change autocorrelations consistent with the findings of subsection A. It also yields further implications for the correlation between public information announcements (such as managers' forecasts or financial reports of sales, cash flows or earnings) and future price changes.

B.1 THE MODEL

We retain the basic structure considered in earlier sections. We assume that the investor has a prior on the precision of his private signal, and uses an updating rule that reflects self-attribution bias. As before, the (unobservable) value of a share of the firm's stock is $\tilde{\theta} \sim \mathcal{N}(0, \sigma_\theta^2)$. The public noise variance σ_θ^2 is common knowledge. At date 1, each informed investor receives a private signal $\tilde{s}_1 = \tilde{\theta} + \tilde{\epsilon}$ where $\tilde{\epsilon} \sim \mathcal{N}(0, \sigma_\epsilon^2)$. At dates 2 through T, a public signal $\tilde{\phi}_t$ is released, $\tilde{\phi}_t = \tilde{\theta} + \tilde{\eta}_t$, where $\tilde{\eta}_t$ is $i.i.d$ and $\tilde{\eta} \sim \mathcal{N}(0, \sigma_\eta^2)$. The variance of the noise, σ_η^2, is also common knowledge. Let Φ_t be the average of all public signals through time t:

$$\Phi_t = \frac{1}{(t-1)} \sum_{\tau=2}^{t} \tilde{\phi}_\tau = \theta + \frac{1}{(t-1)} \sum_{\tau=2}^{t} \tilde{\eta}_\tau. \tag{17}$$

The average public signal Φ_t is a sufficient statistic for the $t-1$ public signals, and $\tilde{\Phi}_t \sim \mathcal{N}(\theta, \sigma_\eta^2/(t-1))$.

As before, an informed investor forms expectations about value rationally (using Bayesian updating) except for his perceptions of his private information precision. The error variance σ_ϵ^2 is incorrectly perceived by the investor. He estimates σ_ϵ^2 using an *ad hoc* rule described below. At time 1, the investor believes that the precision of his signal, $v_{C,1} = 1/\sigma_{C,1}^2$, is greater than the true precision $v_\epsilon = 1/\sigma_\epsilon^2$. At every subsequent release of public information the investor updates his estimate of the noise variance. If the new public signal (ϕ_t) confirms the investor's private signal s_1, and the private signal is not too far away from the public signal, then the investor becomes more confident in his private signal. If the new public signal disconfirms his private signal, the investor revises the estimated precision downwards, but not by as much. Thus, the specific updating rule that we implement is:

$$\text{if}\begin{cases} sign(s_1 - \Phi_{t-1}) = sign(\phi_t - \Phi_{t-1}) \text{ and } |s_1 - \Phi_{t-1}| < 2\sigma_{\Phi,t} \\ \quad \text{then } v_{C,t} = (1+\overline{k})v_{C,t-1} \quad \text{otherwise} \\ \quad v_{C,t} = (1-\underline{k})v_{C,t-1}, \end{cases} \tag{18}$$

where $\sigma_{\Phi,t}$ is the standard deviation of Φ at time t. We impose the restriction that $\overline{k} > \underline{k} > 0$. The ratio $(1+\overline{k})/(1-\underline{k})$ is an index of the investor's attribution bias.[18]

B.2 THE EQUILIBRIUM

Since the investor is risk-neutral and the risk-free rate is zero, at each point in time the stock price is the expectation of its terminal value:

$$P_t = E_C[\tilde{\theta}|s_1, \phi_2, \dots, \phi_t] = E_C[\tilde{\theta}|s_1, \Phi_t]. \tag{19}$$

Define $v_\theta = 1/\sigma_\theta^2$, and $v_\eta = 1/\sigma_\eta^2$. The price of the security at time t is given by:

$$\tilde{P}_t = E_C[\tilde{\theta}|s_1, \Phi_t] = \frac{(t-1)v_\eta\Phi_t + v_{C,t}s_1}{v_\theta + v_\eta + v_{C,t}}. \tag{20}$$

Recall that the precision of Φ_t is $(t-1)v_\eta$.

B.3 SIMULATION RESULTS AND EMPIRICAL IMPLICATIONS

For the simulation we use the parameters $\overline{k} = 0.75$, $\underline{k} = 0.1$, $\sigma_\theta^2 = \sigma_\varepsilon^2 = 1$, and $\sigma_\eta^2 = 7.5$. We also make the investor's initial estimate of his precision equal to the true precision of his private signal. We perform this simulation 50,000 times, each time redrawing the value θ, the private signal $s_1 = \theta + \varepsilon$, and the public information set ϕ_t, for $t = 2, \dots T$.

It is useful to first illustrate the dynamic price path implied by the model for specific realizations of s_1 and θ. Figure 13.2 shows the average price path following a private signal of $s = 1$ when $\theta = 0$, so that the informed investors' signal is unduly favorable. The price initially jumps from 0 up to 0.5, a rational assessment. On average, the price continues moving up, reaching a maximum of 0.7366 in period 16. The average price then declines, and eventually asymptotes to zero. Thus, there is an initial overreaction phase in

---

[18] Several alternative *ad hoc* updating rules consistent with this intuition all lead to roughly equivalent results. For tractability, we assume that the investor forms beliefs as if, at each point in time, he knows his exact signal precision. Rationally he should allow for the fact that $v_{C,t}$ is an estimate. We expect that the essential results are not sensitive to this simplification.

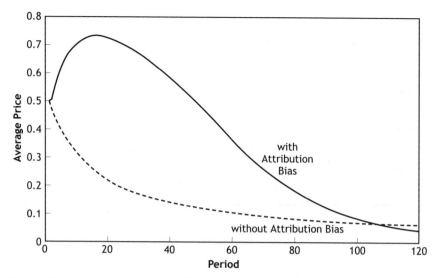

Figure 13.2. Average price path following private information shock. This figure shows average price path calculated using the simulation in Section 3.B.3, following a private information shock $s_1 = 1$. The price-path is shown for the dynamic model with (solid line) and without (dashed line) self-attribution bias.

which the price moves away from the true value as the investor's attribution bias causes him to place more weight, on average, on his private information. Eventually the public information become precise enough that the investor revises his valuation of the security downward. This is the correction phase. A similar hump-shaped pattern holds for an investors' self-perceived precision (confidence) as a function of time. This changing confidence is the source of the overreacting average price trend.

Figure 13.3 presents the *unconditional* average autocorrelations (at lags between 1 period and 119 periods), where now $\tilde{\theta}$ and $\tilde{s}_1$ are resampled for each iteration. This figure confirms the intuition derived from figure 13.2 that short-lag price change autocorrelations should be positive and long-lag autocorrelations should be negative.

Several papers examine "long-horizon" regressions of long period returns on past returns (see, e.g., Fama and French 1988) rather than long-lag autocorrelations of short-period returns. In our model, it is straightforward to show that there is a one-to-one mapping between price change autocorrelations and more standard test statistics such as variance ratios or long-horizon regression coefficients. In unreported simulations, these coefficients exhibit behavior similar to that of the autocorrelations. Short-horizon regression coefficients are positive and long-horizon ones are negative, consistent with empirical literature on momentum and reversals.

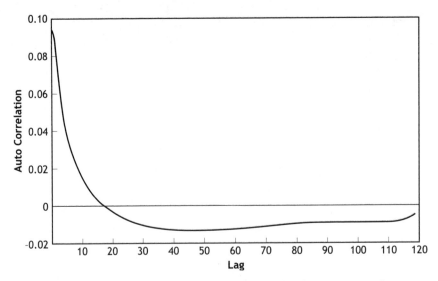

Figure 13.3. Average price-change autocorrelations. This figure presents the unconditional average autocorrelations (at lags between 1 period and 119 periods), calculated using the simulation described in section 3.B.3.

The conclusions of this simulation are summarized as follows:

Result 1. In the biased self-attribution setting of Subsection B, if the true share value $\theta = 0$ and the initial private signal $s_1 = 1$, then with sufficient attribution bias the average price at first rises and then gradually declines. This contrasts with a steadily declining price path if there is no attribution bias. In the biased self-attribution setting, average self-perceived precision also initially rises and then declines.

Result 2. In the biased self-attribution setting of Subsection B, short-lag autocorrelations (correlating single-period price changes with single-period price changes) are positive and long-lag autocorrelations are negative.

Result 3. In the biased self-attribution setting of Subsection B, short-term autocorrelations are positive and long-horizon autocorrelations are negative.

Recent research indicates strong and consistent evidence of momentum in the United States and in European countries, but weak and insignificant evidence of momentum in Japan (see, e.g., Haugen and Baker 1996, and Daniel, Titman, and Wei 2001). There is corresponding evidence of a difference in biased self-attributions in Western versus Asian groups, especially Japan. For example, Kitayama, Takagi, and Matsumoto (1995) review twenty-three studies conducted in Japan that find essentially no evidence of self-enhancing biases in attribution. These findings suggest the more general prediction that cultures in which there is little or no self-enhancing attribution bias (e.g., other Asian countries such as Korea, PRC, and Taiwan; see the references in Kitayama, Takagi, and Matsumoto 1995) should have weak momentum effects.

DeLong, Shleifer, Summers, and Waldmann (1990a) have derived security return autocorrelations in a model with mechanistic positive feedback traders. Our approach differs in explicitly modeling the decisions of quasi-rational individuals. Our model provides one possible psychological foundation for a stochastic tendency for trades to be correlated with past price movements, which can create an appearance of positive feedback trading.

B.4 CORRELATION OF ACCOUNTING PERFORMANCE
WITH SUBSEQUENT PRICE CHANGES

Finally, we consider the implications of this model for the correlation between accounting performance and future price changes. Accounting information (sales, earnings, etc.) can be thought of as noisy public signals about θ, so in this subsection we interpret the ϕs as accounting performance change measures. Consider the first public signal (at $t = 2$). If this is positive, the first private signal was probably also positive. Based on the momentum results in this section, this suggests that prices will continue to increase after the arrival date of the public signal, consistent with empirical evidence on earnings-based return predictability. Eventually prices will decline as the cumulative public signal becomes more precise and informed investors put less weight on their signal. Thus, the analysis of this section suggests that earnings-based return predictability, like stock-price momentum, may be a phenomenon of continuing overreaction.[19] In the long-run, of course, the security price will return to its full-information value, implying long-run negative correlations between accounting performance and future price changes. This conjecture is consistent with the empirical evidence though, from an empirical standpoint, statistical power to detect long-lag autocorrelations is limited.

To evaluate the above conjecture, we again calculate average correlations using our simulation as follows. For each $\tilde{\phi}_t$ (for $t = 2, 120$) we calculate the "earnings" surprise, defined as:

$$\Delta e_t = \tilde{\phi}_t - \Phi_t = \tilde{\phi}_t - E[\tilde{\phi}_t | \phi_2, \phi_3, \ldots, \phi_{t-1}], \qquad (21)$$

the deviation of ϕ_t from its expected value based on all past public signals. Then, we calculate the set of sample correlations between the Δe_t and price

---

[19] The discussion of event-study implications in subsection B.3 describes conditions under which postearnings announcement drift could be an underreaction effect.

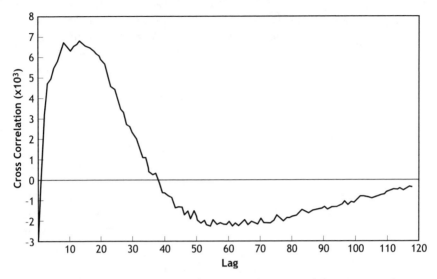

Figure 13.4. Correlation between information changes and future price changes. This figure shows the set of average sample correlations between the Δe_t and price changes τ periods in the future $\Delta P_{t+\tau} = P_{t+\tau} - P_{t+\tau-1}$. These are calculated using the simulated dynamic model of section 3.B.3.

changes τ periods in the future $\Delta P_{t+\tau} = P_{t+\tau} - P_{t+\tau-1}$. These correlations are then averaged over the Monte Carlo draws. The average correlations are plotted in figure 13.4. This simulation yields:

Result 4. In the biased self-attribution setting of subsection B, short-lag correlations between single-period stock price changes and past earnings are positive, and long-lag correlations can be positive or negative.

To summarize, the analysis suggests that the conclusion from the basic model that investors overreact to private signals holds in the dynamic model. While investors underreact on average to public signals, public signals initially tend to stimulate additional overreaction to a previous private signal. Thus, underreaction is mixed with continuing overreaction.

In the model of this section, earnings-based return predictability and momentum both arise from self-attribution bias. Further, the literature cited in subsection B.3 suggests that the magnitude of this bias varies systematically across countries. Based on these observations, the self-attribution model suggests a positive relationship across international markets between the strength of the momentum effect and that of the postearnings announcement drift.

IV. Conclusion

Empirical securities markets research in the last three decades has presented a body of evidence with systematic patterns that are not easy to explain with rational asset pricing models. Some studies conclude that the market underreacts to information, while others find evidence of overreaction. We have lacked a theory to integrate this evidence, and to make predictions about when over- or underreaction will occur.

This work develops a theory based on investor overconfidence and on changes in confidence resulting from biased self-attribution of investment outcomes. The theory implies that investors will overreact to private information signals and underreact to public information signals. In contrast with the common correspondence of positive (negative) return autocorrelations with underreaction (overreaction) to new information, we show that positive return autocorrelations can be a result of continuing overreaction. This is followed by by long-run correction. Thus, short-run positive autocorrelations can be consistent with long-run negative autocorrelations.

The theory also offers an explanation for the phenomenon of average public event stock price reactions of the same sign as postevent long-run abnormal returns. This pattern has sometimes been interpreted as market underreaction to the event. We show that underreaction to new public information is neither a necessary nor a sufficient condition for such event-based predictability. Such predictability can arise from underreaction only if the event is chosen in response to market mispricing. Alternatively, predictability can arise when the public event triggers a continuing overreaction. For example, postearnings announcement drift may be a continuing overreaction triggered by the earnings announcement to preevent information.

The basic noise trading approach to securities markets (e.g., Grossman and Stiglitz 1980, Shiller 1984, Kyle 1985, Glosten and Milgrom 1985, Black 1986, DeLong, Shleifer, Summers, and Waldmann 1990b, and Campbell and Kyle 1993) posits that there is variability in prices arising from unpredictable trading that seems unrelated to valid information. Our approach is based on the premise that an important class of mistakes by investors involves the misinterpretation of *genuine* new private information. Thus, our model endogenously generates trading mistakes that are correlated with fundamentals. Modeling the decision problems of quasi-rational traders imposes restrictions on trade distributions that are not obvious if distributions are imposed exogenously. This structure provides predictions about the dynamic behavior of asset prices which depend on the particular cognitive error that is assumed. For example, *under*confidence also gives rise to quasi-rational trading that is correlated with fundamentals, but gives rise to empirical predictions which are the reverse of what the empirical literature finds. Specifically, if informed investors are underconfident ($\sigma_C^2 > \sigma_\epsilon^2$), there will be insufficient volatility relative to the rational level, long-run return continuation, and negative correlation between selective events such as repurchase and postevent returns. Of course, one could arbitrarily specify whatever pattern of correlated noise is needed to match empirically observed ex post price patterns. Such an exercise would merely be a relabeling of the puzzle, not a theory. Instead, we examine a form of irrationality consistent with well-documented psychological biases, and our key contribution is to show that these biases induce several of the anomalous price patterns documented in the empirical literature.

Some models of exogenous noise trades (e.g., DeLong, Shleifer, Summers, and Waldmann 1990b, Campbell and Kyle 1993) also imply long-run reversals and excess volatility because of the time-varying risk premia induced by these trades. Our approach additionally reconciles long-run reversals with short-term momentum, explains event-based return predictability, and offers several other distinct empirical predictions (see subsections 2.B.1–2.B.3).

As noted in the introduction, a possible objection to models with imperfectly rational traders is that wealth may shift from foolish to rational traders until price-setting is dominated by rational traders. For example, in our model the overconfident informed traders lose money on average. This outcome is similar to the standard result that informed investors cannot profit from trading with uninformed investors unless there is some "noise" or "supply shock." However, recent literature has shown that in the long-run rational traders may not predominate. DeLong, Shleifer, Summers, and Waldman (1990b, 1991) point out that if traders are risk-averse, a trader who underestimates risk will allocate more wealth to risky, high expected return assets. If risk averse traders are overconfident about genuine information signals (as in our model), overconfidence allows them to exploit information more effectively. Thus, the expected profits of the overconfident can be greater than those of the fully rational (see Daniel, Hirshleifer, and Subrahmanyam 2001).

Furthermore, owing to biased self-attribution, those who acquire wealth through successful investment may *become* more overconfident (see also Gervais and Odean 2001). Another distinct benefit of overconfidence is that this can act like a commitment to trade aggressively. Since this may intimidate competing informed traders, those known to be overconfident may earn higher returns (see Kyle and Wang 1997, and Benos 1998).

Recent evidence suggests that event-based return predictability varies across stocks (e.g., Brav and Gompers 1997). Moving beyond the confines of the formal model, we expect the effects of overconfidence to be more severe in less liquid securities and assets. Suppose that all investors are risk averse and that prices are not fully revealing (perhaps because of noisy liquidity trading). If rational arbitrageurs face fixed setup costs of learning about a stock, then large liquid stocks will tend to be better arbitraged (more rationally priced) than small stocks, because it is easier to cover the fixed investigation cost in large, liquid stocks. This suggests greater inefficiencies for small stocks than for large stocks, and for less liquid securities and assets such as real estate than for stocks. Furthermore, since the model is based on overconfidence about private information, the model predicts that return predictability will be be strongest in firms with the greatest information asymmetries. This also implies greater inefficiencies in the stock prices of small companies. Furthermore, proxies for information asymmetry such as the adverse selection component of the bid-ask spread should also be positively related to momentum reversal, and postevent drift.

It is an open question whether the overconfident traders in the model can be identified with a specific category of investor, such as institutions, other investment professionals, small individual investors, or all three. Even small individual investors, who presumably have less information, may still be overconfident. The uninformed investors of the model could be interpreted as being contrarian-strategy investors (whether institutions or individuals). (Some smart contrarian investors could be viewed as rational and informed; including such traders would not change the qualitative nature of the model predictions.) An identification of the confidence characteristics of different observable investor categories may generate further empirical implications, and is an avenue for further research.

APPENDIX A: COVARIANCE AND VARIANCE CALCULATIONS
FOR THE BASIC MODEL

Covariances and Variances of Section 2.B, and Proof of Proposition 3

The calculations of the covariances and variances presented in Section 2.B, and the proof of Proposition 3 follow by routine application of the properties of multivariate normal variables. For details, see Daniel, Hirshleifer, and Subrahmanyam (1998).

Proofs of Some Claims in Section B.3

Part 1 of Proposition 4: Denote the date 2 mispricing as M_2. Suppressing arguments on $P_2^R(s_2)$ and $P_2^C(s_2)$, we have that $M_2 = P_2^R - P_2^C = -E[\theta - P_2^C(s_2)|s_1, s_2]$. By the properties of normal random variables, this implies that the variable $x = \theta - P_2^C + M_2$, which is the residual from the regression of $\theta - P_2^C$ on s_1 and s_2, is orthogonal to s_1 and s_2. Suppose we pick a variable $y = f(s_1, s_2)$ which is orthogonal to M_2. Such a variable will be orthogonal to x, so that we have $\text{cov}(\theta - P_2^C + M_2, y) = 0$. Since $\text{cov}(M_2, y) = 0$ by construction, it follows from the linearity of the covariance operator that $\text{cov}(\theta - P_2^C, y) = 0$. A converse argument shows that if we pick a variable $y' = g(s_1, s_2)$ which is orthogonal to the post event return $\theta - P_2^C$ then $\text{cov}(M_2, y') = 0$. Thus, all functions of s_1 and s_2 are orthogonal to M_2 if and only if they are orthogonal to the post event return $\theta - P_2^C$.

For the specific case when the event depends linearly on s_2, by (6),

$$P_3 - P_2 = \frac{\sigma_C^2 \sigma_p^2 \theta - \sigma_p^2 \sigma_\theta^2 \epsilon - \sigma_C^2 \sigma_\theta^2 \eta}{\sigma_\theta^2(\sigma_C^2 + \sigma_p^2) + \sigma_C^2 \sigma_p^2}. \tag{A1}$$

Since $s_2 \equiv \theta + \eta$, from the above expression, it immediately follows that $\text{cov}(P_3 - P_2, s_2) = 0$, thus showing that events that depend only on s_2 are non-selective.

Part 2 of Proposition 4: By standard results for calculating conditional variances of normal variables (Anderson (1984)),

$$\text{cov}(P_3 - P_2, s_2|s_1) = \text{cov}(P_3 - P_2, s_2|P_1 - P_0)$$
$$= \frac{\sigma_p^2 \sigma_\theta^4 (\sigma_\epsilon^2 - \sigma_C^2)}{[\sigma_C^2(\sigma_p^2 + \sigma_\theta^2) + \sigma_p^2 \sigma_\theta^2](\sigma_\epsilon^2 + \sigma_\theta^2)}, \tag{A2}$$

which is positive under overconfidence ($\sigma_C^2 > \sigma_\epsilon^2$).

Proposition 5: Using standard normal distribution properties,

$$\epsilon^* = E[\epsilon|P_1, \theta + \eta] = \frac{\sigma_\epsilon^2(\sigma_\theta^2 + \sigma_p^2)(\theta + \epsilon) - \sigma_\theta^2\sigma_\epsilon^2(\theta + \eta)}{\sigma_\epsilon^2(\sigma_\theta^2 + \sigma_p^2) + \sigma_\theta^2\sigma_p^2}. \qquad (A3)$$

It is straightforward to show that the ratio of the date 2 mispricing to ϵ^* is

$$\frac{\sigma_\epsilon^2[\sigma_C^2(\sigma_\theta^2 + \sigma_p^2) + \sigma_\theta^2\sigma_p^2]}{\sigma_p^2\sigma_\theta^2(\sigma_C^2 - \sigma_\theta^2)}, \qquad (A4)$$

which is constant (for a given level of confidence). Thus, selective events can alternatively be viewed as events that are linearly related to ϵ^*.

High values of ϵ^* signify overpricing and low values underpricing. The proposition follows by observing that

$$\text{cov}(P_3 - P_2, \epsilon^*) = \frac{\sigma_\epsilon^2\sigma_\eta^2\sigma_\theta^2(\sigma_\theta^2 + \sigma_p^2) + (\sigma_C^2 - \sigma_\epsilon^2)}{[\sigma_\epsilon^2(\sigma_\theta^2 + \sigma_p^2) + \sigma_\theta^2\sigma_p^2][\sigma_C^2(\sigma_\theta^2 + \sigma_p^2) + \sigma_\theta^2\sigma_p^2]} < 0 \quad (A5)$$

and

$$\text{cov}(P_2 - P_1, \epsilon^*) = -\frac{\sigma_C^2\sigma_\epsilon^2\sigma_\theta^4[\sigma_\epsilon^2(\sigma_p^2 + \sigma_\theta^2) + \sigma_p^2\sigma_\theta^2]}{(\sigma_C^2 + \sigma_\theta^2)[\sigma_C^2(\sigma_p^2 + \sigma_\theta^2) + \sigma_p^2\sigma_\theta^2]^2} < 0. \qquad (A6)$$

Since $\text{cov}(P_3 - P_2, \epsilon^*) < 0$, by the conditioning properties of mean-zero normal distributions, $E[P_3 - P_2|\epsilon^*]$ can be written in the form $k\epsilon^*$, where $k < 0$ is a constant. Thus, $E[P_3 - P_2|\epsilon^*] < 0$ if and only if $\epsilon^* > 0$. Since this holds for each positive realization of ϵ^*, $E[P_3 - P_2|\epsilon^* > 0] < 0$. By symmetric reasoning, $E[P_3 - P_2|\epsilon^* < 0] > 0$. The result for event-date price reactions uses a similar method. Since $\text{cov}(P_2 - P_1, \epsilon^*) < 0$, it follows that $E[P_2 - P_1|\epsilon^*] < 0$ if and only if $\epsilon^* > 0$.

Proposition 6: We interpret the "fundamental/price" ratio or "run-up" as $\bar{\theta} - P_1$. For part 1,

$$\text{cov}(\bar{\theta} - P_1, \epsilon^*) = \frac{\sigma_\epsilon^2[\sigma_\epsilon^2(\sigma_p^2 + \sigma_\theta^2) + \sigma_p^2\sigma_\theta^2]}{\sigma_C^2(\sigma_p^2 + \sigma_\theta^2) + \sigma_p^2\sigma_\theta^2} > 0. \qquad (A7)$$

By our assumption that the selective event is linearly related to ϵ^*, the selective event is positively correlated with the mispricing measure, proving part 1.

For part 2, note that $\epsilon^* = k_1 s_1 + k_2 s_2$, where

$$k_1 = \frac{\sigma_\epsilon^2 (\sigma_\theta^2 + \sigma_p^2)}{\sigma_C^2 (\sigma_p^2 + \sigma_\theta^2) + \sigma_p^2 \sigma_\theta^2}, \tag{A8}$$

$$k_2 = -\frac{\sigma_\epsilon^2 \sigma_\theta^2}{\sigma_C^2 (\sigma_p^2 + \sigma_\theta^2) + \sigma_p^2 \sigma_\theta^2}. \tag{A9}$$

This implies that the distribution of ϵ^* conditional on $\theta + \epsilon$ is normal with mean

$$\frac{(k_1 + k_2)\sigma_\theta^2 + k_1 \sigma_\epsilon^2}{\sigma_\theta^2 + \sigma_\epsilon^2} (\theta + \epsilon) \tag{A10}$$

and variance

$$\frac{[(k_1 + k_2)\sigma_\theta^2 + k_1 \sigma_\epsilon^2]^2}{\sigma_\theta^2 + \sigma_\epsilon^2} (\theta + \epsilon). \tag{A11}$$

The complement of the standardized cumulative normal distribution function of a normal random variable with nonzero mean and variance is increasing in its mean. Since $E[\epsilon^* | \theta + \epsilon]$ is proportional to $\theta + \epsilon$, the probability conditional on P_1 that ϵ^* exceeds a given threshold value (indicating occurrence of the positive event) is increasing in $\theta + \epsilon$. The reverse holds for a negative event, proving part (2).

APPENDIX B: DISCRETE MODEL OF OUTCOME-DEPENDENT OVERCONFIDENCE

At time 0, θ has a value of $+1$ or -1 and an expected value of zero. At time 1, the player receives a signal s_1, and, at time 2, a signal s_2. s_1 may be either H or L while s_2 may be either U or D. After each signal, the player updates his prior expected value of θ.

$$Pr(s_1 = H | \theta = +1) = p = Pr(s_1 = L | \theta = -1), \tag{A12}$$

$$Pr(s_2 = U | \theta = +1) = q = Pr(s_2 = D | \theta = -1). \tag{A13}$$

The probabilities that $\theta = +1$, given s_1 and s_2 are

$$Pr(\theta = +1 | s_1 = H) = \frac{Pr(s_1 = H | \theta = +1) Pr(\theta = +1)}{Pr(s_1 = H)}$$

$$= \frac{p/2}{p/2 + (1-p)/2} = p. \tag{A14}$$

When s_2 confirms s_2 (either $s_1 = H$, $s_2 = U$ or $s_1 = L$, $s_2 = D$), the player becomes overconfident and acts as if his precision were p_C instead of p, so

$$Pr(\theta = +1|s_1 = H, s_2 = U) = \frac{Pr(s_1 = H, s_2 = U|\theta = +1)Pr(\theta = +1)}{Pr(s_1 = H, s_2 = U)}$$

$$= \frac{p_C q}{p_C(2q - 1) + (1 - q)}. \tag{A15}$$

When s_2 is informative ($q > 1/2$), this probability exceeds p_C. When s_2 does not confirm s_1, the player does not become overconfident, so

$$Pr(\theta = +1|s_1 = H, s_2 = D) = \frac{Pr(s_1 = H, s_2 = D|\theta = +1)Pr(\theta = +1)}{Pr(s_1 = H, s_2 = D)}$$

$$= \frac{p(1 - q)}{p(1 - q) + q(1 - p)}. \tag{A16}$$

When evaluated with an informative signal s_2 ($q > 1/2$), this probability is less than p. With a risk neutral player, the price of the asset with value θ can be calculated linearly using the above probabilities. The price at time 0 (P_0) is, by definition, equal to 0. As θ can take on a value of +1 or −1, the price is $(\rho)(+1) + (1 - \rho)(-1)$ or, $2\rho - 1$, where ρ is the probability that θ is +1.

$$P_1|_{s_1 = H} = -P_1|_{s_1 = L} = 2Pr(\theta = +1|s_1 = H) - 1 = 2p - 1 \tag{A17}$$

$$P_2|_{s_1 = H, s_2 = U} = -P_2|_{s_1 = H, s_2 = D} = 2Pr(\theta = +1|s_1 = H, s_2 = U) - 1$$

$$= \frac{p_C + q - 1}{p_C(2q - 1) + (1 - q)} \tag{A18}$$

$$P_2|_{s_1 = H, s_2 = D} = -P_2|_{s_1 = H, s_2 = U} = 2Pr(\theta = +1|s_1 = H, s_2 = D) - 1$$

$$= \frac{p - q}{p + q - 2pq}. \tag{A19}$$

The price changes are $\Delta P_1 = P_1 - P_0 = P_1$ and $\Delta P_2 = P_2 - P_1$. $E[P_1] = 0$, so $\text{cov}(\Delta P_1, \Delta P_2) = E[\Delta P_1 \Delta P_2]$. The probabilities of the eight possible outcomes are:

$$Pr(\theta = +1, s_1 = H, s_2 = U) = Pr(\theta = -1, s_1 = L, s_2 = D) = pq/2 \tag{A20}$$

$$Pr(\theta = -1, s_1 = H, s_2 = U) = Pr(\theta = +1, s_1 = L, s_2 = D)$$
$$= (1 - p)(1 - q)/2 \tag{A21}$$

$$Pr(\theta = +1, s_1 = H, s_2 = D) = Pr(\theta = -1, s_1 = L, s_2 = U) = p(1 - q)/2 \tag{A22}$$

$$Pr(\theta = -1, s_1 = H, s_2 = D) = Pr(\theta = +1, s_1 = L, s_2 = U) = (1 - p)q/2. \tag{A23}$$

The product $\Delta P_1 \Delta P_2$ can only take on two values, based upon the various signal combinations:

$$X \equiv [\Delta P_1 \Delta P_2]_{s_1 = H, s_2 = U} = [\Delta P_1 \Delta P_2]_{s_1 = L, s_2 = D}$$

$$= (2p - 1)\left(\frac{p_C + q - 1}{p_C(2q - 1) + (1 - q)} - (2p - 1) \right). \quad (A24)$$

$$Y \equiv [\Delta P_1 \Delta P_2]_{s_1 = H, s_2 = D} = [\Delta P_1 \Delta P_2]_{s_1 = L, s_2 = U}$$

$$= (2p - 1)\left(\frac{p - q}{p + q - 2p} - (2p - 1) \right). \quad (A25)$$

Combining, $E[\Delta P_1 \Delta P_2]$ can be written as $(1 - a)X + aY$, where $a = p + q - 2pq$. After some calculation, the two components of this expression become:

$$(1 - a)X = \frac{2(2p - 1)(2pq - p - q + 1)(p_C p + p_C q + pq - 2p_C pq - p)}{p_C(2q - 1) + (1 - q)} \quad (A26)$$

$$aY = 2p(2q - 1)(2p - 1)(p - 1). \quad (A27)$$

Combining these two terms and a great deal of factoring produces the final result,

$$E[\Delta P_1 \Delta P_2] = \frac{2q(2p - 1)(p_C - p)(1 - q)}{p_C(2q - 1) + (1 - q)} > 0. \quad (A28)$$

When there is no overconfidence ($p_C = p$) this expression is zero and price changes are uncorrelated.

A Second Noisy Public Signal

The model so far shows that overreaction can be exaggerated by a possible rise in confidence triggered by a noisy public signal. We now add a second noisy public signal to consider whether correction of mispricing is gradual. Signal $s_{3'}$ follows s_2 and can take on values G or B. The precision of this signal is as follows:

$$Pr(s_{3'} = G | \theta = +1) = r = Pr(s_{3'} = B | \theta = -1). \quad (A29)$$

This signal does not affect confidence. If the player becomes overconfident (and replaces p with p_C) after s_2, then the player will continue to use p_C as his measure of the precision of s_1, regardless of whether $s_{3'}$ confirms s_1. As there are two possible prices after the first signal and four possible prices after the second, there are eight possible prices after observation of the third signal. As above, by symmetry, only half of these prices need to be calculated. Using the conditional probabilities, the period three prices are:

$$P_{3'}\big|_{s_1=H,s_2=U,s_{3'}=G} = \frac{p_C qr - (1-p_C)(1-q)(1-r)}{p_C qr + (1-p_C)(1-q)(1-r)}; \tag{A30}$$

$$P_{3'}\big|_{s_1=H,s_2=U,s_{3'}=B} = \frac{p_C q(1-r) - (1-p_C)(1-q)r}{p_C q(1-r) + (1-p_C)(1-q)r}; \tag{A31}$$

$$P_{3'}\big|_{s_1=H,s_2=D,s_{3'}=G} = \frac{p(1-q)r - (1-p)q(1-r)}{p(1-q)r + (1-p)q(1-r)}; \tag{A32}$$

$$P_{3'}\big|_{s_1=H,s_2=D,s_{3'}=B} = \frac{p(1-q)(1-r) - (1-p)qr}{p(1-q)(1-r) + (1-p)qr}. \tag{A33}$$

With two possible values for θ, there are now sixteen possible sets of $\{\theta, s_1, s_2, s_3\}$ realizations. Only $\{s_1, s_2, s_3\}$ are observed by the player, resulting in eight sets of possible signal realizations. When calculating the covariances of price changes, only half of these realizations can result in unique products of price changes, so we define

$$A_{ij} \equiv \Delta P_i \Delta P_j\big|_{H,U,G} = \Delta P_i \Delta P_j\big|_{L,D,B}; \tag{A34}$$

$$B_{ij} \equiv \Delta P_i \Delta P_j\big|_{H,U,B} = \Delta P_i \Delta P_j\big|_{L,D,G}; \tag{A35}$$

$$C_{ij} \equiv \Delta P_i \Delta P_j\big|_{H,D,G} = \Delta P_i \Delta P_j\big|_{L,U,B}; \tag{A36}$$

$$D_{ij} \equiv \Delta P_i \Delta P_j\big|_{H,D,B} = \Delta P_i \Delta P_j\big|_{L,U,G}. \tag{A37}$$

Each of these four possible products must then be weighted by their probability of occurrence to calculate the expected value of the products of the price changes (the expected value of each price is zero). The weights for the A_{ij} component of covariance are:

$$Pr(H, U, G|\theta = +1) + Pr(H, U, G|\theta = -1) = pqr/2 \atop + (1-p)(1-q)(1-r)/2, \tag{A38}$$

$$Pr(L, D, B|\theta = -1) + Pr(L, D, B|\theta = -1) = pqr/2 \atop + (1-p)(1-q)(1-r)/2. \tag{A39}$$

Proceeding in this manner, the covariances are:

$$\begin{aligned}
E[\Delta P_i \Delta P_j] = {}& [pqr + (1-p)(1-q)(1-r)]A_{ij} + [pq(1-r) \\
& + (1-p)(1-q)r]B_{ij} \\
& + [p(1-q)r + (1-p)q(1-r)]C_{ij} + [p(1-q)(1-r) \\
& + (1-p)qr]D_{ij}.
\end{aligned} \tag{A40}$$

(Earlier calculations of $E[\Delta P_1 \Delta P_2]$ had $A_{12} = B_{12} = X$ and $C_{12} = D_{12} = Y$, with the r and $1 - r$ factors from $s_{3'}$ summing to one.) To simplify the algebra, temporarily let all signals have the same precision (i.e., $q = r = p$), with p_C replacing p as the perceived precision of the first signal if overconfidence occurs. Direct calculation of the covariances then shows that

$$E[\Delta P_1 \Delta P_2]_{r=q=p} = \frac{2p(1-p)(2p-1)(p_C - p)}{p_C(2p-1) + (1-p)} > 0; \tag{A41}$$

$$E[\Delta P_1 \Delta P_{3'}]_{r=q=p} = \frac{2pp_C(p-1)(p_C - p)(1-p_C)(2p-1)^3}{[p_C(2p-1)+1-p][p_C(2p-1)+(1-p)^2]} < 0; \tag{A42}$$

$$E[\Delta P_2 \Delta P_{3'}]_{r=q=p} = \frac{4p^2 p_C (p-1)^2 (p_C - p)(p_C - 1)(2p-1)^2(2p_C - 1)}{[p_C(2p-1)+1-p]^2 [p_C(2p-1)+(1-p)^2]} < 0. \tag{A43}$$

By direct comparison, $E[\Delta P_1 \Delta P_2]_{r=q=p}$ and $E[\Delta P_2 \Delta P_{3'}]_{r=q=p}$ are related by:

$$E[\Delta P_2 \Delta P_{3'}]_{r=q=p} = -\frac{2p(1-p)p_C(1-p_C)(2p-1)(2p_C - 1)}{[p_C(2p-1)+(1-p)][p_C(2p-1)+(1-p)^2]} E[\Delta P_1 \Delta P_2]_{r=q=p}, \tag{A44}$$

so the covariance between the date 2 and 3 price changes is negatively proportional to the covariance of the date 1 and 2 price changes. Consider the numerator N of the proportionality factor. The first three components, $2p(1-p)$, are maximized when $p = 1/2$ while the next two components, $p_C(1 - p_C)$, are maximized when $p_C = 1/2$. Since the last two components satisfy $(2p - 1)(2p_C - 1) < 1$, the $N \leq 1/8$. In the denominator D, the expression $p_C(2p-1) + (1-p)$ is minimized when $p_C = p = 1/2$, resulting in a minimum of $1/2$. The second component of D is similarly minimized when $p_C = p = 1/2$, resulting in a minimum of $1/4$. So $D \geq 1/8$. Since $N \leq 1/8$, the ratio $N/D \leq 1$. Therefore, the negative covariance between date two and date three price changes must be, in absolute value, less than or equal to the positive covariance between period one and period two price changes, resulting in an overall one-period covariance that is positive.

When $q = r$ differs from p, direct calculation of covariances shows:

$$E[\Delta P_1 \Delta P_2]_{r=q} > 0; \tag{A45}$$

$$E[\Delta P_1 \Delta P_{3'}]_{r=q} < 0; \tag{A46}$$

$$E[\Delta P_2 \Delta P_{3'}]_{r=q} < 0. \tag{A47}$$

Now let the signal $s_{3'}$ have a precision of r that differs from both precisions of p and q. Proceeding as above, the covariance satisfy

$$E[\Delta P_1 \Delta P_2] > 0; \tag{A48}$$

$$E[\Delta P_1 \Delta P_{3'}] < 0; \tag{A49}$$

$$E[\Delta P_2 \Delta P_{3'}] < 0; \tag{A50}$$

$$E[\Delta P_{3'} \Delta P_3] > 0; \tag{A51}$$

$$E[\Delta P_1 \Delta P_3] < 0, \tag{A52}$$

The magnitude of $E[\Delta P_2 \Delta P_{3'}]$ varies nonmonotonically with q. As r rises (the precision of $s_{3'}$ is increased), direct calculation shows that $E[\Delta P_2 \Delta P_{3'}]$ becomes more negative (increases in absolute value). As $r \to 0.5$, this covariance approaches zero. Thus, when the second noisy public signal is not very informative, this negative single-lag covariance becomes arbitrarily small in absolute value.

Confidence increases when s_2 confirms s_1, but its effects are mitigated as s_2 becomes more informative. Thus, an increase in the precision of s_2 has an ambiguous effect on $E[\Delta P_2 \Delta P_{3'}]$. This increase results in a greater likelihood of overconfidence occurring, yet also places greater, rational, confidence in s_2 itself, yielding less leverage to the effects of overconfidence. (At the extreme, a value of q equal to one yields the greatest chances of s_2 confirming s_1 yet results in zero values for all covariances as the perfect information of s_2 entirely determines all subsequent prices.) Based on simulation, it appears that the greater information resulting from higher values of q tends overshadow the increased likelihood of overconfidence, resulting in generally lower absolute values for $E[\Delta P_2 \Delta P_{3'}]$.

Larger values of r, the precision of $s_{3'}$, result in more negative values of $E[\Delta P_2 \Delta P_{3'}]$. In this case, a more informative second noisy public signal can only place less weight on previous signals and result in a stronger correction of the previous overreaction. Thus, the final one-period covariance is more negative as the precision of $s_{3'}$ rises.

REFERENCES

Admati, Anat, and Paul Pfleiderer, 1988, A theory of intraday patterns: Volume and price variability, *Review of Financial Studies* 1, 3–40.

Ahlers, David, and Josef Lakonishok, 1983, A study of economists' consensus forecasts, *Management Science* 29, 1113–25.

Alpert, Murray, and Howard Raiffa, 1982, A progress report on the training of probability assessors, in Daniel Kahneman, Paul Slovic, and Amos Tversky (ed.), *Judgement under Uncertainty: Heuristics and Biases*, Cambridge University Press.

Anderson, Thomas W., 1984, *An Introduction to Multivariate Statistical Analysis*, Wiley.

Barberis, Nicholas, Andrei Shleifer, and Robert Vishny, 1998, A model of investor sentiment, *Journal of Financial Economics* 49, 307–43.

Batchelor, Roy, and Parmi Dua, 1992, Conservatism and consensus-seeking among economic forecasters, *Journal of Forecasting* 11, 169–81.

Baumann, Andrea O., Raisa B. Deber, and Gail G. Thompson, 1991, Overconfidence among physicians and nurses: The micro-certainty, macro-uncertainty phenomenon, *Social Science & Medicine* 32, 167–74.

Bem, Daryl J., 1965, An experimental analysis of self-persuasion, *Journal of Experimental Social Psychology* 1, 199–218.

Benos, Alexandros, 1998, Aggressiveness and survival of overconfident traders, *Journal of Financial Markets* 1, 353–83.

Black, Fischer, 1986, Noise, *Journal of Finance* 41, 529–43.

Brav, Alon, and Paul A. Gompers, 1997, Myth or reality? The long-run underperformance of initial public offerings: Evidence from venture and nonventure capital-backed companies, *Journal of Finance* 52, 1791–1821.

Caballé, Jordi, and József Sákovics, 1996, Overconfident speculation with imperfect competition, Working Paper, Universitat Autonoma de Barcelona.

Campbell, John Y., and John H. Cochrane, 1999, By force of habit: A consumption based explanation of aggregate stock market behavior, *Journal of Political Economy* 107, 205–51.

Campbell, John Y., and Albert S. Kyle, 1993, Smart money, noise trading, and stock price behaviour, *Review of Economic Studies* 60, 1–34.

Christensen-Szalanski, Jay J., and James B. Bushyhead, 1981, Physicians' use of probabilistic information in a real clinical setting, *Journal of Experimental Psychology: Human Perception and Performance* 7, 928–35.

Cooper, Arnold C., Carolyn W. Woo, and William C. Dunkelberg, 1988, Entrepeneurs' perceived chances for success, *Journal of Business Venturing* 3, 97–108.

Cornett, Marcia Millon, Hamid Mehran, and Hassann Tehranian, 1998, Are financial markets overly optimistic about the prospects of firms that issue equity? Evidence from voluntary versus involuntary equity issuance by banks, *Journal of Finance* 53, 2139–60.

Daniel, Kent D., David Hirshleifer, and Avanidhar Subrahmanyam, 1998, Investor psychology and security market under- and over-reactions, *Journal of Finance* 53, 1839–86.

————, 2001, Overconfidence, arbitrage, and equilibrium asset pricing, *Journal of Finance* 56, 921–65.

Daniel, Kent D., and Sheridan Titman, 1999, Market efficiency in an irrational world, *Financial Analysts' Journal* 55, 28–40.

————, and John Wei, 2001, Cross-sectional variation in common stock returns in Japan, *Journal of Finance.*

DeBondt, Werner F. M., 1991, What do economists know about the stock market?, *Journal of Portfolio Management* 17, 84–91.

————, and Richard H. Thaler, 1990, Do security analysts overreact?, *American Economic Review* 80, 52–57.

————, 1995, Financial decision-making in markets and firms: A behavioral perspective, in Robert A. Jarrow, Voijslav Maksimovic, and William T. Ziemba (ed.), *Finance, Handbooks in Operations Research and Management Science,* vol. 9, 385–410, North Holland.

DeLong, J. Bradford, Andrei Shleifer, Lawrence Summers, and Robert J. Waldmann, 1990a, Noise trader risk in financial markets, *Journal of Political Economy* 98, 703–738.

————, 1990b, Positive feedback investment strategies and destabilizing rational speculation, *Journal of Finance* 45, 375–95.

————, 1991, The survival of noise traders in financial markets, *Journal of Business* 64, 1–20.

Einhorn, Hillel J., 1980, Overconfidence in judgment, *New Directions for Methodology of Social and Behavioral Science* 4, 1–16.

Elton, Edwin J., Martin J. Gruber, and Mustafa N. Gultekin, 1984, Professional expectations: Accuracy and diagnosis of errors, *Journal of Financial and Quantitative Analysis* 19, 351–63.

Fama, Eugene F., 1998, Market efficiency, long-term returns and behavioral finance, *Journal of Financial Economics* 49.

Fama, Eugene F., and Kenneth R. French, 1988, Permanent and temporary components of stock prices, *Journal of Political Economy* 96, 246–73.

Fischhoff, Baruch, Paul Slovic, and Sarah Lichtenstein, 1977, Knowing with certainty: the appropriateness of extreme confidence, *Journal of Experimental Psychology* 3, 552–64.

Fischoff, Baruch, 1982, For those condemned to study the past: Heuristics and biases in hindsight, in Daniel Kahneman, Paul Slovic, and Amos Tversky (ed.), *Judgement under Uncertainty: Heuristics and Biases,* Cambridge University Press.

Froot, Kenneth, and Jeffery A. Frankel, 1989, Forward discount bias: Is it an exchange risk premium?, *Quarterly Journal of Economics* 104, 139–61.

Gervais, Simon, and Terrance Odean, 2001, Learning to be overconfident, *Review of Financial Studies* 14, 1–27.

Glosten, Lawrence R., and Paul R. Milgrom, 1985, Bid, ask and transaction prices in a specialist market with heterogeneously informed traders, *Journal of Financial Economics* 14, 71–100.

Greenwald, Anthony G., 1980, The totalitarian ego: Fabrication and revision of personal history, *American Psychologist* 3, 603–18.

Griffin, Dale, and Amos Tversky, 1992, The weighing of evidence and the determinants of overconfidence, *Cognitive Psychology* 24, 411–35.

Grossman, Sanford J., and Joseph E. Stiglitz, 1980, On the impossibility of informationally efficient markets, *American Economic Review* 70, 393–408.

Harris, Milton and Artur Raviv, 1985, A sequential signalling model of convertible debt call policy, *Journal of Finance* 40, 1263–81.

Haugen, Robert A. and Nardin L. Baker, 1996, Commonality in the determinants of expected stock returns, *Journal of Financial Economics* 41, 401–39.

Hirshleifer, David, 2001, Investor psychology and asset pricing, *Journal of Finance* 64, 1533–97.

Hirshleifer, David, Avanidhar Subrahmanyam, and Sheridan Titman, 1994, Security analysis and trading patterns when some investors receive information before others, *Journal of Finance* 49, 1665–98.

Hong, Harrison, and Jeremy C. Stein, 1999, A unified theory of underreaction, momentum trading and overreaction in asset markets, *Journal of Finance* 54, 2143–84.

Hovakimian, Armen, Tim Opler, and Sheridan Titman, 2001, The debt-equity choice, *Journal of Financial and Quantitative Analysis* 36, 1–24.

Jain, Prem C., and Omesh Kini, 1994, The post-issue operating performance of IPO firms, *Journal of Finance* 49, 1699–1726.

Jegadeesh, Narasimhan, and Sheridan Titman, 1993, Returns to buying winners and selling losers: Implications for stock market efficiency, *Journal of Finance* 48, 65–91.

Jung, Kooyul, Yong-Cheol Kim, and René M. Stulz, 1996, Timing, investment opportunities, managerial discretion, and the security issue decision, *Journal of Financial Economics* 42, 159–85.

Kidd, John B., 1970, The utilization of subjective probabilities in production planning, *Acta Psychologica* 34, 338–47.

Kitayama, Shinobu, H. Takagi, and Hisaya Matsumoto, 1995, Causal attribution of success and failure: Cultural psychology of the Japanese self, *Japanese Psychological Review* 38, 247–80.

Kyle, Albert S., 1985, Continuous auctions and insider trading, *Econometrica* 53, 1315–35.

Kyle, Albert, and F. Albert Wang, 1997, Speculation duopoly with agreement to disagree: Can overconfidence survive the market test?, *Journal of Finance* 52, 2073–90.

Langer, Ellen J., and Jane Roth, 1975, Heads I win tails it's chance: The illusion of control as a function of the sequence of outcomes in a purely chance task, *Journal of Personality and Social Psychology* 32, 951–55.

Lichtenstein, Sarah, Baruch Fischoff, and Lawrence Phillips, 1982, Calibration of probabilities: The state of the art to 1980, in Daniel Kahneman, Paul Slovic, and Amos Tversky (ed.), *Judgement under Uncertainty: Heuristics and Biases,* 306–34, Cambridge University Press.

Ljungqvist, Alexander P., 1997, Pricing initial public offerings: Further evidence from Germany, *European Economic Review* 41, 1309–20.

Loughran, Tim, and Jay Ritter, 1997, The operating performance of firms conducting seasoned equity offerings, *The Journal of Finance* 52, 1823–50.

Loughran, Tim, Jay Ritter, and Kristian Rydqvist, 1994, Initial public offerings: International insights, *Pacific Basin Finance Journal* 2, 165–99.

MacKinlay, A. Craig, 1995, Multifactor models do not explain deviations from the CAPM, *Journal of Financial Economics* 38, 3–28.

Mikkelson, W., M. Megan Partch, and Kshiti Shah, 1997, Ownership and operating performance of companies that go public, *Journal of Financial Economics* 44, 281–307.

Miller, Dale T., and Michael Ross, 1975, Self-serving bias in attribution of causality: Fact or fiction?, *Psychological Bulletin* 82, 213–25.

Neale, Margaret, and Max Bazerman, 1990, *Cognition and Rationality in Negotiation*, Free Press.

Odean, Terrance, 1998, Volume, volatility, price and profit when all traders are above average, *Journal of Finance* 53, 1887–1934.

Oskamp, Stuart, 1965, Overconfidence in case study judgements, *Journal of Consulting Psychology* 29, 261–65.

Pagano, Marco, Fabio Panetta, and Luigi Zingales, 1998, Why do companies go public? an empirical analysis, *Journal of Finance* 53, 27–64.

Rees, William P., 1996, The arrival rate of initial public offers in the UK, Working Paper 96/8, Department of Accounting and Finance, University of Glasgow.

Ritter, Jay R., 1991, The long-run performance of initial public offerings, *Journal of Finance* 46, 3–27.

Russo, J. Edward, and Paul J. H. Schoemaker, 1992, Managing overconfidence, *Sloan Management Review* 33, 7–17.

Shefrin, Hersh, 1997, Behavioral option pricing, Working Paper, Santa Clara University.

Shiller, Robert J., 1984, Stock prices and social dynamics, *Brookings Papers on Economic Activity Review* 2, 457–98.

Stael von Holstein, C., 1972, Probabilistic forecasting: An experiment related to the stock market, *Organizational Behavior and Human Performance* 8, 139–58.

Svenson, Ola, 1981, Are we all less risky and more skillful than our fellow drivers?, *Acta Psychologica* 47, 143–48.

Taylor, Shelley E., and Jonathan D. Brown, 1988, Illusion and well-being: A social psychological perspective on mental health, *Psychological Bulletin* 103, 193–210.

Teoh, Siew Hong, T. J. Wong, and Gita Rao, 1998, Are accruals during an initial public offering opportunistic?, *Review of Accounting Studies* 3, 175–208.

Wagenaar, Willem, and Gideoan Keren, 1986, Does the expert know? The reliability of predictions and confidence ratios of experts, in Erik Hollnagel, Giuseppe Mancini, and David D. Woods (ed.), *Intelligent Decision Support in Process Environment*, Springer.

Wang, F. Albert, 1998, Strategic trading, asymmetric information and heterogeneous prior beliefs, *Journal of Financial Markets* 1, 321–52.

Wilson, Pete, 1986, The relative information contents of accruals and cash flows: Combined evidence of the earnings announcement and annual report release date, *Journal of Accounting Research* Supplement, 165–200.

Yates, J. Frank, 1990, *Judgement and Decision Making*, Prentice Hall.

Chapter 14

A UNIFIED THEORY OF UNDERREACTION, MOMENTUM TRADING, AND OVERREACTION IN ASSET MARKETS

Harrison Hong and Jeremy C. Stein

OVER THE LAST several years, a large volume of empirical work has documented a variety of ways in which asset returns can be predicted based on publicly available information. Although different studies have used a host of different predictive variables, many of the results can be thought of as belonging to one of two broad categories of phenomena. On the one hand, returns appear to exhibit continuation, or momentum, in the short to medium run. On the other hand, there is also a tendency toward reversals, or fundamental reversion, in the long run.

It is becoming increasingly clear that traditional asset-pricing models—such as the capital asset pricing model (CAPM) of Sharpe (1964) and Lintner (1965), Ross's (1976) arbitrage pricing theory (APT) or Merton's (1973) intertemporal capital asset pricing model (ICAPM)—have a hard time explaining the growing set of stylized facts. In the context of these models, all of the predictable patterns in asset returns, at both short and long horizons, must ultimately be traced to differences in loadings on economically meaningful risk factors. And there is little affirmative evidence at this point to suggest that this can be done.

As an alternative to these traditional models, many are turning to "behavioral" theories, where "behavioral" can be broadly construed as involving some departure from the classical assumptions of strict rationality and unlimited computational capacity on the part of investors. But the difficulty with this approach is that there are a potentially huge number of such departures that one might entertain, so it is hard to know where to start.

This research is supported by the National Science Foundation and the Finance Research Center at MIT. We are grateful to Denis Gromb, René Stulz, an anonymous referee, and seminar participants at MIT, Michigan, Wharton, Duke, UCLA, Berkeley, Stanford, and Illinois for helpful comments and suggestions. Thanks also to Melissa Cunniffe for help in preparing the manuscript. This is a slightly revised version of a paper of the same title that appeared in the *Journal of Finance* in December 1999. It also incorporates some material from our joint paper with Terence Lim "Bad news Travels Slowly: Size, Analyst Coverage, and the Profitability of Momentum Strategies."

In order to impose some discipline on the process, it is useful to articulate the criteria that a new theory should be expected to satisfy. There seems to be broad agreement that to be successful, any candidate theory should, at a minimum: (1) rest on assumptions about investor behavior that are either a priori plausible or consistent with casual observation; (2) explain the existing evidence in a parsimonious and unified way; and 3) make a number of further predictions which can be subject to "out-of sample" testing and which are ultimately validated. Fama (1998, p. 284) puts particular emphasis on the latter two criteria: "Following the standard scientific rule, market efficiency can only be replaced by a better specific model of price formation, itself potentially rejectable by empirical tests. Any alternative model has a daunting task. It must specify biases on information processing that cause the same investors to under-react to some types of events and over-react to others."

A couple of recent papers take up this challenge. Both Barberis, Shleifer, and Vishny (BSV) (1998) and Daniel, Hirshleifer, and Subrahmanyam (DHS) (1998) assume that prices are driven by a single representative agent, and then posit a small number of cognitive biases that this representative agent might have. They then investigate the extent to which these biases are sufficient to simultaneously deliver both short-horizon continuation and long-horizon reversals.[1]

In this chapter, we pursue the same goal as BSV and DHS, that of building a unified behavioral model. However, we adopt a fundamentally different approach. Rather than trying to say much about the psychology of the representative agent, our emphasis is on the interaction between heterogeneous agents. To put it loosely, less of the action in our model comes from particular cognitive biases that we ascribe to individual traders, and more of it comes from the way these traders interact with one another.

More specifically, our model features two types of agents, whom we term "newswatchers" and "momentum traders." Neither type is fully rational in the usual sense. Rather, each is boundedly rational, with the bounded rationality being of a simple form: each type of agent is only able to "process" some subset of the available public information.[2] The newswatchers make forecasts based on signals that they privately observe about future fundamentals; their limitation is that they do not condition on current or past prices. Momentum traders, in contrast, do condition on past price changes. However, their limitation is that their forecasts must be "simple" (i.e., univariate) functions of the history of past prices.[3]

---

[1] We have more to say about these and other related papers in section 4 below.

[2] Although the model is simpler with just these two types of traders, the results are robust to the inclusion of a set of risk-averse, fully rational arbitrageurs, as shown in section 2.B.

[3] The constraints that we put on traders' information-processing abilities are arguably not as well motivated by the experimental psychology literature as the biases in BSV or DHS, and so may appear to be more ad hoc. However, they generate new and clear-cut asset-pricing predictions, some of which have already been supported in recent tests. See section 3 below.

In addition to imposing these two constraints on the information-processing abilities of our traders, we make one further assumption, which is more orthodox in nature: private information diffuses gradually across the newswatcher population. All of our conclusions then flow from these three key assumptions. We begin by showing that when only newswatchers are active, prices adjust slowly to new information—there is underreaction but never overreaction. As is made clear later, this result follows naturally from combining gradual information diffusion with the assumption that newswatchers do not extract information from prices.

Next, we add the momentum traders. It is tempting to conjecture that because the momentum traders *can* condition on past prices, they arbitrage away any underreaction left behind by the newswatchers; with sufficient risk tolerance, one might expect that they would force the market to become approximately efficient. However, it turns out that this intuition is incomplete, if momentum traders are limited to simple strategies. For example, suppose that a momentum trader at time t must base his trade only on the price change over some prior interval, say from $t-2$ to $t-1$. We show that in this case, momentum traders' attempts to profit from the underreaction caused by newswatchers lead to a perverse outcome: The initial reaction of prices in the direction of fundamentals is indeed accelerated, but this comes at the expense of creating an eventual overreaction to any news. This is true even when momentum traders are risk-neutral.

Again, the key to this result is the assumption that momentum traders use simple strategies—that is, do not condition on all public information. Continuing with the example, if a momentum trader's order at time t is restricted to being a function of just the price change from $t-2$ to $t-1$, it is clear that it must be an increasing function. *On average*, this simple trend-chasing strategy makes money. But if one could condition on more information, it would become apparent that the strategy does better in some circumstances than in others. In particular, the strategy earns the bulk of its profits early in the "momentum cycle"—by which we mean shortly after substantial news has arrived to the newswatchers—and loses money late in the cycle, by which time prices have already overshot long-run equilibrium values.

To see this point, suppose that there is a single dose of good news at time t and no change in fundamentals after that. The newswatchers cause prices to jump at time t, but not far enough, so that they are still below their long-run values. At time $t+1$ there is a round of momentum purchases, and those momentum buyers who get in at this time make money. But this round of momentum trading creates a further price increase, which sets off more momentum buying, and so on. Later momentum buyers—that is, those buying at $t+i$ for some i—lose money, because they get in at a price above the long-run equilibrium.

Thus a crucial insight is that "early" momentum buyers impose a negative externality on "late" momentum buyers.[4] Ideally, one uses a momentum strategy because a price increase signals that there is good news about fundamentals out there that is not yet fully incorporated into prices. But sometimes, a price increase is the result not of news but just of previous rounds of momentum trade. Because momentum traders cannot directly condition on whether or not news has recently arrived, they do not know whether they are early or late in the cycle. Hence they must live with this externality, and accept the fact that sometimes they buy when earlier rounds of momentum trading have pushed prices past long-run equilibrium values.

Although we make two distinct bounded-rationality assumptions, our model can be said to "unify" underreaction and overreaction in the following sense. We begin by modeling a tendency for one group of traders to underreact to private information. We then show that when a second group of traders tries to exploit this underreaction with a simple arbitrage strategy, they only partially eliminate it and, in so doing, create an excessive momentum in prices that inevitably culminates in overreaction. Thus, the very existence of underreaction sows the seeds for overreaction, by making it profitable for momentum traders to enter the market. Or, said differently, the unity lies in the fact that our model gets both underreaction and overreaction out of just one primitive type of shock: gradually diffusing news about fundamentals. There are no other exogenous shocks to investor sentiment and no liquidity-motivated trades.

In what follows, we develop a simple infinite-horizon model that captures these ideas. In section 1, we present and solve the basic model, and do a number of comparative statics experiments. Section 2 contains several extensions. In section 3, we draw out the model's empirical implications. Section 4 discusses related work, and section 5 concludes.

1. THE MODEL

A. Price Formation with Newswatchers Only

As mentioned above, our model features two classes of traders, newswatchers, and momentum traders. We begin by describing how the model works when only the newswatchers are present. At every time t, the newswatchers trade claims on a risky asset. This asset pays a single liquidating dividend at some later time t. The ultimate value of this liquidating dividend can be written as: $D_T = D_0 + \sum_{j=0}^{T} \varepsilon_j$, where all the ε's are independently distributed, mean-zero normal random variables with variance σ^2. Throughout,

---

[4] As we discuss below, this "momentum externality" is reminiscent of the herding models of Banerjee (1992), Bikhchadani, Hirshleifer, and Welch (1992), and Scharfstein and Stein (1990).

we consider the limiting case where t goes to infinity. This simplifies matters by allowing us to focus on steady-state trading strategies—that is, strategies that do not depend on how close we are to the terminal date.[5]

In order to capture the idea that information moves gradually across the newswatcher population, we divide this population into z equal-sized groups. We also assume that every dividend innovation ε_j can be decomposed into z independent subinnovations, each with the same variance σ^2/z: $\varepsilon_j = \varepsilon_j^1 + \cdots + \varepsilon_j^z$. The timing of information release is then as follows. At time t, news about ε_{t+z-1} begins to spread. Specifically, at time t, newswatcher group 1 observes ε_{t+z-1}^1, group 2 observes ε_{t+z-1}^2, and so forth, through group z, which observes ε_{t+z-1}^z. Thus at time t, each subinnovation of ε_{t+z-1} has been seen by a fraction $1/z$ of the total population.

Next, at time $t + 1$, the groups "rotate," so that group 1 now observes ε_{t+z-1}^2, group 2 observes ε_{t+z-1}^3, and so forth, through group z, which now observes ε_{t+z-1}^1. Thus at time $t + 1$ the information has spread further, and each subinnovation of ε_{t+z-1} has been seen by a fraction $2/z$ of the total population. This rotation process continues until time $t + z - 1$, at which point every one of the z groups has directly observed each of the subinnovations that comprise ε_{t+z-1}. So ε_{t+z-1} has become totally public by time $t + z - 1$. Although this formulation may seem unnecessarily awkward, the rotation feature is useful, because it implies that even as information moves slowly across the population, everybody is on average equally well-informed.[6] This symmetry makes it transparently simple to solve for prices, as is seen momentarily.

In this context, the parameter z can be thought of as a proxy for the (linear) rate of information flow—higher values of z imply slower information diffusion. Of course, the notion that information spreads slowly is more appropriate for some purposes than others. In particular, this construct is fine if our goal is to capture the sort of underreaction that shows up empirically as unconditional positive correlation in returns at short horizons. However, if we are also interested in capturing phenomena like postearnings-announcement drift—where there is apparently underreaction even to data that is made available to everyone simultaneously—we need to embellish the model. We discuss this embellishment later on; for now it is easiest to think of the model as only speaking to the unconditional evidence on underreaction.

---

[5] A somewhat more natural way to generate an infinite-horizon formulation might be to allow the asset to pay dividends every period. The only reason we push all the dividends out into the infinite future is for notational simplicity. In particular, when we consider the strategies of short-lived momentum traders below, our approach allows us to have these strategies depend only on momentum traders' forecasts of price changes, and we can ignore their forecasts of interim dividend payments.

[6] Contrast this with a simpler setting where group 1 always sees all of ε_{t+z-1} first, then group 2 sees it second, etc. In this case, group 1 newswatchers are better-informed than their peers.

All the newswatchers have constant absolute risk aversion (CARA) utility with the same risk-aversion parameter, and all live until the terminal date T. The riskless interest rate is normalized to zero, and the supply of the asset is fixed at Q. So far, all these assumptions are completely orthodox. We now make two that are less conventional. First, at every time t, newswatchers formulate their asset demands based on the static-optimization notion that they buy and hold until the liquidating dividend at time T.[7] Second, and more critically, while newswatchers can condition on the information sets described above, they *do not* condition on current or past prices. In other words, our equilibrium concept is a Walrasian equilibrium with private valuations, as opposed to a fully revealing rational expectations equilibrium.

As suggested in the introduction, these two unconventional assumptions can be motivated based on a simple form of bounded rationality. One can think of the newswatchers as having their hands full just figuring out the implications of the ε's for the terminal dividend D_T. This leaves them unable to also use current and past market prices to form more sophisticated forecasts of D_T (our second assumption); it also leaves them unable to make any forecasts of future price changes, and hence unable to implement dynamic strategies (our first assumption).

Given these assumptions, and the symmetry of our setup, the conditional variance of fundamentals is the same for all newswatchers, and the price at time t is given by:

$$P_t = D_t + \{(z-1)\,\varepsilon_{t+1} + (z-2)\,\varepsilon_{t+2} + \cdots\cdots + \varepsilon_{t+z-1}\}/z - \theta Q \qquad (1)$$

where θ is a function of newswatchers' risk aversion and the variance of the ε's. For simplicity, we normalize the risk aversion so that $\theta = 1$ hereafter. In words, Eq. (1) says that the new information works its way linearly into the price over z periods. This implies that there is positive serial correlation of returns over short horizons (of length less than z). Note also that prices never overshoot their long-run values, or equivalently, that there is never any negative serial correlation in returns at any horizon.

Even given the eminently plausible assumption that private information diffuses gradually across the population of newswatchers, the gradual-price-adjustment result in equation (1) hinges critically on the further assumption that newswatchers do not condition on prices. For if they did—and as long as Q is nonstochastic—the logic of Grossman (1976) would imply a fully revealing equilibrium, with a price P_t^*, following a random walk given by (for $\theta = 1$):[8]

$$P_t^* = D_{t+z-1} - Q \qquad (2)$$

---

[7] There is an element of time-inconsistency here, since in fact newswatchers may adjust their positions over time. Ignoring the dynamic nature of newswatcher strategies is more significant when we add momentum traders to the model, so we discuss this issue further in section 1.B.

[8] Strictly speaking, this result also requires that there be an initial "date 0" at which everybody is symmetrically informed.

We should therefore stress that we view the underreaction result embodied in Eq. (1) to be nothing more than a point of departure. As such, it raises an obvious next question: Even if newswatchers are too busy processing fundamental data to incorporate prices into their forecasts, can't some other group of traders focus exclusively on price-based forecasting, and in so doing generate an outcome close to the rational expectations equilibrium of Eq. (2)? It is to this central question that we turn next, by adding the momentum traders into the mix.

B. Adding Momentum Traders to the Model

Momentum traders also have CARA utility. Unlike the newswatchers, however, they have finite horizons. In particular, at every time t, a new generation of momentum traders enters the market. Every trader in this generation takes a position, and then holds this position for j periods—that is, until time $t + j$. For modeling purposes, we treat the momentum traders' horizon j as an exogenous parameter.

The momentum traders transact with the newswatchers by means of market orders. They submit quantity orders, not knowing the price at which these orders will be executed. The price is then determined by the competition among the newswatchers, who double as market-makers in this setup. Thus in deciding the size of their orders, the momentum traders at time t must try to predict $(P_{t+j} - P_t)$. To do so, they make forecasts based on past price changes. We assume that these forecasts take an especially simple form: The only conditioning variable is the cumulative price change over the past k periods, that is, $(P_{t-1} - P_{t-k-1})$.

As it turns out, the exact value of k is not that important, so in what follows we simplify things by setting $k = 1$, and using $(P_{t-1} - P_{t-2}) \equiv \Delta P_{t-1}$ as the time-t forecasting variable.[9] What is more significant is that we restrict the momentum traders to making *univariate* forecasts based on past price changes. If, in contrast, we allow them to make forecasts using n lags of price changes, *giving different weights* to each of the n lags, we suspect that for sufficiently large n, many of the results that we present below would go away. Again, the motivation is a crude notion of bounded rationality: momentum traders simply do not have the computational horsepower to run complicated multivariate regressions.

With $k = 1$, the order flow from generation-t momentum traders, F_t, is of the form:

$$F_t = A + \varphi \Delta P_{t-1} \tag{3}$$

where the constant A and the elasticity parameter φ have to be determined from optimization on the part of the momentum traders. This order flow

---

[9] In the NBER working paper version, we provide a detailed analysis of the comparative statics properties of the model with respect to k.

must be absorbed by the newswatchers. We assume that the newswatchers treat the order flow as an uninformative supply shock. This is consistent with our prior assumption that the newswatchers do not condition on prices. Given that the order flow is a linear function of past price changes, if we allowed the newswatchers to extract information from it, we would be indirectly allowing them to learn from prices.

To streamline things, the order flow from the newswatchers is the *only* source of supply variation in the model. Given that there are j generations of momentum traders in the market at any point in time, the aggregate supply S_t absorbed by the newswatchers is given by:

$$S_t = Q - \sum_{i=1}^{j} F_{t+1-i} = Q - jA - \sum_{i=1}^{j} \varphi \Delta P_{t-i} \qquad (4)$$

We continue to assume that, at any time t, the newswatchers act as if they buy and hold until the liquidating dividend at time T. This implies that prices are given exactly as in Eq. (1), except that the fixed supply Q is replaced by the variable S_t, yielding:

$$P_t = D_t + \{(z-1)\varepsilon_{t+1} + (z-2)\varepsilon_{t+2} + \cdots + \varepsilon_{t+z-1}\}/z - Q$$

$$+ jA + \sum_{i=1}^{j} \varphi \Delta P_{t-i} \qquad (5)$$

In most of the analysis, the constants Q and A play no role, so we disregard them when it is convenient to do so.

As noted previously, newswatchers' behavior is time-inconsistent. Although at time t they base their demands on the premise that they do not retrade, they violate this to the extent that they are active in later periods. We adopt this time-inconsistent shortcut because it dramatically simplifies the analysis. Otherwise, we face a complex dynamic programming problem, with newswatcher demands at time t depending not only on their forecasts of the liquidating dividend D_T, but also on their predictions for the entire future path of prices.

Two points can be offered in defense of this time-inconsistent simplification. First, it fits with the basic spirit of our approach, which is to have the newswatchers behave in a simple, boundedly rational fashion. Second, we have no reason to believe that it colors any of our important qualitative conclusions. Loosely speaking, we are closing down a "frontrunning" effect, whereby newswatchers buy more aggressively at time t in response to good news, since they know that the news will kick off a series of momentum trades and thereby drive prices up further over the next several periods.[10] Such frontrunning by newswatchers may speed the response of prices to information, thereby mitigating underreaction, but in our setup it can never wholly eliminate either underreaction or overreaction.[11]

[10] This sort of frontrunning effect is at the center of DeLong et al. (1990).
[11] See the NBER working paper version for a fuller treatment of this frontrunning issue.

C. *The Nature of Equilibrium*

With all of the assumptions in place, we are now ready to solve the model. The only task is to calculate the equilibrium value of φ. Disregarding constants, optimization on the part of the momentum traders implies:

$$\varphi \Delta P_{t-1} = \gamma E_M(P_{t+j} - P_t)/\text{var}_M(P_{t+j} - P_t) \tag{6}$$

where γ is the aggregate risk tolerance of the momentum traders, and E_M and var_M denote the mean and variance given their information, which is just ΔP_{t-1}. We can rewrite Eq. (6) as:

$$\varphi = \gamma \text{cov}(P_{t+j} - P_t, \Delta P_{t-1})/\{\text{var}(\Delta P)\text{var}_M(P_{t+j} - P_t)\} \tag{7}$$

The definition of equilibrium is a fixed point such that φ is given by Eq. (7), while at the same time price dynamics satisfy equation (5). We restrict ourselves to studying covariance-stationary equilibria. In the appendix, we prove that a necessary condition for a conjectured equilibrium process to be covarian *ce* stationary is that $|\varphi| < 1$. Such an equilibrium may not exist for arbitrary parameter values, and we are also unable to generically rule out the possibility of multiple equilibria. However, we prove in the appendix that existence is guaranteed so long as the risk tolerance γ of the momentum traders is sufficiently small, since this in turn ensures that $|\varphi|$ is sufficiently small. Moreover, detailed experimentation suggests that a unique covariance-stationary equilibrium does in fact exist for a large range of the parameter space.[12]

In general, it is difficult to solve the model in closed form, and we have to resort to a computational algorithm to find the fixed point. For an arbitrary set of parameter values, we always begin our numerical search for the fixed point at $j = 1$. Given this restriction, we can show that the condition $|\varphi| < 1$ is both necessary and sufficient for covariance-stationarity. We also start with a small value of risk tolerance and an initial guess for φ of zero. The solutions in this region of the parameter space are well-behaved. Using these solutions, we then move to other regions of the parameter space. This procedure ensures that if there are multiple covariance-stationary equilibria, we would always pick the one with the smallest value of φ. We also have a number of sensible checks for when we have moved outside the covariance-stationary region of the parameter space. These are described in the appendix.

Even without doing any computations, we can make several observations about the nature of equilibrium. First, we have:

---

[12] Our experiments suggest that we only run into existence problems when *both* the risk tolerance γ and the information-diffusion parameter z *simultaneously* become very large—even an infinite value of γ poses no problem so long as z is not too big. The intuition will become clearer when we do the comparative statics, but loosely speaking, the problem is this: as z gets large, momentum trading becomes more profitable. Combined with high risk tolerance, this can make momentum traders behave so aggressively that our $|\varphi| < 1$ condition is violated.

Lemma 1: In any covariance-stationary equilibrium, $\varphi > 0$. That is, momentum traders must rationally behave as trend-chasers.

The lemma is proved in the appendix, but it is trivially easy to see why $\varphi = 0$ cannot be an equilibrium. Suppose to the contrary it is. Then prices are given as in the all-newswatcher case in Eq. (1). And in this case, $\text{cov}(P_{t+j} - P_t, \Delta P_{t-1}) > 0$, so that Eq. (7) tells us that $\varphi > 0$, establishing a contradiction.

We are now in a position to make some qualitative statements about the dynamics of prices. First, let us consider the impulse response of prices to news shocks. The thought experiment here is as follows. At time t, there is a one-unit positive innovation ε_{t+z-1} that begins to diffuse among newswatchers. There are no further news shocks from that point on. What does the price path look like?

The answer can be seen by decomposing the price at any time into two components: that attributable to newswatchers, and that attributable to momentum traders. Newswatchers' aggregate estimate of D_T rises from time t to time $t + z - 1$, by which time they have completely incorporated the news shock into their forecasts. Thus by time $t + z - 1$, the price is just right in the absence of any order flow from momentum traders. But with $\varphi > 0$, any positive news shock must generate an initially positive impulse to momentum-trader order flow. Moreover, the cumulative order flow must be increasing until at least time $t + j$, since none of the momentum trades stimulated by the shock begin to be unwound until $t + j + 1$. This sort of reasoning leads to the following conclusions:

Proposition 1: In any covariance-stationary equilibrium, given a positive one-unit shock ε_{t+z-1} that first begins to diffuse among newswatchers at time t: (1) there is always overreaction, in the sense that the cumulative impulse response of prices peaks at a value that is strictly greater than one; (2) if the momentum traders' horizon j satisfies $j \geq z - 1$, the cumulative impulse response peaks at $t + j$, and then begins to decline, eventually converging to one; (3) if $j < z - 1$, the cumulative impulse response peaks no earlier than $t + j$, and eventually converges to one.

In addition to the impulse response function, it is also interesting to consider the autocovariances of prices at various horizons. We can develop some rough intuition about these autocovariances by considering the limiting case where the risk tolerance of the momentum traders γ goes to infinity. In this case, Eq. (7) implies that the equilibrium must have the property that $\text{cov}(P_{t+j} - P_t, \Delta P_{t-1}) = 0$. Expanding this expression, we can write:

$$\text{cov}(\Delta P_{t+1}, \Delta P_{t-1}) + \text{cov}(\Delta P_{t+2}, \Delta P_{t-1}) + \cdots + \text{cov}(\Delta P_{t+j}, \Delta P_{t-1}) = 0 \quad (8)$$

Eq. (8) allows us to state the following:

> **Proposition 2**: In any covariance-stationary equilibrium, if price changes
> are positively correlated at short horizons (e.g., if $\text{cov}(\Delta P_{t+1}, \Delta P_{t-1})$
> > 0), then with risk-neutral momentum traders they are negatively
> correlated at a horizon no longer than $j + 1$—that is, it must be that
> $\text{cov}(\Delta P_{t+i}, \Delta P_{t-1}) < 0$ for some $i \leq j$.

It is useful to explore the differences between Propositions 1 and 2 in some detail, since at first glance, it might appear that they are somewhat contradictory. On the one hand, Proposition 1 says that in response to good news, there is continued upward momentum in prices for at least j periods, and possibly more (if $j < z - 1$). On the other hand, Proposition 2 suggests that price changes begin to be reversed within $j + 1$ periods, and quite possibly sooner than that.

The two propositions can be reconciled by noting that the former is a *conditional* statement—that is, it talks about the path of prices from time t onward, conditional on there having been a news shock at time t. Thus Proposition 1 implies that if a trader somehow knows for sure that there is a news shock at time t, he could make a strictly positive expected profit by buying at this time and holding until time $t + j$. One might term such a strategy "buying early in the momentum cycle"—that is, buying immediately on the heels of news arrival. But of course, such a strategy is not available to the momentum traders in our model, since they cannot condition directly on the εs.

In contrast, Proposition 2 is an *unconditional* statement about the auto-covariance of prices. It flows from the requirement that if a trader buys at time t in response to an unconditional price increase at time $t - 1$, and then holds until $t + j$, he makes zero profits on average. This zero-profit requirement in turn must hold when momentum traders are risk-neutral, because the unconditional strategy *is* available to them.

There is a simple reason why an unconditional strategy of buying following any price increase does not work as well as the conditional strategy of buying only following directly observed good news: not all price increases are news-driven. In particular, a trader who buys based on a price increase observed at time t runs the following risk. It may be "late" in the momentum cycle, in the sense that there has not been any good news for the last several periods. Say the last good news hit at $t - i$. If this is the case, the price increase at time t is just due to a late round of momentum buying. And those earlier momentum purchases kicked off by the news at $t - i$ will begin to be unwound in the very near future (specifically, at $t - i + j + 1$) causing the trader to experience losses well before the end of his trading horizon.

This discussion highlights the key spillover effect that drives our results. A momentum trader who is fortunate enough to buy shortly after the arrival of good news imposes a negative externality on those that follow him. He does so by creating a further price increase that the next generation partially misinterprets as more good news. This causes the next generation to buy, and so on. At some point, the buying has gone too far, and the price overshoots the level warranted by the original news. Given the inability of momentum traders to condition directly on the ε's, everybody in the chain is behaving as rationally as possible, but the externality creates an apparently irrational outcome in the market as a whole.

D. Winners and Losers

A natural question is whether the bounded rationality of either the news-watchers or the momentum traders causes them to systematically lose money. In general, both groups can earn positive expected returns as long as the net supply Q of the asset is positive. Consider first the case where $Q = 0$. In this case, it can be shown that the momentum traders earn positive returns, as long as their risk tolerance is finite. Because with $Q = 0$, this is a zero-sum game, it must therefore be that the newswatchers lose money. The one exception is when momentum traders are risk-neutral, and both groups break even.[13]

When $Q > 0$, the game becomes positive-sum, as there is a return to risk-sharing that can be divided between the two groups. Thus even though the newswatchers may effectively lose some money on a trading basis to the momentum traders, this can be more than offset by their returns from risk-sharing, and they can make a net profit. Again, in the limit where the momentum traders become risk-neutral, both groups break even. The logic is similar to that with $Q = 0$, because risk-neutrality on the part of momentum traders dissipates all the risk-sharing profits, restoring the zero-sum nature of the game.

E. Numerical Comparative Statics

In order to develop a better feeling for the properties of the model, we perform a variety of numerical comparative statics exercises.[14] For each set of parameter values, we calculate the following five numbers (1) the equilibrium value of φ; (2) the unconditional standard deviation of monthly returns ΔP; (3) the standard deviation of the pricing *error* relative to a rational expectations benchmark, $(P_t - P_t^*)$; (4) the cumulative impulse response of prices to a one-unit ε shock; and (5) the autocorrelations of returns. The

---

[13] This result is related to the fact that newswatchers have time-inconsistent strategies, so that in formulating their demands they ignore the fact that they will be transacting with momentum traders who will be trying to take advantage of them. Thus in some sense, the newswatchers are more irrational than the momentum traders in this model.

[14] The appendix briefly discusses our computational methods.

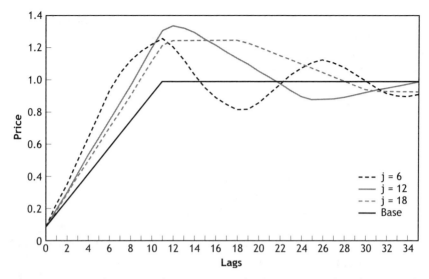

Figure 14.1. Cumulative impulse response and momentum traders' horizon. The momentum traders' horizon j takes on values of 6, 12, and 18. Base is the cumulative impulse response without momentum trading. The other parameter values are set as follows: the information diffusion parameter z is 12, the volatility of news shocks is 0.5 and the risk tolerance gamma is 1/3.

detailed calculations are not shown; rather we use plots of the impulse responses to convey the broad intuition.

We begin in figure 14.1 by investigating the effects of changing the momentum traders' horizon j. We hold the information-diffusion parameter z fixed at 12 months, and set the standard deviation of the fundamental ε shocks equal to 0.5 per month. Finally, we assume that the aggregate risk tolerance of the momentum traders, γ, equals 1/3.[15] We then experiment with values of j ranging from 6 to 18 months. As a baseline, focus first on the case where $j = 12$ months. Consistent with Proposition 1, the impulse response function peaks 12 months after an ε shock, reaching a value of 1.342. In other words, at the peak, prices overshoot the change in long-run fundamentals by 34.2 percent. After the peak, prices eventually converge back to 1.00, although not in a monotonic fashion—rather, there are a series of damped oscillations as the momentum-trading effects gradually wring themselves out.

Now ask what happens as j is varied. As can be seen from the figure, the effects on the impulse response function are nonmonotonic. For example,

---

[15] Campbell, Grossman, and Wang (1993) suggest that this value of risk tolerance is about right for the market as a whole. Of course, for individual stocks, arbitrageurs may be more risk-tolerant, since they may not have to bear systematic risk. As we demonstrate below, our results on overreaction tend to become more pronounced when risk tolerance is increased.

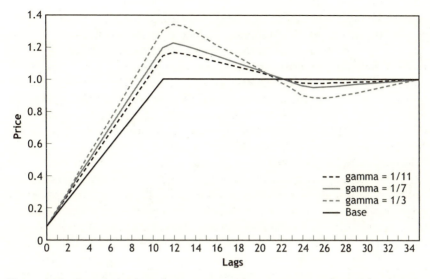

Figure 14.2. Cumulative impulse response and momentum traders' risk tolerance. The momentum traders' risk tolerance gamma takes on values of 1/11, 1/7 and 1/3. Base is the cumulative impulse response without momentum trading. The other parameter values are set as follows: the information diffusion parameter z is 12, the momentum traders' horizon j is 12 and the volatility of news shock is 0.5.

with $j = 6$, the impulse response peaks at 1.265, while with $j = 18$, the peak reaches 1.252, neither as high as in the case where $j = 12$. This nonmonotonicity arises because of two competing effects. On the one hand, an increase in j means that there are more generations of momentum traders active in the market at any one time; hence their cumulative effect should be stronger, all else equal. On the other hand, the momentum traders rationally recognize the dangers of having a longer horizon—there is a greater risk that they get caught trading late in the momentum cycle. As a result, they trade less aggressively, so that φ is decreasing in j.

A more clear-cut result appears to emerge when we consider the effect of j on the time pattern of autocorrelations. As suggested by figure 14.1, the smaller j is, the faster the autocorrelations begin to turn negative. For example, with $j = 6$, the first negative autocorrelation occurs at a lag of 6 months, while with $j = 18$, the first negative autocorrelation occurs at a lag of 12 months. Thus the intuition from Proposition 2 seems to carry over to the case of nonzero risk aversion.

In figure 14.2, we examine the effect of changing momentum traders' risk tolerance. (This Experiment can equivalently be thought of as varying the relative proportions of momentum traders and newswatchers.) We set $j = z = 12$ months, and allow γ to vary. As risk tolerance increases, momentum traders respond more aggressively to past price changes—that is, φ increases. This causes the impulse response function to reach higher peak values. Also, the unconditional volatility of monthly returns rises monotonically.[16] It turns out, however, that the effect of risk tolerance on the pricing error $(P_t - P_t^*)$ is U-shaped: the pricing error first falls, and then rises, as risk tolerance is increased. On the one hand, more momentum trading accelerates the reaction of prices to information, which reduces underreaction and thereby decreases pricing errors. On the other hand, more momentum trading also exacerbates overreaction, which increases pricing errors. Evidently, the two effects interact so as to produce a nonmonotonic pattern.[17]

Finally, in figure 14.3, we allow the information-diffusion parameter z to vary. Increasing z has a monotonic effect on the intensity φ of momentum trade: the slower the newswatchers are to figure things out, the greater the profit opportunities are for momentum traders. In the range of the parameter space where $j \geq z - 1$, the induced increase in φ in turn has a monotonic effect on the peak impulse response—more aggressive momentum trade leads to more pronounced overshooting, and correspondingly, to negative autocorrelations that are generally larger in absolute value during the reversal phase.[18]

2. EXTENSIONS OF THE BASIC MODEL: MORE RATIONAL ARBITRAGE

We now consider a few extensions of the basic model. The overall spirit here is to ask: What happens as we allow for progressively more rational behavior by arbitrageurs?

A. Contrarian Strategies

A.1. CONTRARIANS AND MOMENTUM TRADERS ARE TWO SEPARATE GROUPS

We have emphasized repeatedly that our results are attributable to the assumption that momentum traders make "simple" forecasts—that is, they can only run univariate regressions. But even if one accepts this restriction at face value, it begs the following question: Why do *all* traders have to use the *same* single forecasting variable? Why not allow for some heterogeneity in trading styles, with different groups focusing on different predictive variables?

---

[16] Although volatility rises with momentum trading, it is not necessarily (though it may be) "excessive" relative to a rational expectations benchmark. This is because we are starting from a point where there is underreaction, which leads to *lower* volatility than under a random walk.

[17] The fact that momentum trading can increase both volatility and pricing errors serves as another counterexample to Friedman's (1953) famous claim that profitable speculation must stabilize prices. See also Hart and Kreps (1986), Stein (1987), and DeLong et al. (1990).

[18] When $j < z - 1$, there is no longer a monotonic link between φ and the degree of overshooting. This is because the biggest momentum trades are already being unwound before newswatchers have fully incorporated a news shock into their forecasts.

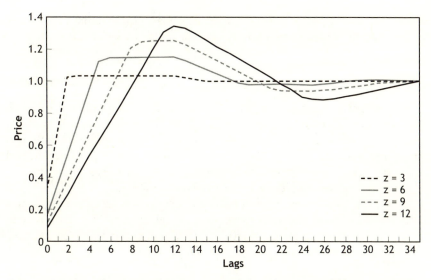

Figure 14.3. Cumulative impulse response and the information diffusion parameter. The information diffusion parameter z takes on values of 3, 6, 9, and 12. The other parameter values are set as follows: momentum traders' horizon j is 12, the volatility of news shocks is 0.5, and momentum traders' risk tolerance gamma is 1/3.

Given the existence of the newswatchers and the underreaction that they create, it is certainly natural to *begin* an examination of simple arbitrage strategies with the sort of momentum-trading style that we have considered thus far. However, once it is understood that the momentum traders must— if they are the only arbitrageurs active in the market—ultimately cause prices to overreact, we then ought to think about the effects of second-round "contrarian" strategies that might be designed to exploit this overreaction.

To incorporate such contrarian strategies into our model, we assume that there is a total risk tolerance of γ available to engage in arbitrage activity. We also continue to assume that all arbitrageurs have horizons of j periods. But there are now two arbitrage styles. A fraction w of the arbitrageurs are momentum traders, who use ΔP_{t-1} to forecast $(P_{t+j} - P_t)$. The remaining $(1 - w)$ are contrarians, who use ΔP_{t-1-c} to forecast $(P_{t+j} - P_t)$. If we choose the lag length c properly, the contrarians will in equilibrium put *negative* weight on ΔP_{t-1-c} in making these forecasts.

Suppose provisionally that one takes the fraction w as fixed. Then the equilibrium is a natural generalization of that seen above. In particular, prices will be given by:

$$P_t = D_t + \{(z-1)\varepsilon_{t+1} + (z-2)\varepsilon_{t+2} + \cdots + \varepsilon_{t+z-1}\}/z$$

$$+ \sum_{i=1}^{j} (\varphi^M \Delta P_{t-i} + \varphi^C \Delta P_{t-c-i}) \tag{9}$$

where φ^M and φ^C now denote the trading elasticities of the momentum traders and the contrarians respectively. These elasticities in turn satisfy:

$$\varphi^M = w\gamma\text{cov}(P_{t+j} - P_t, \Delta P_{t-1})/\{\text{var}(\Delta P)\text{var}_M(P_{t+j} - P_t)\} \qquad (10)$$

$$\varphi^C = (1 - w)\gamma\text{cov}(P_{t+j} - P_t, \Delta P_{t-1-c})/\{\text{var}(\Delta P)\text{var}_C(P_{t+j} - P_t)\} \qquad (11)$$

Equilibrium now involves a two-dimensional fixed point in (φ^M, φ^C) such that prices are given by equation (9), while at the same time (10) and (11) are satisfied. Although this is a more complicated problem than before, it is still straightforward to solve numerically. Of course, this is no longer the end of the story, since we still need to endogenize w. This can be done by imposing an indifference condition: In an interior solution where $0 < w < 1$, the utilities of the momentum traders and contrarians must be equalized, so nobody wants to switch styles. It turns out that the equal-utility condition can be simply rewritten in terms of either conditional variances or covariances of prices (see the appendix for a proof). This gives us:

Proposition 3: In an interior solution with $0 < w < 1$, it must be that:

1. $\text{var}(P_{t+j} - P_t \mid \Delta P_{t-1}) = \text{var}(P_{t+j} - P_t \mid \Delta P_{t-1-c})$; or equivalently

2. $|\text{cov}((P_{t+j} - P_t), \Delta P_{t-1})| = |\text{cov}((P_{t+j} - P_t), \Delta P_{t-1-c})|$; or equivalently

3. $\text{cov}(\Delta P_{t+1}, \Delta P_{t-1}) + \text{cov}(\Delta P_{t+2}, \Delta P_{t-1}) + \cdots + \text{cov}(\Delta P_{t+j}, \Delta P_{t-1}) =$
   $-\text{cov}(\Delta P_{t+1}, \Delta P_{t-1-c}) - \text{cov}(\Delta P_{t+2}, \Delta P_{t-1-c}) - \cdots - \text{cov}(\Delta P_{t+j}, \Delta P_{t-1-c})$.

The essence of the proposition is that in order for contrarians to be active in equilibrium (that is, to have $w < 1$) there must be as much profit opportunity in the contrarian strategy as in the momentum strategy. Loosely speaking, this amounts to saying that the negative autocorrelations in the reversal phase must cumulatively be as large in absolute magnitude as the positive autocorrelations in the initial underreaction phase. Thus adding the option of a contrarian strategy to the model cannot overturn the basic result that if there is underreaction in the short run, there must eventually be overreaction at some later point.

As it turns out, for a large range of parameter values, we can make a much stronger statement: the contrarian strategy is not used at all, for any choice of c. Rather, we get a corner solution of $w = 1$, in which all arbitrageurs endogenously choose to use a momentum strategy. This is in fact the outcome for every set of parameters that appears in figures 14.1–14.3. Thus our previous numerical solutions are wholly unaffected by adding contrarians to the mix.

In order to get contrarian strategies to be adopted in equilibrium, we have to crank up the aggregate risk tolerance γ to a very high value. This does two things: first, it drives down the expected profits to the momentum strategy; and second, it causes the degree of overreaction to increase. Both of these effects raise the relative appeal of being a contrarian to the point

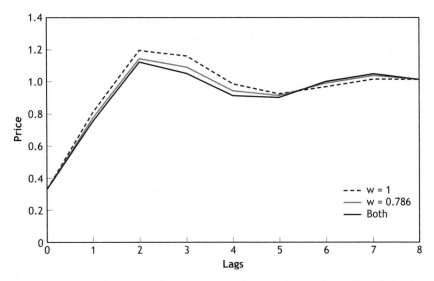

Figure 14.4. Cumulative impulse response and contrarian trading. Cumulative impulse responses for all-momentum trading equilibrium ($w = 1$); the equilibrium in which traders endogenously choose whether to follow either momentum or contrarian strategies ($w = 0.786$); and the equilibrium in which traders can optimally condition on both momentum and contrarian variables ("Both"). The other parameter values are set as follows: the information diffusion parameter z is 3, the momentum traders' horizon j is 1, the volatility of news shocks is 1 and risk tolerance gamma is 1/0.3. The contrarians are assumed to trade based on returns from three periods ago.

that some arbitrageurs eventually switch over from the momentum strategy. Figure 14.4 illustrates by considering a situation where $z = 3$, $j = 1$, where the contrarians trade at a lag that is $c = 2$ periods greater than the momentum traders, and where the risk tolerance takes on the value 1/0.3.

Given these parameter values, $w = 0.786$. That is, 78.6 percent of traders opt to play momentum strategies and the remaining 21.4 percent become contrarians. The contrarians appear to have a modest stabilizing impact—the impulse response function peaks at 1.197 when there are only momentum traders, and this figure declines somewhat, to 1.146, when we allow for contrarian strategies. Nevertheless, price dynamics are still remarkably similar to what we have seen throughout. This underscores our key point: Across a wide range of parameter values, allowing for contrarian strategies need not alter the important qualitative features of our model.

A.2. ARBITRAGEURS CAN RUN BIVARIATE REGRESSIONS

To further relax our assumptions in the direction of rationality, we now ask what happens if every arbitrageur becomes incrementally smarter, and can condition on not one, but two lags of past prices. Said differently, instead of forcing each arbitrageur to choose whether to play a momentum strategy (and condition on ΔP_{t-1}) or a contrarian strategy (and condition on ΔP_{t-1-c}), we now allow them all to play an optimal blended strategy.

The results of this experiment are also illustrated in figure 14.4. Relative to the previous case of segregated momentum and contrarian trading, allowing for bivariate regression-running arbitrageurs is more stabilizing. For example, keeping all other parameters the same as before, the impulse response function now reaches a peak of only 1.125, as compared to the value of 1.146 with segregated momentum and contrarian trading. Nevertheless, its qualitative shape continues to remain similar. Thus while increasing the computational power of arbitrageurs obviously attenuates the results, it does not appear that we are in a knife-edge situation where everything hangs on them being able to run only univariate regressions.

B. Fully Rational Arbitrage

Finally, it is natural to ask whether our basic results are robust to the introduction of a class of fully rational arbitrageurs. To address this question, we extend the baseline model of section 1 as follows. In addition to the newswatchers and the momentum traders, we add a third group of traders, whom we label the "smart money." To give these smart-money traders the best shot at making the market efficient, we consider an extreme case where they can observe and rationally condition on *everything* in the model that is observed by any other trader. Thus, at time t, the smart-money traders observe all the fundamental information that is available to any of the newswatchers—that is, they see ε_{t+z-1} and all preceding news innovations in their entirety. They also can use the complete past history of prices in their forecasts. Like everyone else, the smart money have CARA utility. Finally, each generation has a one-period horizon.

Unlike in the cases with contrarian trading considered in sections 2.A.1 and 2.A.2 above, it is very difficult to solve explicitly for the equilibrium with the smart-money traders, either analytically or via numerical methods. This is because in the context of our infinite-horizon model, the optimal forecasts of the smart money are a function of an unbounded set of variables, as they condition on the entire past history of prices. (They really have to be very smart in this model to implement fully rational behavior.) Nevertheless, as proven in the appendix, we are able to make the following strong general statements about the properties of equilibrium:

> **Proposition 4:** Assume that the risk tolerance of the smart-money traders is finite. In any covariance-stationary equilibrium, given a one-unit shock ε_{t+z-1} that begins to diffuse at time t: (1) there is always underreaction, in the sense that prices rise by less than one at time t; (2) there is active momentum trading; (3) there is always

overreaction, in the sense that the cumulative impulse response of prices peaks at a value that is strictly greater than one.

If the risk tolerance of the smart money traders is infinite, prices follow a random walk, and there is no momentum trading: $\varphi = 0$.

The proposition formalizes the intuitive point—common to many models in this genre—that risk-averse fully rational arbitrageurs attenuate, but do not eliminate, the effects induced by other less-than-rational traders. In our particular setting, all the key qualitative results about the dynamics of prices continue to apply.

3. EMPIRICAL IMPLICATIONS

We will not belabor the fact that our model delivers the right first-order predictions for asset returns: positive correlations at short horizons, and negative correlations at longer horizons. After all, it is designed to do just that. More interesting are the auxiliary implications, which should allow it to be tested against other candidate theories of underreaction and overreaction.

A. In What Stocks Do Momentum Strategies Work Best?

In our model, short-term return continuation is a consequence of the gradual diffusion of private information, combined with the failure of newswatchers to extract this information from prices. This gradual-information-diffusion story is logically distinct from the mechanism in other models, such as BSV's, that emphasizes a conservatism bias (Edwards 1968) with respect to public information. Moreover, it has testable cross-sectional implications. If momentum in stock returns does indeed come from gradual information flow, then momentum strategies of the sort proposed by Jegadeesh and Titman (1993) should be most profitable among those stocks for which information moves most slowly across the investing public.

In research conducted subsequent to the development of the model here, we attempt in Hong, Lim, and Stein (2000), to test this hypothesis. To do so, we consider two different proxies for the rate of information diffusion. The first is firm size. It seems plausible that information about small firms gets out more slowly; this would happen if, for example, investors face fixed costs of information acquisition, and choose to devote more effort to learning about those stocks in which they can take large positions. Of course, one must be careful in drawing inferences because size may also capture a variety of other factors, such as cross-stock differences in arbitrage costs.[19] In

[19] Consequently, one might argue that virtually any behavioral model would be consistent with there being more predictability in small stocks.

light of this concern, we use as a second—and hopefully purer—proxy for information flow a stock's residual analyst coverage, after controlling for size.[20]

The basic findings from Hong, Lim, and Stein are reproduced here as tables 14.1–14.3, and figure 14.5. These findings can be briefly summarized as follows. With respect to size, we find that once one moves past the very smallest-capitalization stocks (where price discreteness and/or very thin market-making capacity are issues) the profitability of Jegadeesh-Titman-style six-month momentum strategies declines sharply with market cap. With respect to residual analyst coverage, not only are momentum strategies substantially more profitable at a horizon of six months in low-analyst-coverage stocks, they are also profitable for *longer*—there is pronounced positive correlation of returns for up to about two years in these stocks, as opposed to less than one year in high-coverage stocks. Size and residual coverage also interact in an interesting and economically plausible fashion: the marginal impact of analyst coverage is most pronounced in smaller stocks, which have fewer analysts to begin with. While it may be possible to come up with alternative interpretations, all these pieces of evidence would seem to be strongly consistent with our emphasis in this work on gradual information flow as the root cause of underreaction.

B. Linking Momentum to Overreaction in the Cross Section

There is also a second, more subtle cross-sectional implication of our model pertaining to the rate of information flow. In figure 14.3 we saw that not only does slower information diffusion lead to higher short-run return correlations, but by making stocks more attractive to momentum traders, it also (for a wide range of parameter values) leads to more pronounced overshooting and stronger reversals in the longer run. In other words, the same stocks that we find in Hong, Lim, and Stein to be most "momentum-prone"—small stocks with relatively few analysts—should also be most "reversal-prone."

Although this prediction has not to our knowledge been subjected to detailed investigation, it is broadly consistent with recent work which finds that much of the long-horizon predictability that has been documented in the stock market is attributable to smaller-cap companies.[21] As noted above, there is the caveat that size may be proxying for a number of other factors so, as in Hong, Lim, and Stein, it would be desirable to create a sharper test, perhaps using analyst coverage or some other nonsize measure of momentum-proneness.

[20] Of course, analyst coverage is not an ideal proxy either, as it may be endogenously related to a number of other stock-specific factors besides size. So in various sensitivity tests, we also control for the correlation between analyst coverage and share turnover, industry factors, beta, and market-to-book.

[21] Fama (1998) argues that this evidence is problematic for existing behavioral models, as they do not clearly predict that overreaction should be concentrated in smaller stocks.

TABLE 14.1

Momentum Strategies, 1/1980–12/1996: Using Raw Returns and Sorting by Size

This table includes all stocks. The relative momentum portfolios are formed based on six-month lagged raw returns and held for six months. The stocks are ranked in ascending order on the basis of six-month lagged returns. Portfolio P1 is an equally weighted portfolio of stocks in the worst performing 30%, portfolio P2 includes the middle 40%, and portfolio P3 includes the best performing 30%. This table reports the average monthly returns of these portfolios and portfolios formed using size-based subsamples of stocks. Using NYSE/AMEX decile breakpoints, the smallest firms are in size class 1, the next in size class 2, and largest in 10. Mean (median) size is in millions. T-stats are in parentheses.

PAST	All Stocks	Size Class (NYSE/AMEX Decile Breakpoints)									
		1	2	3	4	5	6	7	8	9	10
P1	0.01043	0.02106	0.00653	0.00231	0.00194	0.00469	0.00573	0.00606	0.01010	0.00922	0.01258
	(2.44)	(4.44)	(1.37)	(0.52)	(0.43)	(1.05)	(1.32)	(1.43)	(2.51)	(2.25)	(3.37)
P2	0.01378	0.01662	0.01290	0.01280	0.01244	0.01395	0.01374	0.01375	0.01393	0.01401	0.01355
	(4.48)	(4.97)	(3.84)	(3.88)	(3.75)	(4.18)	(4.14)	(4.27)	(4.40)	(4.43)	(4.50)
P3	0.01570	0.01733	0.01507	0.01664	0.01570	0.01655	0.01608	0.01491	0.01436	0.01363	0.01278
	(4.35)	(4.40)	(3.89)	(4.35)	(4.05)	(4.26)	(4.26)	(4.13)	(4.04)	(3.96)	(3.84)
P3 – 1	0.00527	−0.003740	0.00854	0.01433	0.01376	0.01187	0.01035	0.00885	0.00425	0.00441	0.00021
	(2.61)	(−1.77)	(3.60)	(6.66)	(6.10)	(5.32)	(4.80)	(3.72)	(1.90)	(1.73)	(0.08)
P2 – P1 / P3 – P1		—	0.746	0.732	0.763	0.780	0.774	0.869	0.901	1.086	—
Mean Size		7	21	44	79	138	242	437	806	1658	7290
Median Size		7	21	43	78	136	237	430	786	1612	4504
Mean Analyst		0.1	0.5	1.1	2.0	3.2	5.0	7.3	10.6	15.3	21.4
Median Analyst		0.0	0.0	0.7	1.3	2.5	4.4	6.9	10.5	15.7	22.4

TABLE 14.2
Momentum Strategies, 1/1980–12/1996: Using Raw Returns and
Sorting by Residual Analyst Coverage

This table includes only stocks above the NYSE/AMEX 20th percentile. The relative momentum portfolios are formed based on six-month lagged raw returns and held for six months. The stocks are ranked in ascending order on the basis of six-month lagged returns. Portfolio P1 is an equally weighted portfolio of stocks in the worst performing 30%, portfolio P2 includes the middle 40%, and portfolio P3 includes the best performing 30%. This table reports the average monthly returns of these portfolios and portfolios formed using an independent sort on analyst coverage residuals of log size and a NASDAQ dummy. The least covered firms are in Sub1, the medium covered firms in Sub2, the most covered firms in Sub3. Mean (median) size is in millions. T-stats are in parentheses.

		Residual Coverage Class			
PAST	ALL STOCKS	Low: SUB1	Medium: SUB2	High: SUB3	SUB1-SUB3
P1	0.00622	0.00271	0.00669	0.00974	−0.00703
	(1.54)	(0.66)	(1.70)	(2.31)	(−5.16)
P2	0.01367	0.01257	0.01397	0.01439	−0.00182
	(4.40)	(4.20)	(4.58)	(4.29)	(−2.11)
P3	0.01562	0.01402	0.01583	0.01690	−0.00288
	(4.35)	(3.95)	(4.52)	(4.45)	(−2.80)
P3-1	0.00940	0.01131	0.00915	0.00716	0.00415
	(4.89)	(5.46)	(4.64)	(3.74)	(3.50)
Mean Size		962	986	455	
Median Size		103	200	180	
Mean Analyst		1.5	6.7	9.7	
Median Analyst		0.1	3.5	7.6	

C. Differential Dynamics in Response to Public versus Private News Shocks?

As we have stressed repeatedly, the most natural interpretation of the εs in our model is that they represent information that is initially private, and that gradually diffuses across the population of investors. Thus our primary contribution is to show that the equilibrium impulse response to such private information must be hump-shaped, with underreaction in the short run giving way to eventual overreaction. But what about the impulse response to news that is simultaneously observed by all investors, such as earnings announcements?

TABLE 14.3

Momentum Strategies, 1/1980–12/1996: Using Raw Returns and Sorting by Size and Residual Analyst Coverage

This table includes only stocks above the NYSE/AMEX 20th percentile. The relative momentum portfolios are formed based on six-month lagged raw returns and held for six months. The stocks are ranked in ascending order on the basis of six-month lagged returns. Portfolio P1 is an equally weighted portfolio of stocks in the worst performing 30%, portfolio P2 includes the middle 40%, and portfolio P3 includes the best performing 30%. This table reports the average monthly returns to portfolios formed by sorts on size and analyst coverage residuals of log size and a NASDAQ dummy. Size is sorted using NYSE/AMEX breakpoints. The least covered firms are in Sub1, the medium covered firms in Sub2, the most covered firms in Sub3. Mean (median) size is in millions. T-stats are in parentheses.

| Residual Coverage Class | Size Class: | | | |
	1:20th–40th Percentile	2:40th–60th Percentile	3:60th–80th Percentile	4:80th–100th Percentile
Low:Sub1	P3 – P1 = .01511 (6.46)	P3 – P1 = .01057 (4.49)	P3 – P1 = .00605.(3.11)	P3 – P1 =.00092 (0.49)
	Mean Size = 63	Mean Size = 199	Mean Size = 653	Mean Size = 5056
	Median Size = 59	Median Size = 183	Median Size = 592	Median Size = 2363
	Median Coverage = 0.0	Median Coverage = 0.6	Median Coverage = 3.7	Median Coverage = 11.1
Medium:Sub2	P3 – P1 = 0.01389 (5.48)	P3 – P1 = 0.00975 (4.95)	P3 – P1 = 0.00316 (1.62)	P3 – P1 = 0.00009 (0.05)
	Mean Size = 61	Mean Size = 207	Mean Size = 678	Mean Size = 5163
	Median Size = 56	Median Size = 193	Median Size = 629	Median Size = 2853
	Median Coverage = 0.9	Median Coverage = 3.6	Median Coverage = 9.0	Median Coverage = 18.8
High:Sub3	P3 – P1 = 0.01147 (5.10)	P3 – P1 = 0.00730 (3.60)	P3 – P1 = 0.00424 (2.02)	P3 – P1 = 0.00070 (0.33)
	Mean Size = 64	Mean Size = 202	Mean Size = 663	Mean Size = 3650
	Median Size = 61	Median Size = 188	Median Size = 615	Median Size = 2511
	Median Coverage = 3.1	Median Coverage = 7.6	Median Coverage = 14.7	Median Coverage = 24.9
Sub1-Sub3	P3 – P1 = 0.00364(2.13)	P3 – P1 = 0.00327 (1.95)	P3 – P1 = 0.00180 (1.18)	P3 – P1 = 0.00023 (.14)

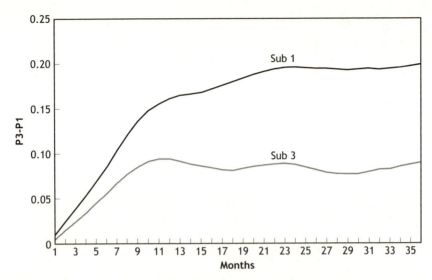

Figure 14.5. Cumulative beta-adjusted returns in event time: Momentum profits for low and high coverage stocks. We assign stocks to performance categories based on six months' prior beta-adjusted returns, and do an independent sort based on the analyst coverage residuals. We then track the cumulative beta-adjusted momentum-portfolio returns (P3-P1) on a month-by-month basis, out to thirty-six months for low coverage (SUB1) and high coverage (SUB3) stocks.

It is easy to embellish our model so that it also generates short-run underreaction to public news. For example, one might argue that although the news announcement itself (e.g., "earnings are up by 10 percent") is public, it requires some other, private, information (e.g., knowledge of the stochastic process governing earnings) to convert this news into a judgement about value. If this is true, the market's response to public news involves the aggregation of private signals, and our previous underreaction results continue to apply.

On the one hand, this sort of patch adds an element of descriptive realism, given the large body of empirical evidence on postevent drift. But the more interesting and subtle question is this: If we augment the model so as to deliver short-run underreaction to public news, what does it have to say about whether there is *overreaction* in the longer run to this same news? Is the impulse response function hump-shaped as before, or do prices drift gradually to the correct level without going too far?

Unlike with private news, the answer is now less clear. This is because the inference problem for momentum traders is simplified. Recall from above that with private news, a momentum trader never knows whether he is buying early or late in the cycle—that is, he cannot tell if a price increase is the result of recent news or of past rounds of momentum trade. But if momentum traders can condition on the fact that there was a public news announcement at some given date t, they can refine their strategies. In particular, they can make their strategies time-dependent, so that they only trend-chase aggressively in the periods right after public news, and lay low at other times. If they do this, there need be no overreaction to public news in equilibrium; rather, the impulse response function may be increasing everywhere.

Of course, it is conceivable that momentum traders are not so sophisticated, and continue to use strategies that do not depend on how recently public news was released. If so, the impulse response to public news is also hump-shaped. But the important point is that the logic of our model admits (even strongly suggests) the possibility that the response to public news looks different than that to private information. This is clearly a testable proposition.

D. Trading Horizons and the Pattern of Return Autocorrelations

One novel feature of our model is that it explicitly links momentum traders' horizons to the time pattern of return autocorrelations. This link is loosely suggested by Proposition 2, and it emerges clearly in the comparative statics results of figure 14.1: the longer the momentum traders' horizon j, the longer it takes for the autocorrelations to switch from positive to negative.

The first thing to note in this regard is that our model seems to get the average magnitudes about right. For example, Jegadeesh and Titman (1993) find that autocorrelations for stock portfolios are positive for roughly twelve months, and then turn systematically negative. According to our calculations (see the appendix), this is what one should expect if j is on the order of twelve to eighteen months, which sounds like a plausible value for the horizon of a trading strategy.[22]

A second observation is that we can make cross-sectional predictions, to the extent that we can identify exogenous factors that influence the trading horizon j. One natural candidate for such a factor is trading cost. It seems plausible to conjecture that as trading costs increase, momentum traders choose to hold their positions for longer. If so, we would expect stocks with relatively high bid-ask spreads to have autocorrelations that stay positive for longer periods of time before turning negative. Or going across assets classes, we would expect the same thing for assets such as houses, and collectibles, where trading costs are no doubt significantly higher.[23] Some evidence on this latter point is provided by Cutler, Poterba, and Summers (1991). They find that, in

[22] As a benchmark, turnover on the NYSE has been in the range of 50 to 60 percent in recent years, implying an average holding period of twenty to twenty-four months. Of course, momentum traders may have shorter horizons than the average investor.

[23] Some care should be taken in testing this prediction, since assets with higher trading costs are likely to have more stale prices, which can induce spuriously positive autocorrelations in measured returns.

contrast to equities, the autocorrelations for house and farm prices are positive at lags of up to three years, and for collectibles, at lags of up to two years.

E. Anecdotal Evidence on Professional Investment Strategies

In our model, momentum traders have two key characteristics: (1) aside from their inability to run multiple regressions, they are rational maximizers who make money on average; and (2) they impose a negative externality on others. The latter feature arises because someone entering the market at any time t does not know how heavily invested momentum traders are in the aggregate at this time, and hence cannot predict whether or not there will be large-scale unwinding of momentum positions in the near future.

Anecdotal evidence supports both of these premises. With regard to the near-rationality of momentum strategies, it should be noted that a number of large and presumably sophisticated money managers use what are commonly described as momentum approaches, that "emphasize accelerating sales, earnings, or even stock prices . . . and focus less on traditional valuation measures such as price-to-earnings ratios."[24] This contrasts with the more pejorative view of positive-feedback trading that prevails in prior academic work such as that of Delong et al. (1990).

With regard to the negative externalities, it seems that other professional investors do in fact worry a lot about the dangers of momentum traders unwinding their positions. The following quotes from money managers illustrate these concerns: "Before I look at a stock, I take a look at the (SEC) filings to see who the major shareholders are. If you see a large amount of momentum money in there, you have to accept that there's a high risk . . ."; "If you're in with managers who are very momentum oriented . . . you have to be aware that's a risk going in. They come barreling out of those stocks, and they're not patient about it."[25]

In addition to these two premises, anecdotal evidence is also consistent with one of our key predictions: that momentum traders are more active in small stocks, where analyst coverage is thinner and information diffuses more slowly. According to a leading pension fund consultant, "most of the momentum players play in the small and mid-cap stocks." And a well-known momentum investor says that he typically focuses on small companies because "the market is inefficient for smaller companies."[26]

---

[24] The quote is from Ip (1997). Among the large investors labeled momentum players are Nicholes-Applegate Capital Management, Pilgrim Baxter & Associates, Friess Associates, and Richard Driehaus, who was ranked first among 1,200 managers of all styles for the five years ending December 1995, by Performance Analytics, a pension advisory firm (see Rehfeld 1996).

[25] See Ip (1997).

[26] The consultant is Robert Moseson of Performance Analytics, quoted in Jereski and Lohse (1996). The momentum investor is Richard Driehaus, quoted in Rehfeld (1996).

More broadly, the extended version of the model with contrarians fits with the observation that there are a variety of professional money-management "styles," each of which emphasizes a different subset of public information. Such heterogeneity cannot be understood in the context of the standard rational model, where there is only one "correct" style, that which processes *all* available information in an optimal fashion. But it is a natural feature of our bounded-rationality framework, which allows multiple styles to coexist and earn similar profits.

4. COMPARISON TO RELATED WORK

As noted in the introduction, this work shares the same goal as recent work by BSV (1997) and DHS (1997)—that is, to construct a plausible model that delivers a unified account of asset-price continuations and reversals. However, the approach taken here is quite different. Both BSV and DHS use representative agent models, while our results are driven by the externalities that arise when heterogeneous traders interact with one another.[27] Consequently, many of the auxiliary empirical implications of our model are distinct.

First, it is impossible for a representative agent model to make predictions linking trading horizons to the temporal pattern of autocorrelations, as we do in section 3.D. Second, neither the BSV nor the DHS model would seem to be able to easily generate our prediction that both continuations and reversals are more pronounced in stocks with thinner analyst coverage (sections 3.A and 3.B). A further difference with BSV is that our model allows for a differential impulse response to public and private shocks (section 3.C), while theirs only considers public news.

In its focus on the interaction of different types of traders—including those who behave in a trend-chasing fashion—this work is closer to earlier models of positive-feedback trading by DeLong et al. (1990) and Cutler, Poterba, and Summers (1990). However, there are significant differences with this work as well. For example, in DeLong et al., the positive-feedback traders are extremely irrational, and get badly exploited by a group of rational frontrunners.[28] In our model, the momentum traders are very nearly

---

[27] BSV develop a regime-switching learning model, where investors wind up oscillating between two states: one where they think that earnings shocks are excessively transitory; and one where they think that earnings shocks are excessively persistent. DHS emphasize the idea that investors are likely to be overconfident in the precision of their private information, and that this overconfidence will vary over time as they learn about the accuracy of their past predictions.

[28] In Cutler, Poterba, and Summers (1990), positive-feedback traders *can* make money, as there is background underreaction, like in our model. However, since the feedback behavior is assumed, rather than derived, their model does not yield many of the predictions discussed in section 3.

rational, and actually manage to take advantage of the other group of traders, the newswatchers. This distinction is closely related to the fact that in DeLong et al, there is never any underreaction. There is short-run positive correlation of returns, but this reflects an initial overreaction, followed by *even more* overreaction.[29]

At a more general level, this chapter revisits several themes that have been prominent in previous theoretical work. The notion that one group of optimizing traders might create a negative informational externality, and thereby destabilize prices even while they are making profits, also shows up in Stein (1987). Stretching a bit further, there is an interesting analogy here with the ideas of Banerjee (1992) and Bikhchandani, Hirshleifer, and Welch (1992) on informational cascades. In these models, agents move sequentially. In equilibrium, each rationally bases his decision on the actions of the agent before him, even though this inflicts a negative informational externality on those that follow. Very much the same thing could be said of the generations of momentum traders in this model.

5. CONCLUSIONS

At the outset, we argued that any new "behavioral" theory of asset pricing should be judged according to three criteria: (1) it should rest on assumptions about investor behavior that are either a priori plausible or consistent with casual observation; (2) it should explain the existing evidence in a parsimonious and unified way; and (3) it should make a number of further predictions that can be subject to testing and that are ultimately validated.

How well have we done on these three scores? With respect to the first, we believe that our particular rendition of bounded rationality—as the ability to process a small subset of the available information in an unbiased way—is both plausible and intuitively appealing. Moreover, in our framework, this sort of bounded rationality implies a widespread reliance by arbitrageurs on simple momentum strategies. As we have discussed, this implication appears to be strongly consistent with what is observed in the real world.

In terms of the parsimony/unity criterion, it should be emphasized that everything in our model is driven by just one primitive type of shock: slowly-diffusing news about future fundamentals. There are no other exogenous sources of investor sentiment, and no liquidity disturbances. Our main conceptual contribution is to show that if there is ever any short-run underreaction to this kind of news on the part of one set of traders, then

[29] Also, the model of DeLong et al. (1990) does not rally endogenously deliver reversals. Rather, prices are just forced back to fundamentals on a terminal date. In our model, the reversal phase is more endogenous, corresponding to the unwinding of momentum traders' positions. It also involves more complex dynamics, with the sort of damped oscillations seen in the figures.

(given the simple nature of arbitrage strategies) there must eventually be overreaction in the longer run as well.

Finally, our model does deliver several testable auxiliary implications. Among the most noteworthy are the following:(1) both short-run continuation and long-run reversals should be more pronounced in those (small, low-analyst-coverage) stocks where information diffuses more slowly; (2) There may be more long-run overreaction to information that is initially private than to public news announcements; and (3) there should be a relationship between momentum traders' horizons and the pattern of return autocorrelations. Evidence supportive of the first prediction is already emerging; we hope to explore some of the others in future work.

Appendix: Proofs

A. ARMA Representation of the Return Process

Let us begin by recalling Eq. (5) from the text (suppressing constants):

$$P_t = D_t + \frac{(z-1)}{z}\varepsilon_{t+1} + \cdots + \frac{1}{z}\varepsilon_{t+z-1} + \sum_{i=1}^{j} \varphi \Delta P_{t-i} \tag{A.1}$$

It follows that

$$\Delta P_t = \frac{\sum_{i=0}^{z-1}\varepsilon_{t+i}}{z} + \varphi \Delta P_{t-1} - \varphi \Delta P_{t-(j+1)}. \tag{A.2}$$

Assuming that φ satisfies proper conditions to be specified, ΔP_t is a covanance stationary process. Let

$$\alpha_k \equiv E[\Delta P_t \Delta P_{t-k}]$$

(i.e., the unconditional autocovariance lagged k periods). When $k = 0$, we have the unconditional variance. The autocovariances of this process satisfy the following Yule-Walker equations.

$$\alpha_0 = E\left[\sum_{i=0}^{z-1}\frac{\varepsilon_{t+i}}{z}\Delta P_t\right] + \varphi\alpha_1 - \varphi\alpha_{j+1}. \tag{A.3}$$

And for $k > 0$, we have

$$\alpha_k = E\left[\sum_{i=0}^{z-1}\frac{\varepsilon_{t+i}}{z}\Delta P_{t-k}\right] + \varphi\alpha_{k-1} - \varphi\alpha_{k-(j+1)}. \tag{A.4}$$

It is not hard to verify that for $k > z - 1$,

$$E\left[\sum_{i=1}^{z-1}\frac{\varepsilon_{t+i}}{z}\Delta P_{t-k}\right] = 0. \tag{A.5}$$

And for $k \leq z - 1$, we have

$$E\left[\sum_{i=0}^{z-1}\frac{\varepsilon_{t+i}}{z}\Delta P_{t-k}\right] = \frac{(z-k)\sigma^2}{z^2} + \varphi E\left[\sum_{i=0}^{z-1}\frac{\varepsilon_{t+i}}{z}\Delta P_{t-(k+1)}\right] - \varphi E\left[\sum_{i=0}^{z-1}\frac{\varepsilon_{t+i}}{z}\Delta P_{t-(k+j+1)}\right]$$

$$\tag{A.6}$$

where σ is the standard deviation of the ε's. Solving the Yule-Walker equations reduces to solving a system of $j + 2$ linear equations. Next, the optimal strategies of the momentum traders are given by

$$\zeta_t^M = \frac{\gamma E[P_{t+j} - P_t | \Delta P_{t-1}]}{Var[P_{t+j} - P_t | \Delta P_{t-1}]}, \tag{A.7}$$

where

$$P_{t+j} - P_t = \Delta P_{t+j} + \cdots + \Delta P_{t+1}.$$

In equilibrium,

$$\zeta_t^M = \varphi \Delta P_{t-1}. \tag{A.8}$$

Finally, it follows that

$$Cov(\Delta P_{t-1}, P_{t+j} - P_t) = \alpha_{j+1} + \cdots + \alpha_2,$$

and

$$Var(P_{t+j} - P_t) = j\alpha_0 + 2(j-1)\alpha_1 + \cdots + 2(j-(j-1)\alpha_{j-1}.$$

Using these formulas, the problem is reduced to finding a fixed point in φ that satisfies the equilibrium condition (A.8). Given the equilibrium φ, we then need to verify that the resulting equilibrium ARMA process is in fact covariance stationary (since all of our formulas depend crucially on this assumption).

B. Stationarity

We next provide a characterization for the covariance stationarity of a conjectured return process. This condition is just that the roots of

$$1 - \varphi x + \varphi x^{j+1} = 0 \tag{A.9}$$

lie outside the unit circle (see, e.g., Hamilton 1994).

Lemma A.1. The return process specified in equation (A.2) is a covariance stationary process only if $|\varphi| < 1$.

Proof. Proof is by induction on j. For $j = 1$, the return process follows an ARMA(2, z). So, the conditions for covariance stationarity are: $-2 \varphi < 1$; and $-1 < \varphi < 1$, (see, e.g., Hamilton 1994). The stated result follows for $j = 1$. Apply the inductive hypothesis and assume the result holds for $j = k$.

From Eq. (A.9), it follows that the roots x of

$$1 - \varphi x + \varphi x^{k+1} = 0$$

must lie outside the unit circle (e.g., $|x| > 1$). It follows that

$$|1 - \varphi x| = |\varphi||x|^{k+1}. \tag{A.10}$$

Hence, as k increases, it follows that $|\varphi|$ decreases for equation (A.10) to hold. The stated result follows for arbitrary j. QED

We use this result to characterize a number of properties of a conjectured covariance stationary equilibrium.

> **Proof of Lemma 1.** We show that $\varphi > 0$ in a covariance stationary equilibrium by contradiction. Suppose it is not, so that $\varphi \leq 0$. It is easy to verify from equation (A.4) and from Lemma A.I that
>
> $$\alpha_k \geq 0 \qquad \forall k \qquad \rightarrow \alpha_2 + \alpha_3 + \cdots + \alpha_{j+1} > 0$$
>
> implying that $\varphi > 0$, leading to a contradiction. QED

C. Existence and Numerical Computation

An equilibrium φ satisfying the convariance stationary condition in Lemma A.1 does not exist for arbitrary parameter values. It is easy to verify however that a covariance stationary equilibrium does exist for sufficiently small γ.

> **Lemma A.2.** For γ sufficiently small, there exists a covariance stationary equilibrium.

> **Proof.** It is easy to show that for γ sufficiently small, we can apply Brouwer's fixed point theorem. QED

In general, the equilibrium needs to be solved numerically. For the case of $j = 1$, we can always verify the resulting φ leads to covariance stationarity. For arbitrary j, we only have a necessary condition although the calculations for the autocovariances would likely explode for a φ that does not lead to a covariance stationary process. So, we always begin our calculations for $j = 1$ and γ small and use the resulting solutions to bootstrap our way to other regions in the parameter space. The solutions are gotten easily. When we move outside the covariance stationary region of the parameter space, autocovariances take on nonsensible values such as negative values for the unconditional variance or autocovariances that do not satisfy the standard property that

$$|\alpha_k| < |\alpha_0|, \qquad k > 0$$

in a covariance stationary equilibrium. In general, we have not had much problem finding fixed points for wide parameter regions around those exhibited in the text.

D. Remaining Proofs

Proof of Proposition 3

The equilibrium condition to determine w is for the utilities from the two strategies to be equal. Given our assumptions on the preferences of the momentum and contrarian investors and the distributions of the εs, it follows from Grossman and Stiglitz (1980) that this is equivalent to the conditional variance of the j-period returns being equal across the two strategies. Given that both momentum and contrarian investors have the same j-period horizon, it follows that this is equivalent to the conditional covariance of the j-period returns being equal across the two strategies. QED

Proof of Proposition 4

Suppose initially that there are only newswatchers and smart money investors (i.e., there are no momentum investors). Smart money investors have finite risk tolerance given by γ^s and maximize one-period returns. We conjecture the following equilibrium price function:

$$P_t = D_t + \frac{(z-1)}{z}\varepsilon_{t+1} + \cdots + \frac{1}{z}\varepsilon_{t+z-1} + \sum_{i=1}^{z-1}\beta_i\varepsilon_{t+i}. \tag{A.11}$$

Note that we are once again suppressing all calculations related to the constant. The holdings of the smart money investors are given by

$$\zeta_t^S = \frac{\gamma^S E[P_{t+1} - P_t|D_t, \varepsilon_{t+1}, \ldots, \varepsilon_{t+z-1}]}{Var[P_{t+1} - P_t|D_t, \varepsilon_{t+1}, \ldots, \varepsilon_{t+z-1}]}. \tag{A.12}$$

At the conjectured equilibrium price given in equation (A.11), we have that

$$\zeta_t^S = \sum_{i=t+1}^{t+z-1}\beta_i\varepsilon_i. \tag{A.13}$$

Eq. (A.13) then gives the following set of equations that determine the β's in equilibrium:

$$\beta_1 = \gamma^s \frac{\dfrac{1}{z} - \beta_1}{\left(\dfrac{1}{z} + \beta_{z-1}\right)^2 \sigma^2} \tag{A.14}$$

and

$$\beta_1 = \gamma^s \frac{\dfrac{1}{z} + (\beta_{i-1} - \beta_i)}{\left(\dfrac{1}{z} + \beta_{z-1}\right)^2 \sigma^2}, \qquad i = 2, \ldots, z-1. \tag{A.15}$$

Using equations (A.14) and (A.15), it is not hard to show that in a covariance stationary equilibrium: (1) the returns still exhibit positive serial correlation for finite levels of smart money risk tolerance, $\gamma^s < \infty$; and (2) when smart money investors are risk neutral, prices follow a random walk.

Since returns are serially correlated when the risk tolerance of smart money is finite, $\varphi = 0$ cannot be an equilibrium when we add momentum traders to the model. Since smart money investors have access to the entire history of past price changes, it follows from the logic of Eq. (A.11) that the conjectured price function with momentum traders is now

$$P_t = D_t + \frac{(z-1)}{z} \varepsilon_{t+1} + \cdots + \frac{1}{z} \varepsilon_{t+z-1} + \sum_{i=1}^{z-1} \beta_i \varepsilon_{t+i}$$

$$+ \sum_{i=1}^{\infty} \kappa_i \Delta P_{t-i} + \sum_{i=1}^{j} \varphi \Delta P_{t-i}. \tag{A.16}$$

Assuming that a covariance stationary equilibrium exists, the holding of the smart money is

$$\zeta_{St}^s = \frac{\gamma^s E[P_{t+1} - P_t | D_t, \varepsilon_{t+1}, \ldots, \varepsilon_{t+z-1}, \Delta P_{t-1}, \Delta P_{t-2}, \ldots, \Delta P_{-\infty}]}{Var[P_{t+1} - P_t | D_t, \varepsilon_{t+1}, \ldots, \varepsilon_{t+z-1}, \Delta P_{t-1}, \Delta P_{t-2}, \ldots, \Delta P_{-\infty}]}. \tag{A.17}$$

while the holding of the momentum investors is given by Eq. (A.7). At the conjectured equilibrium price in Eq. (A.16), we have

$$\zeta_{St}^s = \sum_{i=t+1}^{t+z-1} \beta_i \varepsilon_i + \sum_{i=1}^{\infty} \kappa_i \Delta P_{t-i} \tag{A.18}$$

for the smart money and Eq. (A.8) for the momentum investors.

In general, the βs, κs, and φs in Eq. (A.16) have to be determined numerically as fixed points of equations (A.8) and (A.18) using the same methodology as described above in section A.3. While solving for these parameters is computationally difficult, we can characterize certain behavior in a covariance stationary equilibrium. Given a positive one-unit shock that begins to diffuse among newswatchers at time t, the price underreacts at t for finite smart money risk tolerance, that is,

$$\Delta P_t = \frac{1}{z} + \beta_{z-1} < 1.$$

The price eventually converges to one in a covariance stationary equilibrium. And in a covariance stationary equilibrium, the price must also overshoot one. To see this, suppose it does not. Then the serial correlation in returns would be positive at all horizons. Then this implies that momentum investors would have $\varphi > 0$, which by our previous logic implies that there would be overreaction, thereby establishing a contradiction.

When the risk tolerance of smart money is infinite, it follows from the discussion above that without momentum traders prices follow a random walk. So, the expected return to momentum trading is zero. Hence, when the risk tolerance of smart money is infinite, prices following a random walk and no momentum trading is in fact a covariance-stationary equilibrium. QED

References

Banerjee, Abhijit, 1992, A simple model of herd behavior, *Quarterly Journal of Economics* 107, 797–817.

Barberis, Nicholas, Andrei Shleifer, and Robert Vishny, 1998, A model of investor sentiment, *Journal of Financial Economics*, 49, 307–43.

Bernard, Victor L., 1992, Stock price reactions to earnings announcements, in R. Thaler, ed., *Advances in Behavioral Finance*, Russell Sage Foundation.

Bernard, Victor L., and J. Thomas, 1989, Post-earnings announcement drift: Delayed price response or risk premium?, *Journal of Accounting Research*, 27, 1–48.

———, 1990, Evidence that stock prices do not fully reflect the implications of current earnings for future earnings, *Journal of Accounting and Economics* 13, 305–40.

Bikhchandani, Sushil, David Hirshleifer, and Ivo Welch, 1992, A theory of fads, fashions, custom and cultural change as informational cascades, *Journal of Political Economy* 100, 992–1026.

Campbell, John Y., Sanford J. Grossman, and Jiang Wang, 1993, Trading volume and serial correlation in stock returns, *Quarterly Journal of Economics* 108, 905–39.

Campbell, John Y., and Robert Shiller, 1988, Stock prices, earnings, and expected dividends, *Journal of Finance* 43, 661–76.

Chan, Louis K. C., Narasimhan Jegadeesh, and Josef Lakonishok, 1996, Momentum strategies, *Journal of Finance* 51, 1681–1713.

Chopra, Navin, Josef Lakonishok, and Jay R. Ritter, 1992, Measuring abnormal performance: Do stocks overreact?, *Journal of Financial Economics* 31, 235–68.

Cutler, David M., James M. Poterba, and Lawrence H. Summers, 1991, Speculative dynamics and the role of feedback traders, *American Economic Review Papers and Proceedings* 80, 63–68.

———, 1990, Speculative dynamics, *Review of Economic Studies* 58, 529–46.

Daniel, Kent D., David Hirshleifer, and Avanidhar Subrahmanyam, 1998, A Theory of overconfidence, self-attribution, and security market under- and over-reactions, Northwestern University Working Paper, forthcoming in *Journal of Finance*.

Daniel, Kent D., and Sheridan Titman, 1997, Evidence on the characteristics of cross-sectional variation in stock returns, *Journal of Finance* 52, 1–33.

DeBondt, Werner F. M., and Richard H. Thaler, 1985, Does the stock market overreact? *Journal of Finance* 40, 793–808.

DeLong, J. Bradford, Andrei Shleifer, Lawrence H. Summers, and Robert Waldmann, 1990, Positive feedback investment strategies and destabilizing rational speculation, *Journal of Finance* 45, 379–95.

Edwards, W., 1968, Conservatism in human information processing, in B. Kleinmutz (ed.), *Formal Representation of Human Judgment*, Wiley.

Fama, Eugene F., 1998, Market efficiency, long-term returns, and behavioral finance, *Journal of Financial Economics* 49, 283–306.

Fama, Eugene F., and Kenneth R. French, 1988, Permanent and temporary components of stock prices, *Journal of Political Economy* 96, 246–73.

————, 1992, The cross-section of expected stock returns, *Journal of Finance* 47, 427–65.

————, 1993, Common risk factors in the returns on stocks and bonds, *Journal of Financial Economics* 33, 3–56.

————, 1996, Multifactor explanations of asset pricing anomalies, *Journal of Finance* 51, 55–84.

————, 1998, Value versus growth: The international evidence, *Journal of Finance* 53, 1975–99.

Friedman, Milton, 1953, The case for flexible exchange rates, in *Essays in Positive Economics*, University of Chicago Press.

Grossman, Sanford J., 1976, On the efficiency of competitive stock markets where traders have diverse information, *Journal of Finance* 31, 573–85.

Grossman, Sanford J., and Joseph Stiglitz, 1980, On the impossibility of informationally efficient markets, *American Economic Review* 70, 393–408.

Hamilton, James D., 1994, *Time Series Analysis*, Princeton University Press.

Hart, Oliver D. and David M. Kreps, 1986, Price destabilizing speculation, *Journal of Political Economy* 94, 927–52.

Haugen, Robert A., and Nardin L. Baker, 1996, Commonality in the determinants of expected stock returns, *Journal of Financial Economics* 41, 401–39.

Hong, Harrison, Terence Lim, and Jeremy C. Stein, 2000, Bad news travels slowly: Size, analyst coverage, and the profitability of momentum strategies, *Journal of Finance*, 55(1), 265–96.

Hong, Harrison, and Jeremy C. Stein, 1997, A unified theory of underreaction, momentum trading and overreaction in asset markets, NBER Working Paper #6324.

Ikenberry, David, Josef Lakonishok, and Theo Vermaelen, 1995, Market underreaction to open market share repurchases, *Journal of Financial Economics* 39, 181–208.

Ip, Greg, 1997, Red flag on wall street: Momentum investors, *Wall Street Journal*, February 24.

Jegadeesh, Narasimhan, and Sheridan Titman, 1993, Returns to buying winners and selling losers: Implications for stock market efficiency, *Journal of Finance* 48, 65–91.

Jereski, Laura, and Deborah Lohse, 1996, Momentum-investing fever is sending some mutual funds to their sickbeds, *Wall Street Journal*, July 26.

Lakonishok, Josef, Andrei Shleifer, and Robert Vishny, 1994, Contrarian investment, extrapolation and risk, *Journal of Finance* 49, 1541–78.

Lintner, John, 1965, The valuation of risk assets and the selection of risky investments in stock portfolios and capital budgets, *Review of Economics and Statistics* 47, 13–37.

Loughran, Tim, and Jay R. Ritter, 1995, The new issues puzzle, *Journal of Finance* 50, 23–51.

MacKinlay, A. Craig, 1995, Multifactor models do not explain deviations from the CAPM, *Journal of Financial Economics* 38, 3–28.

Merton, Robert C., 1973, An intertemporal capital asset pricing model, *Econometrica* 41, 867–87.

Michaely, Roni, Richard H. Thaler, and Kent L. Womack, 1995, Price reactions to dividend initiations and omissions: Overreaction or drift? *Journal of Finance* 50, 573–608.

Poterba, James M., and Lawrence H. Summers, 1988, Mean reversion in stock returns: Evidence and implications, *Journal of Financial Economics* 22, 27–59.

Rehfeld, Barry, 1996, Mutual funds: What goes up, might go up more, *New York Times*, February 25.

Ross, Stephen A., 1976, The arbitrage theory of capital asset pricing, *Journal of Economic Theory* 13, 341–60.

Rouwenhorst, K. Geert, 1998a, International momentum strategies, Yale University working paper, forthcoming in *Journal of Finance*.

———, 1998b, Local return factors and turnover in emerging stock markets, Yale University Working Paper.

Scharfstein, David S., and Jeremy C. Stein, 1990, Herd behavior and investment, *American Economic Review* 80, 465–79.

Sharpe, William F., 1964, Capital Asset Prices: A theory of market equilibrium under conditions of risk, *Journal of Finance* 19, 425–42.

Spiess, D. Katherine, and John Affleck-Graves, 1995, Underperformance in long-run stock returns following seasoned equity offerings, *Journal of Financial Economics* 38, 241–67.

Stein, Jeremy C., 1987, Informational externalities and welfare-reducing speculation, *Journal of Political Economy* 95, 1123–45.

Womack, Kent L., 1996, Do brokerage analysts' recommendations have investment value?, *Journal of Finance* 51, 137–68.

PART V

Investor Behavior

Chapter 15

INDIVIDUAL INVESTORS

Brad M. Barber and Terrance Odean

One half of U.S. households invest directly in common stocks or indirectly through mutual funds and other managed assets, and one half of U.S. households have self-directed retirement accounts such as individual retirement accounts (IRAs), Keogh accounts, and 401 (k) accounts (Kennickell, Starr-McCluer, and Surette 2000). The future welfare of these households depends on their ability to make sound investment decisions. While it would be convenient if all investors always made personally optimal decisions, they do not. Investors err, and many would benefit from education and advice. Financial advisors can more effectively help investors avoid common errors if the advisors understand the decision processes that lead to these errors.

In this chapter we review research that we, and others, have done to better understand the decision making of individual investors.[1] We focus on two characteristic behaviors of individual investors and the decision biases that lead to these behaviors. First, we look at the "disposition effect"—the tendency of investors to hold losing investments too long while selling winners too soon. Secondly, we examine the propensity of many investors to trade too actively. The disposition effect is one implication of Kahneman and Tversky's (1979) prospect theory. We believe that excessive trade is due, at least in part, to investor overconfidence.

1. The Disposition Effect

Shefrin and Statman (1985) argue that if investors keep separate mental investment accounts (see Thaler 1985) and treat gains and losses as described by prospect theory (Kahneman and Tversky 1979), they will tend to hold onto their losing investments while selling their winners. Under prospect theory, when faced with choices involving simple two- and three-outcome lotteries, people behave as if maximizing an "S"-shaped value function (see figure 15.1). This value function is similar to a standard utility function except that it is defined on gains and losses rather than on levels of wealth.

[1] This review is updated and revised from "The Courage of Misguided Conviction: Trading Behavior of Individual Investors," that appeared in the Nov./Dec. 1999 *Financial Analysts Journal*.

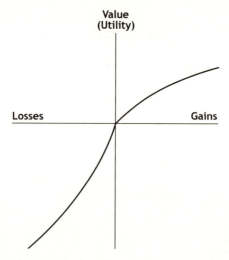

Figure 15.1. Prospect theory value function.

The function is concave in the domain of gains and convex in the domain
of losses. It is also steeper for losses than for gains, which implies that people are generally risk-averse. Critical to this value function is the reference
point from which gains and losses are measured. Usually the status quo is
taken as the reference point; however, "there are situations in which gains
and losses are coded relative to an expectation or aspiration level that differs from the status quo. . . . A person who has not made peace with his
losses is likely to accept gambles that would be unacceptable to him otherwise" (Kahneman and Tversky 1979, p. 287).

For example, suppose an investor purchases a stock that she believes to
have an expected return high enough to justify its risk. If the stock appreciates and the investor continues to use the purchase price as a reference
point, the stock price will then be in a more concave, more risk-averse, part
of the investor's value function. It may be that the stock's expected return
continues to justify its risk. However, if the investor somewhat lowers her
expectation of the stock's return, she will be likely to sell the stock. What if,
instead of appreciating, the stock declines? Then its price is in the convex,
risk-seeking, part of the value function. Here the investor will continue to
hold the stock even if its expected return falls lower than would have been
necessary for her to justify its original purchase. Thus the investor's belief
about expected return must fall further to motivate the sale of a stock that
has already declined rather than one that has appreciated. Similarly, consider an investor who holds two stocks. One is up; the other is down. If she
is faced with a liquidity demand, and has no new information about either
stock, she is more likely to sell the stock that is up.

Odean (1998a) examines the common stock trading of individual investors to see whether these investors tend to sell their winning investments more readily than their losers. A national discount brokerage house provided the data for this study. The data are trading records from January 1987 through December 1993 for 10,000 randomly selected accounts that were active in 1987 (those with at least one transaction). Each record includes an account identifier, a buy-sell indicator, the number of shares traded, the commission paid, and the principal amount.

Throughout the study, investors' reference points are assumed to be their purchase prices. Though the results presented here appear to vindicate that choice, it is likely that for some investments, particularly those held for a long time over a wide range of prices, the purchase price may be only one determinant of the reference point. The price path may also affect the level of the reference point. For example, a homeowner who bought her home for $100,000 just before a real estate boom and had the home appraised for $200,000 after the boom may no longer feel she is "breaking even" if she sells her home for $100,000 plus commissions.

If purchase price is a major component, though not the sole component, of reference point, it may serve as a noisy proxy for the true reference point. Using the proxy in place of the true reference point will make a case for the disposition effect more difficult to prove. It seems likely that if the true reference point were available, the evidence reported here would be even stronger.

A. Taxes

Investors' reluctance to realize losses is at odds with optimal tax-loss selling for taxable investments. For tax purposes, investors should postpone taxable gains by continuing to hold their profitable investments. They should capture tax losses by selling their losing investments, though not necessarily at a constant rate. Constantinides (1984) shows that when there are transaction costs, and no distinction is made between the short-term and long-term tax rates (as is approximately the case from 1987 to 1993 for U.S. federal taxes[2]), investors should gradually increase their tax-loss selling from January to December. Dyl (1977), Lakonishok and Smidt (1986), and Badrinath and Lewellen (1991) report evidence that investors do sell more losing investments near the end of the year.

---

[2] Prior to 1987, long-term capital gains tax rates were 40 percent of the short-term capital gains tax rates; from 1987 to 1993, long-term and short-term gains were taxed at the same marginal rates for lower income taxpayers. The maximum short-term rate at times exceeded the maximum long-term rate. In 1987 the maximum short-term rate was 38.5 percent and the maximum long-term rate was 28 percent. From 1988 to 1990 the highest income taxpayers paid a marginal rate of 28 percent on both long-term and short-term gains. In 1991 and 1992, the maximum long-term and short-term rates were 28 percent and 31 percent. In 1993, the maximum long-term and short-term rates were 28 percent and 39.6 percent.

B. Methodology

To determine whether investors sell winners more readily than losers, it is not sufficient to look at the number of securities sold for gains versus the number sold for losses. Suppose investors are indifferent to selling winners or losers. Then in an upward-moving market, they will have more winners in their portfolios and will tend to sell more winners than losers even though they had no preference for doing so. To test whether investors are disposed to selling winners and holding losers, we must look at the frequency with which they sell winners and losers relative to their opportunities to sell each.

By going through each account's trading records in chronological order, a portfolio of securities is constructed for which the purchase date and price are known. Clearly this portfolio represents only part of each investor's total portfolio. In most accounts there will be securities that were purchased before January 1987 for which the purchase price is not available, and investors may also have other accounts that are not part of the data set. Though the portfolios constructed from the data set are only part of each investor's total portfolio, it is unlikely that the selection process will bias these partial portfolios toward stocks for which investors have unusual preferences for realizing gains or losses.

Each day that a sale takes place in a portfolio of two or more stocks, the selling price for each stock sold is compared to its average purchase price to determine whether that stock is sold for a gain or a loss. Each stock that is in that portfolio at the beginning of that day, but is not sold, is considered to be a paper (unrealized) gain or loss (or neither). Whether it is a paper gain or loss is determined by comparing its high and low price for that day (as obtained from CRSP) to its average purchase price. If both its daily high and low are above its average purchase price, it is counted as a paper gain; if they are both below its average purchase price, it is counted as a paper loss; if its average purchase price lies between the high and the low, neither a gain nor loss is counted. On days when no sales take place in an account, no gains or losses, realized or paper, are counted.

In table 15.1, consider two investors: Daymon and Rosalie. Daymon has five stocks in his portfolio: A, B, C, D, and E. Stocks A and B are worth more than he paid for them; C, D, and E are worth less. Another investor, Rosalie, has three stocks in her portfolio: F, G, and H. Stocks F and G are worth more than she paid for them; H is worth less. On Monday, Daymon sells shares of A and of C. Wednesday, Rosalie sells shares of F. Daymon's sale of A and Rosalie's sale of F are counted as realized gains. Daymon's sale of C is a realized loss. Since B and G could have been sold for a profit but weren't, they are counted as paper gains. D, E, and G are paper losses. So, for these two investors over these two days, two realized gains, one realized loss, two paper gains, and three paper losses are counted. Realized gains,

TABLE 15.1
Example of Calculation of Proportion of Gains Realized (PGR) and
Proportion of Loses Realized (PLR)

	Daymon	Rosalie
Panel A: Positions		
Holdings	A, B, C, D, E	F, G, H
Winners	A, B	F, G
Losers	C, D, E	H
Panel B: Sales		
Sales on Monday	A and C	none
Sales on Wednesday	none	F
Panel C: Calculation of Gains and Losses		
Paper Gains	1(B)	1(G)
Paper Losses	2(D and E)	1(G)
Realized Gains	1(A)	1(F)
Realized Losses	1(C)	0

paper gains, realized losses, and paper losses are summed for each account and across accounts. Then two ratios are calculated:

$$\text{Proportion of Gains Realized (PGR)} = \frac{\text{Realized Gains}}{\text{Realized Gains} + \text{Paper Gains}}$$

$$\text{Proportion of Losses Realized (PLR)} = \frac{\text{Realized Losses}}{\text{Realized Losses} + \text{Paper Losses}}$$

In the example of Daymon and Rosalie, PGR = 1/2 and PLR = 1/4. A large difference in the proportion of gains realized (PGR) and the proportion of losses realized (PLR) indicates that investors are more willing to realize either gains or losses.

Any test of the disposition effect is a joint test of the hypothesis that people sell gains more readily than losses and of the specification of the reference point from which gains and losses are determined. Some possible choices of a reference point for stocks are the average purchase price, the highest purchase price, the first purchase price, or the most recent purchase price. The findings of this study are essentially the same for each choice; results are reported for average purchase price. Commissions and dividends may or may not be considered when determining reference points or profits and losses. Although investors may not consider commissions when they remember what they paid for a stock, commissions do affect capital gains and losses. And because the normative standard to which the disposition effect is being contrasted is optimal tax-motivated selling, commissions are added to the purchase price and deducted from the sales price in this study except where otherwise noted. Dividends are not included when determining which sales are profitable because they do not affect capital gains and losses for tax purposes. The primary finding of these tests, that investors are reluctant to sell their losers and prefer to sell winners, is unaffected by the inclusion or exclusion of commissions or dividends. In determining whether the stocks that are not sold on a particular day could have been sold for a gain or a loss, the commission for the potential sale is assumed to be the average commission per share paid when the stock was purchased.[3] All gains and losses are calculated after adjusting for splits.

C. Results

Figure 15.2 reports PGR and PLR for the entire year, for January through November and for December. We see that for the entire year, investors do sell a higher proportion of their winners than of their losers. Only in December, when the tax year is about to end, does PLR exceed PGR.[4]

It is worth emphasizing that the results described here hold up to a classic principle of scientific inquiry; they are robust to out-of-sample testing. Specifically, subsequent to Odean (1998a), we obtained trading records for 78,000 households from 1991 to 1996 from the same discount brokerage house. (These data are described in more detail in section 4.D.) For this new dataset, the PGR measure is 0.1442 and the PLR measure is 0.0863. During this sample period, stocks that had increased in value were approximately 65 percent more likely to be sold than stocks that had declined in value.

---

[3] If, for potential sales, the commission is instead assumed to be the same percentage of principal as paid when the stock was purchased, the results do not significantly change.

[4] In the reported PLR and PGR calculations, realized and unrealized losses are tabulated on days that sales took place in portfolios of two or more stocks. One objection to this formulation is that, for portfolios that hold only winners or only losers, an investor cannot choose whether to sell a winner or to sell a loser, but only which winner or loser to sell. Another objection is that if an investor has net capital losses of more than $3,000 for the current year (in non-tax-deferred accounts) it may be normative for that investor to choose to sell a winner rather than a loser. The analyses reported in the tables were repeated subject to the following additional constraints: that a portfolio hold at least one winner and one loser on the day of a sale for that day to be counted and that the net realized capital losses for the year to date in the portfolio be less than $3,000. When these constraints are imposed, the difference in PGR and PLR is, for each analysis, greater. For example, for the entire sample and the entire year (as in figure 15.2) there are 10,111 realized gains, 71,817 paper gains, 5,977 realized losses, and 94,419 paper losses. Thus the PLR is 0.060; the PGR is 0.123; their difference is 0.063; and the t-statistic for the difference in proportions is 47.

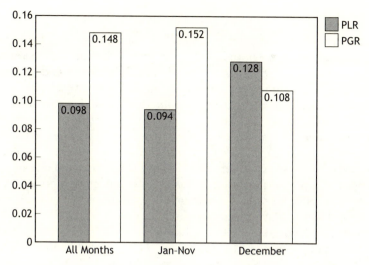

Figure 15.2. Proportion of gains realized and proportion of loses realized.

D. Alternative Reasons to Hold Losers and Sell Winners

Previous research offers some support for the hypothesis that investors sell winners more readily than losers, but this research is generally unable to distinguish among various motivations investors might have for doing so.[5] Recent studies (some of which are discussed in greater detail below) have found evidence of the disposition effect in the exercise of company stock options (Heath, Huddart, and Lang 1999, Core and Guay 2001), the sale of residential housing (Genesove and Mayer 2001), and among professional futures traders (Locke and Mann 1999), Israeli investors (Shapira and Venezia 2001), and Finnish investors (Grinblatt and Keloharju 2001). We believe the disposition effect best explains the tendency for investors to hold losers and sell winners. In this section, we present evidence that allows us to discount competing explanations for this investor behavior.

[5] Starr-McCluer (1995) finds that 15 percent of the stock-owning households interviewed in the 1989 and 1992 Surveys of Consumer Finances have paper losses of 20 percent or more. She estimates that in the majority of cases the tax advantages of realizing these losses would more than offset the trading costs and time costs of doing so. Heisler (1994) documents loss aversion in a small sample of futures speculators. In a study of individual federal tax returns, Poterba (1987) finds that although many investors do offset their capital gains with losses, more than 60 percent of the investors with gains or losses realized only gains. Weber and Camerer (1995) report experimental evidence of the disposition effect. Lakonishok and Smidt (1986) and Ferris, Haugen, and Makhija (1988) find a positive correlation between price change and volume. Bremer and Kato (1996) find the same correlation for Japanese stocks. Such a correlation could be caused by investors who prefer to sell winners and to hold losers, but it could also be the result of buyers' trading preferences.

D.1. ANTICIPATION OF CHANGES IN TAX LAW

One reason investors might choose to sell winners rather than losers is that they anticipate a change in the tax law under which capital gains rates will rise. The tax law of 1986 made such a change. If investors sold off winners in anticipation of higher tax rates, they might have entered 1987 with a larger percentage of losers in their portfolio than usual. Because such stocks are purchased prior to 1987, they would not show up in the portfolios reconstructed here. It is possible therefore that the rate at which winners are being realized relative to losers is lower in the investors' total portfolio than in the partial reconstructed portfolios. As old stocks are sold and new ones purchased, the partial portfolios become more and more representative of the total portfolio. We would expect that if a sell-off of winners in anticipation of the 1986 tax law affects the observed rate at which gains and losses are realized in the partial portfolios, that effect would be greater in the first part of the sample period than in the last. However the ratio PGR/PLR is virtually the same for the periods 1987 to 1990 and 1991 to 1993.

D.2. DESIRE TO REBALANCE

Lakonishok and Smidt (1986) suggest that investors might sell winners and hold onto losers in an effort to rebalance their portfolios. Investors who sell winners for the purpose of rebalancing their portfolios are likely to make new purchases. To eliminate trades that may be motivated by a desire to rebalance, PGR and PLR are calculated using only sales and dates for which there is no new purchase into a portfolio on the sale date or during the following three weeks. When sales motivated by a desire to rebalance are eliminated in this way, investors continue to prefer to sell winners. Once again, investors realize losses at a higher rate than gains in December.

D.3. BELIEF THAT ONE'S LOSERS WILL BOUNCE BACK

Another reason investors might sell winners and hold losers is that they expect their losers to outperform their winners in the future. An investor who buys a stock because of favorable information may sell that stock when it goes up because she believes her information is now reflected in the price. On the other hand, if the stock goes down she may continue to hold it, believing that the market has not yet come to appreciate her information. Investors could also choose to sell winners and hold losers simply because they believe prices may revert. It is possible to test whether such beliefs are justified, ex post.

To test whether the losing stocks investors hold outperform the winners they sell, Odean (1998a) calculates market-adjusted returns for losing stocks held and winning stocks sold subsequent to each sales date. For winners that were sold, he calculates market-adjusted returns (the average return in excess of the CRSP value weighted index) starting the day after the transaction for the next 84 trading days (four months), 252 trading days (one year), and 504 trading days (two years). For the same horizons, he calculates market-adjusted returns subsequent to paper losses. That is, for stocks held for a loss in portfolios on which sales did take place, market-adjusted returns are calculated starting the day after the sale for the next 84, 252, and 504 trading days.

For winners that are sold, the average excess return over the following year is a highly statistically significant 3.4 percent more than it is for losers that are not sold.[6] (Winners sold subsequently outperform paper losses by 1.03 percent over the following four months and 3.58 percent of the following two years.) Investors who sell winners and hold losers because they expect the losers to outperform the winners in the future are, on average, mistaken. The superior returns to former winners noted here are consistent with Jegadeesh and Titman's (1993) finding of price momentum in security returns at horizons of up to eighteen months.[7]

D.4. ATTEMPT TO LIMIT TRANSACTION COSTS

Harris (1988) suggests that investors' reticence to sell losers may be due to their sensitivity to higher trading costs at lower stock prices. To contrast the hypothesis that losses are realized more slowly due to the higher transactions costs with the disposition effect, we can look at the rates at which investors purchase additional shares of stocks they already own. If investors are avoiding the sale of losing investments because of the higher transaction costs associated with selling low-price stocks, we would also expect them to avoid purchasing additional shares of these losing investments. In fact, this is not the case; investors are more inclined to purchase additional shares of their losing investments than additional shares of their winning investments. In this sample, investors are almost one and one half times more likely to purchase additional shares of any losing position they already hold than any winning position.

D.5. BELIEF THAT ALL STOCKS MEAN REVERT

The results presented so far are not able to distinguish prospect theory and the mistaken belief that losers will bounce back to outperform current winners. Both prospect theory and a belief in mean-reversion predict that investors will hold their losers too long and sell their winners too soon. Both predict that investors will purchase more additional shares of losers than of winners. However, a belief in mean-reversion should apply to stocks that

[6] Here and in section 3, statistical significance is determined using a bootstrapping technique similar to those discussed in Brock, Lakonishok, and LeBaron (1992), Ikenberry, Lakonishok, and Vermaelen (1995), and Lyon, Barber, and Tsai (1999). This procedure is described in greater detail in Odean (1998a) and Odean (1999).

[7] At the time of this study, CRSP data were available through 1994. For this reason two-year subsequent returns are not calculated for sales dates in 1993.

an investor does not already own as well as those she does, but prospect theory applies only to the stocks she owns. Thus, a belief in mean-reversion implies that investors will tend to buy stocks that had previously declined even if they do not already own these stocks, while prospect theory makes no prediction in this case. Odean (1999) finds that this same group of investors tends to buy stocks that have, on average, outperformed the CRSP value-weighted index over the previous two years. This would appear inconsistent with a pervasive belief in mean-reversion.

E. Employee Stock Options

Investors are more likely to sell stocks that they are holding for a gain over purchase price than those they are holding for a loss. How do they treat securities for which there is no clear purchase price? Heath, Huddart, and Lang (1999) help to answer this question by examining when employees exercise company stock options. Because employees do not pay for their stock options, there is no purchase price that can serve as a reference point. Options are generally issued with ten years to expiration and are typically exercised for cash. Heath, Huddart, and Lang examine stock option records for over 50,000 employees at seven publicly traded corporations over a ten-year period. For each option grant (options issued on a single date), they calculate the fraction of outstanding options exercised each week. They regress this fraction on several variables including the fraction of options recently vested, the fraction of options soon to expire, the ratio of the option's intrinsic value to its expected value, recent returns, and a dummy variable for whether the current price exceeds the maximum price obtained in the previous year (excluding the previous month). As one would expect, recently vested options, those soon to expire, and those with a greater intrinsic value relative to expected value are more likely to be exercised. Employees are more likely to exercise options when the exercise price is above the stock's previous year's maximum, and they are more likely to exercise options that have recently appreciated. These findings are consistent with the disposition effect and suggest that when purchase price is not an available reference point, many investors focus on recent maximums as a reference point.

F. Finnish Investors

Grinnblatt and Keloharju (2001) examine trading records for 1995 and 1996 for all Finnish stock investors—households, institutions, and foreigners. Estimating logit regressions for the decision to sell rather than continue to hold a stock, Grinblatt and Keloharju find that all investor groups are more likely to sell stocks that have outperformed the market in recent days and weeks. Investors are less likely to sell when faced with a larger (i.e., greater than 30 percent) capital loss than a smaller loss. They pay attention to taxes in December, especially in late December. Controlling for past market returns, investors who are holding a stock for a loss are less likely to sell than those holding for a gain. And investors are more likely to sell a stock that has hit its high price within the last month. Grinnblatt and Keloharju also estimate logit regressions comparing selling decisions to purchase decisions. They find that, generally, high past returns make it more likely that a Finnish investor will sell rather than buy a stock. Finnish investors are also more likely to buy a stock that is at a monthly low and sell a stock that is at a monthly high. High volatility increases the propensity of households to buy, rather than sell, a stock. And, consistent with the life cycle hypothesis, the oldest investors are more likely to sell stocks and the youngest more likely to buy.

G. Real Estate

The reluctance of investors to realize losses is not confined to stock and option losses. Genesove and Mayer (2001) find that homeowners, too, exhibit a disposition effect. Genesove and Mayer examine individual listings for Boston condominiums between 1990 and 1997. Their data track listing dates and prices, exit dates, type of exit (e.g., sale or withdrawal), and property characteristics such as square footage and number of bedrooms, previous appraisal prices, owner occupancy, and mortgage information. They determine which sellers face an expected loss by estimating current condominium values and comparing these to original purchase prices. They find that sellers facing losses set higher asking prices of 25 to 35 percent of the difference between the expected selling price of a property and their original purchase price. On average, these sellers attain higher selling prices of 3 to 18 percent of that difference though their sales come, on average, after more time on the market than those of sellers not facing losses.

2. OVERCONFIDENCE AND EXCESSIVE TRADING

Psychologists find that people tend to be overconfident. That is, they tend to overestimate their abilities and the precision of their information. Odean (1998b) demonstrates theoretically that overconfident investors trade more than those who are not overconfident and, as a result of excessive trading, lower their expected utilities.[8]

Overconfidence increases trading activity because it causes investors to be too certain about their own opinions and to not consider sufficiently the

---

[8] Other theoretical treatments of overconfident investors include De Long, Shleifer, Summers, and Waldmann (1991), Benos (1998), Kyle and Wang (1997), Daniel, Hirshleifer, and Subramanyam (1998), and Gervais and Odean (2001).

opinions of others. This increases the heterogeneity of investors' beliefs—
the source of most trading. Overconfident investors also perceive their actions to be less risky than generally proves to be the case.

In this section, we briefly review psychological studies of overconfidence
and then describe three empirical studies we have done of investor overconfidence.

A. Overconfidence

Studies of the calibration of subjective probabilities find that people tend to
overestimate the precision of their knowledge (Alpert and Raiffa 1982, Fischhoff, Slovic, and Lichtenstein 1977; see Lichtenstein, Fischhoff, and
Phillips 1982 for a review of the calibration literature). Such overconfidence has been observed in many professional fields. Clinical psychologists
(Oskamp 1965), physicians and nurses (Christensen-Szalanski and Bushyhead 1981, Baumann, Deber, and Thompson 1991), investment bankers
(Staël von Holstein 1972), engineers (Kidd 1970), entrepreneurs (Cooper,
Woo, and Dunkelberg 1988), lawyers (Wagenaar and Keren 1986), nego-
tiators (Neale and Bazerman 1990), and managers (Russo and Schoemaker
1992) have all been observed to exhibit overconfidence in their judgments.
(For further discussion, see Lichtenstein, Fischhoff, and Phillips 1982, and
Yates 1990).

Miscalibration is only one manifestation of overconfidence. Researchers
also find that people overestimate their ability to do well on tasks, and
these overestimates increase with the personal importance of the task
(Frank 1935). People are also unrealistically optimistic about future events.
They expect good things to happen to them more often than to their peers
(Weinstein 1980, Kunda 1987). They are even unrealistically optimistic
about pure chance events (Marks 1951, Irwin 1953, Langer and Roth 1975).

People have unrealistically positive self-evaluations (Greenwald 1980).
Most individuals see themselves as better than the average person, and most
individuals see themselves better than others see them (Taylor and Brown
1988). They rate their abilities and their prospects higher than those of
their peers. For example, when a sample of U.S. students—average age
twenty-two—assessed their own driving safety, 82 percent judged themselves to be in the top 30 percent of the group (Svenson 1981). And 81 percent of 2,994 new business owners thought their business had a 70 percent
or better chance of succeeding, but only 39 percent thought that any business like theirs would be this likely to succeed (Cooper, Woo, and Dunkelberg 1988).

People overestimate their own contributions to past positive outcomes,
recalling information related to their successes more easily than that related
to their failures. Fischhoff (1982) writes that "they even misremember their

own predictions so as to exaggerate in hindsight what they knew in fore-sight." And when people expect a certain outcome and the outcome then occurs, they often overestimate the degree to which they were instrumental in bringing it about (Miller and Ross 1975). Taylor and Brown (1988) argue that exaggerated belief in one's abilities and unrealistic optimism may lead to "higher motivation, greater persistence, more effective performance, and ultimately, greater success." These beliefs can also lead to biased judgments.

B. Overconfidence in Financial Markets

In a market with transaction costs, we would expect informed traders who trade for the purpose of increasing returns to increase returns, on average, by at least enough to cover transaction costs. That is, over the appropriate horizon, the securities these traders buy will outperform the ones they sell by at least enough to pay the costs of trading. If speculative traders are in-formed, but overestimate the precision of their information (one form of overconfidence), the securities they buy will, on average, outperform those they sell, but possibly not by enough to cover trading costs. If these traders believe they have information, but actually have none, the securities they buy will perform, on average, about the same as those they sell, before fac-toring in trading costs. Overconfidence in only the precision of unbiased in-formation will not, in and of itself, cause expected trading losses beyond the loss of transaction costs.

If, in addition to being overconfident about the precision of their infor-mation, investors are overconfident about their ability to interpret informa-tion, they may incur average trading losses beyond transaction costs. Sup-pose investors receive useful information but are systematically biased in their interpretation of that information; that is, the investors hold mistaken beliefs about the mean, instead of (or in addition to) the precision of the distribution of their information. If they unwittingly misinterpret informa-tion, they may choose to buy or sell securities that they would not have oth-erwise bought or sold. They may even buy securities that, on average and before transaction costs, underperform the ones they sell.

C. Do Investors Trade Too Much?

To test whether individual investors at a large discount brokerage are over-confident in the precision of their information, Odean (1999) determines whether the common stocks these investors buy outperform the common stocks they sell by enough to cover trading costs. To test for biased inter-pretation of information, he determines whether the securities these investors buy outperform those they sell when trading costs are ignored. The data for the study are the same as are analyzed in Odean (1998a) and described in section 1 above. Return horizons of four months (84 trading days), one year (252 trading days), and two years (504 trading days) following each transaction are examined.[9] Returns are calculated from the CRSP daily return files.

To calculate the average return to securities bought (sold) in these accounts over the T ($T = 84$, 252, or 504) trading days subsequent to the purchase (sale), each purchase (sale) transaction is indexed with a subscript i, $i = 1$ to N. Each transaction consists of a security, j_i, and a date, t_i. If the same security is bought (sold) in different accounts on the same day, each purchase (sale) is treated as a separate transaction. Market-adjusted returns are calculated as the security return less the return on the CRSP value-weighted index. The market-adjusted return for the securities bought over the T trading days subsequent to the purchase is:

$$R_{P,T} = \frac{1}{N} \sum_{i=1}^{N} \left(\prod_{\tau=1}^{T} (1 + R_{j_i, t_i + \tau}) - \prod_{\tau=1}^{T} (1 + R_{VW, t_i + \tau}) \right)_1$$

where $R_{j,t}$ is the CRSP daily return for security j on date t and $R_{VW,t}$ is the daily return for the CRSP value-weighted index on date t. Note that return calculations begin the day after a purchase or a sale to avoid incorporating the bid-ask spread into returns.

In this dataset, the (equally weighted) average commission paid when a security is purchased is 2.23 percent of the purchase price. The average commission on a sale is 2.76 percent of the sale price.[10] Therefore, if one security is sold and the sale proceeds are used to buy another security, the total commissions for the sale and purchase average about 5 percent. The average effective bid-ask spread is 0.94 percent.[11] Thus the average total cost of a round-trip trade is about 5.9 percent. An investor who sells securities and buys others because he expects the securities he is buying to outperform the ones he is selling, will have to realize, on average and weighting trades equally, a return nearly 6 percent higher on the security he buys just to cover trading costs.

The first hypothesis tested here is that, over horizons of four months, one year, and two years, the average returns to securities bought minus the average returns to securities sold are less than the average round-trip trading

---

[9] Investment horizons will vary among investors and investments. Benartzi and Thaler (1995) estimate the average investor's investment horizon to be one year, and, during this period, NYSE securities turned over about once every two years. At the time of this analysis, CRSP data was available through 1994. For this reason, two-year subsequent returns are not calculated for transactions dates in 1993.

[10] Weighting each trade by its equity value, rather than equally, the average commission for a purchase (sale) is 0.9 (0.8) percent.

[11] Barber and Odean (2000) estimate the bid-ask spread of 1.00 percent for individual investors from 1991 to 1996. Carhart (1997) estimates trading costs of 0.21 percent for purchases and 0.63 percent for sales made by open-end mutual funds from 1966 to 1993.

Figure 15.3. Market-adjusted returns subsequent to buys less market-adjusted returns subsequent to sells.

costs of 5.9 percent. This is what we expect if investors are sufficiently overconfident about the precision of their information. The first null hypothesis is that this difference in returns is greater than or equal to 5.9 percent. This null is consistent with rationality. The second hypothesis is that over these same horizons the average returns to securities bought are less than those to securities sold, ignoring trading costs. This hypothesis implies that investors must actually misinterpret useful information. The second null hypothesis is that average returns to securities bought are greater than or equal to those sold.

For all three follow-up periods the average subsequent market-adjusted returns to stocks that were bought is less than that to stocks that were sold. Figure 15.3 provides a graph of the difference between the market-adjusted returns to stocks that were bought and the market-adjusted returns to stocks that were sold. Regardless of the horizon, the stocks that investors bought underperformed the stocks that they sold. (This is also true when actual returns are calculated instead of market-adjusted returns.) Not only do the investors pay transactions costs to switch stocks, but the stocks they buy underperform the ones they sell. Over a four-month horizon, the average market-adjusted return on a purchased stock is 1.45 percentage points lower than the average market-adjusted return on a stock sold. Over a one-year horizon, this underperformance is 3.2 percentage points. Over a two-year horizon the shortfall is only slightly greater, 3.6 percentage points.

The first null hypothesis that the expected returns to stocks purchased are 5.9 percent (the average cost of a round-trip trade) or more greater than the expected returns to stocks sold is comfortably rejected ($p < 0.001$ for all three horizons). The second null hypothesis, that the expected returns to stocks purchased are greater than or equal to those of stocks sold (ignoring transactions costs), is also comfortably rejected ($p < 0.001$, $p < 0.001$, and $p < 0.002$ for horizons of four months, one year, and two years respectively).

These investors are not making profitable trades. Of course investors trade for reasons other than to increase profit. They trade to meet liquidity demands. They trade to move to more, or to less, risky investments. They trade to realize tax losses. And they trade to rebalance; for example, if one stock in her portfolio appreciates considerably, an investor may sell part of her holding in that stock and buy others to rebalance her portfolio.

Odean (1999) examines trades for which these alternative motivations for trading have been largely eliminated. These "speculative" trades include: (1) only sales and purchases in which a purchase was made within three weeks following a sale; such transactions are unlikely to be liquidity motivated since investors who need cash for less than three weeks can borrow more cheaply (e.g., by using credit cards) than by selling and later buying stocks; (2) only sales that were for a profit; so these stocks were not sold in order to realize tax losses (and they were not short sales); (3) only sales of an investor's complete holding in the stock sold; so most of these sales were not motivated by a desire to rebalance the holdings of an appreciated stock; and (4) only sales and purchases in which the purchased stock is from the same-size decile as the stock sold or it is from a smaller-size decile (CRSP size deciles for the year of the transaction). Since size has been shown to be highly correlated with risk, this restriction is intended to eliminate most instances in which an investor intentionally buys a stock of lower expected return than the one he sells because he is hoping to reduce his risk.

When all of these alternative motivations for trading are eliminated, investors actually perform worse over all three evaluation periods. Over a four-month horizon, speculative purchases underperform speculative sells by 2.5 percentage points; over a one-year horizon by 5.1 percentage points; and over a two-year horizon by 8.6 percentage points. Sample size is, however, greatly reduced and statistical significance slightly lower. Nonetheless, both null hypotheses can still be comfortably rejected. (For the first null hypothesis $p < 0.001$ at all three horizons; for the second null hypothesis $p < 0.001$, $p < 0.001$, and $p < 0.02$ for four months, one year, and two years respectively).

As was the case for the tests of the disposition effect, we have been able to replicate these results out-of-sample. Subsequent to Odean (1999), we obtained trading records for 78,000 households from 1991 to 1996 from the same discount brokerage house. (These data are described in more detail in section 4.E.) On average, the 1,082,106 stocks that these households buy reliably underperform ($p < 0.001$) the 887,638 they sell by 2.35 percent over the 252 trading days subsequent to each transaction.

Overconfidence alone cannot explain these results. These investors appear to have some ability to distinguish stocks that will subsequently perform better and worse. Unfortunately, somehow they get the relationship wrong.

D. Trading is Hazardous to Your Wealth

Odean (1998b) predicts that the more overconfident investors are, the more they will trade and the more they will thereby lower their expected utilities. If overconfidence is an important motivation for investor trading, then we would expect that, on average, those investors who trade most actively will most reduce their returns through trading. As reported in Barber and Odean (2000), we find that this is the case.

We examine trading and position records for 78,000 households with accounts at the same discount brokerage house as supplied the data described above. The records are from January 1991 through December 1996 and include all accounts at this brokerage for each household. (See Barber and Odean 2000 for a detailed description of these data.) Of the 78,000 sampled households, 66,465 had positions in common stocks during at least one month; the remaining accounts either held cash or investments in other than individual common stocks. Roughly 60 percent of the market value in the accounts was held in common stocks. There were over 3 million trades in all securities; common stocks accounted for slightly more than 60 percent of all trades. In December 1996, these households held more than $4.5 billion in common stock. In addition to trade and position records, for much of our sample, our dataset identifies demographic characteristics such as age, gender, marital status, and income.

We partition the households into quintiles on the basis of the average monthly turnover of their common stock portfolios. Mean monthly turnover for these quintiles ranges from 0.19 percent (low turnover quintile) to 21.49 percent (high turnover quintile). Households that trade frequently (high turnover quintile) earn a net annualized geometric mean return of 11.4 percent, while those that trade infrequently (low turnover quintile) earn 18.5 percent. Figure 15.4 graphs turnover and net annualized geometric returns for these quintiles.

Our finding that the more investors trade the more they reduce their expected returns is consistent with the prediction that more overconfident traders will trade more actively and earn less. However, we still haven't tested directly whether overconfidence is motivating trading. To do so, we partition our data into two groups which psychologists have shown to differ in their tendency to overconfidence: men and women.

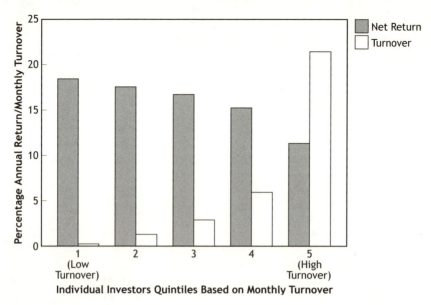

Figure 15.4. Monthly turnover and annual performance of individual investors. The gray bar represents the net annualized geometric mean return from February 1991 to January 1997 for individual investor quintiles based on monthly turnover. The white bar represents the monthly turnover.

E. Boys Will Be Boys

While both men and women exhibit overconfidence, men are generally more overconfident than women (Lundeberg, Fox, and Puncochar 1994).[12] Gender differences in overconfidence are highly task dependent (Lundeberg, Fox, and Puncochar). Deaux and Farris (1977) write, "overall, men claim more ability than do women, but this difference emerges most strongly on . . . masculine task[s]." Several studies confirm that differences in confidence are greatest for tasks perceived to be in the masculine domain (Deaux and Emswiller 1994, Lenney 1977, Beyer and Bowden 1997). Men are inclined to feel more competent than women do in financial matters (Prince 1993). Indeed, casual observation reveals that men are disproportionately represented in the financial industry. We expect, therefore, that men will generally be more overconfident about their ability to make financial decisions than women.

Additionally, Lenney (1977) reports that gender differences in self-confidence depend on the lack of clear and unambiguous feedback. When

[12] While Lichtenstein and Fischhoff (1981) do not find gender differences in calibration of general knowledge, Lundeberg, Fox, and Puncochar (1994) argue that this is because gender differences in calibration are strongest for topics in the masculine domain.

feedback is "unequivocal and immediately available, women do not make lower ability estimates than men. However, when such feedback is absent or ambiguous, women seem to have lower opinions of their abilities and often do underestimate relative to men." The stock market does not generally provide clear, unambiguous feedback. All the more reason to expect men to be more confident than women about their ability to make common stock investments.

Our prediction, then, is clear: We expect men, the more overconfident group, to trade more actively than women and, in doing so, to detract from their net return performance more. As reported in Barber and Odean (2001a), we find that this prediction holds true. Men trade 45 percent more actively than do women (76.9 percent turnover annually versus 52.8 percent). And men reduce their net annual returns through trading by 0.94 percentage points more than do women. (Men underperform their "buy-and-hold" portfolios by 2.652 percentage points annually; women underperform their "buy-and-hold" portfolios by 1.716 percentage points annually.) The differences in the turnover and performance of men and women are highly statistically significant and robust to the introduction of other demographic variables such as marital status, age, and income.

3. BUYING VERSUS SELLING

Our analysis of the trading behavior of individual investors reveals that most investors treat the decision to buy a security quite differently from the decision to sell. Since most investors do not short—less than 1 percent of the positions in our discount brokerage datasets are short positions—those seeking a security to sell need only consider the ones they already own. This is usually a manageable handful; in our discount brokerage datasets the average number of securities, including bonds, mutual funds, and options as well as stocks per account is less than seven. Investors can carefully consider selling each security they own.

When buying securities, investors face a formidable problem. There are well over 10,000 securities to be considered. While the search for potential purchases can be simplified by confining it to a subset of all securities (e.g., the S&P 500), even then the task of evaluating and comparing each security is beyond what most nonprofessionals are equipped to do. Unable to evaluate each security, investors are likely to consider purchasing securities to which their attention has been drawn such as securities that are in the news. In ongoing research (Barber and Odean 2003), we find that investors tend to be net purchasers of attention grabbing stocks, even when it is bad news that catches their attention.

4. The Internet and the Investor

The Internet has brought changes to investing that may bolster the over-confidence of online investors by providing an illusion of knowledge and an illusion of control, while also changing the decision criteria to which they attend (Barber and Odean 2001b, 2002).

By one account, every online investor has access to over three billion pieces of financial data; those who are willing to pay have access to over 280 billion pieces.[13] However, when people are given more information on which to base a forecast or assessment, their confidence in the accuracy of their forecasts tends to increase much more quickly than the accuracy of those forecasts (Oskamp 1965, Hoge 1970, Slovic 1973, Peterson and Pitz 1988). In fact, at some point, actual predictive skill may decline as informa-tion rises, due to information overload (Stewart, Heideman, Moniger and Reagan-Cirincione 1992, Keller and Staelin 1987). Thus, additional infor-mation can lead to an illusion of knowledge.

Online investors—who have access to vast data—are likely to become overconfident. They may believe that they have more ability to perform tasks such as stock-picking than they actually do. Data providers encourage this belief with advertisements such as one (from eSignal) that promises: "You'll make more, because you know more." In theoretical models, over-confident individual investors trade more actively and more speculatively than they otherwise would, they hold underdiversified portfolios, have lower expected utilities, and contribute to increased market volatility (Odean 1998b).

In an empirical study of investors at a large discount brokerage who switched from phone-based to personal computer-based trading, we find that after going online investors tend to trade both more actively and more speculatively (Barber and Odean 2002). Corroborating evidence that the internet encourages trading comes from the behavior of participants in company 401(k) plans. At companies that adopted web-based interfaces for plan participants during the 1990s, turnover in 401(k) accounts in-creased by 50 percent; there was no such increase in trading activity for firms without web-based access (Choi, Laibson, and Metrick, 2002). Per-haps investors that switched from phone-based to online trading antici-pated higher trading levels; though less plausible, perhaps companies that adopted web-based interfaces for 401(k) participants anticipated the greater

[13] This estimate was provided by Inna Okounkova at Scudder Kemper. These estimates are based on financial information readily available on the web. For example, an investor can download daily high, low, closing prices, volume, and returns data from Microsoft's investor website (moneycentral.msn.com) for up to ten years for all publicly traded stocks in the United States. Assuming 10,000 publicly traded stocks with an average history of five years, these data alone represent 63 million bits of information.

trading needs of their employees. Neither of these studies can prove that the Internet causes increased trading, but they do provide preliminary evidence.

The theme of control is pervasive in the advertising of financial e-commerce firms. One Ameritrade advertisement, for example, states that online investing "is about control." Balasubramanian, Konana, and Menon (1999) list "feeling of empowerment" as one of seven basic reasons given for switching to online trading by visitors to an online brokerage house's website. Psychologists find that people behave as if their personal involvement can influence the outcome of chance events—an effect labeled the illusion of control (Langer 1977, Langer and Roth 1975, for a review, see Presson and Benassi 1996). This literature documents that overconfidence occurs when factors ordinarily associated with improved performance in skilled situations—such as choice, task familiarity, competition, and active involvement—are present in situations at least partly governed by chance. The problem is that investors are likely to confuse the control they have—over which investments they make, with the control that they lack, over the return those investments realize. As a result, they are likely to trade too often and too speculatively.

5. CONCLUSION

One of the major contributions of behavioral finance is that it provides insights into investor behavior where such behavior cannot be understood using traditional theories. In this chapter we review tests of two behavioral finance theories—the disposition effect, which emanates from Kahneman and Tversky's Prospect Theory, and overconfidence. Consistent with the predictions of prospect theory, there is compelling evidence that investors tend to sell their winning investments and to hold onto their losers. As a result of overconfidence, investors trade too much. These behaviors reduce investor welfare. Understanding these behaviors is therefore important for investors and for those who advise them.

But the welfare consequences of investor behavior extend beyond individual investors and their advisors. Modern financial markets depend on trading volume for their very existence. It is trading—commissions and spreads—that pays for the brokers and market-makers without whom these markets would not exist. Traditional models of financial markets give us very little insight into why people trade as much as they do. In some models, investors seldom trade or do not trade at all (e.g., Grossman 1976). Other models simply stipulate a class of investors—noise or liquidity traders—who are required to trade (e.g., Kyle 1985). Harris and Raviv (1993) and Varian (1989) point out that heterogeneous beliefs are needed to generate significant trading. But it is behavioral finance that gives us insights into why and when investors form heterogeneous beliefs.

Both behavioral theories tested in this chapter offer insights into trading volume. The disposition effect says that investors will generally trade less actively when their investments have lost money. The overconfidence theory suggests that investors will trade more actively when their overconfidence is high. Psychologists find that people tend to give themselves too much credit for their own success and do not attribute enough of that success to chance or outside circumstance. Gervais and Odean (2001) show that this bias leads successful investors to become overconfident. And, in a market where most investors are successful (e.g., a long bull market), aggregate overconfidence and consequent trading rise. Statman and Thorley (1999) find that over even short horizons, such as a month, current market returns predict subsequent trading volume.

In the past two decades, researchers have discovered many anomalies that apparently contradict established finance theories.[14] New theories, both behavioral (e.g., Barberis, Shleifer, and Vishny 1998, Daniel, Hirshleifer, and Subrahmanyam 1998) and rational (e.g., Berk 1995, Berk, Green, and Naik 1999), have been devised to explain anomalies in asset prices. It is not yet clear what contribution behavioral finance will make to asset pricing theory.

The investor behaviors discussed in this chapter have the potential to influence asset prices. The tendency to refrain from selling losing investments may, for example, slow the rate at which negative news is translated into price. The tendency to buy stocks with recent extreme performance could cause recent winners to overshoot. For biases to influence asset prices, investors must be sufficiently systematic in their biases and sufficiently willing to act on them.[15]

Our common psychological heritage ensures that we systematically share biases. Overconfidence provides the will to act on our biases.

[14] See, for example, Thaler's (1992) collection of "Anomalies" articles originally published in the *Journal of Economic Perspectives*.

[15] Of course, there must also be limits to arbitrage (see Shleifer and Vishny 1997).

References

Alpert, Marc, and Howard Raiffa, 1982, A progress report on the training of probability assessors, in Daniel Kahneman, Paul Slovic, and Amos Tversky (eds.), *Judgment Under Uncertainty: Heuristics and Biases*, Cambridge University Press.

Badrinath, S., Wilber Lewellen, 1991, Evidence on tax-motivated securities trading behavior, *Journal of Finance*, 46, 369–82.

Balasubramanian, S., P. Konana, and N. Menon, 1999, Understanding online investors: An analysis of their investing behavior and attitudes, Working Paper, University of Texas, Austin.

Barber, Brad M., and Terrance Odean, 1999, The courage of misguided convictions, *Financial Analysts Journal*, November/December, 41–55.

———, 2000, Trading is hazardous to your wealth: The common stock investment performance of individual investors, *Journal of Finance*, 55, 773–806.

———, 2001a, Boys will be boys: Gender, overconfidence, and common stock investment, *Quarterly Journal of Economics*, 116(1), 261–92.

———, 2001b, The internet and the investor, *The Journal of Economic Perspectives*, 15(1), 41–54.

———, 2002, Online investors: Do the slow die first?, *Review of Financial Studies* 15, 455–87.

———, 2003, All that glitters: The effect of attention and news on the buying behavior of individual and institutional investors, Working Paper, University of California, Davis.

Barberis, Nicholas, Andre Shleifer, and Robert Vishny, 1998, A model of investor sentiment, *Journal of Financial and Economics Analysts*.

Baumann, Andrea O., Raisa B. Deber, and Gail G. Thompson, 1991, Overconfidence among physicians and nurses: The "Micro-Certainty, Macro-Uncertainty" Phenomenon, *Social Science & Medicine* 32, 167–74.

Benartzi, Shlomo, and Richard Thaler, 1995, Myopic loss aversion and the equity premium puzzle, *Quarterly Journal of Economics* 110, 73–92.

Benos, Alexandros V., 1998, Aggress, Veness and survival of overconfident speculators in call markets: Trade patterns investors, *Journal of Financial Markets* 1, 353–83.

Berk, Jonathan, 1995, A critique of size related anomalies, *Review of Financial Studies* 8, 275–86.

Berk, Jonathan, Richard C. Green, and Vasant Noik, 1999, *Journal of Finance* 54, 1553–1607.

Bremer, Marc, and Kiyoshi Kato, 1996, Trading volume for winners and losers on the Tokyo Exchange, *Journal of Financial and Quantitative Analysis* 31, 127–42.

Beyer, Sylvia, and Edward M. Bowden, 1997, Gender differences in self-perceptions: Convergent evidence from three measures of accuracy and bias, *Personality and Social Psychology Bulletin* 23, 157–72.

Brock, William, Josef Lakonishok, and Blake LeBaron, 1992, Simple technical trading rules and the stochastic properties of stock returns, *Journal of Finance* 47, 1731–64.

Carhart, Mark M., 1997, On persistence in mutual fund performance, *Journal of Finance* 52, 57–82.

Choi, James J., David Laibson, and Andrew Metrick, 2002, How does the internet affect trading, Evidence from Investor Behavior in 401(k) Plans, *Journal of Financial Economics* 64, 317–421.

Christensen-Szalanski, Jay J. and James B. Bushyhead, 1981, Physicians' use of probabilistic information in a real clinical setting, *Journal of Experimental Psychology: Human Perception and Performance* 7, 928–35.

Constantinides, George, 1984, Optimal stock trading with personal taxes: Implications for prices and the abnormal January returns, *Journal of Financial Economics* 13, 65–69.

Cooper, Arnold C., Carolyn Y. Woo, and William C. Dunkelberg, 1988, Entrepreneurs' perceived chances for success, *Journal of Business Venturing* 3, 97–108.

Core, John E., and Wayne R. Guay, 2001, Stock option plans for non-executive employees, *Journal of Financial Economics* 61, 253–87.

Daniel, Kent, David Hirshleifer, and Avanidhar Subrahmanyam, 1998, A theory of overconfidence, self-attribution, and security market under- and over-reactions, *Journal of Finance* 53, 1839–86.

Deaux, Kay, and Tim Emswiller, 1974, Explanations of successful performance on sex-linked tasks: What is skill for the male is luck for the female, *Journal of Personality and Social Psychology* 29, 80–85.

Deaux, Kay, and Elizabeth Farris, 1977, Attributing causes for one's own performance: The effects of sex, norms, and outcome, *Journal of Research in Personality* 11, 59–72.

De Long, J. Bradford, Andrei Shleifer, Lawrence H. Summers, and Robert J. Waldmann, 1991, The survival of noise traders in financial markets, *Journal of Business* 64, 1–19.

Dyl, Edward, 1977, Capital gains taxation and the year-end stock market behavior, *Journal of Finance* 32, 165–75.

Ferris, Stephen, Robert Haugen, and Anil Makhija, 1988, Predicting contemporary volume with historic volume at differential price levels: Evidence supporting the disposition effect, *Journal of Finance* 43, 677–97.

Fischhoff, Baruch, 1982, For those condemned to study the past: Heuristics and biases in hindsight, in Daniel Kahneman, Paul Slovic, and Amos Tversky (eds.), *Judgment Under Uncertainty: Heuristics and Biases*, Cambridge University Press.

Fischhoff, Baruch, Paul Slovic, and Sarah Lichtenstein, 1977, Knowing with certainty: The appropriateness of extreme confidence, *Journal of Experimental Psychology* 3, 552–64.

Frank, Jerome D., 1935, Some psychological determinants of the level of aspiration, *American Journal of Psychology* 47, 285–93.

Genesove, David, and Chris Mayer, 2001, Loss aversion and seller behavior: Evidence from the housing market, *Quarterly Journal of Economics* 116, 1233–60.

Gervais, Simon, and Terrance Odean, 2001, *Review of Financial Studies* 14(1), 1–27.

Greenwald, Anthony G., 1980, The totalitarian ego: Fabrication and revision of personal history, *American Psychologist* 35, 603–18.

Grinblatt, Mark, and Matti Keloharju, 2001, What makes investors trade?, *Journal of Finance* 56, 589–616.

Grossman, Sanford J., 1976, On the efficiency of competitive stock markets where traders have diverse information, *Journal of Finance* 31, 573–85.

Harris, Lawrence, 1988, Discussion of Predicting contemporary volume with historic volume at differential price levels: Evidence supporting the disposition effect, *Journal of Finance* 43, 698–99.

Harris, Milton, and Artur Raviv, 1993, Differences of opinion make a horse race, *Review of Financial Studies* 6, 473–506.

Heath, Chip, Steven Huddart, and Mark Lang, 1999, Psychological factors and security option exercise, *Quarterly Journal of Economics* 114, 601–27.

Heisler, Jeffrey, 1994, Loss aversion in a futures market: An empirical test, *Review of Futures Markets* 13, 793–822.

Hoge, Robert D., 1970, Confidence in decision as an index of perceived accuracy of information processing, *Psychonomic Science* 18, 351–53.

Ikenberry, David, Josef Lakonishok, and Theo Vermaelen, 1995, Market underreaction to open market share repurchases, *Journal of Financial Economics* 39, 181–208.

Irwin, Francis W., 1953, Stated expectations as functions of probability and desirability of outcomes, *Journal of Personality* 21, 329–35.

Jegadeesh, Narasimhan, and Sheridan Titman, 1993, Returns to buying winners and selling losers: Implications for stock market efficiency, *Journal of Finance* 48, 65–91.

Kahneman, Daniel, and Amos Tversky, 1979, Prospect theory: An analysis of decision under risk, *Econometrica* 47, 263–92.

Keller, Kevin L. and Richard Staelin, 1987, Effects of quality and quantity of information on decision effectiveness, *Journal of Consumer Research* 14, 200–13.

Kennickell, Arthur B., Martha Starr-McCluer, and Brian J. Surette, 2000, Recent changes in U.S. Family Finances: Results from the 1998 survey of consumer finances, Federal Reserve Bulletin 86, 1–29.

Kidd, John B., 1970, The utilization of subjective probabilities in production planning, *Acta Psychologica* 34, 338–47.

Kunda, Ziva, 1987, Motivated inference: Self-serving generation and evaluation of causal theories, *Journal of Personality and Social Psychology* 53, 636–47.

Kyle, Albert S., 1985, Continuous auctions and insider trading, *Econometrica* 53, 1315–35.

Kyle, Albert S., and F. Albert Wang, 1997, Speculation duopoly with agreement to disagree: Can overconfidence survive the market test?, *Journal of Finance* 52, 2073–90.

Lakonishok, Josef, and Seymour Smidt, 1986, Volume for winners and losers: Taxation and other motives for stock trading, *Journal of Finance* 41, 951–74.

Langer, Ellen J., 1977, The psychology of chance, *Journal for the Theory of Social Behavior* 7, 185–207.

Langer, Ellen J., and Jane Roth, 1975, Heads I win, tails it's chance: The illusion of control as a function of the sequence of outcomes in a purely chance task, *Journal of Personality and Social Psychology* 32, 951–55.

Lenney, Ellen, 1977, Women's self-confidence in achievement settings, *Psychological Bulletin* 84, 1–13.

Lichtenstein, Sarah, and Baruch Fischhoff, 1981, The effects of gender and instructions on calibration, Decision Research Report 81–5, Decision Research.

Lichtenstein, Sarah, Baruch Fischhoff, and Lawrence Phillips, 1982, Calibration of probabilities: The state of the art to 1980, in Daniel Kahneman, Paul Slovic, and

Amos Tversky (eds.), *Judgment Under Uncertainty: Heuristics and Biases*, Cambridge University Press.

Locke, Peter, and Steven Mann, 1999, Do professional traders exhibit loss realization aversion?, Working Paper, Texas Christian University.

Lundeberg, Mary A., Paul W. Fox, Judith Punccohar, 1994, Highly confident but wrong: Gender differences and similarities in confidence judgments, *Journal of Educational Psychology* 86, 114–21.

Lyon, John, Brad Barber, and Chih-Ling Tsai, 1999, Holding size while improving power in tests of long-run abnormal stock returns, *Journal of Finance* 54, 165–202.

Marks, Rose, 1951, The effect of probability, desirability, and "privilege" on the stated expectations of children, *Journal of Personality* 19, 332–51.

Miller, Dale T., and Michael Ross, 1975, Self-serving biases in attribution of causality: Fact or fiction?, *Psychological Bulletin* 82, 213–25.

Neale, Margaret A., and Max H. Bazerman, 1990, Cognition and Rationality in Negotiation, Free Press.

Odean, Terrance, 1998a, Are investors reluctant to realize their losses?, *Journal of Finance* 53, 1775–98.

———, 1998b, Volume, volatility, price and profit when all trades are above average, *Journal of Finance* 53, 1887–1934.

Odean, Terrance, 1999, Do Investors Trade Too Much?, *American Economic Review* 89, 1279–98.

Oskamp, Stuart, 1965, Overconfidence in case-study judgments, *Journal of Consulting Psychology* 29, 261–65.

Peterson, Dane K., and Gordon F. Pitz, 1988, Confidence, uncertainty, and the use of information, *Journal of Experimental Psychology* 14, 85–92.

Poterba, James, 1987, How burdensome are capital gains taxes? Evidence from the United States, *Journal of Public Economics* 33, 157–72.

Presson, Paul K., and Victor A. Benassi, 1996, Illusion of control: A meta-analytic review, *Journal of Social Behavior and Personality* 11, 493–510.

Prince, Melvin, 1993, Women, men, and money styles, *Journal of Economic Psychology* 14, 175–82.

Russo, J. Edward, and Paul J. H. Schoemaker, 1992, Managing overconfidence, *Sloan Management Review* 33, 7–17.

Shapira, Zur, and Itzhak Venezia, 2001, Patterns of behavior of professionally managed and independent investors, *Journal at Banking and Finance* 25, 1573–87.

Shefrin, Hersh, and Meir Statman, 1985, The disposition to sell winners too early and ride losers too long: Theory and evidence, *Journal of Finance* 40, 777–90.

Shleifer, Andrei, and Robert Vishny, 1997, Limits of Arbitrage, *Journal of Finance* 52, 35–55.

Slovic, Paul, 1973, Behavioral problems of adhering to a decision policy, Working Paper, Oregon Research Institute.

Staël von Holstein, Carl-Axel S., 1972, Probabilistic forecasting: An experiment related to the stock market, *Organizational Behavior and Human Performance* 8, 139–58.

Starr-McCluer, Martha, 1995, Tax losses and the stock portfolios of individual investors, Working Paper, Federal Reserve Board of Governors.

Statman, Meir, and Steve Thorley, 1999, Investor overconfidence and trading volume, Working Paper, Santa Clara University.

Stewart, Thomas R., Kenneth F. Heideman, William R. Moninger, and Patricia Reagan-Cirincione, 1992, Effects of Improved Information on the Components of Skill in Weather Forecasting, *Organizational Behavior & Human Decision Processes* 53, 107–34.

Svenson, Ola, 1981, Are we all less risky and more skillful than our fellow drivers?, *Acta Psychologica* 47, 143–48.

Taylor, Shelley, and Jonathon D. Brown, 1988, Illusion and well-being: A social psychological perspective on mental health, *Psychological Bulletin* 103, 193–210.

Thaler, Richard, 1985, Mental accounting and consumer choice, *Marketing Science* 4, 199–214.

Thaler, Richard, 1992, The winner's curse: Paradoxes and anomalies of economic life, Free Press.

Varian, Hal R., 1989, Differences of opinion in financial markets, in Courtenay C. Stone (ed.), *Financial Risk: Theory, Evidence and Implications* (Proceedings of the Eleventh Annual Economic Policy conference of the Federal Reserve Bank of St. Louis, Boston).

Wagenaar, Willem, and Gideon B. Keren, 1986, Does the expert know? The reliability of predictions and confidence ratings of experts, in Erik Hollnagel, Giuseppe Mancini, David D. Woods (eds.), Intelligent Decision Support in Process Environments, Springer.

Weber, Martin, and Colin Camerer, 1995, The disposition effect in securities trading: An experimental analysis, *Journal of Economic Behavior and Organization* 33, 167–84.

Weinstein, Neil D., 1980, Unrealistic optimism about future life events, *Journal of Personality and Social Psychology* 39, 806–20.

Yates, J. Frank, 1990, *Judgment and Decision Making*, Prentice Hall.

Chapter 16

NAIVE DIVERSIFICATION STRATEGIES IN DEFINED CONTRIBUTION SAVINGS PLANS

Shlomo Benartzi and Richard H. Thaler

THERE IS A WORLDWIDE trend toward defined contribution saving plans in which investment decisions are made by the plan participants themselves (Employee Benefit Research Institute 1997). While the advantages of such plans are numerous (e.g., the plans tend to be fully funded and portable), many have expressed concern about the quality of the decisions being made by the participants (e.g., Mitchell and Zeldes 1996). One of the reasons for concern is the lack of financial sophistication in the general public (B. Douglas Bernheim 1996). To illustrate, a 1995 survey by John Hancock Financial Services found that a majority of respondents thought money market funds were riskier than government bonds, and felt that their own company stock was safer than a diversified portfolio.

Of course, it is possible that poorly informed employees are still making good decisions. How can we evaluate whether plan participants are making good choices in what is arguably the most important financial decision of their lives? We do not attempt to evaluate asset allocations on an individual case-by-case basis because nearly any combination of stocks and bonds could, in principle, be consistent with the maximization of some utility function. Rather, in this paper we look for evidence that participants make decisions that seem to be based on naive (or confused) notions of diversification. One extreme example we discuss is what we call the "$1/n$ heuristic." Someone using this rule simply divides her contributions evenly among the n options offered in her retirement savings plan.

The use of the $1/n$ rule has a long history in asset allocation. In fact, it was recommended in the Talmud. Writing in about the fourth century, a

This project has been sponsored by TIAA-CREF, the U.S. Department of Labor, and the Center for International Business and Economic Research at UCLA. We appreciate valuable comments from Michael Brennan, Colin Camerer, Cade Massey, Dave McCarthy, Steve Lippman, Toby Moskowitz, Terry Odean, Joe Piacentini, Mark Warshawsky, Martin Weber, and Ivo Welch. We thank Captain Joe A. Montanaro from the TWA Pilots Directed Account Plan/401(k), John Ameriks and Mark Warshawsky from TIAA-CREF, and Syl Schieber from Watson Wyatt for sharing data with us. This chapter was originally written as a paper while Thaler was a fellow at the Center for Advanced Study in the Behavioral Sciences. He is grateful for the Center's support. Opinions expressed are the sole responsibilities of the authors and do not represent the views of the U.S. Department of Labor.

Rabbi Issac bar Aha gave the following asset-allocation advice: "A man should always place his money, a third into land, a third into merchandise, and keep a third at hand."[1] There is anecdotal evidence the rule is still in use. For example, for many years TIAA-CREF, the largest defined contribution savings plan in the world, offered two investments: TIAA (bonds) and CREF (stocks). By far, the most common allocation of contributions was 50-50; about half of the participants chose this precise allocation of new funds (Samuelson and Zeckhauser 1988).[2] Indeed, Harry Markowitz, a pioneer in the development of modern portfolio theory, reports that he used this rule himself. He justifies his choice on psychological grounds: "My intention was to minimize my future regret. So I split my contributions fifty-fifty between bonds and equities" (Zweig 1998).

Of course, there is nothing wrong with this allocation per se, but the complete reliance on the $1/n$ heuristic could be costly. For example, individuals who are using this rule and are enrolled in plans with predominantly stock funds will find themselves owning mostly stocks, while those in plans that have mostly fixed-income funds will own mostly bonds. While either allocation could be on the efficient frontier, the choice along the frontier should reflect factors other than the proportion of funds that invest in stocks. As we show below, using calculations based on Brennan and Torous (1999), the choice of the wrong asset allocation can be quite costly in utility terms.

The $1/n$ heuristic is a special case of a more general choice heuristic dubbed the "diversification heuristic" by Read and Loewenstein (1995). The first demonstration of this phenomenon was by Itamar Simonson (1990). He gave college students the opportunity to select among six familiar snacks (candy bars, chips, etc.) in one of two conditions: (1) sequential choice: they picked one of the six snacks on each of three class meetings held a week apart; (2) simultaneous choice: on the first class meeting they selected three snacks to be consumed one snack per week over the three class meetings. Simonson observed that in the simultaneous choice condition subjects displayed much more variety seeking than in the sequential choice condition. For example, in the simultaneous choice condition 64 percent of the subjects chose three different snacks while in the sequential choice condition only 9 percent of the subjects made this choice. Simonson suggests that this behavior might be explained by variety seeking serving as a choice heuristic. That is, when asked to make several choices at once, people tend to diversify. This is sensible under some circumstances (such as when eating a meal—we typically do not order three courses of the same food) but can be misapplied to other situations.

[1] Thanks to Hersh Shefrin and Meir Statman for this quote. Shefrin tells us that the reference to the original Aramaic is "Talmud Bavli, Baba Metzia 42a."

[2] For more recent statistics on the asset allocation of TIAA-CREF participants see TIAA-CREF (1997).

Read and Loewenstein produce the same behavior in an ingenious experiment conducted on Halloween night. The "subjects" in the experiment were young trick-or-treaters. In one condition the children approached two adjacent houses and were offered a choice between two candies (Three Musketeers and Milky Way) at each house. In the other condition they approached a single house where they were asked to "choose whichever two candy bars you like." Large piles of both candies were displayed to assure that the children would not think it was rude to take two of the same. The results showed a strong diversification bias in the simultaneous choice condition: every child selected one of each candy. In contrast, only 48 percent of the children in the sequential choice condition picked different candies. This result is striking since in either case the candies are dumped into a bag and consumed later. It is the portfolio in the bag that matters, not the portfolio selected at each house.[3]

In these experiments with young people choosing snacks we see an inappropriate use of diversification, a strategy that is often sensible. In this work we investigate whether the same behavior can be found in adults choosing how to invest their retirement savings. Namely, we see whether plan participants use naive diversification strategies in making their asset-allocation decisions. We do this using a variety of methods.

We begin our analysis with a set of hypothetical questionnaires, where university employees are asked to allocate their retirement contributions between two funds. Different groups of subjects choose between different pairs of funds; for example, one group chooses between a stock fund and a bond fund while another chooses between a balanced fund (half stocks and half bonds) and a stock fund. We find, consistent with the diversification heuristic, that the pair of funds offered has a strong influence on the asset allocation. Put another way, the participants are not sensitive enough to the options they are being asked to choose among. We also find that if participants are asked to choose one of many blends (that is, combinations of stocks and bonds) they make different choices than if they are allowed to compose their own blend (by allocating between a stock fund and a bond

---

[3] Graham Loomes (1991) also finds evidence consistent with the diversification heuristic. He offers subjects a series of gambles with three possible states of the world A, B, and C where $\text{pr}(A) > \text{pr}(B) > \text{pr}(C)$. If state C occurs the subject wins nothing. The subject can divide £20 between A and B, winning the amount placed on a state if that state occurs. Rational subjects would put all the money on A, thereby maximizing the expected payoff, but very few subjects did this. Instead, most divided the £20 in proportion to $\text{pr}(A)/\text{pr}(B)$. In unpublished research, Daniel Kahneman and Thaler ran a similar experiment. The experimenter had two envelopes, one labeled Heads, the other Tails. Each envelope contained twenty numbered cards. Subjects were given a form with two rows of numbers, also labeled Heads and Tails. They were told to circle five numbers. The experimenter would then flip a coin and pick a number from the indicated envelope. Anyone who had circled the right number in the right row would win a prize: $3 if the coin came up heads, $2 following a tails. Again, rational subjects should only circle numbers in the Heads row but most subjects circled three numbers in the Heads row and two in the Tails row. Repeating the game twenty times did not help.

fund). This result has implications for the design of both retirement saving plans and privatized Social Security systems.

These experiments suggest that the array of funds offered to plan participants can have a surprisingly strong influence on the assets they end up owning. In particular, the allocation to stocks increases as the number of stock funds, relative to bond funds, increases. A comparison of the plan offered to TWA pilots with that offered to University of California (UC) employees dramatically illustrates this point. The TWA plan offers five core stock funds and one core bond fund (a stable value fund to be precise.) The participants in this plan invest 75 percent of their money in stocks, which is well *above* the national average of 57 percent (Greenwich Associates 1996). The University of California plan, on the other hand, offers one stock fund and four bond funds, and employees in this plan invest only 34 percent in stocks, well *below* the national average. Of course, there are many possible explanations for this result. One is that the pilots are more risk-seeking than the UC employees are. To see if this factor drives the results we ran an additional experiment in which the UC employees were asked to make an asset-allocation decision in one of two conditions. They either chose from the array they face in their own plan or the funds available in the TWA plan. We find that when they chose from a set of mostly bond funds the UC employees selected an asset allocation heavy in bonds, but when they chose from a mostly stock mix as in the TWA plan they chose to invest mostly in stocks.

To supplement these controlled experiments, we also analyze the actual choices made by participants in 170 retirement saving plans. Using cross-sectional analysis we again find that the mix of funds in the plan has a strong effect on the asset allocation participants select, across a variety of plans. We also investigate whether the pattern can be explained by other factors such as the plan sponsors choosing an array of funds to match the preferences of the employees. To do this we study the choices of the employees of one firm for which we have been able to obtain quarterly time-series data. This time-series analysis reinforces the conclusions of the cross-sectional study.

The paper proceeds as follows. In section 1, we examine whether individuals use the diversification heuristic with a set of hypothetical questionnaires. In section 2, we use cross-sectional data on retirement saving plans to explore how the set of funds being offered affects the asset allocation participants select. Section 3 summarizes the results and discusses their practical implications.

1. Experimental Evidence on the Diversification Heuristic

We begin our investigation with surveys of the employees of the University of California. The employees were contacted by mail and told that if they replied they would be entered in a lottery in which one respondent would be paid $500. The respondents were asked one short question about how they would allocate their defined contribution retirement funds if they were offered a particular set of investment options. We use two different methods to investigate this question. The first experiment describes the investment strategies of the funds verbally; the second displays historical returns graphically. We also conduct a third experiment that is designed to resemble the actual array of investment options offered by the University of California and TWA. All the experiments use a between-subject design; that is, each subject answered just one version of the question. Comparisons are made across groups.

A. Verbal Savings Questionnaire: Experimental Methods

In the first survey, employees were asked to allocate their retirement contributions between two funds labeled Fund A and Fund B. The manipulation in the experiment was the investment strategies of the two funds. In condition 1, Fund A invested in stocks and Fund B invested in bonds. In condition 2, Fund A was again a stock fund but Fund B was a "balanced fund" investing half its assets in stocks and half in bonds. In the third condition, Fund A was the balanced fund and Fund B was a bond fund. The investment strategies of the funds were described verbally using the language used by TIAA-CREF to describe its stock and bond funds. Thus in condition 1 they were told the following:[4] "Fund A includes almost the entire range of domestic stock investments, large and small companies alike. Fund B holds primarily high- and medium-quality fixed-income securities— bonds of many different companies or government agencies—all with varying maturities." The question we address is whether the set of funds offered influences the asset allocation chosen by the participants (by more than what would be expected by the constraints imposed). We are also interested in how many participants choose exactly the $1/n$ strategy of dividing their money evenly between the two funds offered.

B. Verbal Savings Questionnaire: Results

One hundred and eighty questionnaires were completed, yielding a response rate of 12 percent. The results are described in figure 16.1. The left panel of the figure shows the allocations between the funds in the three conditions as well as the mean allocation to Fund A. In every condition there was a substantial group that elected the 50-50 allocation. In the first two conditions the 50-50 allocation is the modal choice, attracting 34 percent

---

[4] For a complete set of the instructions to all of the experiments reported in this paper, contact Shlomo Benartzi.

Panel A1:
Stock Fund (A) & Bond Fund (B)

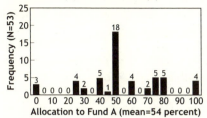

Panel A2:
Stock Fund (A) & Bond Fund (B)

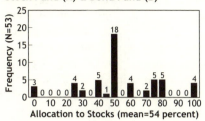

Panel B1:
Stock Fund (A) & Balanced Fund (B)

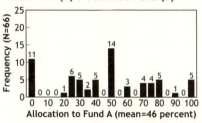

Panel B2:
Stock Fund (A) & Balanced Fund (B)

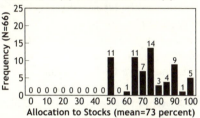

Panel C1:
Balanced Fund (A) & Bond Fund (B)

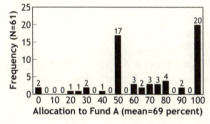

Panel C2:
Balanced Fund (A) & Bond Fund (B)

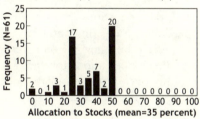

Figure 16.1. Verbal savings questionnaire: Histograms of the allocation to fund A and the resulting allocation to stocks. *Notes:* Three groups of individuals were asked to allocate contributions between two funds, labeled Fund A and Fund B, based on verbal description of the composition of the funds. The first group was asked to allocate contributions between stocks (Fund A) and bonds (Fund B). The second group was asked to allocate contributions between stocks (Fund A) and a balanced fund that was half stocks and half bonds (Fund B). The third group was asked to allocate contributions between a balanced fund (Fund A) and bonds (Fund B). The histograms on the left provide the actual allocation to Fund A by group, and the histograms on the right provide the resulting allocation to stocks.

of the contributions in the first (stocks and bonds) condition and 21 percent in the second (stocks and balanced). In the third condition the allocations are bimodal, with 28 percent selecting the 50-50 allocation and 33 percent putting all of their money in the balanced fund. Note that the popularity of the $1/n$ allocation is not very sensitive to the funds offered.

In contrast, the final asset allocation does depend greatly on the funds offered. When choosing between stocks and bonds, the mean allocation to stocks is 54 percent. When choosing between a stock fund and a balanced fund the allocation to stocks rises to 73 percent, whereas when choosing between the bond fund and the balanced fund the mean percent in stocks falls to 35 percent. Of course, this simple analysis fails to take into consideration that some allocations are not feasible in conditions 2 and 3. (When choosing between the balanced fund and the bond fund, the highest feasible allocation to stocks is 50 percent.) Therefore, to more carefully determine whether the funds offered influence the asset allocation we do the following analysis. We first assume there is no difference in the underlying preferences of the subjects across conditions. We then take the asset allocation selected by each of the subjects in the first (stocks vs. bonds) condition and calculate the closest asset allocation that subject could have selected if in the other conditions. (In condition 2 all allocations between 50 percent and 100 percent stocks are feasible, while in condition 3 all allocations between 0 and 50 percent stocks are feasible.) We then ask what the mean allocation to stocks would be in conditions 2 and 3 if the subjects had the same preferences as those in condition 1 and were not influenced by the funds presented (except when constrained). Finally, we compare this "implied allocation" to the one actually selected. The results are shown in table 16.1. As predicted, the allocations in conditions 2 and 3 are closer to 50-50 than the implied allocations. In condition 2 the implied allocation to the stock fund is 21 percent but they put 46 percent of their money in this fund. In condition 3 the implied allocation to the balanced fund is 87 percent but the subjects only put 69 percent of the money in this fund. Both departures from the implied allocations are highly significant.[5]

C. Graphic Savings Questionnaire: Methods

One of the limitations of the first experiment is the use of the terms "stocks" and "bonds" to describe the investment options. Subjects might have ended up with the 50-50 allocation, simply because they do not know the difference between stocks and bonds. We have therefore replicated the previous study replacing the verbal descriptions of the funds with graphical displays of annual returns. In particular, we presented the subjects with a year-by-year chart of each fund's performance over the last twenty-five years. Stock returns were based on the S&P 500 index, and bond returns were based on the Lehman Aggregate Bond index. The experimental design (i.e., between subjects), the number of investment funds presented to the

---

[5] One concern is that allocations greater than 100 percent or lower than 0 are unfeasible, violating the normality assumption of the t-tests. We have repeated the statistical analysis using bootstrapping techniques that do not assume normality and obtained comparable significance levels. The specific techniques used and the resulting significance levels are available from the authors upon request.

TABLE 16.1
Verbal Savings Questionnaire: Mean Allocation to Fund A

Version	N	Fund A	Fund B	Mean Actual Allocation to Fund A (Median)	Mean Implied Allocation to Fund A (Median)	p-Value for the Difference in Means (Medians)
One	53	Stocks	Bonds	54 percent (50)	54 percent (50)	N/A N/A
Two	66	Stocks	Half stocks and half bonds	46 (50)	21 (0)	0.001 (0.001)
Three	61	Half stocks and half bonds	Bonds	69 (70)	87 (100)	0.001 (0.001)

Notes: Three groups of individuals were asked to allocate contributions between two funds, labeled Fund A and Fund B, based on a verbal description of the composition of the funds. The first group was asked to allocate contributions between stocks (Fund A) and bonds (Fund B). The second group was asked to allocate contributions between stocks (Fund A) and a balanced fund, which was half stocks, and half bonds (Fund B). The third group was asked to allocate contributions between a balanced fund (Fund A) and bonds (Fund B). The table provides the actual allocation to Fund A by group. The table also includes what should have been the allocation to Fund A by the second and third groups to stay consistent with the choices of the first group—i.e., the implied allocation.

subjects, the composition of the funds, and the pool of subjects[6] were all identical to those used in the first experiment.

In addition to replicating the previous conditions we added a fourth condition to this experiment. In this condition, subjects have to choose one fund out of five different multiasset funds, labeled as Fund A, B, C, D, and E. The proportion of stocks in the five funds varies from 0 to 100 percent by 25 percent increments. Fund A, for example, invests all of its assets in stocks whereas Fund E is invested completely in bonds. This means that a subject can choose any asset allocation in 25 percent increments, and thus is formally equivalent (up to rounding error) to the first condition where the subject explicitly divides her assets between stocks and bonds. This condition is motivated by the design of the privatized Chilean Social Security system.[7] In that system participants must choose among an array of funds, each of which is diversified across asset classes.[8] We are interested in

[6] Although the subjects in the various experiments were drawn from the same pool, no subject participated in more than one of the experiments we report in this work.

[7] See Peter Diamond and Salvador Valdes-Prieto (1994) for details on the Chilean retirement system.

[8] We do not use actual data from Chile, because regulatory restrictions result in all the investment funds having similar asset allocations.

whether this formulation of the choice leads to different asset allocations than the more traditional formulation in condition 1. A sample questionnaire, used in the fourth condition, appears in the appendix.

D. Graphic Savings Questionnaire: Results

Four hundred and seventeen questionnaires were completed, yielding a response rate of 21 percent. The results are reported in figure 16.2. When choosing between stocks and bonds, the mean allocation to Fund A (stocks) is 56 percent, quite similar to the 54 percent average we observed in the first experiment (Panel A1). Again we find that the mean allocation to Fund A is not very sensitive to variations in the composition of the funds. When choosing between stocks and a balanced fund, the mean allocation to Fund A (stocks) is 59 percent (Panel B1). Similarly, when choosing between a balanced fund and bonds, the mean allocation to Fund A (balanced) is 57 percent (Panel C1). The differences across the three conditions are statistically insignificant based on an ANOVA test ($p = 0.77$). As in our first experiment, the asset allocation subjects elect depends strongly on the mix of funds they have to choose from. Also, as in the first experiment, a large segment of the respondents in each condition choose the 50-50 allocation in every condition.

Next, we repeat the analysis used in the previous experiment to determine whether the funds offered influence the asset allocation chosen, again correcting for the limited range of choices offered. The results are shown in the right panel of table 16.2. To be consistent with the choices made in condition 1, the subjects in condition 2 (who are choosing between a stock fund and a balanced fund) would invest 29 percent of their funds in the stock fund, the rest in the balanced fund. Instead, they invest 59 percent in the stock fund. Similarly, in condition 3, where the subjects divide their funds between the balanced fund and the bond fund, if they made their constrained choices consistent with the preferences displayed by the subjects in the first experiment, they would place 84 percent of their funds in the balanced fund, rather than the 57 percent they actually select. Again both differences are highly significant.

The results of condition 4, in which subjects must choose a single fund, are displayed in the bottom right panel of figure 16.2, which can be compared to condition 1 shown in the top panel, the simple stock-bond condition. Although the two choices are formally nearly identical, the choices subjects make are quite different. In condition 1, subjects allocated 57 percent of their money to stocks, while in the Chilean condition, subjects put 75 percent in stocks. Most striking is the large number who selected the 100 percent stock allocation (51 percent), compared to only 14 percent in condition 1. We believe this occurs because when investors must choose a single fund there is no opportunity for the diversification heuristic to kick in. Given the graphical displays and the good performance of the stock market over the period shown, many choose to put all their money in

TABLE 16.2
Graphic Savings Questionnaire: Mean Allocation to Fund A

Version	N	Fund A	Fund B	Mean Actual Allocation to Fund A (Median)	Mean Implied Allocation to Fund A (Median)	p-Value of the Difference in Means (Medians)
One	111	Stocks	Bonds	56% (55)	56% (55)	N/A N/A
Two	96	Stocks	Half stocks and half bonds	59 (60)	29 (10)	0.001 (0.001)
Three	105	Half stocks and half bonds	Bonds	57 (60)	84 (100)	0.001 (0.001)

Notes: Three groups of individuals were asked to allocate contributions between two funds, labeled Fund A and Fund B, based on a year-by-year chart of the performance of the funds. The first group was asked to allocate contributions between stocks (Fund A) and bonds (Fund B). The second group was asked to allocate contributions between stocks (Fund A) and a balanced fund that was half stocks and half bonds (Fund B). The third group was asked to allocate contributions between a balanced fund (Fund A) and bonds (Fund B). Stock returns were derived from the S&P 500 index and bond returns were derived from the Lehman Brothers Aggregate Bond index. The table provides the actual allocation to Fund A by group. The table also includes what should have been the allocation to Fund A by the second and third groups to stay consistent with the choices of the first group—i.e., the implied allocation.

stocks. Whether this choice turns out to be a good one, of course, would depend on the future performance of the stock and bond markets.

E. Verbal Savings Questionnaire with Multiple Funds per Asset Class: Experimental Methods

In the experiments reported so far the subjects were asked to allocate their retirement contributions between just two funds. One question is whether the results are applicable to a more realistic scenario where there are multiple funds per asset class. To investigate this question, we conducted a third experiment in which University of California employees were asked to allocate their retirement contributions between five funds labeled Fund A, B, C, D, and E. The manipulation in this experiment is the proportion of fixed-income and stock funds. In condition 1, there are four fixed-income funds and one stock fund, which corresponds to the investment options offered by the University of California. The specific funds are money market, savings (bank deposits), insurance contracts, bonds, and diversified stocks. In condition 2, there is one fixed-income fund and four stock funds that resemble the investment options offered by the TWA Pilots plan. Here the specific funds

Panel A1:
Stock Fund (A) & Bond Fund (B)

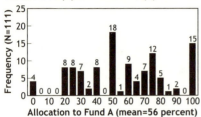

Panel A2:
Stock Fund (A) & Bond Fund (B)

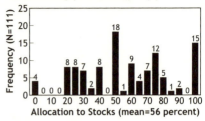

Panel B1:
Stock Fund (A) & Balanced Fund (B)

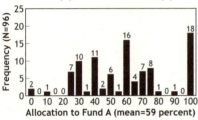

Panel B2:
Stock Fund (A) & Balanced Fund (B)

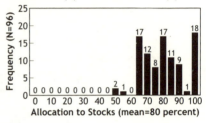

Panel C1:
Balanced Fund (A) & Bond Fund (B)

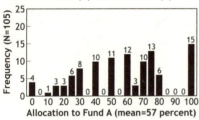

Panel C2:
Balanced Fund (A) & Bond Fund (B)

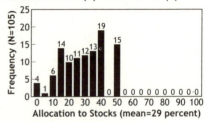

Panel D:
Picking One of Five Funds

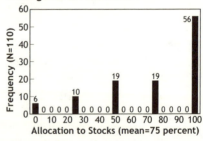

Figure 16.2. Graphic savings questionnaire: Histograms of the allocation to fund A and the resulting allocation to stocks. *Notes:* Three groups of individuals were asked to allocate contributions between two funds, labeled Fund A and Fund B, based on a year-by-year chart of the performance of the funds. The first group was asked to allocate contributions between stocks (Fund A) and bonds (Fund B). The second group was asked to allocate contributions between stocks (Fund A) and a balanced fund

are diversified fixed income, conservative equity income, equity index, growth stock, and international equity. The investment strategies of the funds were described verbally using the language used by the University of California and TWA. The question we address is how would the University of California employees invest their retirement contributions if they were offered a plan dominated by stock funds as opposed to the current plan that is dominated by fixed-income funds.

F. Verbal Savings Questionnaire with Multiple Funds per Asset Class: Results

Three hundred and forty-eight questionnaires were completed, yielding a response rate of 17 percent. The results are described in table 16.3. The top row of the table shows the allocations in the first condition, which includes four fixed-income funds and one stock fund. In this condition, the average allocation to the stock fund is 43 percent. In the second condition, described in the bottom row, another group of subjects selected among one fixed-income fund and four stock funds. Here, University of California employees allocated 68 percent to stocks. The 25 percent difference (68 percent – 43 percent) between the two conditions is statistically significant at the 0.001 level, suggesting that the array of funds offered affects participants selecting between simple sets of two funds and among larger sets of five funds. Furthermore, the choices the university employees made in each condition were closer to the choices made by the actual employees in the respective plans (75 percent for the TWA pilots and 34 percent for the university employees) than to each other.

G. Can the 1/n Heuristic Be a Sensible Strategy?

We have seen that subjects do appear to employ something like the 1/n heuristic in choosing investments. Is this necessarily bad? There are several circumstances in which this strategy might be sensible. First, participants might realize they are not very sophisticated and are counting on the employer to put together a selection of choices that makes sense for them. Still, this strategy may make little sense if the plan sponsor does not anticipate participants choosing this way. A plan that adds equity funds in response to

---

that was half stocks and half bonds (Fund B). The third group was asked to allocate contributions between a balanced fund (Fund A) and bonds (Fund B). A fourth group of individuals was asked to pick one fund out of a list of five funds and invest all the contributions in that fund. The percentage of stocks in each of the five funds was varied from 0 to 100 by 25 increments. Stock returns were derived from the S&P 500 index and bond returns were derived from the Lehman Brothers Aggregate Bond index. The histograms on the left provide the actual allocation to Fund A by group, and the histograms on the right provide the resulting allocation to stocks.

TABLE 16.3

Verbal Savings Questionnaire with Multiple Funds per Asset Class: Mean Allocation to Equities

Version	N	Fund Description and Mean Allocation:					Mean Allocation to Equities (Median)
		Fund A	Fund B	Fund C	Fund D	Fund E	
Multiple fixed-income funds	179	Money markets 14%	Savings 14%	Insurance contracts 11%	Bonds 18%	Diversified equity 43%	43% (40%)
Multiple equity funds	169	Diversified fixed-income 32%	Conservative equity 15%	Equity index 16%	Growth stock 26%	International equity 11%	68% (75%)

Notes: Two groups of individuals were asked to allocate contributions among five funds (A, B, C, D, and E), based on a verbal description of the composition of the funds. The first group was asked to allocate contributions among four fixed-income funds and an equity fund. The specific funds are (A) money markets, (B) saving accounts, (C) guaranteed investment contracts, (D) bonds, and (E) diversified equity. The second group was asked to allocate contributions among one fixed-income fund and four equity funds. The specific funds presented to the second group consist of (A) diversified fixed-income, (B) conservative equity income, (C) equity index, (D) growth stock, and (E) international equity. The table provides the allocation to equities by group.

requests from sophisticated investors who want lots of choices can find that naive new participants are investing more in stocks simply because there are proportionally more equity options available. Also, if employees are heterogeneous in terms of risk attitudes (as might be expected in a diverse setting), then it cannot be the case that the mix of funds in the plan reflects an optional asset-allocation strategy for all of the employees.

Another explanation for our results is that employees increase their equity exposure when more stock funds are added because the additional funds allow them to diversify over active managers, and in so doing gain higher returns at little or no increase in risk. The question that needs to be asked about this explanation is how much we would expect the equity exposure to increase as the number of equity options is increased. This is a complicated question that we investigate using a commercial investment product (Ibbotson's Portfolio Optimizer) and data about the correlation among large-cap funds taken from Catherine Voss Sanders (1997).

We perform two analyses. First, we see how a rational, mean-variance optimizing investor changes his asset allocation as we add funds that invest in different asset classes. We begin by assuming that a plan offers just two options, a large-cap index fund and an intermediate-term government bond fund. We choose the parameters for the utility function so that our rational investor would choose a 50-50 mix of these two funds.[9] We then add a small-cap index fund (that is assumed to perform in line with historic performance of such funds, i.e., higher risk and higher returns than large-cap funds). Next we calculate the utility maximizing mix. The results are shown in Panel A of table 16.4. As we see, the proportion invested in equities actually falls to 43 percent. The intuition for this result is that the addition of the small-cap fund shifts the efficient frontier out. A mean-variance maximizing investor substitutes some small stocks for large stocks, increasing both risk and return, but compensates by decreasing the overall equity exposure, to bring the risk level back down. In contrast, adding an international index fund increases the equity exposure to 56 percent since it offers greater diversification.

---

[9] In most consumption-based asset-pricing models, a 50-50 asset allocation requires extreme levels of risk aversion. This is, of course, the famous equity premium puzzle (Mehra and Prescott 1985). However, there are settings where a 50-50 allocation will be selected by someone who is not extremely risk averse. Using an alternative approach, Benartzi and Thaler (1995), for example, consider a representative investor who is loss averse (i.e., the disutility of losing money relative to a reference point is greater than the utility of making the same amount) and myopic (i.e., focuses on short-term performance). We find that a 50-50 allocation is quite plausible. Furthermore, we find that myopic loss-averse investors are sensitive to their investment horizon, where short horizons are associated with lower equity allocation. In the exercise, we use one-year returns (the default in the Ibbotson optimizer) in combination with a mean-variance utility function. For a mean-variance maximizer, very much like a myopic loss-averse investor, the investment horizon makes a difference. Consequently, in this setting a 50-50 allocation does not require extreme levels of risk aversion. Had we used longer horizons, the mean-variance maximizer would invest more, if not all, in stocks (Siegel 1998).

584 BENARTZI AND THALER

TABLE 16.4
The Effect of Different Plan Structures on the Asset Allocation of a Markowitz
Mean-Variance Optimizing Investor

Scenario	Investment Funds Being Offered	Allocation to Stock Funds
	Panel A: Diversification Across Asset Classes	
1.0	IT gov. (intermediate-term government) bonds and a large-cap index	50 percent
1.1	IT gov. bonds and large and small-cap indices	43
1.2	IT gov. bonds and large and international indices	56
1.3	IT gov. bonds, large, small, and international indices	40
1.4	IT gov. bonds, a large-cap index, and money markets	42
1.5	IT gov. bonds, a large-cap index, and long-term government bonds	49
1.6	IT gov. bonds, a large-cap index, money markets, and long-term government bonds	42
	Panel B: Diversification across Actively Managed Funds within an Asset Class	
2.0	IT gov. bonds and an actively managed large-cap fund	50
2.1	IT gov. bonds and two actively managed large-cap funds	54
2.2	IT gov. bonds and three actively managed large-cap funds	56
2.3	IT gov. bonds and four actively managed large-cap funds	57
2.4	IT gov. bonds and five actively managed large-cap funds	57
2.5	IT gov. bonds and ten actively managed large-cap funds	57

Notes: In this table, we hypothesize a mean-variance optimizing investor who, by assumption, selects 50 percent equities when there are just intermediate-term government bonds and a large-cap index fund. Then, we introduce additional asset classes and calculate how the mean-variance optimizing investor changes her allocation to stocks, using a commercial investment product (Ibbotson's Portfolio Optimizer). The results of this analysis are presented in Panel A. Next, we hypothesize a mean-variance optimizing investor who, again by assumption, selects 50-percent equities when offered intermediate-term government bonds and an *actively managed* large-cap fund. Here, we vary the number of actively managed large-cap funds from one to ten. The resulting allocations to stocks are reported in Panel B.

The second set of simulations investigates what happens if we just add actively managed large-cap funds. The additional funds allow an investor to diversify over manager performance risk, but since the performance of these funds is highly correlated, the benefits of such diversification are small. This fact is revealed in the results. Again we start with just two funds, here a large-cap actively managed fund and an intermediate-term government bond fund. Then we add another actively managed large-cap fund. In this case, an investor who selected a 50-percent equity exposure when offered just one equity fund increases his equity exposure to 54 percent with two funds. When four equity funds are offered, the equity exposure rises to 57 percent, but after that more funds do not increase the amount invested in equities (see Panel B of table 16.4).

What should we conclude from these analyses? The primary conclusion is that adding more equity funds to the plan would not produce a dramatic increase in the proportion of assets invested in equities for a rational, mean-variance optimizing investor. The largest increase we obtain in our simulations is from 50 to 57 percent, and when the additional funds offer new asset categories such as small-cap, a rational investor would choose to *decrease* the proportion held in equities. These results help us interpret the behavior observed in the previous experiment, and the behavior reported in the next section. We will see that, consistent with the diversification heuristic, participants respond much more to changes in the mix of funds in the plan than we would expect based on these calculations.

2. DOES THE ARRAY OF FUNDS OFFERED AFFECT PARTICIPANTS' CHOICES?

The experiments reported in the previous section suggest that the array of funds offered to plan participants can affect the asset allocations they choose. Of course, these experiments are merely survey questions with no real money at stake. Therefore, our next step is to determine whether there is evidence of the same behavior in the actual choices made by plan participants. We also use the actual choices to investigate how employees treat investments in the stock of their own company.

A. Data

To investigate this question we obtained a proprietary database from the Money Market Directories (MMDs). The database covers 170 retirement saving plans (mostly corporations) with 1.56 million participants, annual contributions of \$3.23 billion, and assets of \$49.99 billion. This represents about 5 percent of the universe of defined contributions plans estimated to be \$1,090 billion by the U.S. Department of Labor (1998). The plan sizes in our sample range from 100 participants up to 237,600 participants, and the industry affiliation of the sponsoring corporations consists of thirty-seven different 2-digit SIC codes.

For each plan, the database includes a list of the investment options available to the participants. The database also provides the following information about each investment option: its investment style (i.e., money market, bonds, domestic equity, and so forth), its assets as a percentage of the plan assets, and the year in which it was added to the plan. We should

TABLE 16.5
Mean Asset Allocation for the MMD Sample of 401(k) Plans as of 6/30/96

Type of Investment	Plans Not Offering Company Stock as an Investment Option (N = 103)	Plans Offering Company Stock as an Investment Option(N = 67)	All Plans (N = 170)
Money market	7.06%	3.14%	4.74%
Stable value	33.16	10.24	19.61
Bonds	4.26	9.64	7.44
Company stock	0.00	41.98	24.81
Domestic equity	45.95	27.41	34.99
International equity	3.24	1.85	2.42
Multi-asset	4.63	0.86	2.40
Other	1.66	4.84	3.54
Total	100.00	100.00	100.00

Note: The mean allocation is weighted by plan assets.

note that allocation percentages are based on plan assets as of mid-1996 rather than the contributions made during 1996. The Money Market Directories do not include the allocation of the annual contributions (and we have been unable to locate a source of such data). This limitation creates some problems for our analysis that we discuss below.

The average participant has accumulated retirement funds of $32,044 ($49.99 billion in assets divided by 1.56 million participants), which is remarkably similar to the $32,010 figure reported by Access Research (1996). The average annual contribution per participant is $2,073 ($3.23 billion contributions divided by 1.56 million participants).

The average number of investment options available to the participants is 6.8. Two plans offer one investment fund only, and one plan offers as many as twenty-one funds. (We exclude from our analysis below the eight plans that offer less than four options.) We assume that hybrid funds, such as asset-allocation and multiasset options, are invested half in equities and half in fixed-income securities.[10] The average number of equity-type options offered is 4.2, with a range from 0 to 14.5. Thus, 61.76 percent of all the available investment options are equity options (4.2 divided by 6.8). With three exceptions, it is always the case that at least half of the investment options are equities.

Table 16.5 displays the mean allocation to various asset classes. To examine where the "typical dollar" is invested, the allocations are weighted by plan assets. The mean allocation to equities, defined as the combined

[10] Assuming that hybrid funds are either 25 percent or 75 percent in equities does not affect any of the results reported in this paper.

allocation to company stock, domestic equity, and international equity, is 62.22 percent (24.81 percent +34.99 percent +2.42 percent). The aggregate data offer a crude test of the diversification heuristic: 61.76 percent of the funds invest in equities and the allocation to equities is 62.22 percent. The remarkable similarity between the two percentages is consistent with the diversification heuristic. We provide more detailed tests below.

B. The Time Weighting of Investment Options

We wish to investigate the relation between the funds offered and the asset allocation of the participants. Given that our data consists of total fund assets (rather than new flows), this task is complicated by two factors. First, plans have been changing the mix of funds over time. In the early part of our sample the most popular investments (aside from company stock) were fixed-income funds, especially money market funds and guaranteed investment contracts (GICs). In the more recent years, most of the funds added were equity funds, and the proportion of equity funds, (as a percentage of new funds) has increased over time from 25 percent in 1976 to 68 percent in 1996. Second, participants alter *existing* investments much less often than they change the allocation of new contributions (*Pensions & Investments,* May 12, 1997). Samuelson and Zeckhauser (1988), who document the phenomenon among investors in TIAA-CREF, have dubbed this behavior the "status quo bias." To see the problem these two factors create for our research, compare two hypothetical plans. Plan A offers one fixed-income fund and one equity fund and has done so for ten years. Plan B was identical to Plan A until the last year when it added two more equity funds. Suppose further that every participant in both plans is using the $1/n$ heuristic. Since participants rarely rebalance their existing assets, the mix of assets in the two plans will be very similar (only participants who joined during the last year would be heavily in equities) although the mix of funds would appear to be very different.

To take into account the effect of the status quo bias on the results, we weight the number of each type of investment option by how long it has been in the plan and how well it has performed. The weighting procedure is best illustrated with an example. Consider a retirement saving plan that was established in 1995 with one fixed-income fund and one equity fund. After one year the plan adds another equity fund. Let's suppose that each year investors contribute (at year-end) an aggregate amount of $100 to the plan, and that all investors use the $1/n$ heuristic. In that case at the end of the first year $50 would be in bonds and $50 in stocks. During the second year, 1996, this money would appreciate at the market returns for these two kinds of investments. We use the Lehman Aggregate Bond index and the S&P 500 index as benchmarks for bond and stock returns, respectively. For 1996, the bond and stock returns are 3 percent and 23 percent, resulting in gains of \$1.50 and \$11.50 for the bond and stock funds. Meanwhile, in the second year we assume that new money is being divided evenly among the three options. By the end of 1996, the balances in the fixed-income fund and the equity funds are \$84.50 (\$50 + \$1.50 + \$33) and \$128.50 (\$50 + \$11.50 + \$67). Thus, the *weighted* relative number of equity funds is 0.60 (\$128.50/(\$84.50 + \$128.50)). In the next subsection, we use the relative number of equity funds to explain cross-sectional differences in the percentage of assets invested in equities.

C. Results

We begin with a simple categorical analysis. We use the relative number of equity funds to categorize retirement saving plans into three equal-size groups: low, medium, and high.[11] As reported in table 16.6, the relative number of equity funds for the three groups is 0.37, 0.65, and 0.81, respectively. For a plan with ten investment options, for example, a 0.37 figure

TABLE 16.6
The Relative Number of Equity-Type Investment Options and Asset Allocation
Using the MMD Sample of 401(k) Plans (as of 6/30/96)

Relative Number of Equity-type Investment Options	N	Mean Relative Number of Equity Investment Options	Mean Allocation to Equities
Low	54	0.37	48.64%
Medium	54	0.65	59.82
High	54	0.81	64.07
p-value (ANOVA test)			0.01

Notes: Eight retirement savings plans with less than four investment options were excluded from the initial MMD sample of 401 (k) plans, resulting in a sample of 162 plans. Then, the sample was partitioned into three groups based on the relative number of equity-type investment options: low, medium, and high. The relative number of equity options was based on the following calculation. At the beginning of each year, a contribution of \$1 was allocated evenly among the available investment options. The account balance in each investment option kept growing as additional contributions were made. The account balance also fluctuated with the return on either the S&P 500 index (for equity funds) or the Lehman Aggregate Bond index (for fixed-income funds). The ending balances in the various investment options were used as weights in the calculation of the relative number of equity-type investment options. Hybrid investment options such as multi-asset funds were assumed to be half in equities and half in fixed-income securities. Last, we calculated the average allocation to equities for plans with low, medium, and high relative number of equity-type investment options.

[11] Eight plans with less than four investment options were excluded from the analysis, because they offer very little choice to the participants.

implies that roughly four of the options are equity funds. Next, we calculated the mean allocation to equities for each group: 48.64 percent, 59.82
percent, and 64.07 percent. Consistent with the diversification heuristic,
there is a positive correlation between the relative number of equity funds
and the percentage invested in equities. An ANOVA test for the difference
across the three groups is statistically significant at the 0.01 level. Thus, we
can reject the null hypothesis that participants are unaffected by the array
of funds being offered.

How large is this effect? Participants in our sample increase their equity
exposure from 48.64 to 64.07 percent as the proportion of equity funds goes
from 37 to 81 percent. Calculations, in the spirit of those in table 16.4, suggest that a mean-variance optimizer would increase her equity exposure
from 50 to 53 percent as the proportion of equity funds varied from 33 to
87 percent. This implies that the shifts in equity exposure are much more
strongly influenced by the array of funds in the plan than would be expected in an optimizing framework.

We also examined the relationship between the relative number of equity
funds and asset allocation in a regression framework. The dependent variable is the percentage allocated to equities and the independent variables
are the relative number of equity funds, the logarithm of plan assets as a
control for size, and an indicator for the existence of company stock in the
plan. (The role of company stock in asset-allocation decisions is addressed
in the next section.) The weighted least-squared (WLS) estimation results
with plan assets used as weights are reported in table 16.7.

The main variable of interest is the relative number of equity options.
The diversification heuristic predicts a positive coefficient on this variable,
indicating that the higher the number of equity funds offered the higher the
allocation to equities. Consistent with the diversification heuristic, the coefficient estimate is significantly positive at the 0.01 level in all of the regressions. It ranges from a low of 36.77 to a high of 63.14, depending on the
regression specification.[12] To illustrate the magnitude of the regression coefficients, consider a plan with a mix of fixed-income and equity funds and a
total of ten funds. Replacing one of the fixed-income funds with an equity
fund is expected to increase the allocation to equities by 3.67 to 6.31 percent.

We have also included fixed effects for the total number of funds offered
in the plan, to investigate whether the use of the $1/n$ heuristic might decrease as the number of funds in the plan increases. However, this did not
change the results. This may be due to the fact that the plans in our sample
do not have a very large number of funds (only eight plans out of 170 have
as many as twelve funds in the plan). We suspect that different behavior

[12] We obtain similar results when: (a) we run the analysis on plans with no company stock,
(b) we use OLS rather than WLS regressions, and (c) we exclude observations with a studen-
tized residual above two in absolute value.

TABLE 16.7
The Relative Number of Equity-Type Investment Options and Asset Allocation:
A Regression Analysis
(Dependent Variable: The Percentage of Plan Assets Invested in Equities)

WLS Regression Model	Intercept	Relative Number of Equity Options	Indicator Whether the Plan Offers Company Stock	Log of the Plan Assets in Thousands	Adjusted R^2
Panel A: No Industry Indicators ($N = 162$)
1	22.09	63.14			34.61 percent
	(4.94)	(9.28)			
2	29.72	36.75	15.05		43.45 percent
	(6.73)	(4.49)	(5.10)		
3	10.57	36.77	14.78	1.40	44.16 percent
	(0.89)	(4.52)	(5.03)	(1.74)	
Panel B: Including Industry Indicators Based on 2-Digit SIC Codes ($N = 142$)
4		58.68			55.12 percent
		(8.29)			
5		43.90	12.93		58.91 percent
		(5.39)	(3.26)		
6		47.07	9.09	4.13	61.79 percent
		(5.93)	(2.25)	(2.96)	

Notes: The initial sample consists of the June 1996 MMD sample of 401(k) plans. Eight plans with less than four investment options were excluded, resulting in a sample of 162 plans. When we include industry indicators, the sample is further reduced to 142 plans due to missing industry information. The table reports WLS regression estimates with plan assets as weights (t-statistics are in parentheses).

might be observed in plans that offer the full range of funds from a large mutual fund company such as Fidelity or Vanguard (often called a "Mutual Funds Window"). Such offerings are common in the 403(b) plans at universities and other nonprofits, but not in the corporate 401(k) plans in our sample.

D. Alternative Explanations

So far, we have interpreted the positive correlation between the relative number of equity options and the allocation to equities as supporting the diversification heuristic. One concern, though, is that different equity funds might serve different purposes. For example, adding a second growth fund to a plan that already had a mix of equity funds should probably have little effect on the overall asset allocation of the participants, but adding an international equity fund might provide a rational justification for increasing the total equity exposure. Thus, a positive correlation between the relative number of equity funds and the number of international funds offered could be driving our results. However, this is not what we find. In fact, the presence of an international equity fund in the plan is uncorrelated with the relative number of equity funds in the plan. Furthermore, the percentage invested internationally is small across the board. In plans with a small, average, and large number of equity funds the percentage invested abroad is 2.70 percent, 3.48 percent, and 2.24 percent, respectively. Thus, it does not seem that international diversification drives the results.

A more troubling objection to our analysis is the possibility that firms choose the array of funds in the plan specifically to meet the desires of the plan participants. A plan with a young workforce, for example, might offer many equity funds whereas a plan with a relatively mature workforce would be more likely to emphasize stable value and other fixed-income funds. Thus, the observed association between the relative number of equity funds and asset allocation could be driven by an omitted correlated variable—that is, the underlying risk preferences of the plan participants.

It is difficult to test this explanation directly in our data since we do not have any information on the characteristics or preferences of the plan participants. However, two things argue against this interpretation. First, the experimental results are immune to this critique. Since subjects were assigned randomly to one of the treatment conditions, we would expect no systematic differences in risk preferences or demographics across the groups. The fact that we obtain the same results in these conditions when we know by construction that the array of funds was not selected to match the preferences of the participants supports our interpretation of the later results with actual choices. Second, if demographic differences in risk preferences are driving the array of funds being offered, we might expect those to be stronger between industries rather than within industries. Therefore, we have added industry dummies to the regression analysis using 2-digit SIC codes. The inclusion of the industry controls does not materially affect the results. The coefficient on the relative number of equity funds decreases from 63.14 to 58.68 in the univariate regression and increases from 36.77 to 47.07 in the multivariate regression. Still, the best way to test this alternative explanation is with time-series data. We use this technique in the next section.

E. Time-Series Analysis

The problem of endogeneity (that firms choose the options in the plan to match the preferences of the employees) is greatly reduced if we switch from cross-sectional analysis across firms to a time-series analysis of changes in the asset mix within plans. To this end we have obtained data from Watson Wyatt (a pension consulting firm) for one midsize company. We selected this company to study (*before obtaining the data*) because it made two changes in the options in its savings plan in a relative short (3.5 years) period of time, and quarterly information was available about participants' asset allocations. The ability to study quarterly changes makes it possible to assume that employee preferences have not changed dramatically. This plan was also attractive because it began with a small number of options, making the subsequent alterations to the plan especially significant. Our database includes the investment choices of individual participants from June 1993 through December 1997. The company twice changed the array of funds offered during the sample period, offering two chances to observe any effect on participants' asset allocation. At the beginning of our time period the plan offered just two investment options: a balanced fund (63 percent in stocks) and a bond fund. In the last quarter 1994, a stable value fund and three stock funds were added, and in the last quarter of 1996, the bond fund was dropped.

The number of participants and the mean allocation across the different investment options is displayed quarter by quarter in table 16.8. The discussion focuses on the allocation of future contributions because participants rarely change the allocation of their accumulated balances. The mean allocation between the balanced fund and the bond fund is quite stable from June 1993 through September 1994 with a rough mix of 30/70. The resulting equity exposure is 18 percent. During the last quarter of 1994, three stock funds were added and the allocation to stocks increased from 18 percent to 41 percent. The increase in the allocation to stocks continued to drift upwards thereafter, which probably reflects a combination of employees slowly altering their allocations combined with the strong performance in the stock market over this period.

One concern with this simple analysis is that equity exposures above 63 percent (the proportion in stocks in the balanced fund) were infeasible when the only options were the balanced fund and a bond fund. To explore the magnitude of this effect we calculate the number of participants who allocated 100 percent to the balanced fund and nothing to the bond fund. There were 279 such participants as of September 30, 1994. Next, we assume that all of those participants were constrained and would choose to increase their equity exposure from 63 percent to 100 percent when that became feasible. This behavior only increases the equity exposure by 4 percent.

We also examine participants' reaction to the elimination of the bond fund, which took place at the last quarter of 1996. During that quarter, equity exposure increased from 62 percent to 71 percent. Note that during the prior quarter (Sep. 96) and the following quarter (Mar. 97) equity exposure increased by a mere percent or two. The magnitude of the equity exposure increase during the last quarter of 1996 suggests it is driven by the

TABLE 16.8

Average Allocation of Future Contributions by Quarter for a Midsize Company

Quarter	Number of Plan Participants	Balanced Fund	Bond Fund	Average Allocation of Future Contributions Among the Following Funds:				Equity Exposure
				Stable value Fund	S&P 500 Fund	International Stock Fund	Aggressive Stock Fund	
Jun-93	4,406	29%	71%	N/A	N/A	N/A	N/A	18%
Sep-93	4,413	29	71	N/A	N/A	N/A	N/A	18
Dec-93	3,768	28	72	N/A	N/A	N/A	N/A	18
Mar-94	3,778	29	71	N/A	N/A	N/A	N/A	18
Jun-94	3,837	28	72	N/A	N/A	N/A	N/A	18
Sep-94	2,348	29	71	N/A	N/A	N/A	N/A	18
Dec-94	2,576	25	47	2	8	9	9	41
Mar-95	2,591	25	46	2	8	10	9	43
Jun-95	2,341	24	44	3	9	10	11	44
Sep-95	2,685	24	43	3	9	10	12	45
Dec-95	2,445	23	34	3	13	9	18	55
Mar-96	2,463	23	32	2	13	9	20	58
Jun-96	2,623	23	29	2	14	9	22	60
Sep-96	2,631	23	22	8	15	9	24	62
Dec-96	2,475	20	N/A	21	17	10	31	71
Mar-97	2,479	20	N/A	21	18	10	32	72
Jun-97	2,629	20	N/A	20	19	10	32	73
Sep-97	2,638	20	N/A	19	19	10	31	73
Dec-97	2,358	19	N/A	17	21	10	33	76

Notes: This table reports the mean allocation of future contributions by quarter for an anonymous midsize company. During the first quarter in our sample, the plan included two options: a balanced fund (63 percent in stocks) and a bond fund. In the last quarter of 1994, a stable value fund and three stock funds were added; in the last quarter of 1996, the bond fund was dropped. The last column reports the overall allocation to stocks (i.e., the allocation to individual stock funds plus the stock component of the balanced fund).

elimination of the bond fund rather than a gradual migration into equity funds.

The evidence in this section documents that the array of funds offered to participants can have a strong influence on the asset allocation they select. Using time-series analysis, we are able to keep employee preferences relatively stable and attribute changes in investment behavior to the addition and elimination of specific investment options. We conclude that the greater the relative number of equity funds, the more is allocated to equities.

F. The Mental Accounting of Company Stock

Another aspect of diversification that can be investigated with our database is the role of company stock in retirement saving plans. This is potentially an important question since in the plans that offer company stock as one of the options, this investment captures nearly 42 percent of the assets, more than any other type of investment (see table 16.5).

There are many pros and cons of including the company stock in the saving plan. From the company's point of view it can be attractive since employees who consider themselves stockholders may be better and more loyal workers. On the other hand, from the employees' point of view, tying up a substantial portion of their retirement wealth in an asset that is positively correlated with their primary source of income is a dubious strategy. However, our concern here is not why employees own so much company stock.[13] (There are numerous explanations; for example, owning company stock is often encouraged in some way, and employees may feel [rightly or wrongly] that they have good information about the prospects of their own firm.) Rather, we are interested in a mental accounting (Kahneman and Tversky 1984, Thaler 1985, 1999) question related to our main theme in this work—diversification. We ask how employees with large amounts of company stock choose to invest the rest of their retirement funds. Specifically, do they think of company stock as a substitute for other equities, or do they think of it as an asset in a different category altogether? We investigate this by comparing the investments of employees in plans that do not offer company stock as an option (103 plans) with those that do (67 plans). When company stock is not one of the available investment options, the assets are split evenly between equities (49.19 percent = 45.95 percent domestic + 3.24 percent international) and fixed-income securities. This nearly 50–50 split is similar to that observed in the plans in the public sector. *Pensions & Investments* (1998) reports that public plans were 48.8 percent in stocks at the end of 1996.

As we reported above, when the company offers its own stock in the plan this option captures 41.98 percent of the assets. What happens to the rest?

---

[13] See Benartzi (2001) for a discussion of this question.

If the employees treat this investment as part of their equity portfolio and want a roughly 50-50 asset allocation, then they would invest the bulk of the rest of their assets in fixed income. However, that is not what we observe. Instead the noncompany stock assets are split about evenly between equities and fixed-income securities. Of the remaining 58.02 percent of the assets, 29.26 percent are invested in other equities and the rest (28.76 percent) are invested in fixed-income investments.

It appears that the mental accounting of these investments involves putting the company stock into its own category separate from other equities. The diversification heuristic then pushes people toward the ubiquitous 50-50 split of the remaining assets. The result is that employees in plans that offer company stock have over 71 percent of their assets in equities (including the company stock) while those in plans without company stock have about 49 percent in stock.

A similar result emerges from the regression analysis reported above. When the company stock indicator is included in the analysis, its coefficient is significantly positive. The allocation to equities, defined as the combined allocation to company stock, domestic equity, and international equity, is roughly 15 percent higher for plans with company stock relative to plans without company stock.

G. Is Naive Diversification Costly?

Suppose that people do engage in naive diversification strategies, as the results of this chapter suggest. There are two ways in which such behavior could be costly compared to an optimizing strategy. First, investors might choose a portfolio that is not on the efficient frontier. Second, they might pick the wrong point along the frontier. The cost of the first type of error is almost certainly quite small. Even the very naive $1/n$ strategy will usually end up with a well-diversified portfolio that is reasonably close to some point on the frontier. As one illustration of this point, Canner et al. (1997) estimate that the popular advice of financial planners, while inconsistent with traditional models of portfolio selection, results in portfolios that are only 20 basis points below the efficient frontier. In contrast, the second inefficiency—that is, picking an inappropriate point on the efficient frontier—can potentially be quite significant. Brennan and Torous (1999) report the following calculation. They consider an individual with a coefficient of relative risk aversion of 2, which is consistent with the empirical findings of Friend and Blume (1975). They then calculate the loss of welfare from picking portfolios that do not match the assumed risk preferences. Using a twenty-year investment horizon, an individual who switched from an equity-rich plan that led to an 80 percent investment in stocks to a bond-rich plan that produced a 30 percent allocation to stocks would suffer a utility loss of 25 percent. If the horizon is increased to thirty years then the welfare loss can be as much as

35 to 40 percent. These are clearly significant costs. For an individual who is less risk averse, for example, a coefficient of 1.0, which corresponds to log utility, the *ex ante* welfare costs of investing too little in equities can be much larger. Even larger *ex ante* welfare losses are associated with large holdings of company stock because of the lack of diversification.

3. Summary and Discussion

This chapter examines how individuals deal with the complex problem of selecting a portfolio in their retirement accounts. We suspected that in this situation, as in most complex tasks, many people use a simple rule of thumb to help them. One such rule is the diversification heuristic or its extreme form, the $1/n$ heuristic. Consistent with the diversification heuristic, the experimental and archival evidence suggests that some people spread their contributions evenly across the investment options irrespective of the particular mix of options in the plan. One of the implications is that the array of funds offered to plan participants can have a strong influence on the asset allocation people select; as the number of stock funds increases, so does the allocation to equities. The empirical evidence confirms that the array of funds being offered affects the resulting asset allocation. While the diversification heuristic can produce a reasonable portfolio, it does not as-sure sensible or coherent decision making.

The results highlight difficult issues regarding the design of retirement saving plans, both public and private. What is the right mix of fixed-income and equity funds to offer? If the plan offers many fixed-income funds the participants might invest too conservatively. Similarly, if the plan offers many equity funds the employees might invest too aggressively. Another question is how the plan should deal with differences across participants. If the plan offers many equity funds the participants will end up with a fairly aggressive portfolio, which is consistent with the recommendation of many financial advisors for young workers but not for older ones. Should the plan offer different funds based on age?

In the context of private plans, our results suggest that the increase in re-tirement funds invested in equities over the past decade may be partly ex-plained by the abundance of new equity funds that have been added to these plans (though the booming stock market in the 1990s has also been an important factor). This is a trend that could easily continue, in part be-cause of the greater ease in differentiating the product of equity funds. Eq-uity funds can be segmented by many factors: size of firm (e.g., small cap); style (e.g., active vs. index; value vs. growth); industry or sector (health care, technology); county or region (China, Asia); and so forth. It is some-what more difficult to differentiate fixed-income funds other than by maturity and risk (especially since tax-exempt funds have no role in tax-sheltered pension plans).

It is more difficult to say with any assurance what the ex ante welfare costs to investors are of using simple rules of thumb to make their investment decisions. As the calculations in the previous section show, in some cases these costs can be substantial, even if investors obtain a portfolio close to the efficient frontier. And, though ex ante welfare costs are the proper concept for economists to worry about in designing savings plan, plan administrators (either private or public) may also be worried about ex post regret. A plan that by design encourages investors to put an unusually large or small proportion of assets in equities may suffer later if returns differ from historical norms.

Appendix: Retirement Savings Questionnaire

Figure 16.A1 shows the annual rates of return (or growth rates) for Funds A, B, C, D, and E from 1970 through 1996. These rates indicate the percentage change in the value of your funds in a given year. As you can see, funds on the top of the page had a higher average rate of return, but the returns were more variable. For example, in the best year Fund A grew by 37.5 percent, while in the worst year the fund lost 26.4 percent of its value. The average was 13.4 percent. On the contrary, funds on the bottom of the page had a lower average rate of return, but the returns were less variable. For example, Fund E offered an average return of 9.7 percent but less variability. The annual rate of return was between 32.6 percent and negative 2.9 percent. No adjustment has been made for inflation, which averaged 3.1 percent over this period.

If these funds were my only retirement options, **and I had to choose one fund only,** I would choose the following fund: _A_B_C_D_E.

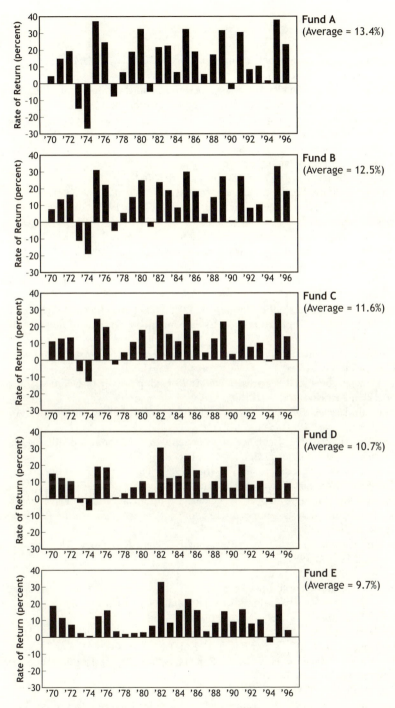

Figure 16.A1. Annual rates of return for funds A, B, C, D, and E from 1970–1996.

References

Access Research, 1996, *Participant attitudes and behavior: Overview and trend analysis*, Access Research.

Benartzi, Shlomo, 2001, Excessive Extrapolation and the Allocation of 401(k) Accounts to Company Stock, *Journal of Finance*, forthcoming.

Benartzi, Shlomo, and Richard H. Thaler, 1995, Myopic Loss Aversion and the Equity Premium Puzzle, *Quarterly Journal of Economics* 110(1), 73–92.

Bernheim, B. Douglas, 1996, Financial Illiteracy, Education, and Retirement Saving, University of Pennsylvania (Pension Research Council) Working Paper No. 96–7.

Brennan, Michael J. and Walter N. Torous, 1999, Individual Decision-Making and Investor Welfare, Working Paper, University of California, Los Angeles.

Canner, Niko, N. Gregory Mankiw, and David N. Weil, 1997, An Asset Allocation Puzzle, *American Economic Review* 87(1), 181–91.

Diamond, Peter, and Salvador Valdes-Prieto, 1994, Social Security Reforms, in Barry P. Bosworth, Rudiger Durnbusch, and Raul Laban (eds.) *The Chilean economy*, Brookings Institution Press, 257–320.

Employee Benefit Research Institute, 1997, *EBRI data-book on employee benefits*, Washington, DC, EBRI.

Friend, Irwin, and Marshall E. Blume, 1975, The Asset Structure of Individual Portfolios and Some Implications for Utility Functions, *Journal of Finance* 30(2), 585–603.

Greenwich Associates, 1996, *Investment management: Statistical supplement*, Greenwich Associates.

John Hancock Financial Services, 1995, 1995 Gallup Survey of Defined Contribution Plan Participants".

Kahneman, Daniel, and Amos Tversky, 1984, Choices, Values and Frames, *American Psychologist* 39(4), 341–50.

Loomes, Graham, 1991, Evidence of a New violation of the Independence Axiom, *Journal of Risk and Uncertainty* 4(1), 91–108.

Mehra, Rajnish, and Edward C. Prescott, 1985, The Equity Premium: A Puzzle, *Journal of Monetary Economics* 15(2), 145–61.

Mitchell, Olivia S., and Stephen P. Zeldes, 1996, Social Security Privatization: A Structure for Analysis. *American Economic Review, (Papers and Proceedings)* 86(2), 363–67.

Pensions & Investments, DuPont Revamps DC Plan: Rebalancing Key Feature of Move, May 12, 1997, p. 1.

——. Top 1,000 Funds, January 26, 1998, p. 60.

Read, Daniel, and George Loewenstein, 1995, Diversification Bias: Explaining the Discrepancy in Variety Seeking between Combined and Separated Choices, *Journal of Experimental Psychology: Applied* 1(1), 34–49.

Samuelson, William, and Richard J. Zeckhauser, 1988, Status Quo Bias in Decision Making, *Journal of Risk and Uncertainty* 1(1), 7–59.

Sanders, Catherine Voss, How Many Funds Do You Need? *Morningstar Investor*, July 1997 5, 1–5.

Siegel, Jeremy, 1998, *Stocks for the long run*, McGraw-Hill.

Simonson, Itamar, 1990, The Effect of Purchase Quantity and Timing on Variety-Seeking Behavior, *Journal of Marketing Research* 27(2), 150–62.

Thaler, Richard H., 1985, Mental Accounting and Consumer Choice, *Marketing Science* 4, 199–214.

——, 1999, Mental Accounting Matters, *Journal of Behavioral Decision Making* 12(3), 183–206.

TIAA-CREF, 1997, Premium Allocations and Accumulations in TIAA-CREF—Trends in Participant Choices Among Asset Classes and Investment Accounts, Research Dialogues No. 51.

U.S. Department of Labor, 1998, Pension and Welfare Benefits Administration, Abstract of 1994 Form 5500 Annual Reports, *Private pension plan bulletin*, U.S. Government Printing Office.

Zwelg, Jason, Five Investing Lessons from America's Top Pension Fund, *Money*, January 1998, 115–18.

PART VI

Corporate Finance

Chapter 17

RATIONAL CAPITAL BUDGETING

IN AN IRRATIONAL WORLD

Jeremy C. Stein

1. Introduction

The last several years have not been good ones for the capital asset pricing model (CAPM). A large volume of recent empirical research has found that (1) cross-sectional stock returns bear little or no discernible relationship to β and (2) a number of other variables besides β have substantial predictive power for stock returns. For example, one variable that has been shown to be an important and reliable predictor is the book-to-market ratio: the higher a firm's B/M, the greater its conditional expected return, all else being equal.[1]

In light of these empirical results, this work addresses a simple, yet fundamental question: What should the academic finance profession be telling MBA students and practitioners about how to set hurdle rates for capital budgeting decisions? Can we still follow the standard textbook treatments with a clear conscience and a straight face, and march through the mechanics of how to do weighted-average-cost-of-capital or adjusted-present-value calculations based on the CAPM? Or should we abandon the CAPM for capital budgeting purposes in favor of alternative models that seem to do a better job of fitting actual stock-return data?

If one believes that the stock market is efficient and that the predictable excess returns documented in recent studies are, therefore, just compensation for risk—risk that is, for some reason, not well captured by β—then

This research is supported by the National Science Foundation and the International Financial Services Research Center at Massachusetts Institute of Technology. Thanks to Maureen O' Donnell for assistance in preparing the manuscript and to Michael Barclay, Doug Diamond, Steve Kaplan, Jay Ritter, Dick Thaler, Luigi Zingales, an anonymous referee for the *Journal of Business*, and seminar participants at the National Bureau of Economic Research for helpful comments and suggestions.

[1] Early work on the predictive power of variables other than β includes Stattman (1980), Banz (1981), Basu (1985), Keim (1983), DeBondt and Thaler (1985), Rosenberg, Reid, and Lanstein (1985), Bhandari (1988), and Jaffe, Keim, and Westerfield (1989). See Fama (1991) for a detailed survey of this literature. More recent papers that have focused specifically on B/M as a predictive variable include Chan, Hamao, and Lakonishok (1991), Fama and French (1992), Davis (1994), Lakonishok, Shleifer, and Vishny (1994), and Chan, Jegadeesh, and Lakonishok (1995).

the answer to the question is simple. According to standard finance logic, in an efficient market the hurdle rate for an investment in any given asset should correspond exactly to the prevailing expected return on the stock of a company that is a pure play in that asset. The only operational question is, Which regression specification gives the best estimates of expected return? Thus the inevitable conclusion is that one must throw out the CAPM and in its place use the "new and improved" statistical model to set hurdle rates. For shorthand, I will label this approach to setting hurdle rates the NEER approach, for new estimator of expected return.

As an example of the NEER approach, consider a chemical company that currently has a low B/M ratio, and hence—according to an agreed-upon regression specification—a low expected return. If the company were considering investing in another chemical plant, this approach would argue for a relatively low hurdle rate. The implicit economic argument is this: the low B/M ratio is indicative of the low risk of chemical industry assets. Given this low risk, it makes sense to set a low hurdle rate. Of course, if the chemical company's B/M ratio—and hence its expected return—were to rise over time, then the hurdle rate for capital budgeting purposes would have to be adjusted upward.

This NEER approach to capital budgeting is advocated by Fama and French (1993). Fama and French couch the predictive content of the B/M ratio and other variables in a linear multifactor-model setting that they argue can be interpreted as a variant of the arbitrage pricing theory (APT) or intertemporal capital asset pricing model (ICAPM). They then conclude: "In principle, our results can be used in any application that requires estimates of expected stock returns. This list includes . . . estimating the cost of capital" (p. 53).

However, it is critical to the Fama-French logic that the return differentials associated with the B/M ratio and other predictive variables be thought of as compensation for fundamental risk. While there seems to be fairly widespread agreement that variables such as B/M do indeed have predictive content, it is much less clear that this reflects anything having to do with risk. Indeed, several recent papers find that there is very little affirmative evidence that stocks with high B/M ratios are riskier in any measurable sense.[2]

An alternative interpretation of the recent empirical literature is that investors make systematic errors in forming expectations, so that stocks can become significantly over- or undervalued at particular points in time. As these valuation errors correct themselves, stock returns will move in a partially predictable fashion. For example, a stock that is overvalued relative to

[2] See, e.g., Lakonishok, Shleifer, and Vishny (1994), Daniel and Titman (1995), and MacKinlay (1995). The Daniel and Titman paper takes direct issue with the Fama-French (1993) notion that the B/M effect can be given a multifactor risk interpretation.

fundamentals will tend to have a low B/M ratio. Over time, this overvaluation will work its way out of the stock price, so the low B/M ratio will predict relatively low future returns.[3]

In a world where predictable variations in returns are driven by investors' expectational errors, it is no longer obvious that one should set hurdle rates using a NEER approach. The strong classical argument for such an approach rests in part on the assumption that there is a one-to-one link between the expected return on a stock and the fundamental economic risk of the underlying assets. If this assumption is not valid, the problem becomes more complicated. Think back to the example of the chemical company with the low B/M ratio. If the low value of the ratio—and hence the low expected return—is not indicative of risk, but rather reflects the fact that investors are currently overoptimistic about chemical industry assets, does it make sense for rational managers to set a low hurdle rate and invest aggressively in acquiring more such assets?

The key point is that, when the market is inefficient, there can be a meaningful distinction between a NEER approach to hurdle rates, and one that focuses on a measure of fundamental asset risk—which I will call a FAR approach. A FAR approach involves looking directly at the variance and covariance properties of the cash flows on the assets in question. In the chemical company case, this might mean assigning a high hurdle rate if, for example, the cash flows from the new plant were highly correlated with the cash flows on other assets in the economy—irrespective of the company's current B/M ratio or the conditional expected return on its stock.

Given this distinction between the NEER and FAR approaches, the main goal of this work is to assess the relative merits of the two, and to illustrate how one or the other may be preferred in a given set of circumstances. To preview the results, I find that, loosely speaking, a NEER approach makes the most sense when either (1) managers are interested in maximizing short-term stock prices or (2) the firm faces financial constraints (in a sense which I will make precise). In contrast, a FAR approach is preferable when managers are interested in maximizing long-run value and the firm is not financially constrained.

The fact that a FAR approach can make sense in some circumstances leads to an interesting and somewhat counterintuitive conclusion: In spite of its failure as an *empirical description* of actual stock returns, the CAPM (or something quite like it) may still be quite useful from a *prescriptive* point of view in capital budgeting decisions. This is because β—if calculated properly—may continue to be a reasonable measure of the fundamental economic risk of an asset, even if it has little or no predictive power for stock returns. However, it must be emphasized that this sort of rationale for

---

[3] For evidence supporting this interpretation, see Lakonishok et al. (1994) and La Porta et al. (1994).

using the CAPM does not apply in all circumstances. As noted above, when managers have short horizons or when the firm faces financial constraints, the CAPM—or any FAR-based approach—will be inappropriate to the extent that it does not present an accurate picture of the expected returns on stocks.

Before proceeding, I should also reiterate that the entire analysis that follows is based on the premise that the stock market is inefficient. More precisely, cross-sectional differences in expected returns will be assumed throughout to be driven in part by expectational errors on the part of investors. I make this assumption for two reasons. First, it strikes me that, at the least, there is enough evidence at this point for one to question market efficiency seriously and to wonder what capital budgeting rules would look like in its absence. Second, as discussed above, the efficient-markets case is already well understood and there is little to add. In any event, however, readers can judge for themselves whether or not they think the inefficient-markets premise is palatable as a basis for thinking about capital budgeting.

Of course, this is not the first work to raise the general question of whether and how stock market inefficiencies color investment decisions. This question dates back at least to Keynes (1936, p. 151), who raises the possibility that "certain classes of investment are governed by the average expectation of those who deal on the Stock Exchange as revealed in the price of shares, rather than by the genuine expectations of the professional enterpreneur."[4] More recent contributions include Bosworth (1975), Fischer and Merton (1984), DeLong et al. (1989), Morck, Shleifer, and Vishny (1990) and Blanchard, Rhee, and Summers (1993). The latter two pieces are particularly noteworthy in that they stress—as does this chapter—the importance of managers' time horizons and financing constraints. The contribution of this chapter relative to these earlier works is twofold: first, it provides a simple analytical framework in which the effects of horizons and financing constraints can be seen clearly and explicitly, and, second, it focuses on the question of what are appropriate *risk-adjusted* hurdle rates, thereby developing an inefficient-markets analog to textbook treatments of capital budgeting under uncertainty.[5]

The remainder of the chapter is organized as follows. In section 2, I examine the link between managers' time horizons and hurdle rates, leaving aside for simplicity the issue of financial constraints. This section establishes that a FAR approach is more desirable when the time horizon is longer. In section 3, I introduce the possibility of financial constraints and show how these have an effect similar to shortening the time horizon—that is, financial constraints tend to favor a NEER approach. In section 4, I take

[4] As will become clear, in terms of the language of this article Keynes is effectively expressing the concern that managers will adopt a NEER approach to capital budgeting.

[5] In contrast, the informal discussion in Blanchard et al. (1993) assumes risk neutrality and, hence, does not speak to the whole issue of risk-adjusted hurdle rates.

up measurement issues. Specifically, if one decides to use a FAR approach, what is the best way to get an empirical handle on fundamental asset risk? To what extent can one rationalize the use of β—as conventionally calculated—as an attempt to implement a FAR approach? Section 5 briefly discusses a number of extensions and variations of the basic framework, and section 6 fleshes out its empirical implications. Section 7 concludes the discussion.

2. Time Horizons and Optimal Hurdle Rates

I consider a simple two-period capital budgeting model that is fairly standard in most respects. At time 0, the firm in question is initially all equity financed. It already has physical assets in place that will produce a single net cash flow of F at time 1. From the perspective of time 0, F is a random variable that is normally distributed. The firm also has the opportunity to invest \$1 more at time 0 in identical assets—that is, if it chooses to invest, its physical assets will yield a total of $2F$ at time 1. The decision of whether or not to invest is the only one facing the firm at time 0. If it does invest, the investment will be financed with riskless debt that is fairly priced in the marketplace. There is no possibility of issuing or repurchasing shares. (As will become clear in section 3, allowing the firm to transact in the equity market at time 0 may in some circumstances alter the results.) There are also no taxes.

The manager of the firm is assumed to have rational expectations. I denote the manager's rational time-0 forecast of F by $F^r \equiv EF$. The firm's other outside shareholders, however, have biased expectations. Their biased forecast of F is given by $F^b \equiv EF (1 + \delta)$. Thus δ is a measure of the extent to which outside investors are overoptimistic about the prospects for the firm's physical assets. This bias in assessing the value of physical assets is the only way in which the model departs from the standard framework. Outside investors are perfectly rational in all other respects. For example, they perceive all variances and covariances accurately. Thus the degree of irrationality that is being ascribed to outside investors is in a sense quite mild. It would certainly be interesting to entertain alternative models of such irrationality, but in the absence of clear-cut theoretical guidance, the simple form considered here seems a natural place to start.

The shares in the firm are part of a larger market portfolio. The net cash flow payoff on the market portfolio at time 1 is given by M, which is also normally distributed. For simplicity, I assume that both the manager of the firm and all outside investors have rational expectations about M. Thus I am effectively assuming that investors make firm-level mistakes in assessing cash flows, but that these mistakes wash out across the market as a whole.[6]

---

[6] Or, said somewhat more mildly, the manager of the firm does not disagree with outside investors' assessment of M.

I denote the price of the market portfolio at time 0 by P_M, and define $R_M \equiv M/P_M - 1$ as the realized percentage return on the market.

The final assumption is that the price of the firm's shares is determined solely by the expectations of the outside investors. This amounts to saying that even though the manager may have a different opinion, he is unable or unwilling to trade in sufficient quantity to affect the market price.

With the assumptions in place, the first thing to do is to calculate the initial market price, P, of the firm's shares, *before* the investment decision has been made at time 0. This is an easy task. Note that we are operating in a standard mean-variance framework, with the only exception being that investors have biased expectations. This bias does not vitiate many of the classical results that obtain in such a framework. First of all, investors will all hold the market portfolio, and the market portfolio will be—in their eyes—mean-variance efficient. Second, the equilibrium return required by investors in firm's equity, k, will be given by

$$k = r + \beta^r (ER_M - r), \tag{1}$$

where r is the riskless rate and β^r is the usual "rate-of-return β," defined as

$$\beta^r \equiv \text{cov}(F/P, R_M)/\text{var}(R_M). \tag{2}$$

Thus, outside investors' required returns are determined as in the standard CAPM. Given the cash flow expectations of these investors, the initial price of the firm's shares, P, satisfies

$$P = F^b/(1 + k). \tag{3}$$

Eq. (3) is not a completely reduced form, however, because P appears in the definition of k and hence is on both sides of the equation. Rearranging terms, we obtain the following expression for P in terms of primitive parameters:

$$P = \{F^b - \beta^d(ER_M - r)\}/(1 + r), \tag{4}$$

where β^d is the "dollar β," defined as

$$\beta^d \equiv \text{cov}(F, R_M)/\text{var}(R_M). \tag{5}$$

It is useful to compare Eqs. (1)–(4) with the analogous expressions that would prevail in a classical setting with rational expectations. Using asterisk superscripts to denote these (unobserved) rational expectations values, we have

$$k^* = r + \beta^*(ER_M - r), \tag{6}$$

$$\beta^* \equiv \text{cov}(F/P^*, R_M)/\text{var}(R_M), \tag{7}$$

$$P^* = F^r/(1 + k^*), \tag{8}$$

and

$$P^* = \{F^r - \beta^d(ER_M - r)\}/(1 + r). \tag{9}$$

From a comparison of Eqs. (4) and (9), it can be seen that in the reduced form, the only difference between P and P^* is the bias in the expected cash flow term.

While outside investors perceive that the firm's stock will yield an expected return of k, that is not the rational expectation of the stock's performance. Rather, the best estimate of conditional expected return, which I will denote by CER, is

$$CER = F^r/P - 1 = (1 + k)/(1 + \delta) - 1. \tag{10}$$

Thus from the perspective of a rational observer such as the firm's manager, the stock may have a CER that is either greater or less than the CAPM rate k. In this sense, the model crudely captures that empirical regularity that there are predictable returns on stocks that are not related to their β's. These predictable returns simply reflect the biases of the outside investors. Note that when $\delta = 0$, so that outside investors have no bias, $CER = k = k^*$. When $\delta > 0$, so that the stock is overpriced, $CER < k < k^*$. And, conversely, when $\delta < 0$, $CER > k > k^*$.

We are now ready to address the question of the optimal hurdle rate. To do so, we have to be clear about the objective function that is being maximized. There are two distinct possibilities. First, one might assume that the manager seeks to maximize the stock price that prevails at time 0, immediately after the investment decision has been made. This is the same as saying that the manager tries to maximize outside investors' perception of value. Alternatively, one might posit that the manager seeks to maximize the present value of the firm's future cash flows, as seen from his more rational perspective.

In principle, one can think of reasons why managers might tend to favor either objective. For example, if they are acting on behalf of shareholders (including themselves) who have to sell their stock in the near future for liquidity reasons, they will be more inclined to maximize current stock prices. In contrast, if they are acting on behalf of shareholders (including themselves) who will be holding for the longer term—for example, due to capital gains taxes or other frictions—they will be more inclined to maximize the present value of future cash flows. In what follows, I treat the managerial time horizon as exogenous, although in a fuller model it would be endogenously determined.[7]

[7] This distinction between maximizing current stock prices vs. maximizing management's perception of long-run value also arises in the literature on investment and financing decisions under asymmetric information. See, e.g., Miller and Rock (1985) and Stein (1989) for a fuller discussion of the forces that shape the trade-off between the two objectives. One potentially important factor has to do with agency considerations. Specifically, shareholders may—in response to agency problems—impose on managers an incentive scheme or corporate policies that have the effect of making the managers behave as if they were more concerned with maximizing current stock prices. This issue is discussed in more detail in sec. 5C below.

Let us first consider the "short-horizon" case, in which the goal is to maximize the current stock price. It is easy to see that in this case, the "value" created by investing is simply $(P - 1)$. Intuitively, as long as the market's current valuation of the assets in question exceeds the acquisition cost, the current stock price will be increased if the assets are purchased. To translate this into a statement about hurdle rates, note that, from management's perspective, the expected cash flow on the investment is F^r. Thus the short-horizon hurdle rate, defined as h^S, has the property that the gross discounted value of the investment, $F^r/(1 + h^S)$, equals P. Using Eq. (10), it follows immediately that

> **Proposition 1.** In the short-horizon case, the manager should discount his expected cash flow F^r at a hurdle rate $h^S = \text{CER}$. In other words, the manager should take a NEER approach and use the conditional expected return on the stock as the hurdle rate.

One way to think about Proposition 1 is that, if the manager is interested in maximizing the current stock price, he must cater to any misperceptions that investors have. Thus if investors are overly optimistic about the prospects for the firm's assets—thereby leading to a low value of CER—the manager should be willing to invest very aggressively in these assets and hence should adopt a low hurdle rate.

Things work quite differently in the "long-horizon" case, in which the manager seeks to maximize his perception of the present value of future cash flows. In this case, the "value" created by investment is $(P^* - 1)$. That is, the manager should only invest if the *rational expectations value* of the assets exceed their acquisition cost. Thus the long-horizon hurdle rate h^L has the property that $F^r/(1 + h^L) = P^*$. Using Eq. (8), this leads to

> **Proposition 2.** In the long-horizon case, the manager should discount his expected cash flow F^r at a hurdle rate $h^L = k^*$. In other words, the manager should take a FAR approach and choose a hurdle rate that reflects the fundamental risk of the assets in question and that is independent of outside investors' bias δ.

Proposition 2 suggests that hurdle rates in the long-horizon case should be set in a "CAPM-like" fashion. This is very close in spirit to the standard textbook prescription. However, the one major caveat is that, unlike in the textbook world, one needs to be more careful in the empirical implementation. According to Eq. (6) and (7), the β^* that is needed for this CAPM-like calculation is the (unobserved) β that would prevail in a rational expectations world, as this is the correct measure of the fundamental risk borne by long-horizon investors. And given that the underlying premise throughout is that the stock market is inefficient, one cannot blithely make the usual assumption that a β calculated in the traditional way—with a regression of the firm's *stock returns* on market returns—will provide an adequate proxy for the β^* that is called for in Proposition 2. Thus there is a nontrivial set of issues surrounding the best way to measure β^*. These issues are taken up in detail in section 6 below.

3. Financing Considerations and Optimal Hurdle Rates

So far, the analysis has ignored the possibility that the firm might either issue or repurchase shares. Given the premise—that the market is inefficient and that managers know it—this is a potentially important omission. First of all, there will naturally be circumstances in which managers wish to engage in stock issues or repurchases to take advantage of market inefficiencies. Second, and more significant for our purposes, there may, in some cases, be a link between these opportunistic financing maneuvers and the optimal hurdle rate for capital budgeting.

The goal of this section is to explore these links between financing considerations and hurdle rates. I begin with a general formulation of the problem. I then consider a series of special cases that yield particularly crisp results and that highlight the most important intuition.

A. A General Formulation of the Problem

When a manager chooses an investment-financing combination in an inefficient market, there are, in general, three considerations that must be taken into account: (1) the net present value of the investment; (2) the "market timing" gains or losses associated with any share issues or repurchases; and (3) the extent to which the investment-financing combination leads to any costly deviations from the optimal capital structure for the firm. Thus, in order to specify an overall objective function, one must spell out each of these considerations in detail.[8]

1. THE NET PRESENT VALUE OF INVESTMENT

As will become clear, to the extent that financing considerations have any consequence at all for hurdle rates, it is to effectively shorten managers' time horizons—that is, to make them behave in more of a NEER fashion. Therefore, to make the analysis interesting, I assume that absent financing concerns, managers take a FAR approach, and seek to maximize the present value of future cash flows.

---

[8] One possibility that I ignore for the time being is that managers might wish to take advantage of market inefficiencies by transacting in the stock of *other* firms. This consideration is taken up in section 5D below, and, as will be seen, need not materially affect the conclusions of the analysis.

For the purpose of doing a bit of calculus, I generalize slightly from the previous section, and allow the amount invested at time 0 to be a continuous variable K. The gross expected proceeds at time 1 from this investment are given by $f(K)$, which is an increasing, concave function. The relevant FAR-based definition of the net present value of investment is thus $f(K)P^*/F^r - K$, or equivalently, $f(K)/(1 + k^*) - K$, where k^* continues to be given by Eqs. (6) and (7).

2. MARKET TIMING GAINS OR LOSSES

Denote by E the dollar amount of equity raised by selling new shares at time 0. Thus, if $E > 0$, this should be interpreted as an equity issue by the firm; if $E < 0$, this should be interpreted as a repurchase. If the firm is able to transact in its own equity without any price-pressure effects, the market timing gains from the perspective of the manager are given simply by the difference between the market's initial time-0 valuation of the shares and the manager's time-0 valuation. For a transaction of size E, this market timing gain is simply $E(1 - P^*/P)$.[9]

Of course, it is extreme and unrealistic to assume that there are no price-pressure effects whatsoever, particularly if the implied equity transactions turn out to be large in absolute magnitude. At the same time, given the premise of investor irrationality, one does not necessarily want to go to the other extreme—represented by rational asymmetric information models such as that of Myers and Majluf (1984)—and assume that the announcement effects of a share issue or repurchase are such that they, on average, completely eliminate the potential for market timing gains.

As a compromise, I adopt a simple, relatively unstructured formulation in which the net-of-price-pressure market timing gains are given by $E(1 - P^*/P) - i(E)$. Here $i(E)$ captures the price-impact-related losses associated with an equity transaction of size E, with $i(0) = 0$. The only other restrictions I impose a priori are, first, when $E > 0$, $di/dE \geq 0$, and, conversely, when $E < 0$, $di/dE \leq 0$; second, $d^2i/dE^2 \geq 0$ everywhere. In words, equity issues tend to knock prices down, while repurchases push prices up, with larger effects for larger transactions in either direction.

The $i(E)$ function can be interpreted in terms of a couple of different underlying phenomena. First, it might be that even irrational investors do update their beliefs somewhat when they see management undertaking an equity transaction. However, in contrast to rational models based on asymmetric information, the updating is insufficient to wipe out predictable excess returns. This interpretation fits with the spirit of recent studies that suggest that the market underreacts dramatically to the information contained in

---

[9] As above, I continue to assume that when the firm issues debt, this debt is fairly priced, so that there are no market timing gains or losses. This assumption can be relaxed without affecting the qualitative results that follow.

both seasoned equity offerings and repurchases.[10] Alternatively, in the case of share repurchases, $i(E)$ might be thought of as reflecting the premium that tendering investors require to compensate them for capital gains taxes.

3. THE COSTS OF DEVIATING FROM OPTIMAL CAPITAL STRUCTURE

Finally, one must consider the possibility that a given investment-financing combination will lead to a suboptimal capital structure. For example, if a firm decides to invest a great deal and to engage in repurchases to take advantage of a low stock price, leverage may increase to the point where expected costs of financial distress become significant. To capture this possibility in a simple way, I assume that the optimal debt ratio for the firm is given by D, and that, prior to the investment and financing choices at time 0, the firm is exactly at this optimum. Thus, after it has invested an amount K and raised an amount of new equity E, it will be overleveraged by an amount $L \equiv K(1 - D) - E$. I assume that this imposes a cost of $Z(L)$.

Again, I do not put too much a priori structure on the $Z(L)$ function. By definition, things are normalized so that $Z(0) = 0$. In principle, straying in either direction from the optimum of 0 can be costly—too little debt may be a problem as well as too much debt. Moreover, to the extent that there are costs of straying, these costs are a convex function of the distance from the optimum. As with the $i(E)$ function, this implies that $dZ/dL \geq 0$ when $L > 0$, and, conversely, $dZ/dL \leq 0$ when $L < 0$; also, $d^2Z/dL^2 \geq 0$ everywhere.

4. OPTIMAL INVESTMENT AND FINANCING DECISIONS

Taking all three considerations together, the manager's objective function is

$$\max f(K)P^*/F^r - K + E(1 - P^*/P) - i(E) - Z(L), \tag{11}$$

subject to

$$L \equiv K(1 - D) - E.$$

The first-order conditions for this problem are

$$df/dK - [1 + (1 - D)dZ/dL]F^r/P^* = 0, \tag{12}$$

$$(1 - P^*/P) - di/dE + dZ/dL = 0. \tag{13}$$

A little algebra shows that optimal investment therefore satisfies

$$df/dK = DF^r/P^* + (1 - D)(F^r/P + di/dE)$$

$$= D(1 + k^*) + (1 - D)(1 + \text{CER} + di/dE). \tag{14}$$

---

[10] See, e.g., Cheng (1995), Loughran and Ritter (1995), and Spiess and Affleck-Graves (1995) on seasoned equity offerings, and Ikenberry, Lakonishok, and Vermaelen (1995) on share repurchases.

B. Case-by-Case Analysis

Since the intuition underlying Eq. (14) may not be immediately apparent, it is useful to go through a series of special cases to build an understanding of the various forces at work.

1. CAPITAL STRUCTURE IS NOT A BINDING CONSTRAINT

The first, simplest limiting case to consider is one in which $dZ/dL = 0$—that is, there are no marginal costs or benefits to changing leverage, other than those that come directly from issuing or repurchasing shares at time 0. This condition would clearly hold in a world with no taxes and no costs of financial distress, where, were it not for the mispricing of the firm's stock, the Modigliani-Miller theorem would apply. But more generally, one need not make such strong assumptions for this case to be (approximately) relevant. All that is really required is that the Z function be flat in the neighborhood of the optimal solution. For example, if price-pressure effects are significant, and diminishing returns to investment set in quickly, the firm will only choose to make small investment and financing adjustments, and thus will never try to push capital structure very far from its initial position of $L = 0$. If, in addition, the Z function happens to be flat in this region near 0, the firm will be left in a position where, for example, incremental increases in leverage would have only a trivial impact on costs of financial distress.

When $dZ/dL = 0$, Eqs. (12) and (13) tell us that investment and financing decisions are fully separable. Intuitively, this is because capital structure can at the margin adjust costlessly to take up the slack between the two. The optimal behavior for the firm in this case is spelled out in the following proposition:

> **Proposition 3.** When capital structure is not a binding constraint, and the manager has long horizons, the optimal policies are always to set the hurdle rate at the FAR value of k^*, as in Proposition 2, and to issue stock if the CER < k^*, but repurchase stock if the CER > k^*.

Figure 17.1 illustrates the optimal investment and financing policies. As can be seen, the two are completely decoupled. When the stock price is low and the CER is high, the firm repurchases shares. However, because capital structure is fully flexible, the repurchase does not affect its hurdle rate. Rather, the firm adjusts to the repurchase purely by taking on more debt. Therefore, at the margin, investment should be evaluated vis-à-vis fairly priced debt finance, exactly as in section 2 above.

Conversely, when the stock price is high and the CER is low, the firm issues shares. However, it does not have to plow the proceeds of the share issue into investment. These proceeds can be used to pay down debt or

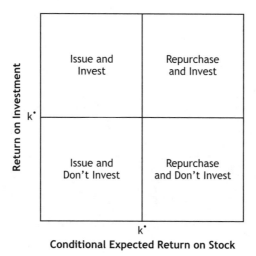

Figure 17.1. Investment and financing policies when capital structure is not a constraint.

accumulate cash. So there is no reason that the issuance of "cheap stock" should lower the hurdle rate for investment.

2. BINDING CAPITAL STRUCTURE CONSTRAINT, NO PRICE-PRESSURE EFFECTS

The next case to examine is one in which the capital structure constraint is binding, but where price-pressure effects are absent—that is, one in which $dZ/dL \neq 0$ and $di/dE = 0$. In this case, Eq. (14) simplifies to

$$df/dK = D(1 + k^*) + (1 - D)(1 + \text{CER}). \qquad (15)$$

Based on Eq. (15), we have:

> **Proposition 4.** When the capital structure constraint is binding and there are no price-pressure considerations, the optimal hurdle rate has the following properties: the hurdle rate is between the NEER and FAR values of CER and k^*, respectively; as D approaches 0, the hurdle rate converges to CER, as in Proposition 1; as D approaches 1, the hurdle rate converges to k^*, as in Proposition 2.

The intuition behind Proposition 4 is very simple. When capital structure imposes a binding constraint, one cannot, in general, separate investment and financing decisions. This is perhaps easiest to see in the case where $\delta < 0$, so that the stock is undervalued and the firm would like to repurchase shares. For each dollar that is devoted to investment, there is less cash available to engage in such repurchases, holding the capital structure fixed.

618   STEIN

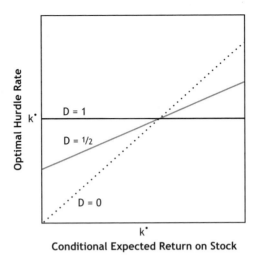

Figure 17.2. Optimal hurdle rates with binding capital structure constraint and no price-pressure effects.

Indeed, in the extreme case where $D = 0$—that is, where the incremental investment has zero debt capacity—each dollar of investment leaves one full dollar less available for repurchases. Hence, in this case, the opportunity cost of investment is simply the expected return on the stock, as in the NEER approach.

Thus, in the limiting case where $D = 0$, financial constraints force managers who would otherwise take a long-run view into behaving exactly as if they were interested in maximizing short-term stock prices. This is simply because, in order to leave capital structure undisturbed, any investment must be fully funded by an immediate stock issue, so all that matters is the market's current assessment of whether the investment is attractive or not.

In the intermediate cases, where $0 < D < 1$, investment need only be partially funded by a stock issue. This implies that the hurdle rate moves less than one-for-one with the CER on the stock. At the other extreme, when $D = 1$ and investment can be entirely debt financed, the hurdle rate remains anchored at the FAR value of k^*, irrespective of the CER on the stock.[11] Figure 17.2 illustrates the relationship between the hurdle rate and the CER on the stock for different values of D.

3. BINDING CAPITAL STRUCTURE CONSTRAINT AND PRICE-PRESSURE EFFECTS

The final case to consider is the most general one where the capital structure constraint is binding and where there are price-pressure effects. This case is most usefully attacked by breaking it down into subcases.

[11] Of course, one should not take this limiting case too literally, given that I have also assumed that the firm can issue fairly priced (i.e., riskless) debt.

Stock is Undervalued: $\delta < 0$. When $\delta < 0$, it is easy to show that $L > 0$. That is, the firm will choose to be overlevered relative to the static optimal capital structure of $L = 0$. However, the sign of E is ambiguous: the firm may either issue or repurchase shares. This ambiguity in E arises because there are two competing effects: on the one hand, the fact that $\delta < 0$ makes a repurchase attractive from a market timing standpoint; on the other, given that the firm is investing, it needs to raise some new equity if it does not wish to see its capital structure get too far out of line. Depending on which effect dominates, there can either be a *net share repurchase* or a *share issue*. In the case of share repurchase ($E < 0$), it is straightforward to verify:

> **Proposition 5.** When the capital structure constraint is binding, there are price-pressure considerations, $\delta < 0$ and $E < 0$, then the optimal hurdle rate has the following properties: the hurdle rate is always between the NEER and FAR values; the stronger the price-pressure effects—that is, the larger is di/dE in absolute magnitude—the lower the hurdle rate, all else equal, and therefore the closer the hurdle rate is to the FAR value of k^*.

Proposition 5 says that this case represents a well-behaved middle ground between the two more extreme cases covered in Propositions 3 and 4. When price-pressure effects are strong, the outcome is closer to that in Proposition 3, where capital structure is not a binding constraint—the hurdle rate is set more according to a FAR approach. This is because price pressure leads the firm to limit the scale of its repurchase activity. Consequently, capital structure is not much distorted, and there is less influence of financial constraints on investment. Of course, when price-pressure effects are very weak, we converge back to the case described in Proposition 4. The outcome with an equity issue ($E > 0$) is a bit more counterintuitive:

> **Proposition 6.** When the capital structure constraint is binding, there are price-pressure considerations, $\delta < 0$ and $E > 0$, then the optimal hurdle rate has the following properties: The hurdle rate no longer necessarily lies between the NEER and FAR values; in particular, it may exceed them both, though it will never be below the lower of the two, namely the FAR value of k^*. The stronger are price-pressure effects—that is, the larger di/dE is in absolute magnitude—the higher the hurdle rate, all else equal.

Thus here is a situation—the first we have encountered so far—where the hurdle rate does not lie between the NEER and FAR values. However, this result has nothing really to do with the market irrationality that is the focus of this article. Rather, it is just a variant on the Myers-Majluf (1984) argument that when investment requires an equity issue, and such an equity issue knocks stock prices down, there will typically be underinvestment. Indeed, the effect is seen most cleanly by assuming that there is no irrationality whatsoever—that is, that $\delta = 0$—so that the NEER and FAR values coincide. Inspection of Eq. (14) tells us that optimal investment will satisfy $df/dK = (1 + k^*) + (1 - D)di/dE$. In other words, the hurdle rate is a markup over the NEER/FAR value of k^*, with the degree of this markup determined by the magnitude of the price-pressure effect.

Stock is Overvalued: $\delta > 0$. When $\delta > 0$, there is no ambiguity about the sign of E. This is because both market timing considerations and the need to finance investment now point in the same direction, implying a desire to sell stock. So $E > 0$. This gives rise to a result very similar to that seen just above:

> **Proposition 7.** When the capital structure constraint is binding, there are price-pressure considerations, $\delta > 0$ and $E > 0$, then the optimal hurdle rate has the following properties: The hurdle rate no longer necessarily lies between the NEER and FAR values. In particular, it may exceed them both, though it will never be below the lower of the two, namely, the NEER value of CER. The stronger the price-pressure effects—that is, the larger di/dE is in absolute magnitude—the higher the hurdle rate, all else equal.

C. Conclusions on the Effects of Financing Considerations

The analysis of this section had shown that financing considerations shape the optimal hurdle rate in three distinct ways. The first factor that matters is the shape of the Z function, which measures the degree to which deviations in capital structure are costly. When such deviations are inconsequential, this tends to favor a FAR-based approach to setting hurdle rates. In contrast, when such deviations are costly, the optimal hurdle rate is pushed in the NEER direction.

The second factor is the debt capacity, D, of the new investment. This second factor interacts with the first. In particular, the lower is D, the more pronounced an effect capital structure constraints have in terms of driving the hurdle rate toward the NEER value.

The third factor is the extent to which share issues or repurchases have price-pressure consequences. In terms of the NEER-FAR dichotomy, the impact of this third factor is somewhat more ambiguous than that of the other two. One can make a clear-cut statement only in the case where the firm engages in a stock repurchase; here price-pressure considerations unambiguously move the hurdle rate closer to the FAR value of k^*. However, when the firm issues equity, all that one can say for sure is that price pressure exerts an upward influence on the hurdle rate; it no longer follows that the hurdle rate is pushed closer to the FAR value.

The overall message of this section is that, while one can certainly argue in favor of a FAR-based approach to capital budgeting, the argument is somewhat more delicate than it might have appeared in section 2, and it does not apply in all circumstances. In order for a FAR-based approach to make sense, not only must managers have long horizons, but they must be relatively unconstrained by their current capital structures.

4. Implementing a FAR-Based Approach: Measuring β^*

Part of the appeal of a FAR-based approach to capital budgeting is that it appears to be very close to the textbook CAPM method. However, as noted in section 2 above, the one hitch is that, in order to implement a FAR-based approach, one needs to know β^*, which is the value of β that would prevail in a rational expectations world; that is, the fundamental risk of the assets in question. And given the underlying premise of the article—that the stock market is inefficient—one cannot simply assume that a β calculated using observed stock returns will yield a good estimate of β^*. Thus the following question arises: as a practical matter, how close to β^* can one expect to get using the standard regression methodology for calculating β?

A. Theoretical Considerations

In order to clarify the issues, it is useful to begin with a more detailed analytical comparison of the value of a β computed from actual stock return data—which I will continue to denote by β^r—versus that of β^*. To do so, I will generalize somewhat from the setting of the previous sections by entertaining the possibility that there is mispricing of the market as a whole as well as mispricing of individual stocks. In addition, and somewhat trivially, I will allow for more than one period's worth of stock returns.

Note that in any period t, for any stock i, we can always make the following decomposition:

$$R_{it} \equiv R_{it}^* + N_{it}, \tag{16}$$

where R_{it} is the *observed* return on the stock, R_{it}^* is the return that would prevail in a rational expectations world—that is, the portion of the observed return due to "fundamentals"—and N_{it} is the portion of the observed return due to "noise." We can also make a similar decomposition for the observed return on the market as a whole, R_{Mt}:

$$R_{Mt} \equiv R_{Mt}^* + N_{Mt}. \tag{17}$$

Clearly, as a general matter, the β calculated from observed stock returns, $\beta_i^r = \text{cov}(R_{it}, R_{Mt})/\text{var}(R_{Mt})$ will not coincide with $\beta_i^* = \text{cov}(R_{it}^*, R_{Mt}^*)/\text{var}(R_{Mt}^*)$. To get a better intuitive handle on the sources of the difference between β_i^r

and β_{i}^{*}, it is helpful to consider a simple case where both R_{it}^{*} and N_{it} are generated by one-factor processes, as follows:

$$R_{it}^{*} = \beta_{i}^{*} R_{Mt}^{*} + \epsilon_{it}, \tag{18}$$

$$N_{it} = \theta_{i} N_{Mt} + \mu_{it}, \tag{19}$$

where $\text{cov}(\epsilon_{it}, \mu_{it}) = 0$.[12] In this formulation, θ_{i} represents the sensitivity of stock i's noise component to the noise component on the market as a whole—that is, θ_{i} is a "noise β" for stock i.

It is now easy to calculate β_{i}^{r}:

$$\beta_{i}^{r} = [\beta_{i}^{*} \text{var}(R_{M}^{*}) + \theta_{i} \text{var}(N_{M}) + (\beta_{i}^{*} + \theta_{i}) \text{cov}(R_{M}^{*}, N_{M})]/ \tag{20}$$

$$[\text{var}(R_{M}^{*}) + \text{var}(N_{M}) + 2\text{cov}(R_{M}^{*}, N_{M})].$$

From (20), one can see how various parameters influence the relative magnitudes β_{i}^{r} and β_{i}^{*}. The most important conclusion for our purposes is that it is not obvious a priori that one will be systematically larger or smaller than the other. Indeed, in some circumstances, they will be exactly equal. For example, if $\text{var}(N_{M}) = 0$, so that all noise is firm specific and washes out at the aggregate level, then $\beta_{i}^{r} = \beta_{i}^{*}$. Alternatively, the same result obtains if there is marketwide noise, but $\theta_{i} = \beta_{i}^{*}$. Although these cases are clearly special, they do illustrate a more general point: a stock may be subject to very large absolute pricing errors—in the sense of $\text{var}(N_{i})$ being very large—and yet one might in principle be able to retrieve quite reasonable estimates of β_{i}^{*} from stock price data.[13] Whether this is true in practice is, then, a purely empirical question.

B. Existing Evidence

In order to ascertain whether a β estimated from stock price data does in fact do a good job of capturing the sort of fundamental risk envisioned in β^{*}, one needs to develop an empirical analog of β^{*}. A natural, though somewhat crude, approach would be as follows. Suppose one posits that the rational expectations value of a stock is the present value of the expected cash flows to equity, discounted at a constant rate. Suppose further that cash flows follow a random walk, so today's level is a sufficient statistic

---

[12] Note that the two-period model used in sections 2 and 3 above does not quite conform to this specification. This is because all mispricing is assumed to disappear after the first period, which in turn implies that there are not enough degrees of freedom to also assume that $\text{cov}(\epsilon_{it}, \mu_{it}) = 0$. However, the simple specification of Eqs. (18) and (19) is merely an expositional device that allows one to illustrate the important effects more clearly.

[13] A second implication of (20) is that if the marketwide noise is stationary, one might be able to obtain better estimates of β_{i}^{*} by using longer-horizon returns. At sufficiently long horizons, the variance of R_{M}^{*} will dominate the other terms in (20), ultimately leading β_{i}^{r} to converge to β_{i}^{*}.

for future expectations. In this very simple case, it is easy to show that for any given stock i:

$$\beta_i^* = \text{cov}(\Delta F_i/F_i, \Delta M/M)/\text{var}(\Delta M/M), \tag{21}$$

where F_i and M are the cash flows accruing to stock i and the market as a whole, respectively. This is a quantity that can be readily estimated and then compared to the corresponding βs estimated from stock prices.

In fact, there is an older literature, beginning with Ball and Brown (1969) and Beaver, Kettler, and Scholes (1970), that undertakes a very similar comparison. In this literature, the basic hypothesis being tested is whether "accounting βs" for either individual stocks or portfolios are correlated with βs estimated from stock returns.[14] In some of this work—notably Beaver and Manegold (1975)—accounting βs are defined in a way that is very similar to (21), with the primary exception being that an accounting net income number is typically used in place of a cash flow.

Subject to this one accounting-related caveat, Beaver and Manegold's (1975) results would seem to indicate that there is indeed a fairly close correspondence between stock market β's and fundamental risk. For example, with ten-stock portfolios, the Spearman correlation coefficient between accounting and stock-return β's varies from about .70 to .90, depending on the exact specification used.

The bottom line is that both theoretical considerations and existing empirical evidence suggest that, at the least, it may not be totally unreasonable to assume simultaneously that stocks are subject to large pricing errors and that a β estimated from stock returns can provide a good measure of the fundamental asset risk variable β^* needed to implement a FAR-based approach to capital budgeting.[15]

5. Extensions and Variations

The analysis in sections 2 and 3 above has made a number of strong simplifying assumptions. In some cases, it is easy to see how the basic framework could be extended so as to relax these assumptions; in other cases, it is clear

[14] The motivation behind this earlier literature is quite different from that here, however. In the 1970s work, market efficiency is taken for granted, and the question posed is whether accounting measures of risk are informative, in the sense of being related to market-based measures of risk (which are assumed to be objectively correct). In addition to the papers mentioned in the text, see also Gonedes (1973, 1975) for further examples of this line of research.

[15] Of course, this statement may be reasonable on average and at the same time be more appropriate for some categories of stocks than for others. To take just one example, some stocks—e.g., those included in the S&P 500—might have more of a tendency to covary excessively with a market index. This would tend to bias measured β's for these particular stocks toward one and thereby present a misleading picture of their fundamental risk. More empirical work would clearly be useful here.

that the problem becomes substantially more complex and that more work is required.

A. Alternative Measures of Fundamental Risk

One assumption that has been maintained until now is that the underlying structure of the economy is such that β^* is the appropriate summary statistic for an asset's fundamental risk. This need not be the case. One can redo the entire analysis in a world where there is a multifactor representation of fundamental risk, such as that which emerges from the APT or the ICAPM. In either case, the spirit of the conclusions would be unchanged—these alternative risk measures would be used instead of β^* to determine FAR-based hurdle rates. Whether or not such FAR-based hurdle rates would actually be used for capital budgeting purposes—as opposed to NEER-based hurdle rates—would continue to depend on the same factors identified above, namely managers' time horizons and financing constraints.

The harder question this raises is how can one know a priori which is the right model of fundamental risk. For once one entertains the premise that the market is inefficient, it may become difficult to use empirical data in a straightforward fashion to choose between, say, a β^* representation of fundamental risk and a multifactor APT-type representation. Clearly, one cannot simply run atheoretical horse races and see which factors better predict expected returns. For such horse races may tell us more about the nature of market inefficiencies than about the structure of the underlying fundamental risk. In particular, a B/M "factor"—à la Fama and French (1993)—may do well in prediction equations, but given the lack of a theroretical model, it would seem inappropriate to unquestioningly interpret this factor as a measure of fundamental risk. (Unless, of course, one's priors are absolute that the market is efficient, in which case the distinction between NEER and FAR vanishes, and everything here becomes irrelevant.)

B. Managers Are Not Sure They Are Smarter than the Market

Thus far, the discussion has proceeded as if a manager's estimate of future cash flow is always strictly superior to that of outside shareholders. However, a less restrictive interpretation is also possible. One might suppose that outside shareholders' forecast of F, while containing some noise, also embodies some information not directly available to managers. In this case, the optimal thing for a rational manager to do would be to put some weight on his own private information and some weight on outside shareholders' forecast. That is, the manager's rational forecast, F^r, would be the appropriate Bayesian combination of the manager's private information and the market forecast. The analysis would then go forward exactly as before. So one does not need to interpret FAR-based capital budgeting as dictating that managers completely ignore market signals in favor of their own beliefs; rather it simply implies that they will be less responsive to such market signals than with NEER-based capital budgeting.

C. Agency Considerations

Suppose we have a firm that is financially unconstrained and whose shareholders all plan to hold onto their shares indefinitely. The analysis above might seem to suggest that such a firm should adopt a FAR-based approach to capital budgeting. But this conclusion rests in part on the implicit assumption that the manager who makes the cash flow forecasts and carries out the capital budgeting decisions acts in the interests of shareholders. More realistically, there may be agency problems, and managers may have a desire to overinvest relative to what would be optimal. If this is the case, and if the manager's forecast F^r is not verifiable, shareholders may want to adopt ex ante capital budgeting policies that constrain investment in some fashion.

One possibility—though not necessarily the optimal one—is for shareholders simply to impose on managers NEER-based capital budgeting rules. An advantage of NEER-based capital budgeting in an agency context is that it brings to bear some information about F that is verifiable. Specifically, under the assumptions of the model above, shareholders can always observe whether or not NEER-based capital budgeting is being adhered to simply by looking at market prices. In contrast, if the manager is left with the discretion to pursue FAR-based capital budgeting, there is always the worry that he will overinvest and explain it away as a case where the privately observed F^r is very high relative to the forecast implicit in market prices. Of course, if shareholders have long horizons, there is also a countervailing cost to imposing NEER-based capital budgeting to the extent that market forecasts contain not only some valid information about F, but biases as well.

This discussion highlights the following limitation of the formal analysis: while I have been treating managers' horizons as exogenous, they would, in a more complete model, be endogenously determined. Moreover, in such a setting, managerial horizons might not correspond to those of the shareholders for whom they are working. If agency considerations are important, shareholders may choose ex ante to set up corporate policies or incentive schemes that effectively foreshorten managerial horizons, even when this distorts investment decisions.[16]

---

[16] This is already a very familiar theme in the corporate finance literature, particularly that on takeovers. For example, it has been argued that it can be in the interest of shareholders to remove impediments to takeovers as a way of improving managerial incentives, even when the resulting foreshortening of managerial horizons leads to distorted investment. See, example, Laffont and Tirole (1988), Scharfstein (1988), and Stein (1988). Note, however, that these earlier papers make the point without invoking market irrationality, but rather simply appeal to asymmetries of information between managers and outside shareholders.

D. Portfolio Trading in the Stock of Other Firms

To this point, I have ignored the possibility that managers might wish to take advantage of market inefficiencies by transacting in stocks other than their own. To see why this possibility might be relevant for capital budgeting, consider a manager who perceives that his firm's stock is underpriced, say, because it has a high B/M ratio. On the one hand, as discussed above, this might lead the manager to engage in repurchases of his own stock. And to the extent that such repurchases push capital structure away from its optimum level of $L = 0$, they will spill over and affect investment decisions—in this particular case, raising the hurdle rate from its FAR value in the direction of the higher NEER value.

On the other hand, the capital structure complications associated with own-stock repurchases lead one to ask whether there are other ways for the manager to make essentially the same speculative bet. For example, he might create a zero net-investment portfolio, consisting of long positions in other high B/M stocks and short positions in low B/M stocks. An apparent advantage of this approach is that it does not alter his own firm's capital structure.

For the purposes of this chapter, the bottom line question is whether the existence of such portfolio trading opportunities changes the basic conclusions offered in section 3 above. The answer is, it depends. In particular, the pivotal issue is whether the other trading opportunities are sufficiently attractive and available that they completely eliminate managers' desire to distort capital structure away from the first-best of $L = 0$. If so, capital structure constraints will become irrelevant for hurdle rates, leading to strictly FAR-based capital budgeting. If not, the qualitative conclusions offered in section 3 will continue to hold, with binding capital structure constraints pushing hurdle rates in the direction of NEER values.

Ultimately, the outcome depends on a number of factors that are not explicitly modeled above. First, while "smart money" managers can presumably exploit some simple inefficiencies—like the B/M effect—by trading in other stocks using only easily available public data, it seems plausible that they can do even better by trading in their own stock. If this is the case, there will be circumstances in which the existence of other trading opportunities does not eliminate the desire to transact in own-company stock, and the basic story sketched in section 3 will still apply. A second unmodeled factor that is likely to be important is the extent to which firms exhibit risk aversion with respect to passive portfolio positions. If such risk aversion is pronounced, it will again be the case that the existence of other trading opportunities is not a perfect substitute for transactions in own-company stock.[17]

---

[17] One can imagine a number of reasons for such risk aversion at the corporate level. For example, Froot, Scharfstein, and Stein (1993) develop a model in which capital market imperfections lead firms to behave in a risk-averse fashion, particularly with respects to those risks—such as portfolio trading—that are uncorrelated with their physical investment opportunities.

E. Richer Models of Irrationality

Finally, and perhaps most fundamentally, another area that could use further development is the specification of investors' misperceptions about key parameters. I have adopted the simplest possible approach here, assuming that all investors are homogeneous and that their only misperception has to do with the expected value of future firm cash flows. In reality, there are likely to be important heterogeneities across outside investors. Moreover, estimates of other parameters—such as variances and covariances—may also be subject to systematic biases. It would be interesting to see how robust the qualitative conclusions of this work are to these and related extensions.

6. EMPIRICAL IMPLICATIONS

Traditional efficient-markets-based models conclude that a firm's investment behavior ought to be closely linked to its stock price. And, indeed, a substantial body of empirical research provides evidence for such a link.[18] At the same time, however, a couple of recent papers have found that once one controls for fundamentals like profits and sales, the incremental explanatory power of stock prices for corporate investment, while statistically significant, is quite limited in economic terms, both in firm-level and aggregate data (Morck et al. 1990, Blanchard et al. 1993). Thus it appears that, relative to these fundamental variables, the stock market may be something of a sideshow in terms of its influence on corporate investment.

This sideshow phenomenon is easy to rationalize in the context of the model presented above. If the market is inefficient, and if managers are for the most part engaging in FAR-based capital budgeting, one would not expect investment to track stock prices nearly as closely as in a classical world. Perhaps more interestingly, however, this chapter's logic allows one to go further in terms of empirical implications. Rather than simply saying the theory is consistent with existing evidence, it is also possible to generate some novel cross-sectional predictions.

These cross-sectional predictions flow from the observation that not all firms should have the same propensity to adopt FAR-based capital budgeting practices. In particular, FAR-based capital budgeting should be more prevalent among either firms with very strong balance sheets (who, in terms of the language of the model are presumably operating in a relatively flat region of the Z function) or those whose assets offer substantial debt capacity. In contrast, firms with weak balance sheets and hard-to-collateralize assets— for example, a cash-strapped software development company—should tend to follow NEER-based capital budgeting. Thus the testable prediction is

---

[18] See, e.g., Barro (1990) for an overview and a recent empirical treatment of the relationship between stock prices and investment.

that the cash-strapped software company should have investment that responds more sensitively to movements in its stock price than, say, an AAA-related utility with lots of tangible assets.

A similar sort of reasoning can be used to generate predictions for the patterns of asset sales within and across industries. For concreteness, consider two airlines, one financially constrained, the other not. Now suppose that a negative wave of investor sentiment knocks airline-industry stock prices down and thereby drives conditional expected returns up. The constrained airline, which uses NEER-based capital budgeting, will raise its hurdle rates, while the unconstrained airline, which uses FAR-based capital budgeting, will not. This divergence in the way the two airlines value physical assets might be expected to lead the constrained airline to sell some of its planes to the unconstrained airline. Conversely, if there is a positive sentiment shock, the prediction goes the other way—the constrained airline will cut its hurdle rates, and become a net buyer of assets.[19]

7. CONCLUSIONS

Is β dead? The answer to this question would seem to depend on the job that one has in mind for β. If the job is to predict cross-sectional differences in stock returns, then β may well be dead, as Fama and French (1992) argue. But if the job is to help in determining hurdle rates for capital budgeting purposes, then β may be only slightly hobbled. Certainly, any argument in favor of using β as a capital budgeting tool must be carefully qualified, unlike in the typical textbook treatment. Nonetheless, in the right circumstances, the textbook CAPM approach to setting hurdle rates may ultimately be justifiable.

This defense of β as a capital budgeting tool rests on three key premises. First, one must be willing to assume that the cross-sectional patterns in stock returns that have been documented in recent research—such as the tendency of high B/M stocks to earn higher returns—reflect pricing errors, rather than compensation for fundamental sources of risk. Second, the firm in question must have long horizons and be relatively unconstrained by its current capital structure. And finally, it must be the case that even though there are pricing errors, a β estimated from stock returns is a satisfactory proxy for the fundamental riskiness of the firm's cash flows.

---

[19] I use the example of airlines because of a very interesting paper by Pulvino (1995), who documents exactly this sort of pattern of asset sales in the airline industry—financially unconstrained airlines significantly increase their purchases of used aircraft when prices are depressed. As Shleifer and Vishny (1992) demonstrate, this pattern can arise purely as a consequence of liquidity constraints and thus need not reflect any stock market inefficiencies. Nonetheless, in terms of generating economically large effects, such inefficiencies are likely to give an added kick to their story.

This chapter was intended as a first cut at the problem of capital budgeting in an inefficient market, and, as such, it leaves many important questions unanswered. There are at least three broad areas where further research might be useful. First, there are the pragmatic risk-measurement issues raised in section 4, namely, just how well do stock return β's actually reflect the fundamental riskiness of underlying firm cash flows? Are stock return β's more informative about fundamental risk for some classes of companies than for others? Does lengthening the horizon over which returns are computed help matters? Here it would clearly be desirable to update and build on some of the work done in the 1970s.

Second, as discussed in section 5, there is potentially quite a bit more that can be done in terms of refining and extending the basic conceptual framework. And finally, as seen in section 6, the theory developed here gives rise to some new empirical implications, having to do with cross-sectional differences in the intensity of the relationship between stock prices and corporate investment.

REFERENCES

Ball, R., and P. Brown, 1969, Portfolio theory and accounting. *Journal of Accounting Research* 7, 300–23.

Banz, Rolf W., 1981, The relationship between return and market value of common stocks, *Journal of Financial Economics* 9, 3–18.

Barro, Robert J., 1990, The stock market and investment, *Review of Financial Studies* 3, 115–31.

Basu, Sanjoy, 1977, Investment performance of common stocks in relation to their price-earnings ratios: A test of the efficient market hypothesis, *Journal of Finance* 32, 663–82.

Beaver, William, Paul Kettler, and Myron Scholes, 1970, The association between market determined and accounting determined risk measures, *Accounting Review* October, 654–82.

Beaver, William, and James Manegold, 1975, The association between market-determined and accounting-determined measures of systematic risk: Some further evidence, *Journal of Financial and Quantitative Analysis* June, 231–84.

Bhandari, Laxmi Chand, 1988, Debt/equity ratio and expected common stock returns: Empirical evidence, *Journal of Finance* 43, 507–28.

Blanchard, Olivier, Changyong Rhee, and Lawrence Summers, 1993, The stock market, profit, and investment, *Quarterly Journal of Economics* 108, 115–36.

Bosworth, Barry, 1975, The stock market and the economy, *Brookings Papers on Economic Activity*, 257–300.

Chan, Louis K. C., Y. Hamao, and Josef Lakonishok, 1991, Fundamentals and stock returns in Japan, *Journal of Finance* 46, 1739–64.

Chan, Louis K. C., Narasimhan Jegadeesh, and Josef Lakonishok, 1995, Evaluating the performance of value versus glamour stocks: The impact of selection bias, *Journal of Financial Economics* 38, 269–96.

Cheng, Li-Lan, 1995, The motives, timing and subsequent performance of seasoned equity issues, Ph.D. diss., MIT, Department of Economics.

Daniel, Kent, and Sheridan Titman, 1995. Evidence on the characteristics of cross-sectional variation in stock returns. Working Paper. University of Chicago.

Davis, James L., 1994, The cross-section of realized stock returns: The pre-COMPUSTAT evidence, *Journal of Finance* 49, 1579–93.

DeBondt, Werner F., and Richard H. Thaler, 1985, Does the stock market overreact. *Journal of Finance* 40, 793–805.

DeLong, J. Bradford, Andrei Shleifer, Lawrence H. Summers, and Robert J. Waldmann, 1989, The size and incidence of the losses from noise trading, *Journal of Finance* 44, 681–96.

Fama, Eugene F., 1991, Efficient capital markets: II, *Journal of Finance* 46, 1575–1617.

Fama, Eugene F., and Kenneth R. French, 1992, The cross-section of expected stock returns, *Journal of Finance* 47, 427–65.

———, 1993, Common risk factors in the returns on stocks and bonds, *Journal of Financial Economics* 33, 3–56.

Fischer, Stanley, and Robert Merton, 1984, Macroeconomics and finance: The role of the stock market, *Carnegie Rochester Conference Series on Public Policy* 21, 57–108.

Froot, Kenneth A., David S. Scharfstein, and Jeremy C. Stein, 1993, Risk management: Coordinating corporate investment and financing policies, *Journal of Finance* 48, 1629–58.

Gonedes, Nicholas J., 1973, Evidence on the information content of accounting numbers: Accounting-based and market-based estimates of systematic risk, *Journal of Financial and Quantitative Analysis* June, 407–43.

———, 1975, A note on accounting-based and market-based estimates of systematic risk, *Journal of Financial and Quantitative Analysis* June, 355–65.

Ikenberry, David, Josef Lakonishok, and Theo Vermaelen, 1995, Market underreaction to open market share repurchases, Working Paper. N.p.

Jaffe, Jeffrey, Donald B. Keim, and Randolph Westerfield, 1989, Earnings yields, market values, and stocks returns, *Journal of Finance* 44, 135–48.

Keim, Donald B., 1983, Size-related anomalies and stock return seasonality, *Journal of Financial Economics* 12, 13–32.

Keynes, John Maynard, 1936, *The General Theory of Employment, Interest and Money*, Macmillan.

Laffont, Jean Jacques, and Jean Tirole, 1988, Repeated auctions of incentive contracts, investment, and bidding parity with an application to takeovers, *Rand Journal of Economics* 19, 516–37.

Lakonishok, Josef, Andrei Shleifer, and Robert W. Vishny, 1994, Contrarian investment, extrapolation, and risk, *Journal of Finance* 49, 1541–78.

La Porta, Rafael, Josef Lakonishok; Andrei Shleifer, and Robert Vishny, 1994, Good news for value stocks: Further evidence on market efficiency, Working Paper, Harvard University.

Loughran, Tim, and Jay R. Ritter, 1995, The new issues puzzle, *Journal of Finance* 50, 23–51.

MacKinlay, A. Craig, 1995, Multifactor models do not explain deviations from the CAPM, *Journal of Financial Economics* 38, 3–28.

Miller, Merton M., and Kevin Rock, 1985, Dividend policy under asymmetric information, *Journal of Finance* 40, 1021–52.

Morck, Randall, Andrei Shleifer, and Robert Vishny, 1990, The stock market and investment: Is the market a sideshow?, *Brookings Papers on Economic Activity*, 157–215.

Myers, Stewart, and N. Majluf, 1984, Corporate financing and investment decisions when firms have information that investors do not have, *Journal of Financial Economics* 13, 187–221.

Pulvino, Todd, 1995, Do asset fire-sales exist? An empirical investigation of commercial aircraft transactions, Working Paper, Harvard University.

Rosenberg, Barr, Kenneth Reid, and Ronald Lanstein, 1985, Persuasive evidence of market inefficiency, *Journal of Portfolio Management* 11, 9–17.

Scharfstein, David, 1988, The disciplinary role of takeovers, *Review of Economic Studies* 55, 185–99.

Shleifer, Andrei, and Robert Vishny, 1992, Liquidation values and debt capacity: A market equilibrium approach, *Journal of Finance* 47, 1343–66.

Spiess, D. Katherine, and John Affleck-Graves, 1995, Underperformance in long-run stock reurns following seasoned equity offerings, *Journal of Financial Economics* 38, 241–67.

Stattman, Dennis, 1980, Book values and stock returns, *Chicago MBA: A Journal of Selected Papers* 4, 25–45.

Stein, Jeremy C., 1988, Takeover threats and managerial myopia, *Journal of Political Economy* 96, 61–80.

———, 1989, Efficient capital markets, inefficient firms: A model of myopic corporate behavior, *Quarterly Journal of Economics* 104, 655–69.

Chapter 18

EARNINGS MANAGEMENT TO

EXCEED THRESHOLDS

FRANÇOIS DEGEORGE, JAYENDU PATEL,
AND RICHARD ZECKHAUSER

1. INTRODUCTION

Analysts, investors, senior executives, and boards of directors consider earnings the single most important item in the financial reports issued by publicly held firms. In the medium to long term (1–10 year intervals), returns to equities appear to be explained overwhelmingly by the firm's cumulative earnings during the period; other plausible explanations—such as dividends, cash flows, or capital investments—have marginal correlations close to zero (Easton, Harris, and Ohlson 1992, Kothari and Sloan 1992). Even for short-term equity returns, earnings are an important explanatory factor.[1]

The rewards to a firm's senior executives—both employment decisions and compensation benefits—depend both implicitly and explicitly on the earnings achieved on their watch (Healy 1985). But such executives have considerable discretion in determining the figure printed in the earnings report for any particular period. Within generally accepted accounting principles (GAAP), executives have considerable flexibility in the choice of inventory methods, allowance for bad debt, expensing of research and development, recognition of sales not yet shipped, estimation of pension liabilities, capitalization of leases and marketing expenses, delay in maintenance expenditures,

We thank the David Dreman Foundation for funding support; Degeorge also thanks the Fondation Hautes Etudes Commerciales for research support. The data on analysts' forecasts of earnings were provided by I/B/E/S International Inc. (post-1984 period) and by Q Prime (pre-1984). We have benefited from helpful comments by Raj Aggarwal, Shlomo Benartzi, Bengt Holmstrom, David King, Todd Milbourn, Clyde Stickney, Richard Thaler, Kent Womack, and a referee. We have also benefited from helpful comments from seminar participants at the Behavioral Finance Working Group of the National Bureau of Economic Research; Boston University; the Centre for Economic Policy Research European Summer Symposium in Financial Markets at Studienzentrum Gerzensee, Switzerland; the European Finance Association meetings, Vienna, 1997; the French Finance Association meetings, Grenoble, 1997; Harvard University; the European Institute of Business Administration (INSEAD); the Q Group; and the Amos Tuck School, Dartmouth College.

[1] Ball and Brown (1968) is the classic early work; see Dechow (1994) and references there for subsequent research that details the relevance of earnings.

and so on. Moreover, they can defer expenses or boost revenues, say, by cutting prices. Thus, executives have both the incentive and ability to manage earnings. It is hardly surprising that the popular press frequently describes companies as engaged in earnings management—sometimes referred to as manipulations.[2]

This chapter studies earnings management as a response to implicit and explicit rewards for attaining specific levels of earnings, such as positive earnings, an improvement over last year, or the market's consensus forecast. We label as "earnings management" (EM) the strategic exercise of managerial discretion in influencing the earnings figure reported to external audiences (see Schipper 1989). It is accomplished principally by timing reported or actual economic events to shift income between periods.

We sketch a model that predicts how executives strategically influence the earnings figures that their firms report to external audiences and then examine historical data to confirm such patterns. Our model incorporates behavioral propensities and a stylized description of the interactions among executives, investors, directors, and earnings analysts to identify EM patterns that generate specific discontinuities and distortions in the distribution of observed earnings.[3]

We do not determine which components of earnings or of supplementary disclosures are adjusted. Nor do we attempt to distinguish empirically between "direct" EM—the strategic timing of investment, sales, expenditures, or financing decisions—and "misreporting"—EM involving merely the discretionary accounting of decisions and outcomes already realized.[4]

We identify three thresholds that help drive EM: the first is to report profits—for example, one penny a share. This threshold arises from the psychologically important distinction between positive numbers and negative numbers (or zero). The second and third benchmarks rely on performance relative to widely reported firm-specific values. If the firm does as well or better than the benchmark, it is met; otherwise it is failed. The two benchmarks are performance relative to the prior comparable period and relative to analysts' earnings projections. Performance relative to each benchmark is assessed by examining the sprinkling of quarterly earnings reports in its neighborhood. A big jump in density at the benchmark demonstrates its importance.

---

[2] See, e.g., the multipage stories "Excuses Aplenty When Companies Tinker with Their Profits Reports," *New York Times* (June 23, 1996), and "On the Books, More Facts and Less Fiction," *New York Times* (February 16, 1997). A further study—Bruns and Merchant (1996, p. 25)—concludes that "we have no doubt that short-term earnings are being manipulated in many, if not all, companies."

[3] DeBondt and Thaler (1995, pp. 385–410) provide a discussion of behaviorally motivated financial decisions by firms.

[4] Foster (1986, p. 224) discusses mechanisms for misreporting transactions or events in financial statements.

Burgstahler and Dichev (1997) examine the management of earnings to meet our first two thresholds, though not in relation to analysts' estimates.[5] Their analysis delves more deeply into accounting issues and identifies the "misreporting" mechanisms—for example, the manipulation of cash flow from operations, or changes in working capital—that permit earnings to be moved from negative to positive ranges. We devote considerably more attention to the motivations for EM, consider direct EM (for example, lowering prices to boost sales) in addition to misreporting, provide an optimizing model on how earnings are managed, and analyze the consequences of management for future earnings. In addition, we explore EM as the executive's (agent's) response to steep rewards—reaping a bonus or retaining a job—that depend on meeting a bright threshold.[6] Finally, we look at the hierarchy among our thresholds.

Earnings management arises from the game of information disclosure that executives and outsiders must play. Investors base their decisions on information received from analysts—usually indirectly, say, through a broker—and through published earnings announcements. To bolster investor interest, executives manage earnings, despite the real earnings sacrifice. Other parties, such as boards of directors, analysts, and accountants, participate in this game as well, but their choices are exogenous to our analysis. For example, the contingent remuneration actions of boards are known to executives. Presumably such pay packages are structured to take distorting possibilities into account and may have been adjusted somewhat to counter EM.[7] If so, finding evidence of management is more significant.

Executives may also distort earnings reports in a self-serving manner, imposing an agency loss that reduces the firm's value if their incentives are not fully aligned with those of shareholders. Full alignment is unlikely. First, while the value of the stock is the present value of dividends stretching to infinity, the executive's time horizon is relatively short. Since it is difficult for boards, shareholders, or the stock market to assess future prospects, executives have an incentive to pump up current earnings at the expense of the hard-to-perceive future beyond their reign. Accordingly, a major benefit of stock options is that they extend the time horizon for executives.

Second, an executive's compensation, including the probability of keeping his job, is likely linked to earnings, stock price performance, or both (see Healy 1985, Gaver, Gaver, and Austin 1995). If accepting lower earnings today might result in a termination or a lost bonus, substantially

[5] Payne and Robb (1997) show that managers use discretionary accrual to align earnings with analysts' expectations.

[6] Burgstahler (1997) adds a model in which earnings are manipulated because the marginal benefit of reporting higher earnings is greatest in some middle range.

[7] Dechow, Hudson, and Sloan (1994) document that compensation committees often override the provisions of incentive plans to avoid providing incentives for executives to behave opportunistically.

greater earnings tomorrow may not represent a desirable trade-off. When earnings are near the unacceptable range, executives' incentives to manage them upward will be significant. However, when bonuses are near maximum, further earnings increases will be rewarded little, generating an incentive to rein in today's earnings—that is, shift them forward—making future thresholds easier to meet.[8] Executives may also be reluctant to report large gains in earnings because they know their performance target will be ratcheted up in the future. Earnings so poor as to put thresholds and bonuses out of reach may also be shifted to the future; the executive saves for a better tomorrow.

Earnings can be managed by actually shifting income over time, which we label "direct management," or by misreporting. A typical misreport, failing to mark down "stale" inventory or incurring extraordinary charges beyond what prudence requires, simply relocates an amount from one year to another. Such misreports must pass through the hands of accountants, who are reliable professionals. Accountants' procedures prevent simple misreporting of earnings; indeed, only their oversight makes earnings reports meaningful. But accountants are neither omniscient nor disinterested. They can be misled, but only at a cost. The executive may need to co-opt the auditor, say, with an unneeded consulting contract. Alternatively, he may make his misreporting hard to detect, but that requires weakening internal control mechanisms, which help the manager in allocating resources or detecting shirking or misappropriation at lower levels in the firm.

Direct management of earnings upward—through delaying desirable training or maintenance expenditures or cutting prices to boost sales—has real consequences and can impose costs beyond today's benefits plus imputed interest. Earnings delays, perhaps, by accelerating costs to this year to pave the way for a brighter future—common behavior when a new team takes over and blames poor initial results on past leadership—are also costly. Both misreporting and direct earnings management, whether pushing earnings forward or back, are costly activities. Their marginal cost increases with scale since cheap transfers are undertaken first.

Section 2 of this chapter reports briefly on relevant literature from psychology, develops a model of EM around threshold targets, and draws inferences for real world data. Section 3 reports on empirical explorations relating to thresholds, studying conditional and unconditional distributions of quarterly earnings over the period 1974 to 1996. Section 4 examines whether

---

[8] Healy (1985, p. 106) reports that "managers are more likely to choose income-decreasing accruals when their bonus plan's upper and lower bounds are binding, and income-increasing accruals when these bounds are not binding." Holthausen, Larcker, and Sloan (1995) find that managers manipulate earnings downward when they are at the upper bounds of their bonus contracts. However, they find no manipulation downward below their contract's lower bounds.

firms that are more likely to have managed earnings upward to attain a threshold in a particular year underperform in the subsequent year. Section 5 suggests future directions and concludes.

2. A Threshold Model of Earnings Management

Executives manage earnings to influence the perceptions of outsiders—such as investors, banks, and suppliers—and to reap private payoffs.[9] In our stylized model, outsiders utilize thresholds as a standard for judging and rewarding executives. When executives respond to these thresholds, distributions of reported earnings get distorted: far too few earnings fall just below a threshold, too many just above it.

A. Why Thresholds?

Executives focus on thresholds for earnings because the parties concerned with the firm's performance do. Executives may also manipulate earnings for their own reasons if, for example, they derive personal satisfaction from making a target; however, the biases of outsiders are our focus.

Beyond boards, investors, and analysts, earnings reports are important to those people concerned with the firm's viability and profitability because they make firm-specific investments, such as customers and suppliers, bankers, and workers. Many of these outsiders exhibit what we call a "threshold mentality," for both rational and perceptual reasons. In a range of circumstances, individuals perceive continuous data in discrete form; indeed "the tendency to divide the world into categories is a pervasive aspect of human thought" (Glass and Holyoak 1986, p. 149). For example, we perceive the continuous color spectrum discretely, recognizing seven primary colors. Similarly, if a diagram shades from dark to light and then remains light, humans perceive a bright line where the shading to light stops (Cornsweet 1974, pp. 276–77). Below we discuss three established demarcations for corporate earnings. Unlike our vision examples, earnings demarcations draw strongly on external cues.

The salience of thresholds arises from at least three psychological effects. First, there is something fundamental about positive and nonpositive

---

[9] Even if EM is costly, it may be in the interest of shareholders ex ante if it increases the information available to important parties. In some settings, manipulated earnings may contain more, not less, information about the firm's true prospects. For example, if a firm's earnings barely meet some threshold, it is likely that the figure has been inflated. But this implies that executives are confident that the cost of manipulation—reduced profits next year—will not be so large as to reduce dramatically the prospect that the firm will meet the threshold next year. Thus, small manipulated profits may contain more information than small unmanipulated profits.

numbers in human thought processes.[10] Hence, this dividing line carries over for the threshold on absolute earnings. When looking at the benchmarks of quarterly earnings a year back and the analysts' consensus forecast, there is a salient dividing line between meeting and failing to meet the norm. Meeting the norm is critical, as opposed to beating it by 10 percent or falling short by 3 percent. Saliency makes the norm itself a focal point, which reinforces its psychological properties.[11]

Second, as prospect theory tells us, individuals choosing among risky alternatives behave as if they evaluate outcomes as changes from a reference point (Kahneman and Tversky 1979). The reference point is usually some aspect of the decision maker's current state (for example, wealth), and it shifts over time, sometimes with how the decision is framed. The amount of shifting can dramatically affect choices for two reasons: there is a kink in the utility function at the reference point (zero change); and the overall curve is S-shaped (that is, it is convex for losses and concave for gains). If the preferences of executives, the boards that review them, or the investors who trade the firm's stock are consistent with the predictions of prospect theory, then executives will have a threshold-related reward schedule and are likely to manage reported earnings in response. The thresholds they will wish to reach are the reference points in the value functions of the participants; such points are likely to be perceptually salient.

Third, thresholds come to the fore because people depend on rules of thumb to reduce transactions costs. The discreteness of actions, whether by investment analysts recommending sell, hold, or buy, rating agencies giving letter grades, bankers making or refusing loans, or boards retaining or dismissing the CEO promotes the use of thresholds of acceptable performance.[12] Banks, for example, may grant loans only to firms that report positive earnings; that is, banks use a threshold of zero earnings as an initial screen since judiciously adjusting interest rates in response to differential performance may be too hard. Earnings management across thresholds can also simplify executives' relations with shareholders and boards of directors. A report to shareholders that earnings have been up six years in a row is cheaply

[10] The symbol for zero came late and with difficulty to mathematicians, except in India. For example, China imported it from India in the eighth century, and "the mathematicians and astronomers of Sumer and Babylon labored for nearly 1500 years before they introduced the notion of a 'zero' symbol." Negative numbers were much harder still, not becoming "generally recognized as 'numbers' until the sixteenth century" (Barrow 1992, pp. 89–90). In contrast, positive numbers appear to be a more directly grasped concept for humans.

[11] Any assessor of earnings will worry about the consistency of his judgment with that of others, which makes focal points critical. When comparing performance to a yardstick, just meeting the standard is a spotlighted property. For a seminal analysis of focal points see Schelling (1960). See Young (1996) for a discussion of conventions.

[12] Burgstahler (1997) shows empirically that the net probability of improvements in outside ratings of both debt and equity are greatest in the neighborhoods of zero earnings and zero changes in earnings.

communicated. A statement that they have been up five out of six years, and only fell by 1 percent in the off year, is less easily understood, so that struggling across the threshold of last year's earnings becomes worthwhile. When a firm falls short of analysts' earnings projections, the board may think that the executives did a poor job; bonuses and stock option awards may suffer. Such doubts are much less likely to arise if the analysts' earnings are just met.[13]

Threshold effects may be important even if few participants respond to them directly. Suppose that only the firm's bankers care directly whether the firm reaches a specific performance threshold but all parties know how the bankers feel. Since analysts and shareholders know that executives cannot lightly risk raising the bankers' ire, they will want to know whether the firm meets the banker's performance threshold. Thus, reaching the threshold caters both to the bankers and to other participants' rational perceptions through inference.

In contrast to a world in which all participants care about thresholds, threshold-regarding (TR) behavior by merely a minority may have a much more than proportional effect. For example, the level of EM in a world where 25 percent of boards of directors respond naturally to thresholds may be much more than 25 percent as great as in a world where all boards are threshold-driven. Consider an executive threatened with modestly negative results who does not know how his board will respond. If it is TR, it will fire him with probability 0.4; otherwise, his job is safe. If he knew he faced a TR board, he would manage earnings to the positive safe zone. But even with only a 25 percent chance it is TR, he may do the same thing. A 10 percent probability of being fired may be sufficient stimulus. Signaling and lemons-type unraveling can also lead to spillovers, for instance, if higher-quality firms are more able and likely to manipulate to the safe range. If so, TR behavior by a modest proportion of boards spills over to affect potentially the behavior of large numbers of executives.

B. Three Thresholds

Reports in the financial press suggest that executives care about three thresholds when they report earnings:

1. to report positive profits, that is, report earnings that are above zero;
2. to sustain recent performance, that is, make at least last year's earnings; and
3. to meet analysts' expectations, particularly the analysts' consensus earnings forecast.

[13] President Clinton, recognizing the role of thresholds, announced that he was seeking to secure 50 percent of the 1996 presidential vote so as to claim a mandate. Not surprisingly, he struggled hard in the final days to get more than 50 percent. (In fact, he won 49.2 percent of the actual vote.)

The analysts' consensus estimate, unlike our other thresholds, is endogenous. Although executives try to report earnings that exceed analysts' forecasts, analysts try to anticipate reported earnings.[14] A complicated game ensues, in which analysts predict an earnings number that will then be manipulated in response to their prediction. Anecdotal evidence suggests that executives, realizing the importance of meeting or exceeding the analysts' consensus, actively try to influence analysts' expectations downward, especially when the earnings announcement date draws near.[15]

C. A Two-period Model with Last Period's Earnings as Threshold

Using earnings management to reach thresholds affects the distribution of reported earnings. We study a simple 2-period model where the threshold to be met is last year's earnings. In each period $t = 1, 2$, the firm gets a random, independent, and identically distributed draw of "latent" or true earnings, L_t. Outsiders cannot observe these latent earnings. They only see reported earnings, R_t. In period 1, executives can manipulate reported earnings R_1 by choosing an amount M_1 (possibly negative) to add to earnings, such that $R_1 = L_1 + M_1$. The cost of manipulation is paid when there is full settling up in period 2:

$$R_2 = L_2 - k(M_1),$$

where $k(0) = 0$ and there are positive and increasing marginal costs for moving away from zero. For simplicity, assume a zero discount rate. Pumping up reported earnings today reduces earnings tomorrow by more than one dollar. If period 1 manipulation is negative (executives rein in earnings), another dollar reduction boosts next year's earnings by less than one dollar.

The executive exits after period 2, and we assume that all is revealed at that point. This produces the trade-off indicated in figure 18.1. Point a corresponds to $M_1 = 0$, and thus $R_1 = L_1$. As shown, the slope of the trade-off curve at a is -1. (More generally, the slope will be $-(1 + r)$, where r is the 1-period interest rate corresponding to a nonzero time value of money.)

We assume that the executive's expected reward schedule falls sharply at one or more thresholds, such as negative earnings, or earnings below last year. Below such thresholds, he or she might risk termination or at least a

---

[14] See Abarbanell and Bernard (1992) and references there on possible biases in analysts' forecasts.

[15] See "Learn to Manage Your Earnings, and Wall Street Will Love You," *Fortune* (March 31, 1997). This article tells the story of a meeting among Microsoft's Bill Gates, his chief financial officer, and financial analysts, during which the Microsoft executives paint a particularly bleak picture of the company's future. At the end of the meeting, Gates and his chief financial officer congratulate each other when they realize that their goal of depressing analysts' expectations has been achieved.

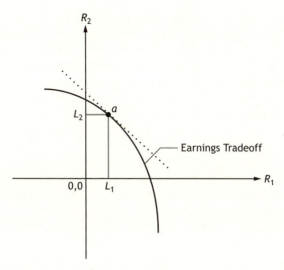

Figure 18.1. Reported earnings in period 2 as a function of those in period 1, holding L_1 and L_2 fixed.

substantial cut in bonus. For simplicity, we assume that at all earnings levels other than at the thresholds the incentives for better performance are positive and constant. (In practice, we suspect that they are steep near a threshold and more tempered at either extreme.)

The self-interested executive manages earnings to maximize his personal payoff. In each period, he receives a payoff $f(R_t, R_{t-1})$, where R_t is the reported earnings performance in period t. If the manager meets or surpasses the benchmark, he receives a bonus $v(R_t, R_{t-1})$.[16] Thus, we posit the following form for f:

$$f(R_t, R_{t-1}) = \beta R_t + v(R_t, R_{t-1}),$$

where

$$v(R_t, R_{t-1}) = \gamma \text{ if } R_t \geq R_{t-1}$$

$$= 0 \text{ otherwise.}$$

The executive's direct rewards for the current period performance (at a rate β) are captured by the first term. The previous period's reported earnings

---

[16] If effort boosts earnings, incentives should be strongest where earnings outcomes, given optimal effort, are most likely. Strong incentives cannot be provided across all outcomes because executives cannot be paid negatively for poor outcomes. Thus, strong incentives will not be provided for very favorable outcomes either lest executives be overpaid on average. The optimal reward schedule will be steeply responsive near the benchmark since such earnings outcomes are most likely.

serve as a benchmark for a second effect. For period 1, the benchmark is R_0, which is normalized to zero for exposition, and the benchmark is R_1 for period 2. Thus the $v(R_t, R_{t-1})$ term induces a ratcheting effect.[17]

Executives are assumed to be risk neutral for convenience; this assumption could easily be relaxed. For our 2-period illustration, the executive selects M_1 to maximize the net present value of the expected payoffs in the two periods, that is, to maximize

$$f(R_1, R_0) + \delta E[f(R_2, R_1)],$$

where E denotes expectation and δ is the discount factor.

Managing earnings is an imprecise science, relying on estimates of both latent earnings and the effects of any attempts to boost earnings. Latent earnings may well prove higher or lower than expected. We analyze two cases, depending on whether the executive knows L_1 precisely or imprecisely when he selects M_1.

Case 1. The executive knows L_1 precisely when he selects M_1. In this setting, the primary element of the executive's strategy is intuitively clear. If $L_1 < R_0$, the executive should select M_1 to achieve the threshold and reap the bonus, unless the entailed loss on L_2 in expected value terms proves too costly.

We set R_0 equal to zero for convenience. If L_1 is slightly below zero, then it will be worthwhile to select a positive M_1—the executive should borrow future earnings to make the bonus. While manipulation will sacrifice a greater amount of second-period earnings and raise the hurdle for the second period, it will allow the executive to earn the bonus for sure now, only sacrificing it with some chance in period 2. The borrowing will prove well worthwhile, except in the unlikely case when it turns out to sacrifice next period's bonus.

If L_1 is significantly below zero, then borrowing to cross the threshold may be too costly. To determine whether it is, the executive compares two quantities. The first is his expected payoff if he manipulates just enough— that is, selects M_1 so that $R_1 = 0$—to secure the bonus. The second is his optimal strategy if he forgoes the bonus. For the second, he actually selects a negative value of M_1, lowering the next period's threshold and pushing earnings forward thus in two ways. We call this "saving for a better tomorrow." Reducing earnings when latent earnings are disappointing is referred to in the literature as "taking the Big Bath."

If L_1 is above R_0, then there is no reason to boost earnings. Indeed, for $L_1 > R_0$, some reining in is desirable since it increases the likelihood that the executive will earn the next period's bonus.

---

[17] Ratcheting of standards is well known in the contexts of worker productivity, procurement, and regulation and is primarily studied for its disincentive effects on first-period effort. See Milgrom and Roberts (1992, pp. 233–36) and Laffont and Tirole (1993, pp. 381–87).

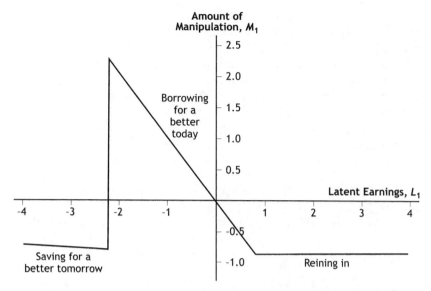

Figure 18.2. Optimal amount of period 1 manipulation, M_1, as a function of latent period 1 earnings L_1. Latent earnings L_1 are normally distributed with mean zero and standard deviation 10. If reported earnings $R_1 = L_1 + M_1$ reach at least $R_0 = 0$, the executive reaps a bonus of 10. The period 2 cost of manipulation is $k(M_1) = e^M - 1$. The executive knows L_1 exactly when choosing the manipulation level M_1.

To illustrate, we choose $R_0 = 0$, $\beta = 1$, $\gamma = 10$, and $\delta = 1$; hence, $f(R_1) = R_1 + v(R_1, 0)$. Earnings have a normal distribution each period, with mean of zero and standard deviation of 10.[18] The second-period cost from manipulation is $k(M) = e^M - 1$, which is greater than M, implying that any manipulation is costly on net. (If $M < 0$, earnings are manipulated downward in the first period and boosted in the second period—but the second-period boost is smaller than the first-period hit.)

Figure 18.2 illustrates the executive's optimal strategy as a function of latent earnings L_1. The initial threshold is achieved where $L_1 + M_1 = R_0 = 0$. Our key finding is that, just below zero, the optimal strategy is to set $M_1 = -L_1$; future earnings are borrowed to meet today's earnings threshold. At point Z, the payoff from choosing $M_1 = -L_1$ (and therefore a positive M_1, indicating borrowing) just equals the payoff from saving for a better

---

[18] We assume stationarity in the latent earnings distribution. This might be considered unrepresentative if the real earnings process has a random walk characteristic. If latent earnings do follow a random walk and we keep the same ratcheting structure in the payoff function, the manipulation behavior will be identical close to the threshold ($M_1 = L_1$). Away from the threshold, firms will manipulate by a constant amount regardless of L_1: ratcheting combined with the random walk assumption ensures that the executive's decision problem is invariant to L_1.

tomorrow (taking the optimal sacrifice in earnings). Left of Z, the optimal bath gives a higher payoff than striving. Right of Z, borrowing gives a higher 2-period payoff. Hence the discontinuity in the graph.

When L_1 is small and positive, it pays to rein in, so that reported earnings just sneak beyond the threshold (recall that in this initial version of the model, R_1 can be targeted perfectly, so there is no risk of missing zero earnings). As L_1 becomes larger, reining in becomes less attractive since ratcheting upward makes the benchmark less likely to be attained in period 2 and the k function is convex. Indeed, for large values of L_1 (not shown), reining in is abandoned since next year's bonus is unlikely to be reaped in any circumstance.[19]

Figure 18.2 identifies three phenomena that arise if executives misreport earnings. First, for a range of values of L_1, a profit just sufficient to meet the threshold is recorded. Second, EM creates a gap in the earnings distribution just below the threshold (zero in this case). Third, the level of reported earnings will be a sharply discontinuous function of latent earnings.[20]

Case 2.   The executive has an imprecise estimate of L_1 when he chooses M_1. The executive has a prior probability distribution on L_1 centered on its true value with variance σ^2. Now, when the executive sets an $M_1 > 0$ seeking to meet or exceed the threshold, he must choose a value higher than in Case 1 to be sure the threshold is met. Also, when by chance L_1 ends up toward the bottom of its expected range, small negative earnings will be recorded.

Case 2 incorporates uncertainty, sets $\sigma^2 = 1$, and uses the same parameter values employed in our prior example. Figure 18.3 shows the distribution of reported earnings for 20,000 draws of latent earnings with a bin width of one unit. The density of reported earnings dips just below zero and piles up above the threshold. The extreme outcome of zero density just below zero, which occurs when the executive has perfect knowledge of L_1, does not appear in Case 2. The maximum hump is shifted to the right of zero because executives hedge against uncertainty by undertaking some positive EM even when the mean of their prior distribution of L_1 is somewhat above the threshold. This simulated distribution of R_1 is the pattern to

---

[19] Healy (1985, p. 90), who focuses on misreporting (discretionary accruals) and does not consider ratcheting, provides intuition for a three-component linear schedule. Whereas our schedule has a jump at the threshold, with a shallow positive slope to either side, Healy assumes a schedule that has a slope over a middle range, with a zero slope to either side. Unlike Healy, we assume improved performance is rewarded everywhere and that there is a sharp reward at the threshold.

[20] This will make reported earnings very difficult to predict. Thus, executives' manipulations could explain why analysts' forecasts are often wrong. Roughly 45 percent of analysts' estimates fall outside a band of 15 percent plus or minus the actual earnings (Dreman and Berry 1995a, p. 39).

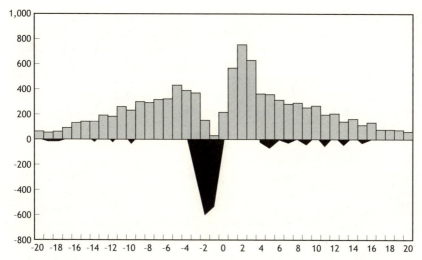

Figure 18.3. Simulated distributing of reported earnings R_1. Latent earning L_1 are normally distributed with mean 0 and standard deviation 10. If reported earnings $R_1 = L_1 + M_1$ reach at least $R_0 = 0$, the executive reaps a bonus of 10. The period 2 cost of manipulation is $k(M_1) = e^M - 1$. The executive knows L_1 imprecisely when choosing the manipulation level M_1 (he has a probability distribution centered on L_1 with a variance of one). The dark shaded areas below the horizontal show shortfalls relative to the equidistant bin on the other side of the threshold of zero.

which we compare the empirical distributions below. The dark shaded areas below the horizontal show shortfalls in the density, if any, relative to the equidistant bin on the other side of the threshold (which, by construction, is at the peak of the latent symmetric distribution).

In results not shown, we explored the consequences of changing the parameter values of the model. We find that the changeover point Z (where L_1 is negative and the payoff from borrowing to meet the threshold just equals the payoff from taking the optimal sacrifice) moves to the left as the discount factor increases since, the higher the executive's discount rate, the more valuable it is to get high earnings this period, and the costlier it is to take a bath.

The more uncertain are second-period earnings, the more the executive will manipulate to secure the bonus in the first period since big borrowings are less likely to sacrifice the second year's threshold. As the bonus for crossing the threshold (indicated by γ) falls in importance relative to the rewards per unit of reported earnings (indicated by β), EM becomes more costly and decreases. For any level of L_1, as β increases, the optimal M_1 moves closer to zero, and the dip below and pile-up above the threshold both diminish. Where borrowing earnings had been most extreme, the executive saves instead for a better tomorrow.[21]

The next two sections relate the results of the model to empirical data on earnings so as to evaluate the evidence of EM. Section 3 examines the distributions (both unconditional and conditional) of reported earnings between 1974 and 1996. Section 4 reports on statistical tests of the hypothesis that future earnings are lower when current earnings are likely to have been manipulated upward to attain a threshold.

3. EVIDENCE OF EARNINGS MANAGEMENT TO EXCEED THRESHOLDS

Theory suggests that simple thresholds will significantly influence executives' management of earnings. It is impossible to monitor manipulation, M, and test the theory directly, so we evaluate the indirect evidence provided by the values of reported earnings, R.[22]

Our empirical analyses explore the extent to which managers manage earnings to attain our three thresholds: (1) to "report profits," that is, to achieve 1 cent or more in earnings per share; (2) to "sustain recent performance," that is, to meet or surpass the most recent level of comparable earnings (which, given seasonal variation, is the corresponding quarter from the previous year); and (3) to "meet analysts' expectations," that is, to meet or exceed the consensus forecast of analysts. We study the density function for earnings near each threshold. If managers do indeed manage earnings to meet a threshold, we expect to observe "too few" earnings reports directly below it and "too many" at or directly above it. We do not expect findings as stark as those our model generates because of numerous additional factors, including heterogeneity among firms in both earnings distributions and EM potential.

Subsection 3A briefly discusses the sample and the construction of variables. Subsection 3B presents three univariate histograms that provide evidence of EM across the three thresholds. For each histogram, we report the results of a statistical test that the discontinuity at the conjectured threshold is significant. Details of the test method are discussed in the appendix. Finally, in subsection 3C, we explore conditional distributions to rank the importance of the three thresholds.

---

[21] We have extended results to a three-period setting in results not shown. With more than two periods, there are factors that make saving earnings from the first period both more and less valuable. They would be more valuable because there would be no danger that they would be "wasted," that is, more than enough to secure the second-period bonus. They would be less valuable because executives could always borrow in the second period to make that period's bonus.

[22] Dechow et al. (1995) address the problems of estimating the level of discretionary accrual activity.

A. Data and Construction of Variables

Our data set consists of quarterly data on 5,387 firms providing partial or complete data over the 1974 to 1996 period. To conveniently align quarterly observations, we drop firms whose fiscal years do not end in March, June, September, or December. While the total number of observations exceeds 100,000, the number of available observations is much smaller for many of the analyses. For the 1974 to 1984 period, the sample includes only the midcapitalization or larger firms for which Abel-Noser (more recently Q-Prime) provides data on analysts' forecasts of earnings. The reported earnings per share are from Compustat item no. 8, which excludes extraordinary items. Our post-1984 sample of more than 83,000 observations draws from the databases provided by I/B/E/S International Inc. The I/B/E/S databases contain analysts' forecasts of quarterly earnings as well as the reported earnings.

We represent analysts' expectations by the mean of the analysts' forecasts for the contemporaneous quarter. Such forecasts are usually available around the middle of the last month of the quarter. (The financial results for a quarter are announced by firms about four weeks into the next quarter—typically slightly later for the fiscal-year-ending quarter and somewhat earlier for the other three quarters.) According to I/B/E/S, analysts' earnings forecasts do not include unusual or nonrecurring charges, and so the reported earnings per share (EPS) variable we use excludes extraordinary items. Thus, any evidence of EM we uncover excludes earnings-shifting strategies employing extraordinary items.[23]

In testing our hypotheses, we pool data from firms that vary widely in size and share price. For example, the median firm size in our sample during the 1980s, as measured by its average market capitalization, is $128 million; the interquartile range of market capitalization is $353 million. The corresponding values based on price per share are $12.77 and $11.88, respectively. We need to address the potential heterogeneity that results from drawing quarterly results from such a wide range of firms.

The literature commonly normalizes EPS by deflators such as price per share or assets per share in an attempt to homogenize the distribution from which the different observations are drawn. However, because EPS is measured (and reported and forecast) rounded to the closest penny, spurious patterns can arise in the distribution of such normalized EPS. (This problem

[23] Philbrick and Ricks (1991) argue that analysts fail to account for special items, especially asset sales, that affect reported earnings. They recommend that the reported earnings before extraordinary items also be purged of the after-tax effects of asset sales. See also Keane and Runkle. There are some large outliers in the set of reported earnings recorded by I/B/E/S in the post-1984 sample that could be corrected by cross-checking with Compustat data. However, since our analysis focuses on observations in a region far from the tails of the distributions, this problem of possibly spurious outliers is not significant for us. In our analyses, we do not make adjustments to the EPS numbers coded by I/B/E/S for the post-1985 sample.

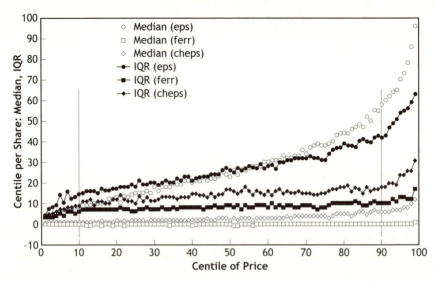

Figure 18.4. Medians and interquartile ranges for EPS, FERR, and ΔEPS as a function of centiles of price per share.

appears to have been overlooked previously.)[24] For example, exactly zero EPS (or change in EPS or forecast error) occur with nontrivial probability because of the rounding (as does any specific value like one penny). However, a zero remaps to zero after deflation compared to, for instance, a one-penny EPS that can remap into a relatively large or small number depending on the deflator. Thus, deflation can lead to a spurious buildup in the density at zero, a critical area of interest for our study. In simulations not shown, this problem proves significant under conditions where EPS is rounded off to the nearest penny (as in practice).

Fortunately, if we exclude the extreme firms in terms of price, then deflation to correct for possible heterogeneity proves unnecessary for the important variables related to EPS that we study. Figure 18.4 shows the medians (represented by hollow symbols) and interquartile ranges (represented by corresponding solid symbols which are connected) of the important variables as a function of centiles of price per share.

[24] This problem is analogous to the "aliasing problem" in the literature on the spectral analysis of time-series data (e.g., see Koopmans 1974, ch. 3). The classic aliasing problem arises when the spectrum of interest is a continuous-time series but the available sample was sampled at discrete intervals. In this situation, either lack of prior knowledge of the specific bounds of the frequency interval in which the spectrum is concentrated, or an inability to sample often enough, results in accurate estimates of the *sampled* process spectrum providing poor or misleading estimates of the original spectrum. In our setting, the estimate of the probability density function risks distortion owing to the initial rounding off (discretization) of EPS and any subsequent renormalization.

The best situation for our study would arise if the measures of location (median) and dispersion (interquartile range) proved to be homogeneous across the different centiles. Consider for instance the analysts' forecast error (FERR), constructed as the reported EPS minus the mean of the analysts' forecasts. In figure 18.4, FERR's median and interquartile range are indicated by squares. These measures are reasonably independent of price per share if we focus on the middle 80 percent of the sample indicated as the region between the two vertical lines drawn at 10 percent and 90 percent in figure 18.4. Consider the case of the change in earnings per share, denoted ΔEPS, which is simply EPS minus EPS of four quarters ago. The distribution of ΔEPS, like FERR, appears stable in the middle 80 percent of the sample given in figure 18.4. In the analysis that follows, we restrict our sample to the middle 80 percent of the sample, which delivers reasonable homogeneity.

We further analyzed the sample for heterogeneity caused by variation across different time periods. For the culled sample of the middle 80 percent, time variation in the distribution proved not to be a major problem.

However, the situation for the basic EPS series itself is not resolved by restricting our sample to the middle 80 percent. Earnings-per-share medians as well as interquartile range increase steadily throughout the centiles of price per share, as is readily seen in figure 18.4. Therefore, in any analysis with EPS, we check whether results obtained for our entire sample hold for each of the quartiles of the middle 80 percent (that is, 11%–30%, 31%–50%, 51%–70%, and 71%–90% from the preculled sample).

B. Historical Evidence of Earnings Management

The hypotheses about threshold-driven EM predict discontinuities in earnings distributions at specific values. As a first cut, we assess empirical histograms, focusing on the region where the discontinuity in density is predicted for our performance variables. Second, we compute a test statistic, τ, that indicates whether or not to reject the null hypothesis that the distribution underlying the histogram is continuous and smooth at the threshold point. Since traditional statistical tests are not designed to test such hypotheses, we developed a test statistic, τ, which extrapolates from neighborhood densities to compute expected density at the threshold assuming no unusual behavior there. The appendix discusses our testing method.

To construct empirical histograms requires a choice of bin width that balances the need for a precise density estimate with the need for fine resolution. Silverman (1986) and Scott (1992) recommend a bin width positively related to the variability of the data and negatively related to the number of observations; for example, one suggestion calls for a bin width of $2(\text{IQR})n^{-1/3}$, where IQR is the sample interquartile range of the variable and n is the number of available observations. Given our sample sizes and

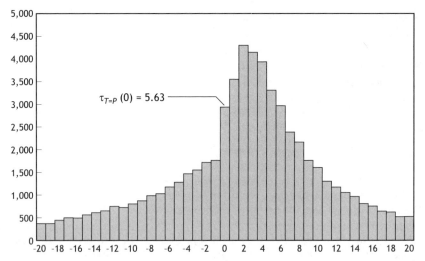

Figure 18.5. Histogram of change in EPS (ΔEPS = EPS$_t$ – EPS$_{t-4}$): exploring the threshold of "sustain recent performance."

dispersions of variables, such formulas imply a bin width of one penny (the minimum resolution for our data).

1. *"Sustain Recent Performance."* Press reports on corporate earnings typically compare current results with those from a year ago. Consistent with this practice, we provide evidence that earnings from one year ago constitute an important threshold for earnings reports, as we posited in our model. The distribution of the change in earnings, denoted ΔEPS, is simply EPS minus EPS of four quarters ago. (The appropriate recent available benchmark proves to be the corresponding quarter from a year ago since earnings exhibit strong annual seasonal variation.) The distribution of ΔEPS is plotted in figure 18.5.

   Since corporate earnings tend to grow (surely in nominal terms), we do not expect the central tendency of the distribution to be close to zero. Indeed, the median and the mode of the distribution of the overall sample are 3 cents, while the mean is 0.81 cents. It is all the more remarkable, then, that we observe a large jump in the distribution at zero. In the region of small negative changes, the distribution appears to have been "shaved," with some density mass transferred to zero or slightly above. This pattern of ΔEPS is consistent with executives' managing earnings to come in at or above the comparable figure for four quarters ago.[25]

---

[25] A qualitatively similar pattern is reported in Burgstahler and Dichev (1997, fig. 1), although, since they deflate earnings, the extreme dip in density just below zero in their distribution of scaled earnings is most likely spurious (as discussed in 3A above).

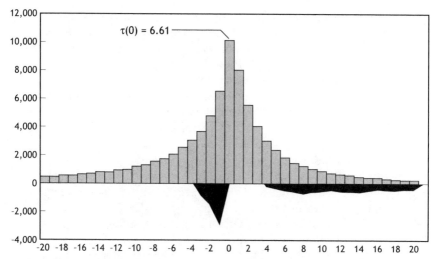

Figure 18.6. Histogram of forecast error for earnings per share: exploring the threshold of meeting analysts' expectations.

The easily discernible pileup of observations at the zero threshold for ΔEPS is confirmed by the τ-statistic of 6.61.[26] The value of 6.61 is the largest for all points in the neighborhood as well as being very significant. These findings are also confirmed with the subsamples of I/B/E/S and Q-Prime (unreported).

2. *"Meet Analysts' Expectations."* Figure 18.6 plots the empirical distribution of the forecast error, FERR (equal to EPS minus the analysts' consensus EPS forecast) in 1-penny bins in a range around zero, using quarterly observations over the 1974 to 1996 period.

Consistent with the notion that "making the forecast" is an important threshold for managers, the distribution of FERR drops sharply below zero: we observe a smaller mass to the left of zero compared to the right. (Note that in the histogram, the bin starting with zero represents observations that are exactly zero.)

There is an extra pileup of observations at zero, although this is hard to see for a distribution like FERR that is centered on zero itself. The pileup is confirmed by the τ-statistic of 5.63, which is very significant.[27] This value exceeds the values of τ for all the neighboring points, none of which exceed 2.0 in absolute value (unreported).

Parallel to figure 18.3 (which, like FERR, had the latent distribution centered at the threshold), we show the shortfall in density

[26] In this case the likely threshold is not at the peak of the distribution although its neighborhood includes the peak; see elaboration A1 discussed in the appendix.

[27] In this case, we compute τ for the case in which the likely threshold is at the peak of the distribution (see elaboration A2 in the appendix).

below the histogram in figure 18.6 for the different outcomes—see the dark shaded areas below the horizontal axis. As predicted by consideration of earnings management to exceed the threshold of analysts' forecasts, we find that (1) the region just below zero exhibits a significant shortfall owing to "borrowing for a better today," and (2) the region of large positive forecast errors shows some shortfall owing to a combination of reduced density of "reining in" and excess density at the mirror bins from "saving for a better tomorrow."[28]

Previous studies on analysts' forecasts have reported an "optimistic bias": analysts' forecasts exceed reported earnings on average. Optimistic bias in the mean of forecasts works against our contention that executives will manage reported earnings to meet or exceed analysts' forecasts. This in turn suggests that a supportive finding will be more meaningful.

Fortunately, the two forces that may explain the data in figure 18.6—EM to attain or exceed the forecast, and a mean optimistic bias in the forecast—can be reconciled. It is sufficient that most of the time executives meet or slightly exceed analysts' forecasts but that they sometimes fall dramatically short. Given those forces, the forecast error distribution will be skewed, with a long left tail. This pattern appears in our sample: the mean of FERR is −5.43 while the median is zero; the skewness measure computes to −43 (whose p-value is near zero under the null hypothesis of a symmetric distribution). This confirms a statistically significant left-skewed distribution of earnings relative to forecast.

3. "*Report Positive Profits.*" Our third possible important threshold is probably the most natural: positive earnings. To know whether this threshold has been reached, investors need no information on the company's performance history or the market's consensus forecast. This threshold also addresses the most important question for shareholders: is this firm profitable? The complication for studying a distribution of EPS, as discussed previously, is that the distribution is not homogeneous with respect to price per share. Thus, while we discuss the results for the overall sample, we confirm that similar findings emerge as well as for subsamples based on quartiles of price per share. In figure 18.7, we show the distribution of EPS in a window around zero.

Two patterns emerge. First, similar to ΔEPS, the EPS distribution appears to be shaved in the negative region, consistent with the hypothesis of loss aversion. Second, the EPS distribution shows a

---

[28] In results not reported, these findings are confirmed with the subsamples of I/B/E/S and Q-Prime.

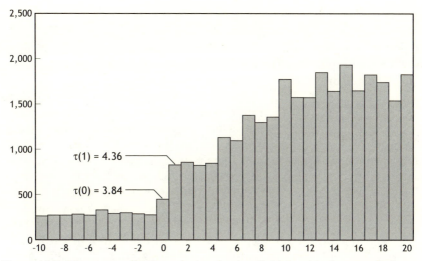

Figure 18.7. Histogram of EPS: exploring the threshold "positive/zero profits"

considerable jump between zero and one (especially the latter); thus it appears that managers strongly desire to be able to report strictly positive earnings—as opposed to just breaking even.[29] The value of the τ-statistic (based on the basic test in the appendix—the case in which the likely threshold is far from the peak of the distribution) confirms the observable pattern: at 1 cent per share, we obtain a τ value of 4.36, confirming a discontinuity in the EPS distribution there.[30]

Finally, we can also detect an upward kink in the EPS distribution from −1 cent/share to 0 cents/share, indicating a secondary threshold at zero, to "avoid red ink." The τ-value for the secondary kink, 3.84, also proves significant, although our visual impression is that the threshold at zero is likely smaller than that at 1 cent/share.

In sum, we have established clear thresholds effects in the reporting of earnings, both visually and through statistical test results. The three thresholds affecting the reporting of earnings are to "sustain recent performance," to "meet analysts' forecasts," and to "report profits."

[29] Note that this figure reinforces the impression of figure 1 in Hayn (1995), who, however, scales EPS by price per share and thus obtains a confounding density estimate at zero (as discussed above in subsection 3A).

[30] Since we have two suspected thresholds adjacent to one another, the neighborhood used in the τ-tests here always excludes the observation corresponding to the other threshold observation.

C. Conditional Distributions: Interaction among Thresholds

If executives pay attention to more than one threshold, as seems likely, is one threshold more important than another? Is there a discernible hierarchy among them?

To investigate interactions between thresholds, an issue that appears to have been ignored by the literature, we analyze the conditional distributions of EPS, ΔEPS, and FERR, when each of the other thresholds is met or failed. For example, suppose that we find a significant threshold in the EPS distribution when we condition it on making the analysts' forecast, as well as when we condition it on failing to reach the analysts' forecast; and suppose that we also find that one of the "parallel" distributions of FERR (that is, FERR conditional on EPS > 0, and FERR conditional on EPS < 0) exhibits no threshold effect: in this hypothetical example, we would conclude that "to report profits" is a more important threshold than "make the analysts' forecast."

Twelve conditional distributions are of interest (three individual distributions × conditioning on the other two × two levels). We attend to the problem that there may be little or no room to meet or fail a threshold when another threshold is met or failed. For example, if the ΔEPS threshold is met, and analysts have predicted earnings below last year, there is no possibility of missing the FERR threshold. We thus focus only on samples where there is at least a 5-cent range within which the threshold could be failed or met. While this conditioning reduces the available sample size, we are assured that inferences in the neighborhood of the threshold are valid.

For our positive earnings threshold, we focus on the case of 1 cent in EPS (though the 0-cent threshold also appears important). Our other two thresholds imply a 0-cent threshold in the distribution of ΔEPS and FERR. Our results appear in the 12 panels of conditional distributions in figure 18.8, where the vertical lines indicate the thresholds.

To illustrate our requirements for inclusion, consider the second panel in the second row of figure 18.8 where we examine the ΔEPS threshold conditional on the EPS being positive. Since we want to have a 5-cent range where the firm could fall short of the ΔEPS threshold in this subsample, we consider only cases where lag(EPS) > 5. This provides a range of 1–5 cents/share where the current EPS can be positive and still fail to attain the ΔEPS threshold. Each of our 12 cases looks at performance relative to one threshold conditional on another threshold having been failed or met. When the conditional threshold is failed (met), we preserve a 5-penny range on the up (down) side.[31]

---

[31] The restrictions we impose on included conditions influences the shape of our histograms. Considering the upper-right-hand diagram, for example. Apart from thresholds, it is unlikely that earnings will be nine cents when the analysts' forecast (AF) < −4, whereas −9 is not so unlikely even though FERR ≥ 0. Our statistical test, which only looks at earnings in a range of 10 cents, mitigates this problem.

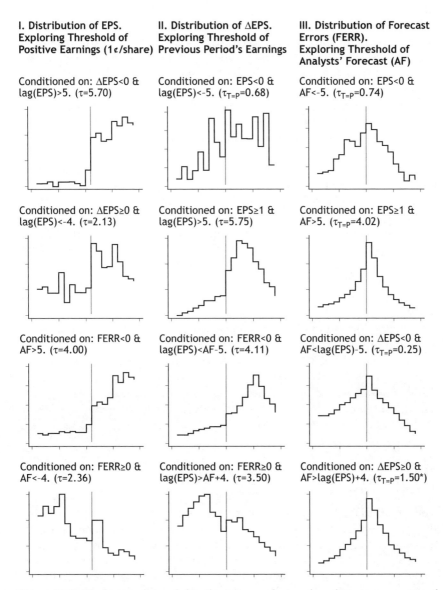

I. Distribution of EPS. Exploring Threshold of Positive Earnings (1¢/share)

Conditioned on: ΔEPS<0 & lag(EPS)>5. (τ=5.70)

Conditioned on: ΔEPS≥0 & lag(EPS)<-4. (τ=2.13)

Conditioned on: FERR<0 & AF>5. (τ=4.00)

Conditioned on: FERR≥0 & AF<-4. (τ=2.36)

II. Distribution of ΔEPS. Exploring Threshold of Previous Period's Earnings

Conditioned on: EPS<0 & lag(EPS)<-5. ($\tau_{T=P}$=0.68)

Conditioned on: EPS≥1 & lag(EPS)>5. (τ=5.75)

Conditioned on: FERR<0 & lag(EPS)<AF-5. (τ=4.11)

Conditioned on: FERR≥0 & lag(EPS)>AF+4. (τ=3.50)

III. Distribution of Forecast Errors (FERR). Exploring Threshold of Analysts' Forecast (AF)

Conditioned on: EPS<0 & AF<-5. ($\tau_{T=P}$=0.74)

Conditioned on: EPS≥1 & AF>5. ($\tau_{T=P}$=4.02)

Conditioned on: ΔEPS<0 & AF<lag(EPS)-5. ($\tau_{T=P}$=0.25)

Conditioned on: ΔEPS≥0 & AF>lag(EPS)+4. ($\tau_{T=P}$=1.50*)

Figure 18.8. Twelve conditional distributions: exploring the relative importance of thresholds. *Note*: the appendix provides motivation and construction details for the τ and $\tau_{T=P}$ statistics. Values in excess of 2.0 reliably reject the null hypothesis of no threshold effect. Whenever the values of the statistics are found to be in excess of 2.0 at the suspected thresholds for the above cases, they also prove to the largest relative to similar computations for all other points; the last panel reporting a $\tau_{T=P} = 1.50$ also obtains the largest value in its neighborhood.

Possible discontinuity in the histograms is evaluated for each of our 12 conditions employing the τ-test used before for the univariate distributions, which is discussed in the appendix. The τ-statistics confirm concretely what we see in figure 18.8. The EPS threshold is highly robust. Whether either of our other two thresholds fails or is met, there is a leap upward in density at our EPS threshold. Our other two thresholds are less robust to the conditioning of whether another threshold is met or failed; that is, under some conditions, they are not significant. Specifically, in row 1 of column 2 in figure 18.8, we observe no clear discontinuity when the EPS earnings are negative. However, a discontinuity in ΔEPS appears in the other three rows of column 2. We conclude that the threshold of the previous period's earnings is "robust" with respect to the threshold of analysts' forecast but not to that of positive earnings.

Similarly, in rows 1 and 3 of column 3 in figure 18.8, we observe no clear discontinuities in the distribution of FERR when EPS < 0 and ΔEPS < 0, respectively. The effect of a FERR threshold reasserts itself when EPS > 1 or ΔEPS > 0, as seen in rows 2 and 4 of column 3. We conclude that the threshold of analysts' forecast matters only if the other thresholds are met.

Overall, a threshold hierarchy emerges. The positive EPS threshold is the most important; it prevails regardless of whether or not the other two thresholds are met. The threshold of previous period's earnings is second in importance; it asserts itself only if the positive EPS threshold is met but is visibly present regardless of whether earnings make the analysts' forecast. The threshold of analysts' forecast is the weakest; it only matters if both the other thresholds are met.

4. THE EFFECT ON FUTURE EARNINGS FROM EARNINGS MANAGEMENT

The previous section showed that executives manage earnings to meet three thresholds. When they do so, as discussed in section 2, current earnings are raised by "borrowing" from future earnings. From an empirical perspective, firms that barely attain a threshold are suspect of having engaged in upward earnings management. This section examines whether the future performance of firms barely meeting thresholds is inferior compared to control groups.

A. The Implication of Earnings Management for Future Earnings

Earnings management to meet thresholds in this period will affect next period's earnings. Thus, we investigate whether following a period with likely EM there is any predictable effect on earnings. Our analysis in this section focuses first on the ΔEPS threshold and then on the positive earnings threshold.[32]

We examine the performance of the suspect firms that just meet the threshold relative to the performance of firms that just miss the threshold or easily surpass it. Accordingly, we divide firms into three groups, depending on their earnings. Group A fails to meet the threshold, B just meets or exceeds it, C beats it easily. Each group has a 5-penny range. Group B is likely to include a number of firms that managed their earnings upward to meet the threshold. Group C is less likely to have boosted earnings and may have reined them in. Denote the average performance of a group by the corresponding lower-case letter, and indicate the period of the performance by a subscript (1 or 2). By assumption, we have $c_1 > b_1 > a_1$. Normally we would expect some persistence in both earnings level and in the change in earnings. Thus, absent any earnings management, we would expect $c_2 > b_2 > a_2$. How might EM affect these inequalities? Earnings recorded by group B are suspect of upward manipulation. Hence, b_2 would move down relative to both c_2 and a_2, giving $c_2 - b_2 > b_2 - a_2$. If EM is substantial, we might even have $a_2 > b_2$; that is, the lower performer in period 1 (those that just fall short of the threshold) would do better in period 2.

To facilitate comparisons, we add a fourth group D that strongly surpasses the threshold. Presumably, manipulation is less prominent for groups C and D, so their difference in performance in some sense provides a benchmark for what we should expect between adjacent groups.

B. Evidence on the "Borrowing" of Future Earnings

Consider first the threshold "sustain recent performance" (that is, ΔEPS = 0). We study the fiscal-year performance of firms since we expect fiscal-year effects to be the most powerful ones. We restrict ourselves to the subset of firms in which the fiscal year ends in December to avoid observations overlapping in time. We also restrict consideration to firms that show an uptick in the last quarter's performance since firms that manage earnings for a given year are likely to show an uptick in the last quarter's performance. (Concerns regarding spurious inferences induced by this artifact of the sample choice are addressed below.)

A widely accepted stylized fact is that a significant component of earnings changes is permanent.[33] But if there is significant mean reversion in

[32] We exclude the analysts' forecast threshold from this analysis. Even if a firm strives to meet the analysts' forecast in a given period, it is unlikely that it will find it harder to meet it in the following period, simply because the analysts' forecast is an endogenous target that will itself move according to firm performance or executives' announcements.

[33] The earnings literature, e.g., Hayn (1995), notes that loss-reporting firms have different time-series properties of EPS. However, all our inferences in this section prove robust to conditioning on the sign of EPS.

ΔEPS, then we may have difficulty discriminating earnings manipulation from overall behavior. Consider the regression of $\Delta EPS_{t+1} = \alpha + \beta \Delta EPS_t$. We estimated this relationship using fiscal-year observations but conditioning on $\Delta EPS_t > 5$ to exclude contamination of threshold effects. The estimated β proved to be close to zero (-0.05) in our sample; thus, a reasonable null hypothesis is that the ranking of firms by ΔEPS over the next year will be unrelated to this year's performance. Moreover, in both the cases below, we find that the "strongly surpass threshold" never underperforms the "surpass threshold" group, reflecting some persistence in earnings growth in the neighborhood of interest.

If there is significant EM, we expect that the "meet threshold" group—many of whose members having presumably borrowed earnings—will underperform the groups immediately above ("surpass threshold") *and* below ("miss threshold"). This conjecture assumes that the EM effect exceeds any normal persistence in performance. This is a sharp and quite unusual prediction.

Table 18.1 column heads show the definitions of our four groups. Then it reports the mean and median of relative performance by group for the year following the formation of the groups. First note that, in our benchmark

TABLE 18.1

Next Year's Relative Performance by Groups Formed around the No-Change Threshold of the Formation Quarter's ΔEPS; Subsample of Firms with ΔEPS ≥ 0 for Formation Quarter

	Groups by Performance in Formation Year			
Annual DEPS (Cents/Share) in Formation Quarter	A. Miss Threshold −5 to −1	B. Meet Threshold 0 to +4	C. Surpass Threshold +5 to +9	D. Strongly Surpass Threshold +10 to +14
No. of Observations	1,143	2,220	3,688	4,049
Performance in following year:				
1. Mean ΔEPS	9.48	7.10	6.53	9.44
2. Median ΔEPS	13	8	9	12
3. Wilcoxon test*	4.02	−.77	−7.54	N.A.
p-values (reporting column relative to next column)	.0001	.4389	.0000	

Note. N.A. = not applicable.

* The Wilcoxon test compares a group's performance in the postformation year with that of the next group. Under the null hypothesis that the distributions of performance of the two groups being compared are the same, the Wilcoxon test is distributed standard normal ($N(0,1)$).

comparison, $d_2 > c_2$ as expected if heterogeneity in earnings growth among firms outweighs regression toward the mean effects. The salient comparisons for our purpose are between B and its neighbors. For both the mean and median, the performance of group B is worse than either of its neighbors, confirming our conjecture $c_2 - b_2 > b_2 - a_2$. In addition, $c_2 > b_2$, which is not surprising since C firms did better in period 1. The salient finding is that $b_2 < a_2$, presumably because of strong EM in the B group. All these differences prove statistically significant under the Wilcoxon test.[34]

Firms that barely attain the threshold of sustain recent performance appear to borrow earnings from the next year.[35] The U-shaped pattern where B firms are outperformed by both A and C firms will be reinforced if groups just missing the threshold "save for a better tomorrow" and if those that surpass it "rein in."[36]

We repeat the analysis for the "report profits" threshold. Now groups are formed based on 4-quarter EPS performance. We divide firms as before using 5-cent bins. Since there are relatively few observations in the region of zero EPS, we do not apply further filters relating to fiscal-year end.

Under the null hypothesis discussed for table 18.1, there is no strongly expected order across groups for relative performance (that is, annual ΔEPS) in the postformation year, except perhaps because of heterogeneity in earnings growth potential among firms, which would predict $d_2 > c_2 > b_2 > a_2$. Summary results are reported in table 18.2.[37] The comparisons in table 18.2 yield one significant result. The meet-threshold group significantly

[34] The Wilcoxon test (also known as the Mann-Whitney two-sample statistic) is distributed standard normal under the null hypothesis that the performances of the two groups being compared have the same distribution. The test assumes independence across observations, which is surely violated in our samples. This implies that the rejection rates using the traditional p-values based on the nominal size of our samples will be too high. However, the observed Wilcoxon test statistics for our sample are sufficiently large that the indicated U-pattern of performance is very unlikely to have arisen by chance.

[35] The patterns are similar if we use a 10-penny range to define groups A, B, C and D, as well as if we use only quarters ending with the fiscal year.

[36] Might the results in table 18.1 be spuriously induced because we select firms that have ΔEPS > 0 in the most recent quarter? For instance, consider the miss-threshold group: it missed the annual threshold despite reporting relatively decent earnings in the latest quarter. This firm might be experiencing a rapid upward performance trend (compared to the meet-threshold group). If so, and given general persistence in earnings changes, the miss-threshold group would outperform the meet-threshold group in the next year absent earnings management. We check for this effect by using selection criterion of ΔEPS > 10 and ΔEPS > 20 for the most recent quarter. Given the construction of our groups, if the observed results in table 18.1 arise purely owing to the ΔEPS > 0 filter, then we expect the meet-threshold group to outperform the surpass-threshold group with the ΔEPS > 10 filter and the surpass-threshold group to outperform the strongly surpass-threshold group with the ΔEPS > 20 filter. Neither turns out to be the case in our sample. The only performance reversal is observed between the miss-threshold group and the meet-threshold group.

[37] Given the problems of heterogeneity for EPS identified in figure 18.4, we also studied the subsample of firms that were in the smallest quartile of price per share. Results (not reported) are qualitatively similar.

TABLE 18.2

Next Year's Relative Performance by Groups Formed around the Zero Threshold
of the Formation Year's EPS; Observations Are Restricted to ΔEPS > 0 for
Formation Quarter

	Groups by Performance in Formation Year			
Annual EPS (Cents/Share) in Formation Quarter	A. Miss Threshold −5 to −1	B. Meet Threshold 0 to +4	C. Surpass Threshold +5 to +9	D. Strongly Surpass Threshold +10 to +14
No. of Observations	157	231	253	277
Performance over following year:				
1. Mean ΔEPS	37.29	10.89	8.36	21.50
2. Median ΔEPS	35	10	18	18
3. Wilcoxon test*	3.44	−.51	−.784	N.A.
p-values (reporting column relative to next column)	.0006	.6074	.4329	

Note. N.A. = not applicable.

* The Wilcoxon test compares a group's performance in the postformation year with that of the next group. Under the null hypothesis that the distributions of performance of the two groups being compared are the same, the Wilcoxon test is distributed standard normal ($N(0,1)$).

underperforms the miss-threshold group in the sample A as well as B, a result indicative of strong EM.

However, the lack of significant difference between the meet and surpass thresholds suggests that evidence on earnings borrowings by the meet-threshold group is less conclusive than for the ΔEPS threshold. While the meet-threshold group significantly underperforms the miss-threshold group, the meet-threshold group is not reliably outperformed by the surpass-threshold groups. In this case of the annual EPS threshold, evidence in earnings borrowings by the suspect meet-threshold group is less conclusive than it is for ΔEPS.

5. CONCLUDING DISCUSSION

Analysts, investors, and boards are keenly interested in financial reports of earnings because earnings provide critical information for investment decisions. Boards of directors charged with monitoring executives' performance recognize the importance of earnings to the firm's claimants and link managerial rewards to earnings outcomes. That this nexus of relations generates strong incentives for executives to manage earnings is hardly surprising. This analysis assesses the importance of thresholds for performance in this arena and the consequences thresholds have for patterns of reported earnings.

In work-in-progress that takes the threshold-based EM documented in this study as a given, we study how the equity market accounts for expected EM in resetting prices on announcement of earnings. Other ongoing investigation includes whether analysts efficiently account for EM in setting and revising their earnings forecasts, the salience of fiscal year thresholds, and whether different types of firms—for example, growth and value stocks—respond to the different incentives to manage earnings that are created because they suffer different penalties from falling short of thresholds.[38]

Our model shows how efforts to exceed thresholds induce particular patterns of EM. Earnings falling just short of thresholds will be managed upward. Earnings far from thresholds, whether below or above, will be reined in, making thresholds more attainable in the future. Our empirical explorations find clear support for EM driven by three thresholds: report positive profits, sustain recent performance, and meet analysts' expectations. We observe discontinuities in the earnings distributions that indicate threshold-based EM. From explorations with conditional distributions, we infer that the thresholds are hierarchically ordered; it is most important first to make positive profits, second to report quarterly profits at least equal to profits of four quarters ago, and third to meet analysts' expectations. We also find evidence that the future performances of firms just meeting thresholds appear worse than those of control groups that are less suspect.[39]

Although earnings are a continuous variable, outsiders and insiders use psychological bright lines such as zero earnings, past earnings, and analysts' projected earnings as meaningful thresholds for assessing firms' performance. Theory suggests, and data document, that executives manage earnings in predictable ways to exceed thresholds.

---

[38] Dreman and Berry (1995b, pp. 23–24) find that low price-to-earnings ratio (P/E) (bottom-quintile) stocks fared better after a negative earnings surprise—actual earnings below the consensus forecast—than did high P/E (top-quintile) stocks. For a 1-year holding period, average annual market adjusted returns were +5.22% for the low P/E stocks but –4.57% for the high P/E stocks. The annualized differential for the quarter in which the surprise occurred was somewhat greater, +7.05% versus –5.69%.

[39] In related work not reported in this work, we have explored whether the special saliency of annual reports creates additional incentives to manipulate earnings. We find that the pressure to sustain recent performance at the fiscal-year horizon induces extra noisiness in fourth-quarter earnings that varies predictably with the temptation to "generate" earnings to meet the threshold.

APPENDIX

TESTING FOR A DISCONTINUITY IN A UNIVARIATE DISTRIBUTION

Let x be the variable of interest, such as the change in earnings per share. The null hypothesis, H_0, conjectures that the probability density function of x, call it $f(x)$, is smooth at T, a point of interest because it may be a threshold under the alternative hypothesis, H. Given a random sample of x of size N, we estimate the density for discrete ordered points $x_0, x_1, \ldots, x_n$, and so on.[40] Suppose the points are equispaced, and without loss of generality set the distance between the points to be of length one. Compute the proportion of the observations that lie in bins covering $[x_0, x_1), [x_1, x_2), \ldots, [x_n, x_{n+1})$, and so on. These proportions, denoted $p(x)$, provide estimates of $f(x)$ at $x_0, x_1, \ldots, x_n$, etc.[41]

1. BASIC TEST

The expectation of $\Delta p(x_n)[\equiv p(x_n) - p(x_{n-1})]$ is $f'(x_n)$, and its variance depends on the higher derivatives of $f(x)$ at x_n as well as the available sample size N. Consider a small symmetric region R_n around n of $2r + 1$ points (i.e., $R_n = \{x_i; i \in (n - r, n + r)\}$); given the smoothness assumption for $f(x)$ under H_0, the distribution of $\Delta p(x_i)$ will be approximately homogeneous.[42]

Use the observations $\Delta p(x_i)$ from R_n, excluding $\Delta p(x_n)$, to compute a t-like test statistic, τ. Specifically, compute

$$\tau_n = \frac{\Delta p(x_n) - \underset{i \in R, i \neq n}{\text{mean}} \{\Delta p(x_i)\}}{\underset{i \in R, i \neq n}{\text{s.d.}} \{\Delta p(x_i)\}},$$

where mean and s.d. denote the sample mean and standard deviation of $\{\cdot\}$. We exclude observations corresponding to $i = n$ in the computation of the mean and standard deviation to increase power in identifying a discontinuity in $f(x)$ at x_n.

Our alternative hypothesis, H_1, conjectures a discontinuity in $f(x)$ at a preidentified threshold T (i.e., zeros in the distributions of ΔEPS or forecast errors of earnings, or 1-penny in the distribution of EPS). The distribution

---

[40] For our analyses the xs are integers, though nothing in our test approach requires this.

[41] Under H_0, improved estimates of $f(x)$are possible using neighborhood bins. However, the power of tests to reject H_0 (especially given our alternative hypotheses discussed below) may be compromised by such an approach. Fortunately in our case, unambiguous results obtain with this most simple estimation strategy.

[42] For our analysis, we selected $r = 5$, which creates 11-penny intervals. Briefly, we explored $r = 7$ and $r = 10$ for ΔEPS, and the qualitative findings remain unchanged.

of τ_T is likely to be well approximated by the Student's t-distribution under H_0 if the distribution of $\Delta p(x_i)$ in R_T is approximately Gaussian. In unreported simulations, working with the log transformation of the estimated density improved the homogeneity of variance (of $\Delta \log\{p(x)\}$) across typical neighborhoods R—thus, all the tests that we report in the text are based on $\Delta \log\{p(x)\}$ rather than on $\Delta p(x)$, though the inferences appear similar. In any case, we do not solely rely on normality. Instead we compare the τ_T to other τ-values computed for nearby points.

We examine the rank of τ_T relative to the other τ's as well as its relative magnitudes to assess whether a discontinuity at T can be established. Fortunately, clear, unambiguous results obtain: using the full sample, the τ_T values always prove to be the largest when compared to the other τ values.[43]

2. Elaborations

The basic test sketched above is satisfactory as long as the point at which the density being examined for a discontinuity (T) falls significantly on one side of the peak of the probability density distribution. Denote the peak by P. Now consider the case when the symmetric construction of R_T sketched above would include P. Since points on different sides of P are likely to have slopes of the density function of opposite signs, the symmetric R_T will no longer be composed of similar points in the sense of similar slopes.

Case A1. Symmetric neighborhood around T would include peak, P, though $T \neq P$. For this case, we construct an asymmetric neighborhood R_T around T. When $T < P$ $(T > P)$, construct R_T to be the most symmetric region possible around T of $2r + 1$ points such that all the points lie at or below (above) P. The intuition for this construction is that by selecting points on the same side of P we obtain a neighborhood with points that have similar slopes of the (log) density function. Given such an R_T, we compute τ_T as in the basic test approach above.

Case A2. Suspected threshold coincides with the peak, that is, $T = P$. Consider the case of the analysts' forecast as the threshold, T. In this case, the distribution of reported earnings is likely centered at this T if analysts forecast the mode or if the latent distribution of earnings is nearly symmetric and forecasters minimize the mean squared forecast error or the mean absolute error. Now, we identify an earnings management effect by testing whether the

---

[43] Given the 10 neighborhood values to which we compare t_T (see n. 3 above), the likelihood of obtaining t_T as the largest value by chance is slightly less than 10 percent. Looking at the magnitudes themselves, the neighborhood t values interestingly always compute to less than $|2|$ while the t_T values always exceed 2.

slope of the density function immediately to the left of T ($= P$) is significantly different from the corresponding slope (adjusted for sign) to the immediate right of T after allowing for any general local skew in the distribution.

Define $\nabla p_j \equiv \Delta \log\{p(x_{T+j})\} - (-1 \times \Delta \log\{p(x_{T-j})\})$. As remarked before, log transformations of the density appear to stabilize variance across nearby j's in simulations as well for our samples (not reported). The test for case B2 amounts to examining whether ∇p_1 is unusual. We use the observations ∇p_j from a small neighborhood R ($j > 1$,) to compute an estimate of the mean of ∇p_1 as well as its standard deviation.[44] As before, we compute a t-like test statistic, say $\tau_{T=P}$, to assess the "unusualness" of ∇p_1.

In simulations that mimic the statistical structure of our sample while assuming a Gaussian distribution for the latent earnings, the statistic $\tau_{T=P}$ proves to be greater than 2.0 less than 5 percent of the time. Nonetheless, since the real distribution is unlikely to be as well behaved as Gaussian in the absence of any discontinuity at $T = P$, the comparison of $\tau_{T=P}$ with the real samples to the reference level of 2.0 is only taken as suggestive of a discontinuity. Thus, we also examine the rank of ∇p_1 to the corresponding values at nearby j's: in our samples, when $\tau_{T=P}$ proves to be larger than 2.0, ∇p_1 is always the largest in the neighborhood.

[44] In the tests reported in the main text of this work the R for computing $\tau_{T=P}$ spans 10 nearby values, that is, $j = 2, 3, \ldots , 11$. Similar results, not shown, obtain with fewer nearby values.

References

Abarbanell, J., and V. Bernard, 1992, Tests of analysts' overreaction/underreaction to earnings information as an explanation for anomalous stock price behavior, *Journal of Finance* 47, 1181–1207.

Ball, R., and P. Brown, 1968, An empirical evaluation of accounting income numbers, *Journal of Accounting Research* 6, 231–58.

Barrow, J. D., 1992, *Pi in the Sky*. Boston: Little, Brown.

Bruns, W., and K. Merchant, 1996, The dangerous morality of managing earnings, *Management Accounting* 72, 22–25.

Burgstahler, D., 1997, Incentives to manage earnings to avoid earnings decreases and losses: Evidence from quarterly earnings, Working Paper, University of Washington.

Burgstahler, D., and I. Dichev, 1997, Earnings management to avoid earnings decreases and losses, *Journal of Accounting and Economics* 24, 99–126.

Cornsweet, T. C., 1974, *Visual Perception*, Academic Press.

DeBondt, W., and R. Thaler, 1995, Financial decision-making in markets and firms: A behavioral perspective, in R. Jarrow, V. Maksimovic, and W. Ziemba (eds.), *Finance*, Vol. 9 of *Handbook in Research and Management Science*, Elsevier.

Dechow, P., 1994, Accounting earnings and cash flows as measures of firm performance: The role of accounting accruals, *Journal of Accounting and Economics* 18, 3–42.

Dechow, P., M. Huson, and R. Sloan, 1994, The effect of restructuring charges on executives' cash compensation, *Accounting Review* 69, 138–56.

Dechow, P., R. Sloan, and A. Sweeney, 1995, Detecting earnings management, *Accounting Review* 70, 193–225.

Dreman, D. N., and M. A. Berry, 1995a, Analyst forecasting errors and their implications for security analysis, *Financial Analysts Journal* 51, 30–41.

———, 1995b, Overreaction, underreaction, and the low-P/E effect, *Financial Analysts Journal* 51, 21–30.

Easton, P., T. Harris, and J. Ohlson, 1992, Aggregate accounting earnings can explain most of security returns: The case of long return intervals, *Journal of Accounting and Economics* 15, 119–42.

Foster, G., 1986, *Financial Statement Analysis*, Prentice-Hall.

Gaver, J. J., K. M. Gaver, and J. R. Austin, 1995, Additional evidence on bonus plans and income management, *Journal of Accounting and Economics* 19, 3–28.

Glass, A. L., and K. J. Holyoak, 1986, *Cognition*, Random House.

Hayn, C., 1995, The information content of losses, *Journal of Accounting and Economics* 20, 125–53.

Healy, P., 1985, The effect of bonus schemes on accounting decisions, *Journal of Accounting and Economics* 7, 85–107.

Holthausen, R. W., D. F. Larcker, and R. G. Sloan, 1995, Annual bonus schemes and the manipulation of earnings, *Journal of Accounting and Economics* 19, 29–74.

Kahneman, D., and A. Tversky, 1979, Prospect theory: An analysis of decision under risk, *Econometrica* 47, 263–91.

Keane, M. and D. Runkle, 1998, Are financial analysts' forecasts of corporate profits rational?, *Journal of Political Economy* 106(4), 768–805.

Koopmans, L. H., 1974, *The Spectral Analysis of Time Series*, Academic Press.

Kothari, S. P., and R. G. Sloan, 1992, Information in prices about future earnings: Implications for earnings response coefficients, *Journal of Accounting and Economics* 15, 143–71.

Laffont, J.-J., and J. Tirole, 1993, *The Theory of Incentives in Procurement and Regulation*, MIT Press.

Milgrom, P., and J. Roberts, 1992, *Economics, Organization, and Management*, Prentice-Hall.

Payne, J. L., and S. W. Robb, 1997, Earnings management: The effect of ex ante earnings expectations, Working Paper, University of Mississippi.

Philbrick, D. R., and W. E. Ricks, 1991, Using Value Line and I/B/E/S analyst forecasts in accounting research, *Journal of Accounting Research* 29, 397–417.

Schelling, T., 1960, *The Strategy of Conflict*, Harvard University Press.

Schipper, K., 1989, Earnings management, *Accounting Horizons* 3, 91–102.

Scott, D. W., 1992, *Multivariate Density Estimation: Theory, Practice, and Visualization*, Wiley.

Silverman, B. W., 1986, *Density Estimation for Statistics and Data Analysis*, Chapman & Hall.

Young, P., 1996, The economics of convention, *Journal of Economic Perspectives* 10 105–22.

Chapter 19

MANAGERIAL OPTIMISM AND

CORPORATE FINANCE

J. B. HEATON

IN THIS CHAPTER, I explore the implications of a single specification of managerial irrationality in a simple model of corporate finance. Specifically, I focus on *managerial optimism* and its relation to the benefits and costs of free cash flow.

Managers are "optimistic" when they systematically overestimate the probability of good firm performance and underestimate the probability of bad firm performance. This assumption finds support in a large psychological literature demonstrating that people are, in general, too optimistic. That literature presents two pervasive findings (e.g., Weinstein 1980) that make optimism an interesting subject of study for corporate finance researchers. First, people are more optimistic about outcomes that they believe they can control. Consistent with this first experimental finding, survey evidence indicates that managers underplay inherent uncertainty, believing that they have large amounts of control over the firm's performance (see March and Shapira 1987). Second, people are more optimistic about outcomes to which they are highly committed. Consistent with the second experimental finding, managers generally appear committed to the firm's success (somehow defined), probably because their wealth, professional reputation, and employability partially depend on it (e.g., Gilson 1989).

The approach taken here departs from the standard assumption of managerial rationality in corporate finance. Behavioral approaches are now common in asset pricing, of course, but little work in corporate finance has dropped the assumption that managers are fully rational.[1] This is somewhat surprising considering that the common objections to behavioral economics have less vitality in corporate finance than in asset pricing. The "arbitrage" objection (rational agents will exploit irrational agents) is

For helpful comments, I thank Gregor Andrade, Alon Brav, Judith Chevalier, Harry DeAngelo, Deborah DeMott, Ed Glaeser, John Graham, Dennis Gromb, Chip Heath, Peter Hecht, Tim Johnson, Steven Kaplan, Adam Long, Cade Massey, Mark Mitchell, Allen Poteshman, Jay Ritter, Andrei Shleifer, Erik Stafford, Jeremy Stein, Richard Thaler, Rob Vishny, Tuomo Vuolteenaho, Richard Willis, Luigi Zingales, Lemma Senbet and Alex Triantis (the editors of Financial Management), two anonymous referees, and participants at the NBER Summer Institute.

[1] The best known exception is surely Roll (1986). See also DeMeza and Southey (1996), and Boehmer and Netter (1997).

weaker, because there are larger arbitrage bounds protecting managerial irrationality than protecting security market mispricing. The most obvious
"arbitrage" of managerial irrationality—the corporate takeover—incurs high
transactions costs, and the specialized investors who pursue takeovers bear
much idiosyncratic risk. Arbitrage strategies short of a corporate takeover
are difficult to implement, because managerial decisions usually concern assets (including human assets) that trade in markets without short sale
mechanisms or other derivative assets that make arbitrage possible (see
Russell and Thaler 1985). The "learning" objection (irrational agents will
learn from experience to be rational) is also weaker, because important corporate financial decisions about capital structure and investment policy are
more infrequent than trading decisions, with longer-delayed outcomes and
noisier feedback. Learning from experience is less likely in such circumstances (see Brehmer 1980).

It is also unclear whether a firm's internal incentive mechanisms or "corporate culture" will eliminate managerial irrationality. Some internal incentive mechanisms (for example, "tournaments") may select *against* rational
managers, in favor of irrational managers. Irrational managers, for example, may take large risks that lower their true expected utility (although not
their perceived expected utility), yet increase the probability that some irrational manager wins the tournament.[2] Further, the interests of principals
may be served best by the design of mechanisms that exploit managerial irrationality rather than quash it. For example, principals may design incentive mechanisms that underpay irrational agents by exploiting the agents'
incorrect assessments of their ability or the firm's risk.

The benefits and costs of free cash flow offer an attractive laboratory for
exploring the implications of managerial irrationality in corporate finance.
Since Jensen's famous 1986 paper, "Agency Costs of Free Cash Flow, Corporate Finance and Takeovers," free cash flow (cash flow above that
needed to fund current positive net present value projects) has been the
focus of a tremendous amount of academic research. The finance profession's views toward the benefits and costs of free cash flow have been
shaped largely by two dominant and often *conflicting* paradigms of corporate finance. The first is the asymmetric information approach typified by
Myers and Majluf (1984). In that approach, free cash flow is beneficial,
because managers loyal to existing shareholders are assumed to have information the market does not have. The main claim is that managers will
sometimes decline new positive net present value investment opportunities
when taking them requires issuance of undervalued securities to the under-
informed capital market. The financial slack provided by large amounts of
free cash flow prevents this socially (and privately) undesirable outcome.

---

[2] This is analogous to the potential survivability and dominance of noise traders in financial
markets for the same reason. See DeLong, Shleifer, Summers, and Waldmann (1991).

In the agency cost approach of Jensen (1986), free cash flow is costly, because of a conflict between managers and shareholders. Managers want to retain free cash flows and invest them in projects that increase managerial benefits like compensation or power and reputation (see Avery, Chevalier, and Schaefer 1998). Shareholders want managers to pay out free cash flows, because the projects that increase managerial benefits often may be negative net present value projects. Thus, Jensen (1986) argues, leverage increasing transactions that bond the firm to pay out free cash flows increase shareholder value and mitigate the conflict of interest between shareholders and managers.

The managerial optimism assumption delivers both of these results in a single framework, implying an underinvestment-overinvestment tradeoff from managerial optimism without invoking asymmetric information or rational agency costs.

On the one hand, managerial optimism leads managers to believe that an efficient capital market undervalues their firm's risky securities. Therefore, managerial optimism leads to a preference for internal funds that can be socially costly. Optimistic managers dependent on external finance sometimes decline positive net present value projects, believing that the cost of external finance is simply too high. Free cash flow can, therefore, be valuable. When the firm has positive net present value projects that optimistic managers would otherwise decline because of incorrectly perceived costs of external finance, free cash flow can prevent social losses from underinvestment.

On the other hand, managerial optimism causes systematically upward biased cash flow forecasts and causes managers to overvalue the firm's investment opportunities. Managers without free cash flow may decline taking a negative net present value project that they perceive to be a positive net present value project, because the cost of external finance seems too high. In this situation, free cash flow is harmful. Free cash flow alleviates the need to obtain external finance and makes it easier to take negative net present value projects mistakenly perceived to be positive net present value projects.

Thus, the managerial optimism theory links the benefits and costs of free cash flow to two variables—the level of managerial optimism and the investment opportunities available to the firm. Optimistic managers want to undertake more projects. The more optimistic the manager, the less likely he is to finance these projects externally. The better are the firm's projects, the more costly this underinvestment is to shareholders. For firms with poor investment opportunities, reliance on the external capital market is beneficial. This implies a shareholder preference for cash flow retention (and cash flow risk management) at firms with both high optimism and good investment opportunity, and a shareholder preference for cash flow payouts at firms with both high optimism and bad investment opportunity.

The basic prediction is not new, but the model is parsimonious—it need not invoke the conflicting possibilities of rational, loyal better informed managers versus rational disloyal (and perhaps no better informed) managers.

Beyond parsimony, managerial optimism provides an independent "as if" foundation for several investment and capital structure phenomena of interest to academic finance. For researchers who are fully content with the "as if" explanations of these phenomena offered by rational agency cost models and asymmetric information models, the theoretical power of managerial optimism may be of little interest. The degrees of freedom offered by both rational agency cost and asymmetric information theories should, in most cases, allow them to capture many of the predictions generated by the optimism assumption (albeit less parsimoniously). The theoretical power of managerial optimism (and other behavioral assumptions) cannot be denied, however, by those who seek to sort out which of several "as if" theories seems best to describe the world, perhaps partly by reference to the realism of assumptions. While a full discussion of this issue is far beyond the scope of this paper, suffice it to say that some important part of the rational-behavioral debate in financial economics can be linked to such inquiries.[3]

The rest of the chapter is structured as follows: Section 1 presents a simple model of managerial optimism. Section 2 presents results, and section 3 concludes.

1. A Simple Model

This section describes the simple three date-two period model. To explore managerial optimism's explanatory power, it is important to isolate its effects from the influence of assumptions made by the two predominant approaches to corporate finance: the asymmetric information approach and the empire-building/rational agency cost approach. Asymmetric information theories (e.g., Myers and Majluf 1984) assume that managers have information that the capital market does not have. Empire-building/rational agency cost theories (for example, Hart 1993 and Jensen 1986) assume that it is impossible (or at least very costly) to write contracts that fully control managerial incentives. Therefore, I make two assumptions that isolate these effects. The first assumption ensures informational symmetry, while the second ensures the absence of rational agency problems.

Assumption 1: Information about the firm's cash flows and investment opportunities is simultaneously available to the capital market and the managers.

[3] The best-known statement of the "as if" principle in economics is Friedman (1953). For one recent analysis of "as if" and "realist" philosophies of science, see Maki (2000).

Assumption 2: Managers take all projects that they believe have positive net present values (including the perceived net present value of financing) and never take projects—including perquisite consumption—that they believe to have negative net present value.

The third assumption ensures that the capital market is rational:

Assumption 3: Security prices always reflect discounted expected future cash flows under the true probability distributions.

While future work with the managerial optimism assumption could relax the third assumption to study the interactions of irrational managers and inefficient markets,[4] assuming that the competitive capital market is *more* rational than the management of a single firm seems the better benchmark. All that really matters for present purposes, however, is that the market is less optimistic than the managers. There are at least two reasons why this is the most plausible case. First, arbitrage is easier against investors in the capital market than against managers in firms, so prices are more likely (even if not certain) to reflect the beliefs of rational investors. Second, even if all investors are also optimistic, they are unlikely to be as optimistic about *this* firm's prospects as its managers. The psychological evidence suggests that optimism is more severe when an individual believes he can control the outcome, and when the outcome is one to which he is highly committed. Both findings suggest that managers would be more optimistic: managers are more likely than investors to believe that they can control the outcome of the firm's investments, and managers have more at stake in the outcomes at this firm than would a diversified investor.

Together, Assumptions 1 and 3 imply that security prices in the model are always strong-form efficient. It is important to note that Assumption 1 does *not* imply that there is no role for managers. Both Assumptions 1 and 3 are statements about *aggregate* information availability and pricing. That the capital market collectively both has and accurately prices this information does not imply that it is possible to contract on this information and force managers always to take the right action. To further simplify the model, I make the following assumption about risk preferences, interest rates, taxes, and costs of financial distress:

Assumption 4: The capital market is risk neutral and the discount rate is zero. There are no taxes and no costs of financial distress.

There are three dates, $t = 0$, $t = 1$, and $t = 2$. The initial project requires investment of K at time $t = 0$. The managers and/or the project's owners

---

[4] Stein (1996) examines the interactions of *rational* managers in an inefficient market.

(who may or may not be the same) have no capital of their own and must finance K by selling some mix of securities in the capital market. The project generates cash flows at date $t = 1$ and date $t = 2$. Cash flow at date $t = 1$ is certain, denoted y_1. Cash flow at date $t = 2$ is uncertain. There is a "good" cash-flow state and a "bad" cash-flow state, denoted $_Gy_2$ and $_By_2$ respectively, where $_Gy_2 > _By_2$. The true probabilities of the time $t = 2$ states are $_Tp_G$ and $_Tp_B$, respectively, where of course $_Tp_G + _Tp_B = 1$. Subscript "T" denotes "True" probability. The True probability distribution can be viewed as the actual probability distribution governing assets in the firm's industry (alternatively, it is the subjective probability distribution that all parties would agree to if no one was affected by the cognitive bias of optimism). The values of y_1, $_Gy_2$, $_By_2$, $_Tp_G$, and $_Tp_B$ are known to the capital market and the managers at time $t = 0$. However, the managers disagree with the capital market about the probabilities (see Definition 1), and do not believe that $_Tp_G$ and $_Tp_B$ are accurate.

The firm receives an unexpected (that is, not expected at time $t = 0$) new investment opportunity at time $t = 1$ that requires investment of i at time $t = 1$ if taken. The project has uncertain time $t = 2$ payoff of either r_H or r_L. Subscript "H" denotes a "high" payoff state to the new investment and subscript "L" denotes a "low" payoff state, where $r_H > r_L$. The true payoff probabilities for the new investment opportunity are $_Tp_H$ and $_Tp_L$, for r_H and r_L. The values of i, r_H, r_L, $_Tp_H$ and $_Tp_L$ are known to the capital market and the managers at time $t = 1$ but the managers once again disagree with the capital market about the probabilities (see Definition 1) and do not believe that $_Tp_H$ and $_Tp_L$ are accurate.

The following definition captures the managerial behavior of interest:

> **Definition 1:** Managers are "optimistic" and exhibit "managerial optimism" when they perceive probabilities $_Mp_G$ and $_Mp_H$ such that $_Mp_G > _Tp_G \Rightarrow _Mp_B < _Tp_B$ and $_Mp_H > _Tp_H \Rightarrow _Mp_L < _Tp_L$.

The "M" subscript denotes managerial perception. Optimistic managers systematically attach too much probability to good outcomes ("good" cash flow at time $t = 2$ and "high" payoffs to new projects at time $t = 2$) and, correspondingly, too little probability to bad outcomes (bad cash flow at time $t = 2$ and "low" payoffs to new projects at time $t = 2$). I rule out "side-bets" on these events. Modeling managerial risk aversion in the model would alleviate this possibility, but add nothing to the intuition of the model. Put another way, I assume that the existence of optimism is not enough to create "money pump" opportunities against managers (for example, Rabin and Thaler 2001).

At date $t = 2$, the firm's operations are wrapped up and cash flows are distributed to security holders according to the rights of their particular security. The following set of securities may be issued by the firm (when feasible) in any combination: (1) risk-free debt, (2) risky debt, and (3) equity. Debt contracts promise a fixed amount in the future in exchange for money today. Debt is risk-free when the probability of repayment of the fixed amount is 1.0. Debt is risky when some probability exists that the firm will be unable to repay the fixed amount. Equity is a security that receives all cash flows left in the firm at time $t = 2$ after debt repayment. Debt may be either short-term, that is, payable at date $t = 1$, or long-term, payable at date $t = 2$.

2. RESULTS

This section presents the chapter's main results. These include the effects of managerial optimism on perceptions of external finance, the effect of optimism on cash-flow forecasts, the benefits and costs of free cash flow, and additional testable implications.

A. Managerial Perceptions of External Finance

The prices of risky securities reflect the capital market's probabilities of good versus bad states of the world. Because optimistic managers systematically attach higher probabilities to good outcomes than the capital market, optimistic managers believe that the capital market undervalues the firm's risky securities. To optimistic managers in an efficient market, issuing a risky security is always perceived to be a negative net present value event (without considering the possibly greater perceived positive net present value of the project being financed).

This induces a pecking order capital structure preference, where managers attempt to minimize costs of external finance by minimizing the amount of risky securities issued.[5] Safer securities are less sensitive to probabilistic beliefs and, thus, (managers believe) are less undervalued by the capital market. Whenever the managers can use internal cash or risk-free debt, both of which are insensitive to probabilistic beliefs, they strictly prefer this to issuing any risky security. Risky debt is preferred to all equity financing, since any issuance of risky debt is a weighted average of risk-free

[5] The pecking order is thus a testable prediction of the managerial optimism model. Harris and Raviv (1991) summarize the empirical evidence suggesting that many firms in fact have "pecking order" capital structure preferences. Survey evidence also bears out this prediction. Surveys by Pinegar and Wilbricht (1989; Fortune 500 firms) and Kamath (1997; NYSE firms) find that roughly twice as many firms report following a pecking order as report attempting to maintain a target capital structure. Nearly 85 percent of financial managers in the Kamath (1997) study reported a first preference for internal equity, with straight debt second, and equity (of any form) a distant third. More recently, Graham and Harvey (2001) present survey evidence of a pecking order effect that, importantly, does not seem well-explained by traditional asymmetric information theories.

debt and equity, and the risk-free component is insensitive to probabilistic beliefs. Therefore, risky debt (that puts positive weight on risk-free debt) must have lower perceived borrowing costs than all equity financing, and the preference results.

Formally, assume there is no $t = 1$ cash flow. The firm can be financed if and only if $E_T(y_2) \geq K$. That is, the firm can be financed if and only if the expected value of the time $t = 2$ payoff is greater than the required investment. If $_By_2 \geq K$, the manager can issue risk-free debt sufficient to finance the firm, since the debt is repaid in either state of the world. The manager correctly perceives the cost of this financing to be $K/K = 1$. To finance the firm entirely by equity requires selling fraction $\alpha = K/E_T(y_2)$ of the firm's equity to the capital market. The manager incorrectly perceives the cost of all-equity financing to be:

$$\left(\frac{K}{E_T(y_2)} \right) \left(\frac{E_M(y_2)}{K} \right) > 1$$

since $E_M(y_2) > E_T(y_2)$. $K/E_T(y_2)$ is the fraction of the firm that is sold to raise K, and $E_M(y_2)$ is the total value of the firm perceived by the manager. The manager believes the required equity flotation should be smaller, specifically:

$$\alpha_M = \frac{K}{E_M(y_2)} < \frac{K}{E_T(y_2)} = \alpha.$$

It follows that since the manager can issue risk-free debt, he will not issue equity. The result for risky debt is analogous. Any issue of risky debt is equivalent to a weighted average of risk-free debt and equity. The managers are indifferent between this weighted average (risky debt) and the individual components. Letting "w" denote the amount raised by risk-free debt, the cost of any combination of risk-free debt and equity is:

$$\frac{w}{K} + \left(\frac{K-w}{K} \right) \left(\frac{K-w}{E_T(y_2)-w} \right) \left(\frac{E_M(y_2)-w}{K-w} \right)$$

$$= \frac{w}{K} + \left(\frac{K-w}{K} \right) \left(\frac{E_M(y_2)-w}{E_T(y_2)-w} \right) > 1$$

for any $w < K$ since $E_M(y_2) > E_T(y_2)$.

Now assume that $_By_2 < K$ so that cash flow in the bad state is now insufficient to pay the required initial investment and the manager can no longer issue risk-free debt to finance the entire amount K. The financing combination that maximizes the risk-free debt component issues $_By_2$ of risk-free debt and then equity (obviously, this is equivalent to an issue of risky debt). The manager perceives the cost of this financing to be:

$$
\frac{_By_2}{K} + \left(\frac{K - _By_2}{K} \right)\left(\frac{K - _By_2}{E_T(y_2) - _By_2} \right)\left(\frac{E_M(y_2) - _By_2}{K - _By_2} \right)
$$

$$
= \frac{_By_2}{K} + \left(\frac{K - _By_2}{K} \right)\left(\frac{E_M(y_2) - _By_2}{E_T - _By_2} \right)
$$

To see that the manager will prefer this to any financing combination that places greater weight on equity, simply note that:

$$
\frac{_By_2}{K} + \left(\frac{K - _By_2}{K} \right)\left(\frac{E_M(y_2) - _By_2}{E_T(y_2) - _By_2} \right) < \frac{w}{k} + \left(\frac{K - w}{K} \right)\left(\frac{E_M(y_2) - w}{E_T(y_2) - w} \right)
$$

That is, the perceived weighted average cost of capital under issue of $_By_2$ of risk-free debt is less than any lower issue, since $w < {_By_2}$ means that more weight is placed on a term greater than one.

It is easy to see that nothing changes significantly if there is certain cash flow at time $t = 1$. Assume that the time $t = 1$ cash flow y_1 is certain. Consider first the case where the manager can raise risk-free debt to finance the entire investment K, because $(y_1 + {_By_2}) \geq K$. That is, certain cash flow to the project is enough to pay back K. Then the manager will always strictly prefer an issue of risk-free debt to any issue that includes equity. Considering the case where $(y_1 + {_By_2}) < K$, that is, where the manager must issue some risky security to finance the project, it also follows that the manager will issue the security with the largest component of risk-free debt, equivalent to a preference for risky debt over equity.

B. Managerial Cash-flow Forecasts

Cash-flow forecasts are the most important inputs to project valuation and selection. Optimism leads the managers' forecasts to be biased. Consider the manager who forecasts time $t = 2$ cash flow at time $t = 0$. While the best forecast is $E_T(y_2) = {_Tp_G} * {_Gy_2} + {_Tp_B} * {_By_2}$, the optimistic manager forecasts $E_M(y_2) = {_Mp_G} * {_Gy_2} + {_Mp_B} * {_By_2}$. By Definition 1, $E_M(y_2) > E_T(y_2)$, since ${_Gy_2} > {_By_2}$. This provides a very sharp testable prediction: if managers are optimistic, average realized cash flows fall short of managerial forecasts. Downward biased forecasts would present strong evidence against the managerial optimism theory. Indeed, upwardly biased cash flow forecasts may be the sharpest testable prediction of the managerial optimism model, particularly against asymmetric information and rational agency cost theories that make no such sharp predictions.

Available evidence is consistent with the managerial optimism prediction of upwardly biased cash flow forecasts. Kaplan and Ruback (1995) study long run cash-flow forecasts made in connection with management buyouts and recapitalizations. They find statistically significant upward bias of both operating income and operating margins. While they attribute some of this bias to the fact that a recession began in 1990, a year included in part of the sample, similar evidence is presented by Kaplan (1989) who studied the performance of a large sample of management buyout firms not affected by the 1990 recession. Hotchkiss (1995) finds similar results for the performance of firms exiting bankruptcy. Even short-term earnings forecasts seem biased. While McNichols (1989) finds no statistically significant bias in managerial earnings forecasts (which are short-term, less than one year), the direction of the statistically insignificant bias is upwards in every year of her sample, strongly suggesting the presence of managerial optimism, albeit at statistically insignificant levels. While short-term earnings (at time $t = 1$) in the model here are known, the introduction of any uncertainty would deliver biased short-term earnings forecasts as well.[6] Additional tests of the sharp prediction on managerial cash-flow forecasts would benefit by the introduction of proxies for the *level* of managerial optimism.[7]

C. Benefits of Free Cash Flow

The perception that risky securities are undervalued can lead to social losses that are alleviated by sufficient amounts of free cash flow. Consider what happens when the managers face a new investment opportunity. If the managers have internal cash flow of y_1, then it is clear that they will use this before raising external funds. Denote any necessary external funds by E and let $C_M(E)$ denote the additional cost of external funds perceived by the managers, that is, the perceived wedge between the cost of internal funds and the cost of external funds. Since prices are always efficient in the model, there is never any overvaluation of the firm's external securities, and so $C_M(E) \geq 0$ (that is, since the markets are efficient, the manager never perceives a *gain* from selling securities). Of course, the true cost is zero; there is

---

[6] These upward biased forecasts also appear to manifest themselves in dividend changes. DeAngelo, DeAngelo, and Skinner (1996), for example, find no evidence that dividend increases signal superior future earnings. They attribute this result to the fact that managers are too optimistic about future earnings and make dividend decisions consistent with those optimistic expectations that are not borne out by later results. Loughran and Ritter (1997, p. 1824) find analogous evidence for seasoned equity offerings, suggesting that "managers are just as overoptimistic about the issuing firms' future profitability as are investors." See also Lee (1997), and Schultz and Zaman (2001).

[7] For example, in a recent extension and test of the underinvestment hypothesis developed below, Malmendier and Tate (2001) use option exercise behavior and stock purchases to proxy for chief executive optimism.

no additional cost of external financing since by assumption there is no informational asymmetry and prices are efficient. Faced with a new project that requires investment of i where $i > y_1$, the managers' decision rule (see Assumption 2) is:

invest if: $\quad\quad\quad\quad\quad$ $E_M(r) - i - C_M(E) > 0$
do not invest if: $\quad\quad$ $E_M(r) - i - C_M(E) \leq 0$

When $E_T(r) - i > 0$, but $E_M(r) - i - C_M(E) \leq 0$, the manager passes up a positive NPV project because he believes the cost of external financing is too high, despite the fact that he believes the project has a positive NPV (he must believe this since by Definition 1, $E_M(r) > E_T(r)$).

Free cash flow alleviates this problem by eliminating the perceived costs of external funds from the decision. This may help explain the appearance of a positive correlation between investment and cash flow, after controlling for investment opportunities (see Fazzari, Hubbard, and Petersen 1988, and Kaplan and Zingales 1997). For any given project perceived to be positive net present value, the managers always take the project if they have sufficient internally generated cash flow or can issue risk-free debt. However, if risky securities must be issued to finance the project, managers will perceive $C_M(E) \geq 0$. *Ceteris paribus*, more projects will be rejected by firms that do not have sufficient cash flow to finance them internally (or cannot issue risk-free debt), inducing a positive correlation between cash flow and investment. Note that the correlation is unrelated to any *actual* costs of external financing. This is important, since Kaplan and Zingales (1997) find large cash-flow sensitivities for most firms, but no reliable relationship between those sensitivities and the actual cost of external financing for a given firm.

D. Costs of Free Cash Flow

Optimistic managers sometimes want to take negative net present value projects that they believe are positive net present value projects. This can lead to social losses that are lessened when free cash flow is paid out of the firm.

A simple way to think about the effects of optimism on project selection is to imagine a ranking of all projects by their net present values. In this simple model, the optimistic managers' ranking will be the same as the rational one, but their optimism will lead to the perception of a "cutoff" that is too low. Put another way, the managers will want to take too many projects from the ranking. In terms of the model, the true expected cash flow for a given new project is $E_T(r) = {}_T p_H * r_H + {}_T p_L * r_L$. The managers' perceived expected cash flow is $E_M(r) = {}_M p_H * r_H + {}_M p_L * r_L$. Optimistic managers believe that negative net present value projects are positive net present value projects when $E_M(r) > i > E_T(r)$. This range of projects occurs for probabilistic beliefs where:

$$1 \geq {}_M p_H > \frac{(i - r_L)}{(r_H - r_L)} > {}_T p_H \geq 0.$$

It is important to note, therefore, that there is a *limited* set of bad decisions that will be made by optimistic managers. When the investment cost i exceeds the high cash-flow state r_H, then the optimistic managers never take the project. In other words, there are projects that are bad enough that even the most optimistic managers will not take them, because optimism about the probability of the good state can never overcome the fact that the good state is never good enough to cover the investment costs of the project. Nevertheless, the range of negative NPV projects that the optimistic manager will accept can be large.

This is why free cash flow has costs, as well as possible benefits. Jensen (1986) defines free cash flow as "cash flow in excess of that required to fund all projects that have positive net present values when discounted at the relevant cost of capital." Whenever $E_M(r) > i > E_T(r)$, the optimistic manager wants to take negative net present value projects that he perceives have positive net present value. He will not use outside financing (leaving a possible marginal role for free cash flow) in two circumstances. First, and trivially, he will not use outside financing when it is unavailable, because the firm (objectively) will generate insufficient cash flow to provide the necessary return to the security; thus, the market will refuse to buy the newly issued securities. Second, he will not use outside financing when the perceived negative net present value of that financing outweighs the perceived positive net present value of the project, that is, when $C_M(E) > E_M(r) - i > 0$. Assuming one of these conditions holds, it follows that free cash flow in the amount i will allow the manager to accept the project, he will accept it, and the value of the firm will fall. In this case, access to free cash flow is harmful. Forcing the optimistic manager to the capital market might not prevent all bad investments, but it will prevent those where $E_M(r) - i - C_M(E) \leq 0$. Without free cash flow, the misperceived cost of external financing actually prevents some value destruction by the optimistic managers.

E. Some Additional Testable Implications

In addition to the pecking-order capital structure preferences and biased cash-flow forecasts predicted by the managerial optimism model (and largely supported by the available evidence), the overinvestment-underinvestment tradeoff described in sections C and D provide a basis for additional new tests of the theory.[8] Recall that $C_M(E)$ is the additional cost of external financing perceived by the optimistic manager. While this term is capable of both deterring bad overinvestment and causing value destructive underinvestment, it is clear that managers—none of whom believe they undertake value destroying overinvestment (see Assumption 2)—will seek to reduce their reliance on external funds. Retaining cash flow and avoiding high debt levels are two ways of doing so. Employing risk management techniques to protect the firm's cash flow is another. The hedging motive to protect corporate cash flow to avoid actual high costs of external finance is the subject of two papers by Froot, Sharfstein, and Stein (1993, 1994). There, the authors argue for cash flow-based hedging that protects investment opportunities from high marginal costs of external finance. The theory rests, of course, on an assumption that asymmetric information can drive a wedge between internal and external costs of funds.

By allowing for a false, but perceived, wedge between the internal and external cost of funds, the managerial optimism model provides a new testable theory of cash-flow risk management motives. In this model, proxies for optimism (such as those employed by Malmendier and Tate 2001) should predict the extent of cash-flow risk management. This prediction may help sort out whether or not *actual* information asymmetries play a role in cash-flow risk management. In Geczy, Minton, and Schrand (1997), for example, the authors find evidence of cash-flow based risk management, but their proxies for "growth opportunities" (such as research and development) are not necessarily good measures of information asymmetry. Managerial optimism provides a testable theory of why firms hedge, a question that logically precedes questions of whether they should and how they should do it (see Culp 2001).

Other testable implications are also apparent. Consider corporate merger and acquisition activity. The role of optimism in corporate takeovers is, of course, the subject of the first significant paper to address optimism in corporate finance—Roll (1986). Roll argues that managerial hubris (essentially a heuristic way of describing optimism) might explain corporate takeovers. In particular, Roll argues that managerial hubris helps explain why *acquirers* fail to make significant gains on takeover announcement. But managers are also *targets* of corporate takeovers, and agency conflicts arise between managers and shareholders when managers refuse to sell assets at a price higher than their current price. This resistance may be explained in a measurable way by managerial optimism, which predicts that optimistic managers make suboptimal decisions to resist takeovers.

---

[8] In direct extension and test of the underinvestment result presented above, Malmendier and Tate (2001) find evidence that cash-flow sensitivities of investment to cash-flow can be explained by optimism of the chief executive officer. Their measures of CEO optimism (options exercise and patterns of own-stock acquisition) provide promising candidates for future research.

Consider a date $t = 1$ bid B for which the firm can be sold. This value may in general exceed $E_T(y_2)$. This may be true because of operational synergy, economies of scale or scope, the incompetence of current management, or because other optimistic managers believe the firm will be worth more in their hands. That incumbent managers may resist this bid suboptimally in the view of current shareholders follows simply from the fact that optimality, from the shareholders' perspective, requires that the firm be sold when future expected cash flow is less than the bid. That is, (assuming no new project is taken at time $t = 1$) the firm should be sold when $B > E_T(y_2)$. Since the managers will acquiesce to the takeover attempt only when $B > E_M(y_2)$, and since $E_M(y_2) > E_T(y_2)$, the managers' resistance decision may be suboptimal. This offers a prediction for the study of corporate control contests where managers fight for independence (often at very high financial and personal cost), even when takeovers would leave the incumbent managers with large post-takeover wealth through stock gains and golden parachute provisions. Proxies for top executive optimism such as those employed by Malmendier and Tate (2001) are well-suited to tests of this hypothesis, which would logically focus on the degree to which takeover resistance (poison pill adoption and rescission; deal failure, extra) is explained by proxies for managerial optimism.

3. Conclusion

This chapter adopts an explicitly behavioral approach in a simple corporate finance model, and examines its implications for the free cash-flow debate. Two dominant features emerge. First, optimistic managers believe that capital markets undervalue their firm's risky securities and may pass up positive net present value projects that must be financed externally. Second, optimistic managers overvalue their own corporate projects and may wish to invest in negative net present value projects even when they are loyal to shareholders. These results imply an underinvestment-overinvestment tradeoff related to free cash flow, without invoking asymmetric information or (rational) agency cost theories.

The model suggests that the effects of free cash flow are ambiguous. Optimistic managers will sometimes decline *positive* NPV projects if those projects require outside financing. Free cash flow in an amount required to fund positive net present value projects can prevent socially costly underinvestment. In a world with optimistic managers, therefore, it is unclear that mechanisms that force the firm to pay out all cash flow and acquire external finance are necessarily good mechanisms. This is true both for debt (as in Jensen 1986) and dividends (as in Easterbrook 1984). Whether the savings in preventing bad investment outweighs the social costs of underinvestment is likely to vary by firm. If all managers are optimistic, and markets are efficient (or at least are less optimistic about particular firms than their managers), then shareholders may prefer large amounts of free cash flow to be retained by firms with good investment opportunities.

The managerial optimism model generates several new additional testable predictions as well. First, managerial optimism predicts the existence of biased cash-flow forecasts. Second, managerial optimism predicts pecking order capital structure preferences. Third, managerial optimism predicts efforts to hedge corporate cash flow, even in the absence of significant asymmetric information, by generating a false, but perceived wedge between the internal and external cost of funds. Fourth, managerial optimism predicts takeover resistance. Using proxies such as those presented in recent work by Malmendier and Tate (2001), each of these predictions provides significant future challenges to the managerial optimism theory of corporate finance.

The managerial optimism approach may also shed light on numerous institutional mechanisms. For example, managerial optimism may help explain the role of outsiders in corporate governance. Kahneman and Lovallo (1993) argue that organizational optimism is best alleviated by introducing an "outside" view, one capable of realizing all the reasons the "inside" view might be wrong. Outsiders are capable of drawing managerial attention to information that might indicate that their perceptions are wrong. The recent push in corporate governance circles for outside directors and outside chairmen of the board is consistent with this prescription. This also suggests that the most effective prescription for managerial optimism combines strong incentives with strong outside monitoring. In his study of Kohlberg, Kravis, and Roberts ("KKR"), for example, Anders (1992, p. 179) describes KKR's role in monitoring managerial decisions, particularly to ensure that managers receive constant feedback against targets:

> Even the executives who prospered in KKR's regimen knew that if their companies fell badly short of the bank-book projections, their wonderful rapport with the partners and associates of KKR could vanish. The chief executive and chairman of Owens-Illinois in the late 1980's, Robert Lanigan, described the underlying message from KKR as follows: ' "If you miss the targets, we don't want to know about the dollar, the weather, or the economy." KKR wanted results, not excuses. "There are negatives if we don't meet those targets," Lanigan confided in an interview. He paused, as if afraid to say more. Then he concluded: "That's 90 percent of what drives us."

Of course, managerial optimism may have limits as a complete theory of corporate finance. On its own, and without some amount of asymmetric information, it may not explain the rich results on announcement effects, nor can it account for the importance of legal mechanisms that target rational agency problems and problems of managerial loyalty. Nevertheless, the results presented here suggest that managerial irrationality may play a role in future corporate finance research, delivering some results more parsimoniously and as plausibly as competing theories.

REFERENCES

Anders, G., 1992, *Merchants of Debt*, Basic.

Avery, C., J. A. Chevalier, and S. Schaefer, 1998, Why Do Managers Undertake Acquisitions? An Analysis of Internal and External Awards for Acquisitiveness, *Journal of Law, Economics, and Organizations* 14, 24–43.

Boehmer, E., and J. M. Netter, 1997, Management Optimism and Corporate Acquisitions: Evidence from Insider Trading, *Managerial and Decision Economics* 18, 693–708.

Brehmer, B., 1980, In One Word: Not from Experience, *Acta Psychologica* 45, 223–41.

Culp, C. L., 2001, *The Risk Management Process: Business Strategy and Tactics*, Wiley.

DeAngelo, H., L. DeAngelo, and D. J. Skinner, 1996, Reversal of Fortune: Dividend Signaling and the Disappearance of Sustained Earnings Growth, *Journal of Financial Economics* 40, 341–71.

DeLong, J. B., A. Shleifer, L. H. Summers, and R. J. Waldmann, 1991, The Survival of Noise Traders in Financial Markets, *Journal of Business* 64, 1–19.

DeMeza, D., and C. Southey, 1996, The Borrower's Curse: Optimism, Finance, and Entrepreneurship, *The Economic Journal* 106, 375–86.

Easterbrook, F. H., 1984, Two Agency-Cost Explanations of Dividends, *American Economic Review* 74, 650–59.

Fazzari, S. R., G. Hubbard, and B. Petersen, 1988, Financing Constraints and Corporate Investment, *Brookings Papers on Economic Activity* 1, 141–95.

Friedman, M., 1953, The Methodology of Positive Economics, in *Essays in Positive Economics*, University of Chicago Press.

Froot, K. A., D. S. Scharfstein, and J. C. Stein, 1993, Risk Management: Coordinating Investment and Financing Policies, *Journal of Finance* 48, 1629–58.

———, 1994, A Framework for Risk Management, *Harvard Business Review* 72, 91–102.

Geczy, C., B. A. Minton, and C. Schrand, 1997, Why Firms Use Currency Derivatives, *Journal of Finance* 52, 1323–54.

Gilson, S., 1989, Management Turnover and Financial Distress, *Journal of Financial Economics* 25, 241–62.

Graham, J. R., and C. R. Harvey, 2001, The Theory and Practice of Corporate Finance: Evidence from the Field, *Journal of Financial Economics* 60, 187–243.

Harris, M., and A. Raviv, 1991, The Theory of Capital Structure, *Journal of Finance* 46, 297–355.

Hart, O., 1993, Theories of Optimal Capital Structure: A Managerial Discretion Perspective, in M. Blair (ed.), *The Deal Decade: What Takeovers and Leveraged Buyouts Mean for Corporate Governance*, Brookings, 19–53.

Hotchkiss, E. S., 1995, Postbankruptcy Performance and Management Turnover, *Journal of Finance* 50, 3–21.

Jensen, M. C., 1986, Agency Costs of Free Cash Flow, Corporate Finance, and Takeovers, *American Economic Review* 76, 323–29.

Kahneman, D., and D. Lovallo, 1993, Timid Choices and Bold Forecasts: A Cognitive Perspective on Risk Taking, *Management Science* 39, 17–31.

Kamath, R. R., 1997, Long-Term Financing Decisions: Views and Practices of Financial Managers of NYSE Firms, *Financial Review* 32, 331–56.

Kaplan, S. N., 1989, The Effects of Management Buyouts on Operating Performance and Value, *Journal of Financial Economics* 24, 217–54.

Kaplan, S. N., and R. S. Ruback, 1995, The Valuation of Cash Flow Forecasts: An Empirical Analysis, *Journal of Finance* 50, 1059–93.

Kaplan, S. N., and L. Zingales, 1997, Do Investment-Cash Flow Sensitivities Provide Useful Measures of Financing Constraints, *Quarterly Journal of Economics* 112, 169–215.

Lee, I., 1997, Do Firms Knowingly Sell Overvalued Equity, *Journal of Finance* 52, 1439–65.

Loughran, T., and J. R. Ritter, 1997, The Operating Performance of Firms Conducting Equity Offerings, *Journal of Finance* 52, 1823–50.

Maki, U., 2000, Reclaiming Relevant Realism, *Journal of Economic Methodology* 7, 109–25.

Malmendier, U., and G. Tate, 2001, CEO Overconfidence and Corporate Investment, Working Paper, Harvard University.

March, J. G., and Z. Shapira, 1987, Managerial Perspectives on Risk and Risk Taking, *Management Science* 33, 1404–18.

McNichols, M., 1989, Evidence of Informationational Asymmetries from Management Earning Forecasts and Stock Returns, *Account Review* 1, 1–27.

Myers, S. C., and N. S. Majluf, 1984, Corporate Financing and Investment Decisions When Firms Have Information That Investors Do Not Have, *Journal of Financial Economics* 13, 187–221.

Pinegar, J. M., and L. Wilbrecht, 1989, What Managers Think of Capital Structure Theory: A Survey, *Financial Management* 18, 82–91.

Rabin, M., and R. H. Thaler, 2001, Anomalies: Risk Aversion, *Journal of Economic Perspectives* 15, 219–32.

Roll, R., 1986, The Hubris Hypothesis of Corporate Takeovers, *Journal of Business* 59, in R. H. Thaler, (ed.), *Advances in Behavioral Finance*, Russell Sage, 197–216.

Russell, T., and R. H. Thaler, 1985, The Relevance of Quasi Rationality in Competitive Markets, *American Economic Review* 75, 1071–82.

Schultz, P., and M. Zaman, 2001, Do The Individuals Closest To Internet Firms Believe They Are Overvalued?, *Journal of Financial Economics* 59, 347–81.

Stein, J. C., 1996, Rational Capital Budgeting in an Irrational World, *Journal of Business* 69, 429–55.

Weinstein, N., 1980, Unrealistic Optimism about Future Life Events, *Journal of Personality and Social Psychology* 39, 806–20.

CONTRIBUTORS

Richard H. Thaler is the Robert P. Gwinn Professor of Economics, Finance, and Behavioral Science at the University of Chicago's Graduate School of Business, where he is the director of the Center for Decision Research. He is also a research associate at the National Bureau of Economic Research, where he codirects the behavioral economics project. Thaler is considered one of the pioneers in the attempt to fill the gap between psychology and economics. Among the problems he has worked on are self control, savings, mental accounting, fairness, the endowment effect, and behavioral finance. He is the author of the books *The Winner's Curse and Quasi Rational Economics*, and is an editor of the collection *Advances in Behavioral Finance*. He writes a series of articles in the *Journal of Economics Perspectives* under the heading "Anomalies."

Brad M. Barber is a Professor of Finance at the UC-Davis, Graduate School of Management. His recent research focuses on analyst recommendations and investor psychology. His research has been covered extensively in the popular press, including *Business Week, Time, The Wall Street Journal*, ABC News, NBC Nightly News, CNN, CNNfn, and CNBC. Professor Barber has written numerous scholarly articles, which have appeared in many publications including the *Journal of Finance, Journal of Financial Economics, Review of Financial Studies Journal of Political Economy, Quarterly Journal of Economics, American Sociological Review, Journal of Financial and Quantitative Analysis*, and the *Financial Analyst Journal*. He is a regular speaker at academic and practitioner conferences. He currently serves on the Investment Advisory Committees for Mercer Global Advisors and the Market Surveillance Committee of the California Independent System Operator. Professor Barber received his Ph.D. in finance from the University of Chicago in 1991. He also received an MBA from the University of Chicago and a BS in economics from the University of Illinois. At UC-Davis, he teaches courses in investment analysis and corporate financial policy.

Nicholas Barberis is Professor of Finance at the Yale School of Management and a Faculty Research Fellow at the National Bureau of Economic Research. His research focuses primarily on behavioral finance and, in particular, on psychology-based models of investor preferences and investor beliefs. He has received the FAME Prize for Research, the Paul A. Samuelson Prize for Outstanding Scholarly Writing on Lifelong Financial Security, as well as several teaching awards. Prior to his arrival at the Yale School of Management, he taught for many years at the University of Chicago's

Graduate School of Business, and has also held visiting professorships at Harvard University and the London Business School. He received his Ph.D. from Harvard University in 1996 and his BA from Cambridge University in 1991.

Shlomo Benartzi is an associate professor at UCLA's Anderson Graduate School of Management. Dr. Benartzi received his Ph.D. from Cornell University's Johnson Graduate School of Management. His research investigates participant behavior in defined contribution plans. In particular, his current work examines how do individuals make financial decisions in retirement saving plans? In addition, he is developing behavioral prescriptions to assist employees make better financial decisions including the "Save More Tomorrow" program. Dr. Benartzi's work has been published in the *American Economic Review, Journal of Political Economy, the Quarterly Journal of Economics, the Journal of Finance, the Accounting Review and Management Science.* His work been discussed in the *Economist, Financial Times, Investor's Business Daily,* the *Los Angeles Times, Money Magazine,* the *New York Times, Plan Sponsor, Pensions and Investments, The Wall Street Journal and CNBC.* Benartzi served on the ERISA Advisory Council of the U.S. Department of Labor, the Investment Advisory Council of the Alaska State Pension and the advisory board of Morningstar.

John Y. Campbell is the Otto Eckstein Professor of Applied Economics at Harvard University. He did his undergraduate work at Oxford University, obtained his Ph.D. in Economics from Yale University in 1984, and taught at Princeton University for ten years before moving to Harvard in 1994. He is a research associate and former director of the program in asset pricing at the National Bureau of Economic Research, a former co-editor of the American Economic Review and the Review of Economics and Statistics, a fellow of the Econometric Society and the American Academy of Arts and Sciences, and the 2004 president-elect of the American Finance Association. Campbell serves on the board of the Harvard Management Company and is a partner of Arrowstreet Capital, LP, a quantitative asset management firm. Campbell's work concerns asset markets and their relation to the macroeconomy, and the normative analysis of portfolio choice. He is the author of two books, *The Econometrics of Financial Markets* (with Andrew Lo and Craig MacKinlay) and *Strategic Asset Allocation: Portfolio Choice for Long-Term Investors* (with Luis Viceira), both of which have won Paul Samuelson Awards from TIAA-CREF for outstanding scholarly writing on life-long financial security.

Emil M. Dabora received his Bachelors of Science at the Massachusetts Institute of Technology in 1991, and his Ph.D. in economics from Harvard University in 1996. After spending six years at Morgan Stanley in proprietary trading, he is currently a portfolio manager heading the event-driven investing group at Caxton Associates, a global, multistrategy hedge fund.

Kent Daniel is the Helen and John L. Kellogg Professor of Finance at the Kellogg School of Management at Northwestern University. Prior to joining Kellogg, Daniel taught at the University of Chicago and at the University of British Columbia. Professor Daniel has published widely. His work has examined tests of asset pricing models, in particular tests of models attempting to explain cross-sectional predictability of asset returns and the magnitude and predictability of the equity premium. He has done both theoretical and empirical studies on psychology-based asset pricing theories. His papers have twice won the Smith-Breeden Award for the best paper published in the *Journal of Finance*. He is a Research Associate of the National Bureau of Economic Research. He is an Associate Editor of the *Journal of Finance*. He received his Ph.D. in Finance from UCLA in 1992.

François Degeorge is a professor of finance at the University of Lugano, Switzerland. He received his Ph.D. from Harvard University. He taught finance at HEC Paris from 1993 to 2003. His research focuses on corporate finance, and has been published in the *Journal of Business*, the *Journal of Finance*, the *Journal of Financial Economics*, and the *Journal of Risk and Uncertainty*. He has received the following awards: Merton Miller Prize (2000); Inquire Europe First Prize (1998 and 2003); the HEC Foundation Prize in 1994; and in 1993 he was nominated for the Smith Breeden Prize.

Kenneth A. Froot is André R. Jakurski Professor of Business Administration at Harvard University's Graduate School of Business Administration. He teaches courses in Capital Markets, International Finance, and Risk Management. Professor Froot received his B.A. from Stanford University and his Ph.D. from the University of California at Berkeley. He spent the 1988–89 academic year as an Olin Fellow at the National Bureau of Economic Research, where he is Research Associate and Chair of the NBER's Insurance Group. His research on a wide range of topics in finance, risk management, and international economics has been published in many journals and books. He is editor of the *Journal of International Financial Management and Accounting*, associate editor of the *Journal of International Economics*, and of *The Financing of Catastrophe Risk, Foreign Direct Investment*, and *The Transition in Eastern Europe, Vols. 1 and 2*. He is a member of the American Finance Association, the American Economics Association, and the Behavioral Finance Working Group, and served as a term member of the Council on Foreign Relations.

J. B. Heaton is a litigation partner with Bartlit Beck Herman Palenchar & Scott LLP in Chicago. He earned a B.A. in Liberal Arts & Sciences at the University of Illinois in 1990 and earned J.D., M.B.A., and Ph.D. (finance) degrees from the University of Chicago in 1999. He has taught corporate restructuring at Duke University's Fuqua School of Business and received Duke's Excellence in Teaching Award in 2003. He has published articles in many areas of law and finance and in 2003 received (with Alon Brav) the Barclay's Global Investors/Michael Brennan Award for the best paper published in the *Review of Financial Studies* for work analyzing the difficulty of distinguishing rational and behavioral asset pricing theories.

David Hirshleifer is the Ralph W. Kurtz Chair in Finance at the Fisher College of Business, Ohio State University. He previously taught at the Anderson School at UCLA and held the Waterman Chair at the University of Michigan Business School. His research in finance and economics has won several awards, and has been profiled in media outlets. He is considered a leading researcher in the field of behavioral economics and finance, has served as editor of the *Review of Financial Studies*, and as associate editor and coeditor of several journals in finance, economics, and corporate strategy. His recent research emphasizes psychology in firms and markets, including analysis of mood and stock prices, limited investor attention and the misuse of accounting information, the design of trading strategies to exploit stock market mispricing, imitation and fads, and takeovers and managerial investment decisions.

Harrison Hong is a Professor of Economics at Princeton University, where he teaches courses in finance in the undergraduate, masters and Ph.D. programs. Before coming to Princeton in 2002, he was on the finance faculty of Stanford University's Graduate School of Business, most recently as an Associate Professor of Finance. He received his B.A. in economics and statistics with highest distinction from the University of California, Berkeley in 1992 and his Ph.D. in economics from M.I.T. in 1997. Hong's research has covered a range of topics including: behavioral finance and stock-market efficiency; asset pricing and trading with market imperfections; social interaction and investor behavior; career concerns and herd behavior; mutual funds; and security analysts and investor relations. He is on the editorial board of the *Journal of Financial Intermediation* and has received various research grants and awards.

Ming Huang is professor of finance at Cheung Kong Graduate School of Business, Beijing, China, and is currently on leave from the Stanford Graduate School of Business, where he is associate professor of finance. He has conducted research in areas of behavioral finance, credit risk, liquidity, and auctions, and he has published in the *Journal of Political Economy*, the *Quarterly Journal of Economics*, the *American Economic Reviews*, the *Journal of Economic Theory*, and the *Journal of Finance*. He has won the Year 2000 FAME Award, and M.B.A. teaching awards at both Stanford and University of Chicago.

Narasimhan Jegadeesh is the Dean's Distinguished Professor of Finance at the Goizueta Business School, Emory University. He is also a research associate at the National Bureau of Economic Research Asset Pricing Group. Professor Jegadeesh teaches courses on Empirical Research Methods, Portfolio Management and Fixed-Income Securities. His research focuses on investments, stock market efficiency, analysts' forecasts and recommendations, and fixed-income securities. Professor Jegadeesh has published extensively in the *Journal of Finance*, the *Journal of Financial Economics*, the *Review of Financial Studies* and other leading academic journals. He is on the editorial board of the *Journal of Finance* and the *Journal of Financial Markets*. His research has been featured in the *Economist, Money, New York Times, Smart Money*, Boston WPIX radio and CNNFn.

Owen A. Lamont is Professor of Finance at Yale School of Management and a Research Associate at the National Bureau of Economic Research. He obtained a B.A. in Economics and Government from Oberlin College in 1988, and a Ph.D. in Economics from the Massachusetts Institute of Technology in 1994. Before moving to Yale in 2003, he previously taught at Princeton and the University of Chicago. He has received numerous prizes and awards, including fellowships from the National Science Foundation and the Alfred P. Sloan Foundation. His research is in asset pricing and corporate finance, and has published academic papers on short-selling, stock returns, bond returns, closed-end funds, and corporate diversification. At Yale he teaches a course in Behavioral Finance.

Josef Lakonishok is the Karnes Professor of Finance at the University of Illinois at Urbana-Champaign, a Research Associate at the National Bureau of Economic Research (NBER), and a principal at LSV Asset Management. Previously he was a Professor of Finance at Tel Aviv University. He received his Ph.D. in Finance from Cornell University. Josef Lakonishok specializes in empirical investment research. He has published more than eighty papers. His papers cover a broad range of investment topics such as performance evaluation, analysts' forecasts, share repurchases and fundamental and momentum based trading strategies. Dr. Lakonishok served and is serving as an associate editor of many leading journals in financial economics. Recently he was featured in the book *Investment Titans*, published by Mc-Graw Hill.

Roni Michaely is the Rudd Family professor of Management and a professor of finance at the Johnson Graduate School of Management at Cornell University. He is also affiliated with the Interdisciplinary Center (IDC) in Herzliya, Israel. Professor Michaely's research interests are in the areas of corporate finance, capital markets, and valuation. His current research focuses on conflict of interest in the capital markets, corporate payout policy,

690

CONTRIBUTORS

and securities' valuation. His research has appeared in such scholarly journals as the *Journal of Finance, Review of Financial Studies, Journal of Financial and Quantitative Analysis, Journal of Financial Intermediation,* and *Financial Management*. His research has been also frequently featured in *The Wall Street Journal, New York Times,* the *Economist, Investor's Business Daily, San Francisco Chronicle, BusinessWeek, Forbes, Barrons, Money, Reuters, Worth,* and others. Professor Michaely was a director of the Israeli Securities Authority (ISA) from 1998 to 2003. He consults in the area of securities valuation, restructuring, and conflict of interest in the banking industry.

Terrance Odean is an associate professor of Finance at the Haas School of Business at the University of California, Berkeley. He earned a B.A. in Statistics at UC Berkeley in 1990 and a Ph.D. in Finance from the university's Haas School of Business in 1997. He taught finance at UC Davis from 1997 through 2001. As an undergraduate at Berkeley, Odean studied judgment and decision making with Daniel Kahneman. This led to his current research focus on how psychologically motivated decisions affect investor welfare and securities prices. During the summer of 1970, he drove a yellow cab in New York City.

Jayendu Patel leads ChoiceStream's team of research scientists whose expertise span micro-econometrics, Bayesian statistics, choice modeling, collaborative filtering, library science/taxonomy, and search. He received his Ph.D. from the University of Chicago. Prior to joining ChoiceStream as Chief Scientist in 2001, Dr. Patel was a professor at Boston University, Harvard University, and Boston College. His current interests relate to consumer choice, judgment and decision-making, and corporate finance.

Tano Santos is the 1967 Associate Professor of Business at the Finance and Economics division of Columbia Business School. He obtained his Ph.D. in Economics at the Department of Economics of the University of Chicago. His thesis focused on the timing and real side effects of financial innovations. Before coming to Columbia University he was in the faculty of the Chicago Business School. Santos current research focuses on asset pricing and the institutions of financial markets.

Robert J. Shiller is the Stanley B. Resor Professor of Economics, Cowles Foundation for Research in Economics, Yale University, and fellow at the International Center for Finance, Yale School of Management. He received his Ph.D. in economics from the Massachusetts Institute of Technology in 1972, and his since been awarded several honorary doctorates/professorships. He is Research Associate of the National Bureau of Economic Research, a fellow of the American Academy of Arts and Sciences, a fellow of the Econometric Society, a recipient of a Guggenheim fellowship, and a member of the American Philosophical Society. He has written widely on financial markets, financial innovation, behavioral economics, macroeconomics, real estate, statistical methods, and on public attitudes, opinions, and moral judgments regarding markets. His 1989 book *Market Volatility* (MIT Press) was a mathematical and behavioral analysis of price fluctuations in speculative markets. His 1993 book *Macro Markets: Creating Institutions for Managing Society's Largest Economic Risks* (Oxford University Press) proposed a variety of new risk-management contracts, such as futures contracts in national incomes or in real estate that would revolutionize the management of risks to standards of living. This book won the 1996 Paul A. Samuelson Award, TIAA-CREF. His book *Irrational Exuberance* (Princeton University Press, 2000, Broadway Books 2001) is an analysis and explication of the stock market boom from 1982 to 2000. This book won the Commonfund Prize, 2000, was translated into 15 languages, and was a *New York Times* Nonfiction Bestseller. His book *The New Financial Order: Risk in the 21st Century* (Princeton University Press, 2003), which is being translated into eight languages, is an analysis of an expanding role of finance, insurance, and public finance in our future. The book won the Financial Times-getAbstract Award for Best Business Book and the Wilmott Prize 2003, and was named as one of the Ten Best Business Books of 2003 by *Business Week* magazine. He is co-founder of Case Shiller Weiss, Inc., an economics research and information firm, which was sold to Fiserv, Inc. in 2002. He is also co-founder of Macro Securities Research, LLC, a firm devoted to the securitization of new risks.

Andrei Shleifer is the Whipple V. N. Jones Professor of Economics at Harvard University and holds an undergraduate degree from Harvard and a Ph.D. from MIT. Before coming to Harvard in 1991, he has taught at Princeton and the Chicago Business School. Shleifer's has worked in the areas of comparative corporate governance, law and finance, behavioral finance, as well as institutional economics. He has published four books, including *The Grabbing Hand* (with Robert Vishny), and *Inefficient Markets: An Introduction to Behavioral Finance*, as well as over a hundred articles. Shleifer has served as the editor of the *Quarterly Journal of Economics* between 1989 and 1999, and as an associate editor of both the *Journal of Finance* and *the Journal of Financial Economics*. He is currently the editor of the *Journal of Economic Perspectives* and an Advisory Editor of the JFE. Shleifer is a fellow of the Econometric Society and of the American Academy of Arts and Sciences. In 1999, Shleifer won the John Bates Clark medal of the American Economic Association.

Jeremy C. Stein is a Professor of Economics at Harvard University, where he teaches courses in finance in the undergraduate and Ph.D. programs. He is also a research associate at the National Bureau of Economic research. Before coming to Harvard in 2000, he was for ten years on the finance faculty of M.I.T.'s Sloan School of Management, most recently as the J.C. Penney

Professor of Management. Prior to that, he was an assistant professor of finance at the Harvard Business School from 1987–1990. He received his B.A. in economics summa cum laude from Princeton University in 1983, and his Ph.D. in economics from M.I.T. in 1986. Stein's research has covered such topics as: behavioral finance and stock-market efficiency; corporate investment and financing decisions; risk management; capital allocation inside firms; financial intermediation; and monetary policy.

Avanidhar Subrahmanyam ("Subra") is currently a Professor of Finance at UCLA. He received his Ph.D. in finance from the Anderson School in 1990. He was Assistant Professor at Columbia University from 1990 to 1993, and Visiting Associate Professor at Anderson in 1993–1994. His current research interests range from the relationship between the trading environment of a firm's stock and the firm's cost of capital to behavioral theories for asset price behavior to empirical determinants of the cross-section of equity returns. Professor Subrahmanyam is the author or coauthor of numerous refereed journal articles on these and other subjects in leading finance and economics journals. He is a member of the Working Research Group on Market Microstructure recently established by the National Bureau of Economic Research (NBER) in Cambridge, Mass. He has received best paper awards at the *Journal of Finance*, the *Journal of Financial Economics*, Western Finance Association meetings and the International Conference of Finance in Taiwan, and has been nominated several times for the best paper at the *Journal of Finance*. He is a co-editor of the *Journal of Financial Markets* and a past associate editor of the *Journal of Finance* and the *Review of Financial Studies*. He has served as a consultant for several firms including the NASDAQ Stock Exchange, the National Stock Exchange in Mumbai (Bombay), India, San Jose Mercury News, Irwin/McGraw-Hill, Law and Economics Group, and Deutsche Bank.

Sheridan Titman holds the McAllister Centennial Chair in Financial Services at the University of Texas and is a research associate of the National Bureau of Economic Research. He has a B.S. from the University of Colorado and an MS and Ph.D. from Carnegie Mellon University. Professor Titman taught at UCLA for over ten years where in addition to his teaching and research activities he served as the department chair for the finance group and as the Vice Chairman of the UCLA management school faculty. Between 1992 and 1994 Professor Titman was one of the founding professors of the School of Business and Management at the Hong Kong University of Science and Technology where he was the vice chairman of the faculty and the chairman of the faculty appointments committee. From 1994 to 1997 he served as the John J. Collins, S. J. Chair in Finance at Boston College. In the 1988–89 academic year Professor Titman worked in Washington D.C. as the special assistant to the Assistant Secretary of the Treasury for Economic Policy. He has served on the editorial boards of the leading academic finance journals, was an editor of the *Review of Financial Studies*, and is the founding editor of the *International Review of Finance*. He has served as a director of the American Finance Association, the Asia Pacific Finance Association, the Western Finance Association and the Financial Management Association. Professor Titman has won a number of awards for his research excellence, including the Batterymarch fellowship in 1985, which was given to the most promising assistant professors of finance, and the Smith Breeden prize for the best paper published in the *Journal of Finance* in 1997. In addition, in 2001 he was inducted as a Fellow of the Financial Management Association. Professor Titman has published numerous articles on both investments and corporate finance and coauthored a leading advanced corporate finance textbook entitled "Financial Markets and Corporate Strategy."

Robert W. Vishny is the Eric J. Gleacher Distinguished Service Professor of Finance at the University of Chicago Graduate School of Business where he has taught since 1985. He is also a founding partner of LSV Asset Management, an institutional value equity money management firm. Vishny has previously served as director of the program in corporate finance at the National Bureau of Economic Research as well as a trustee of the College Retirement Equities Fund (CREF). He has published extensively in the areas of corporate finance, corporate governance, law and finance, and behavioral finance. He is a fellow of the American Academy of Arts and Sciences.

Kent Womack is an associate professor of Finance at the Tuck School of Business at Dartmouth College. He received his Ph.D. from Cornell University and began his academic career at Tuck in 1994. He is also a graduate of Yale University (B.A., 1978) and Stanford University (M.B.A., 1982). Before academia, Kent was a vice president at Goldman, Sachs & Co. and, earlier, a CPA with Price Waterhouse. His research focuses on the value of sell-side security analysis, security analysts' conflicts of interest, and the underwriting process. He is a co-editor of FEN Educator.

Richard Zeckhauser is Frank P. Ramsey Professor of Political Economy at the John F. Kennedy School of Government, Harvard University. His entire academic career has been at Harvard. He graduated summa cum laude from the College in 1962, was a junior fellow of the Society of Fellows from 1965–68, received a Ph.D. in economics in 1968, then served as a junior faculty member until appointed as a full professor in 1972. He teaches courses on economics and analytic methods (Kennedy School), risk (joint Kennedy & Law Schools), and regulation (joint Kennedy & Law Schools). Zeckhauser has been elected to membership in the Institute of Medicine of the National Academy of Sciences, and as a fellow of the Association for Public Policy and Management, the Econometric Society, and the American Academy of Arts and Sciences. He is a research associate of the National Bureau of Economic Research and the Japan–U.S. Center (NYU), and sits on the editorial boards of eight professional journals. He serves as a Group Insurance Commissioner (State of Massachusetts), as a trustee of the Commonwealth School, and has been the director of a number of high technology companies. He is a member of the Academic Advisory Committee of the American Enterprise Institute, and the Behavioral Economics Roundtable of the Russell Sage Foundation. He has won numerous contract bridge championships at the regional and national levels. In pairs competition, he won the 1966 United States championship, and was a finalist in the 1998 World Bridge Federation championship. Often working with others, Professor Zeckhauser has authored 180 articles, three books and eight edited books. His most recent edited books are *Principals and Agents: The Structure of Business* (1985), *American Society: Public and Private Responsibilities* (1986), *Privatization and State-Owned Enterprises: Lessons from the United States, Great Britain, and Canada* (1989), *Strategy and Choice* (1991), and *Wise Choices: Games, Decisions, and Negotiations* (1996). The challenges of creating appropriate commitments and making effective decisions under uncertainty, motivate his major ongoing research projects. His current major studies address early admissions to colleges, trust on the Internet, and the intricate game between stock market analysts and the stock market.

INDEX

Abreu, D., 6n
ACT. *See* Advance Corporate Tax
Advance Corporate Tax (ACT), 121, 125
Affleck-Graves, J., 428
Aha, Rabbi Issac bar, 571
aliasing problem, 648n
Allen, Franklin, 81
Allen, Jeffrey W., 162
Almazan, Andres, 165
ambiguity aversion, 21–22, 30–31, 51–52
anchoring bias, 15, 408n
Anders, G., 681
Anderson, E., 30–31
Andreassen, P., 432–33
APT. *See* arbitrage pricing theory
arbitrage: anomalies and, 96–99; arbitrage
    resources, markets attracting, 94–96; de-
    scribed, 2, 3–4, 79–80; law of one price
    and, 131 (*see also* law of one price, viola-
    tions of); limits to (*see* limits to arbitrage);
    managerial irrationality and, 667–68;
    modern financial theory and, 131; in the
    newswatcher/momentum trader model,
    516–21; noise trader risk and, 5–7, 9–10,
    82, 88–91, 95–97, 424; performance-
    based (*see* performance-based arbitrage);
    risks associated with, 3–7, 80, 131–32,
    148
arbitrage pricing theory (APT), 502, 606,
    624
Arrow, Kenneth, 64
asset pricing: alternative framework for,
    224–27; consumption-based approach to,
    224–27, 254; equilibrium prices derived in
    an alternative framework for, 239–47; eq-
    uity premium puzzle (*see* equity premium
    puzzle); formal proofs of alternative
    framework for, 266–68; investor behavior
    and, 564; investor preferences in an alter-
    native framework for, 227–36; loss aver-
    sion and questions regarding, 264–65;
    prior outcomes, importance of in an alter-
    native framework, 260–64; prospect
    theory in an alternative framework for,
    236–39; results of analysis within an alter-
    native framework for, 247–60

attribution bias/theory, 463, 465. *See also*
    biased self-attribution
availability biases, 15

Badrinath, S., 545
Baker, M., 56, 57–59, 61
Bakshi, Gurdip S., 190n.16
Balasubramanian, S., 563
Ball, R., 36n, 623
Banerjee, Abhijit, 505n, 530
Banz, Rolf W., 35, 290, 317n.1
Barber, Brad M.: bid-ask spread for individ-
    ual investors, estimate of, 556n.11; boot-
    strapping technique, 551n; brokerage stock
    recommendations, 397–99, 402; the buy-
    ing decision, 55; event studies, 38; exces-
    sive trading, 52; investor behavior, contri-
    bution to understanding, xv; investor
    overconfidence, 559, 561
Barberis, Nicholas: comovement of returns,
    50; conservatism bias and the momentum
    effect, 371; earnings growth, irrational ex-
    trapolation of, 190n.17; empirical testing
    of models, 65; the equity premium puzzle,
    xiii, 28–29; investor behavior and asset re-
    turns, 227; overreaction/underreaction,
    contribution to theories of, xv; overreac-
    tion/underreaction, explanation of, 464;
    overreaction/underreaction, unified theory
    regarding, 503, 521, 529; returns, belief-
    based models explaining, 41–43; returns,
    preference-based model explaining, 46;
    stock market puzzles, explanation of, 34
Barsky, Robert B., 32n.19, 190n.17, 436–37
base rate neglect, 13
Basu, S.: cross-sectional variation in stock re-
    turns, explanation of, 317n.1; predictive
    power of scaled-price ratios, 36; price/
    earnings ratio, value strategy and, 281–83;
    value strategies, success of, 273
Bayes's law, 13
Beaver, William, 623
behavioral finance: criteria for a theory to
    satisfy, 503; optimism regarding the future
    of, xvii; progress in, 63–65; Rational Ex-
    pectations Equilibrium framework and,